Lecture Notes in Computer Science 9754

Commenced Publication in 1973
Founding and Former Series Editors:
Gerhard Goos, Juris Hartmanis, and Jan van Leeuwen

More information about this series at http://www.springer.com/series/7409

Jia Zhou · Gavriel Salvendy (Eds.)

Human Aspects of IT for the Aged Population

Design for Aging

Second International Conference, ITAP 2016
Held as Part of HCI International 2016
Toronto, ON, Canada, July 17–22, 2016
Proceedings, Part I

 Springer

Editors
Jia Zhou
Chongqing University
Chongqing
China

Gavriel Salvendy
Purdue University
West Lafayette, IN
USA

ISSN 0302-9743   ISSN 1611-3349   (electronic)
Lecture Notes in Computer Science
ISBN 978-3-319-39942-3   ISBN 978-3-319-39943-0   (eBook)
DOI 10.1007/978-3-319-39943-0

Library of Congress Control Number: 2016940107

LNCS Sublibrary: SL3 – Information Systems and Applications, incl. Internet/Web, and HCI

Printed on acid-free paper

This Springer imprint is published by Springer Nature
The registered company is Springer International Publishing AG Switzerland

Foreword

The 18th International Conference on Human-Computer Interaction, HCI International 2016, was held in Toronto, Canada, during July 17–22, 2016. The event incorporated the 15 conferences/thematic areas listed on the following page.

A total of 4,354 individuals from academia, research institutes, industry, and governmental agencies from 74 countries submitted contributions, and 1,287 papers and 186 posters have been included in the proceedings. These papers address the latest research and development efforts and highlight the human aspects of the design and use of computing systems. The papers thoroughly cover the entire field of human-computer interaction, addressing major advances in knowledge and effective use of computers in a variety of application areas. The volumes constituting the full 27-volume set of the conference proceedings are listed on pages IX and X.

I would like to thank the program board chairs and the members of the program boards of all thematic areas and affiliated conferences for their contribution to the highest scientific quality and the overall success of the HCI International 2016 conference.

This conference would not have been possible without the continuous and unwavering support and advice of the founder, Conference General Chair Emeritus and Conference Scientific Advisor Prof. Gavriel Salvendy. For his outstanding efforts, I would like to express my appreciation to the communications chair and editor of *HCI International News*, Dr. Abbas Moallem.

April 2016   Constantine Stephanidis

HCI International 2016 Thematic Areas
and Affiliated Conferences

Thematic areas:

- Human-Computer Interaction (HCI 2016)
- Human Interface and the Management of Information (HIMI 2016)

Affiliated conferences:

- 13th International Conference on Engineering Psychology and Cognitive Ergonomics (EPCE 2016)
- 10th International Conference on Universal Access in Human-Computer Interaction (UAHCI 2016)
- 8th International Conference on Virtual, Augmented and Mixed Reality (VAMR 2016)
- 8th International Conference on Cross-Cultural Design (CCD 2016)
- 8th International Conference on Social Computing and Social Media (SCSM 2016)
- 10th International Conference on Augmented Cognition (AC 2016)
- 7th International Conference on Digital Human Modeling and Applications in Health, Safety, Ergonomics and Risk Management (DHM 2016)
- 5th International Conference on Design, User Experience and Usability (DUXU 2016)
- 4th International Conference on Distributed, Ambient and Pervasive Interactions (DAPI 2016)
- 4th International Conference on Human Aspects of Information Security, Privacy and Trust (HAS 2016)
- Third International Conference on HCI in Business, Government, and Organizations (HCIBGO 2016)
- Third International Conference on Learning and Collaboration Technologies (LCT 2016)
- Second International Conference on Human Aspects of IT for the Aged Population (ITAP 2016)

Conference Proceedings Volumes Full List

Human Aspects of IT for the Aged Population

Program Board Chairs: **Gavriel Salvendy, USA and P.R. China, and Jia Zhou, P.R. China**

- Ronald M. Baecker, Canada
- Marc-Eric Bobillier Chaumon, France
- Jeff K. Caird, Canada
- Alan H.S. Chan, Hong Kong, SAR China
- Judith Charlton, Australia
- Neil Charness, USA
- Fausto Colombo, Italy
- Sara Czaja, USA
- Richard Darin Ellis, USA
- Hua Dong, P.R. China
- Mireia Fernández-Ardèvol, Spain
- Mohammad Anwar Hossain, Saudi Arabia

- Jiunn-Woei (Allen) Lian, Taiwan
- Eugene Loos, The Netherlands
- Lisa J. Molnar, USA
- Richard Pak, USA
- Denice C. Park, USA
- Joseph Sharit, USA
- Marie Sjölinder, Sweden
- António Teixeira, Portugal
- Wang-Chin Tsai, Taiwan
- Gregg C. Vanderheiden, USA
- Brenda Vrkljan, Canada
- Jonathan Wallace, UK
- Martina Ziefle, Germany

The full list with the program board chairs and the members of the program boards of all thematic areas and affiliated conferences is available online at:

http://www.hci.international/2016/

HCI International 2017

The 19th International Conference on Human-Computer Interaction, HCI International 2017, will be held jointly with the affiliated conferences in Vancouver, Canada, at the Vancouver Convention Centre, July 9–14, 2017. It will cover a broad spectrum of themes related to human-computer interaction, including theoretical issues, methods, tools, processes, and case studies in HCI design, as well as novel interaction techniques, interfaces, and applications. The proceedings will be published by Springer. More information will be available on the conference website: http://2017. hci.international/.

General Chair
Prof. Constantine Stephanidis
University of Crete and ICS-FORTH
Heraklion, Crete, Greece
E-mail: general_chair@hcii2017.org

http://2017.hci.international/

Contents – Part I

Technology Use and Acceptance by Older Users

Psychological and Cognitive Aspects of Interaction and Aging

Mobile and Wearable Technologies for the Elderly

Contents – Part II

Aging, Learning, Training and Games

Aging, Mobility and Driving

Designing for and with the Elderly

Technologically Mature
but with Limited Capabilities

Yvonne Eriksson[✉]

Information Design, Mälardalen University, Västerås, Sweden
yvonne.eriksson@mdh.se

Abstract. A growing population of elderly people with an extensive knowledge of ICT is to be expected – a generation that has several decades of daily experience from using computers, cell phones and other devices at work situations and in their spare time. Today the discussion of elderly people and technology is dominated by the perception that the elderly are comparatively inexperienced with regard to digital technology. The challenge for the future is, however, to overcome the gradual loss of the senses with the help of technical devices that fulfill the needs of older technologically mature users.

Keywords: Users · Categorization · Design thinking · Phenomenology

1 Introduction

Interaction Design, Ergonomic Design and Information Design are only a few examples of fields that claim they use a human-centered perspective in order to take the users' needs into consideration while designing e.g. interfaces, work spaces or information that support people's ability to access information, and to support communication between artifacts and individuals. Even though the human-centered perspective is crucial for these areas and for putting the user in focus, it is necessary to problematize the concept of user. The ISO standards for users (ISO 134 07) and usability (ISO 9241-11) reflect the complexity when it comes to human-centered design and user-centered design in relation to usability [1]. In order to avoid a too limited perspective on users and situations, it is necessary to take both cognitive and sociocultural aspects into consideration.

The lack of a definition of user has been discussed by some scholars [2], but there is no discussion regarding the categorizations of users in terms of factors such as age, sex, and ethnicity. While conducting research where users are involved in different ways, one has to start by identifying the context and the situation before identifying the user. Sometimes the group of users is more limited than it appears at first glance. Websites showing train timetable will be visited by very few categories of users if only the situations are taken into consideration: people that travel often and want to make sure that the timetable has remained the same, the ones traveling only now and then, and the very infrequent travellers. What they all have in common, no matter their age, sex, ethnicity or disability, is their wish to find out when the train is leaving. This trivial example will work as an introduction to a discussion about the problem of categorizing

© Springer International Publishing Switzerland 2016
J. Zhou and G. Salvendy (Eds.): ITAP 2016, Part I, LNCS 9754, pp. 3–12, 2016.
DOI: 10.1007/978-3-319-39943-0_1

users without adopting a holistic perspective. In some cases it is obvious who the users are, especially if the research is done in collaboration with an organization, but still the users' needs have to be identified.

Even though the concept of user is not defined, user- and human-centered perspectives claim that they focus on users' needs [3, 4]. Since a definition of user and a deeper analysis of user is missing in most cases, there is a tendency to group people into several categories such as sex, age, sexuality, ethnicity or with regard to disabilities. Users are often chosen ad hoc and rarely problematized in relation to categories such as those just mentioned [3, 4]. These categories make sense for some situations but not for most. When taking a theoretical and interdisciplinary perspective on human- and user-centered design, it is easy to find the pitfalls, especially if this is combined with design thinking where the purpose is to create new value, with no prior assumption as to what and how an artifact should be created [5]. This requires a focus on a specific situation or system rather than fixed categories of users.

From a theoretical perspective, this paper will discuss the problem of categorizing users in general and in relation to age and ICT. Age is a very vague category and based on the mapping of both visible characteristics and behavior. Age means ageing, but how this is experienced is individual and could be explained from a phenomenological perspective [6]. By bringing up some aspects of how the understanding of gender, age, sexuality, and ethnicity or disabilities have an impact not only on how we perceive a group but also the self image, this paper will problematize how well-intention can contribute to stigmatization of groups.

2   Categorization and Mapping

Getting older is not only to reach a new age; it is connected to the experience of the environment and of limitations of various kinds. How such limitations will affect people is dependent on individual bodily changes, which have an emotional impact on individuals since they will affect daily life, but also behavior. The changes take different forms and do not necessarily involve intellectual capacity, but also aspects such as hearing, eyesight and fine motor skills. It is a continuous oscillation between the experience of bodily limitations and environmental expectations. It also includes self-reflection [7] and the ability to live up to the environment's expectations. When defining a group and then involving them in the design process or in a testing situation, they will know that they belong among the intended users of the product or service. The people that are addressed will either do their best to fulfill the environment's expectations based on the category they are selected for, or try to perform as well as possible, or disqualify the product or service. It could also be a combination of these behaviors, but the classification based on age, sex or ethnicity will have an impact on their self-reception as well as the designers' or researchers' understanding of the individuals in the categorized group. While selecting criteria for users, one relates to a historical tradition of grouping and categorization.

Mapping and categorizing is a way to understand the environment, in a systematic way that facilities learning about different phenomena and identifying criteria for research. There has been an interest in the meaning of the concept of mapping and its impact on our way of thinking and how it influences understanding and behavior. Denis Cosgrove wrote: To map is in one way or another to take the measure of a world, and more than merely take it to figure the measure so taken in such a way that it may be communicated between people, places or time. The measure of mapping is not restricted to the mathematical; it may equally be spiritual, political or moral. By the same token, the mapping's record is not confined to archival; it includes the remembered, the imagined, the contemplated [8]. By systematic categorization of users (e.g. within ICT, Ergonomics, Information Design) into predefined categories that rest on stereotypic preconceptions, the user that designers or design researchers are looking for could easily be missed or left out.

Mapping and categorization have been a powerful and influential tool for the organization of knowledge, thinking, planning and conducting research. To understand the impact of categorization one has to adopt a historical perspective. In the 17th century, while the need to understand the environment grew, and science with it, categorization and mapping became tools to organize and define important historical phenomena as well as species and objects vital for S&T. This took place in universities and in cabinets for collections (Peter the Great's cabinet in St Petersburg is one example) and the very first science museums. According to the French philosopher Michel Foucault, categorization was a way to control the field of knowledge and by extension science and thinking [9]. In order to map and categorize living species and objects, the single parts or artifacts needed to be defined beforehand. The species or parts that did not fulfill the criteria were either left out or given a description that fit a specific criterion [9] On the basis of description, depiction and placing in a specific category the species or object would then be perceived as belonging to that category [9]. The artifacts/species that did not fit into a specific category tended to become 'non-existing' and were forgotten [10]. This is very typical when it comes to historical events or objects, especially when it comes to artifacts created by groups with less influence in society, like women and people from non-western countries [10]. Leaving out artifacts made by groups with less status in society is a kind of stigmatization. By keeping this in memory one can ask what happens when we define users in terms of age and assign certain qualities to an age group. From history we can learn about the risks of using definitions of users that are too strict and stereotypical. While loosening the categories the mapping system will become more complex and several mappings of groups and phenomena are required.

3 Defining Users

When a designer or a design researcher defines an intended user for his or her product they need to narrow down the group of users, e.g. to one defined in terms of sex or special needs caused by disabilities. The needs or requirements for the defined group could be found in previous research made in other areas such as cognitive psychology or behavior psychology where average living conditions and needs are defined. It should be kept in mind, however, that the intentions with this kind of research are different from those in design situation. Since the description of different groups is widely flowering, even the groups themselves adapt the understanding of their needs or limitations. It is a part of the internalization of external expectations.

Pre-understanding and assumptions about people affect not only how we understand other groups but also how we understand ourselves. Claims such as "young people do not read manuals but look for instructions on YouTube" imply that the elderly do it differently. This in turn raises questions about the definition of "young people" and until what age someone is young and when one becomes elderly. These are concepts that are used with a considerable confidence but based on old definitions. In some contexts, e.g. advertising, life will start after retirement, or at least retirees are assumed to be active consumer of travels, exclusive dinners etc., but when it comes to ICT the same age group is often defined as an immature user of such technology.

If you can't make it, fake it. The saying is about more than pretending that you are better than you are; it also says something about how we create our identity. To create an identity takes time; it is something one grows into, step by step, but it also changes over time. Every age, profession, civil status, living area etc. affects an individual's identity. This could be explained by the fact that we interact with our environment and the tools that surround us; everything we do is cognitively situated. But it takes time: we do not adopt to an identity by going from one age to another, or by moving or changing job; the new role has to be internalized in the interaction between the individual and the environment, but also with the expectations that come from a specific age, position or social status – expectations that are often based on fixed categories and specifications. To internalize an age in the sense that one gets a deeper understanding of other needs than earlier in life takes time. It is not for sure that one recognizes a hearing problem or even bad eyesight, for example, until it causes other problems.

3.1 Categorization and Expected Behavior

Categorization is not exclusively related to static characteristics such as, appearance but also very much to behavior and expected behavior. Grouping people in terms of age, sex or ethnicity often implies that a specific behavior is expected. When an individual accepts to be involved in a design process or testing situation, they also agree to the classification and will often act as a representative for the group. This can be expressed in different ways, e.g. this is not something I care for but I am sure that others in my age/situation etc. do. This could also be explained by that they are taking a role as. When Goffman brought up the idea about the performative self, he was focusing on people's need to perform well and to play a role to impress or please people they meet [11] doing so he brought the meaning of roles in daily life, and this includes a testing situation or when individuals take part in a design process. In many situations people protect themselves against failure by telling from the very beginning that they are not interested or capable. The excuses they give are often based on preconceptions regarding aspects such as age or sex. Since different categories are associated with specific behavior, such excuses are accepted and will not affect the interpretation/understanding of the concrete individual. This also entails the opposite: if, for example, a young person tells that (s)he is not familiar with ICT, this will not be accepted as a natural statement.

3.2   Individuals vs. Groups

The relationships between a group of users and individuals are complex. Interestingly, in discussions of groups of users, it is often brought up that every single individual has different needs, yet at the same time users are categorized in groups. In that context it is often pointed out that a person may have a disability but is not disabled because cause of that. Such a statement is often regarded as politically correct, but not necessarily taken seriously. In research with a focus on human interaction or human- or user-centered design, it is important to take such a statement seriously, however. Otherwise there is a risk of users being regarded as the other, to use a term from gender and post-colonial studies [10] i.e. someone with supposedly fixed characteristics that will be looked at from an outside position. Instead, it is necessary to find new ways to define users and to group people in other ways than earlier. Consider sex and gender, where sex is biological while gender is a social construction based on expectations of specific behavior in relation to biological sex (though later research indicates that it is problematic even to define sex on biological grounds) [12]. If the elderly could be defined as more experienced in a specific area, we will have groups of users with different ages but more or less the same user history, and other criteria will become more crucial, such as what talent is needed for a specific activity. The user group will in such cases be more heterogeneous in terms of, for example, biological age, gender, ethnicity and disabilities. The focus will be on how to facilitate for the users and make an interface for ICT, an artifact or a service useable.

4   Phenomenology and Situated Experience

From a phenomenological perspective, we perceive and orient ourselves in the environment by using our body; in that sense the condition of the body affects how we understand the environment [6]. That means that getting older also changes the way that we experience life in terms of what we perceive and how we interact with the environment. What we perceive and how depends on an interaction between physiological conditions, previous knowledge, culture and context. This will have consequences for users' involvement, if tests and studies are carried out in a lab. By bringing users out of their natural contexts, they will experience a given design or product in a different way [14].

The difference between a test situation and a daily context/situation will have impact on the users' experiences of a product. The relation between test or design situations and a future implementation will have an effect on e.g. digital factory layout and planning (on going project). The experience of the environment is a bodily one. By combining a phenomenological perspective with working memory, episodic memory and semantic memory, it is obvious that a person that has long experience of something is also more mature in many respects. We learn to see and interpret visuals, but the adequate interpretation of visual representations of milieus requires experience. To be a skilled computer game player does not automatically create visual interpretation skills outside of the game. It is something that one learns over time. A mature user of ICT or one familiar with a specific kind of visuals could feel uncomfortable in new contexts, which could negatively affect the desire or ability to change behavior. Since all memory is not stored intellectually but in the body, it is sometimes hard to change a physical behavior [13].

Experience from real environments and work situations is required, as it visual literacy, i.e. the ability to relate a visual representation/presentation to a planned reality. Sizes, relations, level of noise or lightning are often hard to transpose from the screen into reality with the help of the imagination. The theory of situated cognition maintains that human thoughts and actions are adapted to the environment. It is situated because what people perceive and how they perform is affected by the context and the situation [14]. That is to be taken into consideration when using age as a category in connection with ICT usage: there are those who lack experience and those who don't.

4.1   Ageing

If ageing is regarded as a phenomenological process, it is something that individuals grow into. Emotionally, most people do not feel that they become older, but at the same time they experience changes such as physical limitations and altered appearance. The change in appearance is not something that individuals recognize daily while looking in the mirror; what most people see when they meet their face in the mirror is the mental image of themselves. Often they recognize ageing only when looking at pictures of themselves that provide them with an external perspective. That means that the self-image does not always agree with how the environment perceives an individual, and there can also be a mismatch between self-expectations and expectations from the environment.

Ageing is a slow process for most people. Single individuals do not necessarily realize that they have bad eyesight or limited hearing. What they experience is annoyance when using ICT, for example. The interface is badly designed and the sound is not clear enough. That leads to frustration in many cases and less interest in using different devices, but also in watching television or listening to the radio. What we are dealing with here is challenges with regard to loss in sensorial capabilities.

The share of the population that is over 65 years old increases in Western countries. This is caused by the baby boom after the Second World War and because of an improved standard of living: people live longer and have an active life after retirement. The average education level of the generation born during the 1940s is high, and they also belong to the first generation that was introduced to and used computers. They have experience from the first Internet connections made by phone, and later from broadband and now Wi-Fi. Upon turning 65, they suddenly belong to a group that is looked upon as digitally immature. They had previously also been introduced to television and have experience of many generations of telephones from rotary phones to smartphones, so the number of technical innovations they have been through during their lifetime is considerable. How come, then, that they are regarded as digitally immature after turning 65? Note that the opposite also applies, i.e. the expectation that all young people are technically mature since they are assumed to play computer games.

It has recently been stated that the elderly are typically defined as those 65 years old or older and that they are the fasted growing segment of the population [15]. Their share is expected to increase over the next 25 years: in the USA alone they will increase by 80 % [15]. If this trend continues, a digitally mature population over 65 years is to be expected, including people that have used digital devices of different kinds since they were children. In addition, we will probably have growing numbers of elderly people that are still active and even work full time. Therefore, the challenge for the future is not to develop devices for technologically immature elderly ICT users but for mature ones.

5 Intended Users and Actual Users

How can we know that the intended users will be the actual users? Is it because they believe so themselves? Or do the users live up to the designer's expectation of the users' needs for the redesign of a product or a new one? Research indicates that people are not aware of why they make decisions and especially not when they are put into situations where they are asked to make choices [16]. In design situations where users are involved either as part of a reference group or in the design process, they are often told why they are chosen. The challenge is to identify the actual needs and the usability of a product or service. Since most people are aware of conventional expectations of specific groups they will probably live up to the expectation by giving voice to the group and putting their own experience aside.

As early as 1985, Harker and Eason [17] brought up the problem with user involvement when it comes to identifying their needs. They identified three areas, which are critical:

- The extent of task uncertainty or task entropy, enabling an assessment of variability in the task on different occasions. This variability may be due to stimulation conditions, goals, users' discretion or task environment.
- The openness of the task, which, apart from other considerations, will mean that the as can continue to provide opportunities for the task performer to learn no matter how skilled he may become.
- Task discretion as reflection by the level and extent of choice available to the performer of the task.

They found that a much broader view of user requirements must be taken if usable and acceptable systems are to result [17]. ISO 13407 was established in 1999 and provides guidance for human-centered design processes for interactive systems [1]. It describes use abilities at the level of principles rather than in detail, as compared to the literature on methodology [1]. The relationship between human-centered and user-centered design and usability is complex. In addition, usability is also connected to motivations among users; this is often crucial when introducing new devices or systems for people that are satisfied with a current product or system. This is often mixed up with the ability to learn and use new devices or systems. The standard definition of usability is effectiveness, efficiency and satisfaction, aspects that have to be evaluated in the situation where the system is used. Effectiveness is considered the accuracy and completeness with which users achieve specified goals, while efficiency can be defined as the resources expended in relation to the accuracy and completeness with which users achieve goals. Satisfaction, finally, is understood to be freedom from discomfort and a positive attitude to using the product [1]. Also important are the context and the situation of use; this is often defined as the characteristics of the user in relation to the organizational and physical environment [1]. Following the analysis of ISO 13407 and ISO 9241-11 by Jokela et al. [1] which problematize the vague definition of user, usability and human-centered and user-centered design, it becomes obvious that age is a non-accurate way to characterize users, but also that a holistic perspective is missing.

5.1 Design Thinking and User Involvement

Design thinking strives for a holistic perspective. It is an iterative process making use of prototyping and mock-ups. It includes the user in the process, and sometimes the users themselves can come up with design suggestions, where the designer's role will be to fulfill the users' ideas. What is crucial for design thinking is the desired value. It could be inclusive accessible ICT. What does inclusive mean? It means that everyone can use software or devices or have access to a webpage since the interface is possible to navigate independent of sight problems, dyslexia or motoric limitations, for example.

The first step using a design thinking perspective is to define the problem. This could also be described as framing, which is considered unique for design theory. There exist two ways of defining a frame in a design context: as a product of mental knowledge and meaning structures or as a product of social symbolic structures [5]. Why are people not satisfied with a product or situation? What is the problem? It is not always what one thinks. Do the pay channels have a complicated interface or is it the remote control that has too small buttons and unreadable text on the buttons that make the pay channels inaccessible for people of advanced age? The next step is to identify many options or ideas for how to solve the problem, while a third step includes refining the solutions or ideas. It is a cycle that involves the ideation and refinement of solutions, which adds to the problem content, and refining or re-framing the understanding of the problem. The last part is to execute the best solution for the problem [5, 18]. This is an iterative process and requires openness from the very beginning while formulating the problem. If one gets stuck in categorizations, e.g. if a user group is defined in terms of age, it is easy to explain the problem from the perspective that they are digitally immature and therefore have problems with accessing the pay channels; yet it could easily be the design of the remote control that causes the problem.

6 Conclusions

With good intentions, human-centered design and user-centered design focus on different groups of users, often with the idea to include and involve larger groups of people as users of ICT. The result is less successful since categorizations build on stereotypic ideas about what could be expected from people of different age or with some kind of disability. By focusing on the situation instead of the context the user situation will be narrowed down and using a design thinking perspective will provide a more holistic perspective where the problem is the first to the first thing to be identified, as well as the desired value, rather than trying to solve what is expected to be the problem. When developing digital devices and creating interfaces with a focus on elderly people, it is necessary to take a holistic perspective and realize that the challenge for the future is to over bridge the lost of senses capacity and the need of technical devices that full fill the needs among older technical mature users.

By bringing together different perspectives on users and users' expected needs in relation to the categorization and mapping of different target groups, this paper has brought up a range of problems that need to be taken into consideration. Human- and user-centered design need to broaden their concepts and involve a design thinking perspective that involves framing of the problem: a holistic perspective that combines the cognitive and perceptual aspects involved in the interpretation and use of artifacts or systems with phenomenological and socio-cultural perspectives. By adopting a holistic perspective and problematizing defined categories we avoid ending up in stigmatizing groups by describing them with characteristics built on presumptions. In addition, we will have groups of users that can contribute to an inclusive ICT design that will be accessible for elderly people with great knowledge in the area as well as immature ICT users of young age. To avoid falling into a stereotypic classification it is necessary to define a products or service use, but also what is required of users to use a product or service, but especially in what situations. By focusing on situations where e.g. an ICT platform is expected to be used, it is possible to redefine the intended user. The group of users may not be age homogenous it could be the level of technology maturity that is needed for the situation. While the circumstances for the use in the specific situation requires keyboard with large keys, large screen and text to speech to fulfill the needs for an elderly person. This will not bother a young person with no perception limitations but will help elderly people who are technology experienced with some supporting needs.

References

1. Jokela, T., Iivari, N., Matero, J., Karukka, M.: The standard of user-centered design and the standard definition of usability: analysing ISO 13407 against ISO 9241-11. In: CLIHC (2003)
2. Law, E., Roto, V., Vermeeren, A.P.O.S., Kort, J., Hassenzahl, M.: Towards a shared definition of user experience. In: CHI 2008 Extended Abstracts on Human Factors in Computing Systems, pp. 2395–2398. ACM (2008)
3. Vredenburg, K., Isensee, S., Righi, C.: User Centered Design: An Integrated Approach. Prentice Hall, Upper Saddle River (2002)
4. Burdick, A., Willis, H.: Digital learning, digital scholarship and design thinking. Des. Stud. 32, 546–566 (2011)
5. Paton, B., Dorst, K.: Briefing and reframing: a situated practice. Des. Stud. 32, 573–587 (2011)
6. Merleau-Ponty, M.: Phenomenology of Perception, pp. 346–365. Routledge, London (1962/1979)

7. Gillespie, A.: Becoming Other: From Social Interaction to Self-Reflection. Information Age Publishing, Greenwich (2006)
8. Cosgrove, D. (ed.): Mapping, pp. 1–2. Reaction Books, London (1999)
9. Foucault, M.: The Order of Things: An Archeology of the Human. Routledge, London (1966/1994)
10. Pollock, G.: Differencing the Canon: Feminist Desire and the Writing of Art's History. Routledge, London (1999)
11. Goffman, E.: The Presentation of Self in Everyday Life. Penguin, London (1959/1990)
12. Butler, J.: Bodies that Matter: On the Discursive Limits of "Sex". Routledge, London (1993)
13. Baddely, A.: Working memory: looking back and looking forward. Nat. Rev. Neurosci. **4**, 829–839 (2003)
14. Clancey, W.J.: Situated Cognition: On Human Knowledge and Computer Representations. Cambridge University Press, Cambridge (1997)
15. Williams, D., Ahamed, S.I., Chu, W.: Designing interpersonal communication software for the abilities of elderly users. In: 2014 IEEE 38th Annual International Computers, Software and Applications Conference Workshops, pp. 282–287 (2014)
16. Hall, L., Johansson, P., de Léon, D.: Recomposing the will: distributed motivation and computer mediation extrospection. In: Vierkant, T., Clark, A., Kiversterin, J. (eds.) Decomposing the Will, vol. 481. Oxford University Press, Oxford (2013)
17. Harker, S., Eason, K.: Task analysis and the definition of users needs. In: IFAC Man-Machine System, Varese, Italy (1985)
18. Adams, R.S.: Being a profession: three lenses into design thinking, acting, and being. Des. Stud. **32**, 588–607 (2011)

Designing Poker Time: Older People as Fixpartners in a Co-design Process

Linna Hu and Hua Dong[✉]

College of Design and Innovation, Tongji University, Shanghai, China
hulinna25657@126.com, donghua@tongji.edu.cn

Abstract. An effective way to involve older people in design is to include them as equally important partners in co-design practices. This paper illustrates how students applied design knowledge and interaction skills to collaborate with older people to fix their real life problem. It was found that many older people have specific needs of communication, which depend heavily on their lifestyle and preferences. The design solution tackled the entertainment and communication issues for an old couple, through creating a better experience of their everyday poker time. Older people played an active role in the project and contributed positively to the final solution. It concludes that working with older people as design partners could lead to better products that are more appropriate for them.

Keywords: Older people · Co-design · Fixpert

1 Introduction

An effective way to involve older people in design is to include them as equally important partners in the co-design process (Newell et al. 2007). 'Fixperts' projects adopt such a practice. 'Fixperts' (www.fixperts.org) is a social project and an open knowledge-sharing platform, which promotes creative and social values through design. Designers and users work together to identify a problem, explore possible solutions and finally make prototypes, thus solving a practical everyday problem by the use of imagination and design skills. In the postgraduate course 'User Research and Design Innovation' at Tongji University, the Fixperts format were adopted as the assignment. 21 master students were divided into 10 groups of 2 or 3 students as Fixperts. Each group needed to find a person aged over 60 to be the design partner (the Fix partner) who would actively engage in the whole project process. Upon completion of the course, the students were required to deliver a final design (Dong and Vanns 2009), typically a product, and a mini film recording the design process.

1.1 People Involved in Fixperts

This paper will illustrate a Fixperts case study on how postgraduate students (Fixperts) applied design and communication skills to collaborate with older people (Fixpartners) and eventually solve real life problems for older people through design.

© Springer International Publishing Switzerland 2016
J. Zhou and G. Salvendy (Eds.): ITAP 2016, Part I, LNCS 9754, pp. 13–22, 2016.
DOI: 10.1007/978-3-319-39943-0_2

Fixperts and Film Makers (Students). Fixperts are those who are ready to apply their academically trained design skills and knowledge to make and improve things, say design learners or designers. A Film Maker is also a storyteller as he/she captures the whole story and translates the conversations between Fixperts and Fixpartners into a mini documentary film to share the journey with others and showcase the inspiring results.

Fixpartner (Older People). Fixpartners are someone with a fixing challenge, who is happy to invite a Fixpert to help fix problems.

1.2 Fixpartners

The Fixpartners of this project are an old couple, Mr. and Mrs. LI, who have known each other for over 60 years. Their profile is summarized in Table 1.

Table 1. Profile of fixpartners

Introduction	LI Shuzhi (Grandpa)	YUAN Lili (Granny)
Age	83	82
Birthplace	Nantong, Jiangsu	Shanghai
Personality	Intelligent, hard-working, tenacious	Passionate, humorous, optimistic
Occupation	Chinese Medicine Pharmacist	Electric Welder in Shipyard
Hobby	Dance, Watching TV	Music, Mahjong
Life Habit	Seldom go out except daily shopping	Keep Indoors, Love Cleanliness
Condition	Senile Chronic Bronchitis Minor Impairment in Hearing Oxygen Therapy Twice a Day Medication and Spray Avoid Spicy and Salty Food No Strenuous Exercise	High Blood Pressure Vascular Occlusion A Big Surgery 3 Years Ago 5 Different Types of Medication Each Day Pay Attention to Rest and Diet

2 Design Process

The participants in the project included 2 industrial design master students (known as Fixperts and also Film Makers) and 2 older people, the Fixpartners. To identify a problem in older people's life and explore possible solutions that are appropriate for them, the design process was conducted with a user-centered method, and followed 5 stages, i.e. discover, define, design, develop and deliver. The project used these stages as a way to equip both Fixperts and Fixpartners with guidance to refine the final solution. At the beginning of the design process, it was important to discover the needs and wants of the Fixpartners as much as possible. The second part of the process involved in-depth interviews and discussions to support defining an everyday problem that Fixpartners meet. The analysis of issues and needs were then presented, and followed by the initial design, feedback from the Fixpartners, iterative design improvement, and the final solution. The development session finished with presentation where participants delivered their work. The whole process was video recorded.

2.1 Initial Visit and Observation

Fixpartners introduced their daily life routine and basic information regarding the relevant activities including their typical day, bathing, health management, meal preparation, home maintenance, activities, hobbies, communication in community and within family. Fixperts acted as listeners and observers, making efforts to find potential problems to allow later analysis of issues and needs. The initial visit involved the following 6 parts (Lindsay et al. 2010):

1. Information Gathering
2. Scenario Discussion
3. Issue Identification
4. Analysis of Needs and Requirements
5. Envisioning
6. Idea Generation

2.2 Discovering

Fixpartners were asked to verbalize their concerns about their daily life and perform some activities, such as doing laundry and playing a card game, so that Fixperts could find emotional and functional issues as well as physical ones. Some of the everyday life issues were identified, including:

- Fixpartner's hands tremble a lot, especially when holding something
- Having difficulties in hanging out the clothes
- Inconvenience in taking medicine
- Often forgetting to bring Seniors Travel Cards when going out
- Difficulties in storing poker cards and coins

The Fixperts and Fixpartners brainstormed together to answer how to change the situations outlined, which is the most productive part of the discovering process.

2.3 Defining

Fixpartners play Paodekuai, a type of Chinese poker game, from 2 pm to 4 pm every afternoon. This poker game, serving as a means to train older people's memory and logical inference, is also a somewhat competitive indoor entertainment that involves money in order to create a feeling of achievement for Fixpartners. It was found that Mr. LI puts the coins in a wooden small drawer while Mrs. LI puts her money in a leather purse. The process of playing poker was divided successively into 5 steps, i.e. taking cards out, shuffling, dealing cards, playing, and paying, as shown in Fig. 1.

Based on the observation, it was found that the couple did not talk to each other while playing cards, and the two hours of poker time was strangely quiet.

Fig. 1. The process of playing poker

Through deep interviews, it was realized that the Fixpartners were interested to talk about their past but there was no such effective props in the poker game to provoke conversations about their shared memory. A crucial feature of older people was that they have to deal with various aging challenges that life brings (Sustar et al. 2013) and thus would lack opportunities to have focused discussion on a specific topic. In addition, the accelerating pace of work and modern lifestyle leave young people with little time for spending with older relatives (Waterworth and Waterworth 2006). It is essential to facilitate communication between the two generations, for family connection is known to be vital for emotional as well as physical and psychological health for older people (Waterworth and Waterworth 2006).

In summary, the Fixpartners' emotional needs of playing poker cards are:

- To elicit conversation
- To experience much happiness in displaying the memories of the past
- To share and enjoy memories of past decades in an instant, easy, vibrant and amusing way
- To tell stories to younger people and spend some quality time together

And their functional needs include:

- To make cards easier to find and to take out
- Better to place two packs of cards and coins together
- Ingenious, simple and convenient to use
- To be able to store a certain number of coins

2.4   Design

Spending time with the old couple and participating in their daily activities in a real setting provided the students with many clues on which to make design decisions. Older people's confidence in their ability to use new products can be fragile due partly to their unfamiliarity and potential fear of new things (Newell et al. 2007). If the Fixperts tried to change something completely, they would face considerable opposition from the Fixpartners.

To meet the Fixpartners' emotional needs, many well-conceived ideas were produced, one of which was eventually accepted by the old couple with satisfaction, that is, the Conversation-Trigger-Cards (Fig. 2).

Fig. 2. Conversation trigger card

The Conversation-Trigger-Cards aimed to trigger intimate conversation regarding everyday life, career, likes and dislikes, historical events, and old stories. The items presented on the poker cards were grouped into 4 categories:

- Hearts: Career and Hobby
- Diamonds: Story, History and Experience
- Clubs: Life and City Memory
- Spades: Old Items and Culture

Furthermore, a Storage Case was designed to better integrate poker cards with coins. The first prototype was produced as quickly as possible in order to get something tangible and low-cost to facilitate discussions with the old couple and get their feedback (Waterworth and Waterworth 2006). The iterative development of different prototypes was conducted with a user-centered approach. Throughout the development Fixperts tested diverse mocks-ups and prototypes with Fixpartners so as to obtain feedback for the next development process. A wide range of possible forms of Storage Case (Fig. 3) was presented to the Fixpartners.

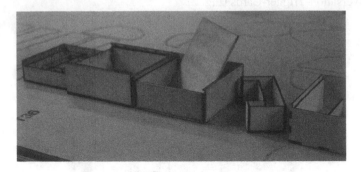

Fig. 3. The iterative development of prototypes

2.5   Development

It is advised that both the Fixperts and Fixpartners should be involved in concept development and prototype stage of the design process, so that both sides can positively affect early design decisions (Newell et al. 2007). The best method was the in-home interview, demonstrating prototypes in Fixpartners' home and offering detailed instruction for them to test (Bagnall et al. 2006). The Fixperts visited Fixpartners' home for the second time with the prototype of the Conversation-Trigger-Cards and the Storage Case. During the visit, Fixpartners were asked to try out the sample cards and later examine the usability of the Storage Case. The old couple became excited, and gave a lot of feedback on prototypes. The evaluation (Fig. 4) was effective in eliciting more stories about how an old item was used in home, how people thought about a famous historical event, who influenced their life attitude and lifestyle, and the sharing of a range of good and bad experiences (Fig. 5).

Fig. 4. The evaluation of the conversation-trigger-cards

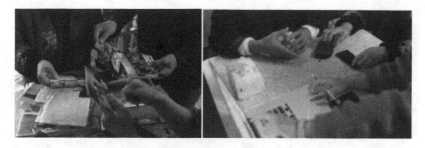

Fig. 5. The sharing of past stories

Fixpartners offered more items that could be added to the cards, explaining the information through language and drawings, which contributed a lot to completing the Conversation-Trigger-Cards. The items include but were not limited to:

1. Influential People in their lives
2. Traditional Custom and Food
3. Classic Films and Songs
4. Old Games
5. Old Fashions
6. Old Brands

As for the Storage Case, the Fixpartners provided suggestions on aesthetics and the size of the Storage Case, and expressed their material preferences. They preferred wood rather than plastic or metal. The feedback helped the redesign of the prototype.

The development stage played a crucial role in the design process, as it addressed the difficulty of presenting intangible concepts in design through the use of sketches, prototypes and mock-up for working with Fixpartners, which stimulated creative thinking and user-centered innovation. This session also allowed Fixperts to observe the difference between what Fixpartners said and what actually happened. Tied to this is the generation of many constructive suggestions from both Fixperts and Fixpartners to improve the design in every aspect.

2.6 Delivering

Concerns about interrupting each other led Fixperts to the idea of triggering conversation that Fixpartners both interested in, as an appealing way of inviting communication. The inconvenience of placing coins sparked creativity of integrating the poker box with the coins container. The design was named Poker Time. It consisted of Conversation-Trigger-Cards and a Storage Case (Fig. 6).

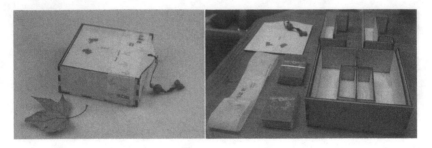

Fig. 6. Prototype of poker time (final version)

A major challenge of this project was to design and develop a systematic product for the Fixpartners that was convenient and intuitive to use for fulfilling their daily activities (Waterworth and Waterworth 2006). Consequently, the Storage Case was made out of 4 parts, i.e. 2 coins containers inside, a box cover and a wooden box. The 2 coins containers where Fixpartners put their coins could be taken out while playing poker, served as the moneybox. The 2 packs of Conversation-Trigger-Cards could be placed in the middle of the Storage Case. It is important that the Conversation-Trigger-Card and the Storage Case complement each other and fit together seamlessly.

The Conversation-Trigger-Cards were designed to encourage communication in a form that Fixpartners would find easy to assimilate and act upon. It is thus suggested that the size of each card is 57 mm * 87 mm, the same as the size of a normal poker card on market. The reverse side of cards, which was inspired from dragon and phoenix in Chinese art, the symbol of love and good marriage, was selected by Fixpartners, from the 8 designers offered by the design students. In the testing session, the Fixpartners enjoyed the new cards and the Storage Case with delight and appreciation (Fig. 7).

Fig. 7. Fixpartners' using the new design solution

The Poker Time is a customized product for the Fixpartner, with aesthetics and full functionality, solving the communication and storage problem in playing poker. The design is based on a great deal of user research and prototype making as well as aesthetics consideration.

3 Discussion

The discovery stage of the design process ensured that Fixpartners' needs and requirements were explored extensively early in the design cycle (Newell et al. 2007), and that Fixperts became more aware of the issues which they were supposed to address, that is, the communication and storage issues in their daily poker time. The final version of the prototype was given to Fixpartners as a gift. Overall the Conversation-Trigger-Cards were found to be a very useful way for provoking discussions on the topics shown on the cards which the Fixpartner find interesting and enjoyable, and the feedback gained from them was sufficient to ascertain the usefulness of the Storage Case.

The Fixperts project is more like a process rather than a service. The final result at first is likely to be a temporary solution, but in the long term the process might be a part of a better and bigger solution for others and probably even lead to production of the product. The Fixperts project has proved to positively influence the students' creative capability and their user research skills.

Older people as Fixpartners should be seen as an equally important part of the team rather than just subjects of experimentation (Newell et al. 2007), because while Fixperts contribute knowledge in design field, Fixpartners contribute their life experience and an understanding of what would be appropriate for other peers. The voices of users must be heard in the design process, but this brings significant challenges to designers faced with older users. Therefore, cooperation with older people has to be done with much more care and patience, even within limited time and resources.

4 Conclusions

This case study has demonstrated the value of gaining a comprehensive understanding of older people's daily life. While the original intention was to design an entertainment product that older people could benefit from, the result was that they needed a more attractive and appropriate way of communication when they play poker cards every day. In addition, older people and younger people can be better connected to each other by the use of the design, as the older people can tell the stories triggered by the cards while they play the game.

A large proportion of older people have specific needs of communication, which depend heavily on their lifestyle and preference. The phenomenon of aging population is creating expanding markets for products that can be used by older people with a broader range of needs and wants (Newell and Gregor 2002). It is believed that design coupled with the needs of older people could stimulate better design methods and lead to better products for everyone (Newell and Gregor 2002).

Acknowledgements. Thanks go to Yiyuan LIU for cooperation, Shu YUAN for her guidance on working with users, and Jingyi LI for her introduction to Mr. and Mrs. LI. Also thanks to www.fixperts.org for its useful design brief and project guidelines.

References

Newell, A.F., Arnott, J., Carmichael, A., Morgan, M.: Methodologies for involving older adults in the design process. In: Stephanidis, C. (ed.) UAHCI 2007. LNCS, vol. 4554, pp. 982–989. Springer, Heidelberg (2007)

Dong, H., Vanns, N.: Designing an innovative pill dispenser: an undergraduate level case study of inclusive design. Des. J. **12**(2), 95–116 (2009)

Lindsay, S.C., Robinson, A.L., Olivier, P.L., Brittain, K.: Design with older users and people with dementia – methodologies, practical lessons and challenges. In: 28th Annual CHI Conference on Human Factors in Computing Systems (2010)

Sustar, H., Jones, S., Dearden, A.: Older people as equal partners in creative design. In: Holzinger, A., Ziefle, M., Hitz, M., Debevc, M. (eds.) SouthCHI 2013. LNCS, vol. 7946, pp. 649–656. Springer, Heidelberg (2013)

Waterworth, E.L., Waterworth, J.A.: Designing IT for older people. Gerontechnology **5**(2), 99–105 (2006)

Bagnall, P., Onditi, V., Rouncefield, M., Sommerville, I.: Older people, technology and design a socio-technical approach. Gerontechnology **5**(1), 46–50 (2006)

Newell, A., Gregor, P.: Design for older and disabled people – where do we go from here? Univ. Access Inf. Soc. **2**(1), 3–7 (2002)

A Preliminary Exploration of Technology Necessities Among Elderly Living Alone

Lin-Ya Huang[✉] and Chang-Franw Lee

Graduate School of Design, National Yunlin University of Science
and Technology, Douliu, Yunlin, Taiwan
carrie_huang@outlook.com

Abstract. There were three in five of the elderly living alone in Taiwan considered continue living alone would be an ideal way of living in the future. Products and services not only support elderly living alone have the ability to live independently, but also to influence social network to the elderly living alone. Due to the lack of product and service targeting especially for elderly living alone that related to care and assist them to live independently, this research was designed as a preliminary exploration of technology necessities to provide insight into the issue. The findings suggest that (1) Life of living alone need to be simple for the elderly. (2) Sharing behavior might be the most opportunities to care . No matter how form of the product or service was, only in association with the encourage from stakeholders that elderly living alone would have more courage to try new things or to accept assistance.

Keywords: Elderly living alone · Living technology · Caring

1 Introduction

As aging society has been on a rise, and under the background of society with fewer children, marriage status, refuse to go to the care center, living apart with family, or personal choice, more and more elderly living alone. According to the statistics by National Development Council, Taiwan would reach "super-aged" societies in 2025 which means more than one in five of the population is 65 or older.

Particularly, with the rapid development of the internet, communication technology and smart device, lifestyle and the needs of care had changed into multivariate ways. There were three in five of the elderly living alone in Taiwan considered continue living alone would be an ideal way of living in the future (Ministry of Health and Welfare 2013). Elderly living alone would like to live without relatives, and would put less effort on them. Even in response to this trends, technology turns out to be one kinds of socialization pipeline, and this would help the formation of a new individual thinking value at the same time (Shun-Hsiang 2015).

Even though elderly living alone can stay contact with society at home, most of them went out to do activities (Klinenberg 2013). Due to the lack of product and service targeting especially for elderly living alone, this research was designed as a preliminary exploration of technology necessities to provide insight into the issue. The purpose of this study was to investigate whether the technology necessities and lifestyle difference influence the social network of elderly living alone or not.

© Springer International Publishing Switzerland 2016
J. Zhou and G. Salvendy (Eds.): ITAP 2016, Part I, LNCS 9754, pp. 23–31, 2016.
DOI: 10.1007/978-3-319-39943-0_3

2 Literatures

2.1 Difference Between Elderly Living Alone and Living with Others

Definition of Elderly Living Alone. By the definition from WHO, the United Nations, and recently research (Bishop 1986; Cabinet Office of Japa 2014; WHO 2015), most developed world countries have accepted the chronological age of 65 years as a definition of 'elderly' or older person. We define that the "elderly living alone" as the older person above 65 years and lived alone, or, elderly lived with relatives but the people lived together frequently not at home for at least three days a week.

The Potential Risk of Elderly Living Alone. One of the more intriguing issues prevailing throughout the last few decades of elderly living alone research is the question of how much focus in the mental and physiological status should be placed on quality of life (QOL). Nowadays, elderly living alone encounters more risk of cognition problems, chronic diseases, dementia, loneliness, depression, low income or disability than elderly living with others. These reasons were related to high suicide risk, bad quality of life and non-interaction of social network especially on rural community and woman (Arslantaş et al. 2015; Fukunaga et al. 2012; Ortman et al. 2014; Poudel-Tandukar et al. 2011; Klinenberg 2013; Cabinet Office of Japan 2014; Paddock 2015; Shih 2010; WHO 2015).

2.2 Research Related to Elderly Living Alone

The Importance of Social Support. The research mentioned above indicated that social support has gathered great importance in recent years. To date, within many care service studies of elderly living alone, ICT, ZigBee 3D accelerometer sensor network, human-type communication robot, WSN technology (Hung et al. 2013; Peruzzini and Germani 2014; Shimokawara et al. 2013; Tanaka et al. 2012) have been used to build or create interaction with others.

In recent years, United States and European countries had implemented services like home care/home help, home nursing, meals on wheels, day club, day care or emergency wiring (the health care system - life rescue, firefighting or police - police or security alarm connection, civil society contractor) or formal government agencies and types of organizations involved in providing care and other services, income-based subsidies (Huang et al. 2010; Kim 2015). Such services not only let elderly living alone have the ability to live independently, but also improve the willingness for elderly to live alone.

Technology Applied on Elderly Living Alone. As result of living apart with children, elderly living alone releases responsibility of family then frequently involve in social participation (Teerawichitchainan and Pothisiri 2015). Some studies use sensors to detect behavior patterns so the caregivers, family and elderly could interact with each other with the aspect of health (Live!y 2015). Furthermore, this method was applied to daily necessities such as blender, toaster grilled in the kitchen, heater, TV, telephone, bed in the dorm (Bruzek et al. 2014). No matter which ways, caring for elderly living alone would affect by the factors of culture, experience, region, social economy or social network (Suryadevara and Mukhopadhyay 2012).

Thus, the product or service designed for elderly living alone could be a chance to technology, which could meet needs of social support and improve social connection of elderly living alone and the society.

3 Method

This research adopted service design process to study technology necessities among elderly living alone. The method was proposed by Service Science Society of Taiwan (Taiwan 2015), which combined "hear - create – deliver (HCD)" process from IDEO and the Double-Diamond Design Process Model (discover - define – develop - deliver) from UK Design Council. Our process mainly focused on the stage between "discover service area", "analyze and collect thoughts" to "define design problem."

3.1 Participants

The participants for this research were selected from the population of elderly living alone lived at least three days without relatives the in Douliu city and Kaohsiung city in Taiwan. Six of the elderly living alone participated in the study (one of the participants were male and five were female). Their ages ranged from 65 to 92 years. One of the participants (subject a.) involved in this study can be further categorized by the independent living ability (need someone to take care of the daily life). Most of them were lived alone more than 15 years and half of them would use smart devices (internet) in daily lives. Participants were given a $10 honorarium. Every subject was randomly named from alphabet a–f. The Table 1 is participants' basic information survey.

Table 1. Basic information survey of the participants

Subject	a	b	c	d	e	f
Gender	F	F	M	F	F	F
Age	92	65	79	78	75	81
Education	None	College	None	Junior high school	Senior high school	Junior high school
Income (economic independently or rely on allowance[a])	N	Y	N	N	Y	Y
Years of living alone	32	20	20	34	15	26
Usage of Internet and Smart devices	N	Y	N	N	Y	Y

[a]N (No): Economic Independently, Y (Yes): Rely on Allowance

3.2 Procedure

We used a semi-structured interview with averaging 40 min to collect qualitative data of each subject. Additionally, participants took interviews at a local day club or at home. The following were the content of the interview questions:

1. Basic information survey included Gender/Age/Education/Income (economic independently or rely on an allowance)/Years of living alone/Internet and Smart devices usage situations – this helped researcher to find out if different lifestyle had related to social networks.
2. The reason why they live alone/interaction ways of family and social network or any relationships with others – in this step, knowing stakeholders of elderly living alone matters to the service/product they used.
3. Understanding participants' social participation situation about eating (cooking and eating habits/behaviors), shopping (frequency or the place buying things and what they shopped), housing (used home care service or not), transportation (how would they move and what transportation they used), learning activities (interest/volunteering), entertainment (leisure activities), and other suggestion to improve or difficulties of service/product – by collecting the information, we discovered the service/product could be the new chance of technology necessities.

After the interviews, we used affinity diagram to classification and collect needs. Then analysis the reason why elderly living alone had the need. Finally, gather similar insight together to form several topic about technology needs.

4 Results

4.1 Diet Situations

In this aspect, elderly living alone more or less had some diet preference. Among the duration of diet, elderly living alone kept connection to different kinds of products or service' stakeholders. Hence, diet could help subjects maintain certain scope of their social networks. The following can help enlighten us on this:

1. Elderly living alone prefered to enjoy the diet in a convient and simple way regardless of cooking at home or going out to eat: While cooked at home, the majority of elderly living alone (4 of 6) tended to buy much quantities of ingredients like fish, meat and vegetables for several meals. With this way, they could reduce cooking and buying frequency to save time and eat whatever they want. As two subjects separately said, "If I cooked for every meal, it would be not much food for one meal but wasted times." Or "I only cooked one time and ate the dishes for three times a day." For the most important of all, 5 of 6 subjects were used to take out the dishes already cooked from refrigerator and then re-heating it by using kitchenware such as wok, electric rice cooker or microwave oven, so that they could eat right away. By contrast to diet at home, went out to eat not only can change moods but to have diversity selections of food and restaurants that consistent with their diet

habitations ("I went to some restaurants because I don't need to cook and the food there were relatively fresh and easy to chew").

2. Activities could gather elderly living alone and their relatives or social organizations' caregivers together: Family reunion specially on holidays, were one of the significant days to diet with relatives together. At that period of time, included friends, femilies or social organizations' caregivers turned out to be interact more often than usual with elderly living alone. One subject who joined day club commented that, "Every time I went to day club, my friends would bring foods here and we just have tea time there. I even carried my steam cooker with motorcycle, so that everyone could taste the taro cake I made, and it's still hot! They enjoy my snake very much. Other friends' food were always cold." Another subject a, who were not able to walk to long, "My grandchildren would buy vegetable and other ingredients I need for me, if my condition turned well, I would go out to eat." Subject a accepted home care service, the caregivers cooked lunch included rice and one dish, but the subject would eat the food within three meals.

4.2 Shopping Situations

Of all the subjects, the most place they went for shopping were traditional market (to buy food, ingredients and groceries), the second was local supermarket like PXmart (to buy daily necessities) in Taiwan. The others such as convenient store (to pay bill, telephone fee and buy newspapers at 7–11), night market (to buy daily supplies, hardware), retailer (Carrefour). Each place was unique in terms of the communities it located and the demand of which it solved.

4.3 Housing Situations

In regard to housing issues, elderly living alone mostly concerned about cleaning their house and fixing household facilities.

1. Home maintenance were complex to the elderly living alone: "If there were too dirty or under a mess than I won't let my friends come inside my house. Sometimes I just so lazy that I didn't hope anyone else know, it's not a good thing to say." The elderly living alone with friends stated that "I cared every little thing of my house. Once I hired a housekeeper on clean, but I didn't like the way she did of my house. Unfortunately, the one corresponded to my request didn't willing to come because it's far away from her home."

2. Household facilities' status were associated with fixing and basic life smoothness among elderly living alone: When product broke, elderly living alone would change light bulb or try to fix other things. However, subject a usually forgot which button should her push on washing machine to do laundry. Thus, her grandson mark the button for her. Even occasionally happened the situation that she needed to rely on calling grandson to help her activating the machine. As she couldn't recognize, she would afraid to miss use.

3. Couldn't get used to different living environment: Elderly living alone didn't get accustomed to new dwelling place. For instance, even though traveled with relatives, subjects couldn't get used to new places to sleep and couldn't sleep well. Moreover, moved house were inconvenient and difficult. Therefore, local life experience was what they expected.

4.4   Transportation Situations

Limited mobility influences elderly living alone with social network. Once elderly fell down or encountered knee degeneration, the interaction frequency became less than their life before. Subject a had limited mobility and couldn't go out to find friends. Only family would take her out or fiends would came to visit her with some gifts. Additionally, the subject couldn't join community activities as usual, as result of lumbago and pains on knee. In contrast to the elderly living alone with motorcycle or still used public transportation, they could be more initiative on relationships. Besides the problems mentioned above, if there were emergency situations, elderly living alone needed to recruit housekeeper or ask other relatives for help.

4.5   Learning Situations

Participated in activities hold for the elderly will be the mainly social life of all day long of the elderly people living alone. Apart from this, the subjects almost did not participated in other activities. Being alone have created more time of life, which gain the opportunities to them into learning. By dedicated the time to community involvement, subject felt a sense of pride. Owing to the sense of substantial, elderly living alone could teach the skill they were good with to last the learning passion onto other elderly. Subject were likewise absorb health knowledge that kept them stay more and more healthy.

4.6   Entertainment Situations

Most subjects had daily entertainments and social participation experiences. We separated entertainment into two main topics as following:

1. Entertainment could help enrich common sense and inner beauty: Watching foreign traveling channels on TV, reading books or listening to the radio news report would gain the lively sound in the house. When those electronic device or equipment broken, some of the subject could fix by themselves, but those who didn't would need to rely on relatives or neighborhoods. In some condition, a problem of the karaoke machine at home could reduce the opportunities elderly living alone being together with friends. Additionally, recite scriptures (religion factor), volunteering in school or society, could straighten inner peacefulness, honor and confidence.
2. Social activities could be chances to encourage elderly living alone participated in societies or to trouble the willing of social interaction: "When I went to a volunteer,

there were some else (direct seller) just want to grab benefit from us, this was not correct on account of we didn't have too money to waste."

3. Visiting relatives and friends could enhance the opportunities elderly living alone went out to travel: "I seldom went to travel, but I'll attend my grandson's wedding ceremony." Or the condition like" I can go hiking with my family or visit my friends who lived far away from me." Thank to every family member had different kinds of interest, elderly living alone would choose the schedule they had abilities to do. Therefore, they trust the travel plan made by day club instead.

4. Maintained relationships well may have contributed to the instant messaging apps usage on smart phones: Without smart device, half of the subjects use home phone to contact. The other half used internet on mobile or computer. For those who had smart phone with internet, thought that instant messaging app such as Line, was an ideal way to share things with relatives and friends. Due to the free call function design in the instant message, video phone shorten the distance between elderly living alone and the relatives and friends. In one subject word, "By using video-phone, I can see my cute grandson far away from me, and they can say hello to me too." In addition, some of the subject would ask the sellers to questions of operating the app function and setting up personal preferences like big font to view content on the screen clearly and loud sounds to listen more directly while buying smart phones. Therefore, as the new era for them to adapt, elderly living alone started to send messages, read article, learn songs and watch video through the apps. Yet this might put them to the danger of privacy or scam, although some relatives support elderly living alone to use instant messaging apps to interact with others, they couldn't know the detail privacy settings or the way to protect themselves. The situation happened to them really increased uncertainty and safety issues from using smart phone without liberty.

5 Discussion

5.1 Life of Living Alone Need to Be Simple for the Elderly

Simple ways of living are the first of this findings worth summarizing. The results indicated that elderly living alone had regular and routine life. On one hand, the issue of life privacy, liberty and self-dignity are important concerns of having safe life. On the other hand, this could be a great chance for product or service provider to use technologies to meet the unmet needs. The ability to balance safety and danger will result to totally different consequence. With regard to hosing situation, our findings match to the concept of aging in place, although there are differences regarding other aspect of the life style.

5.2 Sharing Behavior Might Be the Most Opportunities to Care

At the moment of sharing, are also the opportunity to care each other. Sometimes subjects considered that caring would bother life of other people. The major finding is that elderly living alone feel concern about the wayt hey do or the appearance people think about them. Activities let elderly connect to the communities and mainly, to the social support and social networks. Despite technologies' advantages, it does have some points we need to improve, such as the invisible computing or data analyzing behind screen cause complex situation and the misuse of app function that confuse the elderly living alone and without instant assistance.

6   Conclusions

To conclude, the resource of local communities where elderly living alone are important, but for them, living conveniently are the biggest challenge. Much more also needs to be known about the household facilities, belongings, communities service and even behaviors from different culture.

These findings lead us to believe that technologies from the aspect of diet, shopping, housing, transportation, learning or entertainment, were beneficial to build the relationships into the life of elderly living alone. No matter how form of the product or service was, only in association with the encourage from stakeholders that elderly living alone would have more courage to try new things or to accept assistance.

Finally, this kind of preliminary exploration of technology necessities though discovered unmet needs, but much more has yet to be done. There is a continuing need for more extensively investigation for the detail part into care product or products. Further research is therefore warranted in different life style unmet of technologies.

References

Arslantaş, H., Adana, F., Ergin, F.A., Kayar, D., Acar, G.I.: Loneliness in elderly people, associated factors and its correlation with quality of life a field study from western Turkey. Iran. J. Publ. Health **44**(1), 43–50 (2015). http://ijph.tums.ac.ir/index.php/IJPH/article/view/8210.pdf

Bishop, C.: Living arrangement choices of elderly singles effects of income and disability. Health Care Financing Rev. **7**(3), 65–73 (1986). http://www.ncbi.nlm.nih.gov/pmc/articles/PMC4191527/

Bruzek, A.: Smart Home Sensors Could Help Aging Population Stay Independent, vol. 145. Scientific American website (2014). http://www.scientificamerican.com/article/smart-home-sensors-could-help-aging-population-stay-independent/

Teerawichitchainan, J.K.B., Pothisiri, W.: What does living alone really mean for older persons? a comparative study of Myanmar, Vietnam, and Thailand. Demographic Res. **15**(48), 1329–1360 (2015). http://www.demographic-research.org/special/15/48/

Fukunaga, R., Abe, Y., Nakagawa, Y., Koyama, A., Fujise, N., Ikeda, M.: Living alone is associated with depression among the elderly in a rural community in Japan. Psychogeriatrics **12**(3), 179–185 (2012). doi:10.1111/j.1479-8301.2012.00402.x

Huang, S.-L.Y., Cheng, Q.-Y., Wu, S.-C.: Care services for the elderly living alone-An example of home care services usement between elderly living alone and elderly live with others in Taiwan. In: paper presented at the Social Welfare Conference of Two Sides Across the

Taiwan Strait 2010 - An Aging Population and Pension Services, Taipei, Taiwan (2010). http://www.ccswf.org.tw/S_7100_detail.asp?booksn=11

Hung, Y.-S., Chen, K.-L.B., Yang, C.-T., Deng, G.-F.: Web usage mining for analysing elder self-care behavior patterns. Expert Syst. Appl. **40**(2), 775–783 (2013). doi:10.1016/j.eswa. 2012.08.037

Ortman, J.M., Velkoff, V.A., Hogan, H.: An Aging Nation: The Older Population in the United States - Population Estimates and Projections. U.S. Department of Commerce Economics and Statistics Administration (2014). https://www.census.gov/prod/2014pubs/p25-1140.pdf

Poudel-Tandukar, K., Nanri, A., Mizoue, T., Matsushita, Y., Takahashi, Y., Noda, M., Tsugane, S.: Differences in suicide risk according to living arrangements in Japanese men and women – the Japan public health center-based (JPHC) prospective study. J. Affect. Disord. **131**(1–3), 113–119 (2011). doi:10.1016/j.jad.2010.11.027

Kim, E.H.-W.: Public transfers and living alone among the elderly: a case study of Korea's new income support program. Demographic Res. **S15**(50), 1383–1408 (2015). http://www. demographic-research.org/special/15/50/

Klinenberg, E.: Going Solo: The Extraordinary Rise and Surprising Appeal of Living Alone. Azoth Books, Taipei (2013)

Lively. How it works (2015). http://www.mylively.com/

Cabinet Office of Japan: The Aging Society: Current Situation and Implementation Measures Japan: Economic and Social Research Institute, Government of Japan http://www8.cao.go.jp/ kourei/english/annualreport/2014/2014pdf_e.html

Paddock, C.: WHO: society needs to think differently about aging (2015). http://www. medicalnewstoday.com/articles/300459.php

Peruzzini, M., Germani, M.: Designing a user-centred ICT platform for active aging. In: 2014 IEEE/ASME 10th International Conference on Mechatronic and Embedded Systems and Applications (Mesa 2014), vol. 6, <Go to ISI>://WOS:000348664800102. IEEE (2014)

Shih, J.-H.: Regional differences in social characteristics among the elderly living alone in Taiwan. (Master), National Cheng Kung University. Airiti AiritiLibrary database (2010)

Shimokawara, E., Kaneko, T., Yamaguchi, T., Mizukawa, M., Matsuhira, N.: Estimation of basic activities of daily living using ZigBee 3D accelerometer sensor network. In: 2013 International Conference on Biometrics and Kansei Engineering (Icbake), pp. 251–256. IEEE (2013). doi:10.1109/icbake.2013.36

Shun-Hsiang, C.: Aging Society - Technology help living independently determines four kinds of business opportunities. chinatimes (2015). http://www.chinatimes.com/newspapers/20150826 000331-260207. Accessed 25 July 2015

Suryadevara, N.K., Mukhopadhyay, S.C.: Wireless sensor network based home monitoring system for wellness determination of elderly. IEEE Sens. J. **12**(6), 1965–1972 (2012). doi:10. 1109/Jsen.2011.2182341

Taiwan S.S.S.O. Service Science: Service System and Value Co-creation (1 ed.). Future Career, Taipei (2015)

Tanaka, M., Ishii, A., Yamano, E., Ogikubo, H., Okazaki, M., Kamimura, M., Watanabe, Y.: Effect of a human-type communication robot on cognitive function in elderly women living alone. Med. Sci. Monit. **18**(9), CR550–CR557 (2012). <Go to ISI>: // WOS:000308607100009

Ministry of Health and Welfare: The elderly condition survey report Taipei. Ministry of Health and Welfare, Taiwan (2013)

WHO. World report on ageing and health (2015). http://apps.who.int/iris/bitstream/10665/ 186463/1/9789240694811_eng.pdf?ua=1

Understanding the Critical Needs of Older People:
An Aging Perspective

Ying Jiang[1,2], Timothy Joseph Jachna[1(✉)], and Hua Dong[2]

[1] School of Design, The Hong Kong Polytechnic University, Hong Kong, China
my.jiang@connect.polyu.hk, timothy.joseph.jachna@polyu.edu.hk
[2] College of Architecture and Urban Planning, Tongji University, Shanghai, China
donghua@tongji.edu.cn

Abstract. Much of the existing research on older people's needs is based upon a popular understanding that older people are defined by age strata. However, from the perspective of the multidimensional meaning of aging, people's age is a state that represents a process of change. It cannot be simply defined in years. This concept motivates us to explore the needs of older people from the perspective of aging. This study aims first, to provide a literature review on different aspects of aging in order to better understand the aging process. Second, having considered aging, a critical needs model was proposed. As a result, a design suggestion was made in order for designers to focus their attention on helping people find the meaning of life as a first principle.

Keywords: Critical needs · Aging · Older people · Design

1 Introduction

Understanding the genuine needs of older people is an integral part of designing for older adults and is crucial to the success of any such design. Designing for older people can be understood as designing for older people's needs.

Much of the existing research within design regards the needs of older people based on a popular understanding that older people are defined by age strata[1] [1, 2]. The ages of 60 or 65 years are often used to define the age at which people might be considered as old [4]. However, according to the study of gerontology[2], people's age cannot be simply defined in years. Although people usually use chronology (years) as a metric of age, this is not a good predictor of functional status in biological, psychological and social processes [7]. Age is not a number; it is a state that represents multiple aging processes including chronological aging, biological aging, psychological aging and social aging. In some sense, designing for older people means to design for people who

---

[1] According to the life course dimension, age strata may be defined by chronological age or by stages in the life cycle (e.g. infancy, childhood, adolescence, early adulthood, etc.) [3].
[2] In 1903, Elie Metchnikoff was the first person to use the term "gerontology" [5]. The term gerontology is defined in the Concise Oxford Dictionary as 'the scientific study of old age and the process of aging, and of old people's special problems' [6].

© Springer International Publishing Switzerland 2016
J. Zhou and G. Salvendy (Eds.): ITAP 2016, Part I, LNCS 9754, pp. 32–41, 2016.
DOI: 10.1007/978-3-319-39943-0_4

are experiencing aging processes. Therefore, the needs of older people should be identified and must then be placed in the context of these aging processes.

Dealing with the issue of older people's needs from the perspective of aging is not only related to surviving but also to death. As a result of the irreversible aging process, death is the final event for older people. From this perspective, some critical needs may emerge from the common needs. These 'critical needs' can be seen as making older people's lives meaningful and alleviating fear of death.

This paper aims at exploring design for the critical needs of older people based on gerontology studies. Firstly, understanding aging is important. It is a multidimensional concept consisting of within-person aging and between-person aging. Secondly, identifying the needs of older people should be based upon the meanings of aging. A critical needs model is proposed. As a result, a design proposition is developed. It must be emphasized that designers do not need exhaustive knowledge of gerontology. They need to understand the consequences of aging rather than the causes of aging so as to help them understand what to focus on.

2   Aging: A Process of Change

Aging is a continuous and process of change that begins the day we are born and only ends when we die [8]. We can recognize aging as a demonstration of time and an expression of the fundamental reality of change. All the changes follow the flow of time. By studying time and the process of change, we can understand the real meaning of aging.

2.1   Time

To a great extent, time as chronometric time is indicated by clocks and calendars [9], which is measured in seconds, minutes, hours, days, weeks, months, years, etc. Time as a general tool can represent the duration of a process or locate in time an event like the birth of a baby, a future appointment, or the death of a person [10]. But our personal estimates of time tend to be unreliable because in certain situations they are relative to our physical states or emotional attitudes [11].

Time is an irreversible vector consisting of past, present and future as a whole. The past and the future are represented, but the present can only be known as past. People cannot capture the present, as it is passing in every second. One cannot go back and repeat the past. Therefore, aging is an irreversible process that we are experiencing in every moment.

2.2   A Process of Change

Time is infinite, but the process of aging is finite. Birth is where the aging process begins and death is the final event.

Aging can be defined as a process of change over time. To speak of our aging is also to speak of the process of change. Changing is constituted in 'becoming from' one state and 'becoming to' another. The material world is always in a state of change that never ceases. The only thing constant is change itself as Heraclitus held. On biological, psychological, and sociological levels, aging involves a process of continuing differentiation [12]. In other words, as long as we are alive, we are all in a process of change, which has an effect on our bodily, mental and emotional functioning, and social interactions.

Under the guidance of these concepts, designing for older people can be viewed as designing for people experiencing the changing process in different aspects. Actually all people are experiencing this process. Older people are those who are in a particular period within this process, but none of us are outside the process. This also coined the concept of "designing for our future selves" [13].

3   The Multidimensional Meanings of Aging

Aging is a complex process of change that involves many different factors. Historically, the concept of 'aging' refers to change resulting from some combination of logical, psychological, and social mechanisms [14]. The 'life-span developmental' perspective is a somewhat broader framework [15, 16], as it considers 'aging' to begin at birth and conceptualizes human development as multidimensional and multidirectional processes of growth involving both gains and losses [14]. Aging is often identified simply as "age-related change" [17, 18].

Based on the study of gerontology, two dimensions of ageing in four distinct processes are identified: the within-person aging dimension and the between-person aging dimension. 'Within-person aging' refers to the age-related changing process in a person, including chronological aging, biological aging and personality development. 'Between-person aging' indicates people's various roles, which are established by interacting with other people in different stages of the lifecycle.

3.1   Within-Person Aging

3.1.1   Chronological Aging

Chronological aging is the definition of aging on the basis of a person's years from birth [3]. Its development is parallel with the progression of time.

Chronological age or calendar age is a measure of an individual's age based on the calendar date on which he or she was born.

3.1.2   Biological Aging

Biological aging (or physiological aging) can be defined as the normal process of changes in the body and its components over time. By and large, most functions begin to decline linearly after reaching peak performance in the third decade of life [19]. The changes in different biological abilities occur at varied rates and degrees.

However, the speed of the decline is largely determined by factors related to one's adult life style – such as smoking, alcohol consumption and diet; and the environment where one lives [20]. Maintaining functional capacity is the concept throughout the life course (Fig. 1).

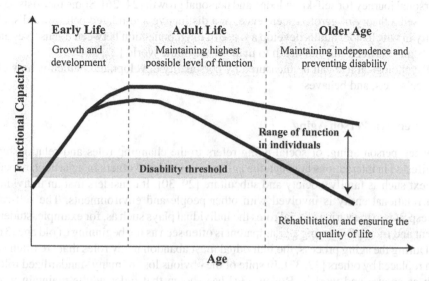

Fig. 1. Maintaining functional capacity over the life course (Source: Kalache and Kickbusch [21]).

Biological age (or physiological age) shows how your body is developing or breaking down compared to the average.

3.1.3 Psychological Aging

Psychological aging mainly means that the aging process influences cognitive abilities and personality. Cognition (to think) refers to mental process such as intelligence, learning and memory. The ways that we all perceive, recall, reason, make decisions, solve problems, and make sense of the world around us are all cognitive processes [22]. Personality can be defined as a unique pattern of innate and learned behaviors, thoughts and emotions that influence how each person responds and interacts with the environment [3].

Aging does not affect all people's psychological functions in the same way. Hooyman and Kiyak [3] provided considerable evidence that normal aging does not result in significant declines of cognitive functioning. Although some decline in cognitive ability occurs with aging, these symptoms are not a normal part of aging [23]. Therefore, this article mainly focuses upon studying personality development as a normal part of aging, which is a positive ego-development process.

Personality development is considered as a process of personal growth and a self-transformative journey, moving to maturation and gaining wisdom. It is also an irreversible process such that the individual cannot repeat a previous developmental stage. Erik Erickson and Carl Jung examined the individual's confrontation with death in the last stage of life. Jung suggested that the aging person must find meaning in inner exploration and in an afterlife [3].

In recently years, scholars have built upon the work of Erikson and Jung to expand the definition of spirituality more broadly than religious belief [7]. Spirituality refers to a personal journey for self-knowledge and personal growth [24–26]. Some theorists have proposed a theory of gerotranscendence, or a distinctive age-related path toward spirituality in which older adults develop a sense of interconnection between themselves and others and between life and death to make sense of the world [27, 28].

Psychological age can be measured by personality development, which is how old one feels, acts, and behaves.

3.2   Between-Person Aging

Between-person aging, or social aging refers to the changing roles and relationships manifested in interactions between the aging individual and others in a particular social context such as family, society and subculture [29, 30]. It considers that an individual as a relational entity is involved with other people and environments. The self-role corresponds to the various social roles the individual plays such as, for example, student, parent and friend. Becoming a grandparent is often seen as the beginning of old age [31].

During the aging process, the individual must abandon many roles that are often not then replaced by others [32, 33]. In spite of the obvious loss of many standardized roles, such as spouse and worker, Rosow [34] has shown that older adults maintain more informal roles [34].

An individual's social roles are embedded in personal networks. A personal network is generally defined as all persons (network members) with whom a focal individual has a direct relationship [35]. The network used in gerontology focuses on the older adult's ties to society through participation in network and social roles [36]. Older people's networks reflect a transition from the roles they held earlier in life. From this viewpoint, between-person aging or social aging suggests a process of change in a personal network.

Sociology defines age by one's role in society [8]. In other words, social age also refers to an individual's role in her or his networks.

3.3   Key Insights Related to Aging and Age

Based on an understanding of the four types of aging processes presented, the following insights related to aging and age are revealed:

3.3.1   Insights Related to Aging
- Understanding the meaning of aging requires the consideration of the four processes simultaneously. It seems as if there are four 'clocks' all running at a different pace, measuring the individual's four aging processes. All of these processes are interconnected, and each affects the others.
- The process of growing old is unique to each individual [37]. There is no single and uniform way in which adults grow old [38].
- Under the concept of within-person aging, biological aging and personality development tend to have an opposite relationship with one another. However, they do

still share some interdependency. Biological aging is considered as a gradual declining and an inevitable process that begins in early adulthood. The process is universal, deleterious and progressive [3]. Age-related change in appearance and physical functioning is most highly correlated with chronological age. Conversely, psychological aging is not necessarily a process of decline over time. It should be a positive process, especially taking into account people's personality development.

- In addition, an individual's biological aging and personality development do not progress at the same rate. For example, a person can have a psychological age that exceeds his or her biological age if he or she has a mature personality.
- Although people can slow down the progress of biological aging, the overall trend is an irreversible decline that cannot be changed. However, personality development can be controlled by people's intentions and actions.
- Biological aging can have an effect on social aging. For example, a decline in biological functions such as hearing impairment can impose restrictions upon older people's ability to engage in interaction with others.
- Positive psychological changes have effects on physical health [39] and interpersonal relationships including quality of marital relationships and friendship relationships [40].
- Under the concept of between-person aging, social aging is regarded as a process of change in personal networks. The personal networks of individuals reflect their social opportunities and personal choices to maintain a specific set of relationships with relatives, neighbours, friends, acquaintances, and so on [41, 42]. Social aging can be potentially influenced by individuals to meet their needs.

3.3.2   Insights Related to Age

- The meaning of age includes four dimensions consisting of chronological age, biological age, psychological age and social age. Chronological age is easy to measure in years, but others are difficult to evaluate. A person's age cannot be simply calculated in years. Age is not a number; it is a state representing four aging processes.
- Each individual has a unique aging process [37, 38]. If age is a state representing one's position in these various aging processes, each person can be said to have a distinctive age such that there is no absolute equivalent between the ages of any two people.
- Although people usually use chronology (years) as a metric of age, it is not a good predictor of functional status in biological, psychological and social processes [7]. This means that biological age, psychological age and social age cannot be clearly defined by chronological age. For example, we may know a 70-year-old person has a younger appearance and a good physical condition very much like a 60-years-old. For another example, a 30-year-old may have the facial features of a 40-year-old, yet behave and dress more like a 20-year-old. Some may perceive this person to be "old" for his or her age, while others may perceive the person to be "immature" [30]. Moreover, social age is not the same as chronological age. For instance, the passage into the role of being grandparents may occur at age 50 or age 70, or never.

- Biological age is not necessarily equal to psychological age and social age. For example, we may remark that a person acts older (or younger) than his or her biological age. For another example, different norms, roles and expectations for people of different biological ages exist in different societies and cultures.

4 Designing for Critical Needs

4.1 Critical Needs of Older People

Critical needs can be distinguished from common needs by reviewing the multidimensional meaning of aging. Critical needs and common needs are defined using two different perspectives; one in which age is understood to be a process and, conversely, another in which age is seen as a number. Common needs are proposed on the basis of surviving and living. The better life quality a person wants to achieve, the more needs they have. But critical needs are identified from the perspective of aging processes. Critical needs help people to face death with the knowledge that it is part of aging.

The individual's psychological state, especially personality development, is considered to be the most critical aspect and is what motivates and guides older people in living a meaningful life. It helps people to experience aging and face death calmly by achieving self-realization and to understand the meaning of life. It also influences the individual's biological condition and social relationships. For example, positive psychological states would help people to keep healthy and promote interpersonal relationships. On the contrary, psychological and social stresses can cause a change in nutrition and a decline in health; or the changing deep-sleep patterns of the elderly may be due to depression rather than physical changes [43, 44].

Maintaining biological condition is another critical concern. Although the ultimate result of the biological aging process is a progressive loss of function, age-related biological changes can be slowed down. As the severity of age-related changes in the body can be affected by disease, injury, exercise, nutrition, smoking, environmental pollution, and other lifestyle factors [45], avoiding some bad habits and improving one's living environment could slow down the aging process or prevent the detrimental effects of aging. For example, the natural decline in cardiac function can be accelerated by smoking, leaving the individual with a functional capacity level lower than what would normally be expected for his or her age [20].

Personal networks are regarded as sources of support, contributing to older people's functioning and wellbeing [35]. If we acknowledge that psychological need is the most critical concern for people who are growing old, then social interaction can be viewed as a kind of support for people to develop their personality.

Most people have these three interdependent needs as long-term requirements concurrently. The arrangement of these needs can be represented as a structure of concentric circles (as shown in Fig. 2). It is not in a hierarchical structure such that a lower basic need is submerged and a new and higher need emerges as postulated by western psychologists such as Maslow. Rather, this model presents that three critical needs are simultaneously demanded and that the psychological needs should be the highest priority for a person's attention.

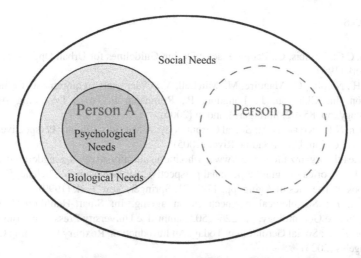

Fig. 2.   A critical needs model of older people

4.2   A Suggestion for Design

This model of critical needs suggests a strategy for helping to meet older people's requirements. Design for older people can be understood in terms of design for their critical needs including biological need, psychological need and social need. The purpose of design is not only to help older people adjust to aging, but also to assist them in finding meaning in life. Designers should seek to design in a way so as to inspire older people to achieve self-realization. It also can help people maintain their physical ability and promote harmonious relationships with others.

If designers focus on older people's chronological aging and biological aging as processes of decline, they will emphasize on improving the physical environment, to make it inclusive and cater for different disabilities. If designers acknowledge the primary importance of psychological aging among the different dimensions of the aging process, they will try to support older people's personality development which may bring these older people real wellbeing and happiness.

5   Conclusions

The main aim of this study is to identify the critical needs of older people. These critical needs are viewed as the most important requirements for older people facing death as part of aging. It suggests that design should help older people in finding the meaning of life as its main priority.

This study identifies the need for a design pattern related to the critical needs of older people, but there is a need for further research in this area, in order to define such a pattern in detail. Further studies are required to articulate these needs in a way that could inform design, and future empirical research is needed to guide such design practice.

References

1. Marcus, C.C., Francis, C.: People Places: Design Guidelines for Urban Open Space. Wiley, New York (1997)
2. Boyle, H., Nicolle, C., Maguire, M., Mitchell, V.: Older users' requirements for interactive television. In: Clarkson, J., Langdon, P., Robinson, P. (eds.) Designing Accessible Technology, pp. 85–92. Springer, London (2006)
3. Hooyman, N.R., Kiyak, H.A.: Social Gerontology: A Multidisciplinary Perspective, 7th edn. Pearson education, Upper Saddle River (2005)
4. World Health Organization. http://www.who.int/healthinfo/survey/ageingdefnolder/en/
5. Birren, J.: Theories of aging: a personal perspective. In: Bengtson, V., Schaie, K.W. (eds.) Handbook of Theories of Aging, pp. 459–471. Springer, New York (1999)
6. Davidson, K.: Sociological perspectives on ageing. In: Stuart-Hamilton, I. (ed.) An Introduction to Gerontology, pp. 226–250. Cambridge University Press, Cambridge (2011)
7. Markson, E.W.: Social Gerontology Today: An Introduction. Roxbury Publishing Company, Los Angeles (2003)
8. Woodrow, P.: What is ageing? In: Woodrow, P. (ed.) Ageing: Issues for Physical, Psychological and Social Health, pp. 1–11. Whurr Publishers, London (2002)
9. Baars, J.: Aging and the Art of Living. The Johns Hopikins University Press, Baltimore (2012)
10. Baars, J.: Introduction: chronological time and chronological age – problems of temporal diversity. In: Baars, J., Visser, H. (eds.) Aging and Time: Multidisciplinary Perspectives, pp. 1–14. Baywood, Amityville (2007)
11. McFadden, S.H., Atchley, R.C.: Aging and the Meaning of Time: A Multidisciplinary Exploration. Springer, Heidelberg (2001)
12. Beattie, W.M.: The relevance of communication for professionals involved with the elderly. In: Oyer, H.J., Oyer, E.J. (eds.) Aging and Communication. Baltimore Press, University Park (1976)
13. Coleman, R.: Designing for Our Future Selves. Royal College of Art, London (1993)
14. Alwin, D.F.: Social structure, cognition, and ageing. In: Dannefer, D., Phillipson, C. (eds.) The Sage Handbook of Social Gerontology, pp. 265–279. SAGE Publication, London (2010)
15. Baltes, P.B.: Theoretical propositions of life-span developmental psychology: on the dynamics between growth and decline. Dev. Psychol. 23, 611–626 (1987)
16. Featherman, D.L.: Life-span perspectives in social science research. In: Baltes, P.B., Brim Jr, O.G. (eds.) Life-Span Development and Behaviour, vol. 5, pp. 1–57. Academic Press, New York (1983)
17. Bengtson, V.L., Schaie, K.W. (eds.): Handbook of Theories of Aging. Springer, New York (1999)
18. Hofer, S.M., Alwin, D.F. (eds.): Handbook of Cognitive Aging: Interdisciplinary Perspectives. Sage, Thousand Oaks (2008)
19. Strehler, B.L.: Time, Cells, and Aging. Demetriades Brothers, Larnaca (1999)
20. Kalache, A., Barreto, S.M., Keller, I.: Global ageing: the demographic revolution in all cultures and societies. In: Johnson, M.L. (ed.) The Cambridge Handbook of Age and Ageing, pp. 30–46. Cambridge University Press, Cambridge (2005)
21. Kalache, A., Kickbusch, I.: A global strategy for healthy ageing. World Health 4(1), 4–5 (1997)
22. Smith, A.D.: Cognitive processes. In: Maddox, G.L., Atchley, R.C., Evans, J.G., et al. (eds.) Encyclopedia of Aging, 2nd edn, pp. 186–188. Springer, New York (1995)
23. Yoost, B.L., Crawford, L.R.: Fundamentals of Nursing: Active Learning for Collaborative Practice. Elsevier, Philadelphia (2016)

24. Wink, P.: Addressing end-of-life issues: spirituality and inner life. Generations **23**(1), 75–80 (1999)
25. Zinnbauer, B.J., Pargement, K.I., Cole, B., Rye, M.S., et al.: Religious and spirituality: unfuzzying the fuzzy. J. Sci. Stud. Relig. **36**(4), 549–564 (1997)
26. Chaffers, J.: Spirituality—the missing "i" in mass product (i) on: or why "mass quality" need not be an oxymoron. In: Conference Proceedings of the Association of Collegiate Schools of Architecture European Conference: The Urban Scene and the History of the Future, London (1994)
27. Tornstam, L.: Late-life transcendence: a new developmental perspective on ageing. In: Thomas, L.E., Eisenhandler, S. (eds.) Religion, Belief, and Spirituality in Later Life, pp. 178–202. Springer, New York (1999)
28. Fowler, J.W.: Stages of Faith Development. HarperCollins, New York (1981)
29. Bigby, C.: Ageing with a Lifelong Disability: A Guide to Practice, Program and Policy Issues for Human Services Professionals. Jessica Kingsley Publishers, London (2004)
30. McPherson, B.D.: Aging as a Social Process: An Introduction to Individual and Population Aging. Harcourt Brace & Company Canada, Toronto (1998)
31. Newton, N.J., Stewart, A.J.: Personality development in adulthood. In: Whitbourne, S.K., Sliwinski, M.J. (eds.) The Wiley-Blackwell Handbook of Adulthood and Aging. Blackwell Publishing, New York (2012)
32. Phillips, B.S.: A role theory approach to adjustment in old age. Am. Sociol. Rev. **22**, 212–217 (1957)
33. Riley, M.W., Foner, A., Hess, B., Toby, M.L.: Socialization for the middle and later years. In: Goslin, D. (ed.) Handbook of Socialization: Theory and Research. Rand McNally, Chicago (1969)
34. Rosow, I.: Status and role change through the life span. In: Binstock, R.H., Shanas, E. (eds.) Handbook of Aging and the Social Sciences. Van Nostrand Reinhold, New York (1976)
35. Van Tilburg, T.G., Thomese, F.: Societal dynamics in personal networks. In: Dannefer, D., Phillipson, C. (eds.) The Sage Handbook of Social Gerontology, pp. 215–225. SAGE Publication, London (2010)
36. Rosow, I.: Social Integration of the Aged. Free Press, New York (1967)
37. Smith, L., Gestorf, D.: Ageing differently: potential and limits. In: Daatland, S.O., Biggs, S. (eds.) Ageing and Diversity: Multiple Pathways and Cultural Migrations, pp. 13–28. Policy Press, Bristol (2004)
38. Tamir, L.M.: Communication and the Aging Process: Interaction Throughout the Life Cycle. Pergamon Press, New York (1979)
39. Bower, J.E., Low, C.A., Moskowitz, J.T., Sepah, S., Epel, E.: Benefit finding and physical health: positive psychological changes an enhanced allostasis. Soc. Pers. Psychol. Compass **2**, 223–244 (2008)
40. Lopez, S.J., Snyder, C.R.: The Oxford Handbook of Positive Psychology. Oxford University Press, Oxford (2009)
41. Adams, R.G., Allan, G.: Placing Friendship in Context. Cambridge University Press, Cambridge (1998)
42. Hall, A., Wellman, B.: Social networks and social support. In: Cohen, S., Syme, S.L. (eds.) Social Support and Health, pp. 23–41. Academic Press, Orlando (1985)
43. Looft, W.R.: Egocentrism and social interaction across the life span. Psychol. Bull. **78**, 73–92 (1972)
44. Marsh, G.R., Thompson, L.W.: Psychophysiology of aging. In: Birren, J.E., Schaie, K.W. (eds.) Handbook of the Psychology of Aging. Van Nostrand Reinhold, New York (1977)
45. Aiken, L.R.: Human Development in Adulthood. Kluwer Academic Publishers, New York (2002)

Designing Tablet Computers for the Elderly
A User-Centered Design Approach

Nicole Jochems[✉]

University of Lübeck, IMIS, Lubeck, Germany
jochems@imis.uni-luebeck.de

Abstract. The fast aging of many western and eastern societies and their increasing reliance on information technology create a compelling need to reconsider older users' interactions with computers. Changes in perceptual and motor skill capabilities that often accompany the aging process bring important implications for the design of information and communication technologies. This paper summarizes different methods integrated into a user-centred design approach to develop design concepts for a tablet computer, focussing on the needs and wishes of the elderly. Therefore, current tablet computers were compared respective their applicability und usability. Furthermore, based on the results of a questionnaire, elevating the needs of the user group two design concepts were developed and evaluated.

Keywords: Demographic change · Aging computer users · Tablet computers · User centered design

1 Introduction

Our society is currently characterized by two major trends: The demographic change and the mechanization and automation of processes in the working environment as well as in the private sector. The usage of computers often represents a barrier for older users due to changes of the perceptual, cognitive and psychomotor system (Czaja 1997; Hawthorn 2000) as well as their attitude towards new interaction technologies (Brickfiled 1984). This leads to a digital divide between older and younger users (Selwyn 2002). However, the rapid development in the mobile sector could lead to significant improvements in the usage for older users and reduce the digital divide. The users require less implicit knowledge of computers and direct input with a touch sensitive screen simplifies the interaction with the system (Luczak et al. 2011; Jochems et al. 2010; Caprani et al. 2012; Stößel et al. 2010). Nevertheless, there is a conflict for producers in the mobile sector between the intuitiveness of usage and exploiting technical possibilities. The features of the terminals increase with the rapid growth of the mobile market at the expenses of easy usage especially for elderly users. Is it necessary to develop mobile systems especially for elderly users because of these age-related changes and, if so, how should they look like?

J. Zhou and G. Salvendy (Eds.): ITAP 2016, Part I, LNCS 9754, pp. 42–51, 2016.
DOI: 10.1007/978-3-319-39943-0_5

1.1   State of the Art

The first tablet computers, coming into market in the 1990s, were developed to support tasks like managing contacts or appointments as well as administrative tasks. After the rollout of the first tablet from Apple, the so called iPad, a rapid distribution of tablet computer started. Especially the touch-sensitive display and the corresponding inter-action with gestures were ground-breaking technological innovations. By now there are a multitude of tablet computers of diverse providers, based on different software like Android, iOS or Microsoft Phone.

Considering the frequency of use of the elderly (65 plus), effective 10 % of this group use up-to-date tablet computers (BITKOM 2015). Looking at products designed specific for this user group, currently no tablet exits on the European market. There are just a few possibilities to adapt current systems, regarding luminance or font size. Therefore, the users have to know about these possibilities and also need the ability to execute the adaptation. First applications (for example Big Buttons, Keyboard Deluxe, BigDialer and mElderly) for mobile systems could be found considering elderly users. However, these applications are not integrated into an overall concept and the main focus is as well just the adaption of the font size.

In a time when the aging population have become global trends, we cannot afford to exclude an increasing number of people by design, for ethical *and* financial reasons.

2   Method

For the development of a tablet computer especially focussing on the elderly a user-centered design (UCD) approach was chosen (DIN EN ISO 9241-210:2010 2011). Therefore, different methods and analysing steps were combined. In Fig. 1 the different aspects and methods as part of the UCD process are visualized.

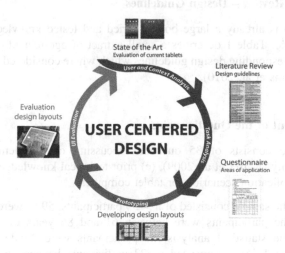

Fig. 1. User-centered design process

The approach consists of the following parts (1) evaluation of current tablet computers, (2) literature review regarding design aspects focusing the elderly, (3) questionnaire to identify suitable areas of application, (4) developing design concepts and (5) evaluating the developed concepts.

In a first step current tablet computers were compared and evaluated regarding their usability, especially focusing on the needs of elderly computer users. In a next step general age specific design guidelines as well as results of own user studies (see Schlick et al. 2013) were analysed regarding their fitting for the age-specific design of mobile systems, especially tablet computers. In order to understand the needs and wishes of the elderly computer users a questionnaire with 35 items was developed. Afterwards based on the results of the literature review as well as the questionnaire two different concepts were designed and evaluated.

2.1 Evaluation of Current Tablet Computers

Primarily two of the most commonly used tablet computers (Samsung Galaxy Tab with Android software and Apple iPad with iOS) were compared respective their usability for elderly computer users. Therefore, the subjects have to work with the two systems, executing typical tasks like editing or sending emails. Thereby suggestions, ideas and problems while working with the systems were collected with the thinking aloud method (Boren and Ramey 2000). Afterwards the subjects rated the overall performance of both systems on a scale from 1 = excellent to 6 = insufficient.

Test Subjects. The sample consisted of nine subjects between 61 and 75 years (M = 69.8, SD = 5.2). Their previous technical knowledge was rated by the subjects on a scale from 1 to 6 with 3 (SD = 1.1).

2.2 Literature Review – Design Guidelines

Fortunately, there is already a large body of tried and tested knowledge and design principles available. Table 1 describes a small extract of age-related changes of performance and corresponding design guidelines which where considered. For the overall results (see Jochems et al. 2010).

2.3 Development of the Questionnaire

The questionnaire consists of 35 questions focussing on (a) demographic data, (b) technical affinity (Karrer et al. 2009), (c) prior technical knowledge, (d) frequency of use and (e) application scenarios for tablet computers.

Test Subjects. The sample consisted of n = 54 participants. 59 % were female and 41 % were male. The participants were between 61 and 86 years of age (M = 71.2, SD = 5.5). For the statistical analysis the participants were divided into two age groups. Age group I (AGI) consisted of 22 participants between 61 and 68 years

Table 1. Age-related changes and corresponding HCI guideline

Age-related changes	Corresponding HCI guidelines
Decrease accommodation ability	Increase duration of presenting objects
Degradation depth perception	Simple two-dimensional consistent visualization
Reduction visual acuity	Adaption of font size
Limitation color perception	High-contract colors
Reduction contrast sensitivity	Maximize contrast between font and background
Problem to record information in memory	Highlighting of important information, for example arrangements in groups
Reduction of memory span to 5,5 items	Elimination of nonrelevant information, highlighting important information
Loss of information (working memory) especially complex information	Reduce complex visualizations, improve recognition by uniform design
Reduction of spatial sense	Assistance for spatial orientation like directory of available information, adaption of the menu, assistance to navigate for example overview map
Problems learning new skills regarding attended time, number of mistakes, number of repetition and so on	Reduce complexity of required skills and present suitable training material
Reduction of fine motor skills	Alternative input devices, large buttons, adaption of the menu structure

(M = 65.6, SD = 1.9). Age group II (AGII) consisted of 31 participants between 71 and 86 years (M = 75.1, SD = 3.3).

In terms of educational level 27.5 % of the subjects had certificate of secondary education, 35 % general certificate of secondary education, 7.5 % advanced technical college entrance qualification and 30 % final secondary-school examinations. Regarding their current working situation 85.2 % were pensioners while 14.8 % are still employed.

2.4   Development of Different Design Concepts

Based on the findings thus obtained, two different interface layouts were designed and mock-ups were implemented. Both mock-ups contain the essential features based on the results of the questionnaire. The main differences are the visual illustration of the structure (categories or applications with corresponding icons) and the implementation of individual functions as well as interaction concepts. Concept 1 is based on an interaction concept similar to tablet computers while concept 2 is based on interaction concepts of personal computers.

2.5   Evaluation of the Design Concepts

The evaluation was conducted in two steps. In a first step the systems were introduced to a possible user group during a senior event for analysing advantages and disadvantages of the two concepts. Afterwards the subjects rated the overall impression of the two concepts on a scale from 1 = excellent to 6 = insufficient.

In the second step a task-based evaluation inside a usability lab was executed. The subjects have to work with the application photo gallery (see Fig. 4). Therefore, typically tasks like searching and editing of photos have to be performed.

Test Subjects. In the first evaluation step 12 subjects (60 plus) filled in the questionnaire and rated the two layouts. In the second step nine subjects between 61 and 75 years of age (M = 69.8, SD = 4.83) took part in the usability study.

3   Results

3.1   Evaluation of Current Tablet Computers

Based on the thinking aloud method many usability problems (for this specific user group) appeared. Neither of the subjects had the ability to solve the tasks unassisted. Major functions were not found, buttons und functions misinterpreted and problems with the touch-sensitive screen appeared. In Fig. 2 (right) the main aspects are summarized. Overall four of the subjects preferred the android tablet because of its simple symbols and its layout, four subjects preferred the iOS systems because of its similarity to well-known systems and one subject preferred either of them.

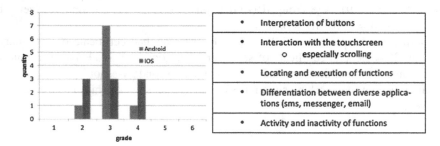

Fig. 2. Results of the evaluation, total score of the two system (left), usability problems (right) (Color figure online)

3.2   Questionnaire

Overall 54 subjects filled in the questionnaire. Focussing on the use of information and communication technologies especially the use of mobile technologies, 17 subjects use a smartphone while nine persons are daily users and seven subjects didn't even know it. Regarding tablet computers 11 subjects use it, six subjects are daily users and seven didn't know this technology.

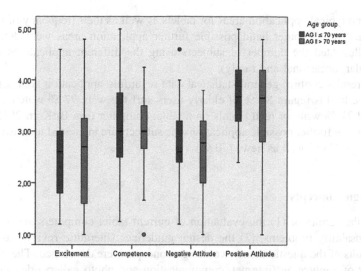

Fig. 3. TA subscales regarding age group (Color figure online)

Considering the technical affinity (TA, see Karrer et al. 2009) among the elderly, no significant correlation between age and TA could be found. Figure 3 visualised trends between age group and the TA subscales (excitement, competence, negative attitude and positive attitude).

Concerning the correlation between ICT use and technical affinity, significant positive correlations could be found between the use of smartphones and TA (r = .48). Interestingly there are no significant correlations between the use of a tablet computer and technical affinity.

Another important goal of the questionnaire was the investigation of suitable application areas for the development of an age-specific tablet computer. Therefore, on

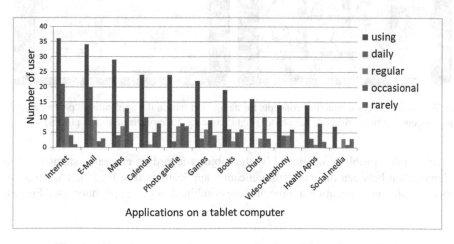

Fig. 4. Using frequency of common applications (Color figure online)

the one hand typical application areas for tablets as well as their frequency of use were analysed and on the other hand possible further application areas were determined. Figure 4 illustrated the number of subjects using the different applications (overall, daily, regular, occasional and rarely).

These results confirm general statistical data regarding application areas of elderly tablet users. In this regard 84 % of elderly users surf the web, 77 % watch videos or photos and 77 % write or read emails on a tablet computer (see BitKom 2015).

Looking for further possible applications the subjects are interested in music (57 %), gardening (44 %) as well as news (70 %).

3.3   Design Concepts

Based on the results of (1) the evaluation of current tablet computers and the corresponding usability problems, (2) the design guidelines (literature review) as well as (3) the results of the questionnaire two design concepts were developed. Therefore, the main areas of application (internet, communication and photo gallery) desired by the subjects, were implemented. In the following some main aspects of the two concepts are described. One aspect that is implemented similarly for both concepts is the possibility of adaption respective luminance and font size. The possibility of adaption of these dimensions is the first step when working with the tablet.

One aspect that differentiated between the two concepts is the interaction with the touch-sensitive display. In the first concept the user could thump though the data while in the second one they have to scroll (see Fig. 5).

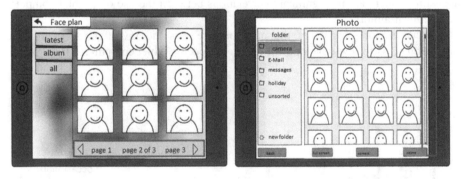

Fig. 5. Two different interaction concepts for navigation within the application "photo gallery", left: concept 1 (thumb through the photos) right: concept 2 (scroll through the photos)

One further problem mentioned by the subjects regarding current systems was the differentiation between diverse communication applications (see Fig. 2). Therefore, in concept 1 all communication approaches are combined in one application (see Fig. 6).

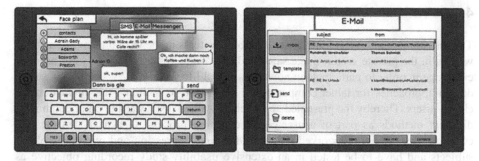

Fig. 6. Two different concepts for communication. Left: concept 1 integrated different communication applications, right: concept 2 based on a classical separated design

3.4   Evaluation of the Design Concepts

First the two concepts were evaluated by 12 subjects during a senior event. The overall evaluation of both concepts is described in Fig. 7. To this effect the two concepts were valuated approximately equal with a tendency for concept 2. If the subjects have to select one of the two concepts 50 % preferred concept 2 because of its clearly arranged design, whereas only 17 % preferred concept 1. Some positive and negative aspects as well as improvements mentioned by the subjects are summarized in Fig. 7.

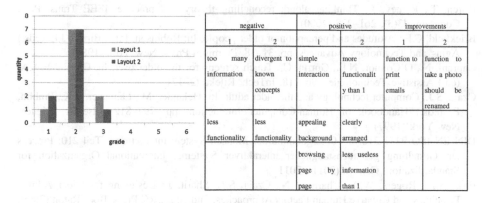

negative		positive		improvements	
1	2	1	2	1	2
too many information	divergent to known concepts	simple interaction	more functionality than 1	function to print emails	function to take a photo should be renamed
less functionality	less functionality	appealing background	clearly arranged		
		browsing page by page	less useless information than 1		

Fig. 7. First evaluation results for both concepts (Color figure online).

The next evaluation step was a task-based usability study. Following first impressions of the subjects based on the differences between the both concepts are summarized:

- Scrolling is preferred compared to browsing page by page
- Stepwise presentation and zooming of photos is favoured
- Pop-up windows are desired instead of inconspicuous windows
- Navigation in full screen is preferred

4 Discussion

The distribution and the common use of mobile systems in the working environment as well as in the private sector, make safe handling of the systems necessary for users of every age in order to participate in nowadays social life. Within the scope of this study, design approaches for tablet computers are developed to facilitate the interaction for elderly users. Thereby the presented approach described just a starting point combining different methods as part of a user centered design process. In a next step the two concepts have to be overworked regarding the first impression and references of the subjects and have to be tested in an extensive usability study recording objective as well as subjective data. The overall goal should be the transformation of the results into general design guidelines for information and communication systems designed for elderly users.

Acknowledgements. The questionnaire and aspects of the layouts were development as part of a student work. Thanks to Daniel Grosche, Adrian Göbbels, Marco Schwandt and Florian Thaeter as well as Prof. Martin Leucker.

References

Bitkom 2015: Zukunft der Consumer Electronics-2015

Boren, T., Ramey, J.: Thinking aloud: reconciling theory and practice. IEEE Trans. Prof. Commun. **43**(3), 261–278 (2000)

Brickfield, C.F.: Attitudes and perception of older people. In: Robinson, P.K., Birren, J.E. (eds.) Aging and Technology Advances, pp. 31–38. Premium Press, New York (1984)

Caprani, N., O'Connor, N.E., Gurrin, C.: Touch screens for the older user. In: Cheein, F.A.A. (ed.) Assistive Technologies, 96–118. InTech, Rijeka (2012)

Czaja, S.J.: Computer technology and the older adult. In: Helander, M., Landauer, T.K., Prabhu, P. (eds.) Handbook of Human-Computer Interaction, pp. 797–812. Elsevier Science, New York (1997)

DIN EN ISO 9241-210: 2010: Ergonomie der Mensch-System-Interaktion – Teil 210: Prozess zur Gestaltung gebrauchstauglicher interaktiver Systeme. International Organization for Standardization, Geneva (2011). 2011

Fisk, A.D., Rogers, W.A., Charness, N., Czaja, S.J., Sharit, J.: Designing for Older Adults: Principles and Creative Human Factors Approaches, 2nd edn. CRC Press, Boca Raton (2009)

Hawthorn, D.: Possible implications of aging for interface designers. Interact. Comput. **12**, 507–528 (2000)

Jochems, N.: Altersdifferenzierte Gestaltung der Mensch-Rechner-Interaktion am Beispiel von Projektmanagementaufgaben. Dissertation RWTH Aachen, Shaker Verlag (2010)

Karrer, K., Glaser, C., Clemens, C., Bruder, C.: Technikaffinität erfassen – der Fragebogen TA-EG (Measure affinity to technology –the questionnaire TA-EG). In: Lichtenstein, A., Stößel, C., Clemens, C. (eds.) Der Mensch im Mittelpunkt technischer Systeme 8. Berliner Werkstatt Mensch-Maschine-Systeme 7. bis 9. Oktober 2009 (ZMMS Spektrum Band 22), vol. 29, pp. 196–201. VDI, Düsseldorf (2009)

Luczak, H., Schlick, C., Jochems, N., Vetter, S., Kausch, B.: Touch screens for the elderly: some models and methods, prototypical development and experimental evaluation of human-computer interaction concepts for the elderly. In: Haftor, D., Mirijamdotter, A. (eds.) Information and Communication Technologies, Society and Human Beings: Theory and Framework, pp. 116–135. IGI Global, Hershey (2011)

Pedell, S., Vetere, F., Kulik, L., Ozanne, E., Gruner, A.: Social isolation of older people: the role of domestic technologies. In: Proceedings of the 22nd Conference of the Computer-Human Interaction Special Interest Group of Australia on Computer-Human Interaction-OZCHI 2010. ACM Press, New York (2010)

Schlick, C., Vetter, S., Bützler, J., Jochems, N., Mütze-Niewöhner, S.: Ergonomic design of human-computer interfaces for aging users. In: Schlick, C.M., Frieling, E., Wegge, J. (eds.) Age-Differentiated Work Systems, pp. 347–368. Springer, Heidelberg (2013)

Selwyn, N.: Defining the 'digital divide': developing a theoretical understanding of inequalities in the information age. Occasional Paper 49. Cardiff University, Cardiff (2002)

Stößel, C., Wandke, H., Blessing, L.: Gestural interfaces for elderly users: help or hindrance? In: Kopp, S., Wachsmuth, I. (eds.) GW 2009. LNCS, vol. 5934, pp. 269–280. Springer, Heidelberg (2010)

Lowering the Threshold: Reconnecting Elderly Users with Assistive Technology Through Tangible Interfaces

Suhas Govind Joshi[✉] and Heidi Bråthen

Department of Informatics, University of Oslo, Oslo, Norway
{joshi,heibr}@ifi.uio.no

Abstract. In this paper, we discuss tangible interfaces as an alternative to touch-based interfaces and report from a study where we ported traditional screen-based solutions to physical solutions in order to make information more accessible. Our research approach targets the needs of elderly users who struggle with using, or are unable to use, existing touch-based interfaces currently available in municipal care homes. In an attempt to make assistive technology more readily available to this group, we aim to draw on their existing knowledge, competence and habits when designing alternative assistive technology. We present a tangible alternative to an existing touch-based interface, and discuss how tangible interfaces can help assistive technology become more available and familiar, thereby lowering the threshold for use and making information more accessible.

Keywords: Tangible interfaces · Assistive technology · Elderly users

1 Introduction

There is an increasing availability of welfare technology designed to assist elderly people. Elderly users of assistive technology constitute a heterogeneous group of users with varying degrees of capacity and function. The design of new technology does not always take into consideration this diverse user group's needs and varying degree of function. Our research targets the needs of elderly users who struggle with using, or are unable to use, existing touch-based interfaces currently available in municipal care homes in Norway. We present a tangible prototype named GLiMT that aims to support existing competences and habits by porting selected functionality from a traditional screen-based solution to a physical solution. GLiMT attempts to make information more accessible to users struggling with touchscreen interfaces by allowing them to interact trough a physical interface. We included a total of 42 elderly participants (aged 67 to 92 years old). The prototype serves as a demonstrative artifact and allows us to compare current touchscreen-based interaction with a tangible alternative. We draw on the results of our interviews and usability tests to discuss the potential role of tangible interaction in the context of assistive technology. We use the case of GLiMT to discuss how tangible interfaces can help users experience assistive technology as available and familiar, and thereby help to lower the threshold for use and make information more accessible.

© Springer International Publishing Switzerland 2016
J. Zhou and G. Salvendy (Eds.): ITAP 2016, Part I, LNCS 9754, pp. 52–63, 2016.
DOI: 10.1007/978-3-319-39943-0_6

The paper is organized as follows. Section 2 provides a brief overview of related work on tangible user interfaces and frameworks in the context of elderly people. We then outline our empirical context and research methods of our study in Sects. 3 and 4, before we present the results in Sect. 5. In Sect. 6, we present a discussion of the implications of our study, and the potential of opportunities that arises when moving from screen-based to tangible interaction.

2 Related Work

One of the three dimensions of aging defined by Spreicer [1] is biological age. Reduction of bodily capacities, such as loss of fine motor movements, limits our ability to interact with certain interfaces. Prior research has demonstrated that screen-based interaction introduces new of challenges due to bodily changes [2, 3]. Spreicer [1] further argues that cognitive aging changes our cognition and information processing abilities, and thereby makes it difficult to adapt to new problems without extensive training.

There has been some relevant research on tangible interaction as a way to overcome the challenges of traditional screen-based interfaces. Gamberini et al. [4] introduces Eldergames, an interactive physical apparatus that provides social cognitive training. Cognitive rehabilitation has also been the goal of the work of de la Guía, Lozano and Penichet [5] who used a NFC-based solution to accompany touch-screens in a game-based setting. Iversen and Joshi [6] introduces various tangible and embodied prototypes for helping elderly deal with declining bodily and cognitive skills. The work of Häikiö et al. [7] presents a solution similar to ours as it relies on NFC-based interfaces in order to help elderly people solve daily tasks such as ordering meals. Findings from their paper suggest that decline in motor abilities does not necessarily prevent or complicate the use of the system.

Cho et al. [8] present a framework for tangible user interfaces tailored for elderly users. The framework introduces two dimensions; tangible interface properties and supportive interface properties. We draw on four of these categories in the discussion to understand the tangible properties of our prototype. More precisely, from tangible interface properties, we include manipulation and intuitiveness; from supportive interface properties, we have elicited accessibility and simplicity as the main implication relevant for our research. Simplicity is described as easy to understand in this framework, however designing for simplicity in the context of elderly people and assistive technology is not a simple matter, and our prior research has demonstrated how screen-based interaction, in particular, may become too challenging for the users [3]. Thus, our understanding of simplicity introduces a more tailored understanding of the term; simplicity is to be understood only through the experience of the user, rather than something context-detached, and it should build on mastery and context to support users.

3 Empirical Context

Our study is part of a larger research project focusing on assistive technology in cooperation with Oslo Municipality. Two local care homes served as our primary locations for understanding the problem area and gather data for user requirements. In addition to these two local care homes, we used a third activity center to recruit participants for our control group. The care home offers residency to elderly users with cognitive and physical impairments. As a part of the Municipality's welfare program, each apartment comes preinstalled with a set of assistive technologies. One of these assistive technologies is a customized tablet installed in the apartment [3]. The tablet is portrayed in Fig. 1 (left) and served as the touch-based device which we used as a basis when porting functionality to our proposed tangible prototype.

3.1   GLiMT

The GLiMT prototype, illustrated in Fig. 1 (right), is a small wooden cube that receives a stream of four categories of online information through a wireless configuration. The information is identical to the information offered through the existing touchscreen-based tablet. The cube has four sides with corresponding symbols to represent the four categories of information. Incoming messages are signaled by having the corresponding side of the cube light up. Messages can be displayed on any bigger screen that the residents are comfortable with, e.g., tablet, cell phone or TV, by placing the lit side of the cube next to the back of the device or remote control (TV). The topside displays a small screen where a thumbnail of the sender of the message is shown inside a frame with the corresponding color. The bottom side has an inductive charger unit to charge the cube whenever it's placed on its base. It is designed not to be confined to each apartment, but to be carried around in the whole local care home. A battery icon indicates charging, and this icon is repeated on the charging station. While charging, a battery icon symbolizes the charging status on the small screen on the top of the cube.

Fig. 1.   The current touch-based tablet (left) and the GLiMT prototype (right).

4   Research Methods

The research was conducted over three months during the autumn of 2015. The main goal of our mixed-method approach was to gain insight into challenges with current touchscreen-based interfaces and to compare the device to our tangible alternative. Table 1 presents an overview of all participants included in our study. We conducted six individual interviews, and two sessions of group interviews with a combined total

Table 1. Overview of research methods and participants.

Research Method	Participants	
	Experiment group	Control group
Interviews	6	–
Group interviews	5	5
Usability test – formative	11	8
Usability test - summative	3	4
Total	25	17

of 10 participants. We carried out formative testing on the GLiMT prototype and held a summative test to compare real-task differences between the tangible prototype and the existing touchscreen-based interface.

The participants involved in this study were residents at the local care homes. We also recruited participants for the usability test from an independent activity center for a control group to reduce the likeliness of contextual bias. Most of the visitors at the activity center resided in private homes and came to the activity center during daytime to participate in scheduled activities such as dinner and board games.

The total number of participants was 42 people, with 25 in the experiment group and 17 in the control group. The age ranged from 67 to 92 years (M = 80). We recruited our participants through the method of convenience sampling by visiting both care facilities and joining activities in the common rooms. We aimed to achieve a balanced and representative distribution of age and gender within the target population, but the gender distribution was skewed towards women (61 %). While we did recruit several users with physical impairments, there were also instances where people declined to participate because of physical impairments.

4.1 Interviews and Group Interviews

We used semi-structured interviews and group interviews to capture the daily life in the common rooms of the care home to understand the problem space and establish an understanding of current challenges. The interviews were conducted in the common rooms of the care home over the course of three weeks. We spent the time visiting the care home on five separate occasions to take part in daily activities like dinner in the cafeteria, afternoon coffee, and reading group in the library of the care home. We asked questions about what technological devices they used regularly, as well as related questions regarding social aspects, daily activities, routines, and communication with relatives. We also complemented the interviews with observations of their daily life in these common rooms and discussed their current assistive technological devices, like digital pill organizers, safety alarms, and the customized tablet. Figure 2 portrays some of the interview and observations activities conducted.

To more accurately present the results of the interviews and group interviews, as well as provide a more detailed analysis, we end this section by providing an overview of all participants who contributed to these activities in Table 2. Three participants (#5, #10, and #16) chose not to disclose their age.

Fig. 2. Examples of conversations, interviews and walkthroughs with participants.

Table 2. Overview of participants in interviews and group interviews.

Interviews					
Participant #	Sex	Age	Participant #	Sex	Age
1	F	83	4	W	87
2	M	84	5	M	?
3	M	79	6	W	86
Group interview – *experimental*			*Group interview –* *control*		
Participant #	Sex	Age	Participant #	Sex	Age
7	F	92	12	M	84
8	F	83	13	M	86
9	F	79	14	W	67
10	F	?	15	W	89
11	F	68	16	M	?

4.2   Usability Tests

We conducted two rounds of usability testing, one formative and one summative. All tests were conducted in the common rooms of the two institutions during times where there were organized activities such as dinner and afternoon coffee. The formative usability testing was conducted on an earlier version of the GLiMT prototype in order to get feedback on performance. More precisely, we registered the number of attempts and error-rate as participants, who struggled with the existing touchscreen tablet or were unable to use it, carried out a set of 10 daily tasks that encompassed all major aspects of the interaction. 19 users participated in this formative evaluation, 11 in the experiment group and 8 in the control group.

In the summative evaluation, we compared performance when using GLiMT vs. touchscreen-based devices. This usability test required participants to be capable of using any touchscreen-based device (e.g., provided a tablet or own mobile phone), and being familiar with common tasks and main interaction mechanisms. Thus, the number of participants was lower during this test. Seven users participated in the summative test, 3 in the experiment group and 4 in the control group. The participants were asked to perform 11 daily tasks during the evaluation.

Fig. 3. Elderly users participating in the summative usability test.

The tasks used during the two tests provided insight into several aspect of the design such as (1) understandability of the concept of interaction, signals and messages; (2) perception of representation, typography and icons; (3) volume and quality of auditory feedback; and (4) difficulty with operational tasks (handling, manipulating, and charging). Participants were encouraged to think out loud while performing the tasks in order to capture any additional opinions. Examples of tasks included reading daily activities, identify the sender of a picture, and charging the device. The participants were given instructions and demonstrations of all tasks included before initiating the test, and the task order in both rounds was randomized to negate any learning effects. Figure 3 shows two of the elderly residents that participated in the summative evaluation, and how they used different touchscreen-based interfaces based on preference.

5   Results

5.1   Interviews and Group Interviews

We performed a thematic analysis of the gathered data from both the individual and group interviews. We categorized the data into four thematic areas by using an inductive approach [9] with two levels of clusters for each identified thematic area. Table 3 presents an overview of the four thematic areas that emerged from the data collected during the interviews and group interviews.

In our interviews, the customized tablet was repeatedly brought up as a topic of interests to the participants. 4 out of 6 participants from the individual interviews reported difficulties with the touch-based interaction. For certain residents, the touch-based interaction felt unfamiliar: *"It is strange to use your hand like this [demonstrating with a sweeping motion with the hand], so I don't really care much for it, haven't really used at all"* (Participant # 3). Connectivity problems led to the content of menu and activity calendars not being updated on a daily basis: *"It has been [the same dish] on the menu for a week, one has to go down [to the common rooms] when the tablet does not work"* (Participant #7). Two of the users reported that they preferred to go to the common room to read the poster on the wall because they found it easier than using the tablet. The manager of the care home reported that the tablet was of "limited use to the residents" because of these usability problems. The charging unit for the tablet was mounted on a wall in the kitchen of the apartments. This led to the tablet

Table 3. Overview of elicited thematic areas.

Thematic area	Reported by participant #:
Contextual factors (e.g., configuration of assistive technology)	#1, #8, #9, #10, #11, #12, # 13, #15
Challenges with touchscreen-based devices	#1, #2, #3, #10, #12
Delivery and accessibility of assistive technology	#1, #3, #4, #5, #7, #8, #9,#11, #12 #15
Technological development and expectation to adapt	#2, #6, #14

not always being available to the users who depended on assistance to get out of bed in the morning, or used wheelchairs, walkers or other aids.

Regarding the participants use of technology, in general, we found that all of the participants owned and used a TV regularly. The use of cell phones and tablets was common but to a varying degree. Some participants also had a personal computer that they used. Participation in social media and the internet varied considerably, from daily use to no use. Also, all residents had assistive technology such as automatic control of lighting and heating in their apartments. This increasing number of assistive technological devices was also a topic of interest for the residents. This was brought up by participants both in individual interviews and in the two group interviews; the participants expressed a feeling of being overwhelmed by the number of technology devices and concern regarding the implications for the quality of intrapersonal relationships between caretakers and the elderly people in need of assistance. 9 of the 16 participants in the individual and group interviews expressed a feeling of being overwhelmed by the increasing number of assistive technology devices in their daily lives, e.g., *"It can be too much of a good thing"* (Participant #6), and *"Technology is fine, but many are not using it at all"* (Participant #9).

Three participants reported that they thought it was difficult to follow the technological development in their personal use of technology: *"I will attend a course next fall. It will be good to learn to use it [the tablet]. It's easy for those who know it"* (Participant #2). During both group interviews, there were participants who were uncomfortable with giving an opinion on the use of technology because they did not feel that they knew enough about it. Also, not all the participants who reported feeling overwhelmed by the amount of assistive technology had difficulties using the technology. Two of the participants actively used smartphones, computers and the tablet, but expressed a general interest in the development of the caretaking technologies. A third participant had a professional background where she had worked with computer systems since the early eighties and were interested in following new developments as well as their impact on the community.

5.2   Usability Tests

During the formative test, we registered error rates during task-solving for the 12 participants with the GLiMT prototype. Every participant in both the experiment group

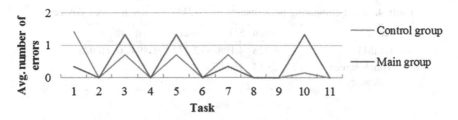

Fig. 4. Average number of errors

and control group was able to grip fully and manipulate the object, and there were no apparent challenges with handling the cube for any participant. 6 out of 12 participants struggled with at least one of the screen-specific tasks (e.g., reading a message from the screen). The reasons varied from small letters and weak contrasts to navigation and interaction challenges.

As Fig. 4 demonstrates, the average number of errors per task peaked at 1.428 (for task #1 and #10), yet remained below 1.0 as average errors per task for the 12 participants. Out of the 120 tasks solved by the 12 participants, 19 errors were registered. One participant in particular (male, 81 years) made 5 of the total 19 errors. Thus, most participants made it through all tasks without making a single error. Only one task was solved by everyone without making errors, but we did not register any significant reasoning for this one error-free task.

During the summative test, we ran comparative tests on the GLiMT prototype vs. the touch-screen device. Figure 5 presents an overview of the time spent during task solving for the 7 participants. The red-colored line illustrates the number of seconds spent per user with their currently preferred touch-screen device, which in this case was their mobile phones; the blue-colored line illustrates the similar performance time with GLiMT. An independent-sample t-test was conducted to compare the performance time, and the results from the t-test are reported in Table 4. While only three of the participants were above the average for the touch-screen device, we still registered a significant difference in time spent when using the touch-screen device vs. GLiMT (p = .028). The average time spent per user was significantly lower for users of GLiMT (M = 8.428, SD = 4.198) compared to the touch-screen devices (M = 23.14, SD = 16.608), and no single participant performed faster with their existing device than with the GLiMT prototype despite this being a novel and previously unexperienced interface for most participants.

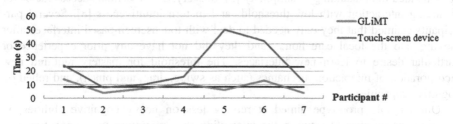

Fig. 5. Time spent on task solving for GLiMT and touch-screen device

Table 4. *t*-test comparing performance on GLiMT vs. touch-screen device

Device	n	Mean	SD	t-stat	t-crit	df	p
GLiMT	7	8.428	4.198	-2.272	1.894	6	0.028
Touch-screen device	7	23.14	16.607				

6 Discussion

GLiMT has served as an interesting prototype in the exploration of how tangible interfaces can open up new interaction opportunities in the context of assistive technology. For elderly people who are unable to use touchscreen-based interfaces for various reasons, our demonstrative prototype has provided empirical evidence of how porting functionality over to new interfaces can reconnect users with important assistive technologies. Furthermore, it demonstrated how using familiar movements and actions as input rather than screen-based commands enabled participants to operate new interfaces with a very low error rate (as illustrated in Fig. 4). Moving beyond the particular functionality of our prototype, this study has presented some new opportunities for interaction through tangible interfaces. In this section, we discuss aspects of interaction with assistive technology supported by our empirical results.

Considering the category of accessibility from the framework of Cho [8], the interviews revealed a strong general opinion of touch-screen devices being inaccessible due to high thresholds of use; the interface was too difficult to use and required too much effort to understand for most people to get started. Increased complexity raises the threshold for interaction, something that may scare away elderly users [10]. Participants also stated that the touch-based interface felt unfamiliar to them, contributing to their feeling of being overwhelmed. These results confirmed similar trends in our previous research [3], where a similar interface was perceived as complex. One of the significant effects of porting functionality over to a tangible interface in this study was the effect on how the users perceived technology and digital information. The tangible interface was perceived as more familiar and thereby more accessible to most users. Both the interviews (Table 3) and results (Fig. 5) demonstrated fewer errors and faster completion time for daily tasks when using GLiMT. By porting selected functionality to a tangible user interface, we aimed to simplify the interaction and build on the users' existing experiences of bodily interaction and manipulation of physical objects. With our extended understanding of simplicity [3], mastery is an essential success factor for achieving interaction with low thresholds and in turn intuitiveness [8]. Several participants claimed that they only needed to deal with touchscreen-based interfaces after moving into the local care home, and they did not have any prior experience or particular desire to learn new interfaces. The threshold for mastery required new incorporation of interaction mechanics (such as swipe, drag, and pinch), and relied on cognitive capacities.

Our tangible prototype aimed at relying less on heavy cognitive abilities by reducing the number of steps in the interaction to a minimum (as demonstrated in Table 4), as well as building on familiar gestures and movements for interactions that had been a part of their prior experience. Past experiences, along with cognitive capabilities, have been demonstrated to have an influence on task performance [11]. Reduction in memory load is a significant advantage of the proposed design in [5]. Building new technologies on familiar metaphors and experiences was also the strategy of [10, 12] when designing for elderly people. Another aspect of mastery is allowing elderly people to engage in interactions that respect their bodily capacities. With bodily changes, a lot of touch-based interfaces became inaccessible due to physical or psychomotor disabilities or reduction in capacity. This point was also made by [2]. One particular participant stated that physical capacities complicated the interaction: « *I'm not very good at that, I can't make it work, it is difficult to start [the interaction], to press* » (Participant #2). GLiMT was designed to offer more flexibility with regards to the bodily configuration in order to acknowledge the importance of manipulation [5, 8] also argues for more flexibility. By designing the interface as a light-weight cube, we opened up new interactions mechanisms that were unavailable to the users when interacting with the tablet. For instance, people with only one good hand were in most cases unable to use the tablet in any other configuration that on a table, while they were fully able to operate GLiMT. The four leveled sides provided good stability, and its non-fragile components did not break like glass if the user were to drop it.

One challenge with the design of our tangible prototype was the consistency which affected the intuitiveness. Intuitiveness has been an important part of the design of similar studies, e.g., [4]. Several participants in the usability tests expected the device to charge by putting the charging icon on the screen down towards the charging icon on the base station. This indicated a perceived break in intuitiveness; they did not notice the battery icon on the bottom of the device at first. Similarly, we found that not all elderly users were familiar with commonly used iconography representing functions in technological devices, such as the battery icon. Some participants did not recognize the icon and did not understand the interface metaphors: *"It reminds me of a remote control or something, maybe a temperature regulator. Maybe if the tip was more articulated... it wouldn't take much"* [elaborating on what the icon represented to him and how it could be altered to remind him more of a battery]. Again, this demonstrates how building on familiar metaphors and gestures is an important implication as there might be breaches in the cultural knowledge of representations [2], thereby violating the intuitiveness. Furthermore, by involving the users in the design process and explore what different representations means to these users, one can tailor representations that build on their existing knowledge [13]. Not designing the cube of our tangible prototype after the concept of tailoring became an evident limitation of the design. While our prototype outperformed the existing touchscreen-based interface, we do not claim this prototype to be a definite piece of technology; instead, it serves as a demonstrative prototype that illustrates the potential of utilizing the key concept of tangible interaction, for instance, tailored representation.

We also registered how the tangible interface incorporated better with the contexts of use, most notably how the elderly users perceived the technology as a part of the home. Familiarizing the technology helped us re-establish interaction, yet we still saw how it also needed to align with the surroundings of the homes of each participant. One participant said that the design of the existing technology should be *"black or light so it could go with anything. Then it would be more appropriate in my home"*. However, most elderly people in our empirical context had a different aesthetic in their homes and did not feel that the black, chrome, edgy and flashy screen-based devices blended well with the context. The wall-mounted tablet stood out in most wooden-furnished homes as an exterior addition to the household. Thus, we aimed at developing a wooden cube that would embed well in the households and reduce the chance of disrupting daily activities. This idea of embedding technology into the everyday environment is also advocated by [7]. This was also the reason for extending the functionality of GLiMT to televisions which were a piece of technology all participants in our study had and used regularly. Building on top of existing technology already incorporated into daily routines further increased the accessibility and did not introduce any major changes to their spatial setup. This also increased the freedom to refrain from adapting to new undesired technology and instead continue relying on familiar technologies such as TV.

7 Conclusion

This paper has used GLiMT as a demonstration of how tangible interfaces building on habits and prior experiences can help elderly users of assistive technology reconnect with lost interactions. The aesthetic nature of the tangible interface allowed the design to immerse better with the contexts of use, as well as to signal a more appealing and accessible interface. We have applied a thematic analysis as well as traditional usability tests to compare the performance of the tangible alternative with existing solutions, and demonstrated the potential of porting screen-based functionality to tangible interfaces.

References

1. Spreicer, W.: Tangible interfaces as a chance for higher technology acceptance by the elderly. In: Proceedings of the 12th International Conference on Computer Systems and Technologies. ACM (2011)
2. Culén, A.L., Bratteteig, T.: Touch-screens and elderly users: a perfect match? In: ACHI 2013, The Sixth International Conference on Advances in Computer-Human Interactions (2013)
3. Joshi, S.G.: Designing for experienced simplicity. Why analytic and imagined simplicity fail in design of assistive technology. Int. J. Adv. Intell. Syst. 8(3&4), 324–338 (2015)
4. Gamberini, L., et al.: Eldergames project: an innovative mixed reality table-top solution to preserve cognitive functions in elderly people. In: 2nd Conference on Human System Interactions, 2009. HSI 2009. IEEE (2009)
5. de la Guía, E., Lozano, M.D., Penichet, V.R.: Cognitive rehabilitation based on collaborative and tangible computer games. In: 2013 7th International Conference on Pervasive Computing Technologies for Healthcare (PervasiveHealth). IEEE (2013)
6. Iversen, T.R., Joshi, S.G.: Exploring spatial interaction in assistive technology through prototyping. Procedia Manuf. 3, 158–165 (2015)
7. Häikiö, J., et al.: Touch-based user interface for elderly users. ACM (2007)
8. Cho, M.E., Kim, M.J.: Characterizing the interaction design in healthy smart home devices for the elderly. Indoor Built Environ. 23(1), 141–149 (2014)

9. Braun, V., Clarke, V.: Using thematic analysis in psychology. Qual. Res. Psychol. **3**(2), 77–101 (2006)
10. Al Mahmud, A., et al.: Designing social games for children and older adults: Two related case studies. Entertainment Comput. **1**(3), 147–156 (2010)
11. Blackler, A., Mahar, D., Popovic, V.: Older adults, interface experience and cognitive decline. In: Proceedings of the 22nd Conference of the Computer-Human Interaction Special Interest Group of Australia on Computer-Human Interaction. ACM (2010)
12. Marques, T., Nunes, F., Silva, P., Rodrigues, R.: Tangible interaction on tabletops for elderly people. In: Anacleto, J.C., Fels, S., Graham, N., Kapralos, B., Saif El-Nasr, M., Stanley, K. (eds.) ICEC 2011. LNCS, vol. 6972, pp. 440–443. Springer, Heidelberg (2011)
13. Hornecker, E., Buur, J.: Getting a grip on tangible interaction: a framework on physical space and social interaction. In: Proceedings of the SIGCHI Conference on Human Factors in Computing Systems. ACM (2006)

Development of the Accessibility Evaluation Platform Beyond Digital Divide

Junji Ohyama[✉]

National Institute of Advanced Industrial Science and Technology 1-1-1, Higashi,
Tsukuba City, Ibaraki 305-8566, Japan
j.ohyama@aist.go.jp

Abstract. We developed a web-based experiment platform for psychological experiments and questionnaire surveys to evaluate accessibility, especially for elderly participant studies. Our proposing system is an accessible experiment platform for experimenters and participants, which has necessary and sufficient functions for studies to solve many open questions of aging society, especially for evaluating accessible design. This system has three advantages. (1) No programming knowledge is needed for users. This system makes surveys and experiments possible only by inputting essential values and words such as a sentence of question, a file name of image to present, a numerical value of presentation time. (2) The System requirements are less severe than other systems. The user can run experiments on a PC, tablet, or mobile, without installing any specific software. If the study does not require strict control of environmental conditions, elderly people can join the survey at home or anyplace. Moreover, this system enables studies for elderly people without a lot of costs, since it is web-based and does not need to have many licenses. (3) Our proposing system has essential functions for basic psychological experiments. It is compatible with personal information protection, confirmation of written consent, design of the task procedure (randomize, block, shuffle), input and response (e.g., free description, evaluation axis, selection, coordinates of mouse click, and response time). The proposing experiment platform is useable for the accessibility study to fill in the gap of digital divide, especially the studies of human computer interaction in aging society.

Keywords: Accessible design · Evaluation tool · Cognitive technology · Experimental psychology · Questionnaire survey

1 Introduction

There are usually three problems for studies in accessibility with elderly people. One is that elderly people's answer and reaction are varying widely from individual to individual, in comparison with the most of the young adults' experiments. A large number of participants are needed to see a distribution of findings' average and individual differences among elderly people in the whole society [1, 2].

Second problem is the difficulty to recruit a large number of elderly people. There are many studies supporting that increase of risk of involved an accident in living

© Springer International Publishing Switzerland 2016
J. Zhou and G. Salvendy (Eds.): ITAP 2016, Part I, LNCS 9754, pp. 64–73, 2016.
DOI: 10.1007/978-3-319-39943-0_7

environment is related to aging of cognitive and physical functions [3, 4]. Therefore, experimenters can recruit only small number of healthy elderlies who have not so much difficulties in accessibility in daily lives, although the target of many aging studies in accessibility is focusing on people who have interrupted their social activity by difficulty of accessibilities.

The third problem is the research environment. It costs a lot of time and money to gather many participants to a lab for experiments. And also it costs a lot of time and money to prepare and conduct paper-based questionnaire survey on many participants.

To solve these three issues, we built a web-based experiment platform that makes psychological experiments and paper-based questionnaire survey easy, especially for elderly participants in aging studies. This system has three advantages. (1) No programming knowledge is needed for users. Most of the previous systems need computer programing technics and technical knowledge about information technologies [5–7], and/or require installation of OS dependent software for each devices [8–11]. This system makes surveys and experiments possible only by inputting essential values and words such as a sentence of question, a file name of image to present, a numerical value of presentation time. (2) The system requirements are less severe than other systems. The user can run experiments on a PC, tablet, or mobile, without installing any specific software. If the study does not require strict control of environmental conditions, elderly people can join the survey at home or anyplace. Moreover, this system enables studies for elderly people without a lot of costs, since it is web-based and does not need to buy many licenses. (3) Our proposing system has essential functions for basic psychological experiments. Moreover, it is compatible with personal information protection, confirmation of written consent, design of the task procedure (randomize, block, shuffle), input and response (e.g., free description, evaluation axis, selection, coordinates of mouse click, response time).

2   Concept of the Envisioned Approach

Figure 1 shows a conceptual structure of our proposing accessibility evaluation platform. Our proposing barrier-free experiment platform is consisted of two main components; the experiment building system (EBS) and the participant experiment system (PES). The main programs of both systems are in the server computer that connected to the Internet. Experimenter can make general psychology tasks and/or questioners by connecting to the EBS on the server without any knowledge of machine languages (see Sect. 3 in detail). Participants can participate the experiment from any places by accessing the PES through the Internet (see Sect. 4 in detail).

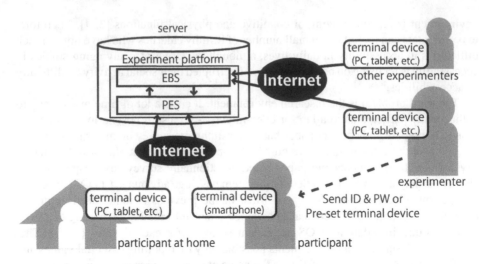

Fig. 1. Conceptual structure of our proposing accessibility evaluation platform

3   The Experiment Building System (EBS)

In this section, we explain how to build experimental settings by the EBS on the server. Functions and procedures are in the following subsections. Figure 2 shows an example of the main window of the EBS, which is simple and similar to a file server.

Back   **Experiment Building System manager**

root/Experiments/Demo_exp1

File name	Update time	Delete
index.csv	2015/05/13 13:38:44	✗
task.csv	2015/05/13 13:38:41	✗
trial.csv	2015/05/13 13:38:37	✗

Create new experiment

Upload new file

Fig. 2. Example of the main window of the EBS

3.1   Making a List of Participants

The researcher who conducts the experiment sets a login ID and password of this developed system for each participant. The list will be used for the participants' identification when they participate in the experiment and also for the experiment log. We do not need to input any the participants' personal information in both EBS and PES. We control the personal information separately and link it to the login ID, so that we can avoid the risk that personal data leak from this system.

3.2   Making an Experiment

An experiment will be created by making an experiment folder in the server specified directory. The name of the experiment folder will be the name of the experiment. The experiment will be created by uploading the files that contain each experiment's information to the experiment folder.

3.3   Uploading Written Informed Consent for the Experiment

Make "written informed consent" by PDF format, which mentions the purpose and content of the experiment and confirmation of consent, and then upload it to the corresponding experiment folder.

3.4   Making an Experiment Program

Experimenter can create an experiment program only by writing the experimental conditions in the text file of the comma separated value (CSV), without knowledge of machine languages or computer programing. The program has three layer composition: "Index" which settles upper whole experiment structure, "Task" which executes tasks in the experiment, and "Trial" which is used in the tasks.

3.5   Making Index

Setting the followings: display conditions throughout the experiment (background color, font color, font size), the unit of size [visual degrees/points] used in the setting description for the whole experiment, and the tasks that will be executed in the experiment and their execution order. If the experimenter arranges the task file names in the Index file simply, the order of tasks that will be executed will be performed in order of the description. Also, it is possible to execute them in random order, by using the task name list.

3.6   Making Tasks

Describe the setting for each task in the experiment. Setting the followings: display conditions throughout the task (background color, font color, font size), the unit size [visual degrees/points] used in the setting description for the whole task, and the trials that will be executed in the task and their execution order. The order of Trial executed will be performed in order of the description, if the experimenter arranges the trial file names simply in the task file. Also, it is possible to execute them in random order, by using the trial name list.

3.7 Making Trials

Describe the setting for each trial in the experiment. Setting the followings: display conditions throughout the task (background color, font color, font size), the unit size [visual degrees/points] used in the setting description for the each trial.

4 The Participant Experiment System (PES)

In this section, we explain how participants access and participate in the experiment by the PES.

4.1 Preparation Before Starting Experiment

The experimenter who conducts the experiment informs the login ID and password of this developed system to each participant in advance.

4.2 Login

The participant inputs the login ID and password given in advance in login screen and does the experiment system.

4.3 Choosing the Experiment

After login, the list of experiment titles that the participant can participate in will be shown. The participant clicks the experiment name that he or she will participate in and starts the experiment.

4.4 Explanation of Experiment Content and Confirmation of Consent to Participation

The PES can show written informed consent that mentions the purpose and content of the experiment and confirmation of consent. Participant reads the content of experiment and agreement, checks the "agree" check box at the lower left. If the participant agrees, the "next" button (at the lower right) color will change from gray to blue, then the participant can click it for decision of agreement and can proceed to the next step (see Fig. 3).

4.5 Setting to a Full Screen Mode

The participant is asked to set the PES window to a full screen mode by following the displayed instruction. Proceed to the next step by clicking "next" button.

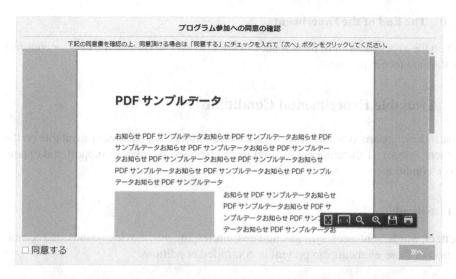

Fig. 3. Demo of the informed consent display. PDF written informed consent is presented at the center. Left bottom is a check box for agreement. If the participant inputs check in the check box, the "next" button (at the right bottom) will change from gray to blue.

4.6 Setting the Screen Size

The participant is instructed to input the exact size of display. Proceed to the next step by clicking "next" button.

4.7 Checking the Sound Volume

The participant is asked to check the volume of sound. Click "play the sample sound" button and check the volume. You can play it any number of times. Adjust the volume for PC and speakers and click "next" button to proceed to the next.

4.8 Ready Screen

Ready screen will be presented at the end of the setting of the experiment. If you click "next" button, the experiment will start.

4.9 Experiment

The experiment will be executed as it was set by the PES. The participant does the operation as displayed. Available experimental conditions are explained in Sect. 5.

4.10   The End of the Experiment

When the experiment ends, participant can select to end and logout the PES, or continue to start another experiment.

5   Available Experimental Conditions

The followings are available stimuli, procedures, and tests that already available on the present system. If there are needs from experimenters, we plan to support and extend more conditions.

5.1   Stimuli

Letters, words, sentences, symbols, squares, circles, images, movies, sounds, and combination of these elements can present in controlled conditions.

5.2   Conditions of Stimuli Presentation

Following conditions are available to control stimuli presentation.

Display position. The stimuli can be shown at the specified positions for specified duration. Space resolution depends on resolution of the screen.

Presentation timing. The stimuli can be shown in specified timing and duration. Also, it can be shown until the participant does operations such as key press. Time resolution depends on the drawing speed of the device. The Table 1 shows the inspection result of the stability of two devices.

Table 1.   Results of stability verification tests in two devices

Device	OS	Stability verification: maximum refresh ratio
iPad	iOS 9.2	◎: max 30 Hz
DELL core i5	Windows 7	◎: max 80 Hz

Presentation order. Not only in the fixed controlled order, but also random selection or shuffled order can be set for the multiple stimuli presentation.

Responses. Key operation and mouse click coordinates are valid during the experiments. Also, you can record the Response Time (RT) of such operations. RT synchronizes with the update of the monitor refresh timing; therefore RT resolution depends on the display refresh ratio.

5.3 Components for Tests and Questionnaires

Image selection component. Image selection component can display a question sentence and multiple image choices. If you click on one of the images, the selected image will be highlighted by a surrounding yellow frame (see Fig. 4). If you select designated number of choices, the confirmation button will become active. Click the confirmation button to decide the selection.

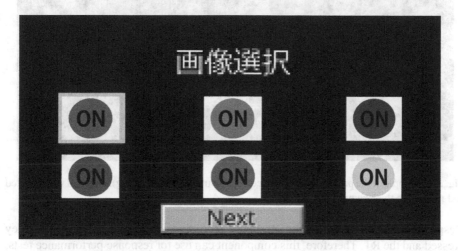

Fig. 4. Example of the presentation of item selection

Text selection component. Text selection component can display a question sentence and multiple text choices. If you click on one of the texts choices, the selected text will be highlighted by a yellow underline. If you select designated number of choices, the confirmation button will become active. Click the confirmation button to decide the selection.

Free description component. Free description component can display a question sentence and free description answer column. Click the confirmation button to decide the input.

Subjective evaluation (Grade rating) component. Subjective evaluation (Grade rating) component can display a subjective evaluation question and sparse evaluation axis (see Fig. 5). Labels can be presented at each grade point on the evaluation axis. If you click one of the grades on the evaluation axis, a mark will be shown above the grade point. Then, the select button will become active. Click the button and decide the input.

Subjective evaluation (Continuous axis) component. Subjective evaluation (Continuous axis) component can display a subjective evaluation question and continuous evaluation axis. Labels can be presented at the both ends on the evaluation axis, and by clicking on the axis with a mouse, a mark will be shown on the axis at the position. Then, the select button will become active. Click the button and decide the input.

Fig. 5. Example of the presentation of subjective evaluation (Grade rating). Left end was selected and marked in this example.

Response recording component. Response recording component can record the key pressed and the RT. Therefore, this component can use for response performance tests, such as the two alternative forced choice (2AFC).

Search test component. Search test component can display multiple stimuli, search a specified item, and perform a search test by answering it with a mouse and keys.

6   Discussion and Conclusion

In this paper, we proposed essential needs and technical specification for accessible experimental platform for aging studies. This system can prevent risks for elderly people to move from their house to the lab to participate experiments. We also developed a prototype system of the proposed accessible experiment platform. Experimenters who want to develop this system might be anxious about the primary creation cost. However, we estimated the cost by developing the prototype system and confirmed that this system can order from outside suppliers by the cost similar to the cost that achieves common questionnaires or evaluation test two times. And also, the development cost of our proposing system is similar or less than outsourcing the experiment using other fee-charging web-research systems. Therefore, development of this proposing experimental platform would be more reasonable solution than planning to call many elderly people to achieve more than two studies, or planning to outsource the experiment to a fee-charging research company.

The proposing experiment platform is useable for the accessibility study to fill in the gap between demographics and regions that have access to modern information and communication technology, and those that don't or have restricted access, especially the evaluation studies of human computer interaction in aging society.

References

1. Sagawa, K., Kurakata, K.: Estimation of legible font size for elderly people. Synthesiology **6**(1), 24–33 (2013)
2. Ohyama, J., Itoh, N., Kurakata, K., Sagawa, K.: Time reduction design method for cognitive assist technology. In: Zhou, J., Salvendy, Gavriel (eds.) ITAP 2015. LNCS, vol. 9193, pp. 94–103. Springer, Heidelberg (2015)
3. Ishimatsu, K., Miura, T., Shinohara, K.: Age influences visual attention characteristics among accident-free and accident-involved drivers. Jpn. Psychol. Res. **52**(3), 186–200 (2010)
4. Kitajima, M., Kumada, T., Akamatsu, M., Ogi, H., Yamazaki, H.: Effect of cognitive ability deficits on elderly passengers' mobility at railway stations: Focusing on attention, working memory, planning. Gerontechnology **3**(4), 231 (2005)
5. Guide, M.U.S.: The mathworks. Inc., Natick, MA, 5, 333 (1998)
6. Python.org. https://www.python.org
7. Straw, A.D.: Vision egg: an open-source library for realtime visual stimulus generation (2008)
8. Presentation. http://www.neurobs.com
9. SuperLab. http://www.superlab.com
10. WebExp, The University of Edinburgh. http://groups.inf.ed.ac.uk/webexp/index.shtml
11. Spruyt, A., Clarysse, J., Vansteenwegen, D., Baeyens, F., Hermans, D.: Affect 4.0: a free software package for implementing psychological and psychophysiological experiments. Exp. Psychol. **57**, 36–45 (2010)

Scaffolding Digital Game Design Activities Grouping Older Adults, Younger Adults and Teens

Margarida Romero[✉] and Hubert Ouellet

Faculté des Sciences de l'Éducation, Université Laval, Québec, Canada
{margarida.romero,hubert.ouellet}@fse.ulaval.ca

Abstract. Digital game design is a complex activity relying on multiple skills of the 21st century as such creativity, problem solving, collaboration in interdisciplinary teams and computational thinking. The complexity of the knowledge modelling and creation process, game design is a powerful learning activity that could benefit in learning from childhood to older adults. Our experiences take advantage of the digital game design as a complex learning activity and engages learners from different age groups in a joint activity. In this paper, we analyze the scaffolding process of intergenerational game design activities as an instructional learning strategy. We argue that the process could help learners from different ages and backgrounds to collaborate together in doing progressive steps through their game design process.

Keywords: Older adults · Digital game design · Intergenerational learning · Knowledge creation

1   Introduction

Digital ageism is a form of discrimination appearing through the use of technologies that have not been adapted for older adults or that conveys a negative image of older adults through their representation of older adults. For instance, digital games tend to convey negative images of older adults and often misrepresent this age category [1]. Intergenerational participatory game design could help overcome those issues by engaging older adults in the game design process through a collaborative approach with game designers of other age groups. Engaging teens, young and older adults in a joint game design activity allows each of the age groups to know each other better and ensure their own representativeness in the game design process and product they develop together [2, 3]. In order to explore the intergenerational game design activities as a way to avoid digital ageism and promote intergenerational learning through game design, we introduce in this paper the organization of two intergenerational game design workshop activities that have been developed during the Silver Gaming Intergenerational Summer School (SGISS) in Québec City. First, we introduce participatory game design and the learning opportunities that are introduced by this approach. Second, we describe the different phases of the game design workshop and the way each one of them has been scaffolded to better support the objectives of the activity in terms of social participation, representation of older adults and intergenerational learning [4].

© Springer International Publishing Switzerland 2016
J. Zhou and G. Salvendy (Eds.): ITAP 2016, Part I, LNCS 9754, pp. 74–81, 2016.
DOI: 10.1007/978-3-319-39943-0_8

2   Intergenerational Participatory Game Design

Games are mostly designed by white young males, including only 11.5 per cent of females in the field in 2009 and 22 per cent in 2016 (International Game Developers Association, 2016). Different initiatives trying to question the diversity in the game industry has led to highly violent campaigns; in 2014, the #gamergate put into their collective crosshairs several women working within the video game industry, including well-known game developers Zoë Quinn and Brianna Wu and cultural critic Anita Sarkeesian. Women in gaming have been victims of sexism, misogyny and harassment within the video game culture [5]. At our knowledge, older adults have not been the object of harassment; still, they remain an age group not only underrepresented but also misrepresented. This is especially true of older women, who are often appearing as maleficent antagonists [1, 6]. Our research [7, 8] points towards a need for a more participatory design process which could allow social participation and a better representation of different age groups, sexual and gender diversity. Participatory design aims to engage individuals from different disciplines and backgrounds in the design decision-making process. In the field of information systems (IS), participative design "promises IS quality while empowering the participants and fostering relationships among developers and users" [9, p. 1]. The participatory game co-design blurs the boundary between game players and the professional game designers [10]. Co-design strategies could include making games from scratch, modifying or 'modding' existing games [11] through a shared-decision making process. Opening the participative design to individuals from different social groups, ages and background aims at improving social representation through a critical perspective.

3   Intergenerational Game Design Workshops

Game creation could be used as a participatory activity in the pursuit of developing and strengthening the link between different generations of participants [12, 13]. In this section, we introduce the intergenerational game creation activities that were held during the *Silver Gaming International Summer School* (SGISS) in August, 2015. The game creation workshops teamed participants from different age groups (18 to 80 years old) from secondary-level students (n = 2) to adults (n = 32). The workshops were held in French and in English. Our main objective was to engage participants in an intergenerational game design experience in order to develop a better awareness of each age group game design preferences. Their contact with each other enabled them to learn together about different aspects of game design. In order to ensure the success of such innovative activities, the scaffolding of the different phases of the game design workshop were the object of an important preparation during several weeks. The researchers needed to ensure both the zone of proximal development (ZPD) [14] and the zone of proximal innovation and complexity (ZPIC) were at the reach of all the intergenerational teams engaged in the task. In the next sections, we introduce the different phases of the workshop and how the intergenerational game design activity was scaffolded and supported to enable the social participation of all the members of the intergenerational teams.

3.1 Scaffolding the Group Forming for the Highest Intergenerational Diversity

The intergenerational workshop game design activity is structured in teams which aims to be the more diverse possible in terms of age and self-declared gender. In order to create teams with the highest quotient of intergenerational participation, we introduced a team-constitution activity based on a pyramid of age representation. As the first activity within the workshop we asked the participants to position themselves on an age and gender pyramid (Fig. 1).

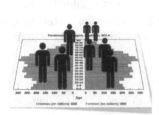 

Fig. 1. Age pyramid distribution of the workshop participants

The purpose of this exercise was to help us put together teams with the higher intergenerational diversity possible.

3.2 Scaffolding the Team Selection and Exploration of a Topic for Their Game Creation Activity

The second activity of the workshop was oriented towards the team decision making for selecting a topic to be developed as a game. Each intergenerational team had to determine what topic they would work on. The two workshop facilitators oriented the decision making towards topics related to the modernization of the province of Québec in the French group and towards topics related to the recent world history for the international English group. The workshop facilitators listed a series of events that could be explored (i.e. the electrification of the province, women's suffragette, Expo 67, the Baby Boom, etc.). We noticed that the choice of topic was strongly influenced by the older member of the teams as they used their own life narrative, having had first-hand memories of some of those events. The three secondary-level students were aware of these topics as they studied them in their prior school year. When asked what they knew about this content, they positioned themselves as "non-experts". Interestingly, they stated that the in-class teaching strategy used was magisterial and that the topics were greatly simplified, not only in their transmission but also in the conversations it generated. The intergenerational approach to the chosen event helped create more diversity and complexity as no effort was made to abridge the topic. They also remained fully focused during the conversations, asking questions and commenting on the topic or the life experiences of the older adult(s) (Fig. 2).

Fig. 2. Teams during the topic selection decision making.

3.3 Scaffolding the Game Design Process

In order to support the game design process, we suggested to develop a short narrative based on a first-person character. The workshop facilitators introduced the objectives of creating an interactive process where the objective was to put together a short narrative sequence centered on the decisions of a real, significant political figure that helped shape a particular historical event. It is this semi-fictional "character" that will communicate directly to the players by asking them questions on the chosen event. As each question constitutes a scene of the game, deciding what to ask is an integral part of the writing process; mobilizing and conceptualizing prior information are an important part of creating new knowledge. In the storyboard example below, Team 2 has decided to focus on the topic of the liberation of Nelson Mandela. He is also the main character of their mini-game. The group has identified a first question for their mini-game "Who made his release possible?" and has imagined (and verified in a second step) three different answers, one of which is correct (Fig. 3).

- We scaffold the game creation process through four steps: (1) identification of a character central to the historic event of the mini-game, (2) identification of the question to be asked by the character, (3) developing hypotheses on the possible answers to the questions formulated in the second step and (4) verifying the validity of the hypothetical answers through an information search. The selection of the character aims to engage the intergenerational team in a discussion during which they explore together who they consider to be one ofthe main proponent in the historical event of their choice. The decision to focus on a character's aims also help humanizing the decision making related to historical event.

- The second step to undertake is to identify what questions they could ask the student. We suggest that each team write what they spontaneously know about their topic of choice. Then, they identify what could be rephrased as potential questions and assemble the information in a chronological order to determine a sequence plan.
- The third step is to formulate possible answers (or hypothesis) to the questions they chose, hence render explicit their prior knowledge. In most cases, their preconceptions are erroneous; making them explicit enables the knowledge deconstruction and its reconstruction.
- The fourth step is to research information regarding the hypotheses formulated before and find the right answer about the topic. As the erroneous possible answers and knowledge that were formulated by the team could be shared by other learners, none of them were to be discarded; instead, they constituted possible wrong answers for the student to select. To further explain why they were not the desired answer, we asked the teams to write a short text hinting at the right answer.

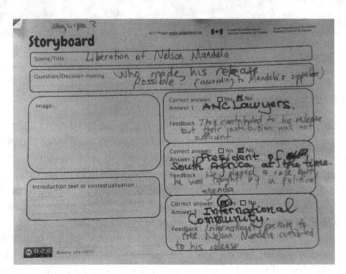

Fig. 3. Template distributed to the teams for supporting their game design process

3.4 Scaffolding the Game Creation Process in a Visual Programming Environment

Once the game design steps were completed, teams were asked to create a storyboard explaining what would constitute their game. They could create it by using either analog (pen and paper, post-its, blackboards, etc.) or digital tools. Each scene had to contextualize a key question developed in step 3.3 (Fig. 4).

Fig. 4. From game design templates to visual programming through Scratch

Now in possession of a storyboard, teams started digitally recreating their ideas in the visual programming tool Scratch (https://scratch.mit.edu/). Scratch is a visual, drag-and-drop programming software that allows the creation of interactive scenes and mini-games. Its appeal is broad, as it was created to be used by individuals from 7 to 107 years old. Scratch can support the creative programming approach — which goes well beyond the learning to code movement — to engage participants in creating new digital media, stories and artefacts through the use of programming [7, 15]. After a short intro-duction in how to use Scratch, each intergenerational team had less than an hour to code a mini-game. In order to scaffold the game creation process we provided a mini-game template to the students. As a team, they could explore the code of the mini-game and decide if they wanted to reuse the example as a template (changing the characters, decorum, texts and interactions) or if they wanted to start anew. In coherency with the growing research on ICTs, we observed that the programming part of the workshop was seen differently by the students and the older adults. While the younger members of the teams were trying to program through "trial and error", adults used a more reflexive approach; some asked for tutorials and many were trying to understand "why" it worked as it was before starting the design process (Fig. 5).

Fig. 5. Scratch game creation based on a game character

3.5 Peer Playing the Mini-Games Created by the Intergenerational Teams

Towards the end of the workshop, we invited the intergenerational teams to demonstrate their work to the other teams. Despite the different aspects that were not finished or not functioning, the participants enjoyed showing their creations to their peers. As a synthesis and a closing comments, participants gave their impressions of the workshop and of coding, its limits and the opportunities it generates as a pedagogical tool. For most of the participants, this intergenerational game design activity was a first both in terms of game design, intergenerational team-based process and coding. Despite the degree of novelty in the tasks to accomplish and the knowledge and competences related to the intergenerational participatory digital game design, the participants enjoyed the experience and were not uncomfortable despite being permanently out of their zone of proximal development and innovation.

4   Conclusion and Discussion

We found that using a highly guided approach to scaffold the intergenerational game creation workshop was a key element for its successful development. Having a predetermined topics list also helped in getting the teams to work quickly. In the same line, making explicit all the tasks that were to accomplish was beneficial to the flow of the workshop and ensured to achieve the pedagogical and intergenerational learning objectives.

As for the difficulties that rose, we noted that in one workshop held at the SGISS, one team had two computers to work on instead of one, shared by the whole team. The result was that this separated the team into two independent groups; each produced their own game without communicating with each other. This split hindered both teamwork and fun for the participants. We should also consider the important time investment required to prepare the intergenerational game creation workshops in terms of participants' recruitment and the preparation with the pedagogical staff in the different educational settings (i.e. high schools and community centers). Despite the efforts required to deploy the intergenerational game creation workshop, the intergenerational learning and cross-age social bonding are extraordinary, as all the actors engaged (learners, teachers, pedagogical experts, game designers, researchers) in these experiences appreciated at the highest level the experiences. Their feedback highlighted the benefits in terms of education, social participation and fun; this has propelled and encouraged us to continue enabling these experiences.

All participants in the workshops experienced an enjoyable and valuable intergenerational learning experience where they developed a joint knowledge creation activity through game design. In these activities, the final game product is not the objective, but an intergenerational facilitator; the game design process in itself is the core of the research as it is enabling participants from different ages and backgrounds to exchange about a certain topic and engage in a joint creative task where the competences and specific know-how of each one is valued and mobilized towards the objective. We invite the digital game industry to introduce intergenerational game design and game evaluation activities when developing new products in order to better represent the needs and interests of different generations and genders.

References

1. Romero, M.: Intergenerational learning, life narratives and games - SGISS 2015 Proceedings, vol. 1. Université Laval. Centre de recherche et d'intervention sur la réussite scolaire (2015)
2. Loos, E.: Designing meaningful intergenerational digital games. In: International Conference on Communication, Media, Technology and Design, pp. 46–51 (2014)
3. Romero, M.: Intergenerational digital storytelling pairing teens as multimedia facilitators with an elder as narrative director. In: International Conference Qualitative Research in Communication 2015. Book of abstracts, Bucharest, Romania, p. 30 (2015)
4. Newman, S., Hatton-Yeo, A.: Intergenerational learning and the contributions of older people. Ageing Horiz. **8**(10), 31–39 (2008)
5. Heron, M.J., Belford, P., Goker, A.: Sexism in the circuitry: female participation in male-dominated popular computer culture. ACM SIGCAS Comput. Soc. **44**(4), 18–29 (2014)
6. Schneider, E.: A tale of damsels and heroes: gender and age in bioshock infinite. In: Intergenerational Learning, Life Narratives and Games, Québec, vol. 1, pp. 25–29 (2015)
7. Romero, M., Loos, E.: Intergenerational Game Creation. Engaging elders and secondary level students in intergenerational learning about immigration through participative game design. In: European Distance and E-Learning Network 2015, Barcelona, 2015, vol. Book of Abstracts Including the Collection of Synergy Synopses, p. 167 (2015)
8. Romero, M.: Creating computer-based life narratives: engaging elders and secondary level students in intergenerational learning about immigration. In: Capital Ideas, Ottawa, Canada (2015)
9. Lukyanenko, R., Parsons, J.: Extending participatory design principles to structured user-generated content. In: Scandinavian Conference on Information Systems, Oulu, Finland (2015)
10. Stewart, J., Bleumers, L., Van Looy, J., Mariën, I., All, A., Schurmans, D., Willaert, K., De Grove, F., Jacobs, A., Misuraca, G.: The Potential of Digital Games for Empowerment and Social Inclusion of Groups at Risk of Social and Economic Exclusion: Evidence and Opportunity for Policy (2013)
11. Sotamaa, O.: When the game is not enough: motivations and practices among computer game modding culture. Games Cult. **5**(3), 239–255 (2010)
12. Kayali, F., et al.: Participatory game design for the INTERACCT serious game for health. In: Göbel, S., Ma, M., Hauge, J.B., Oliveira, M.F., Wiemeyer, J., Wendel, V. (eds.) Serious Games. LNCS, vol. 9090, pp. 13–25. Springer, Heidelberg (2015)
13. Khaled, R., Vanden Abeele, V., Van Mechelen, M., Vasalou, A.: Participatory design for serious game design: truth and lies. In: Proceedings of the First ACM SIGCHI Annual Symposium on Computer-Human Interaction in Play, pp. 457–460 (2014)
14. Vygotsky, L.S.: Mind and Society: The Development of Higher Mental Processes. Harvard University Press, Cambridge (1978)
15. Romero, M., Lambropoulos, N.: Digital game creation as a creative learning activity. In: 2015 International Conference on Interactive Mobile Communication Technologies and Learning (IMCL), pp. 338–342 (2015)

RERC TechSAge: Making a Difference to the Lives of Older Adults with Disability Through Design and Technology

Jon A. Sanford and Elena T. Gonzalez[✉]

Center for Assistive Technology and Environmental Access (CATEA),
Georgia Institute of Technology, Atlanta, GA, USA
{jon.sanford,elena.gonzalez}@coa.gatech.edu

Abstract. As with people who are experiencing normal aging, there is great potential for technology to provide supportive solutions for people aging with disability. Yet, while little is known about the needs and abilities of people aging with disability, universal design (UD), which is an approach that promotes usability for all, regardless of ability or impairment promising, offers great promise in developing effective technologies for people aging with disability. The *Rehabilitation Engineering Research Center on Technologies to Support Successful Aging with Disability* (RERC TechSAge) takes the unique approach of applying UD principles to rehab engineering research and the development of new technologies for older adults. This paper will provide an overview of TechSAge's mission and conceptual framework and highlight three projects: User Needs research, the App for Locational Intelligence and Geospatial Navigation project (ALIGN) and the SmartBathroom. These and other TechSAge projects provide exemplars of how incorporating UD in front-end research and development, versus accommodating specific limitations after the fact, can extend usability of technology and environments for broad use, and particularly people aging with disability.

Keywords: Universal design · Aging with disability · Technologies for aging

1 Introduction

People with disabilities are living longer than ever before. For individuals with long-term impairments, the addition of normal age-related declines, such as loss of vision or hearing, can present unique challenges that can further inhibit their ability to carry out daily living activities and live independently. Historically, research in disability and aging has emphasized the impact of either increasing levels of chronic illness and functional losses in late life (aging into disability) or aging and congenital or acquired impairments from early to middle life (aging with a disability). The former has been primarily the purview of geriatrics/gerontology (e.g., U.S. National Institute on Aging), and has an aging research approach (i.e., understand and control factors that affect aging) more than a disability research approach (i.e., understand and compensate for factors that affect disability). In contrast, the latter, which has been the interest and focus

© Springer International Publishing Switzerland 2016
J. Zhou and G. Salvendy (Eds.): ITAP 2016, Part I, LNCS 9754, pp. 82–91, 2016.
DOI: 10.1007/978-3-319-39943-0_9

of rehabilitation engineering under the National Institute on Disability, Independent Living and Rehabilitation Research (NIDILRR) priorities, has focused primarily on understanding the consequences of life-long impairments in old age and early-onset of aging due to disability.

Although both approaches are important, each only addresses half of the aging problem in that they both overlook the 29.5 million Americans aged 21–64 who are now growing older with a long-term impairment or disability [1] and who will likely experience newly acquired and pervasive age-related functional losses, comorbidities and secondary conditions [2–7]. For these individuals, the additive effects of age-related conditions may mean the difference between their current impairment or disability and aging into disability or multiple disabilities, respectively.

There are few published studies about the effects of rehab interventions for people with age-related deficits in function among the population of people aging with impairment or disability. Evaluation of existing rehabilitation engineering interventions, usability testing, and research devoted to increasing the availability of technologies for this population is lacking; therefore, little scientific evidence exists with which to inform practice. Thus, despite comprising the majority of the population of seniors with disabilities, individuals who are experiencing age-related limitations beyond their primary impairment/disability are also the most underserved and understudied target population. Although many older adults with long-term impairments already use (or have access to) assistive technologies (AT), it is crucial to determine how to adapt and integrate technology as the both the user and their devices age [8].

2 TechSAge Overview

To address this need, the mission of the Rehabilitation Engineering Research Center on Technologies to Support Successful Aging with Disability (RERC TechSAge) is to support people with chronic conditions and long-term impairments who are at risk of disability or increased disability due to comorbid age-related losses; by empowering these individuals to sustain independence; maintain health; engage safely in basic activities at home and in the community; and fully participate in society; through increasing knowledge about, availability of, and access to effective, universally-designed technologies. Working within a universal design paradigm that drives all RERC activities, RERC TechSAge serves as a catalyst for a major shift in the understanding and design of home and community technologies for people aging with impairment and disability in order to achieve the goal of influencing rehabilitation engineering practice by assessing the impact of age-related changes on the activity and participation needs and outcomes of people growing older with impairments and/or disabilities.

2.1 Theoretical Framework

RERC TechSAge is grounded in the idea that disability is not an inevitable outcome for people with impairments. The Person-Environment Fit model suggests that disability occurs when the demands of one's environment exceeds their abilities [9].

Integrating this framework within the World Health Organization's International Classification of Functioning, Disability and Health (ICF) paradigm [10], TechSAge projects focus on understanding the environmental impact of pre-existing and age-related impairments and addressing needs through the development of supportive technologies. While an impairment does not necessarily lead to disability, the potential interaction of multiple comorbidities and impairments on top of a pre-existing impairment will compound the effects of environmental demands. As such, people aging with disability are more likely to encounter barriers in the home and community than they did prior to the onset of age-related declines. As with people who are experiencing normal aging, there is great potential for technology to provide supportive solutions for people aging with disability.

Figure 1 demonstrates the differences in environmental interaction and performance outcomes between individuals with age-related changes and existing impairment compared to those with either age-related changes or impairment. Even when the environment is held constant, when age-related deficits (e.g., loss of strength) are added to one's existing condition (e.g., uses a wheelchair), environmental factors that were previously facilitators (e.g., the slope of a ramp), can become barriers (e.g., slope is too steep). As a result, people aging with a disability are more likely to encounter more environmental challenges than individuals with either an impairment or an age-related change. In comparison to be people with an impairment OR and age-related decline (top row), those with an impairment AND an age-related decline (bottom row) are more likely to encounter barriers (Bs) and less likely to find facilitators (Fs), increasing their risk of disability and decreasing their likelihood of achieving successful performance. Headers at the top represent the integration of Person-Environment Fit constructs (i.e., person, context and performance) with those within the ICF (i.e., body structure and function, contextual barriers and facilitators, and activity and participation). For example, an age-related decline alone, such as hearing loss, can create barriers that prevent an individual from participating or fully participating in an activity. However, this barrier can be overcome with the appropriate support, or facilitator, such as a hearing aid, to perform the activity. Imagine a person who has been blind since childhood. They have become accustomed to using assistive devices with sound based cues, such as screen readers and white canes, to navigate their environment and carryout everyday activities. As an older adult, they are now experiencing age-related hearing loss. The combination of impairments is likely to result in more, and perhaps larger, barriers in their environment. Moreover, the facilitators that previously worked for them are no longer working and have, in essence, become barriers, decreasing the likelihood of successful performance and increasing the likelihood of disability.

2.2 R&D Activities

Currently in year 3, the RERC TechSAge has already made important strides in setting the foundation for strategic research and development (R&D) projects to achieve the goals and mission of the center. Research activities are underway to provide converging evidence necessary to design integrated technology supports for seniors aging with disability. Specifically, RERC TechSAge is developing an evidence-based taxonomy

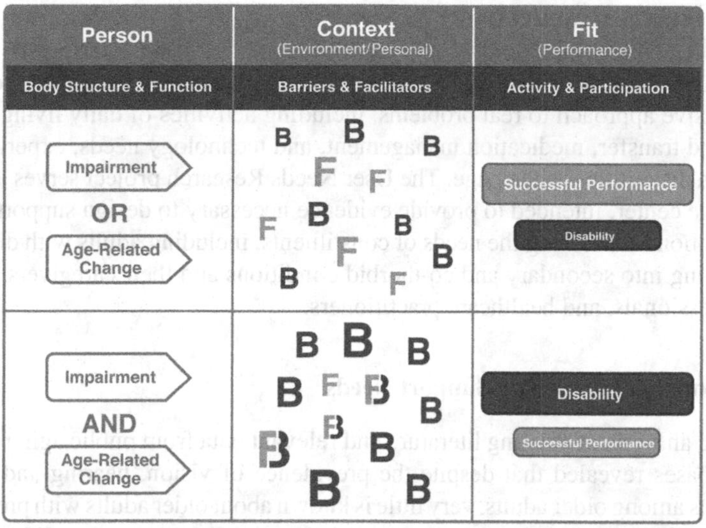

Fig. 1. Differences in person-environment fit and task performance between people with age related changes OR impairment compared to those with age-related changes AND impairment (TechSAge target population).

of user needs, stratified by functional loss, identifying needs and predictors of interventions for home-based tasks, and demonstrating feasibility of using functional performance data to predict task performance within and across activities. The RERC has developed a participant registry of people aging with disability to provide efficient, study-specific recruitment for projects as well as the Minimum Battery assessment to standardize measures across all TechSAge participants. A large-scale database has been developed to integrate both assessment and project-specific data to identify patterns of ability, performance, and technology needs. These are described in greater detail below.

Development activities, including mobile applications and smart technologies have short-term and longer-term outputs and outcomes, respectively. Two projects, representing each of these activities are described in this paper. The ALIGN project, which is a route planning application for people with mobility limitations who are experiencing comorbid vision loss, is intended to advance the rapid and cost-effective deployment of software development and evaluation. In addition, for individuals with unstable abilities due to variable conditions (e.g. arthritis, multiple sclerosis), the SmartBathroom project, will create a context-aware, fully automated bathroom with continuous monitoring of a user's functional status (e.g., gait, balance, posture) and task performance (e.g., toilet and tub transfers) that will synchronously adjust environmental features (e.g., grab bars, fixtures) based on a user's needs at any point in time.

3   User Needs Research

To ensure relevance, all TechSAge activities have a basis in user needs. Projects take a comprehensive approach to real problems, including activities of daily living (ADLs), mobility and transfer, medication management, and technology needs, experienced by people with disabilities as they age. The User Needs Research project serves as a foundation of the center, intended to provide evidence necessary to design supportive technology solutions addressing the needs of constituents, including adults with disabilities who are aging into secondary and co-morbid conditions and their caregivers, rehabilitation professionals, and healthcare practitioners.

3.1   Taxonomy of Everyday Support Needs

An archival analysis of existing literature and relevant data from public aging and disability databases revealed that despite the prevalence of vision, hearing and mobility impairments among older adults, very little is known about older adults with pre-existing impairments specifically [11]. Available statistics and resources were limited to the broader population of older adults with impairments and did not differentiate between individuals with a pre-existing impairment vs those who acquired an impairment in older age. Moreover, the sparse information regarding difficulty in task performance and use of assistive technology among older adults with impairments typically focused on select Activities of Daily Living (ADLs) and Instrumental Activities of Daily Living (IADLs) and failed to capture Enhanced Activities of Daily Living, such as leisure, in which older adults spend a large proportion of their time [12]. Findings confirmed the research gap and the need to comprehensively explore everyday task challenges, what makes these tasks difficult, current strategies and solution, and ultimately unmet support needs for this understudied population of older adults aging with disability.

Addressing this need, TechSAge researchers are currently developing a comprehensive User Needs assessment tool for older adult participants with long-term vision, hearing, and mobility impairments. Specific emphasis will be placed on capturing how the individual responds to task challenges with daily activities in relation to the Selection Optimization and Compensation framework [13]. The User Needs assessment incorporates findings from an interview study wherein subject matter experts with a range of professional and/or personal experiences and roles with older adults with these specific impairments (e.g., caregivers, family members, medical professionals) gave their perspectives on challenges experienced by these populations [14]. Focusing on three domains, including technology use, access to community resources, and housing, this study revealed themes of challenges that were specific to certain impairment groups as well as cross-cutting. For instance, one technology challenge specific to visually impaired older adults was difficulty adapting to popular touch screen devices, as they are used to relying on devices with buttons that provide tactile cues. Across impairment groups, subject matter experts discussed that the small size of phones created operational challenges. Findings from this study and other related studies in the User Needs Project are driving the content and specific questions of the assessment, which will be administered to approximately sixty participants in each target population, stratified by age.

3.2   Home-Based User Needs

In addition to investigating everyday support needs via interviews and survey data, TechSAge investigators are working to establish ground truth by exploring user needs in the home. The Home-Based User Needs project is geared toward understanding how individuals with pre-existing impairments who are experiencing age-related losses co-morbidly carry out activities in the home related to home mobility and medication management, often essential for maintaining independence and aging in place. For the first in-home study researchers interviewed older adults with long-term mobility impairments about their process for select activities of daily living, such as bathing and toileting, in context and documented photos of barriers and supportive solutions in their environment [15]. Researchers continue to analyze the rich interview and photo data, which is driving a follow-up study with participants to gauge longitudinal changes in needs and assistive technology use. The Home-Based User Needs team also conducted an in-home interview with older adults with vision, hearing and mobility impairments focused specifically on issues with medication adherence and current strategies. Through further analysis, researchers hope to identify which strategies or technological solutions are associated with higher rates of adherence for specific combinations of primary impairment and secondary functional loss and the underlying human factors at play.

4   ALIGN

The App for Locational Intelligence and Geospatial Navigation project, or ALIGN, entails the development and evaluation of a mobile app to inform outdoor route planning for people aging with ambulatory impairments who are experiencing additional age-related declines in vision. People aging with long-term mobility impairments generally use familiar outdoor routes that accommodate their functional abilities and assistive technologies (AT). For these individuals, the addition of age-related declines (e.g., vision loss, hearing loss) create a new set of environmental challenges that often exceed the abilities of these individuals, even on long-used routes [16, 17]. Despite these challenges, the real barrier to outdoor mobility is the lack of information with which to plan safe and appropriate alternative routes.

4.1   App Functionality and User Interface

To effectively promote community mobility among the target population, the ALIGN app not only incorporates a range of environmental factors that impact accessibility and safe mobility, but also take into account personal and social preferences of the user. Unlike other accessibility applications that identify predetermined "accessible" routes based on a few "standard" features (e.g., 1:12 slope, smooth sidewalks and curb cuts), ALIGN will include critical information about accessibility factors both static (e.g., land uses, vegetation, street connectivity) and dynamic (e.g., traffic volumes, timing of lights) that can be uploaded (as needed) close to real time. This will enable users to determine for themselves what routes are accessible and acceptable to them based on their own abilities, the demands of the situation, and what they prefer.

An online survey of older adults with mobility impairment was undertaken to identify important parameters for the app. The survey yielded priority factors, such as presence of sidewalks, types of intersections, and obstructions/lanscape overgrowth, which will be incorporated in the app. A weighting system was applied to each factor based on an Analytical Hierarchy Process (AHP) in order to generate mobility scores for route segments, and ultimately develop and implement a routing algorithm.

To address the variety of abilities in the senior population, the ALIGN user interface (Fig. 2) was designed to accommodate a range of abilities. The interface continues to be iteratively refined with upgrades such as featuring more intuitive icons and providing alternative and redundant forms of guidance (e.g., voice and visual) for mapped routes and turn-by-turn directions.

Fig. 2. Screenshots of the ALIGN route planning app show how the user can create pedestrian routes that best suit their needs based on desired environmental characteristics.

4.2   Data Acquistion

Integrating a wide range of environmental information, the development of the ALIGN app's functional capabilities required creative data sourcing strategies. Where possible, relevant public datasets were obtained from national and local organizations, such as the U.S. Census Bureau, Georgia Department of Transportation (DOT), Atlanta Regional Commission, and Atlanta Police Department. In some cases, real time data, such as pedestrian volumes and timing of crossing signals, could not be found with the possibility that such data is not publically available or doesn't yet exist. For these data alternative solutions, including crowd sourcing, are being explored. Data has been acquired to create a working prototype for a small area of Georgia Tech's campus. The prototype is currently being evaluated under conditions of actual use to determine feasibility and practicality.

5   SmartBathroom

Historically, toilet accessibility has primarily consisted of a set of <u>fixed</u> grab bars and raised toilets that are based on the abilities of young male wheelchair users with good upper body strength [18]. However, as people with disabilities grow older, their functional limitations are exacerbated by age-related decrements. Increasingly, existing transfer solutions cannot compensate for age-related frailty. To compound the problem, functional abilities not only vary both across individuals, but also within individuals over time due to progressive chronic conditions, such as arthritis. As a result, fixed transfer systems are only able to support some abilities some of the time.

A number of studies have been undertaken to determine the optimum design for toilet transfer; however only one study has evaluated a flexible system [19] with a user adjustable height and tilt toilet. Although the adjustable toilet was effective, the lack of an adjustable grab bar was problematic. Moreover, user control of the adjustments may not be effective for individuals who are not aware of the specific adjustments they need at a particular time. To provide a more flexible environment that will accommodate a range of abilities at any time, the SmartBathroom project will to develop a bathroom environment capable of assessing an individual's abilities at any point in time and spontaneously adjusting supportive environmental features to accommodate those abilities.

5.1   Lab Construction

An existing bathroom in the Georgia Tech Aware Home Laboratory is being renovated to create a fully functional modular and motorized environment that will provide the flexibility for fixtures (i.e., toilet, tub and sink), supportive devices (e.g., grab bars) lighting and cabinetry to be rearranged or removed. An array of sensing technologies will be embedded in the environment (e.g., floor, walls, ceiling fixtures) to measure biomechanical data (e.g., gait, balance, posture, grip strength and speed, accuracy, and efficiency of movement), forces exerted on the toilet, bathtub, sink, and grab bars, and locations where fixtures and grab bars are used. A vision system (e.g. Kinect) and smart floor sensors will track movement and gait. In addition, motorized hardware will make adjustment to the various fixtures.

5.2   Next Steps and Long-Term Goals

To develop the predictive algorithms that will control the environment, 25 individuals with a mobility impairment will participate in two test sessions at Time 1 (T1) and Time 2 (T2). Functional measures of static and dynamic stability, posture, balance, gait speed, forward and side reaches, grip strength and range of motion will be taken using standardized instruments. Participants will transfer on/off or in/out of the fixtures. In T1 subjects will perform the tasks with the fixtures set up in the same locations and positions (e.g., height, distance from walls) as in their own bathroom. At T2, an occupational therapist (OT) will help subjects adjust the fixtures and grab bars to set up their optimum configuration. The configuration will then be tested, followed by a post-trial rating to determine if any of the dimensions require further adjustment. If so, the dimensions will be reset and the trial repeated. These procedures will be repeated until no adjustments are made.

Given the general absence of integrative technologies in the design of bathroom products, we anticipate that the smart technologies developed in this project are at least 10 years from commercialization. However, within the 5-year project we expect to develop and market, a range of interim, "smarter" technologies that will provide a more universal design system through feedback that will enable users to adjust their transfer behaviors to optimize use of a fixed environment.

6 Discussion

The goal of the RERC is to develop new knowledge and tools that can promote and increase community mobility, health, safety, and independence of people with disabilities even as the onset of new functional limitations result in new and pervasive barriers. However, the RERC's efforts are only beginning to scratch the surface of understanding the problems and developing solutions for our target populations. In fact, the premise of much of the basic research undertaken by the RERC is to identify the set of questions to be addressed by future efforts in this space.

The current RERC development projects have been designed to test usability and utility with pilot data on effectiveness. Longer term there is a need for translational research of these evidence-based interventions to identify intervention efficacy on health, activity and participation of people aging with disability. In research there is the need to examine the use of technology supports and changes in adoption strategies over time as older adults with impairments and some disability age into either disability or greater disability. Because much of the RERC's target audience has historically been underserved by traditional technology interventions, it is important to examine indigenous, individualized solutions that will scale up to customizable universal design solutions. Finally, there is need to understand and develop universally designed, smart interventions that not only compensate for disability, but are capable of effecting behavior change that enhances the acceptance and effectiveness of the interventions.

Acknowledgements. This research was supported in part by a grant from the National Institute on Disability, Independent Living, and Rehabilitation Research (Department of Health & Human Services, Administration for Community Living) Grant 90RE5016-01-00 under the auspices of the Rehabilitation and Engineering Research Center on Technologies to Support Successful Aging with Disability (TechSAge; www.techsage.gatech.edu). The authors would like to Amy Lambeth, HCI graduate student at Georgia Tech, for her assistance creating a visual depiction of differential environmental barriers and performance outcomes between individuals with age-related changes and existing impairment compared to those with either age-related changes or impairment (Fig. 1).

References

1. Brault, M.W.: Americans with disabilities: 2010, U.S. Census Bureau, U.S. Department of Commerce (2012)

2. Freid, V.M., Bernstein, A.B., Bush, M.A.: Multiple chronic conditions among adults aged 45 and over: trends over the past 10 years. National Center for Health Statistics, Hyattsville, MD (2012)

3. Institute of Medicine: Secondary conditions and aging with disability. In: Field, M.J., Jette, A.M. (eds.) The Future of Disability in America. The National Academies Press, Washington, D.C. (2007)

4. Jensen, M.P., Molton, I.R., Groah, S.L., Campbell, M.L., Charlifue, S., Chiodo, A., Forchheimer, M., Krause, J.S., Tate, D.: Secondary health conditions in individuals aging with SCI: terminology, concepts, and analytic approaches. Spinal Cord **50**(5), 373–378 (2011)

5. Kailes, J.I.: A user's perspective on midlife (ages 18–65) aging with disability. In: Workshop on Disability in America: A New Look, pp. 194–204. The National Academies Press, Washington, D.C. (2006)

6. Kemp, B.J., Mosqueda, L. (eds.): Aging with a Disability: What the Clinician Needs to Know. The Johns Hopkins University Press, Baltimore (2004)

7. Kinne, S., Patrick, D.L., Doyle, D.L.: Prevalence of secondary conditions among people with disabilities. Am. J. Public Health **94**(3), 443–445 (2004)

8. Agree, E.: The potential for technology to enhance independence for those aging with a disability. Disabil. Health J. **7**(S), 33–39 (2014)

9. Lawton, M.P., Nahemow, L.: Ecology and the aging process. In: Eisdorfer, C., Lawton, M.P. (eds.) Psychology of Adult Development and Aging. American Psychological Association, Washington, D.C. (1973)

10. World Health Organization (WHO): International Classification of Functioning, Disability and Health. World Health, Organization, Geneva (2001)

11. Harrington, C.N., Mitzner, T.L., Rogers, W.A.: Understanding the role of technology for meeting the support needs of older adults in the USA with functional limitations. Gerontechnology **14**, 21–31 (2015)

12. Rogers, W.A., Meyer, B., Walker, N., Fisk, A.D.: Functional limitations to daily living tasks in the aged: a focus group analysis. Hum. Factors **40**(1), 111–125 (1998)

13. Baltes, P.B., Baltes, M.M.: Psychological perspectives on successful aging: the model of selective optimization with compensation. In: Baltes, P.B., Baltes, M.M. (eds.) Successful Aging: Perspectives from the Behavioral Sciences, pp. 1–34. Cambridge University Press, New York (1990)

14. Preusse, K.C., Gonzalez, E., Singleton, J., Mitzner, T.L., Rogers, W.A.: Needs assessment of individuals aging with impairment: findings from Subject Matter Expert Interviews. In: Proceedings of the Human Factors and Ergonomics Society Europe (HFES Europe) (2015)

15. Gonzalez, E., Fausset, C.B., Foster, A., Cha, G., Fain, W.B.: Moving in, out and around the home: solutions from older adults with long-term mobility impairments. In: Proceedings of the Rehabilitation Engineering Society of North America (RESNA) 2015 Annual Meeting (2015)

16. Rantakokko, M., Iwarsson, S., Mänty, M., Leinonen, R., Rantanen, T.: Perceived barriers in the outdoor environment and development of walking difficulties in older people. Age Ageing **41**(1), 118–121 (2012)

17. Rosso, A.L., Auchincloss, A.H., Michael, Y.L.: The urban built environment and mobility in older adults: a comprehensive review. J. Aging Res., Article ID 816106, 10 (2011). doi: 10.4061/2011/816106

18. Sanford, J.A.: Design for the Ages: Universal Design as a Rehabilitation Strategy. Springer, New York (2012)

19. Gentile, N., Edelmayer, G.: FRR-field-test (2005). http://www.is.tuwien.ac.at/fortec/reha.e/projects/frr/conference/1555_Real_life_test_at_a_day_care_centre_en.pdf. Accessed 24 Mar 2014

To Meet the Needs of Aging Users and the Prerequisites of Innovators in the Design Process

Lessons Learned from Three Pilot Projects

Marie Sjölinder[1(✉)], Isabella Scandurra[2], Anneli Avatare Nöu[1], and Ella Kolkowska[2]

[1] SICS Swedish ICT, Box 1263, 164 29 Kista, Sweden
{marie,anneli}@sics.se
[2] School of Business, Örebro University, 701 82 Örebro, Sweden
{Isabella.Scandurra,Ella.Kolkowska}@oru.se

Abstract. The aim of this paper is to analyze cases where participatory design with different stakeholder groups was a beacon in the development of innovations. An important aspect was a strong foundation both in the needs of the elderly and in the feasibility from the market side. Three cases were analyzed from aspects as: environment and development phase of product; participation of different stakeholders; and proxy involvement of care professionals. The impact of this approach is a benefit for aging end-users as well as increased feasibility for the innovation companies, as a result when collaboration of different stakeholders focuses on balancing the demands of the users and the prerequisites of the industry.

Keywords: Participatory design · Professional-patient relations · Community-based participatory research · Elderly · Social technology · Welfare technology

1 Introduction

User involvement in general is often considered a time consuming process. Therefore it is important to improve the understanding of how this process can be made more effective and efficient in an industrial view. Especially small companies find it difficult to adopt such methods as they value time in respect to both manpower and a fast developing market [1]. The authors believe that existing methods of user involvement in design may be refined to *both* address the needs of the end-users *and* the prerequisites of other stakeholders, such as innovators. When studying participation, different levels of involvement are discussed, often in relation to the end-users' approach and effects on the outcome. The authors were inspired by an article by Östlund [2] remodeling the idea of the "citizen participation ladder" by Arnstein from 1969 [3] to suit older people in the innovation and design process. Östlund [2] states that whether the users are considered as objects or subjects, they get different roles in the design process. Using them as research objects, the designer is seeking generalizations to be applied in design. As a subject they participate themselves in the development process [2]. This is probably valid also for other stakeholder groups participating in an innovation process. Additionally, more active participation is often desired of the stakeholder group of developers

© Springer International Publishing Switzerland 2016
J. Zhou and G. Salvendy (Eds.): ITAP 2016, Part I, LNCS 9754, pp. 92–104, 2016.
DOI: 10.1007/978-3-319-39943-0_10

[4]. New approaches to stakeholder involvement may also contribute to support compa-nies in broadening their market without reducing focus on specific user needs. One recurring example is when technology reaches the hands of real users and is contex-tualized; its real value turns out [5]. Also, studies point out that technology often starts to be used in new ways, different from what the innovator had in mind [2, 6]. Sometimes this comes as a result of the methods that the researchers bring into the process [7].

We present experiences from three information technology and technology (IT&T) projects where stakeholders from industry, care givers and researchers were actively involved together with aging users. Collaboration of those stakeholders while focusing on balancing the demands of the users and the prerequisites of the industry is analyzed and discussed.

1.1 Research Approach and Methodological Background

Human-computer interaction (HCI) research has come a long way in understanding the importance of involving users in the process of developing new technology. The presented cases are all action research projects that adhere to Participatory Design (PD) [8, 9], as one of the HCI theories that regards system development with user participation and that considers designing a social process. The degree of user participation may vary. Regardless of activation degree, in PD, developers and practitioners/users are seen as actively cooperating partners. Together they aim to reduce uncertainty and risk in the development of innovations, where a detailed conception of exactly which future needs should be supported, often lacks [8, 9]. We also know from HCI research that usability aspects should be brought in early in the development process [10]. Previous research presents several methods to engage users with the aim to create future environments, e.g. so-called Future workshops [11]. Other methods to bring analysis of future needs into system development are iterative prototyping and scenario-based design, preferably applied together with potential users in a collaborative approach [12].

PD is highly context-dependent and each application struggles with the under-standing of how to involve different user groups in an optimal way. In this study, the authors have selected cases where the research team has been working as mediators between care professionals and developers from the industry. The approach of the researchers was also the extension of a Triple Helix setting (society working closely with industry and academia) to a Quadruple Helix model (Fig. 1) by involving the main stakeholders, the aging users. Using older adults' extensive experience when trying to meet their needs can result in more adequate solutions and lead faster to the goal [2], rather than relying on interaction patterns based on the computer paradigm [13].

In this Quadruple Helix model, problem-owners in the health and social care sector, aging users, health informatics researchers and developers of novel IT&T work together in a user-centered and participatory design approach, aiming to support aging users by their co-created solutions.

It is important to reach an equivalent balance between these stakeholder groups already from the beginning, especially when designing services for aging users. Many user groups cannot or do not want to participate in design of new IT&T-support, although they are invited as potential end-users of the product. This model relies on aging users

Fig. 1. Quadruple Helix setting

willing and being able to participate, as well as on their health and social care staff that daily works with the potential end-users. Equally important is to align industry into the working model, as they also are seen as supporting actors to the aging users. Experience remarks that the mediating researchers need to "teach user-centered design and participatory methods" before and during the actual project [14, 15]. Once initiated, it is beneficial for the results if the developers also are present in the daily practice that their innovation will be part of. Observation activities as well as sharing knowledge in the form of e.g. demos and being responsive to feedback regarding iteratively presented prototypes create a fruitful environment, where all participants are willing to jointly improve the elderly care situation [12].

To increase the likelihood that a product or service in health and social care of elderly will reach a successful implementation and a usage situation where the users are satisfied with the innovation, it is important to work towards a balance between the demands of the users and the prerequisites of the industry.

The objective of this study was to analyze PD cases with focus on *different* stakeholder groups and their prerequisites to be able to find how this Quadruple Helix PD approach affects the balance between end-user needs and the prerequisites of the innovators. The selected pilot projects were different, but all aimed for a strong foundation in both the needs of the elderly as well as in the co-created result, based on the conditions from the market side, e.g. feasibility.

2   Method

This study used a qualitative case study method containing thorough analyses of the pilot projects in several aspects to investigate effects on the implementation due to the Quadruple Helix PD approach. Apart from aspects of the *innovation*: "environment" and "development phase of the product", the *participation* of Quadruple Helix stakeholders was analyzed in three sub-aspects; "extent of participation of aging users", "Triple Helix joint work", and "proxy involvement of care professionals". A source of inspiration for the analysis was the rework of the "participation ladder" [3] with focus on older people made by Östlund [2]. For each Quadruple Helix aspect different criteria were used to define an adequate range. Degrees of participation were described using two scales, both of them reworked on the idea of the "Participation ladder" by Arnstein [3]. Care professionals as advocates of the aging end-user needs were used in some of the cases. When so, the level was measured in terms of "proxy involvement".

2.1   Analysis of Level of Participation – Older People

The ladder defined by Östlund [2] illustrates the degree of participation of older people in innovation projects, as part of the Aging and Design program at a Swedish university. Here the ladder starts on the highest level, with

1. Older people are co-actors and are themselves driving the changes they want to accomplish.
2. Older people participate as the experts on their own life situation.
3. Older people contribute with their own views in consultation together with others.
4. Older people receive information and/or are being the subject to different types of operations.
5. Manipulation – people are objects for other's actions [2].

These criteria were used to analyze the aspect of the Participation of aging users on an individual level.

2.2   Analysis of Level of Participation – Triple Helix Joint Work

This analysis model, defined by Scandurra [16] and refined by Scandurra and Sjölinder, is inspired by Lindholm and Moritz [17]. Their "participation staircase" is acknowledged by the Swedish Association of Local Authorities and Regions (SALAR). It has been used since 2011 to represent citizen dialogue techniques ranging from the level where citizens are given information to the level where citizens get a direct role in decision-making [18]. Our remodeled staircase illustrates how different stakeholders in a Triple Helix constellation work together in an innovation process. Starting with the lowest level of joint work, the model increases the cooperation step by step.

1. No Communication.
2. Conversation – Mutual telling what you do, as an information or dialogue.
3. Common view – shared goals, common understanding. Requires an agreement between actors.
4. Coordination – the structure of how activities are carried out; procedures, rules and regulations as a basis for Cooperation and Collaboration.
5. Cooperation – Activities carried out by individuals that exceed the organizational boundaries.
6. Collaboration – coordination + cooperation. Activities carried out by organizations, which exceed the boundaries within or between organizations.

These criteria were used to analyze the aspect of Triple Helix Participation on a joint work or group level where all actors from Society, Industry and Academia participate.

2.3 Proxy Involvement

Despite efforts from the developer team, when trying to deploy technology to aging user groups, the technology may be perceived too difficult or cumbersome to use. A challenge for research is therefore to continuously examine when and how to best use the engagement and knowledge of the aging users in the design process, as well as to understand when and how other stakeholders, e.g. social care staff, correctly could define and transfer the needs of the aging users. Inspired by Boyd-Graber et al. [19] and their work regarding using people close to the intended user in the design process, we investigated the extent of "Proxy involvement". The amount of Proxy involvement was weighted in relation to the extent other stakeholders as e.g. the social care staff or next of kin spoke on the aging end-users' behalf. The terms High/Medium/Low referred to a weighted percentage where the activity of the proxies was decreasing: high proxy involvement ~80 %, medium ~50 % and low proxy involvement ~20 %.

3   Materials - The Three Cases in the Study

Many aging users suffer from age-related decline, both with respect to physical and cognitive abilities, which make it difficult to be involved in the design process as well as to use new services and new technology. This was no exception in the cases presented in this paper. Thus, some of the aging users got replaced by others during the projects, resulting in not well defined numbers regarding aging participants.

Each of the cases is described according to the following structure: description of the setting; study design and methods used; results and lessons learned.

3.1   Case 1: Development of a Communication Tool – Usage at a Nursing Home

Short description of the setting: In this project a communication tool and its services were tested [14]. The tool was an innovative mobile communication device connected to the TV, which worked as a remotely controlled large interactive screen. The aim with the study was to find potential users and target groups. During a 1.5 year project in a nursing home outside Stockholm, Sweden five residents (aged 75–88) participated, although suffering from age-related decline, both with respect to physical and cognitive abilities. There were nine persons participating from the care staff were nurse assistants, registered nurses and housing/department managers. The industry participants were four, and their roles were project manager, CTO and developers. The three research participants mediated and supported the project work. Their specialist domains were health informatics, HCI, technology & elderly research.

In the study usage testing was carried out with five devices placed in the residents' apartments and five in public areas. The care staff was deeply involved during the entire project; they recruited residents, gave information to relatives, to users and supported other care personnel in the role of tech ambassadors.

Study design and methods used: The care professionals were invited to co-design services as they are experienced in age-related impairments. Actual test phase lasted six months and every two weeks the project team was gathered at the nursing home in 2–4 h workshops with different content, led by researchers and industry partners. Three aging user profiles were created by the staff based on characteristics such as social situation, preferred hobbies, previous life in terms of work and family situation as well as medical history, current conditions, medication etc.; brainstorming techniques [20] and semi-structured interviews were used to gather information from the different groups about themselves, but also to gather what they thought about the needs and attitudes of the other groups. The researchers gathered information from the residents in individual semi-structured interviews.

Results and lessons learned: The material was analyzed with regard to differences and similarities; what the residents had described and what the care professionals had thought about them as aging users. One lesson learned was that developing the three aging user profiles together with the care personnel forced them to reflect on their residents in a salutogenic [21] or health promotive manner, beyond all medical conditions and as possible users of new technology. The user profiles were useful also for the developers' understanding of the environment and users that the services should support. The workshops revealed that the care personnel underestimated the technology experience and overlooked that many of the elderly once had worked with technology in different environments. The staff initially placed large focus on the importance of technology experience for using the device and it was clear that they did not quite understand for which resident the technology could be useful. Later, the devices were given to residents with little previous experience of new technology, but curious to get a communication channel with people outside the nursing home, and the technology became useful. On the other hand, thanks to the continuous engagement by the staff, devices were placed in the dining areas. It turned out that the main benefit of the device was social interaction between the residents, and not as expected, interaction with people outside the nursing home. This resulted in positive effects by both residents and staff, when realizing how technology can be used and appropriated when aging users were given the opportunity to start using technology in their own ways, as stated previously by e.g. Wyatt [5] and Östlund [2]. Using the technology together with other residents or with care professionals was not at all considered by the developers. Therefore the device needed to be re-designed in several ways to fit new user groups. The engagement by the staff also contributed to the creation of new content and new services [14].

3.2   Case 2: User Study with a Prototype Aiming at Broadening the Target Group

Short description of the setting: This study was conducted within a project that developed a Kinect™ sensor tool for stroke rehabilitation at home [22], and aimed to investigate whether or not usage could be broadened to other user groups than stroke patients. The number of seniors that participated was nine (aged 68–98). They suffered from physical decline due to diagnoses as Parkinson's disease, stroke and back problems, but their cognitive abilities were less affected. Some of the participants were just old and suffered from normal age-related physical decline. Five care personnel participated: nurses, physiotherapists and occupational therapists. The industry professionals were five and their roles were developers of technology and marketing. The three researchers mediated and supported the process. Their specialist domains were Technology & Elderly (1) and HCI (2).

Study design and methods used: The system was installed at three activity centers for elderly and there the aging users tested a Kinect sensor for conducting exercises, although the technology was designed for home usage. Each center had responsible care personnel doing observations during tests. The system provided video communication between patient and physiotherapist. Therefore patients could either do the exercises on their own or use the video communication to get direct feedback from the physiotherapist while doing the exercises.

After the session both aging users and staff filled in a questionnaire about usage of the system and the exercises. Aging users answered from their perspective and the staff based on the support given to the users to use the system. Questions regarded whether the exercises were relevant or if they had preferred some other exercise; the level of the exercises; different levels; and if increasing difficulty should have been performed in another way.

Results and lessons learned: Many of the aging users suffered from severe difficulties in being able to move, and some of the exercises were found too difficult. The aging users and the care professionals suggested more simple exercises, but they also expressed a need for a wide range of exercises since some aging users are physically active. The care professionals also requested less demanding exercises that could be performed sitting down and they suggested more exercises based on real life situations and tasks.

It worked well to evaluate the technology in the present environment. Even though it was a prototype containing flaws, the aging users managed to test it and contributed with suggestions for improvements. According to the questionnaires, there were no direct contradictions between the answers given by aging users and care professionals. However, the care professionals provided a deeper insight since they had a more holistic perspective on the situation. They provided valuable information about how and why features and interaction should be changed. The shared experience between care professionals and aging users contributed to a similar view of the situation and of the usage of the technology. The importance of providing exercises and services on different levels and possibilities to personalize the settings became clear i.e. adjusting the technology to fit larger numbers of aging users as well as broader target groups.

3.3 Case 3: An Innovator and Aging Users Develop New Services Together

Short description of the setting: In the project [6], a communication tool and its services were investigated. An innovative mobile communication device connected to the TV worked as a remotely controlled large interactive screen. The study was conducted at a senior center with eight aging users (aged 64–78). They did not suffer from age-related physical or cognitive decline. Three municipality staff participated: physiotherapist, administrator and manager at the center. There were four industry participants, and their roles were project manager, CTO and developers. Three researchers mediated and supported the project. Their specialist domains were Health informatics, HCI, Technology & Elderly research. The aim of this study was twofold: firstly to investigate novel eHealth services for elderly citizens together with less disabled aging users. Secondly, to examine different methods for combining what seniors perceived as meaningful services in relation to what was feasible by the innovator.

Study design and methods used: The device was tested by eight volunteers who visited a senior center during the 1.5 year project. Formative evaluations consisted of two parts, design workshops and future-oriented workshops where all stakeholders participated with great interest. Seven design workshops elicited demands regarding existing and new services. At the end of the project, the participants' experiences were elaborated in three future-oriented workshops with the purpose to get ideas for improved or new meaningful services, based on what aging users thought would be useful in relation to feasibility of the ideas as viewed by the innovator. Five phases of future-oriented workshops covered a process from user requirements to jointly prioritized services by aging users and innovators.

Results and lessons learned: Case 3 demonstrated how a group of active aging users could contribute in suggesting new services for a company to develop. Besides valuable input, the importance of a social context around such work was clear. The users were very engaged throughout the project and workshops were frequently visited and the participants became friends. The high amount of input from the participants could be explained in terms of social inclusion; they belonged to a group and each member was considered important for the work.

The future workshops contained an iterative process of moving from a large number of new suggested services towards fewer but highly needed services. The requirement list of future services resulted in four categories: cognitive; social; and physical activities as well as information and news,, all high-priority proposals with a strong foundation in both user needs and feasibility for the innovator [6].

4   Comparison Based on Different Aspects of the Cases

Aspects to compare data from the cases were based on the *innovation*: type of innovation; type of environment in which it should work; the project owner and the development phase; as well as the *participation* of the Quadruple Helix stakeholders, divided in three aspects: aging users; triple helix joint work; and proxy involvement. Effects related to user needs and industry prerequisites were described (Table 1).

By working in a Quadruple Helix PD setting where focus was on the joint stakeholder work to balance the outcome between user needs and feasibility, the teams working with the three cases were satisfied with the results: increased common understanding of goals; user needs met by improved technology; new usage situations found; new/other content; Improved social interaction; improved knowledge about other stakeholder interests; and about ways of achieving the goals.

Table 1. Comparison between the cases

Aspects	Case 1	Case 2	Case 3
Type of innovation	Communication tool and services	Rehab tool (extended Kinect)	Communication tool and services
1. Type of environment	Vallentuna Nursing Home	Örebro Activity Center for Elderly	Täby Senior center
2a. Project Owner	Industry	Research	Industry
2b. Development phase	Prototype in late stage	Refinement of prototype	Refinement of prototype
3a. Participation of Aging users[a]	From receiver of information (4) to experts on own life situation (2)	(3) consultant role	(2) experts own life situation
3b. Triple Helix joint work[b]	(6)	(6)	(6)
4. Proxy involvement[c]	High	Medium	No Care professional Proxy
EFFECTS related to user needs/industry prerequisites	User needs met. New usage not yet leading to increased effort from industry part	Improved system, new/other content. Will lead to increased effort by industry (development)	Improved interaction, new/other content. Will lead to great effort by social care staff (creating content)

[a] Participation of older people based on Östlund [2], see criteria in Sect. 2.1.
[b] Assessment of Triple Helix cooperation, see criteria Sect. 2.2.
[c] Proxy Involvement: to which extent staff acted on behalf of aging users, see Sect. 2.3.
[*] Reversed table numbers 5-1: here we use both the number and the textual description.

5   Analysis and Discussion

Each aspect of the Quadruple Helix PD cases is described from the point of view of the "balance between end-user needs and the prerequisites of the innovators".

Type of environment: The analyzed cases consisted of different contexts in terms of way of working with users and investigating user needs. Case 3 had a focus on developing new services and the participants were younger, aiming to design for elderly, under the label "When I get older". The participants in case 1 and 2 had age-related physical and/or psychical impairments but the cases differed with respect to the environment. Case 1 was conducted at a nursing home and case 2 was conducted at three activity centers for elderly. Case 1 and 2 also differed with respect to duration of usage. In case 1 the aging users tested the services for a longer period of time and had the opportunity to use the technology in different ways. In case 2 the participants tested and evaluated the technology at one occasion when they visited the activity center. These different usage situations had an impact both on how the aging users were able to provide feedback on the technology and on the role of the care professionals as proxies for the aging users.

Project owner: In cases 1 and 3 the participating company led the project, which may explain the large effort in finding the balance between needs of aging users and feasibility of the development. However, this may not always be the case. In many research and development projects several companies participate and it is not clear who is responsible for taking the product to market. Uncertainties may lead to a struggle to find a balance between the different companies' needs rather than between the end-user needs and the feasibility of the development.

Development phase: Depending on the possibility to involve aging users in a theoretical discussion, it may be more feasible to involve aging users at a nursing home in the later stages of the development where there is a well-functioning prototype to test, use and discuss. This was shown in case 2 where aging users of high age tested an almost ready technology and provided good feedback from just one test occasion, in consultation together with others (participation ladder stage 3).

Participation of aging users: The degree of participation of the aging users differed. In case 1 the aging users increased their degree of participation along with the increasing possibilities to test the technology in different ways. On the older people participation ladder [2] the participants went from performers (4) to initiators (2) when they were able to use the technology in their own way. The younger users in case 3 gave feedback related to own life situation (2) and how they perceived the technology could improve their own aging.

Triple Helix joint work: All three cases reached high grades on the Triple Helix participation ladder with close cooperation and activities crossing the boarders of the organizations (6). The Triple Helix participation was especially strong in case 1 and 3 where the company played an active role and worked close to the aging users, the care professionals and the researchers. Using researchers as mediators between other stakeholders was important since double competence (e.g. IT&T development plus aging or health context, and analysis methods) was required to work towards a common understanding. Researchers with knowledge from several of the involved areas facilitated communication and pinpointed important issues to be addressed.

Proxy involvement: The cases revealed interesting effects of proxy involvement. In case 1, initially the care professionals did not quite understand for which resident the device could be useful. This is in line with previous studies [2, 5, 7, 15] and may show that sometimes care professionals act as gatekeepers preventing without any clear reason that the elderly are exposed to new technology. Further, the care professional proxies later elicited different usage areas and needs, thereby creating a basis for a new context of usage and more meaningful services.. Another proxy effect was seen in case 2: Other results regarding use of proxies show difficulties in understanding user needs [14] but in case 2, proxies and users provided similar feedback. From an observing perspective, care professional proxies could see what caused problems and provide suggestions to solutions, thereby deepening the understanding. This may indicate that, when using proxies, benefits could be gained by assuring that users and proxies will share the situation and experience it together.

Further work will elaborate this Quadruple Helix PD approach to provide a deeper insight regarding in which development stage it is suitable to test the technology, how and with which type of stakeholder, aging users themselves and/or together with care professionals.

6   Conclusion

The impact of this Quadruple Helix PD approach is improved benefit for aging end-users as well as increased feasibility for the innovation companies, as a result when collaboration of different stakeholders focuses on balancing the demands of the users and the prerequisites of the industry. The involvement of aging users in finding the balance between user needs and feasibility in the development, as well as an active involvement of the industrial partner, may contribute to a common understanding in developing realistic and meaningful services. Another important aspect for the companies was finding a market that is large enough to motivate the costs for development. Often there is a tradeoff between addressing user needs of specific groups and developing IT&T solutions that can be offered to a larger market.

The researchers stress the importance of engaging aging user groups based on situation and possibilities to contribute. The situation and possibilities to contribute is also important regarding proxy involvement. Proxies seems to be better suited in the work with testing existing devices in new contexts than working with or describing user needs in an early phase. Another relevant situation to use proxies could be when working with broadening a concept to find additional areas of usage.

Key to the success of the re-designed IT&T was the responsiveness of the developers. This can probably only be reached by a true engagement and by participation in settings where all stakeholders are encouraged and guided to perform at their best. Methods used that worked well were e.g.: observation of real usage performed by the entire Triple Helix team; creation of user profiles together with care personnel and IT&T developers; workshops guided by researchers; as well as enough time to test and to increase the common understanding for all stakeholders. This study found that the Quadruple Helix PD approach with focus on different stakeholder groups and their prerequisites results in improved possibilities to keep the balance between end-user needs and the prerequisites of the innovators, potentially contributing to improved IT&T solutions for aging users.

Acknowledgements. We would like to thank all participants at collaborating sites for their hard work and engagement. We also would like to thank the entire project teams and the developers of the devices as well as the Swedish Agency for Innovation Systems, Vinnova and RnD Seniorium for supporting the pilot projects with funding and resources.

References

1. Robetson, T.: Participatory design and participative practices in small companies. In: Proceedings of PDC 1996, Cambridge, MA USA, 13–15 November 1996
2. Östlund, B.: The benefits of involving older people in the design process. In: Zhou, J., Salvendy, G. (eds.) ITAP 2015. LNCS, vol. 9193, pp. 3–14. Springer, Heidelberg (2015)
3. Arnstein, S.: A ladder of citizen participation. Am. Inst. Planners J. **35**(4), 216–224 (1969)
4. IEEE Std 1471-2000: Recommended Practice for Architectural Description of Software-Intensive Systems. IEEE Architecture Working Group (2000)
5. Wyatt, S.: Non-users also matter: the construction of users and non-users of the Internet. In: Oudshoorn, N., Pinch, T. (eds.) How Users Matter: The Co-construction of Users and Technology, Cambridge, MA, USA, pp. 67–79 (2003)
6. Östlund, B., Lindén, K.: Turning older people's experiences into innovations: ippi as the convergence of mobile services and TV viewing. Gerontechnology **10**(2), 103–109 (2011)
7. Scandurra, I., Sjölinder, M.: Participatory design with seniors: design of future services and iterative refinements of interactive eHealth Services for Old Citizens. Med 2.0 2013 **2**(2), e12 (2013). http://www.medicine20.com/2013/2/e12/. doi:10.2196/med20.2729
8. Greenbaum, J., Kyng, M.: Design at Work: Cooperative Design of Computer Systems, pp. 3–24. Lawrence Erlbaum Associates, New Jersey (1991)
9. Schuler, D., Namioka, A.: Participatory Design Principles and Practices. Lawrence Erlbaum Associates Inc., London (1993)
10. Constantine, L., Lockwood, L.: Software for Use: A Practical Guide to the Essential Models and Methods of Usage-Centered Design. Addison-Wesley, Reading (1999)
11. Jungk, R., Müllert, N.: Future Workshops: How to Create Desirable Futures. Institute for Social Interventions, London (1987)
12. Scandurra, I., Hägglund, M., Koch, S.: From user needs to system specifications: multi-disciplinary thematic seminars as a collaborative design method for development of health information systems. J. Biomed. Inform. **41**(4), 557–569 (2008)
13. Dickinson, A., Dewsbury, G.: Designing computer technologies with older people. Gerontechnology **5**(1), 1–3 (2006)
14. Sjölinder, M., Scandurra, I.: Effects of using care professionals in the development of social technology for elderly. In: Zhou, J., Salvendy, G. (eds.) ITAP 2015. LNCS, vol. 9194, pp. 181–192. Springer, Heidelberg (2015). doi:10.1007/978-3-319-20892-3
15. Scandurra, I.: Sustainable and Quality-Based Communication Services in Elderly Care. R&D Seniorium Report (2011) (in Swedish) 2011:03. Stockholm
16. Scandurra, I.: Sustainable health for modern aging. Vinnova 2011-02834 (2012)
17. Lindholm, T., Moritz, M.: Handbook of Participation (2007). (in Swedish)
18. Castell, P.: Dialogues and citizen initiatives in stigmatized urban areas: reflections on the development of participatory planning principles in Gothenburg. Paper Presented at IFHP 56th World Congress: Inclusive Cities in a Global World. Gothenburg, 16–19 September 2012
19. Boyd-Graber, J., Nikolova, S.S., Moffatt, K.A., Kin, K.C., Lee, J.Y., Mackey, L.W., Tremaine, M.M., Klawe, M.M.: Participatory design with proxies: Developing a desktop-PDA system to support people with aphasia. Computer-Human Interaction (2006)
20. Shneiderman, B., Plaisant, C.: Designing the User Interface: Strategies for Effective Human-Computer Interaction, 5th edn. Pearson Addison-Wesley, Boston (2009)

21. Antonovsky, A.: The salutogenic model as a theory to guide health promotion. Health Promot. Int. **11**(1), 11–18 (1996). doi:10.1093/heapro/11.1.11
22. Sjölinder, M., Ehn, M., Boman, I.-L., Folke, M., Hansson, P., Sommerfeld, D.K., Nylander, S., Borg, J.: A multi-disciplinary approach in the development of a stroke rehabilitation tool. In: Proceedings of HCI International 2014, Crete, Greece, 22–27 June, 2014

HCI Challenges for Consumer-Based Aging in Place Technologies

Marjorie Skubic[1](✉), Anup Mishra[1], Bradford Harris[1], Carmen Abbott[2], Andrew Craver[3], Katy Musterman[3], and Marilyn Rantz[3]

[1] Electrical and Computer Engineering, University of Missouri, Columbia, MO, USA
{skubicm,harrisbh}@missouri.edu, anupmishra@mail.missouri.edu
[2] Physical Therapy, University of Missouri, Columbia, MO, USA
abbottc@missouri.edu
[3] Sinclair School of Nursing, University of Missouri, Columbia, MO, USA
{cravera,mustermank,rantzm}@missouri.edu

Abstract. New, innovative technologies provide promise in helping older adults to age in place. However, the success of the technology and acceptance of it by the target users will be dependent on both function, i.e., whether it provides a worthwhile service, and the user experience, i.e., how easy it is to achieve the intended function. In this paper, we discuss the challenges in human-computer interaction (HCI), in the context of our experience with two applications designed to support older adults. The first is an in-home sensor system for detecting early signs of health changes and managing chronic health conditions. The second is an interactive remote physical therapy system that connects a therapist in the clinic with an older adult in the home. An overview of each application is presented. We discuss HCI challenges across these two applications.

Keywords: Aging · Technology acceptance

1 Introduction

We envision a time when sensor technology and smart healthcare systems are routinely used to capture subtle changes in health and activity that may represent early signs of illness and functional decline. Seniors are able to receive early treatment when health problems are still small and manageable; healthcare is more effective and efficient, because health problems are caught early. Remote family members can easily stay in touch with their aging loved ones, and, if the seniors allow access, can see pertinent information about their activity and health. Seniors are able to better manage their own chronic health conditions, with aid from automated technology, care coordinators, physical therapists, and family members. When needed, they use technology to connect with a healthcare professional from the comfort of their homes. As a result, seniors are able to maintain a high functional ability, which promotes independence. Thus, Aging in Place is a finally a reality. Seniors have real options on where to live, including staying in their own home.

© Springer International Publishing Switzerland 2016
J. Zhou and G. Salvendy (Eds.): ITAP 2016, Part I, LNCS 9754, pp. 105–116, 2016.
DOI: 10.1007/978-3-319-39943-0_11

As described above, our vision includes the operational use of various smart technologies across a range of housing options in urban, suburban, and rural settings. These include in-home sensors embedded in the environment, wearable sensors such as smart watches, sensors embedded in clothes or shoes, and smartphones for those that carry them. Intervention technology includes automation to help maintain good health and/or manage chronic health conditions, such as health change alerts, fall detection alerts, personalized models, tools to support personalized exercise and health coaching, socially assistive technology such as screen agents or robots, and other innovations that might be developed in the future. These capabilities would benefit anyone battling chronic health problems; however, older adults are particularly vulnerable and may lose their independence if their health problems are not managed appropriately.

This vision comes with a variety of challenges, many of which are related to how users interact with the technology. In this paper, we discuss these challenges in the context of our experience with two applications designed to support older adults. Section 2 first discusses background and related work. In Sect. 3, we consider an in-home sensor system used for clinical decision support to recognize very early health changes and manage chronic health conditions. In Sect. 4, we present an interactive remote physical therapy system designed to connect an older adult in the home with a therapist in the clinic. Section 5 then includes a discussion of challenges across these two applications.

2   Background and Related Work

Previous studies have shown the importance of the user interface when designing for consumers such as older adults and their family members. In particular, older adult users bring new challenges with regards to delivering useful information in easy to interpret formats. In addition to new models of healthcare that may be unfamiliar to consumers, there are difficulties, due to typical aging effects on vision, hearing, and haptic sensing as well as attention and working memory [1]. In spite of these challenges, older adults report that they are willing to use technology as long as it provides a worthwhile function and the interface considers their sensory limitation [2].

There have been a number of studies investigating the efficiency of graphical user interfaces and other new technologies for older adults [3–11]. Demiris et al. have several investigations on determining the usability of data representation techniques for older adults [3, 5, 11]. In [11], experiments with four focus groups and 31 older participants investigate the usability of smart home data visualizations for wellness assessment and cognitive processing abilities of older adults. Their analysis showed that older adults prefer integrated data visualizations rather than raw smart home data. In addition, the group has conducted studies to determine the current status and future trends of patient centered care and observed the growth and significance of informatics systems and electronic health records for patient-centered care models [4, 6].

Other research studies have explored technology acceptance for older adults in different fields [7–10]. In [8], Czaja et al. conducted experiments to determine the performance of older adults in using internet based health care applications. Results show that the older adults that received training, performed better on the tasks with more accuracy and efficiency. The study also indicates that a simpler interface design is necessary for improving the performance.

Among the emerging technologies in healthcare and wellness, telemedicine as a means for healthcare is one of the fastest, time efficient, and most reliable way to provide services [12]. The American Association of Retired Persons survey in 2008 shows that three-fourths of the survey respondents are ready to accept telemedicine as a part of their primary healthcare, for health diagnosis and monitoring [13].

3   In-Home Sensor System

The main function of our in-home sensor system is to recognize early signs of illness and functional decline so that early interventions can be offered when health problems are more manageable [14]. The system includes a collection of bed, motion, and depth sensors installed in the home, a data logger computer in the home, automated alert generation software, a database for storing data on a secure server, and a web interface for viewing the data and alerts [15]. Data are encrypted and sent to the server via Wi-Fi or wired network connection. Falls are detected on the home computer based on depth data; fall alerts are immediately sent to designated individuals [16, 17]. Health alerts are processed once a day on the server and sent to clinical care coordinators, as these do not require immediate attention. Specialized algorithms detect changes in sensor data patterns that might indicate impending health problems which may lead to serious health events if left unattended [15]. With proper interventions, small problems can be addressed before they become major health problems, thus maintaining a high level of functionality and a high quality of life for older adults as they age. The work thus far has relied on the clinical staff to determine whether an intervention is needed. In future work, we plan to investigate the older adults' use of the system for managing their own chronic health conditions.

A web interface includes several graphical visualizations of the sensor data, which were originally developed to support the research team and clinical staff [18, 19]. Figure 1 shows one view of motion and bed sensor data. Passive infrared (PIR) motion sensors are placed in each room to capture activity. Motion events are generated every seven seconds if there is continuous motion in the detection cone. In addition to the bar graphs shown in Fig. 1, motion sensor data are also shown as motion density (number of events from all motion sensors per unit time). An example of a motion density map showing overall activity patterns is shown in Fig. 2. During this period, the older adult slept through the night on most days, woke about 7 am, left the apartment (black regions) for activities and some meals, and went to sleep around 10 pm most days. Several nights show unusual bathroom visit activity (middle section of red bars). Three health alerts were generated over this period, shown as the red vertical bars on Fig. 2. Changes in daily patterns are often vividly illustrated in these activity maps [20, 21].

A depth sensor is used to compute gait parameters and detect falls (initially, the Microsoft Kinect). The depth sensor produces a sequence of images in which each pixel value stores the distance to the nearest object at that pixel. Individuals in the home

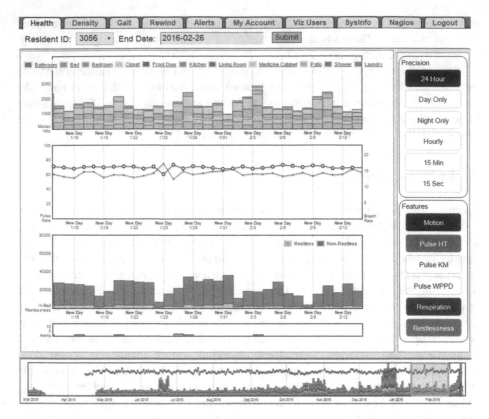

Fig. 1. The Health tab of the web interface showing motion data from each room in the older adult apartment (top) and pulse (in red), respiration (in blue), and restless computed from bed sensor data. Buttons on the right toggle options on/off. The bottom slider bar selects a date range. (Color figure online)

are automatically segmented and tracked in the depth images. They appear as shadowy three-dimensional silhouettes, which users have found to be acceptable [22]. Detected falls result in immediate fall alerts with a link to a short depth video clip showing the fall [16, 17]. Examples of older adult falls detected in the home can be found at https:// www.youtube.com/watch?v=TFB7YOUmIIho. The embedded video link allows receivers to confirm that a fall did happen and to see what happened leading up to the fall. Gait parameters are estimated based on purposeful walks that are observed in the home. The height and other gait parameter estimates are used to distinguish a resident from visitors or one resident from another resident so that gait trends can be tracked [23]. The system sends alerts for changes in walking speed, stride time, and stride length [24]. Examples of older adult walks in the home can be found at https://www.youtube.com/watch?v=MF6yZyLuuII. Figure 3 shows the web interface Gait tab, in this case showing declines in gait speed and stride length.

The in-home sensor systems have been installed in TigerPlace apartments, an aging in place housing site, and in many assisted living apartments elsewhere. For these older

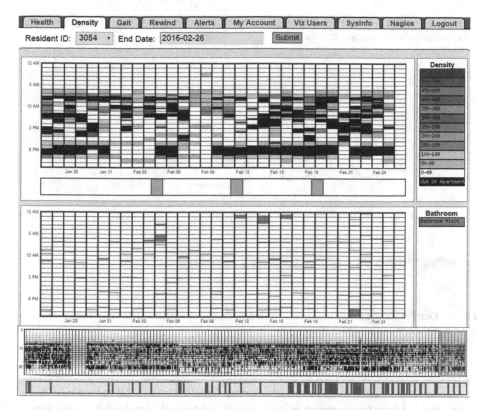

Fig. 2. Density tab showing a motion density map (top) and bathroom visit map (middle). Each column represents a day, starting from midnight at the top to 11 pm at the bottom. Density colors shown on the right indicate the level of activity (higher density represents more activity); black is out of the home, e.g., for meal times and other activities. The slider bar on the bottom selects the date range. The red vertical bars below the motion density map and on the bottom show health alert days. Hovering over the alert bar shows the type of alert. (Color figure online)

adults, the clinical staff receive the alerts as email and use the web interface to determine whether an intervention is warranted. The health alerts include an embedded link to the web interface for that older adult, making it easy for clinical staff to view sensor data around the time of the alert. If further investigation is needed, staff talk to the older adults directly. We have also begun to use the system in private homes. Again, a clinical care coordinator receives the alerts. However, she uses FaceTime as a video conferencing tool to talk with the older adult remotely. In one case, the older adult user had difficulties managing the iPad and FaceTime and had trouble in hearing the voice communication. The iPad was set up for her, with the Wi-Fi connection and applications. The older adult was trained in using the iPad and FaceTime but still had difficulties until she went to visit her children and was able to spend some concentrated and repetitive time practicing. After this visit, she was able to successfully have FaceTime calls. The sound is still a little troublesome for her but she is able to make due. She seems motivated to learn and use FaceTime, because she knows that she can communicate with her family with

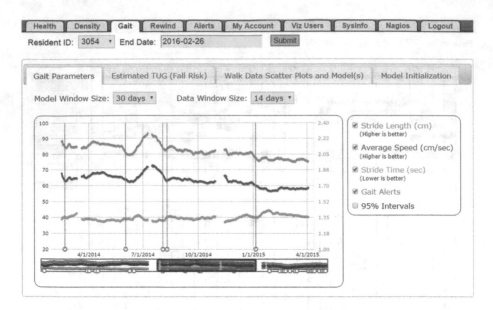

Fig. 3. Gait tab showing walking speed, stride length, and stride time. The graphs show declines in walking speed and stride length.

this technology. Without this motivation, she might not have wanted to learn the interface.

We have also begun to show the sensor data visualizations to the older adults being monitored and their family members as an initial step towards developing a more appropriate interface for consumers. As a start, the older adults and family members have seen motion data and depth videos of falls. Anecdotally, several older adults have shown little interest in seeing the data. The general feeling is that they are too old to bother with it, and they already have clinicians who are looking after them. A couple have expressed interest in seeing more motion data. They are all impressed by the fall sensing technology; the fall depth videos provide the easiest output for them to interpret, as the silhouettes rendered from the depth videos look like people. The floor plane is segmented and colored to help interpret the depth videos; segmented people are also colored in distinct colors. For viewing motion sensor data, older adults prefer the 24-hour motion density maps because they can clearly see their pattern of daily activity, and the bathroom density maps showing bathroom visits. The histogram graph of the motion sensor data is difficult for them to interpret, as the y axis metric (number of motion sensor events) is not meaningful.

4   Interactive Remote Physical Therapy System

The remote physical therapy (PT) system was developed to augment in-clinic time by connecting a therapist in the clinic with a PT client in the home for remote quantitative assessments [12]. The system has two different interfaces, one for the PT client in the

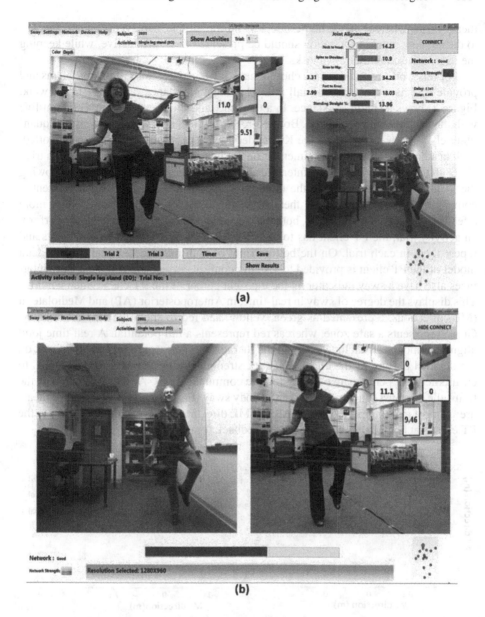

Fig. 4. Interactive remote physical therapy system (a) Therapist interface for the clinic; (b) Home interface

home and another for the therapist; they are connected through a high speed network connection. The interfaces were developed with iterative feedback provided by a therapist and five older adults participants acting as PT clients. Figure 4 shows the final interfaces, which use the Microsoft Kinect for video conferencing as well as for quantitative assessments. The therapist's interface has more detailed real-time and post therapy data, whereas on the home side, less information is displayed. A challenge was to decide how much information should be presented to be productive, while keeping the users focused in their own tasks.

For this work, two tasks were chosen that can both assess for fall risk problems and provide exercises to overcome fall risk: (1) single leg stance, and (2) tandem walk. Figure 4 shows a single leg stance. In a tandem walk, the user walks in a straight line with the feet touching heel to toe. Both exercises test balance, which is measured quantitatively as body sway, using the Kinect depth camera. Multiple trials are supported, each lasting for 20 s. A (green) timer bar on the interface shows the time left for a trial.

Both the therapist and home interfaces have two video feedback elements, showing the local and remote views. In the therapist's interface, the remote video element is comparatively larger to help the therapist evaluate the PT client's performance more effectively. In the home interface, both the video elements are the same size. To perform an activity trial, the PT client has to carefully observe the therapist's movements and repeat them in each trial. On the bottom right of both interfaces, a real-time skeletal model of the PT client is provided to visually confirm correct skeletal data. Both interfaces also have a sway indicator on the top right corner of the PT client video window. This displays the degree of sway in real-time, in Anteroposterior (AP) and Mediolateral (ML) directions, represented as green, yellow, and red to show the amount of sway. Green represents a safe zone, whereas red represents a fall potential. A real-time joint alignment module is included only in the therapist's interface, to provide feedback on the detailed posture of the client. Network strength is also shown to the therapist, to ensure network performance during remote communications. At the conclusion of the trials, the therapist can view traces of the body sway (Fig. 5) and see quantitative measurements of maximum sway in the AP and ML directions. These were not shown to the PT clients at home but could be used as feedback for them to track progress.

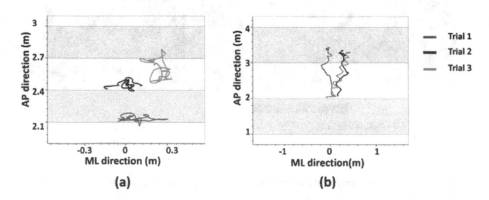

Fig. 5. Traces showing body sway (a) Single leg stance trials, (b) tandem walk trials

The hardware platform used for both the therapist and the home consisted of a 32-inch wide television mounted on a 5-foot high stand with a computer mounted on the side. The Kinect was positioned directly below and in front of the television. This large scale monitor allowed easy viewing at distances required to perform the exercises.

A keyboard and mouse was required at the beginning of each session on both ends, to set up the network connection. After this was established, video conferencing was activated to allow voice communications. A researcher brought the equipment into the home for each session and set up the network connection to begin the session. We did not expect the older adult user to manage this step. In addition, voice commands were implemented for the therapist to allow for easy control through the different exercises and trials without requiring a keyboard or mouse.

The system was tested with five independent older adults, located in Kansas City, MO. The Google Fiber network was used to connect the homes with a physical therapist located on the campus at the University of Missouri in Columbia, MO. Survey results were collected from the older adults in the home and the therapist. The final session showed very high ratings from the therapist for video and audio quality at 4.7/5. The older adult participants rating the video and audio quality at 4.0/5. The average user satisfaction rating from the therapist was 4.8/5, whereas the older adult participants rated it 3.7/5. Lower scores were given by the older adults for categories of (1) using the system with confidence, (2) readily available, and (3) easy to use. These lower ratings were most likely due to the complicated network set-up required at this stage of development. An average rating of 4.25/5 was given by participants for (1) accuracy of remote movements on the interface and (2) senior following the remote activity demonstration. A minimal training time on the interface was apparently sufficient for the older adults to interpret the information on the PT interface. If they did experience problems, the therapist was there to answer questions and provide guidance.

5   Discussion

Although the in-home sensor system and the remote PT system represent different types of systems with much different functionalities, there are common HCI research challenges for both. We consider HCI challenges in the following areas:

- Turning the system on. How should the system operation be initiated?
- Methods for controlling operation and navigating through an interface. Hardware platforms are considered here also, as some control methods are dependent on the platform.
- Output displays. This includes both the format and the level of detail displayed.

Other challenge areas include training (on how to use the system and how to act on the information displayed by the system) and personalization (should the system adapt to the user and will this make it easier to use or harder as it changes?). Although not considered here, these too should be investigated for older adult users.

The challenge of how to turn the system on was not addressed for older adults in either the in-home sensor interface or the remote PT interface. Thus far, we have avoided this issue by having a researcher start the system and show it to the older adult user. However, it will need to be addressed for a system to be accepted and used. Two main options are to require the user to start the system use, e.g., by pressing a button, or to have the system automatically prompt the user. This was shown to be a challenge for one user even in the seemingly simple use of FaceTime, when the call was initiated by the care coordinator. The fact that more training solved the problem is consistent with the study in [8]. For the researchers and clinical staff that currently use the web interface, they often open the system by clicking on a link in an email. However, for older adults that do not use email, this will be yet another barrier to using the system.

The challenge of what control methods to use is somewhat tied to the hardware platform. A tablet supports touch. If large buttons and large type are used, this could provide an effective control method as long as the choices are limited. Likewise, keyboard and mouse can be effective, especially for users already familiar with them, as long as the interface is not too busy. The current sensor data interface has many tabs, options, buttons, and charts that could easily overwhelm an older adult wanting to view their own health related information. A simpler control interface will be necessary for consumers, both older adults and their family members. The remote PT system did not require control by the older adult user; the system was driven completely by the therapist. Because the system was built on synchronous video conferencing, the older adult could talk to the therapist directly if there were any problems with the system.

Speech is another option for application control. In studies investigating interfaces to robots, older adults have stated their preference for speech [25]. However, speech recognition for older adults can be problematic if the recognition is not reliable. One study showed a 10 % reduction in recognition rates for older adults compared to younger adults [26]. The speech interface for the remote PT system worked very well for the therapist but was not tried for the older adult users. Each command to the PT system was begun with "Mizzou Steps" so the system was not confused by the normal conversation between the therapist and client in the home. A similar strategy could be used by the older adult in the home for other applications. For example, the user might provide a name for the system to support a command such as "Buddy, show me my gait for the last week." If it works reliably, this could be an effective control method.

The third challenge is on how to display the output, that is, what format should be used and at what level of detail. In the remote PT system, we obtained feedback from users to determine how much detail to include. It was clear that the older adult users required less detail than the therapist. More investigation is needed to determine whether we really got it right. For the sensor data web interface, the current configuration offers too much detail for consumers. Many of the options and charts have been included to help ensure the system is operating properly. Viewing these charts gives the research team confidence in trusting the data, but many of them would likely confuse consumers. Our initial investigation with older adults was consistent with the study in [11]; older adult users preferred the motion density visualizations over the histograms of the raw motion sensor data.

Other format types are also available. Our research team has been exploring sensor data summaries in the form of textual descriptions. For example, a summary of bed sensor data could be "The bed restlessness tonight is a lot higher than most of the nights in the past two weeks" [27, 28]. This could be used as a text message sent to a family member or it could be used as an explanation of a graph, e.g., as part of training in how to use the system. It might also be used to start an automated discussion with the older adult to investigate further. For example, this could initiate a string of questions to find out if the user is in pain or is having problems with a chronic health condition. In any case, further study is needed to determine the appropriate level of detail in the message and the best time period (day, week, month, etc.).

In summary, we have reviewed two application designed to help older adult age in place and have discussed HCI challenges with respect to the older adult user. Addressing these challenges will provide new opportunities to engage older adults with technologies that can help them better manage their own chronic health conditions, address health problems, maintain function, and ultimately retain independence which is so crucial for aging in place. Getting the interface right will be essential to achieving this vision.

References

1. Pak, R., McLaughlin, A.: Designing Displays for Older Adults. CRC Press, Boca Raton (2011)
2. Demiris, G., Rantz, M.J., Aud, M.A., Marek, K.D., Tyrer, H.W., Skubic, M., Hussam, A.A.: Older adults' attitudes towards and perceptions of "smart home" technologies: a pilot study. Med. Inform. Internet 29(2), 87–94 (2004)
3. Bock, C., Le, T., Samuel, A., Huang, D., Thompson, H.J., Demiris, G.: Visualizing sensor data through an open platform for connected devices. St. Heal. T. 216, 964 (2015)
4. Demiris, G., Kneale, L.: Informatics systems and tools to facilitate patient-centered care coordination. Yearb. Med. Inform. 10(1), 15–21 (2015)
5. Le, T., Thompson, H., Demiris, G.: A comparison of health visualization evaluation techniques with older adults. IEEE Comput. Graph Appl. (2015)
6. Backonja, U., Kneale, L., Demiris, G., Thompson, H.J.: Senior tech: the next generation: health informatics solutions for older adults living in the community. J. Gerontol. Nurs. 42(1), 2–3 (2016)
7. Mitzner, T.L., Boron, J.B., Fausset, C.B., Adams, A.E., Charness, N., Czaja, S.J., Dijkstra, K., Fisk, A.D., Rogers, W.A., Sharit, J.: Older adults talk technology: technology usage and attitudes. Comput. Hum. Behav. 26(6), 1710–1721 (2010)
8. Czaja, S.J., Sharit, J., Lee, C.C., Nair, S.N., Hernández, M.A., Arana, N., Fu, S.H.: Factors influencing use of an e-health website in a community sample of older adults. J. Am. Med. Inform. Assn. 20(2), 277–284 (2013)
9. Hickman, J.M., Rogers, W.A., Fisk, A.D.: Training older adults to use new technology. J. Gerontol. B-Psychol 62(Special Issue 1), 77–84 (2007)
10. Mitzner, T.L., Rogers, W.A., Fisk, A.D., Boot, W.R., Charness, N., Czaja, S.J., Sharit, J.: Predicting older adults' perceptions about a computer system designed for seniors. Univ. Access Inf. Soc., 1–10 (2014)
11. Le, T., Reeder, B., Yoo, D., Aziz, R., Thompson, H.J., Demiris, G.: An evaluation of wellness assessment visualizations for older adults. Telemed. J. E Health 21(1), 9–15 (2015)
12. Mishra, A.K., Skubic, M., Abbott, C.: Development and preliminary validation of an interactive remote physical therapy system. In: 2015 37th Annual International Conference of the IEEE Engineering in Medicine and Biology Society (EMBC), 25–29 August, pp. 190–193 (2015)
13. American Association of Retired Persons: American Association of Retired Persons (Aarp) Healthy @ Home (2008)

14. Rantz, M.J., Skubic, M., Popescu, M., Galambos, C., Koopman, R.J., Alexander, G.L., Phillips, L.J., Musterman, K., Back, J., Miller, S.J.: A new paradigm of technology-enabled 'vital signs' for early detection of health change for older adults. Gerontology **61**(3), 281–290 (2015)

15. Skubic, M., Guevara, R.D., Rantz, M.: Automated health alerts using in-home sensor data for embedded health assessment. IEEE J. Transl. Eng. Health Med. **3**, 1–11 (2015)

16. Stone, E.E., Skubic, M.: Testing real-time in-home fall alerts with embedded depth video hyperlink. In: Bodine, C., Helal, S., Gu, T., Mokhtari, M. (eds.) ICOST 2014. LNCS, vol. 8456, pp. 41–48. Springer, Heidelberg (2015)

17. Stone, E.E., Skubic, M.: Fall detection in homes of older adults using the microsoft kinect. IEEE J. Biomed. Health Inform. **19**(1), 290–301 (2015)

18. Alexander, G., Rantz, M., Skubic, M., Koopman, R., Phillips, L., Guevara, R., Miller, S.: Evolution of an early illness warning system to monitor frail elders in independent living. J. Healthc. Eng. **2**(3), 337–364 (2011)

19. Sheahen, M., Skubic, M.: Design and usability of a smart home sensor data user interface for a clinical and research audience. In: Bodine, C., Helal, S., Gu, T., Mokhtari, M. (eds.) ICOST 2014. LNCS, vol. 8456, pp. 13–20. Springer, Heidelberg (2015)

20. Galambos, C., Skubic, M., Wang, S., Rantz, M.: Management of dementia and depression utilizing in-home passive sensor data. Gerontechnology: Int. J. Fundam. Aspects Technol. Serve Ageing Soc. **11**(3), 457–468 (2013)

21. Wang, S., Skubic, M., Zhu, Y.: Activity density map visualization and dissimilarity comparison for eldercare monitoring. IEEE Trans. Inf. Technol. Biomed. **16**(4), 607–614 (2012)

22. Demiris, G., Oliver, D.P., Giger, J., Skubic, M., Rantz, M.: Older adults' privacy considerations for vision based recognition methods of eldercare applications. Technol. Health Care **17**(1), 41–48 (2009)

23. Stone, E.E., Skubic, M.: Unobtrusive, continuous, in-home gait measurement using the microsoft kinect. IEEE Trans. Biomed. Eng. **60**(10), 2925–2932 (2013)

24. Stone, E.E., Skubic, M., Back, J.: Automated health alerts from kinect-based in-home gait measurements. In: 2014 36th Annual International Conference of the IEEE Engineering in Medicine and Biology Society (EMBC), pp. 2961–2964 (2014)

25. Scopelliti, M., Giuliani, M.V., Fornara, F.: Robots in a domestic setting: a psychological approach. Univ. Access Inf. Soc. **4**(2), 146–155 (2005)

26. Alexenko, T., Biondo, M., Banisakher, D., Skubic, M.: Android-based speech processing for eldercare robotics. In: Proceedings of the Companion Publication of the 2013 International Conference on Intelligent User Interfaces Companion, pp. 87–88 (2013)

27. Jain, A., Keller, J.M.: Textual summarization of events leading to health alerts. In: 2015 37th Annual International Conference of the IEEE Engineering in Medicine and Biology Society (EMBC), pp. 7634–7637 (2015)

28. Wilbik, A., Keller, J.M., Alexander, G.L.: Linguistic summarization of sensor data for eldercare. In: 2011 IEEE International Conference on Systems, Man, and Cybernetics (SMC), pp. 2595–2599 (2011)

Towards Characteristics of Accessibility and Usability Issues for Older People - A Brazilian Case Study

Sandra Souza Rodrigues[1]([⊠]), Renata Pontin de Mattos Fortes[1], and André Pimenta Freire[2]

[1] ICMC University of São Paulo, São Carlos, São Paulo, Brazil
ssrodrigues@usp.br, renata@icmc.usp.br
[2] Federal University of Lavras, Lavras, Minas Gerais, Brazil
apfreire@dcc.ufla.br

Abstract. The constant evolution of the Web is a worldwide phenomenon that needs to deal quickly with the various segments of current
society. Thus, Web content should be accessible to the different user profiles. In this century, the aging population has presented a high rate of
demographic growth. Older people (aged 60+) have some of their capacities limited and may face barriers to interact with services and content
available on the Web. Despite of legislation and recommendations concerning how to make Web content more accessible and usable, there are
still many problems related to accessibility and usability to be solved,
especially those related to recent technological advances of current Web
resources. The purpose of this study was to investigate the main accessibility and usability issues on websites. The study involved a sample of
20 Brazilian older people. Results showed the most common issues found
and participants manifested their main difficulties.

Keywords: Web accessibility · Web usability · Website · Older people

1 Introduction

The Web has undergone substantial technological innovations, and its adoption
in various segments of current society has proved to be irreversible, especially
in segments such as e-government, online banking, entertainment and others.
Although novel Web browsing facilities have arisen, there is still a great challenge
related to Web accessibility and usability. It is very important that different user
profiles must be considered at the system's design, in order for information to
be accessible in the broadest possible way [20]. In addition, an accessible Web
has the potential to help people with disabilities and older people to participate
more actively in society [14].

According to the ISO 9241-171 standard, accessibility is "the usability of a
product, service, environment or facility by people with the widest range of capabilities" [5]. In particular, Web accessibility enables people with disabilities to

J. Zhou and G. Salvendy (Eds.): ITAP 2016, Part I, LNCS 9754, pp. 117–128, 2016.
DOI: 10.1007/978-3-319-39943-0_12

perceive, understand, navigate and interact with the Web, and thus to contribute with it [4]. These requirements are also relevant to older people, which may have their abilities affected by aging, with possible influences in their physical, mental and learning capacities [18].

In this context, older people are identified as a profile to be included in accessibility and usability issues. As people become older, their sensory, physical and cognitive abilities are affected in general, gradually. The aging process naturally brings to them difficulties when interacting with resources of computer systems [17].

Population aging is a worldwide phenomenon. The United Nations (UN) [2] and the World Health Organization (WHO) [8] showed that the world population is in a unique and irreversible transitional demographic process which will result in older populations everywhere. While fertility rates decline, the proportion of people aged 60 or older will double by 2025 and will reach virtually two billion by 2050. According to the National Census data from 2010, conducted by the Brazilian Institute of Geography and Statistics (IBGE) [6], population aging has been occurred at an accelerated way due to factors such as increased life expectancy. Furthermore, according to the population projections, based the on Census, the Brazilian population of people aged 65 or older will be four times greater by 2060. By this time, this number will reach the percentage of 26.8 % of the population, while in 2013 it was only 7.4 %.

Despite the existence of accessibility and usability guidelines such as the Web Content Accessibility Guidelines (WCAG) [9], The National Institute of Aging's (NIA) guidelines [7] and the Brazilian Electronic Government Accessibility Model (e-MAG) [1], further studies are needed in order to reach a better understanding of the needs of older people as users of computer systems. Additionally, the barriers that those users face to interact with websites should be better characterized [10]. Often, websites are not designed aiming at older people. The percentage of these users has been increasing in significant proportions, boosting mechanisms to Web adaptation for taking into account this user profile.

In this context, the purpose of the present study was to investigate the main accessibility and usability issues on websites encountered by Brazilian older people. We first conducted an initial survey to investigate which websites older people access more frequently, which was answered by 87 participants aged 60–90.

Then we selected four websites to the next phase of this study: evaluating their usability and accessibility with the participation of older users. A total of 20 older people agreed to participate in this phase. Their ages ranged from 61 to 84 years, with a mean age of 67.5 years. They were all residents of the city of São Carlos, state of São Paulo, Brazil. We asked each participant to attempt to perform three tasks for each one of the four websites.

All participants had many difficulties during interacting with the websites. After the test sessions, every participant was dissatisfied with the evaluated sites, and almost all have failed to successfully complete the required tasks. We used the guidelines proposed in the literature, by [15,16,19] to define our set of issues for guiding the process of identifying usability and accessibility issues that occurred during the tests. The proposed issues were grouped in sets according to the similar topics, and their overlap was removed. In addition, the issues that refer to the barriers and difficulties that older people face when interacting with the Web were identified.

The remainder of the paper is structured as follows: in Sect. 2, we examine the previous works related to this paper. In Sect. 3, we describe the usability test of the websites, in Sect. 4 we present the results and discussion. The main conclusions and future work are described in Sect. 5.

2   Related Work

Several studies have discussed the main barriers and difficulties that older people encounter while they interact with the Web. Such studies employed methods such as interviews and usability tests, conducted in field studies or in controlled environments. These barriers show that many websites are not designed keeping in mind the profile of older users, making Web access, sometimes, impossible.

Some research studies have investigated the usability and accessibility of websites by older people. Arfaa and Wang [11] performed a study with 22 elderly users aged 65 or older, with none to advanced computer experience, utilizing social networking sites. The results showed that their previous computer experience and the design of the sites affected the usability and accessibility for those users. Furthermore, they identified that social networking sites are difficult for elders to use because of computer illiteracy, lack of knowledge of Web 2.0 concepts, navigation and other usability issues.

Similarly, in another research study which also involved social networking sites, Braun [13] aimed to understand the factors that influence to the use social networks, such as Facebook. In that study, 124 older adults (aged 60–90) who used the Internet were surveyed. The survey focused specifically on factors related to technology adoption and measured attitudes about perceived ease of use and perceived usefulness of social networking websites, as well as other factors related to technology acceptance. The analyses carried out showed that the use of social networks was associated with trust in their abilities and the Internet use frequency. Unlike what was expected, factors like ease of use and social pressures were not significant predictors.

Bergstrom et al. [12] conducted five independent website usability studies that included younger and older participants and examined age-related differences in them using noninvasive eye tracking. The studies highlighted the potential for age-related differences in performance while navigating websites, such as differences in eye movement and performance during use of some of the sites. The older participants had lower accuracy in one study and took longer to complete tasks in two studies compared to younger participants. In addition, the research inferred that when a website has distracting visual elements, older people pay attention at those areas more than to the rest of the screen.

According to Finn and Johnson [16], many web designers still ignore usability and accessibility design guidelines. The authors of that study conducted a usability study in three travel websites with 9 elderly users aged 55–80 and encountered some problems like: text too small and not easily enlargeable, difficulty returning to Home page, confusing terminology, hard-to-operate menus, poor marking of links, among others. That study showed that companies which target older adults may be failing to follow such guidelines.

In the present paper we investigated the main accessibility and usability issues on sites frequently visited by Brazilian older people in the town of São Carlos. In contrast to research conducted by [16], we have carried out an initial survey that showed that the travel websites were not very accessible for elderly Brazilians. In addition, participants in our study had 60 years or more, because Article 1 of the Brazilian Statute of the Elderly (Law 10.741) considers old people as those who are aged more than 60 years [3].

3   Methodology

In order to investigate the accessibility and usability issues on websites for Brazilian older people, we followed the methodological procedures as described in next subsections, detailing the data collected and the usability tests performed.

3.1   The Evaluated Websites

We first conducted an initial survey to investigate which websites older people accessed most frequently. The survey was conducted by means of interviews with 7 open-ended questions: the first 6 questions asked for the main websites the participant accessed in each of the following categories - search engines, social network sites, video sites, email services, news sites and blogs. The last question asked for any other website not previously categorized in the interview, such as shopping sites, Wikipedia, health sites, food sites, banking sites and others.

The survey was answered by 87 participants, aged 60–90, of the educational program of the University of the Third Age in the São Carlos Educational Foundation (UATI - FESC), in the town of São Carlos, in the state of São Paulo, Brazil.

From the initial survey results, we applied a criterion for selecting websites for inclusion in this study. We chose the most accessed websites and government websites, both at national and regional area.

The 4 selected websites for the study, were:

- UOL - Universo Online - http://www.uol.com.br;
- São Carlos Agora - http://www.saocarlosagora.com.br;
- Previdência Social (Social Security services for Brazilian people) - http://www.previdencia.gov.br;
- FESC - http://www.fesc.com.br.

The websites were downloaded with HTTrack Website Copier Tool[1] version 3.48-21, on 6th May 2015 and hosted on the server of our research group for use in the usability test sessions.

---

[1] Available online at https://www.httrack.com/.

3.2   Participants

Twenty participants aged 60 or older participated in the study, out of 53 invited from senior activity centers, as UATI - FESC and the University of Sao Paulo (USP). They were 5 men and 15 women, with ages ranging from 61 to 84 years, with a mean age of 67.5 years. They all lived in the town of São Carlos, in the state of São Paulo. On average, participants had used the web for 5–10 years. Participants reported average daily web use of one to three times per day.

All the 4 websites were evaluated by 17 participants, and three participants evaluated only two websites each. Due to equipment failure, the data of two of the older participants were lost and one participant gave up to do it. According to the responses of the pre-test questionnaire, the participants were divided into 2 groups:

- Group of experts (**GE**): those who use the Internet for over 10 years - 9 seniors
- Group of novices (**GN**): those who use the Internet for less than 10 years - 11 seniors

The distribution of the participants in each group with respect to gender, age and education level is shown in Table 1.

Table 1. Number of participants in each group, according to their characteristics

Distribution of the participants in groups		GE	GN
Gender	Female	6	9
	Male	3	2
Age	60–69	8	8
	70–79	1	1
	80–89	0	2
Education Level	Elementary school	1	1
	High School	2	2
	Graduate	6	9

3.3   Tasks Undertaken

Each participant was asked to perform three tasks in each website, the tasks were different for each website.

The set of tasks devised for each website was related to typical and common tasks that older people could perform on each website. The tasks were organized in a scenario to find specific news for news sites and search for important information by the elderly in government sites.

The websites were evaluated in different cycles, and the order was reshuffled at each cycle to avoid any ordering or fatigue effects.

3.4 Equipment and Software

The evaluations were performed using a HP Pavilion laptop with Microsoft Windows 7 Operating System with processor AMD Dual-Core 2.30 GHz, 4 GB RAM, equipped with speakers, keyboard, a 14 in LCD screen, a webcam and a 2-button mouse.

Participants accessed their assigned website using the Web browser with which they were most familiar. In this study, all participants used Firefox 40.0.3. The computer also ran a screen capture program, Morae 3.2.1[2], that recorded the screen and voice of participant and researcher. Morae was set to record keystrokes and mouse events.

3.5 Procedure

The usability test sessions were conducted in the laboratories of the senior activity centers: the UATI - FESC and USP, where the older people take Internet courses (University of the Third Age). Each session lasted around 46 min, depending on the number of sites each participant chose to evaluate.

Participants were first briefed about the purpose of the study, the process of the evaluation and were asked to read and sign an informed consent form. Next, they completed a brief questionnaire about their age, educational competencies, profession, how long they use the web and the frequency of use of the Internet per day.

After all the settings on the computer have been made, the researcher opened the browser with the link that downloaded sites were hosted in the research group of the server and began the recording session with Morae. For each site, the researcher read the description of the task to the participant and gently asked participants to think aloud protocol, indicating the usability problems they encountered. While the participants performed the tasks, the researcher noted all comments, questions and reactions from the participants during each session.

After usability test sessions were finished, the researcher asked participants to report what tasks had greater difficulty, which sites have suggestions for improvements and summarize the important aspects for them on the evaluated sites.

4 Results and Discussion

The results from the usability tests showed that all participants had many difficulties to interact with the sites. After the test sessions, participants showed dissatisfaction with the evaluated sites, and many failed to successfully complete the requested tasks. Following, the accessibility and usability issues observed during the evaluation of four websites are discussed.

To define our set of issues, we based the analyses on the guidelines proposed by Dias et al. [15], Finn et al. [16] and Lara et al. [19]. The following 7 sets

---

[2] Available online at https://www.techsmith.com/morae.html.

of issues were proposed, regarding to the issues that refer to the barriers and difficulties that older people faced when interacting with the Web. In addition, the identification of accessibility and usability issues was conducted by means of observations by the researcher and manifestation of users during the tests.

Issue 1 - Location of the Requested Information. All participants (both GE and GN) had many difficulties to find the requested information. The sites of FESC and São Carlos Agora had drop-down menus very close, which caused confusion to participants. In addition, important information for the population, such as the opening hours of FESC and program of courses were not easy to find, which made users to give up searching the site. They said they preferred to go or call FESC to obtain this information. The same happened to the site of Previdência Social, which did not present the information in an easy-to-find manner, making users go to another website (The National Social Security Institute - INSS) seeking information that was not clear on the site.

A few comments from participants are transcribed as follows, and show the difficulty in finding the information requested during the tests:

"It is quite difficult to find the opening hours of the FESC Vila Prado."

"The FESC site should facilitate the way in which information is placed there, we have difficulties because of our age, we forget things."

Issue 2 - Site Map Use. Only the FESC and Previdência sites had a site map. In the GE, 44.5 % of the participants used the site map. In the GN, 9 % of the participants used the site map. The fact that GE used the site map more frequently should probably be related to their greater experience. They had more familiarity and had learned how to use this option on sites.

Issue 3 - Forgetting or Inattention. Only one participant in each group did not show any kind of forgetting or inattention. The highest incidence of forgetting episodes and lack of attention was in relation to what had to be done on the task. While performing a task, participants lost attention browsing the site and at any given time, requested help to the researcher to remind them about what should be done on the task. Another occurrence of forgetting what happened was related to what task he/she had already conducted and ended up doing it again.

Issue 4 - Presentation of Links Activation Problems. Participants (both GE and GN) reported having difficulty understanding some links that were not clear for them, for example, the link "Leia Mais" (read more) in the FESC website (Fig. 1). This link caused confusion to participants who did not understand it as a link but as part of the text to which it belonged. In addition, another problem reported was the proximity of the links on the UOL website. Some participants had trouble clicking a few links that were too close together.

Issue 5 - Information Overload and Links. The selected sites had a large amount of information and advertisements that made participants feel overwhelmed with the choices. Participants of GE and GN reported that the UOL

Fig. 1. Screen capture of option "Leia Mais" (read more) of homepage

site had a lot of advertising that appeared and flashed on their screen, numerous windows, endless scrolling, as well as information and very close links, making it difficult to navigate and distracting their attention. In addition, the São Carlos Agora site also presented lack of contrast between text and background colors, making it difficult to search for information. Another reported issue was the need to improve the content and organization of the information on the 4 sites, to make it clear and direct, especially on sites like FESC and Previdência Social, which had older people as their main target audience. A few comments from participants about this issue:

"The São Carlos Agora site is not very familiar to me, I was lost, too much information."

"The São Carlos Agora and FESC sites are very polluted!! The São Carlos Agora has too much advertising."

Issue 6 - Difficulties to Return to the Homepage of the Site. 88.8 % participants of the GE and 90.9 % participants of the GN found it difficult to return the site's home page on FESC, especially to find the schedule of the courses in one of the requested tasks. In this site, it was necessary to get the schedules of the courses offered by clicking on them, and open a new page with the PDF of times. Participants did not know how to get back to the home page. The other sites also had no clear breadcrumbs, creating difficulties for participants, especially to the inexperienced (GN) during navigation.

Issue 7 - Confusing Terminology and Understanding of Abbreviations. The FESC site presented terms that were not clear to participants (both GE and GN), such as the Institution term to indicate the different campi of FESC. Another problem was the menu with abbreviations without their definitions (Fig. 2), which caused confusion for participants who were lost with this menu and requested assistance from the researcher. A few comments about site are described as follows:

"On the website of FESC, the term institution is very formal, I can not understand that refers to differences campus FESC."

"Information needs to be clearer on the FESC site, these abbreviations are not accompanied by their definitions, it left me lost."

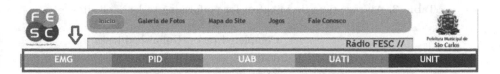

Fig. 2. Screen capture of menu with abbreviations of homepage

Failures (Unfinished Tasks). In each of the sites selected there were tasks that participants had more difficulty and abandoned or performed incorrectly. The most difficult task and most abandoned by users was the task 3 of Previdência Social, related searching for a video. This task was more difficult because the site showed the videos at the bottom, requiring participants to go throughout the entire website content to find the option that directed the videos. In addition, the site did not present the video's names, only one could see it hovering over the video. Task 2 also had a number of abandonment because the search of the FESC opening hours and the term used by the site to refer to different FESC campi was not clear. It also refers to the issue 7 already described.

Task Completion Rates and Time to Complete Tasks. In order to observe the behavior of groups according to the complexity of the evaluated sites for these analyzes, the four sites were divided into two groups:

1. **Simple sites (SS):** regional sites, which have less content and fewer links - FESC and São Carlos Agora
2. **Complex sites (CS):** national sites, with the greatest amount of content, different areas of information and greater amount of links - UOL and Previdência Social

An analysis considering all the sites and the completion of their tasks by the group showed that experienced participants (GE) a task completion rate of 84.4 % and novice participants (GN) had a task completion rate of 69.8 %. A Chi-Square test found a significant difference between the completion rates when comparing the two groups in all websites ($X^2 = 6.439, df = 1, p - value = 0.01$) (Table 2).

Table 2. Percentage of participants that completed or were unable to finish tasks in all sites

Groups	Completed tasks	Unfinished tasks
Experienced users (GE)	84.4 %	15.6 %
Novice users (GN)	69.8 %	30.2 %

According to Table 3, participants in GE spent more time to complete tasks and also more time give up on them. Since they were more experienced, it created

Table 3. Average time (in minutes) for performing tasks in all sites

Group	Completed tasks	Unfinished tasks
Experienced users (GE)	00:02:57	00:08:40
Novice users (GN)	00:02:40	00:05:49

an expectation that they would spend less time to perform the tasks. However, participants in GE tended to more persistent and ended up spending more time in unfinished tasks than participants in GN. More studies would be necessary to increase the number of participants and tasks in order to show this difference with statistical significance.

Task Completion in Simple and Complex Websites. A second analysis was performed splitting the data into simple and complex websites. This analysis was performed in order to verify whether the complexity of the sites in this sample had any effect on task completion rates. Table 4 shows the percentage of tasks completed and unfinished in simple sites. Table 5 shows the same information for complex websites.

Table 4. Percentage of participants that completed or were unable to finish tasks in the SS

Group	Completed tasks	Unfinished tasks
Experienced users (GE)	81.5 %	18.5 %
Novice users (GN)	66.7 %	33.3 %
Total	73.5 %	26.5 %

Table 5. Percentage of participants that completed or not the tasks in the CS

Group	Completed tasks	Unfinished tasks
Experienced users (GE)	88.1 %	11.9 %
Novice users (GN)	72.7 %	27.3 %
Total	78.7 %	21.3 %

Surprisingly, in the evaluations performed with this sample of websites, a Chi-Square test found no significant difference between task completion rates when comparing simple and complex websites ($X^2 = 0.832$, $df = 1$, $p-value = 0.36$). Considering the limited website sample size, further studies with a larger sample of websites would be necessary to analyse the influence of website complexity in task completion rates by experienced and novice older computer users.

5 Conclusions and Future Work

This study presented an evaluation of four websites that Brazilian older people frequently access and showed accessibility and usability issues regarding the design and presentation of content. The issues investigated and the statistical analysis showed that the sites need to improve the way they organize their content and information.

The analyzed Brazilian sites still have problems to present clear links and the links are very near to click, information overload and many advertisements, difficulties to return to the homepage, confusing terminology and abbreviations without their definitions. In addition, more experienced older users succeeded in navigation, suggesting that users more familiar with Internet can navigate more easily.

The results reinforced known accessibility and usability issues related to existing knowledge guidelines from previous studies. Despite the existing guidelines, there are still sites with accessibility and usability problems. Brazilian sites whose target audience are mainly older people, such as the FESC and Previdência Social were not accessible and usable to them. From the results of this research, it is possible to address the problems and redesign the sites interfaces to improve accessibility and usability for older people.

Finally, the suggestions and conclusions of this study can be used as a baseline for the development of sites considering the profile guidelines of accessibility and usability in order to provide better access to information by older people, mainly for Brazilian citizens.

Acknowledgments. We thank all volunteers that took part in the interview, CAPES and University of São Paulo for their great support. We also thank Rafael J. Geraldo for his great help at the analysis in this study.

References

1. Brazilian Government. Accessibility Model for e-Government (e-MAG) - version3.1.   http://www.governoeletronico.gov.br/acoes-e-projetos/e-MAG/o-que-e-acessibilidade. Accessed 28 Feb 2016
2. United Nations (UN). http://www.un.org/en/globalissues/ageing/index.shtml. Accessed 28 Feb 2016
3. Law 10.741 - (Statute of the Elderly) - Estatuto do Idoso do Brasil (2003). http://www.planalto.gov.br/ccivil_03/leis/2003/L10.741.htm. Accessed 28 Feb 2016 (in Portuguese)
4. World Wide Web Consortium (W3C). Introduction to Web Accessibility (2005). http://www.w3.org/WAI/intro/accessibility.php. Accessed 28 Feb 2016
5. International Standards Organization: ISO 9241-171: Ergonomics of human-system interaction–Part 171: Guidance on software accessibility (2008). http://www.iso.org/iso/iso_catalogue/catalogue_tc/catalogue_detail.htm?csnumber=39080. Accessed 28 Feb 2016
6. Brazilian Institute of Geography and Statistics (IBGE) (2015). http://goo.gl/DLhLXV. Accessed 28 Feb 2016

7. National Institute on Aging (NIA). Making Your Website Senior Friendly. National Institute on Aging (2015). https://www.nlm.nih.gov/pubs/staffpubs/od/ocpl/agingchecklist.html. Accessed 28 Feb 2016
8. World Health Organization (WHO) (2015). http://www.who.int/ageing/events/idop_rationale/en/. Accessed 28 Feb 2016
9. World Wide Web Consortium (W3C). Web Content Accessibility Guidelines (WCAG2.0) (2015). http://www.w3.org/WAI/intro/wcag. Accessed 28 Feb 2016
10. Arch, A.: Web accessibility for older users: successes and opportunities (keynote). In: Proceedings of the 2009 International Cross-Disciplinary Conference on Web Accessibililty (W4A), W4A 2009, pp. 1–6 (2009)
11. Arfaa, J., Wang, Y.K.: A usability study on elder adults utilizing social networking sites. In: Marcus, A. (ed.) DUXU 2014, Part II. LNCS, vol. 8518, pp. 50–61. Springer, Heidelberg (2014)
12. Bergstrom, J.C.R., Olmsted-Hawala, E.L., Jans, M.E.: Age-related differences in eye tracking and usability performance: website usability for older adults. Int. J. Hum. Comput. Interact. 29(8), 541–548 (2013)
13. Braun, M.T.: Obstacles to social networking website use among older adults. Comput. Hum. Behav. 29(3), 673–680 (2013)
14. Costa, D., Fernandes, N., Neves, S., Duarte, C., Hijón-Neira, R., Carriço, L.: Web accessibility in africa: a study of three african domains. In: Winckler, M. (ed.) INTERACT 2013, Part I. LNCS, vol. 8117, pp. 331–338. Springer, Heidelberg (2013)
15. Dias, A.L., de Mattos Fortes, R.P., Masiero, P.C.: Heua: A heuristic evaluation with usability and accessibility requirements to assess web systems. In: Proceedings of the 11th Web for All Conference, W4A 2014, NY, USA, pp. 18:1–18:4 (2014). http://doi.acm.org/10.1145/2596695.2596706
16. Finn, K., Johnson, J.: A usability study of websites for older travelers. In: Stephanidis, C., Antona, M. (eds.) UAHCI 2013, Part II. LNCS, vol. 8010, pp. 59–67. Springer, Heidelberg (2013)
17. Hayflick, L.: How and why we become older, Campus, Rio de Janeiro–RJ (1996). In Portuguese
18. Kurniawan, S.: Age-related differences in the interface design process. In: Universal Access Handbook, pp. 8:1–8:12. CRC Press (2009)
19. Lara, S.M.A., de Mattos Fortes, R.P., Russo, C.M., Freire, A.P.: A study on the acceptance of website interaction aids by older adults. Univ. Access Inf. Soc. 15, 1–16 (2015)
20. Power, C., Freire, A.P., Petrie, H.: Integrating accessibility evaluation into web engineering processes. Int. J. Inf. Technol. Web Eng. 4(4), 54–77 (2009)

Board Games and Regulars' Tables — Extending User Centred Design in the Mobia Project

Johannes Tröger[1], Jan Alexandersson[1(✉)], Jochen Britz[1], Maurice Rekrut[1],
Daniel Bieber[2], and Kathleen Schwarz[2]

[1] DFKI GmbH, Saarbrücken, Germany
{johannes.troeger,jan.alexandersson,jochen.britz,maurice.rekrut}@dfki.de
[2] Iso-Institut e.V, Saarbrücken, Germany
{bieber,schwarz}@iso-institut.de
http://www.iso-institut.de
http://www.dfki.de

Abstract. To allow persons with mobility issues to remain mobile, the three-year project Mobia set out to develop a technology-supported human-based service within public transport: mobility guides provide a helping hand for passengers with mobility issues. The Mobia system can be positioned within the field of AAL and consists of multiple user interfaces and actors to coordinate and realise the point of service. This paper introduces two extension to the User-Centred Design methodology which were successfully applied during the course of the project. The first is the development of a large board game like demonstrator that allows for simulation of realistic scenarios within the scenario during which observation of user behaviour can take place. The second – regulars' table – is a monthly face2face meeting between developers, passengers and mobility guides serving as a platform for exchanging experiences, testing and discussing new ideas. Results from the Mobia project are discussed.

Keywords: User-centred design · AAL · Board game · Public transport

1 Introduction

Within two recent German funding schemes by the Federal Ministry for Economic Affairs and Energy (BMWi) *Door to Door* (Tür zu Tür) and Federal Ministry of Education and Research (BMBF) *Mobile up until high ages* (Mobil bis ins hohe Alter), about 25 projects set out to address mobility issues within the scope of Ambient Assisted Living (AAL). The officially demanded objectives were to develop integral concepts for elderly persons by combining various public transport systems into intermodal transport systems and beyond that include human based services to develop holistic transportation concepts. The projects additionally focussed on a number of adjacent topics like indoor and/or outdoor navigation or social community aspects [1]. Although a majority opted for bringing innovative concepts somehow close to the market, few, if any, really succeeded in doing so. Indeed, some of the projects were rather basic research

© Springer International Publishing Switzerland 2016
J. Zhou and G. Salvendy (Eds.): ITAP 2016, Part I, LNCS 9754, pp. 129–140, 2016.
DOI: 10.1007/978-3-319-39943-0_13

oriented projects and in the case of other projects, crossing the *valley of death*[1] would had required more investment which is not always granted. Bearing all this in mind, still a relatively low success rate in bringing the project results into the market can be observed.

One conducive approach in analysing this phenomena is to take a closer look at the research methodology used. The mobility projects are basically AAL projects and thus geared towards the users' needs. Within the last 40 years several methodological approaches have been evolving ensuring that development meets the users needs. One of them is user-centred design (UCD) [5,8] which has been deployed by mobility projects like SIMBA, SenioMobil, Dynamo, Campagno or Mobia [1,2]. Although applying UCD in the case of mobility projects seems both straight forward and well backed by research, there is a great number of interpretations how UCD should be actually implemented [9]. This very fact leads to a big degree of freedom in applying this methodology, potentially overseeing some major challenges arising especially when it comes to adapting UCD [15]. In the case of the afore mentioned AAL mobility projects systems are meant to comprise multiple *actors* and *artefacts* [18] – a user interface is only one artefact of multiple – suggesting different approaches like socio technical design (STD) [19]. STD advocates for the direct participation of the end-user in the design process and is therefore closer related to so called participatory design (PD) approaches which were deployed in mobility projects like PASSAge or S-Mobil 100 [1,3]. But especially in PD, it can be difficult for end-users to participate in innovative solutions given their special needs [15]. Juxtaposing UCD STD and PD there is a large conceptual overlap in the sense of putting the users' needs at the center of the development including generic challenges within this area which this paper is going to discuss from a UCD perspective.

Below, two main challenges are briefly discussed in order to pave the way for a detailed description of how they could be tackled. Within the mobility projects, developing new intermodal transport systems and possibly augmenting them with an additional service concept multidisciplinary teams have to overcome two major challenges:

1. Enabling the user an easy **comprehension** of the innovative system as a whole.
2. **Maintaining** the iterative manner of the chosen methodology and thereby being accompanied by the users throughout the whole project's lifetime and beyond.

Enabling an Easy Comprehension. UCD amongst the other outlined methodologies typically starts with a comprehensive and careful analysis of the users' needs. Derived from this analysis, functional as well as technical requirements are worked out [14] which are then often incorporated by *personas* and

---

[1] Especially in Europe there is a gap between development of science and development of commercial products – the so called valley of death – which results in large problems with knowledge exploitation [4].

scenarios [17]. In a second step the requirements are implemented into user-test ready mock-ups or products which are in a third step evaluated by the actually addressed users. Of course there are multiple variations in labelling the steps included in UCD and this is just an abstract description of how UCD methodology is typically applied [5, 7]. Still there is always a conceptual break between the theoretical analysis of the users' needs and the practical implementation of innovative solutions which should be evaluated by the user in the adjacent step. In most cases users are not disturbed by this break and perceive a certain usefulness of the novel solution. As the *Technology Acceptance Model* (TAM) predicts, the perceived usefulness and the perceived ease of use are the two key predictors for novel technical solutions to be accepted by the user [13]. Ensuring a perception of usefulness can be very challenging in technologically novel systems though. This might be due to the reason that targeted users are either restrained by own mental abilities or – as outlined above intermodal mobility concepts build upon multi-artefacts and multi-actor architectures – proposed new systems are to difficult to understand with reasonable effort [15]. Additionally, the challenge may arise from the fact that UCD was initially developed within the community of user interface designers [16] and therefore "traditional user-centred design methods provide little guidance in how to involve the elderly in [...] ambient assisted living scenarios" [10, p. 334].

Maintaining the Iterative Shape. There is a certain risk that a UCD cycle stays a one-time activity, which is performed at the beginning of the project and gets cut out approaching the final project phase typically running on a tight schedule [7]. This is by definition poor UCD, as UCD methodology builds upon an iterative procedure which should be maintained throughout the project's whole lifetime.

To conclude, having mentioned that development methodologies focusing on users' needs are very popular upon AAL applied research, but still a highly flexible methodology, two frequently overlooked challenges are connected to user acceptance and **comprehension** of novel intermodal concepts and **maintaining** an iterative approach throughout the whole development. The scope of this paper is to suggest extensions to UCD methodology and to provide implementation insights from the Mobia project – one of the afore named mobility projects – which addressed the above mentioned challenges early on. To conclude this paper will discuss the implemented method's efficacy.

2   Mobia

The research project Mobia aimed at reducing barriers within public transport in central Saarbrücken[2] by developing and validating a technology-supported human-based service system. Mobia augments public transport internal physical means (e.g. existing accessibility features in means of transport like fold out

---

[2] Saarbrücken is the capital of the German state Saarland: 180.000 habitants.

wheelchair ramps) and internal digital means (e.g. interface for accessing time tables) by a public transport comprehensive mean: *mobility guides* (German: Mobilitäts-Lotsen) providing a service chain by helping passengers from door to door, or at particular points or even during sub-parts of the journey during which the passenger – of some reason – needs help. This includes for example entering the bus at a particular bus stop (because the bus and bus stop do not match), changing from bus to tram (because the way is too long), walk from the tram to the entrance of the passenger's doctor (because the passenger is afraid of getting lost) or helping a young father with a child, buggy and shopping bags to enter the bus (because he cannot handle that many things at the same time). The technology consists of a software for intelligent disposition and coordination of the mobility guides and front-ends for pilots and passengers. The coordination software directs the mobility guides to the requested point of service. The passenger front-end needed to be implemented flexibly so that all passengers can interact with it. In addition to telephone calls, personalised and adaptable user interfaces running on smartphones that allow their users not only to order trips, but to receive real-time support during the trip were envisioned. This includes tracking service as well as notifications and alerts. The Mobia system was hypothesised to be capable of delivering coordinate personalised interaction and service that allow – in principle – everyone to utilise public transport.

3   Methodology

There are two common challenges using UCD within the domain of AAL mobility projects, which are connected to user acceptance and **comprehension** of novel intermodal concepts and **maintaining** an iterative UCD approach throughout the whole project's lifecycle. This paper claims that noticing these challenges and addressing them upfront can help to increase the probability of succeeding in bringing the envisioned solution close to market. Therefore this paper introduces two methodological extensions to UCD and provides evidence for their effectiveness from Mobia project.

The Mobia project included two traditional iterations of UCD development, an extended iteration including a fully working simulation of the system and a one year lasting longitudinal field test which included monthly feedback iterations. The two first comprehensive UCD iterations were following the widely recognised UCD methodology and included a paper prototype evaluation of first interfaces and a mock-up version of the user interface on a smartphone (see Fig. 1). After these two iterations plenty of feedback concerning the user interface was collected but the overarching Mobia system implementing the service concept was still unreviewed by the user group.

Considering this, one could expect that potential users would be overstrained and have concerns when testing the whole system in a real field test. This issue is of great importance, as the requirement phase at the beginning of the UCD

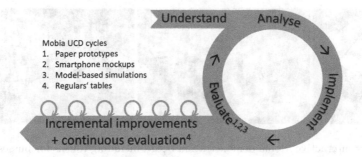

Mobia UCD cycles
1. Paper prototypes
2. Smartphone mockups
3. Model-based simulations
4. Regulars' tables

Fig. 1. User centred design as used in the Mobia project including two cycles of mock-ups based evaluation, the demonstration board workshops and the project's 12 month lasting field test.

revealed that many users avoid using public transport due to its confusing complexity; this is of course a subjective statement and sometimes related to limitations on the user side. Therefore the project included a third UCD cycle whose evaluation phase was geared towards evaluating the Mobia system as a whole and which dealt with the challenge of making complex systems understandable.

Easy Comprehension Through Board Game Based Simulation. The Mobia system includes multiple actors, as well as multiple artefacts including different interfaces and technological components To ensure a certain feasibility of evaluations breaking the system's concept down to simple easy to grasp benefits for the user is nevertheless of vital importance. This becomes especially articulated within the domain of AAL, as users often bring in plenty of different needs due to age or disease related decline in senses or cognitive abilities [22]. Especially cognitive impairments make it very challenging to run an evaluation of a complex system within AAL [18]. Tackling this issue the Mobia project drew upon rich insights from former projects [6] and existing research [11] successfully using simulators in the context of AAL for development of user interfaces as well as for demonstration purposes. Therefore it was decided to use a large board game like demonstrator dedicated for user evaluations within the UCD cycle (Fig. 2).

The Mobia demonstration board is composed of an excerpt of the street-map of Saarbrücken, including public transport (busses and trams) stops and tracks, serving as the board on top of which various figurines simulate passengers and mobility guides. Various small 3D-printed vehicles depict busses and trams. To make the model an interactive simulator, both board and vehicles were equipped with sensors: the buses and trams with three magnets; reed switches are mounted in the board under every public transport stop. Combining this information and the number and the arrangement of the magnets under the vehicles enables one to automatically determine which vehicle is at which stop. Therefore, sensor data are fed to an Arduino Mega micro controller which is connected via USB to a PC. This information is then transmitted by a simulation of the actual timetable

Fig. 2. The interactive Mobia demonstration board including tokens for busses, trams, mobility guides and passengers. The board measures 2.1 m times 1.1 m and is equipped with reed sensors tracking the position of the vehicles.

information system of Saarbrücken's public transport to the backend which also coordinates the front-ends of passengers and mobility guides. In this way it is possible to simulate the trip in a virtual time. RFID tags are attached to every stop and vehicle so passengers and guides can sign up with the help of their near-field-communication-ready front-ends at the stops and at the vehicles and thus transmit their position with one touch to the system.

This demonstration board draws upon two major benefits commonly found in the aria of serious board games: Breaking down the complexity of real life systems makes them easier to understand and enabling direct manipulation through tangible objects reduces the barrier and fear for interaction (see also [6]).

Board games can be used to simulate complex real world systems and make them easier to understand via means of abstraction and reduction of cognitive load[3]. In the Mobia project the challenge was to make the complexity of a technology supported service concept building upon public transport of a whole city comprehensible. This concept includes the interaction of different types of trams and busses, different actions with the system, such as registering at stops or booking trips and different roles such as mobility guides and passengers. Right from the beginning it was clear that only by understanding complex interaction of all parts of the system the project could ensure the important perception of usefulness to pave the way for user acceptance of this novel service concept. Building upon scenarios and personas from the requirement phase of the UCD, the aim was to simulate a realistic scenario of a complete Mobia service chain through an abstract easy-to-understand but not oversimplifying model.

Evaluating interaction of touchscreen based interfaces, designers often encounter hesitation and fear by older users. One explanation for this phenomena is the fact that the age related decline in sensitivity to vibration [20] limits the haptic feedback provided by touchscreens and thereby prevents elderly users from a comfortable quality of interaction [23]. This is why another declared aim of the Mobia demo board was to ensure the haptic experience of classic board games taking into account that older users have special needs for haptic interaction.

---

[3] Board games are effectively used in professional training programs simulating complex scenarios like humanitarian crises https://paxsims.wordpress.com/aftershock/.

In summary, the Mobia demo-board is a model-based simulation of public transport in the style of a classic tangible board game and provides the testing ground for evaluation and acquisition of rich qualitative data within the UCD cycles.

Accompanying the User on His/Her Journey. The Mobia project set out to comprehensively evaluate a running system within the UCD methodology. Therefore it was necessary to build upon a strong basis of users which would regularly use the system and agree to attend recurrent meetings to evaluate and give feedback. For this purpose the Mobia project included a one year lasting field test which was accompanied by evaluative monthly meetings, so called regulars' tables. This approach is promising because of two aspects: The longitudinal evaluation is a perfect indicator for the maturity of a system and the long time period and the personal contact to the user help to set up a project friendly user base which helps to finalise a running prototype.

By the means of a multiple month lasting longitudinal evaluation, projects can prove a certain maturity of a technology based system. Building a prototype and testing it in the real environment within a one year lasting longitudinal study typically represents a *Technology Readiness Level* (TRL) of six or seven [21]. This TRL can be used to rate a system and therefore can serve as indicator of a project's success. A longitudinal study also allows the developers to finalise the system as the main functionality remains fix but the team can focus on smaller features based on the users' feedback.

At regulars' tables on a monthly basis, developers can keep up the personal contact to the user and profit from a well cultivated relationship with an established friendly user base. Especially the fact that there is room for the user to understand the perspective of the developers makes the cooperation more efficient. In addition to that, the physical presence of project members, typically technology experts, can serve as an support structure for technological problems occurring during the field test. This is especially important as most users in AAL contexts are not that tech savvy and therefore need some attention addressing their issues while interacting with the system [12]. Those aspects in combination with the ambient hospitality[4] a regulars' table helps building a strong project friendly user base which can be the basis of efficient cooperation.

Including a longitudinal field evaluation while accompanying the user at regulars' tables combines the benefit of proving a certain technology maturity and also getting constant feedback from a friendly user base which can be fed back into feature adjustment and finalisation of the system.

4   Results and Discussion

Havnig identified two major challenges within UCD for complex AAL mobility systems related to **comprehension** of complex systems and **maintaining**

---

[4] Within the Mobia project fine torte from one of the high quality local confectioneries was povided.

Table 1. User feedback (subsumed in core topics) acquired during the WSs classified according to *aspect of the system* (horizontal) and *type of feedback* (vertical).

	Public transport	User Interface	Service concept
General	– Delays	– Wording	– Locations of high need
	– Connections	– Technical device's barriers	– Office hours
	– Safety at stops		– Customer support
Interaction	– Drivers' behaviour	– In-app navigation principle	– Service manners
	– Complex ticket machines	– Notifications & Alerts	– Registration at stops
		–Booking process	– Request handling duration
		– Help functions	
Representation	– Stops' bad condition	– Buttons & Icons	– Guides' recognisability
	– Stops' equipment	– Trip representation	– Guides' behaviour in public

the iterative shape of UCD, this paper described two extensions to the UCD methodology which were successfully applied within the project.

Results. Within the third UCD cycle of the Mobia project, in February 2013, there were eight two hours lasting workshops (WS) including the demo board visited by the project internal usability experts and around three target users each time ($\Sigma = 20$) as well as two mobility guides. The acquired feedback can be subsumed and plotted in a three times three matrix with the axis *aspect of the system* (public transport, user interface & service concept) and *type of feedback* (general, interaction & representation), see Table 1.

The one year lasting field test took place from November 2013 until Oktober 2014 and set out with a number of 27 subjects participating which grew up to a total number of 71 subjects having used the service at least once (compare Table 2).

Table 2. Number of users showing up to regulars' tables (RT), total number of users enrolled and at least once active (ΣU), number of users active on a monthly basis (U/M) and number of trips conducted per month.

	Nov	Dec	Jan	Feb	Mar	Apr	May	Jun	Jul	Aug	Sep	Oct
RT			25	16	19	19	15	16	13		14	23
ΣU	27	33	41	41	45	49	57	62	66	70	71	71
U/M	26	18	28	28	28	29	30	28	34	24	21	17
Trips	40	12	65	65	109	193	139	162	205	67	110	136

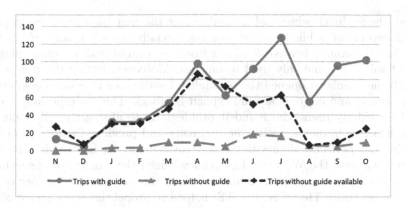

Fig. 3. Trips conducted within the one year field test, lasting from November 2013 (N) until Oktober 2014 (O), with the help of a mobility guide (blue), without the help of a mobility guide but within their working hours (orange) and outside normal working hours (black). (Color figure online)

Plotting the user interactions during the field test clearly shows an increase in total number of trips conducted using the Mobia interface which reached its peak in the summer and then slightly dropped towards the end of the field test (see Table 2). This development aligns with a growing total number of users enrolled into the field test; these are users which conducted at least one trip during the field test. Correcting this total number of users for their monthly activity, shows a relatively constant number of users which were active on a monthly basis.

Further analysis of the number of trips booked reveals that the demand for mobility guidance constantly grew during the whole period, the dip in August is due to holidays. The number of trips not demanding for help of mobility guides varied a lot. Due to the fixed service hours of the Mobia service, there are two cases counting as trip without assistance: trips where mobility guides were available but the user decided not to demand for help and trips outside of service hours but the user decided to conduct the trip anyway. The latter kind of unassisted trips followed the same bell curve as the total number of trips mentioned above, whereas the number of trips refusing available assistance stayed on a low level throughout the whole testing period (see Fig. 3). This bell curve distribution can be interpreted as a season effect as the number of self-conducted trips drops in autumn and winter due to less daylight and worse weather conditions.

Discussion. The demo-board workshops were geared towards improving the core UCD development whereas the regulars' tables were geared towards supporting the longitudinal field test. The former revealed a rich variety of qualitative feedback illustrating how this tool helped the users to quickly understand and to look at the whole system from different angles. This becomes clear through the feedback which did not only cover the user interfaces, but in principle all aspects of public transport and additionally the whole service concept. Therefore, the comprehensive feedback from such quasi-realistic game playing can add value to commonly used techniques. Moreover, letting the user interact with the simulator opened the possibility for the user interface designers to simply observe and not only acquire explicit feedback. This got especially accentuated for elderly users who found it problematic to abstractly reflect on the system which is in one line with the literature and previous findings [6,11,15]. These insights perfectly align with the need for evidence for how to visualise STS [19]. Furthermore, the WS attendees acknowledged the amount of engagement of the project and consortium as made explicit through the *get-together* of the whole project team. Therefore, the WSs helped to propel the development of the system in the midterm and thus legitimated the relatively high monetary and organisational expenses.

The longitudinal study was meant to serve as a realistic benchmark of the system and to help jointly further improving it through dialog and collaboration between all stakeholders. One of the regulars' tables' main advantage was to circumvent users' discouragement which would eventually cause them to leave the project. The regulars' table was open for any passenger which lead to a relatively high fluctuation sometimes threatening the meetings to loose track. Therefore, users were split into small groups discussing similar topics. Especially the technical support for the not very tech-savvy users was of extreme high value and helped keeping a strong *friendly* user base.

The initial tables turned out to become a forum for users' negative experiences and complaints which caused a very unproductive atmosphere, although much of the complaints did not target the project objectives, but the public transport as provided. To tackle this, the project introduced a *passenger's diary* where the passenger would write down positive and negative experiences of any kind. This helped to absorb and buffer negative experiences and helped the users to stay focused on the improvement of the system. All this lead to a throughout constant participation during the long lasting field test without which the degree of matureness probably would have not been achieved.

5   Conclusions

This paper set out to discuss possible solution for common challenges for UCD within the context of complex AAL systems. The identified challenges are: enabling the user an easy **comprehension** system as a whole and **maintaining** the iterative manner throughout the project's whole lifetime. In order to tackle these challenges two extensions to UCD methodology as described in literature [8] were proposed which can be also transferred to other development methodologies focusing on users' needs like PD or STD. Innovative service concepts within the field of AAL, like in Mobia, are designed for vulnerable persons as main users. Developing for or with this user group, experience has shown a mandatory requirement concerning continuous interaction between developers and users [2,6]. Taking this into account, this paper described a way of making complex AAL systems comprehensible for the users during initial development and showed how to maintain the iterative character of UCD and at the same time allow for a continuous development during the whole lifetime of a project. The first extension is the early stage usage of a large board game serving as a simulator of, in this case, public transport allowing both the users to experience and developers to observe the users in a quasi-realistic setting. The second extension is a longitudinal field test accompanied by regular meetings with a project friendly user base.

Evidence for the efficacy of these two extensions is provided by data from the Mobia project which applied the proposed methodology. The simulator provided an easy way to understand the multi-actor multi-artefact AAL system and enabled the acquisition of rich qualitative data concerning not only interfaces but overarching interaction within the whole system. Moreover, the descriptive statistics from the longitudinal study show how recurrent evaluative meetings – regulars' tables – helped to accompany and keep a fixed user base on the one year lasting operational test. Building upon this promising use case, one can say that extended UCD methodology is still an excellent choice where research focusses on users' need. Correctly applied, it has the potential to move innovative ideas into mature and sustainable systems.

Building upon these results, a five-year project started in late 2015 – MobiSaar – with a larger consortium extending the Mobia system to cover the whole federal state of Saarland[5]. This includes particularly finding ways to provide transportation within and outside the public transport spine for everyone.

References

1. Wichert, R., Klausing, H. (eds.): Ambient Assisted Living: 7. AAL-Kongress 2014, Berlin, Germany, January 21-22, 2014. Springer International Publishing (2015)
2. Alexandersson, J., et al.: Oil in the machine: technical support for a human-centred service system for public transport. In: Wichert, R., Klausing, H. (eds.) Ambient Assisted Living. Advanced Technologies and Societal Change, pp. 157–167. Springer, Heidelberg (2015)
3. Bähr, M., et al.: PASSAge: personalized mobility, assistance and service systems in an ageing society. In: Wichert, R., Klausing, H. (eds.) Ambient Assisted Living. Advanced Technologies and Societal Change, pp. 109–119. Springer, Heidelberg (2014)
4. Barr, S.H., Baker, T., Markham, S.K., Kingon, A.I.: Bridging the valley of death: lessons learned from 14 years of commercialization of technology education. Acad. Manage. Learn. Educ. 8(3), 370–388 (2009)
5. ISO/DIS 9241-210. (2010). Ergonomics of Human System Interaction-Part 210: Human-Centred Design for Interactive Systems. International Standardization Organization (ISO), Switzerland (2009)

---

[5] See https://en.wikipedia.org/wiki/Saarland. Saarland has ~1 Mi habitants, 390 habitants per km^2 and one of the highest ratios cars per habitant in Europe.

6. Frey, J., Bergweiler, S., Alexandersson, J., Gholamsaghaee, E., Reithinger, N., Stahl, C.: Smartcase: a smart home environment in a suitcase. In: 2011 7th International Conference on Intelligent Environments (IE), pp. 378–381, Best Demo Award. IEEE (2011)
7. Gulliksen, J., Göransson, B., Boivie, I., Blomkvist, S., Persson, J., Cajander, Å.: Key principles for user-centred systems design. Behav. Inf. Technol. 22(6), 397–409 (2003)
8. Harper, R., Rodden, T., Rogers, Y., Sellen, A. (eds.): Being Human: Human-Computer Interaction in the Year 2020. Microsoft Research Ltd., Cambridge (2007)
9. Iivari, J., Iivari, N.: Varieties of user-centredness: an analysis of four systems development methods. Inf. Syst. J. 21(2), 125–153 (2011)
10. Kanis, M., Alizadeh, S., Groen, J., Khalili, M., Robben, S., Bakkes, S., Kröse, B.: Ambient monitoring from an elderly-centred design perspective: what, who and how. In: Keyson, D.V., et al. (eds.) AmI 2011. LNCS, vol. 7040, pp. 330–334. Springer, Heidelberg (2011)
11. Kanis, M., Robben, S., Kröse, B.: Miniature play: using an interactive dollhouse to demonstrate ambient interactions in the home. In: Proceedings of DIS (2012)
12. Kleinberger, T., Becker, M., Ras, E., Holzinger, A., Müller, P.: Ambient intelligence in assisted living: enable elderly people to handle future interfaces. In: Stephanidis, C. (ed.) UAHCI 2007 (Part II). LNCS, vol. 4555, pp. 103–112. Springer, Heidelberg (2007)
13. Lee, Y., Kozar, K.A., Larsen, K.R.: The technology acceptance model: past, present, and future. Commun. Assoc. Inf. Syst. 12(50), 752–780 (2003)
14. Lowdermilk, T.: User-Centered Design: A Developer's Guide to Building User-Friendly Applications. O'Reilly Media Inc., Sebastopol (2013)
15. Marti, P., Bannon, L.J.: Exploring user-centred design in practice: some caveats. Knowl. Technol. Policy 22(1), 7–15 (2009)
16. Norman, D.A., Draper, S.W.: User Centered System Design. Lawrence Erlbaum Associates, Hillsdale (1986)
17. Pruitt, J., Grudin, J.: Personas: practice and theory. In: Proceedings of the 2003 Conference on Designing for User Experiences, pp. 1–15. ACM (2003)
18. Salvi, D., Colomer, J.B.M., Arredondo, M.T., Prazak-Aram, B.: A framework for evaluating ambient assisted living technologies and the experience of the universAAL project. J. Ambient Intell. Smart Environ. 7(3), 329–352 (2015)
19. Scacchi, W.: Socio-technical design. Encycl. Hum. Comput. Interact. 1, 656–659 (2004)
20. Verrillo, R.T.: Age related changes in the sensitivity to vibration. Chin. J. Gerontol. 35(2), 185–193 (1980)
21. Wikipedia: Technology Readiness Level (2016). https://en.wikipedia.org/wiki/Technology_readiness_level. Accessed 7 Feb 2016
22. Zajicek, M.: Interface design for older adults. In: Proceedings of the 2001 EC/NSF Workshop on Universal Accessibility of Ubiquitous Computing: Providing for the Elderly, pp. 60–65. ACM (2001)
23. Zhang, X., Carré, M., Rowson, J.: Effect on frequency changing of tactile feedback on touchscreen devices. In: Design 4 Health, 3–5 July 2013, Sheffield, UK Sheffield Hallam University, pp. 316–322 (2014)

User Involvement in Design: The Four Models

Bin Zhang[1] and Hua Dong[2(✉)]

[1] Xiamen University of Technology, Xiamen, People's Republic of China
2012112202@xmut.edu.cn
[2] College of Design and Innovation, Tongji University, Shanghai, People's Republic of China
donghua@tongji.edu.cn

Abstract. User studies and user involvement in design have been heavily discussed but lacks a systematic theory, thus causing confusion for novice designers and researchers. Through extensive literature review, this paper identifies three approaches of user studies, i.e. 'empirical studies' which tends to 'learn from the past'; 'experimental studies' which tends to 'learn from the present', and 'scenario-based studies' which tends to 'focus on the future'. It also summarises four models of user involvement in design, i.e. designers representing users, designers consulting users, users participating in the design process, and users as designers. These syntheses will help designers and researchers understand user involvement in a more structured manner, thus making the application of the theory and practice easier.

Keywords: User studies · User involvement · User participation · Models

1 Introduction

Users are often referred in the context of their existing relations with something, which can be a natural thing (e.g. a cave), a man-made artefact (e.g. a chair), a kind of service (e.g. healthcare) which might involve other human being(s) (e.g. a doctor) or social systems (e.g. legislation). The continuous changing relations build, construct and develop our environments and ourselves.

User studies firstly appeared in 1940s and they are one of the most researched areas in library and information science (Siatri 1999). In that field, researchers tend to focus on users' behavioural and cognitive responses to the natural and man-made world in order to understand their physical, sensory, cognitive and emotional needs and interactions.

In innovation and management fields, research shows that users were referred to contribute from 10 % to nearly 40 % per cent of the innovative ideas and products (Von Hippel 2006, pp. 19–22). From a postphenomenological point of view, there are four fundamental relations between the user, artefact and the world, where phenomenological analysis can be applied to each relation for revealing the structure of our daily life (Zhang and Dong 2013).

Understanding users/customers' needs and requirements in design studies is regarded as the first and most essential step for designers and manufacturers to take.

J. Zhou and G. Salvendy (Eds.): ITAP 2016, Part I, LNCS 9754, pp. 141–152, 2016.
DOI: 10.1007/978-3-319-39943-0_14

Users are one of the human roles who put artefacts to use, the other two are designers and manufacturers 'who stand to have their activity and experience transformed' (Carroll and Rosson 2007). In user-innovation studies, users are 'firms or individual consumers that expect to benefit from *using* a product or a service', while manufacturers 'expect to benefit from *selling* a product or a service' (Von Hippel 2006, p. 3). In post-phenomenology, users are those who get different experiences and perceptions through interacting with artefacts. In this paper, 'users' refer to individuals or a group of people using products or services. 'Artefacts' refer to man-made products. Users and artefacts are both in a context, a background which is the users' daily life.

User studies and user involvement in design have been heavily discussed but lacks a systematic theory, thus causing confusion for novice designers and researchers. In this paper, the authors will review literature from a broad range of disciplines, aiming to offer a structured view on user involvement in design.

2   Approaches of User Studies

In his book '*The Sciences of the Artificial*', Simon (1996) points out that to fulfill or adapt a goal involves a relation among three things: 'the purpose or goal, the character of the artefact, and the environment in which the artefact performs'. He gives two examples, one is that whether a clock will tell the time depends on its character (inner construction) and the environment (where it is placed); the other is whether a knife will cut depends on the material and the hardness of the substance. Influenced by Human-Computer Interaction (HCI) studies and social movements, designers in architecture, public service and industrial design gradually formed an opinion that designers have the ability and should be responsible to solve problems through getting to know users and their various needs and requirements.

These concerns have resulted in a series of approaches/methods of involving various users, e.g.

- **Participatory design**, **user design**, and **open design** (*Design Studies Special Issue* 2007; *CoDesign Special Issue* 2008; Björgvinsson 2008; Von Abel et al. 2011; Simonsen and Robertson 2012; Wilkinson and De Angeli 2014; Taffe 2015)
- **Empathy design** (*The Design Journal Special Issues* 2011; Newell et al. 2011)
- **Universal design** (Wolfgang and Korydon 2010; Lidwell et al. 2010; McAdams and Kostovich 2011; Aragall and Montaña 2012)
- **Inclusive design** (Coleman et al. 2007; *Journal of Engineering Design Special Issue* 2010; McGinley and Dong 2011; Heylighena and Bianchinb 2013; *Applied Ergonomics Special Issue* 2015)
- **Design for all** (Bühler 2008; Aragall et al. 2013; Bendixen and Benktzon 2015)
- **Service design** (Erl 2007; Roberto and Alexis 2008; Meroni and Sangiorgi 2011; Beaumont et al. 2014)

These developments of user-involvement research challenge the traditional design approaches, and the users' roles and user-designer relations become a phenomena thrive (Bihanic 2015, pp. vi–vii). Based on the classification of user models and the way of knowing the user, user studies in the design field can be categorised into three approaches:

The first is **empirical studies**, focusing on literature and relevant data. Designers learn from the existing studies of design theories and former practices. They also use data and references from other different disciplinary studies, e.g. ergonomics studies (physical data), medical research (health reports), economics and management studies (market research, innovation studies), psychology (emotions), and sociology (behaviour, habits, beliefs, culture); or from various surveys and reports (e.g. World Health Statistics annual reports 2005–2015; The International Classification of Functioning, Disability and Health, ICF 2015); or from Standards(e.g. British Standards 7000-6 2005 and regulations, e.g. Americans with Disabilities Act 1990; Disability Discrimination Act 1995). This approach can be characterized as "to learn from the past".

The second is **experimental studies**, focusing on real individuals (potential users, target users, focus groups, or designers themselves and their friends, colleges) to get the first hand data and materials. Designers usually borrow qualitative and quantitative methods from ethnography, and they "typically work in teams and use prototypes during fieldwork to create dialog with the people" (Koskinen et al. 2012, pp. 69–70). This type of user studies can be categorised into three basic forms according to how designers interact with the real user: Forum—to ask, Representation—to observe, and Co-design —to participate (Dong et al. 2007). This approach can be characterized as "to learn from the present".

The third is **scenario-based studies**, focusing on certain sets of 'stories', 'narratives' to build a context of use which involves an actor, various backgrounds, and a series of events. It is "a relatively lightweight method for envisioning future use possibilities." (Rosson and Carroll 2003, p. 1033). Designers "can have a prospective approach and can imagine all sorts of events with many alternative interface ideas" (Hasdoğan 1996). This approach also includes computer simulations, and developers tended to think in terms of two kinds of user: one who was exploring the system with no particular goal in mind and one who knew as much as the developer (Blandford et al. 2007). It is "the imagination of the future".

User studies in design are multi-disciplinary. The three approaches can be mixed in the design process, and in each approach the data gathered can be divided into four types: physical, cognitive, performance and psycho-social. Based on the three approaches of user studies and the four types of typical data, we have developed four models of user involvement in design practice.

3   Models of User Involvement

Due to different ways that designers involve users in the design process, there are various levels of users' activities: At one extreme, users are represented by designers or marketers; at the other extreme, users are the designers who are developing products themselves. Between the two are user consultation and user participation. These four models of user involvement are shown in Fig. 1.

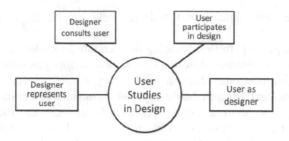

Fig. 1. Models of user involvement

Norman's model (see Fig. 2) will be used to further explain user involvement in design. The model shows the interactions and relationships between the designer, the user, and the system. The design model means the conceptualization that the designer has in mind; the user's model is what the user develops to explain the operation of the system. It depends on not only the system that the designer has designed, but also the various abilities of the users; the system is the only means that designers and users communicate with each other, which often has an interface for operation and responding, and the associated manuals and instructions.

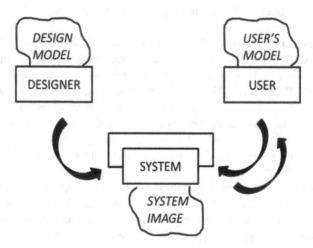

Fig. 2. Three aspects of mental models (Source: Norman 2002, pp. 189–190)

3.1 Designers Representing the Users

In this context, designers are the only users who are 'involved' in the design process, interacting with the device (see Fig. 3). It contains a premise that professional designers are those who know what is best for everyone, no matter who they really are.

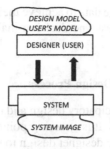

Fig. 3. Designers representing the users

Designers in this model are often users of their own designs, and often think themselves as (typical) users at the early stage of design. In some specific circumstances, this representation can be powerful in getting an insight into the users, the use contexts and the user experiences. Patricia Moore, in the 1970s, made up and acted as an old woman to visit a number of cities in North American with artificial restrictions to her joints, hearing and vision. Her personal experiences show that in the late 1970s there were much discrimination towards old people and people with disabilities in America, especially when using products and public services (Moore 1985). This 'representation' revealed different experiences and conditions that various users encounter, which has made a huge influence on the growing universal design movement.

3.2 Designers Consulting the Users

This model of user involvement is most prevalent in design practice (see Fig. 4). The consultation can take place at any stage of the design process: from conceptual design to detail design. It is helpful for designers to gain access to users, to understand users' needs, requirements, and their responses. There are many different conventions of consulting users in different design disciplines, e.g. product design and architectural design.

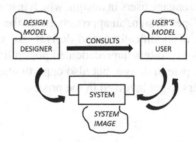

Fig. 4. Designers consulting the users

User consultation can be regarded as a scientific experiment (Newell et al. 2011). The designers are viewed as scientists, and users are the experimental subjects. Scientists pick up and chose what they need from the experimental subjects when doing research in their lab, then collect and analyse data to achieve their goals. In this model, users play a passive role in the design process and decision-making; they are only regarded as information providers.

3.3   Users Participating in the Design Process

This model is represented by participatory design and user design, where users become stakeholders in the design process. It is a turning point from the information providers to the design participants, from the designer design to the designer-user co-design. It is also a co-creation design process of sharing knowledge, skills and experiences of all the participators (Fig. 5).

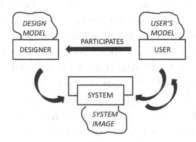

Fig. 5.   Users participating in design

Many methods of this kind of user involvement have been developed (Hanington and Martin 2012; LUMA Institute 2012), such as webpage design and software development (Frick et al. 2001), customized computers (Randall et al. 2007), UTOPIA project (Newell et al. 2011), product design (Kostovich et al. 2009; McAdams and Kostovich 2011; Goodman-Deane et al. 2014). Several approaches and platforms provide supports for user participation in design, e.g. the 'critical user forums' (Dong and Cassim 2007) organized at the Helen Hamlyn Centre at the Royal College of Arts since 2000. Through bringing designers and users with disabilities together, the forums provide designers with an effective method to engage users in design, which inspires designers to develop more inclusive solutions. Open design, an approach that is the 'free distribution, documentation and permission of modifications and derivations' of an object, product or service (Von Abel et al. 2011), offers unprecedented possibilities for not only the end users or amateurs to participate in design, but also opportunities for more professional designers and manufacturers to get involved in the process.

3.4   Users as Designers

This model can be regarded as Do It Yourself (DIY). Through creative thinking and practice to make functional items for themselves, users become designers and innovators. According to Von Hippel's studies, the user firms and individual customers develop or modify products for their own use, and this ranges from 10 per cent to nearly 40 per cent of the innovative ideas and products. "Users as designers are a combination of existing and customized participatory and empathic design methods that help to facilitate the dialogue needed to illicit personal and contextual information that helps define the user's needs and wants" (Resink et al. 2011) (Fig. 6).

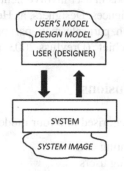

Fig. 6. Users as designers

In this model, users are designers themselves and their creativity often leads to personalized products for themselves in daily use. Because of the lack of expertise and skills, it is rare for users to make the products standardised and then mass-produced.

4   Challenges of User Involvement

User involvements in design are facing three challenges: users' conventions, different cultures and contexts, and company's constrains. Firstly, users' conventions or natural mappings lead users to get an immediate understanding of the relationship between any two kinds of things. Some of them are cultural or biological, and some of them follow the principles of perception. This requires designers to fully recognise what the natural mappings are, and how to apply them correctly.

Secondly, the differences between various cultures result in consumers' different knowledge, experiences, tastes and habits. These differences result in various contexts of use/consumption, which challenge designers when involving the user. Designers might get lost and make mistakes if they fail to choose appropriate methods to understand the users.

Thirdly, user research can be constrained and delayed whether in Small to Medium-sized Enterprises (SMEs) or big companies, because of the limited resources (financial or time pressures).

Several methods have been developed to deal with the challenges, e.g. the Methods Lab (Aldersey-Williams et al. 1999) aims to help designers and other stakeholders to weigh and choose the proper and efficient design methods in design practice or research; The Make Tools (Sanders 2002), regarded as a 'design language' not only for designers, but also for users, are 'built upon an aesthetics of experience rather than an aesthetics of form... and there are many different types of Toolkits that facilitate the expression of a wide range of artefacts and/or models'. The IDEO Human-Centred Design Toolkit provides methods for each HCD phase (i.e. to hear, to create and to deliver), guidance for role-playing workshops, storytelling sessions, scenario building, and prototyping; it gives voice to communities and allows their desires to guide the creation and implementation of solutions.

Various challenges and methods in user involvement require designers' wide range of abilities, knowledge and experiences. Designers, as Henry Dreyfuss once said, 'must be part engineer, part businessman, part salesman, part public-relations man, artist, and almost, it seems at times, Indian chief' (Dreyfuss 2003, p. 24).

5   Discussions and Conclusions

User studies in design can be categorised into four models of user involvement:

- Model (1): Designers representing users
- Model (2): Designers consulting users
- Model (3): Users participating in the design process
- Model (4): Users as designers

In Models (1), (2) and (3), designers with participating users are usually the first batch of 'users' from early concepts to final products. The roles that designers and users play in these three models are distinguishable, but not rigorously distinct. For example, Model (1) is often mixed with Models (2) and (3). When designers do not have the direct experiences and knowledge that the specific users have, e.g. people with disabilities, the Models (2) and (3) will be adopted. Model (4) is less discussed in existing design literature, but more and more emerging design practice adopts this model.

The four models of user involvement show different relations of designers, users and systems. They will help designers and researchers understand user involvement in a more structured manner, thus making the application of the theory and practice much easier.

Acknowledgments. This research has been sponsored by the project FJ2015C008 of Fujian province: the research challenges of postphnomenology in modern western society and the way out, and the project XYS201405 of Xiamen Technology of University: the philosophical meanings of inclusive design.

References

ADA: American with Disabilities Act, US Public Law, pp. 101–336 (1990)

Al-Zu'bi, Z.B.M.F., Tsinopoulos, C.: Suppliers versus lead users: examining their relative impact on product variety. J. Prod. Innov. Manag. **29**(4), 667–680 (2012)

Aldersey-Williams, H., Coleman, R., Bound, J.: The Methods Lab. Royal College of Art, London (1999)

Aragall, F., Montaña, J.: Universal Design: The HUMBLES Method for User-Centred Business. Gower, Hampshire (2012)

Aragall, F., Neumann, P., Sagramola, S.: Design for All in Progress from Theory to Practice (ECA 2013). Info-Handicap-Conseil National des Personnes Handicapées, Luxembourg (2013)

Baldwin, C., von Hippel, E.: From producer innovation to user and open collaborative innovation. Org. Sci. **22**(6), 1399–1417 (2011)

Beaumont, L.C., Bolton, L.E., McKay, A., Hughes, H.P.N.: Rethinking service design: a socio-technical approach to the development of business models. In: Schaefer, D. (ed.) Rethinking Service Design: A Socio-Technical Approach to the Development of Business Models, pp. 121–141. Springer International Publishing, Switzerland (2014)

Bendixen, K., Benktzon, M.: Design for all in Scandinavia: a strong concept. Appl. Ergon. **46**(1), 248–257 (2015)

Bihanic, D. (ed.): Empowering Users through Design: Interdisciplinary Studies and Combined Approaches for Technological Products and Services. Springer International Publishing, Switzerland (2015)

Björgvinsson, E.B.: Open-ended participatory design as prototypical practice. Co-Design **4**(2), 85–99 (2008)

Blandford, A., Keith, S., Butterworth, R., Fields, B., Furniss, D.: Disrupting digital library development with scenario informed design. Interact. Comput. **19**(1), 70–82 (2007)

Bogers, M., Afuah, A., Bastian, B.: Users as innovators: a review, critique, and future research directions. J. Manag. **36**(4), 857–875 (2010)

Brey, P.: Philosophy of technology after the empirical turn. Techné: Res. Philos. Technol. **14**(1), 36–48 (2010)

BS 8300: Design of Buildings and their Approaches to Meet the Needs of Disabled People. Code of Practice. British Standard Institution, London (2001)

BS 7000–6: Guide to Managing Inclusive Design. British Standard Institution, London (2005)

Bühler, C.: Design for all – from idea to practise. In: Miesenberger, K., Klaus, J., Zagler, W.L., Karshmer, A.I. (eds.) ICCHP 2008. LNCS, vol. 5105, pp. 106–113. Springer, Heidelberg (2008)

Büttgen, M., Schumann, J.H., Ates, Z.: Service locus of control and customer coproduction: the role of prior service experience and organizational socialization. J. Serv. Res. **15**(2), 166–181 (2012)

Carroll, J.M., Rosson, M.B.: Participatory design in community informatics. Des. Stud. **28**(3), 243–261 (2007)

Churchill, J., von Hippel, E., Sonnack, M.: Lead User Project Handbook: A practical Guide for Lead User Project Teams (2009). <https://evhippel.files.wordpress.com/2013/08/lead-user-project-handbook-full-version.pdf>

Coeckelbergh, M.: Humans, animals, and robots: a phenomenological approach to human-robot relations. Int. J. Soc. Robot. **3**(2), 197–204 (2011)

Coleman, R., Clarkson, J., Dong, H., Cassim, J.: Design for Inclusivity: A Practical Guide to Accessible, Innovative and User-Centred Design. Gower, Hampshire (2007)

DDA: Disability Discrimination Act. Department for Education and Employment, London (1995)

DeMonaco, H.J., von Hippel, E.: Reducing medical costs and improving quality via self-management tools. PLoS Med. **4**(4), e104–e611 (2007). doi:10.1371/journal.pmed.0040104

Dong, H., Cassim, J.: Critical user forums for inclusive design. Ergon. Des.: Q. Hum. Factors Appl. **15**(4), 4 (2007)

Dong, H., Nicolle, C., Brown, R., Clarkon, J.: Design-orientated user research methods. In: Coleman, R. (ed.) Design for Inclusivity: A Practical Guide to Accessible, Innovative and User-Centred Design, pp. 131–147. Hampshire, Gower (2007)

Erl, T.: SOA: Principles of Service Design. Prentice Hall PTR, Upper Saddle River (2007)

Feenberg, A.: Active and passive bodies: Don Ihde's phenomenology of the body. In: Selinger, E. (ed.) Postphenomenology: A Critical Companion to Ihde. SUNY Press, Albany (2006)

Franke, N., Piller, F.: Value creation by toolkits for user innovation and design: the case of the watch market. J. Prod. Innov. Manag. **21**(6), 401–415 (2004)

Goodman-Deane, J., Ward, J., Hosking, I., Clarkson, J.: A comparison of methods currently used in inclusive design. Appl. Ergon. **45**(4), 886–894 (2014)

Granieri, M., Renda, A.: Innovation Law and Policy in the European Union. Springer, Milan (2012)

Hanington, B., Martin, B.: Universal Methods of Design: 100 Ways to Research Complex Problems, Develop Innovative Ideas, and Design Effective Solutions. Rockport Publishing, Massachusetts (2012)

Hasdoğan, G.: The role of user models in product design for assessment of user needs. Des. Stud. **17**(1), 19–33 (1996)

Heylighena, A., Bianchinb, M.: How does inclusive design relate to good design? Designing as a deliberative enterprise. Des. Stud. **34**(1), 93–110 (2013)

Hienerth, C., Lettl, C., Keinz, P.: Synergies among producer firms, lead users, and user communities: the case of the lego producer–user ecosystem. J. Prod. Innov. Manag. **31**(4), 848–866 (2014)

Jaakkola, E., Alexander, M.: The role of customer engagement behavior in value co-creation: a service system perspective. J. Serv. Res. **17**(3), 247–261 (2014)

Jeppesen, L.B.: User toolkits for innovation: consumers support each other. J. Prod. Innov. Manag. **22**(4), 347–362 (2005)

Kostovich, V., McAdams, D.A., Moon, S.K.: Representing user activity and product function for universal design. In: Proceeding of 2009 ASME Design Engineering Technical Conferences and Computers and Information in Engineering, San Diego, CA, USA (2009)

Koskinen, I., Zimmerman, J., Binder, T., Redstrom, J., Wensveen, S.: Design Research through Practice: From the Lab, Field, and Showroom. Elsevier, Amsterdam (2012)

Lidwell, W., Holden, K., Butler, J.: Universal Principles of Design: 125 Ways to Enhance Usability, Influence Perception, Increase Appeal, Make Better Design Decisions, and Teach Through Design. Rockport Publishers, Beverly (2010)

Institute, L.U.M.A.: Innovating for People, Handbook of Human Centred Design Methods. LUMA Institute, Pittsburgh (2012)

Mahr, D., Lievens, A., Blazevic, V.: The value of customer cocreated knowledge during the innovation process. J. Prod. Innov. Manag. **31**(3), 599–615 (2014)

McAdams, D.A., Kostovich, V.: A framework and representation for universal product design. Int. J. Des. **5**(1), 29–42 (2011)

McGinley, C., Dong, H.: Designing with information and empathy: delivering human information to designers. Des. J. **14**(2), 187–206 (2011)

Menguc, B., Auh, S., Yannopoulos, P.: Customer and supplier involvement in design: the moderating role of incremental and radical innovation capability. J. Prod. Innov. Manag. **31**(2), 313–328 (2014)

Meroni, A., Sangiorgi, D.: Design for Services. Gower, Hampshire (2011)

Mitcham, C.: From phenomenology to pragmatism: using technology as an instrument. In: Selinger, E. (ed.) Postphenomenology: A Critical Companion to Ihde, pp. 21–36. SUNY Press, Albany (2006)

Moore, P.: Disguised. Word Books, Waco (1985)

Newell, A.F., Gregor, P., Morgan, M., Pullin, G., Macaulay, C.: User-sensitive inclusive design. Univers. Access Inf. Soc. **10**(3), 235–243 (2011)

Nishikawa, H., Schreier, M., Ogawa, S.: User-generated versus designer-generated products: a performance assessment at Muji. Int. J. Res. Mark. **30**(2), 160–167 (2013)

Norman, D.: The Design of Everyday Things. Basic Books, New York (2002)

Nørskov, M.: Revisiting Ihde's fourfold "technological relationships": application and modification. Philos. Technol. **28**(2), 189–207 (2015)

Wolfgang, P., Korydon, S. (eds.): Universal Design Handbook, 2nd edn. McGraw-Hill Education, New York (2010)

Oudshoorn, N., Pinch, T.: User-technology relationships: some recent developments. In: The Handbook of Science and Technology Studies, 3rd edn, pp. 541–565. The MIT Press, Cambridge (2008)

Ponty, M.M.: Phenomenology of Perception. Humanities Press, New York (1962). (Smith, C. (Trans.))

Ponty, M.M.: Signs. Northwestern University Press, Evanston (1964). (McCleary, R., Trans.)

Randall, T., Terwiesch, C., Ulrich, K.T.: User design of customized products. Mark. Sci. **26**(2), 268–280 (2007)

Resink, E., Van Dijk, D., Reitenbach, M.: Waag Society (2011). <http://waag.org/nl>

Roberto, M.S., Alexis, P.G.: Service design: an appraisal. Des. Manag. Rev. **19**(1), 10–19 (2008)

Rosenberger, R.: Multistability and the agency of mundane artifacts: from speed bumps to subway benches. Hum. Stud. **37**(3), 369–392 (2014)

Rosson, M.B., Carroll, J.M.: Scenario-based design. In: Jacko, J.A., Sears, A. (eds.) The Human-Computer Interaction Handbook. Fundamentals, Evolving Technologies and Emerging Applications, pp. 1032–1050. Erlbaum, Mahwah (2003)

Salge, T.O., Farchi, T., Barrett, M.I., Dopson, S.: When does search openness really matter? A contingency study of health-care innovation projects. J. Prod. Innov. Manag. **30**(4), 659–676 (2013)

Sanders, E.B.-N.: From user-centered to participatory design approaches. In: Frascara, J. (ed.) Design and the Social Sciences: Making Connections, pp. 1–7. Taylor & Francis Books Limited, London (2002)

Schreier, M., Prügl, R.: Extending lead-user theory: antecedents and consequences of consumers' lead userness. J. Prod. Innov. Manag. **25**(4), 331–346 (2008)

Schweisfurth, T.: Embedded Lead Users inside the Firm. Gabler Verlag, Berlin (2013)

Schweisfurth, T., Raasch, C.: Embedded lead users—the benefits of employing users for corporate innovation. Res. Policy **44**(1), 168–180 (2015)

Siatri, R.: The evolution of user studies. LIBRI **49**(3), 132–141 (1999)

Simon, A.H.: The Sciences of the Artificial, 3rd edn. The MIT Press, Cambridge (1996)

Simonsen, J., Robertson, T.: Routledge International Handbook of Participatory Design. Routledge, New York (2012)

Taffe, S.: The hybrid designer/end-user: revealing paradoxes in co-design. Des. Stud. **40**(9), 39–59 (2015)

Tripathi, A.: Postphenomenological investigations of technological experience. AI Soc. **30**(2), 199–205 (2014)

Van Den Eede, Y.: In between us: on the transparency and opacity of technological mediation. Found. Sci. **16**(2–3), 139–159 (2011)

Verbeek, P.P.: Cyborg intentionality: rethinking the phenomenology of human-technology relations. Phenomenol. Cogn. Sci. **7**(3), 387–395 (2008)

Verbeek, P.P.: Expanding mediation theory. Found. Sci. **17**(4), 391–395 (2012)

Von Abel, B., Evers, L., Klaassen, R., Troxler, P.: Open Design Now: Why Design Cannot Remain Exclusive. BIS Publishers, Amsterdam (2011)

Von Hippel, E.: Perspective: user toolkits for innovation. J. Prod. Innov. Manag. **18**(4), 247–257 (2001)

Von Hippel, E.: Democratizing Innovation. The MIT Press, Cambridge (2006)

Von Hippel, E.: Users rule. Technol. Rev. **114**(2), 14–15 (2011)

Von Hippel, E., Nikolaus, F., Reinhard, P.: Pyramiding: efficient search for rare subjects. Res. Policy **38**(9), 1397–1406 (2009)

Wellner, K.: User Innovators in the Silver Market. Springer Fachmedien Wiesbaden, Hessen (2015)

WHO: World Health Statistics (2005–2015). <http://www.who.int/gho/publications/world_health_statistics/en/index.html>

WHO: The International Classification of Functioning, Disability and Health, ICF (2015). <http://www.who.int/classifications/icf/en/>

Wilkinson, C., De Angeli, A.: Applying user centred and participatory design approaches to commercial product development. Des. Stud. **35**(6), 614–631 (2014)

Zhang, B., Dong, H.: User-mobile phone interactions: a postphenomenology analysis. In: Marcus, A. (ed.) DUXU 2013, Part I. LNCS, vol. 8012, pp. 171–180. Springer, Heidelberg (2013)

Technology Use and Acceptance by Older Users

Risk and Benefit Perceptions:
Resistance, Adoption and Uses of ICT
Among the Italian Elderly

Simone Carlo[1](✉) and Matteo Vergani[2]

[1] Università Cattolica del Sacro Cuore, Largo Gemelli 1, 20121 Milan, Italy
simone.carlo@unicatt.it
[2] Deakin University, Geelong, Victoria 3800, Australia
vergani.matteo@gmail.com

Abstract. This paper presents the main results of a national survey on active aging, with a sample of 900 Italians between 65 and 74 years of age. The research attempted to understand the role of ICT in the daily life of the elderly, in the attempt to answer the following questions: (1) What are the differences between the connected and not connected elderly? (2) What are the perceived risks and opportunities identified by older ICT users? This paper investigates the complex relationship between the elderly and technology, going beyond both deterministic approaches and optimistic analyses of the use (and non-use) of the Internet among elderly Italians.

Keywords: Elderly · ICT · Active ageing · Risks

1 Introduction

Despite a growing academic debate on the relationship between young people and risks (and opportunities) of the Internet [1], the issue of the risks of the Internet for adults seem to have much less resonance echo in scientific debate and public opinion. If the adoption of information and communications technology (ICT) by the elderly is a well-established field of study [2, 3], the literature has mostly focused on the role of digital technology in providing social and cultural resources for active aging and in improving older people's quality of life [4]. It is however crucial to highlight the need, especially when discussing policies aimed to promote active aging, to carefully consider the complex nature of media and ICT, both in terms of opportunities and in potentially perceived risks for the elderly.

The research aimed to understand the role of ICT in the daily life of the elderly, in the attempt to answer the following questions:

(1) What are the differences between the connected and not connected elderly?
(2) What are the perceived risks and opportunities identified by older ICT users?

This article discusses the results of a survey conducted in the fall of 2013 (as part of a larger national research project regarding active aging) that reached a sample of 900 Italians between the ages of 65 and 74 years old.

© Springer International Publishing Switzerland 2016
J. Zhou and G. Salvendy (Eds.): ITAP 2016, Part I, LNCS 9754, pp. 155–166, 2016.
DOI: 10.1007/978-3-319-39943-0_15

2 The Internet: Opportunities and (Perceived) Risks

2.1 The Internet: Risks and Inequalities

The debate around risks and opportunities of the Internet is as old as the Web itself and has been based on the value (or detriment) given to the role of computers and ICT in enhancing or inhibiting communication and social relationships. In particular, since the 90s, forms of mediated communication in daily life [5] have become an increasing object of study. Later on a deterministic approach (the Internet as a tool to break down barriers of space and time, or to threaten the social order) was applied at the beginning of Internet Studies, [6] Internet research has been focused not on "what" happens in the Internet, but on "how" social actors incorporate the Internet into everyday life [7]. Such research has been gradually distancing itself from more pessimistic approaches, discussing the risks that particular groups of users experience (such as children and young people [8]) but also emphasizing, on the contrary, the risks arising from non-use of ICT and the risk of isolation (social, cultural, economic) affecting people who are unable to use the computer and to connect to the Internet. From the 90s onward, several studies have investigated the effects of unequal distribution of digital devices on the population [9]. If the literature of the late 90s was strongly influenced by the idea that ICT would, by itself, be able to enhance economic and social progress, and it was therefore necessary to spread the technology [10], following research on the digital divide has strongly criticized the technological determinism of previous studies, especially the excessive emphasis given to physical access (for example the presence of connection and ICT [11]). The digital divide is not a matter of owning technological devices, but rather of skills people require using technology as a socially and culturally significant practice. The lack of access to ICT and digital skills is a likely source of personal and social inequality [12]. If inequalities of material access to technologies are going to be overcome in developed countries, the gap in terms of skills is destined to grow [12]. Both public and private bodies are involved at different levels in developing policies and interventions that promote the expansion of digital skills. They belief that educational and civic resources require owning devices and using media skills.

2.2 Internet and Risks

As aforementioned, concerns in the scientific literature related to the non-use of the Internet and ICT have in recent years exceeded the dystopic position related to the negative (social and individual) effects in the use of the web. Overcoming the critical view towards Internet access and usage is however a break in the debate related to Internet use among young people and children. Reasons for the continual increase in attention to risks related to Internet use among children are different. On the one hand there is increasing attention on the educational responsibility of adults (teachers, trainers, but also scholars, politicians, professionals) towards young people. On the other hand the debate on the role of ICT in the daily life of young people is taken into account by the media. For the media, the Internet is a place full of interesting stories but also of concerns [13]. Taking into account these issues and the role that the Internet plays in society, in the last 20 years a wide range of research has identified the balance between risks and opportunities related to ICT use by children and young people; and ICT's role not only in their education, but also in their free time. High expectations for the role of the Internet in the lives of young people and children are accompanied by strong concerns about exposure to harmful and unsuitable content.

Livingstone et al. [1] identified the main factors affecting the, negative and positive, online browsing experience, of young people. In particular:

- The more children use the Internet, the more their digital skills and "range of opportunities" grow.
- Not all uses of the Internet have benefits: benefits depend on age, gender, socio-economic status and help from relatives.
- Use, skills and opportunities are also linked to online risks: the more opportunities and skills, the more risks: the growing use of the Internet implies increased efforts to prevent children from these risks.
- Not all risks end up hurting: the possibility that children get hurt because of their online experiences depend on their age, gender and socio-economic status, and also by their resources and resilience in dealing with the Internet.

Going beyond a broader critical analysis of the role of the Internet in today's society [14], the risks associated with the use of the Internet by adults seem to be particularly focused on two fields of analysis:

- The role of Internet users as "consumers" rather than "individuals": personal data theft, fraud, phishing, viruses, worms, spyware, and spam represent, according to public opinion, the major risks associated with the Internet.
- The psychological and psychiatric disorders associated with the use of the Internet: for adults, risks associated with the Internet mainly revolve around the understanding of those psychopathologies related to excessive Internet use. In particular, certain scholars have regarded the Internet as a major cause of increased sexual disorders [15], aggression [16], and addictions [17]. This strongly alarmist literature - with similarities to dystopian reflections on the role of the Internet in the 90s – has been represented by the media in order to reward an "eccentric" use of the Web [18]. But beyond the alarmist approach, it seems to be lacking, in both academic debate and public opinion, a broader reflection on the risks and opportunities of the Internet for adults and the elderly.

3   The Elderly, ICT, and Active Aging

As the western population continues to age, media and communication technology seem to be increasingly important for the elderly, thanks to those services and devices that would help people age actively [19]: the role media and communication technology play in improving the quality of life [20], health and health care [21] of the elderly is a key issue both politically and academically speaking. Political institutions have regarded digital technology as a way to avoid a new kind of divide among the elderly, hence promoting policies designed to build technological literacy among the elderly – and/or setting policy plans to increase digital ICT adoption among older groups. Policy discourse has mainly focused on ICT use as a tool to assist with physical or cognitive (or relational) deficiencies of the elderly. In some cases these policies are often quite optimistic: ICT would (deterministically) compensate for physical and cognitive disability, diseases and loneliness typically related to older age [22]. Policy discourse on 'e-inclusion' and 'digital inclusion' have been characterized by a belief that today's ICT can improve the lives and life chances of disadvantaged groups [23]. Concerning policies about digital inclusion of older people, the risk is to use, in some way, rhetoric and (digital) myths which can be seen to echo the first period of policies to address or reduce or narrow the digital divide: the digital divide was simply a problem of diffusion of technologies and skills and not an element to frame in the context of social, cultural, personal inequalities [24]. Within the broader discussion about the digital divide and digital competences, after years of technological determinism, the multi-dimensional approach is now well established: it is not possible to identify a single element determining the digital divide, but rather a "constellation of differences" [24] (social, cultural, personal) influencing the use of technology. This multi-layered approach does not yet seem to be fully applied in terms of research and reflection on the relationship between ICT and the elderly: age seems to represent, for many theoretical approaches, a key element to explain the aforementioned gaps and to determine the use of ICT by the young elderly (65–74 y/o). Age is regarded as such a crucial element in making laggards of the elderly when compared to younger digital users [19]. The issue of risks is an additional element demonstrating a dangerous simplification in the academic debate about the role between ICT and the elderly. The complex relationship between ICT and risks/benefits for users appears to be marginalized in the study reflection of silver users. ICT is often meant to be used as a deterministic tool, positively impacting the lives of the elderly. There are in fact limited and outdated studies that seek to investigate the impact of ICT use on the daily lives of the elderly, assuming that the use of ICT for the elderly has positive effects in terms of well-being [22].

4   The Italian Digital Elderly

4.1   Methods

This article presents data from a survey with a sample of Italians between the ages of 65 and 74 years old representative of the Italian population. The questionnaires were collected via face-to-face domestic interviews between December 2013 and January 2014. The participants were selected according to a random, proportional and stratified division defined by region and by city size and population. 1,600 names were extracted from an electoral list of 90 municipalities, using a systematic method. There were 900 respondents. Error sample: 3 %. Confidence error: 0.05 %, 56 % response rate.

4.2   What are the Differences Between the Connected and not Connected Elderly?

Possession and use of digital media involve only part of the sample, since only 21.3 % of the participants possess or use a computer, laptop and/or desktop. This is even more interesting when looking at age subgroups (distinguishing between participants between 65–69 and 70–74 years of age) and gender. The subgroup between 65–69 years of age has greater access to information technology (use of PC and Internet access) than the subgroup between the ages of 70 and 74. Additionally, men of both age groups use PCs and go online more than women.

Another interesting result is that 45 % of the elderly who today use a computer started using it before turning 50, 28.2 % between 50 and 59, 19.1 % between 60 and 64 years old. Only 9.1 % of users are "late" ICT users (who started using the computer after 64 y/o, in their senior years and during retirement), with a difference between males and females: new users are mostly elderly women, with 12.8 % of females, as opposed to 6.8 % of males that started to use the computer after 2005.

These data show that elderly digital users already have a history of Internet use: they are not "natives" to the digital world, but rather long-time immigrants, who are nearing the evolution of ICT with their own skills, approaches, and resistance, which are influenced by their history as digital users. Conversely, in our sample, new elderly users are rare, with an interesting proportion of women who are only beginning to approach ICT in recent years, if not months. There is also an interesting significant inverse correlation between first use of personal computers and different income levels ($r = -.31$, $p < .01$). People who have recently started using ICT might have a lower income than users who have used the Internet for several years: this is a possible signal, in our perspective, of a progressive diffusion of ICT among the elderly with lower incomes. As for the frequency of use, 71 % of the elderly who access the Internet do so almost every day. In other words, the majority of elderly people who have access to the Internet are heavy users. Participants with lower income, (Chi-$square$ = 156.87, $p < .01$), lower education (Chi-$square$ = 268.01, $p < .01$), and not working (Chi-$square$ = 28.88, $p = <.01$) reported lower (or no) use of the PC and the Internet (see Table 1).

Table 1. PC and Internet use by age and gender

	65–69 y/o	70–74 y/o	Male	Female	Total
Laptop user	114	43	94	64	158
	24 %	10,2 %	22,6 %	13,3 %	17,6 %
Laptop not users	361	379	322	417	739
	76 %	89,8 %	77,4 %	86,7 %	82,4 %
Desktop user	96	54	96	54	150
	20,3 %	12,8 %	23,1 %	11,3 %	16,7 %
Desktop not users	337	369	320	426	746
	79,7 %	87,2 %	76,9 %	88,8 %	83,3 %
Internet use	113	48	101	61	162
	23,9 %	11.4 %	24,3 %	12,7 %	18 %
Internet not users	359	374	314	419	733
	76,1 %	88,2 %	75,7 %	87,3 %	81,9 %

BASE: Elderly Italians aged between 65 and 74 years of age.

Table 2. PC and Internet use related to employment status, degree and income.

Use	Employment status		Education			Income			
	No Job	Working	Primary	Secondary	Tertiary	Low	Lowermid	Lowerhigh	High
None	487	52	392	245	18	118	361	87	22
	72.9 %	48.1 %	93.1 %	63.6 %	19.8 %	93.7 %	81.7 %	53.7 %	34.4 %
Limited	53	16	11	50	9	2	36	9	6
	7.9 %	14.8 %	2.6 %	13 %	9.9 %	1.6 %	8.1 %	5.6 %	9.4 %
High	128	40	18	90	64	6	45	66	36
	19.2 %	37 %	4.3 %	23.4 %	70.3 %	4.8 %	10.2 %	40.7 %	56.3 %
Total	668	108	421	385	91	126	442	162	64
	100 %	100 %	100 %	100 %	100 %	100 %	100 %	100 %	100 %

The data show that the Internet appears to be linked to existing social resources. Specifically, the larger the family, the more participants use the Internet, although the difference in proportion is only marginally significant (*Chi-square* = 7.79, p = .10). It follows that the elderly who live by themselves are less connected to the Internet (Table 2).

Moreover, the digitized elderly, as compared to the not digitized elderly, are generally characterized by a greater curiosity, higher interest and significant investment in family and social relations. The elderly who attend at least one association have a higher use of the Internet (31.7 %) compared to those not attending any association (12.2 %). In addition, older digitized people generally attribute more importance to "values" (apart from "Religion", to which the participants who are not connected to the Internet show more attachment), in all aspects of private and social life (Tables 3 and 4).

Table 3. PC and Internet use related to family members

PC and Internet use	Alone	2 members	3 or more members	Total
None	128	332	198	658
	81.5 %	72.5 %	69.7 %	73.2 %
Limited	9	38	23	70
	5.7 %	8.3 %	8.1 %	7.8 %
High	20	88	63	171
	12.7 %	19.2 %	22.2 %	19 %
Total	157	458	284	899
	100 %	100 %	100 %	100 %

Focusing more on physical, mental, and social well-being of the digital elderly, the following table (Table 5) shows the differences in distribution measuring quality of life (i.e. physical activity, friendship networks, perceived age, index of personal

Table 4. Importance given to values[a] among PC users and non-users (Descriptive statistics and ANOVA)

Value	PC use	N	Mean	SD	SE	F	p-value
Work	None	653	3.54	.74	.03	8.31	.06
	High	172	3.66	.64	.05		
Family	None	657	3.92	.30	.01	8.88	.15
	High	172	3.95	.21	.02		
Friendship	None	657	3.08	.69	.03	2.72	<.01
	High	172	3.26	.66	.05		
Free time	None	654	2.86	.73	.03	6.19	.01
	High	170	3.02	.67	.05		
Politics	None	654	1.96	.90	.04	3.48	<.01
	High	170	2.50	.92	.07		
Religion	None	657	3.10	.89	.04	9.97	<.01
	High	169	2.89	1.01	.08		

[a]The perceived importance given to values was measured with a Likert scale where 4 was "very important" and 1 "not important at all".

Table 5. Chi-square coefficients and p-values measuring quality of life and use of ICT-

	Technological equipment[a]	PC and Internet Use	Use of SNS
Physical activity	93.35 (p < .01)	102.72 (p < .01)	56.98 (p < .01)
Friendship network	52.37 (p < .01)	51.72 (p < .01)	23.77 (p < .01)
Perceived age	18.9 (p < .01)	20.1 (p < .01)	13.02 (p < .05)
Personal satisfaction	21.82 (p < .01)	17.9 (p = .05)	3.70 (p = .16)

[a]The index is composed of the processing answers regarding personal possession and use of ICTs (Laptop or Netbook, Desktop computer, tablet, eBook reader, Video Games, Smartphone, WiFi, MP3 player).

satisfaction) and the use of ICT[1]. Chi-square tests show that participants who use new technologies and the Internet the most are also the ones who show higher indicators of well-being.

---

[1] For a wider overview of these data and index see [22].

4.3   What are the Perceived Risks and Opportunities Identified by Older ICT Users?

This survey aimed at investigating opportunities and risks perceived by the digital elderly in regard to their use of ICT. A first level of analysis concerns the perception of (positive and negative) changes introduced by the Internet and the related opportunities and risks. (Table 6)

Table 6. Perception of changes introduced by Internet use (ordered by frequency)

Since I use the Internet:	% Yes
I am more informed about current issues	63,7
I can learn more about my interests and passions	60,7
I can deepen my knowledge about my health and well-being	40,3
I stay more in touch with my friends and relatives	36,3
I feel more active than my peers without the Internet	31,6
I can get updated about diseases	29,9
I watch less TV	24,8
I am afraid to make mistakes	22,0
I fear that my data might fall into the hands of the wrong people	21,8
I have new topics to chat about with my children/friends	21,0
I'm not confident of the reliability of sources on the Internet	18,7
I have new interests, thanks to the Internet	18,0
I feel less alone	13,7
I waste a lot of time on the computer	13,5
I save money buying online	13,4
I meet up with old friends online	13,4
I came across offensive and inappropriate content	12,9
I feel more active in my local community	12,5
I feel more active in my country's political process	9,4
I am more deskbound	8,5
I spend more time at home	8,0
I get in touch online with new and interesting people	5,7
I am overwhelmed by information	5,3
Through SNSs I can freely express my point of view	4,1
Through SNSs I more often express my feelings and memories	3,0
I spend less time with my loved ones	2,2
I have met someone in-person that I previously met online	1,4
I feel judged by the things that I write on SNSs	1,2

Two-thirds of elderly users in our sample felt that the Internet has caused positive changes in their knowledge (information on current topics −63.7 %, and personal interests −60.7 %), while about one-third noted positive changes in the sphere of relationships (staying in touch with friends and relatives −36.3 %) and a comparative perception about being active (feeling more active than peers without the Internet

−31.6 %). For a large number of the elderly, the Internet is a source of knowledge for their own health and well-being (40.3 %) and for the treatment of their diseases (29.9 %). There is also a perceived change in the management of time: about 25 % perceived a decrease in the time spent watching television, while 13.5 % say they spend too much time on the computer and about 8 % feel they are more deskbound and/or spend more time at home; 2.2 % of respondents declare spending less time with their loved ones. Although the use of the Internet is generally accompanied by a perception of increased activity and socialization, online and offline participation remains a decidedly minor practice (from 12.5 % of those who feel "more active in their local community" to 4.1 % of those who more freely express their views on SNSs). Among the most common fears associated with Internet use appear to be making mistakes (22 %), having their privacy violated (21, 8 %), or not knowing how to assess the reliability of online sources (18, 7 %). A secondary concerns are those most related to perceived opportunities and risks. Experience has an important role in making the elderly more or less confident Internet users: those who started to use computers later are more afraid of making mistakes. The higher the age of first-time use of a computer and the Internet, the more difficult ICT seems to be. Conversely the more experienced (those who started earlier than others), having overcome any technical concerns, are more concerned about offensive content (offensive words, images, videos). As for the concerns related to "wasted time," those who spend more time on the Internet have a higher perception of the risks involved in terms of "misspent time". The increased frequency of use increases, reflexively, the perception of excessive Internet and computer use. In general, increased Internet use involves an increasing general concern: the higher the frequency of use, the greater the perception of online risks[2] (small correlation: $r = .18$, $p < .01$). What is clear is that the frequency of use not only correlates to increased risk perception, but also greater awareness of the opportunities[3] (small to medium correlation: $r = .29$, $p < .00$) also in terms of sociability[4] (medium correlation: $r = .31$, $p < .00$). There is a stronger correlation when looking at the average of online activities: the greater number of activities carried out, the greater

---

[2] The risk index is a scaled item that combines responses to the following 9 questions (1 = yes; 0 = no): "Since I have been using the Internet" I am afraid to make mistakes, I fear that my data could fall into the hands of the wrong people, I waste a lot of time on the computer, I came across offensive and inappropriate content, I am more deskbound, I spend too much time at home, I am overwhelmed by too much information, I spend less time with my loved ones, I feel judged by the things that I write on SNSs.

[3] The opportunity index is a scaled item that combines responses to the following 9 questions (1 = yes; 0 = no): "Since I have been using the Internet": I am more informed about current issues, I can learn more about my interest and passions, I feel more active, I watch less television, I have new interests thanks to the Internet, I feel less alone, I save money by buying online, I feel more active in my local community, I feel more active in my country's political process.

[4] The sociability index is a scaled item that combines responses to the following 7 questions (1 = yes; 0 = no): "Since I have been using the Internet": I stay more in touch with my friends and family, I have new topics to chat about with my children/friends, I have met someone in-person that I previously met online, I get in touch online with new and interesting people, Through SNSs I can freely express my point of view, Through SNSs I more often express my feelings and memories.

the perceived risk (medium to large correlation: r = .40, p < .00), opportunities (large correlation: r = .63, p < .00) and sociability (large correlation: r = .64, p < .00).

5 Conclusion

The analysis attempts to investigate the main features of the Italian digital elderly and their perception of the risks and opportunities related to the use of ICTs. The results of the survey allow us the opportunity to answer the following research questions:

(1) *What are the differences between the connected and not connected elderly?*

Digitized elderly people are a minority of the Italian population between the ages of 65 and 74, with good economic standing and secure employment, higher cultural sensitivity, strong family and social bonds and better physical health than non-digitized citizens. Men are more digitized than women, and the 65–69 year old sub-cohort is more connected than the 70–74 year old sub-cohort. These data confirm a "classical" dynamic of the digital divide influenced by socio-economic dimensions [24] in which economic, social and cultural capital give rise to processes of digital inclusion-exclusion. Above all, the data indicate that possession and use of ICT is accompanied by a better socio-economic condition, better physical activity, a larger network of friends, a lower perception of being old, a general personal satisfaction, as well as interests and self-confidence. The Italian digital elderly belong mainly to the wealthy minority over 65 years of age, with typical characteristic traits as innovators and early adopters [26]: high social and economical status.

(2) *Which are risks and opportunities perceived by older ICT users?*

One clearly emerging piece of data is a general perception by the elderly that ICT has primarily brought a feel of more positive than negative changes into their lives. Risk awareness is however not absent: the perception and the different nature of the risks are not divided evenly in the sample. In particular, in line with results of research on the relationship between children and ICTs [8], there is a positive correlation between the use and the perceived level of risk: the more ICT is used the more risks but also opportunities are perceived. Additionally, with more use the risk perceptions change: if "new" digital users are particularly afraid of making technical mistakes, more experienced digital users are more concerned with increasingly complex risks, such as exposure to offensive content, data theft, or wasted time on the Internet.

   The results presented provide a starting point on two reflections. First of all, results show that among the elderly, the perception of risks tends to be even higher than the initial enthusiasm towards ICT and the essential role given in their daily lives. Nevertheless, the issue of risks has been widely underestimated by both academic observation and public policies, hence the need to discuss the skills needed for a proper and safe use of ICT. As more access to the Internet spreads, greater importance has to be given to the kind of skills and awareness that the elderly need to acquire in terms of taking advantage of information and participation. These skills depend on their social, economic and cultural resources. With the diffusion of ICT among the "late majority" of older Italians [26], future waves of less "exclusive" (in terms economic, cultural, social resources) elderly users are likely to have less opportunities to take full advantage of the use of ICT. New issues will not be related to elderly peoples procurement of ICTs, but rather the actual technical skills and also critical skills in the selection of information, management of relationships and of new opportunities for active aging.

A second issue regards everyday contexts of use of the ICTs and current policy initiatives to promote active aging: studies on aging, digital inclusion, and risks require reflections that go beyond the benefits of ICT to recognize the importance of the ramifications of the technologies in adoption of contexts at the micro level and for different individuals, and groups. The processes of (digital) inclusion should aim to promote social inclusion and an individual's quality of life, not just the spread of ICT, which in some cases, may be paradoxically counterproductive. If it is true that children who have serious problems in their offline life are also likely to meet the same problems online [28], could the adoption of immersive and personal technologies increase loneliness and isolation of the elders or be an opportunity to overcome these problems? To better understand the processes of aging in the coming decades, politics and academic research are responsible for answering this question in the short term.

References

1. Livingstone, S., Haddon, L., Görzig, A. (eds.): Children, Risk and Safety on the Internet: Research and Policy Challenges in Comparative Perspective. Policy Press, Bristol (2012)
2. Haddon, L.: Social exclusion and information and communication technologies: lessons from studies of single parents and the young elderly. New Media Soc. 2(4), 387–406 (2000)
3. Saunders, E.J.: Maximizing computer use among the elderly in rural senior centers. Educ. Gerontol. 30(7), 573–585 (2004)
4. Sourbati, M., Carlo, S.: The mutuality of age and technology in digital divide policy. In: International Conference on Partnership for Progress on the Digital Divide, Scottsdale (Phoenix), Arizona, USA, 21–22 October 2015
5. Wellman, B.: The three ages of Internet studies. New Media Soc. 6(1), 123–129 (2004)
6. Fox, R.: Newstrack. Commun.ACM 38(8), 11–12 (1995)
7. Bakardjieva, M.: Internet Society: The Internet in Everyday Life. Sage, London (2005)
8. Livingstone, S., Haddon, L. (eds.): Kids Online. Opportunities and Risks for Children. Policy Press, Bristol (2009)
9. Warschauer, M.: Reconceptualizing the digital divide. First Monday 7(7), 114–123 (2002). http://firstmonday.org/issues/issue7_7/warschauer/index.html
10. DiMaggio, P.J., Hargittai, E., Celeste, C., Shafer, S.: From unequal access to differentiated use: a literature review and agenda for research on digital inequality in social inequality. In: Neckerman, K. (ed.) Social Inequality, pp. 355–400. Russell Sage Foundation, New York (2004)
11. Gumpert, G., Drucker, S.: Privacy, predictability or serendipity and digital cities. In: Tanabe, M., Besselaar, P., Ishida, T. (eds.) Digital Cities 2001. LNCS, vol. 2362, pp. 26–40. Springer, Heidelberg (2002)
12. van Dijk, J.A.G.M.: The Deepening Divide. Sage, London (2009)
13. Aroldi, P.: Prefazione all'edizione italiana. In: Livingston, S. Ragazzi online, pp. IX–HVIII. Vita e Pensiero, Milano (2010)

14. Fuchs, C.: Social Media: A Critical Introduction. Sage, London (2014)
15. Schneider, J.P.: Effects of cybersex addiction on the family: results of a survey. In: Cooper, A. (a cura di) Cybersex: The Dark Side of the Force, pp. 127–144. Bruner Routledge, Philadelphia (2000)
16. Kraut, R., Lundmark, V., Patterson, M., Kiesler, S., Mukopadhyay, T., Scherlis, W.: Internet paradox: a social technology that reduces social involvement and psychological well-being. Am. Psychol. 53(9), 1017–1031 (1998)
17. Griffiths, M.: The social impact of internet gambling. Soc. Sci. Comput. Rev. 20(3), 312–320 (2002)
18. Pasquali, F., Carlo, S.: Divertisti da morire: la rappresentazione mediale di Internet sulla stampa italiana. Comunicazioni sociali 3, 423–433 (2008)
19. European Commission Ageing well in the Information Society - an i2010 Initiative - Action Plan on Information and Communication Technologies and Ageing. EU publishing, Bruxelles (2010)
20. Sourbati, M.: On older people, internet access and electronic service delivery. a study of sheltered homes. In: Loos, E., Haddon, L., Mante-Meijer, E. (a cura di) The Social Dynamics of Information and Communication Technology, pp. 95–104. Ashgate, Aldershot (2008)
21. Olve, G.N., e Vimarlund, V.: Elderly Healthcare, Collaboration and ICTs - Enabling the Benefits of an Enabling Technology. VINNOVA, Stockholm (2006)
22. Dickinson, A., e Gregor, P.: Computer use has no demonstrated impact on the well-being of older adults. Int. J. Hum. Comput. Stud. 64(8), 744–753 (2006)
23. Colombo, F., Aroldi, P., Carlo, S.: New elders, old divides: ICTs, inequalities and well being amongst young elderly Italians. Comunicar 23(45), 47–55 (2015)
24. Gunkel, D.J.: Second thoughts: toward a critique of the digital divide. New Media Soc. 5(4), 499–522 (2003)
25. Smith, A.: Older Adults and Technology Use. Pew Research Center. (http://goo.gl/6nMNra)
26. Rogers, E.M.: Diffusion of Innovations. Free Press, New York (1983)
27. Hargittai, E.: Second-level digital divide: differences in peoples online skills. First Monday 7 (4), 1–20 (2002). http://firstmonday.org/issues/issue7_4/hargittai/
28. Shannon, D.: Vuxnas sexuella kontakter med barn via Internet [Adults' Sexual Contacts with Children Online]. Brottsförebyggande rådet, Stockholm (2007)

A Tale of Two Divides: Technology Experiences Among Racially and Socioeconomically Diverse Older Adults

Shelia R. Cotten$^{(\boxtimes)}$, Jessica Francis, Travis Kadylak, R.V. Rikard, Tim Huang, Christopher Ball, and Julia DeCook

Department of Media and Information,
Michigan State University, East Lansing, MI, USA
{cotten, franc202, kadylakt, rvrikard,
huangkul, ballchr3, jdecook}@msu.edu

Abstract. Using information and communication technologies (ICTs) can improve older adults' overall well-being and can be a catalyst for social integration and inclusion into society. While older adults are often compared to other age cohorts, based on previous digital divide research, there may be a significant amount of variation *within* older adult populations with regards to their ICT experiences, attitudes, and uses. Our study seeks to explore the potential gap by examining and comparing ICT uses, views, and experiences among older adults from diverse racial/ethnic and socioeconomic backgrounds. Four semi-structured focus groups (n = 40) were conducted with older adults from two separate cities in Mid-Michigan in the United States: Greater Lansing area and Detroit. Our findings reveal that older adults' experiences, uses, and perceptions about ICTs differ down racial and socio-economic lines. Our study demonstrates that there are potential sub-divides within traditionally digitally divided populations.

Keywords: Older adults · Digital divide · ICTs · Race · Socioeconomic status

1 Introduction

Using information and communication technologies (ICTs) can improve older adults' overall well-being and can be a catalyst for social integration and inclusion into society [1–5]. Despite the potential benefits afforded by ICTs, older adults (i.e., adults age 65 and older) have the lowest computer ownership and Internet use among all age cohorts [6]. Only 59 % of older adults report they use the Internet compared to 85 % of all American adults age 18 to 64 years of age. [7]. Additionally, only 47 % of older adults in the United States report access to broadband service [7]. The digital divide literature traditionally focuses on the various gaps between those who do and do not have access to the benefits of digital inclusion. These divides are tied to factors such as age, race, gender, socioeconomic status, and population density [6, 8–10].

To categorize older adults' ICT use by age, however, may be too simplistic a descriptor for such a vast and diverse population. For instance, older racial/ethnic minorities report using ICTs less and having less experience with ICTs than white older adults [11].

© Springer International Publishing Switzerland 2016
J. Zhou and G. Salvendy (Eds.): ITAP 2016, Part I, LNCS 9754, pp. 167–177, 2016.
DOI: 10.1007/978-3-319-39943-0_16

Moreover, older adults' attitudes toward and use of ICTs are driven by past experiences with ICTs, which may be fundamentally different from both an inter-generational and intra-generational perspective [11, 12]. In other words, while older adults are often compared to other age cohorts, based on previous digital divide research, there may be a significant amount of variation within older adult populations with regards to their ICT experiences, attitudes, and uses. Our study seeks to explore the potential gap by examining and comparing ICT uses, views, and experiences among older adults from diverse racial/ethnic and socioeconomic backgrounds.

1.1 Diversity of ICT Usage Among Older Adults: Racial and SES Differences

Previous research indicates that digital inequalities, such as the adoption of ICTs, may replicate other social inequalities [14]. For instance, older adults with an annual household income of $75,000 or more are nearly five-times more likely to own a tablet than older adults with an annual household income lower than $30,000 [7]. Older adults age 65 and older are also much less likely to have home broadband (43 %) compared other age groups (18–29: 80 %; 30–49: 78 %; 50–64: 69 %) [14].

Moreover, racial differences regarding ICT use and adoption also receives limited attention. Prior research indicates that racial digital divides continue to exist: African-Americans (64 %) are less likely to have home broadband compared to White individuals (74 %) [14]. African American (12 %) and Hispanic American (13 %) adults are more likely to rely on their smartphones for Internet access, compared to only 4 % of White smartphone owners [15]. Yet, some findings suggest that older African American and White adults have similar rates of cellphone adoption [7].

Furthermore, African American adults are less likely to go online, for any purpose, especially when they have not attended college. For example, when holding constant socioeconomic status (SES), 45 % of African American seniors use the Internet compared to 63 % of White adults [7]. Racial differences have been identified regarding other types of ICT use as well: 19 % of White older adults and 12 % of African American older adults use tablets; 19 % of White older adults, compared to 11 % of African American older adults, use E-readers, such as a Kindle [7]. Despite these descriptive differences, in-depth research exploring a more nuanced understanding of racial and SES divides, related attitudes, experience, and ICT use is lacking.

1.2 Importance of Digital Inclusion for Older Adults

ICT use yields various benefits for older adults' well-being, by facilitating access to social support networks, information to make life decisions, and promoting independence [4, 11]. ICT use among older adults is linked to reduced feelings of isolation, loneliness, and depression [1–5]. Older adults reporting such benefits from ICT use, perceive ICTs to be positive for their personal relationships by increasing their feelings of social connectedness to family and friends [2, 5]. Moreover, older adults use ICTs for inclusion into modern social networks [1]. To this end, ICTs afford older adults the means to facilitate meaningful relationships with both their geographically close and distant social ties. However, no research has examined how these benefits may vary among racially and socioeconomically diverse older adults.

Older adults' ICT use and the perceived benefits of ICT use are driven by experience [11, 12]. Perceived usefulness, enjoyment, social influence, confidence, and ease of use are drivers of ICT use among older adults [1, 6]. Furthermore, self-efficacy and experience with ICTs leads to lower levels of anxiety regarding ICT use [6, 11]. As ICTs are such an integral part of social connectedness and well-being for older adults, it is imperative to understand older adults' experiences with ICT use and how those experiences promote or detract from further adoption of ICT use across various demographic lines. Almost no research has examined these processes among diverse racial and socioeconomic groups of older adults. To facilitate a deeper understanding of how racial and SES differences may affect older adults' experiences with and use of ICTs we pose the following question:

What are the ICT experiences among racially and socioeconomically diverse older adults?

2 Methods

Four semi-structured focus groups (n = 40) were conducted with older adults from two separate cities in Mid-Michigan in the United States: Greater Lansing area and Detroit. U.S. Census Bureau [17] estimates indicate that approximately 9.7 % of Lansing residents are 65 years of age and older and that 51.6 % are female. Nearly 24.7 % of Lansing residents attained a Bachelor's, master's, professional, or doctorate degree. In terms of race/ethnicity, 61.2 % of Lansing residents are white and 23.7 % are African American and the median household income is $36,054. Census Bureau [17] estimates indicate reveal that a slightly larger percent of Detroit residents are 65 years of age and older (11.5 %) and 52.7 % are female. In contrast to Lansing residents, roughly 12.7 % of Detroit residents attained a Bachelor's, master's, professional, or doctorate degree. Moreover, 10.6 % of Detroit residents are white and 82.7 % are African American and the median household income is $26,325.

The focus groups were held in November and December of 2015 and February of 2016. Participants were recruited using several different strategies. Participants from the Greater Lansing area were recruited using the online SONA community pool, which allows local residents to view opportunities to participate in research conducted by Michigan State University graduate students and faculty. Participants from the Metro-Detroit area were recruited by a coordinator from a prominent local senior center. Each focus group had between 8 and 12 participants and lasted approximately 90–120 min. Participants were compensated $20 for their involvement in the focus group.

During the semi-structured focus groups, participants were probed to discuss their views, experiences, and use of information and communication technologies. Questions assessed the types, frequencies, and participants' motivation for using ICTs. Participants were asked how they decide on what type of communication channel and device they use to contact specific social ties (i.e., spouse, friends, children, grandchildren, etc.).

Additionally, participants were encouraged to discuss how they feel ICT use impacts their relationships with others, as well as the ways they feel ICT use is beneficial or potentially harmful.

Prior to each focus group session, participants completed a questionnaire that consisted of 15 total questions. Questions assessed sociodemographic characteristics, ICT access and ownership, how often participants use ICTs to communicate with various types of social ties (i.e., family members, close friends, and acquaintances), as well as participants' relationship satisfaction. The ICT use question used a 4-point Likert scale response options.

2.1   Data Analysis and Procedure

During each focus group session, audio was recorded using smartphones & tablets, while two of the focus groups were also recorded using a high definition 360 degree video recording device. The audio from each session was transcribed by a third party service. Additionally, research assistants were present in each session and recorded detailed field notes. Upon completion of each focus group session the moderator and research assistants participated in an informal debrief to discuss their observations and potential themes. Field notes, audio and transcriptions were reviewed independently by research assistants to identify themes (i.e., similarities and differences between sites in how participants use and benefit from using ICTs), which were relevant to the focus of this investigation. Data from the questionnaires was coded and entered into an SPSS dataset. Descriptive analysis was used to compare participants from the two sites.

2.2   Results

Table 1 shows the demographic descriptive results of the focus groups. Demographic characteristics for the two locations were divergent; however, the ages are relatively similar. The mean age of Greater Lansing area participants was 70 years old, while the mean age of Detroit participants was 73 years old. Both locations consisted of mostly females (Lansing: 68 %, Detroit: 95 %). The racial composition of Greater Lansing area participants was 84 % White, 11 % Hispanic, and 5 % African American, while the racial composition of Detroit participants was 86 % African American and 14 % identified as "other."

A single item question was used to assess perceived economic hardship, which contained three response choices— "more than enough financial resources to get by," "just enough financial resources to get by," and "not enough financial resources to get by." As shown in Table 1, participants from the Greater Lansing area were more likely to report having more than enough to get by than participants from Detroit. The participants from Detroit perceived more economic hardship, with 45 % reporting that they do not have enough financial resources to get by compared to only 11 % of those from the Greater Lansing area.

The Greater Lansing area participants were also more likely to report being married, while the majority of Detroit participants reported that they were divorced (42 %).

Table 1. Demographics

Location	Greater lansing area	Detroit
Age		
Age range	65-76	62-88
Mean age	70	73
Gender		
Male	32 %	5 %
Female	68 %	95 %
Race		
White	84 %	0 %
Hispanic	11 %	0 %
African American	5 %	86 %
Other	0 %	14 %
Perceived Economic Hardship		
More than enough	47 %	15 %
Just enough	42 %	40 %
Not enough	11 %	45 %
Education		
Less than high school diploma	0 %	10 %
High school graduate	0 %	19 %
Some college	47 %	28 %
College degree	32 %	19 %
Graduate school degree	21 %	24 %
Martial Status		
Married	74 %	21 %
Single	0 %	11 %
Widowed	0 %	26 %
Divorced	26 %	42 %

Level of education was also more diverse in Detroit, with 29 % reporting a high school degree or less, while all the Lansing participants reported having some college or more.

2.3   ICTs and Connectedness

As shown in Table 2, participants from both focus group locations reported using a variety of ICTs to communicate with family, close friends & acquaintances. Descriptive results suggest that, compared to the Detroit participants, a larger portion of Greater Lansing area participants used mobile phones, Internet enabled laptops & tablets, and desktop computers to communicate with others.

Meanwhile, a larger portion of Detroit participants reported using landline phones to communicate with others (90 %), while only 53 % of the greater Lansing area participants use landlines to communicate with others. Preferred ICT was one of a few areas where results suggest differences among older adults from different racial and SES backgrounds.

Table 2. ICT Use characteristics

Location	Greater lansing area	Detroit
Landline		
Yes	58 %	86 %
No	42 %	10 %
Missing data	–	4 %
Mobile phone		
Yes	100 %	81 %
No	0 %	14 %
Missing data	–	5 %
Desktop computer		
Yes	68 %	48 %
No	26 %	43 %
Missing data	6 %	9 %
Internet enabled laptop computer		
Yes	74 %	43 %
No	21 %	38 %
Missing data	5 %	19 %
Internet enabled tablet		
Yes	79 %	33 %
No	21 %	57 %
Missing data	–	10 %

2.4   ICT Experiences, Use, and Perceived Usefulness

An interesting divergent trend emerged between older adults from the two cities with regards to ICT experience and perceived utility of ICT devices. Participants from the Greater Lansing area tended to discuss a wide range of ICT device ownership and use. Descriptive results suggest that in comparison to the Detroit participants, a larger portion of the Greater Lansing area participants used mobile phones, Internet enabled laptops & tablets, and desktop computers to communicate with others. Meanwhile, a larger portion of Detroit participants reported using landline phones to communicate with others (90 %), while only 53 % of Greater Lansing area participants used landlines to communicate with others. One Greater Lansing area participant stated:

> I'm from San Diego. We would've never made it to Michigan as efficiently as we did, without our smartphones and the GPS because we would, we would find out the hotels, we'd find out the best price, we could negotiate the room rates, we'd find a restaurant that we liked.

In addition to utility aspects of ICTs, other female Greater Lansing area participants discussed how ICT & eBooks have impacted their leisure time:

> I like my Kindle. I have never been a real big reader, and I've gotten hooked on my Kindle. I love to read at night now, and I think I could get the same thing on my tablet though. So I think I'm overlapping myself, but I really like just holding it, and I like the light, I can turn it on when he's sleeping and it doesn't bother him.

When the Greater Lansing area participants were prompted to discuss their favorite ICT, one male participant stated:

Well, the GPS gets me to the spot that I had previously marked in that there as a waymark, and then my fish-finder tell me whether or not I should be staying there or be moving on or whatever. So that old trick about putting a big X on the bottom of the boat doesn't work. [Laughter].

Another greater Lansing area participant stated other advantages of ICTs:

[My favorite ICT is] a pen on my iPad because I have the old technology and I would rather write than type. And just keeping up in how you integrate the new with the old.

Conversely, participants in both of the Detroit focus groups unanimously claimed that their favorite ICT is their landline phone, while only a couple of participants in each group maintained that their cellphone was their favorite device. Although a few participants in both Detroit sessions indicated that the cellphone was their preferred ICT, most replied that their favorite ICT in general and their favorite ICT used to communicate with others was:

Landline! I love my Landline! Landline!

When probed for why landlines are their favorite ICT, one respondent stated:

You don't have to worry about charging it. You don't have to worry about dropping a call. Landlines are more convenient.
The landline does not cut you off. The landline does not travel, no signals. The landline doesn't go through all of that.
…But the point is with the landline, you don't have to worry about charging it unless you've got a cordless phone. We had a three day black out or two and a half day black out. The towers was down you couldn't use this [cellphone]. But you could use the landline as long as it didn't need to be charged. And sometimes you don't feel like getting tied up with trying to learn the technology cause it's time consuming like she was saying, … she trying to figure out how do I text, how do I communicate with this thing. And the benefits too with this new technology; you can reach so many people. But like I said it's pros and cons.
…you don't have to charge the landline. It's on, the phone automatically, you can put a voice message on it and it'll record the message. If you're busy or something, you don't have to get the phone call. Each, all these different things you have to charge 'em and make sure they're running.

These quotes illustrate the myriad reasons why older adults from Detroit relied upon the landline phone.

Other Detroit participants, though fewer in number, felt that cellphones offered them similar benefits regarding convenience:

Convenience too for me, its convenience. You know you don't have to be tied at home to receive confirmation that you need. I do like the text feature when somebody needs to give you an address or something. I just tell them to go ahead and text me the address. It is very convenient.
I agree with everybody but it has this pros and cons. The reason I like the cellphone is for convenience because you can pick it up wherever you at, as long as it's charged…
I was very happy to have my cellphone because I'm able to do business and check with the doctors, and the doctors call you, and you got to call them and everything. And we can have conference calls and take care of business even when I'm out in the street, and that type of thing so… But I don't… A lot of people that know me they will say "You didn't answer you phone when I called." And I say, "I'm not a slave to my phone."
And I said, "That's why I have voice mail."

When detailing their salient experiences with ICTs, one Greater Lansing participants discussed memories and experiences related to recreational activities and travel. One Greater Lansing participant stated:

> I was afraid to drive in a big city. I was afraid of certain streets. I never could figure out when my turn was coming up, and I'm a good driver in general. I never had an accident. I'm a good driver, but certain things really come unglued, repeatedly, and now that I have a GPS, I call her Evelina, [laughter] I stick her on my dashboard, and she keeps me up to speed on traffic and doing all the right turns. And limit my ETA. I text my husband, my ETA. It's totally given me freedom. I'm not afraid to drive at night anymore.

Another Greater Lansing participant added:

> I do a lot of Walleye fishing, so I can find the shoals where the forage is and so forth, and we know that's a hotspot, so we'll waymark it. A couple years ago we went out on the ice in the UP, we went out about two and a half miles and a little baby knock, the ice is like 3–4 feet thick. I mean, I had no idea where we're at. And then you take your ice fi... Or fishfinders, down on the ice and there they are.

Other Greater Lansing participants described experiences with ICTs that enabled them to connect with family. One Greater Lansing participant said:

> When I Skype with my grandson, I can at least see him. Because I think there is more of a... [Again], you don't misread what the communication is, because you can see them versus texting or emailing. So that, to me, is helpful to feel connected because my kids live out of state. So that has helped to feel connected.

Greater Lansing focus group participants recognized the amplifications provided to them through the use of ICTs, whether these involved helping them navigate roads or their lives, or communicate in more realistic modes given the two-way visual communication made possible through Skype, Facetime, and other ICTs. Participants from Detroit, on the other hand, spoke of ICT experiences involving anxiety and concerns. One Detroit participant recalled an experience involving learning how use ICTs for work:

> On the job we have to keep up with today's times. And I didn't know anything but I wanted this job. I needed this job, so I went to school for it. I didn't know how to turn on the computer. It was very scary cause it was just something strange out of this world, a monster standing here I have to tackle. And I'm like well I have to learn this. So I was very fearful, and I was very timid. But once I got the hang of it, you can constantly apply it and keep on applying it to newer and later technology out there. But it was very fearful and I was so bad, when I graduated, the whole class gave me a standing ovation.

Other Detroit participants discussed specific concerns to information security with regard to ICTs and online banking. One Detroit participant stated:

> I listen to what they're saying about how they can steal all of your information. Therefore, I don't do it online. You know what I do it for? I do it through my checking account. I do the E-F-T, transfer. That's how they get my money out of my checking account. End of the month my check come, everything's covered. To me, that's better.

Another Detroit participant followed and stated:

> And what I do is, I have a separate account for paying bills, and I had all of my bills come out of one account. Now, if they steal out of that one, some of those checks are gonna bounce. My savings and stuff, I don't have that information online.

Other Detroit participants cited negative experiences with upgrading ICTs and concerns of cost as salient experiences that had affected their attitudes toward ICTs. One Detroit participant stated:

> Upgrading. Every time you turn around, you can't hardly get a phone without it being obsolete, and there's nothing wrong with the phone. I mean it works perfectly. It does... A smartphone does most of the stuff, might have some more features but you feel you're always compelled to upgrade and spend more money unnecessarily.

Another Detroit participant echoed the previous sentiment and said:

> And initially when stuff comes out the prices... And the one thing I really hate is that the retailers are just so driven by that almighty dollar. That they... They're always up.

To summarize, participants in the Detroit and Greater Lansing focus groups had distinct perspectives, uses, and experiences regarding ICTs. Participants from the Greater Lansing focus group reported a wider variety of ICTs used than the Detroit participants. Detroit participants reported landlines and mobile phones as their primary ICTs of choice due to perceived convenience and reliability. The participants from Greater Lansing experienced less economic hardship, were more educated, and they reported a wider variety of uses of ICTs for maintaining and amplifying aspects of their lives. Further implications of these results are discussed presently.

3 Discussion

Our results show that older adults' experiences, uses, and perceptions about ICTs differ down racial and socio-economic lines. The digital divide was originally conceptualized as the unequal distribution of ICT hardware [18, 9]. However, over the course of the past decade this conceptualization of the digital divide as one simple hardware based divide has shifted to include a series of more complex divides. In particular, it has been posited that there are four distinct access gaps, which can have an influence on an individual's likelihood to use and benefit from ICTs: material access gap, mental access gap, usage access gap, and skills access gap [9]. Our findings echo earlier digital divide research suggesting that older adults' ICT use and perceptions may be driven by past experience [11, 12]. Furthermore, our findings show that older adults appear to find themselves differently divided based on various demographic factors.

While the digital divide has been closing for certain populations (i.e., women) [9], our findings indicate and confirm that the differential impacts of the digital divide remains [17, 18], particularly for older adults. To elaborate, the Detroit based older adults reported very different experiences and attitudes towards ICT compared to the more affluent East Lansing group. The experiences and circumstances of the Detroit group may have prompted a shift from simply being "information have-nots" to becoming "information want-nots" [9]. In order to truly understand this traditionally digitally divided population, we must first begin to understand the digital differences, or sub-divides, that exist within older adults.

Our findings suggest that more disposable income may promote greater opportunity to use a wider variety of ICTs and experience various benefits associated with ICT use. The predominantly White and higher SES of older adults from the Greater Lansing area reported using ICTs to facilitate a wider variety of activities that lend themselves to positive experiences with ICTs (i.e., Travel, Skyping with family, recreational excursions). The predominantly African American and lower SES older adults from Detroit appear to be driven in their ICT use by more negative experiences or fear of technological failure. Such experiences may promote a strong loyalty to older ICTs such as landlines and simpler mobile phones and may serve as barriers to adoption of a wider variety of ICTs. In essence, for individuals from lower SES groups, the perceived unreliability of certain ICTs may have an inverse relationship with their motivations and financial ability to adopt and use ICTs.

4   Conclusion and Limitations

Previous digital divide research demonstrates that the likelihood of ICT access is affected by various demographic factors such as age, race, and SES. Later digital divide literature expands to include a number of divides, rather than just access to ICTs. Our study demonstrates that there are potential sub-divides within traditionally digitally divided populations. In other words, factors such as race and SES, can compound to result in different levels of ICT experience, uses, and attitudes. While older adults are the age group with the lowest level of ICT adoption, there are stratified layers of access and use within this large and diverse group. The results indicate there is a great deal of experiential variation within this generation, which could be just as important as intergenerational differences.

One potential limitation of our study is that we focused specifically on older adults from suburban and urban locations. Furthermore, all participants currently reside in Michigan. Future research should consider older adults from more rural locations and from various regions throughout the United States in order to improve generalizability of the results.

Despite some potential limitations, our research indicates that in order to effectively promote older adults' digital inclusion researchers must first develop an understanding of the digital sub-divides that exist within the population of older adults. Moving forward, it is important to realize that older adults comprise a vast and varied population, which has a great diversity of ICT uses, experiences, and attitudes. Differences in older adults' ICT uses, experiences, and attitudes should be accounted for when attempting to design interventions or create policies that affect this particular population.

References

1. Blit-Cohen, E., Litwin, H.: Elder participation in cyberspace: a qualitative analysis of israeli retirees. J. Aging Stud. **18**(4), 385–398 (2004). doi:10.1016/j.jaging.2004.06.007
2. Cotten, S.R., Anderson, W.A., McCullough, B.M.: Impact of internet use on loneliness and contact with others among older adults: cross-sectional analysis. J. Med. Internet Res. **15**(2), e39 (2013)
3. Cotten, S.R., Ford, G., Ford, S., Hale, T.M.: Internet use and depression among retired older adults in the united states: a longitudinal analysis. J. Gerontol. Ser. B: Psychol. Sci. Soc. Sci. **69**(5), 763–771 (2014)
4. Winstead, V., Anderson, W.A., Yost, E.A., Cotten, S.R., Warr, A., Berkowsky, R.W.: You can teach an old dog new tricks: a qualitative analysis of how residents of senior living communities may use the web to overcome spatial and social barriers. J. Appl. Gerontol. **32**(5), 540–560 (2013). doi:10.1177/0733464811431824
5. McMellon, C.A., Schiffman, L.G.: Cybersenior empowerment: how some older individuals are taking control of their lives. J. Appl. Gerontol. **21**(2), 157–175 (2002). doi:10.1177/07364802021002002
6. Tsai, H.-y., Shillair, R., Cotten, S.R., Winstead, V., Yost, E.: Getting grandma online: are tablets the answer for increasing digital inclusion for older adults in the U.S.? Educ. Gerontol. **41**, 695–709 (2015)
7. Smith, A.: Older adults and technology use: usage and adoption. Pew Research: Internet Project, pp. 1–7 (2014). https://www.pewinternet.org/2014/04/03/usage-and-adoption/
8. van Deursen, A.J., Helsper, E.J.: A nuanced understanding of Internet use and non-use among the elderly. Eur. J. Commun. **30**(2), 171–187 (2015)
9. Van Dijk, J., Hacker, K.: The digital divide as a complex and dynamic phenomenon. Inf. Soc. **19**(4), 315–326 (2003)
10. Van Dijk, J.: Digital divide research, achievements and shortcomings. Poetics **34**(4), 221–235 (2006)
11. Czaja, S.J., Charness, N., Fisk, A., Hertzog, C., Nair, S., Rogers, W., Sharit, J.: Factors predicting the use of technology: findings from the center for research and education on aging and technology enhancement (CREATE). Psychol. Aging **21**(2), 333–352 (2006)
12. Czaja, S.J., Sharit, J.: Age differences in attitudes toward computers. J. Gerontol. Ser. B: Psychol. Sci. Soc. Sci. **53B**(5), P329–P340 (1998). doi:10.1093/geronb/53B.5.P329
13. Robinson, L., Cotten, S.R., Ono, H., Quan-Haase, A., Mesch, G., Chen, W., Schulz, J., Hale, T.M., Stern, M.J.: Digital inequalities and why they matter. Inf. Commun. Soc. **18**(5), 569–582 (2015). doi:10.1080/1369118X.2015.1012532
14. Zickuhr, K., Smith, A.: Pew Research: Internet Project: Home Broadband 2013 (2013). http://www.pewinternet.org/2013/08/26/home-broadband-2013/
15. Anderson, N.: Digital technologies and equity: gender, digital divide and rurality. In: Teaching and Digital Technologies: Big Issues and Critical Questions, p. 46 (2015)
16. US Census Bureau State & County QuickFacts (2015). http://quickfacts.census.gov/qfd/states/26/2646000.html
17. DiMaggio, P., Hargittai, E., Celeste, C., Shafer, S.: From unequal access to differentiated use: a literature review and agenda for research on digital inequality. In: Neckerman, K., Shafer, S. (eds.) Social Inequality, pp. 355–400. Russell Sage Foundation, New York (2004)
18. van Deursen, A., Van Dijk, J.: The digital divide shifts to differences in usage. New Media Soc. **16**(3), 507–526 (2013)

The Role of Technology in Supporting Family Caregivers

Sara J. Czaja[1](✉), Dolores Perdomo[1], and Chin Chin Lee[2]

[1] Department of Psychiatry and Behavioral Sciences,
University of Miami Miller School of Medicine, Miami, FL, USA
{sczaja,dperdomo}@med.miami.edu
[2] Center on Aging, University of Miami Miller School of Medicine, Miami, FL, USA
c.lee7@med.miami.edu

Abstract. In the United States and in many other countries, family members represent the primary source of support for older adults with a chronic disease or disability. While caregiving is associated with positive outcomes such as personal growth or the sense of helping someone in need, evidence has shown that caring for a relative/friend with an illness or disability causes distress in family caregivers and compromises their health and survival. Thus, there have been many intervention programs designed to aid family caregivers and many of these programs have proven beneficial in terms of alleviating caregiver burden and distress. Unfortunately, due to lack of awareness of the existence of these programs or logistic problems accessing these programs, many caregivers do not take advantage of or receive the benefits of evidenced-based interventions. This paper will discuss and demonstrate with examples from our research, how Information and Communication Technology (ICTs) can support family caregivers.

Keywords: Family caregiving · Social support · Information and communication technology

1 Introduction

The growth in the number of older people, especially the old-old, in both developed and developing countries has important implications for society and the healthcare system. Worldwide, the number of older persons was 841 million in 2013, and will almost triple by 2050, when it is expected to surpass the two billion mark [1]. The likelihood of developing a chronic disease or disability and the need for support and healthcare services generally increases with age. For example, about 36 million people worldwide have Alzheimer's disease (AD) or some other form of dementia and this number is expected to increase to 66 million by 2030 [2] (Fig. 1). In the U.S. alone about 92 % of older adults (aged 65 +) are living with one chronic condition such as high blood pressure, diabetes or heart disease and many 77 % have at least two [3].

Most people with a chronic condition such as AD or a disability are cared for at home by family. Although caregiving can have positive benefits, caregiving often creates negative consequences for the caregiver. Overall, the existent literature indicates that caregiving can result in psychological distress, the adoption of poor health habits, sleep disruption, psychiatric and physical illnesses, and mortality. Caregiving also often disrupts social

© Springer International Publishing Switzerland 2016
J. Zhou and G. Salvendy (Eds.): ITAP 2016, Part I, LNCS 9754, pp. 178–185, 2016.
DOI: 10.1007/978-3-319-39943-0_17

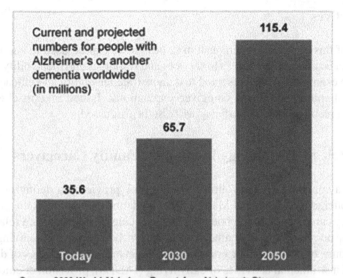

Source: *2009 World Alzheimer Report*, from Alzheimer's Disease
International (ADI), a London-based nonprofit, international federation of 71
national Alzheimer organizations including the Alzheimer's Association.

Fig. 1. Projected increase in the number of people with Alzheimer's Disease worldwide

and other family relationships and employment activities [4, 5]. Given these consequences, there has been a broad range of intervention studies aimed at decreasing caregiver stress and enhancing the caregiver experience. Several of these intervention studies have demonstrated beneficial effects for the caregiver such as in reductions in caregiver burden and depression and enhanced caregiving skills and social support. In fact, many of these programs such as the Resources for Enhancing Alzheimer's Caregiver Health (REACH II) [6], are now considered to be an evidenced-based interventions and are being broadly implemented in the community. However, despite the proliferation of these interventions many caregivers are unaware of or do not have access to these programs. For example, services are not always available to caregivers in some communities or their availability is not well advertised, further many caregivers are unwilling to use services that are available because of issues such as cost, logistic problems, or lack of help from others to care for the older adults when they are engaging in an activity such as attending a community support group. Information and Communication Technologies (ICTs) offer the potential of removing these barriers and providing support and delivering services to caregivers. Existing evidence suggests that the use of technology to deliver intervention programs and support to family caregivers is feasible and acceptable to caregivers and technology-based interventions can prove to beneficial. However, this issue is just beginning to be explored and there is a need for a more robust evidence-based with diverse populations of caregivers. This paper will explore this issue and provide examples of technology-intervention programs.

2   Objectives

The focus of this paper is on demonstrating how ICTs can be used to support family caregivers and enhance their access to services and resources and their ability to provide care. A case example will be presented to demonstrate feasibility and efficacy of using technological interventions for caregiver populations. Issues of cost-effectiveness, barriers to implementation and privacy will also be discussed.

3   The Role of Technology in Support Family Caregivers

To provide a context for what follows we being by providing a definition of family caregivers offered by Schulz and Martire [7], who define caregiving as the provision of extraordinary care outside of the bounds of what is consider typical for a relationship – e.g., a spouse does not typically bathe, feed and dress their partner. Caregiving typically involves a range of task such care coordination, assistance with activities of daily living (ADLs) and instrumental activities of daily living (IADLS), provision of emotional and in some cases (e.g., dementia) provision of cognitive support. Caregiving also increasingly involves assistance with healthcare tasks previously performed by trained specialist such as delivering injections or interacting with a blood glucose monitor or an infusion pump. Thus, caregiving involves tasks that may be unpleasant and uncomfortable; are psychologically stressful and physically exhausting; and involve significant expenditures of time, effort, energy, and financial resources over potentially extended periods of time. Further, the demands of caregiving are not static and many change over the course of their loved ones illness.

Due the increased reliance on family caregivers to help manage the growing population of older adults and the documented consequences of caregiving on the caregiver, there have been a broad range of intervention trials aimed at decreasing the burden of caregiving and providing support to the family caregiver. These interventions included counseling, skills training, case management, and social support. They are also delivered in a variety of formats and contexts such as individual and group sessions delivered in the home or in clinical settings. Unfortunately because many caregivers remain unaware of these programs or confront barriers to accessing these programs, the benefits of these programs are often not experienced by many family members in the caregiving role. Thus there is a need for innovative methods to bring services and support to caregivers – clearly ICTs offer this potential.

Overall, ICTs hold several advantages over more traditional methods of intervention delivery such as: increased ability to deliver and access information on demand and in a time efficient manner, over long distances and asynchronously; increased access to resources and healthcare providers; and increased flexibility with respect to information format. For example, the Internet and mobile devices can enhance caregivers' access to information and resources. A challenge facing many caregivers is having the necessary knowledge about the care recipient's illness or disability, how to provide care, and how to access and utilize available services. There are a vast number of websites available that can provide caregivers with information on illnesses/diseases, medications and treatments, healthcare providers and health resources. These applications can also enhance direct access to experts and professional organizations, which can also facilitate decision-making by the caregiver. Recent data from the Pew Internet and American Life Report [8] indicates that among caregivers in the U.S. who have access to the Internet, 84 % indicated that they went online to research health topics such as information about their loved ones illness, medication safety, and medical procedures. Fifty-nine percent of these caregivers said that the online resources enhanced their ability to provide care and 52 % indicated that these resources have been helpful in their ability to cope with caregiver stress. Of course a concern is the quality, quantity and usability of the information offered by Internet resources. Our data shown that Internet health information can be challenging to use and understand (e.g., [9, 10]).

Network applications can also link caregivers to other family members or long distant caregivers to the person for whom they are providing care. They also offer caregivers the opportunity to engage with other caregivers and participate in support groups.

Monitoring and sensing technologies are increasingly being used to monitor the functional health and activities of older adults, and to assist with the management of chronic conditions, may also be beneficial to family caregivers. Develops in microelectronics and digital wireless technology now make it possible to integrate wireless sensors and network capabilities so that the information collected from the sensors can be transferred to clinicians and family caregivers at remote locations. These systems include a wide variety of technologies such as home-based safety monitoring systems (e.g., fall detection systems, sensor-embedded environmental systems); embedded or integrated activity-monitor sensory systems that track behaviors such as movement patterns, sleep behaviors or simpler systems that track activities such as medication adherence; and systems that monitor vital signs and other health indicators or provide reminders about health-related activities.

However, despite these benefits there are also potential challenges associated with technology use such as lack of "meaningful access" to technology systems for some segments of the population (e.g., older adults, individuals of lower socio-economic status), usability problems, the dynamic and constant evolution of technology, cost and reimbursement, and the possibility that using technology to deliver an intervention may not be a comparable substitute to the face-to-face interactions between caregivers and interventionists, other caregivers, or healthcare providers [11, 12]. To overcome these challenges requires larger robust trials to gather evidence about the benefits and pitfalls of technology and the consideration of caregiver characteristics, needs, and preferences.

3.1 Case Study: The Videocare Study [13]

The VideoCare Study was a randomized pilot trial that evaluated the feasibility and efficacy of a technology-based intervention among an ethnically diverse sample of family caregivers of patients with Alzheimer's disease. Following a baseline assessment a sample of 110 caregivers (56 Hispanic Americans and 54 African Americans) were randomized into: (1) the videophone intervention condition; (2) a nutrition attention control condition; or (3) an information only control condition. Those assigned to the intervention group received a Cisco videophone that was installed in their home and connected to a DSL line and a secure server at the host site (Fig. 2). The Videophones were used to conduct individual skill building sessions with a certified interventionists and facilitator led support groups. The support groups were conducted via the video-phone in English and Spanish and followed a structured education/supportive format. This included an introduction to and discussion of themes related to the caregiving experience. The group themes included: (1) Introduction to Dementia; (2) Managing Behavioral Problems; (3) Caregiver Well Being; and (4) Communication; and Planning for Life Transition. The support group sessions were closed, 60 min in duration, and were interspersed with the individual videophone skill building sessions. The caregivers participated from their own homes via videophone. Other features available on the videophones included an annotated resource guide, caregiver tips: educational seminars. The features were presented in hierarchical menus in a multi-modal format (speech and text). Caregivers received training in the use of the videophone, were provided with a help card and access to technical support. There was also a help feature on the menu. All features were available in English and Spanish (Fig. 3). The intervention duration was 5 months, followed by a post intervention assessment.

Fig. 2. The Videophone technology

The results of the study are encouraging and indicate that the intervention was bene-ficial in terms of alleviating caregiver distress and increasing social support and positive feelings about caregiving among the caregivers assigned to the Videocare intervention arm (Czaja et al. 2014). The majority of caregivers (82 %) also found participating in the on-line support groups was valuable, and that participation in the groups improved their knowledge about caregiving and their caregiving skills. All of the caregivers

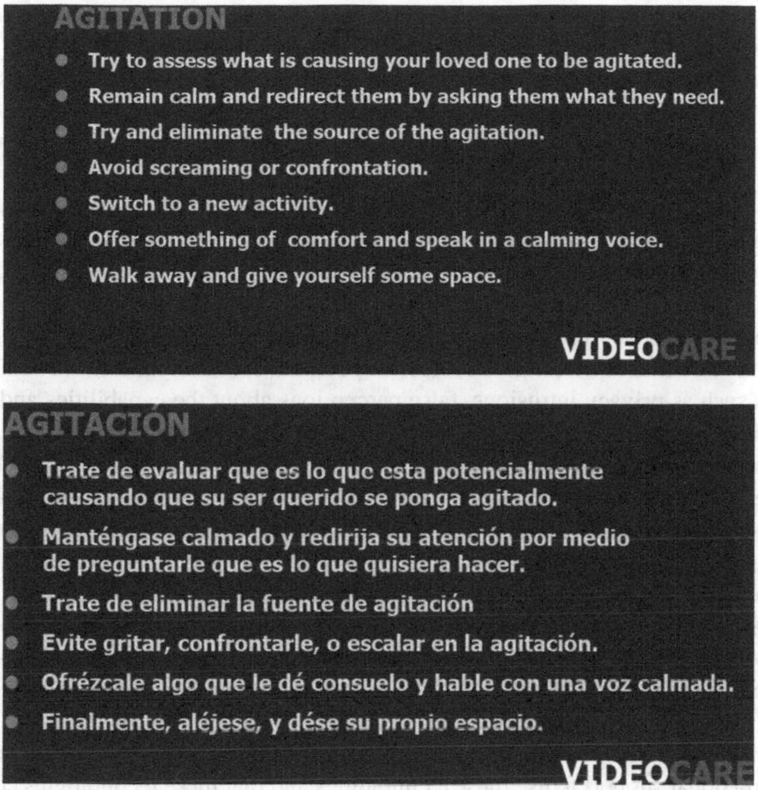

AGITATION

- Try to assess what is causing your loved one to be agitated.
- Remain calm and redirect them by asking them what they need.
- Try and eliminate the source of the agitation.
- Avoid screaming or confrontation.
- Switch to a new activity.
- Offer something of comfort and speak in a calming voice.
- Walk away and give yourself some space.

VIDEOCARE

AGITACIÓN

- Trate de evaluar que es lo que esta potencialmente causando que su ser querido se ponga agitado.
- Manténgase calmado y redirija su atención por medio de preguntarle que es lo que quisiera hacer.
- Trate de eliminar la fuente de agitación
- Evite gritar, confrontarle, o escalar en la agitación.
- Ofrézcale algo que le dé consuelo y hable con una voz calmada.
- Finalmente, aléjese, y dése su propio espacio.

VIDEOCARE

Fig. 3. A sample of a caregiver tip screen in English and Spanish

(100 %) indicated that participation in the groups helped them share their feelings about being a caregiver. In addition, the caregivers were able to use the videophone system and the majority indicated that the videophone was understandable and easy to use. Overall, the findings from the study demonstra that technology is a viable and valuable option for delivering intervention programs and conducting support groups with diverse caregiver populations. The caregivers were enthusiastic about the program and were able to use the technology. They also found it useful in terms of enhancing their access to resources.

4 Conclusions

This paper provides examples of various technologies and their potential benefits for family caregivers. However, for the benefits of these technologies to be realized by caregivers, it is important that the technology is useful and useable by these populations and that systems are reliable and responsive. If a system is unavailable it cannot be used, and if it is unreliable users will become frustrated and avoid using the technology regardless of potential benefits. All technology involves potential barriers to acceptance that must be overcome to facilitate widespread acceptance, adoption and continued use. These include a broad range of user characteristics (socio-demographics, health status, social support, experience with and attitudes towards technology) and resources (sensory, cognitive, psychomotor); system characteristics (user interface, instructional support, aesthetics, engagement, functionality); and the fit between the user and the system.

One issue that remains is technology access. Although the rate of technology adoption is increasing across age groups existing data indicate that there are still age-related gaps in usage especially among caregivers and older adults of lower socio-economic status.

Other issues relate to privacy issues and data integration, management and sharing issues. It is essential to investigate sources of potential for harm inherent in some technologies such as privacy intrusions, false perceptions about the capabilities and safety of technology systems, the proliferation of too much and inappropriate information and miscommunications between caregivers, patients and healthcare providers. Optimal strategies for combining technology with other types of interventions and healthcare interactions need to be identified. More rigorous studies are also needed to evaluate the effectiveness of technology-based interventions with large and diverse caregiver populations and on the cost effectiveness of technological interventions.

It is also important to note that many caregivers are also increasingly need to perform medical/nursing tasks, which also means that they have to interact with complex medical technologies such as catheters blood glucose monitors, and injection equipment. In addition, they may have to interact with telemedicine technologies and Personal Health Records (PHRs). Thus it is important to insure that caregivers have the requisite skills and instructional support to use these technologies and that these technologies conform to usability guidelines. All to often ICT technologies are designed without consideration of user populations.

References

1. United Nations, Department of Economics and Social affairs, Population Division: World Population Ageing 2013. ST/ESA/SER.A/348 (2013)
2. World Alzheimer Report 2010. http://www.alz.co.uk/research/files/WorldAlzheimerReport2010.pdf
3. National Council on Aging: Healthy Aging Facts. https://www.ncoa.org/news/resources-for-reporters/get-the-facts/healthy-aging-facts/
4. Pinquart, M., Sörensen, S.: Correlates of physical health of informal caregivers: a meta-analysis. J. Gerontol. B Psychol. Sci. Soc. Sci. **62**, P126–P137 (2007)
5. Schulz, R., O'Brien, A.T., Bookwala, J., et al.: Psychiatric and physical morbidity effects of dementia caregiving: prevalence, correlates, and causes. Gerontologist **35**, 771–791 (1995)
6. Belle, S.H., Burgio, L., Burns, R., Coon, D., Czaja, S.J., Gallagher-Thompson, D., et al.: Enhancing the quality of life of dementia caregivers from different ethnic or racial groups: a randomized, controlled trial. Ann. Intern. Med. **145**, 727–738 (2006)
7. Schulz, R., Martire, L.M.: Family caregiving of persons with dementia: prevalence, health effects, and support strategies. Am. J. Geriatr. Psychiatry **12**, 240–249 (2004)

8. Fox, S., Duggan, M., Purcell, K.: Family Caregivers are Wired for Health. Pew Research Center. http://www.pewinternet.org/files/old-media//Files/Reports/2013/PewResearch_FamilyCaregivers.pdf

9. Czaja, S.J., Sharit, J., Nair, S.N.: Usability of the medicare health web sites. J. Am. Med. Assoc. **300**, 790–791 (2008)

10. Taha, J., Sharit, J., Czaja, S.J.: Use of and satisfaction with sources of health information among older internet users and nonusers. Gerontologist **49**, 663–673 (2009)

11. Berkowsky, R., Czaja, S.J.: The use of technology in behavioral intervention research: advantages and challenges. In: Gitlin, L., Czaja, S.J. (eds.) pp. 119–136. Springer Publishing Company, LLC, New York (2016)

12. Czaja, S.J., Lee, C.C., Schulz, R.: Quality of life technologies in supporting family caregivers. In: Schulz, E. (ed.) Quality of Life Technology Handbook, pp. 245–260. Taylor & Francis, New York (2012)

13. Czaja, S.J., Loewenstein, D., Schulz, R., Nair, S.N., Perdomo, D.: A videophone psychological intervention for dementia caregivers. Am. J. of Geriatr. Psychiatry **21**, 1071–1081 (2013)

Acceptance of Cloud-Based Healthcare Services by Elderly Taiwanese People

Wen-Tsung Ku[1] and Pi-Jung Hsieh[2(✉)]

[1] Department of General Affairs,
St. Martin De Porres Hospital, Chia-Yi, Taiwan, ROC
kib56265@gmail.com
[2] Department of Hospital and Health Care Administration,
Chia Nan University of Pharmacy and Science, Tainan, Taiwan, ROC
beerun@seed.net.tw

Abstract. With the increasingly aging population and the advances in information technology (IT), cloud service has become an important health informatics topic. Cloud-based healthcare services have significant potential to enable the elderly to live independently and to access health-care services with ease. Despite this potential, there are gaps in our understanding of how the elderly decide to use such services. A field survey was conducted in Taiwan to collect data from the elderly, and the structural equation model was used to examine the data. The results indicated that attitude, subjective norm, perceived behavioral control, perceived risk, and trust are key determinants in the elderly's usage intentions. The results also indicated that perceived risk and trust integrated with the theory of planned behavior (TPB) model provides an improved method for predicting the elderly's intentions to use cloud-based health-care services. Finally, the implications of this study are discussed.

Keywords: Cloud-based healthcare services · Technology acceptance · Perceived risk · Trust

1 Introduction

Population aging is a pressing problem for many countries, especially for developing countries such as Taiwan. The proportion of the population aged 65 and over was 10.7 % in 2010 and 12 % in 2013, and it is estimated that the elderly population will double to 20 % in only 20 years [1, 2]. In Taiwan, nearly 90 % of people over 65 years of age have one chronic condition, and 50 % have three chronic diseases [3]. Chronic diseases, such as cancer, stroke, respiratory disease, diabetes, and heart diseases, are among the leading causes of death in the country. According to the statistics, nearly 35 % of the total health-care expenditure of the National Health Insurance (NHI) in Taiwan was utilized by elderly people aged 65 and over [4]. As the population ages, more of the elderly are expected to have a greater demand for medical services. To deliver a more comfortable and complete health-care service, cloud-based health services have been proposed to help diagnose, monitor, and provide services to deal with the chronic diseases faced by the elderly in recent years [5, 6].

© Springer International Publishing Switzerland 2016
J. Zhou and G. Salvendy (Eds.): ITAP 2016, Part I, LNCS 9754, pp. 186–195, 2016.
DOI: 10.1007/978-3-319-39943-0_18

Cloud-based healthcare services are capable of handling data in the form of text and images, thereby making it possible to maintain complete health databases. This allows health professionals to access health records and make clinical decisions; upload prescriptions; provide healthcare suggestions, including health education and self-health management; and even make emergency calls. Through cloud-based healthcare services, the elderly can obtain healthcare services anytime and anywhere, using mobile devices. These healthcare services have great potential in terms of enabling the elderly to live independently, as well as allowing for the early detection of symptoms and easy access to healthcare services. Hence, many healthcare organizations are looking closely at cloud-based applications for the delivery of healthcare services to the elderly. Despite this potential, there are gaps in our understanding of how the elderly decide to use such cloud-based healthcare services.

Health information technology (IT) use behavior differs in certain ways from typical user behavior with regard to general applications, including the following: (a) health care is not only a type of service but also a lifesaving mechanism, and (b) concerns exist regarding the reliability of the open Internet infrastructure that healthcare service providers employ to interface with users [7]. To elicit the trust of the elderly, cloud-based healthcare service providers must implement more than mere electronic linkages. These differences emphasize the uncertainty of the online environment, the importance of risk, and the significance of new health IT adoption. Thus, the existing variables of the technology acceptance model cannot fully reflect the users and their motives, and, consequently, a study of other intrinsic motivational factors is required. Prior studies have maintained that risk and trust are essential for understanding interpersonal behavior in the field of medical informatics [8, 9]. Based on social psychology theory and the healthcare literature, we have developed an extended version of the theory of planned behavior (TPB) [10] to predict the behavior of the elderly. From a practical standpoint, understanding why the elderly's intention to use the cloud based healthcare service can help government agencies and healthcare administrators to devise appropriate implementation strategies and cloud-based healthcare services to minimize the elderly's resistance to, and any adverse effects on, the healthcare management system.

2 Background

According to the 2014 Healthcare Information and Management Systems Society Analytics Cloud Survey, 92 % of health-care providers see the value of cloud-based services for their organizations now and in the future [11]. Thus, cloud-based healthcare services has been a critical research topic in the field of medical informatics. Previous studies have investigated the factors influencing IT acceptance by patients through the use of several information technologies, such as remote health monitoring [12], Telecare [13], and mobile health services [14, 15]. Compared with previous studies, we specifically highlight the factors driving the elderly's intention to use cloud-based healthcare services.

2.1 Cloud-Based Healthcare Services

Cloud-based healthcare services enable the elderly to access personalized and inter-active health services according to their mobility, portability, and ubiquity. Mobile devices typically include smartphones, personal digital assistants, tablets, notebooks, and health-monitoring devices. Most cloud-based healthcare services use mobile phone platforms. Cloud-based healthcare services have several functions: (a) they improve self-health management and disease diagnosis, treatment, and monitoring; (b) they offer preventive services in health promotion and treatment compliance; and (c) they enhance healthcare processes. For example, the elderly can upload their vital sign data to a cloud platform, via which health professionals can access health records in real time, thus providing a reliable basis for diagnosis. However, for these IT-enabled benefits to materialize, elderly people must first adopt the cloud-based healthcare service. A number of previous studies regarding the health IT adoption behaviors of elderly users developed elderly-specific characteristic constructs to better understand the unique features of the elderly [6, 14, 15]. However, studies that have examined the elderly's willingness to use cloud-based health services are rare.

2.2 Technology Acceptance Theories

Social psychological theories, such as the theory of reasoned action (TRA) [16] and the TPB [10] have been applied to the study of technology acceptance or adoption. TRA is a well-established intention-based theory, according to which behavioral intention is explained by people's attitudes toward that behavior and subjective norms. Although TRA has been evaluated and supported in numerous contexts, it is weak with regard to explaining the essence of behavior. Ajzen [10] found that attitude and sub-jective norm determine intention and further proposed that perceived behavioral control (PBC) reflects the degree to which a person feels that successfully engaging in a behavior is completely under his or her control. Behavioral intention (BI) measures the strength of the user's willingness to exert effort when performing certain behaviors. Attitude is the individual's general feeling about the desirability or undesirability of a particular behavior. Subjective norm (SN) refers to the individual's perception of important people's opinions about performing or not performing the behavior. PBC reflects a person's perception of the ease or difficulty of performing a specific activity. Ajzen [17] proposed that TPB eliminates TRA limitations on managing behavior over which people have incomplete volitional control. Prior studies have shown that the TPB model has good explanatory power for predicting the health IT acceptance of users [15, 18]. Therefore, this study applies the TPB model to explain the elderly's intention to use cloud-based health services.

2.3 Trust

Trust is one party's confident belief that the other party will behave in a dependable, ethical, and socially appropriate manner [19]. In the cloud-based healthcare context, the elderly are the trustors and the cloud services providers are the trustees because the elderly provide sensitive information, such as individual identifiers and health records, to the health professionals. The elderly have a limited ability to monitor or control the use of their personal information, which is why trust is required. Under these circumstances, the elderly's concerns about sufficient security for protecting individual data privacy are likely to slow the diffusion of such IT cloud-based healthcare services. Our literature review revealed that further research is necessary to clarify the role of trust perceptions in user acceptance of health IT [8, 9]. This study uses measures of trust to address the elderly's perceptions of the existence of favorable conditions that are conducive to the situational success of using cloud-based healthcare services.

2.4   Perceived Risk

Perceived risk is defined as the uncertainty that is experienced regarding the possible negative consequences of using a product or service [20]. When the level of uncertainty is more substantial, the level of perceived risk increases [21]. From the perspective of the elderly, there are several different kinds of perceived risk involved with the use of cloud-based healthcare services. These include performance, financial, privacy, and psychological risk. Performance risk is the probability of the health personnel harming a patient because of an incorrect decision based on inadequate information. Financial risk is the financial burden they place on the individual practices. Privacy risk for the elderly is the lack of control over personal information. Psychological risk is the potential that using the cloud-based healthcare services may cause psychological discomfort and tension because it could have a negative effect on the elderly's self-perception. Perceived risk has been used to aid in the understanding of users' adoption of, or resistance to, health IT [7]. Thus, perceived risk is an important factor that can potentially impact an elderly person's perception of cloud-based healthcare services. This study integrates perceived risk into the TPB model to gain a more comprehensive understanding of the behavioral intention of the elderly with regard to cloud-based healthcare services.

3   Research Model

Prior studies have argued that usage intentions are more appropriate than actual behavior because the former are measured contemporaneously with beliefs [22–24]. Certain studies have also chosen usage intention instead of actual usage as a dependent variable to investigate the health IT acceptance of users [25, 26]. Therefore, we considered the application of elderly people's intentions to use the cloud-based healthcare services as a dependent variable as adequate and desirable. Further, the cloud-based health services is a cloud platform for delivering health services, and activities are performed online and are processed virtually. Personal privacy data that hackers might steal are transmitted online. These concerns require a high level of trust and a low level of perceived risk before the elderly are willing to use the cloud-based healthcare services. The literature review indicated that numerous studies have provided empirical support indicating the significance of trust and perceived risk as a direct factor

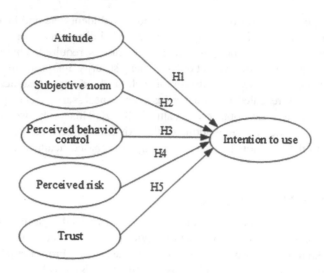

Fig. 1. Research framework

influencing the intentions of the user to engage in health activities [8, 9]. Thus, we extended the TPB model by adding trust and perceived risk construct to the research model. Figure 1 presents a pictorial depiction of the research model, which offers a description of the different dimensions and the development of theoretical arguments.

According to the TPB perspective, attitude, SN, and PBC are three direct antecedents for determining behavioral intention to use. We argue that, in the context of healthcare for Taiwanese senior citizens, there are three other potential linkages between attitude and behavioral intention, SN and behavioral intention, and PBC and behavior intention to use. Deng et al. [15] empirically used the TPB model to explain the behavioral intentions of older people toward mobile health services. Thus, we posit the following hypotheses:

H1. Attitude is positively related to the intention to use the cloud-based healthcare services.

H2. SN is positively related to the intention to use the cloud-based healthcare services.

H3. PBC is positively related to the intention to use the cloud-based healthcare services.

Trust is generally defined as one party's confidence. Trust has been identified as a predictor of usage intention [27]. Prior studies have provided empirical support indicating the importance of trust as a direct factor influencing an individual's intention to engage in healthcare activities [8, 9]. The elderly's use of healthcare services is subject to uncertainty and risk, which require improving the trust of cloud-based healthcare services. Consequently, this study proposes the following:

H4. Trust is positively related to the intention to use the cloud-based healthcare services.

Perceived risk increases the anticipation of negative outcomes, thereby leading to an unfavorable attitude that typically results in a negative effect on a user's intention to use [28, 29]. During the adoption process of cloud-based healthcare services, the elderly verify their perceptions of risks. If healthcare services are perceived to have a large risk, the elderly may resist using the cloud-based healthcare services. Thus, we propose the following hypothesis:

H5. Perceived risk is negatively related to the intention to use the cloud-based healthcare services.

4 Research Method

4.1 Questionnaire Development

The construct measures shown in Fig. 1 were all adopted from previous studies and were rated using a 5-point Likert scale; the anchors ranged from "strongly agree" to "strongly disagree." Although previous studies have validated the questionnaire items, we conducted pretests by requesting several healthcare professionals to evaluate each item. To ensure validity and reliability, we conducted a pilot test with a sample that was representative of the actual respondents. We conducted structural equation modeling using partial least squares (PLS) estimations for the data analysis, because the PLS method requires a minimal sample size and has few residual distribution requirements for model validation [30].

4.2 Sample and Data Collection

The target participants were the elderly in Taiwan. Ten community care centers were successfully contacted to secure their collaboration. A total of 250 questionnaires were distributed through an administrator of the community care center, and 185 questionnaires were returned. We assessed nonresponse bias by comparing early and late respondents (e.g., those who replied during the first three days and the last three days). We found no significant difference between the two respondent groups based on the sample attributes (e.g., gender and age).

5 Research Results

The resulting 178 valid questionnaires constituted a response rate of 70 %. The majority of the questionnaire respondents were females (57.87 %) between the ages of 65 and 74 years (58.99 %). We tested the reliability and validity of the proposed model. Reliability was assessed based on a construct reliability greater than 0.8 [31]. Convergent validity was assessed based on the following three criteria: (a) item loading greater than 0.7 and statistically significant, (b) composite construct reliability (CR) greater than 0.80, and (c) average variance extracted (AVE) greater than 0.5 [32]. The discriminant validity between the constructs was assessed based on the criterion that the square root of the AVE

Table 1. Reliability and validity of the scale

Construct	Item loading	CR	AVE	Correlation					
				AT	SN	PBC	PR	TR	US
AT	.81–.89	.91	.70	**.84**					
SN	.85–.88	.90	.74	.41	**.86**				
PBC	.84–.90	.91	.77	.57	.51	**.88**			
PR	.81–.91	.89	.73	-.38	-.31	-.44	**.85**		
TR	.79–.96	.86	.76	.11	.01	.08	-.02	**.87**	
US	.89–.94	.94	.85	.46	.54	.55	-.36	.13	**.92**

Note: Leading diagonal shows the square root of AVE of each construct

Attitude (AT), Subjective norm (SN), Perceived behavior control (PBC), Perceived risk (PR), Trust (TR), intention to use (IN)

for each construct should be greater than the corresponding correlations with all the other constructs [31]. In this study, the construct reliabilities are all greater than 0.85. For the convergent validity, the item loadings are all greater than 0.7, and the AVEs range from 0.70 to 0.85. For the discriminant validity, the square root of the AVE for a construct is greater than its corresponding correlations with the other constructs. Table 1 shows the descriptive statistics of the principal constructs and the correlation matrix, respectively. These results indicate acceptable reliability, convergent validity, and discriminant validity.

The testing results in the structural model are indicated in Fig. 2. In this empirical study, we analyzed the elderly's intention to use cloud-based healthcare services. The statistical testing conclusions support this research model. In this study, intention to use a cloud-based healthcare service was jointly predicted by attitude ($\beta = 0.14$,

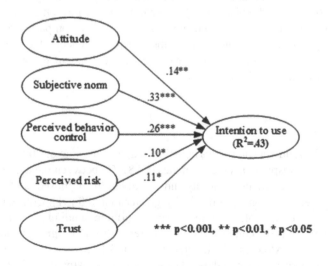

Fig. 2. Results of the structural model

standardized path coefficient, p < 0.01), SN (β = 0.33, p < 0.001), PBC (β = 0.26, p < 0.001), perceived risk (β = −0. 10, p < 0.05), and trust (β = 0.11, p < 0.05). Together, these variables explained 43 % of the variance of intention to use. As a result, hypotheses 1, 2, 3, 4, and 5 were all supported.

6 Discussion

The results indicate that attitude, SN, and PBC are key determinants in the elderly's usage intentions. These findings are consistent with the results obtained by Ryu et al. [25] and Deng et al. [15]. The effects of these usage intention variables were significant in explaining the elderly's usage behavior because they are consistent with Ajzen [17], who maintained that the relative importance of attitude, SN, and PBC in predicting usage intention varies across behaviors and situations. The results showed that of all the main determinants, SN had the strongest effect on behavioral intention. When an elderly person has a greater perception that most people who are important to them think that they should use a new technology, they are more likely to commit to this perceived pressure and are more willing to use a cloud-based healthcare service. PBC was the influential factor in usage intentions toward the cloud-based healthcare services. This result coincides with the findings of previous studies on technology adoption [7, 26] and suggests that the elderly are likely to engage in cloud-based healthcare services when they believe they have the ability to use the new technology. Attitude was an influential factor in the elderly's intention to use cloud-based healthcare services, although its effect was smaller than that of either SN or PBC. Trust was also found to have a significant positive effect on the intention to use cloud-based healthcare services. To increase the acceptance of cloud-based healthcare services, healthcare service providers need to develop strategies that improve the elderly's trust in the underlying technology. As hypothesized, perceived risk increases the anticipation of negative outcomes, thereby leading to an unfavorable attitude that typically results in a negative effect on the elderly's intention to use such a healthcare service.

In summary, the main contribution of this study is that it is the first to explore the elderly's usage behavior using existing social psychology theories. The TPB approach, which was adopted for the model, provides a more complete set of antecedents that better explain the intention to employ a specific technology (i.e., cloud-based healthcare services), thereby enhancing the practical contributions of this study. We extended the model by incorporating trust and perceived risk and examined its influence on the elderly's intentions to adopt a new health IT. All the main constructs, including the new constructs (i.e., trust and perceived risk), were found to have a significant effect on elderly people's intentions to use cloud-based healthcare services. The results indicate that the model provides a good understanding of the factors that influence the intention to use cloud-based healthcare services. We offer implications regarding medical practice and academic research that are based on our findings. We hope to encourage future researchers to (a) further examine the relative effectiveness of the existing, legally binding, and personal information protection act and to (b) improve the effectiveness of the information security mechanism in the healthcare context.

References

1. Council for Economic Planning and Development.: Health and Vital Statistics (1): General Health Statistics. Taiwan: Department of Health, Executive Yuan Republic of China (2015)
2. Ministry of Interior, Executive Yuan, Taiwan. General Population Profile of Taiwan (2012). http://www.moi.gov.tw
3. Chen, C.S., Peng, Y.I., Lee, P.C., Liu, T.C.: The effectiveness of preventive care at reducing curative care risk for the Taiwanese elderly under National Health Insurance. Health Policy **119**, 787–793 (2015)
4. National Health Insurance Administration.: National Health Insurance Research Database (2011). http://www.nhri.org.tw/nhird/. Accessed 08 Sept 2015
5. Chen, H., Cheng, B.C., Liao, G.T., Kuo, T.C.: Hybrid classification engine for cardiac arrhythmia cloud service in elderly healthcare management. J. Vis. Lang. Comput. **25**(6), 745–753 (2014)
6. Lai, J.Y., Wang, J.: Switching attitudes of Taiwanese middle-aged and elderly patients to-ward cloud healthcare services: an exploratory study. Technol. Forecast. Soc. Change **92**, 155–167 (2014)
7. Hsieh, P.J.: Physicians' acceptance of electronic medical records exchange: an extension of the decomposed TPB model with institutional trust and perceived risk. Int. J. Med. Inform. **84**(1), 1–14 (2015)
8. Tung, F.C., Chang, S.C., Chou, C.M.: An extension of trust and TAM model with IDT in the adoption of the electronic logistics information system in HIS in the medical industry. Int. J. Med. Inform. **77**(5), 324–335 (2008)
9. Egea, J.M.O., González, M.V.R.: Explaining physicians' acceptance of EHCR systems: an extension of TAM. Comput, Hum. Behav. **27**, 319–332 (2011)
10. Ajzen, I.: From intentions to actions: a theory of planned behaviour. In: Kuhl, J., Beckmann, J. (eds.) Action-Control: From Cognition to Behavior, pp. 11–39. Springer, Heidelberg (1985)
11. Health IT Industry Research.: 2014 HIMSS Analytics Cloud Survey (2014). http://www.himss.org/ResourceLibrary/genResourceDetailPDF.aspx?ItemNumber=41958
12. Huang, J.C.: Remote health monitoring adoption model based on artificial neural networks. Expert Syst. Appl. **37**, 307–314 (2010)
13. Huang, J.C., Lee, Y.C.: Model construction for the intention to use telecare in patients with chronic diseases. Int. J. Telemed Appl. **2013**, 1–6 (2013)
14. Sun, Y., Wang, N., Guo, X., Peng, Z.: Understanding the acceptance of mobile health services: a comparison and integration of alternative models. J. Electron. Commer. Res. **14**(2), 183–200 (2013)
15. Deng, Z., Mo, X., Liu, S.: Comparison of the middle-aged and older users' adoption of mobile health services in China. Int. J. Med. Inform. **83**(3), 210–224 (2014)
16. Fishbein, M., Ajzen, I.: Belief, Attitude, Intention, and Behavior: An Introduction to Theory and Research. Addison-Wesley, Reading (1975)
17. Ajzen, I.: The theory of planned behavior. Organ. Behav. Hum. Decis. Process. **50**(2), 179–211 (1991)
18. Holden, R.: Physicians' beliefs about using EMR and CPOE: in pursuit of a contextual-ized understanding of health IT use behavior. Int. J. Med. Inform. **79**(2), 71–80 (2010)
19. Hosmer, L.T.: Trust: the connecting link between organizational theory and philosophical ethic. Acad. Manag. **20**(2), 379–403 (1995)
20. Featherman, M.S., Pavlou, P.A.: Predicting e-services adoption: a perceived risk facets perspective. Int. J. Hum. Comput. Stud. **59**(4), 451–474 (2003)

21. Ayanso, A., Herath, T.C., O'Brien, N.: Understanding continuance intentions of physicians with electronic medical records (EMR): an expectancy-confirmation perspective. Decis. Support Syst. **77**, 112–122 (2015)
22. Agarwal, R., Prasad, J.: Are individual differences germane to the acceptance of new information technologies? Decis. Sci. **30**(2), 361–391 (1999)
23. Chang, M.K.: Predicting unethical behavior: a comparison of the theory of reasoned action and the theory of planned behavior. J. Bus. Ethics **17**(16), 1825–1834 (1998)
24. Chau, P.Y.K., Hu, P.J.H.: Investigating healthcare professionals' decisions to accept telemedicine technology: an empirical test of competing theories. Inform. Manag. **39**(4), 297–311 (2002)
25. Ryu, M.H., Kim, S., Lee, E.: Understanding the factors affecting online elderly user's participation in video UCC services. Comput. Hum. Behav. **25**(3), 619–632 (2009)
26. Hung, S.Y., Ku, Y.C., Chien, J.C.: Understanding physicians' acceptance of the medline system for practicing evidence-based medicine: a decomposed TPB model. Int. J. Med. Inform. **81**(2), 130–142 (2011)
27. Hampton-Sosa, W., Koufaris, M.: The effect of web site perceptions on initial trust in the owner company. Int. J. Electron. Commerce. **10**(1), 55–81 (2005)
28. Benlian, A., Hess, T.: Opportunities and risk of software-as-a-service: findings from a survey of IT executives. Decis. Support Syst. **52**(1), 232–246 (2011)
29. Polites, G.L., Karahanna, E.: Shackled to the status Quo: the inhibiting effects of incumbent system habit, switching costs, and inertia on new system acceptance. MIS Q. **36**(1), 21–42 (2012)
30. Chin, W.W., Marcolin, B.L., Newsted, P.R.: A partial least squares latent variable modeling approach for measuring interaction effects: results from a Monte Carlo simulation study and an electronic-mail emotion/adoption study. Inform. Syst. Res. **14**(2), 189–217 (2003)
31. Chin, W.W.: Issues and opinion on structural equation modelling. MIS Q. **22**(1), 7–16 (1998)
32. Fornel, C., Larcker, D.: Structural equation models with unobservable variables and measurement error: algebra and statistics. J. Mark. Res. **18**(3), 382–388 (1981)

Over 60 and ICT: Exploring Factors that Affect Older Adults' ICTs Usage

Qi Ma[1(✉)], Alan Hoi Shou Chan[1], Pei-Lee Teh[2],
and Shun-Nam Poon[1]

[1] Department of Systems Engineering and Engineering Management,
City University of Hong Kong, Kowloon Tong, Hong Kong
qima22-c@my.cityu.edu.hk
[2] School of Business, Monash University, Selangor Darul Ehsan, Malaysia
teh.pei.lee@monash.edu

Abstract. This study aimed to describe the use of information and communication technologies (ICTs) by Hong Kong older adults (over 60 years of age), and to explore the factors affecting their intention to use ICT innovations in future. A questionnaire survey was conducted with 109 older adults in Hong Kong. Exploratory factor analysis was used to extract important factors. Hierarchical regression was used to assess the associations between factors and intention to use ICT innovations in the future. The results showed that the older adults mainly used ICTs for entertainment and social communication. Education, perceived benefits, and security and privacy were applications and issues that were significantly and positively associated with the intention that older adult had towards use of ICT innovations in the future.

Keywords: Older adults · ICT · Usage · Factors

1 Introduction

The Population Division of United Nations recently reported that in 2015 there were 901 million people in the world above 60 years of age. This number is projected to grow to 1.4 billion by 2030, and to 2.1 billion by 2050 [1]. The rapid growth of the aging population is a global phenomenon: virtually every country in the world will experience a substantial increase in the size of the population aged 60 years or over between 2015 and 2030. The growth of the older population is expected to be especially rapid in Asia, with increases of more than 60 % between 2015 and 2030 [1]. In Hong Kong, population ageing is expected to be very marked with the proportion of elderly aged 65 and over projected to increase from 15 % in 2014 to 23 % in 2024 and 30 % in 2034, and further rise to 36 % in 2064 [2]. Globally, 40 % of older persons aged 60 years or over live independently i.e. alone or with only their spouse. As countries develop and their populations continue to age, living alone or with a spouse only will become more common among older people in the future [3]. However, older people may face various difficulties when trying to live independently and safely as a result of age-related decline in physiological and psychological functions that affect physical, sensory and cognitive abilities [4]. The United Nations ageing report [1]

© Springer International Publishing Switzerland 2016
J. Zhou and G. Salvendy (Eds.): ITAP 2016, Part I, LNCS 9754, pp. 196–208, 2016.
DOI: 10.1007/978-3-319-39943-0_19

addressed the importance of improving access for older people to public services in both urban and rural settings, including ensuring that infrastructure and services are accessible to persons with limited mobility, vision, hearing or other impairments which tend to increase with age. The proliferation of technologies, such as mobile devices, offer a variety of new channels to reach older people, for example, by delivering messages related to health, security or environmental hazards via SMS (Short Messaging Service). The digital divide is the gulf between those who have ready access to information and communication technologies (ICT) and those who do not. It is vital to bridge the digital divide for older people by addressing differences in educational background and ICT skills through technology training courses, programmes and learning hubs tailored to their needs [1].

Fortunately, with the rise of the silver market, there are various innovative products and services to help to support older people to live conveniently and independently and to enable them to lead healthy and active lives. There are products such as tailored mobile phones and apps for older adults. However, previous research shows that relative to younger people, older people lag behind in adoption of technology due to factors such as perceived usefulness and ease of use of technology, age-related characteristics in health and cognitive ability, and difficulties in finding technical support to solve interface operation problems [5]. In the case of information and communication technologies such as computers and the Internet, there are many human computer interaction factors that influence decisions for older adults to adopt such technologies [6]. The problem of adoption by older people is exacerbated by the fast rate of introduction of technological innovations such as, the multi-touch user interface used in iPhones and other devices, or most recently, motion-activated user interfaces. These innovations obviously changed the way people interact with technology and have improved the quality of life and work efficiency, for example, simple hand motions on touch panels are easier and quicker than a traditional mouse which need accurate moves and clicks. However, it is not necessarily the case that older people will be ready to learn or to be able to use and adopt innovations with ease. Various age-related factors which are regarded as essential determinants in the process of design and operation should be taken into consideration when trying to enhance the penetration of information and communication technologies among older adults. When studying the acceptance of information and communication technology, the factors related to human-computer interaction are suggested to include perceived usefulness, perceived ease of use, Internet dependence, self-efficacy towards technologies, technology anxiety or technophobia, intrinsic motivations, information reliability and some others [2, 3].

Older adults, especially 'younger' seniors, may now understand the necessity of using ICT products and services in their life [7], and that they are now expected to use some common ICT products and services such as computer, smartphone, and the internet more frequently than before in order to manage daily activities. Thus, it is timely and important to explore what needs to be done now to ensure effective implementation and adoption of ICTs among older adults in the future. The success of innovative technologies and services for older people is based on a comprehensive understanding of their current usage and future needs.

Research around ICT acceptance and usage among older adults is currently receiving an increasing amount of attention, not only in the developed countries but also in developing countries. A variety of factors have been explored by earlier researchers in different contexts. In a review study by some of the current authors [6], these factors were qualitatively categorized into: Perceived usefulness (perceived impact on life, needs satisfaction, perceived convenience and perceived benefits and usefulness); Subjective norms (children/family influence, caregiver influence, social influence); Perceived behavior control (self-efficacy, anxiety, facilitating condition, support availability); Perceived usability (perceived ease of use, age-centered interface, system reliability); Affections, and Socio-demographic mediators (gender, age, education, income, health and past experience). However, the classification and definition of factors were based on qualitative analysis rather than on empirical studies. When considering geographical factors and technological domains, all the potential factors need to be further validated for their effects on the usage of ICTs for older adults in Hong Kong.

The aim of this study was to understand the usage and adoption of ICT products and services by older adults in Hong Kong. This study also explored human computer interaction (HCI) related factors that influence the intentions of older adults to use ICT innovations in the future.

2   Methodology

This cross-sectional study of Hong Kong adults over 60 years of age was conducted through a questionnaire survey, consisting of three major parts: (1) demographic characteristics; (2) usage behavior concerning ICT products and activities; (3) attitudes and perceptions towards ICT. The language of the questionnaire was traditional Chinese. Considering education background variety, the questionnaire was administered through face-to-face interview instead of being self-administered. The interviewer presented the questions and repeated the responses back to the interviewees to confirm that their answers were accurately documented.

2.1   Participants

A total of 109 Hong Kong Chinese adults aged over 60 (47 males and 62 females) from six local elderly service centers participated this study. Background information including gender, age, education, marital status, living arrangement, work status, year income, and means of living was collected.

2.2   Measurements of Usage Behavior: Products and Activities

Based on our previous study [6], a total of three categories of ICT products, services and systems were included in the questionnaire, namely (1) Internet explorer; (2) Phones (telephone/feature phone/smart phone/geriatric cellular phone); (3) Computers (desktop/laptop/tablet). The measurement scale for usage experience towards the three categories of IT products was from one to three (1 = have never heard of the technology or services, 2 = have heard of but not used, 3 = have been using or used) [8]. Six categories containing a total of 21 items of activities using ICT products were listed in this section accordance with the previous review [6]. The six categories were (1) Remote monitoring; (2) E-Health care activities; (3) Social communication; (4) Online services; (5) Entertainment; (6) Daily routine activities. A four-point scale was used to measure usage frequency (4 = Frequent, 3 = Often, 2 = Rare, 1 = Never).

2.3   Acceptance Constructs

The acceptance constructs used in the questionnaire were selected by three experts in this field based on the available sources of previous studies. First, measurement constructs in previous studies which were focused on the adoption of the Internet, computers, mobile phones and related activities by older adults were included; second, constructs related to human-computer interaction (HCI) were included, such as perceived usefulness, perceived ease of use, Internet dependence, self-efficacy towards technologies, technology anxiety or technophobia, intrinsic motivations, and information reliability; then, in order to maintain a higher reliability and validity, the constructs with relatively lower factor loadings (< 0.7) in previous studies were dropped; as a result, 24 acceptance items were retained in the questionnaire (Table 1).

Table 1. Potential acceptance constructs and sources

No.	Potential constructs	Sources
1	Perceived impact on life	[9]
2	Perceived usefulness	[7, 10] [11–13]
3	Needs satisfaction	[14, 15]
4	Perceived benefits	[16]
5	Perceived convenience	[16]
6	Children's/families' influence	[17, 18]
7	Social influence	[18–21]
8	Subjective norm	[7, 11]
9	Self-efficacy	[22, 23]
10	Facilitating condition	[22–24]
11	Anxiety	[9, 22, 25]
12	Support availability	[14, 26]
13	Perceived ease of use	[7, 11, 27]
14	Age-centered interface	[21, 28, 29]
15	Relevance of living style	[15, 17]
16	Technology compatibility	[21]
17	Cost & Economics compatibility	[30, 31]
18	Perceived usability	[14]

(*Continued*)

Table 1. (*Continued*)

No.	Potential constructs	Sources
19	System reliability	[9, 16]
20	Quality of visual presentation	[32]
21	Data protection	[10]
22	Personal privacy	[33]
23	Security and safety	[10]
24	Uncertainty risk	[9, 16, 20]

2.4 Method of Analysis

An exploratory factor analysis (EFA) was conducted to extract the most relevant affecting factors based on the 24 potential acceptance constructs. One of the greatest advantages of EFA is that all the factors extracted through this method are not assumed ahead by the authors. Hierarchical regression analysis was performed to examine the relationships between the independent factors extracted through EFA and the intentions that older adults had towards further usage of IT products. The hierarchical regression method allows researchers to diagnose and control confounding variables which may also influence the dependent factors in the first stage model, such as the demographic characteristics of the older adults.

3 Results

3.1 Demographics

The majority of older adults in the sample were aged 70–74 (54.1 %), with primary education (47.7 %) and secondary education (41.3 %), married (96.3 %), living with household member (64.2 %), retired (61.5 %), living with support of relatives (59.6 %) and with annual income less than $30,000 HKD (93.6 %). Detailed characteristics of the sample are shown in Table 2.

3.2 Usage Behavior: Products and Services

Usage experience towards ICT products was measured by asking the older adults whether they had heard of or personally used the products. The results are shown in Table 3. 100 % of them have been using or had used a phone (smart and non-smart phone, telephone), especially, 42 out of 109 older adults have been using or had used a smartphone. Also, every older adult participating in this survey had heard about computers. However, only 38.5 % of them have been using or had used computers. Regarding Internet explorer, 13.9 % had never heard about it, and 32.9 % have been using or had used it. The usage rates for the Internet and computers were quite similar.

3.3   Usage Behavior: Activities

Experiences of activities were measured by asking the usage frequency for different activities involving the use of ICT products, services and systems over the last 12 months. The results are shown in Table 4. In total, six categories of ICT related activities were summarized as follows; remote monitoring, health care, social communication, online services, entertainment, and routine activities. As shown in Fig. 1, among the six categories, more than half of the older adults had never used ICTs for health care (67.27 %), remote monitoring (81.33 %) or online services (85.55 %). Correspondingly, they often use ICTs for entertainment (23.57 %), social communication (15.54 %), and for routine activities (14.40 %) such as, for example, calendar and alarm clock.

Table 2. Demographic profile (N = 109)

	Frequency	Percentage (%)
Gender		
Male	47.0	43.1
Female	62.0	56.9
Age		
60–64	8.0	7.3
65–69	36.0	33.0
70–74	59.0	54.1
Over 75	6.0	5.5
Education		
Pre-primary	12.0	11.0
Primary	52.0	47.7
Secondary	45.0	41.3
Post-Secondary	0.0	0.0
Marital status		
Married	105.0	96.3
Divorced/Separated	2.0	1.8
Widowed	2.0	1.8
Living arrangement		
With household member	70.0	64.2
Living alone	24.0	22.0
In nursing home	15.0	13.8
Work status		
Full-time work	10.0	9.2
Part-time work	32.0	29.4
Retired	67.0	61.5
Never worked	0.0	0.0
Year income (HKD)		

(*Continued*)

Table 2. (*Continued*)

	Frequency	Percentage (%)
<$30,000	102.0	93.6
$30,000–$49,999	1.0	0.9
$50,000–$74,999	3.0	2.8
>$75,000	3.0	2.8
Primary means of living		
Salary	1.0	0.9
Retirement wages	2.0	1.8
Relatives support	41.0	59.6
Community subsidy	65.0	37.6

Table 3. IT products

	Never heard of (%)	Heard of but never used (%)	Have been using or used (%)
1. Internet Explorer	13.9	53.2	32.9
2. Phones	0.0	0.0	100.0
3. Computers	0.0	61.5	38.5

Table 4. Activities of using ICT over 12 months

Category	Never (%)	Rare (%)	Often (%)	Frequent (%)
1. Remote monitoring	81.33	15.57	2.73	0.30
2. Health care	67.27	18.97	13.77	0.00
3. Social communication	53.02	26.04	15.54	5.32
4. Online services	85.55	12.15	2.08	0.23
5. Entertainment	32.73	37.60	23.57	6.13
6. Routine activities	48.03	35.17	14.40	2.43

3.4   Factor Analysis

Principal factor analysis was used as the extraction method in this study. Kaiser-Meyer-Olkin measure of sampling adequacy was 0.619 ($p < 0.001$) which indicated that factor analysis was an appropriate method here. All constructs were rotated using Varimax with Kaiser Normalization, and the constructs with factor loading over 0.5 were supposed to belong to a certain factor [34].

As shown in Table 5, 17 out of 24 potential constructs were retained (factor loading > 0.5).

Based on the descriptions of those retained constructs, they were classified into 5 factors. According to retained constructs 13, 14, 18, and 20, the first factor was taken to reflect the ease of physical and cognitive use of technology, thus it was named

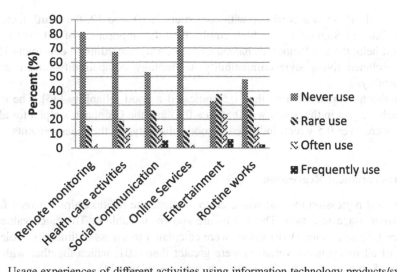

Fig. 1. Usage experiences of different activities using information technology products/systems

Table 5. Principal factor analysis results: factor loading and reliability (N = 109)

No. of constructs	Factor name	Cronbach's alpha	Factor 1	Factor 2	Factor 3	Factor 4	Factor 5
13	Perceived	.511	**.611**	−.022	.322	−.095	.051
14	Affordances		**.682**	.150	.130	.276	.083
18			**.527**	.173	−.093	−.036	.119
20			**.591**	−.065	.064	.254	.385
2	Perceived	.558	.075	**.799**	.077	−.026	−.023
4	Benefits		.038	**.744**	.058	.112	-.063
5			.077	**.591**	.048	.202	.298
19	Security and	.541	.212	−.067	**.498**	.251	−.201
22	Privacy		−.115	−.220	**.609**	.357	.182
23			.006	−.054	**.633**	.078	.175
24			−.018	.305	**.513**	−.209	−.027
7	External Support	.506	−.262	.070	−.049	**.602**	.069
10			−.077	.186	.018	**.540**	.179
12			.169	.117	.108	**.630**	.097
15	Compatibility	.512	−.038	.164	.040	.077	**.568**
16			.051	−.154	.089	.062	**.555**
17			.147	.048	−.049	.084	**.614**

Perceived Affordances (PA); the second factor was named Perceived Benefits (PB) in accordance with constructs 2, 4, and 5, which reflected perceived usefulness and outcome expectancy for ICTs; the third factor was named Security and Privacy (SP) because constructs 19 and 22−24 were focused on the protection of personal security and safety; in accordance with constructs 7, 10, and 12, the fourth factor was named External Support (ES) which emphasized the importance of external facilitations and help; the last factor was named Compatibility according to constructs 15−17, which included living style compatibility, technology compatibility, and economic compatibility.

Cronbach's alpha of more than 0.5 indicated a good reliability [35]. The overall Cronbach's alpha in this study was 0.562 (> 0.5) and the Cronbach's alpha for all five factors were over 0.5 which indicated a good reliability for the measurements.

3.5   Hierarchical Regression

Hierarchical regression method was used to evaluate the relationships between factors and further usage intention. The results are shown in Table 6. Tolerance values and variance inflation factor (VIF) values were calculated to assess collinearity. Tolerance values of all independent variables were greater than 0.01, which together with VIFs less than 5, indicated that collinearity was not a problem [34].

Table 6. Hierarchical regression results for usage intention (N = 109)

Model		Model summary	Standardized coefficients	t	Sig.	Collinearity statistics	
						Tolerance	VIF
1	(Constant)	Adjusted R square = 0.043 R square change = 0.052*		17.638	.000		
	education		.228*	2.420	.017	1.000	1.000
2	(Constant)	Adjusted R square = 0.674 R square change = 0.641***		1.836	.069		
	education		.027	.465	.643	.868	1.152
	PA		−.081	−1.330	.187	.818	1.222
	PB		.119*	2.105	.038	.940	1.064
	SP		.823***	14.117	.000	.888	1.127
	ES		−.085	−1.429	.156	.850	1.177
	PC		.028	.478	.634	.899	1.112

*$p < 0.05$; **$p < 0.01$; ***$p < 0.001$

As suggested by prior studies, demographics should be considered when the relationships between acceptance factors and usage intention are evaluated. Demographic variables such as age [36, 37], education [22], health status [23, 28] were entered in the first stage regression model. However, only education was significantly associated with usage intention and was therefore was retained in the first stage model. The result indicated that older adults with higher education levels were more likely to use ICT innovations.

In the second stage model (model 2), education level was controlled and the five extracted factors were entered. The explanation power of the regression model was obviously much enhanced (R2 = 0.674). Among the factors, perceived benefits and security and privacy were significantly associated with usage intention and had standardized coefficients equal to 0.119 (p < 0.05) and 0.823 (p < 0.001) respectively. This result suggested that older adults with higher score on perceived benefits and stronger trust on security and privacy towards ICTs will be more willing to further adopt ICT innovations.

4 Discussions

4.1 Usage Behaviors

In the present study, it was found that ICTs were mainly used by older adults for communication, entertainment, and some routine activities. The most commonly used product was the phone, including smart and non-smartphone, and telephone. However, for computers and the Internet, more than half of the older adults indicated that they had heard of but never used these technologies. For older adults particularly, computers are more complex than mobile phones both physically and cognitively. Also, older adults may not intend to use internet explorer because it always requires typing which is difficult for them.

The results also showed that older adults rarely used ICTs to do remote monitoring, healthcare, or online services activities. Older adults are not familiar with these relatively complex or innovative activities using ICTs. Social communication and entertainment are the two most frequent activities that older adults in Hong Kong use ICTs for. The findings here are consistent with Mitzner et al. [16] who found that older adults mainly use technology for the basic purposes of communication and entertainment. It seems that adoption of technology may be affected by the level of technological innovativeness and complexity.

4.2 Perceived Benefits

This study validated the idea that perceived benefits positively affect the intention of older adults to make further use of ICT innovations. It has been found that most older adults acknowledged the positive impact of ICTs on their quality of life, and the benefits that ICTs could provide [9]. Older adults have also been found to recognize the benefits of technological devices as well as the importance and usefulness of these for everyday life [38]. Perceived usefulness has also been found to be a significant predictor of Internet use intention [11]. Positive attitudes were most frequently related to how the technology supported activities, enhanced convenience, and contained useful features. Consistent with prior studies, older people in this study incorporated ICT in their daily lives according to its usefulness, they use technology with specific aims in mind for each device but it has been shown that they do not make extensive use of these tools [26].

4.3 Security and Privacy

This study also validated the significant effects of perceived security and privacy on use of ICTs by older adults. It is necessary to consider the concerns of older adults towards the security and privacy aspect of ICTs because it plays an important role in the acceptance and usage of technologies [39]. Older adults have the idea that the aggregation of all the personal data collected by ICT devices and systems may challenge personal information safety, especially when concerning health-related data. Privacy may be considered to be composed of the right to seclusion, autonomy, control of property (including personal data), spatial boundaries, and the ability to see, verify, and correct personal data. It seems that concerns over privacy are contextual, individualized, and influenced by the psychosocial motivations of later life [10]. Older adults generally lack practical and relevant knowledge concerning online privacy and data protection.

5 Conclusions

This study investigated the use of ICT products, services, and systems by older adults in Hong Kong. It also explored and validated two HCI related factors that may affect intention of older adults to further adopt and use ICT. This study collected data from 109 adults over 60 years of age in Hong Kong using a survey questionnaire administered through face-to-face interviews.

It was found that older adults in Hong Kong mainly used ICTs for communication and entertainment. It was also found that education, perceived benefits, and security and privacy were significant factors influencing the intention older people had towards making use of ICT innovations in the future. Older adults with higher education were found to be more likely to adopt ICT innovation in the future. Consistent with the findings of previous studies, older adults in this study were very interested in the benefits that they can gain through the use of ICT products and services. They also reported anxiety about individual privacy protection when using ICT products and services. Previous studies have suggested that attending training programmes can help elderly people to build confidence in using technology, thereby gaining positive attitudes toward and increasing their intention to use ICT [40]. It is important to eliminate the anxiety that older adults feel towards ICTs and to enhance their knowledge about the benefits of ICTs.

References

1. United Nations, Department of Economic and Social Affairs, Population Division. World population ageing 2015 highlights. United Nations, New York (2015)
2. Census and Statistics Department, Hong Kong Special Administrative Region Hong kong population projections for 2015 to 2064. Hong Kong Monthly Digest of Statistics, October 2015

3. United Nations, European Aviation Safety Agency, Population Division. World population ageing, New York (2013)
4. Wellner, K.: The silver market phenomenon. In: User innovators in the silver market, pp 9–25. Springer, Heidelberg (2015)
5. Chen, K., Chan, A.H.-S.: Use or non-use of gerontechnology—a qualitative study. Int. J. Environ. Res. Public Health 10, 4645–4666 (2013)
6. Ma, Q., Chen, K., Chan, A.H.S., Teh, P.-L.: Acceptance of ICTs by older adults: a review of recent studies. In: Zhou, J., Salvendy, G. (eds.) ITAP 2015. LNCS, vol. 9193, pp. 239–249. Springer, Heidelberg (2015)
7. Hong, S.-J., Lui, C.S.M., Hahn, J., Moon, J.Y., Kim, T.G.: How old are you really? cognitive age in technology acceptance. Decis. Support Syst. 56, 122–130 (2013)
8. Chen, K., Chan, A.H.S.: Predictors of gerontechnology acceptance by older Hong Kong Chinese. Technovation 34, 126–135 (2014)
9. Steele, R., Lo, A., Secombe, C., Wong, Y.K.: Elderly persons' perception and acceptance of using wireless sensor networks to assist healthcare. Int. J. Med. Inform. 78, 788–801 (2009)
10. Lorenzen-Huber, L., Boutain, M., Camp, L.J., Shankar, K., Connelly, K.H.: Privacy, technology, and aging: a proposed framework. Ageing Int. 36, 232–252 (2010)
11. Pan, S., Jordan-Marsh, M.: Internet use intention and adoption among chinese older adults: from the expanded technology acceptance model perspective. Comput. Hum. Behav. 26, 1111–1119 (2010)
12. Nayak, L.U.S., Priest, L., White, A.P.: An application of the technology acceptance model to the level of internet usage by older adults. Univ. Access Inf. Soc. 9, 367–374 (2010)
13. Sharit, J., Czaja, S.J., Perdomo, D., Lee, C.C.: A cost-benefit analysis methodology for assessing product adoption by older user populations. Appl. Ergon. 35, 81–92 (2004)
14. Wang, L., Rau, P.-L.P., Salvendy, G.: Older adults' acceptance of information technology. Educ. Gerontol. 37, 1081–1099 (2011)
15. Courtney, K.L., Demiris, G., Rantz, M., Skubic, M.: Needing smart home technologies: the perspectives of older adults in continuing care retirement communities. Inf. Prim. Care 16, 195–201 (2008)
16. Mitzner, T.L., Boron, J.B., Fausset, C.B., Adams, A.E., Charness, N., Czaja, S.J., Dijkstra, K., Fisk, A.D., Rogers, W.A., Sharit, J.: Older adults talk technology: technology usage and attitudes. Comput. Hum. Behav. 26, 1710–1721 (2010)
17. Fausset, C.B., Harley, L., Farmer, S., Fain, B.: Older adults' perceptions and use of technology: a novel approach. In: Stephanidis, C., Antona, M. (eds.) UAHCI 2013, Part II. LNCS, vol. 8010, pp. 51–58. Springer, Heidelberg (2013)
18. Giger, J.T., Pope, N.D., Vogt, H.B., Gutierrez, C., Newland, L.A., Lemke, J., Lawler, M.J.: Remote patient monitoring acceptance trends among older adults residing in a frontier state. Comput. Hum. Behav. 44, 174–182 (2015)
19. Mahmood, A., Yamamoto, T., Lee, M., Steggell, C.: Perceptions and use of gerotechnology: implications for aging in place. J. Hous. Elderly 22, 104–126 (2008)
20. Lian, J.-W., Yen, D.C.: Online shopping drivers and barriers for older adults: age and gender differences. Comput. Hum. Behav. 37, 133–143 (2014)
21. Lam, J.C., Lee, M.K.: Digital inclusiveness–longitudinal study of internet adoption by older adults. J. Manag. Inf. Syst. 22, 177–206 (2006)
22. Chen, K., Chan, A.H.S.: Gerontechnology acceptance by elderly Hong Kong Chinese: a senior technology acceptance model (STAM). Ergonomics 57, 635–652 (2014)
23. Heart, T., Kalderon, E.: Older adults: are they ready to adopt health-related ICT? Int. J. Med. Inform. 82, e209–e231 (2013)
24. Nägle, S., Schmidt, L.: Computer acceptance of older adults. Work: J. Prev. Assess. Rehabil. 41, 3541 (2012)

25. Guo, X., Sun, Y., Wang, N., Peng, Z., Yan, Z.: The dark side of elderly acceptance of preventive mobile health services in China. Electron. Markets **23**, 49–61 (2013)
26. Hernández-Encuentra, E., Pousada, M., Gómez-Zúñiga, B.: ICT and older people: Beyond usability. Educ. Gerontol. **35**, 226–245 (2009)
27. Guo, X., Sun, Y., Wang, N., Peng, Z., Yan, Z.: The dark side of elderly acceptance of preventive mobile health services in China. Electron. Markets **23**, 49–61 (2012)
28. Sayago, S., Blat, J.: Telling the story of older people e-mailing: an ethnographical study. Int. J. Hum Comput Stud. **68**, 105–120 (2010)
29. Demiris, G., Thompson, H., Boquet, J., Le, T., Chaudhuri, S., Chung, J.: Older adults' acceptance of a community-based telehealth wellness system. Inform. Health Soc. Care **38**, 27–36 (2013)
30. Olsson, A., Skovdahl, K., Engström, M.: Using diffusion of innovation theory to describe perceptions of a passive positioning alarm among persons with mild dementia: a repeated interview study. BMC Geriatr. **16**, 1–6 (2016)
31. Ma, Q., Chan, A.H., Chen, K.: Personal and other factors affecting acceptance of smartphone technology by older chinese adults. Appl. Ergon. **54**, 62–71 (2016)
32. Olivier, B., Vilcocq-Merjagnan, C.: Online administration of a quantified self-questionnaire for elderly people: a user satisfaction survey. J. Am. Geriatr. Soc. **63**, 194–195 (2015)
33. Marchibroda, J.M.: New technologies hold great promise for allowing older adults to age in place. Generations **39**, 52–55 (2015)
34. Hair, J.F., Black, W.C., Babin, B.J., Anderson, R.E., Tatham, R.L.: Multivariate Data Analysis, vol. 6. Pearson Prentice Hall, Upper Saddle River (2006)
35. Cronbach, L.J.: Coefficient alpha and the internal structure of tests. Psychometrika **16**, 297–334 (1951)
36. Niehaves, B., Plattfaut, R.: Internet adoption by the elderly: employing is technology acceptance theories for understanding the age-related digital divide. Eur. J. Inf. Syst. **23**, 708–726 (2014)
37. Himmel, S., Ziefle, M., Arning, K.: From living space to urban quarter: acceptance of ICT monitoring solutions in an ageing society. In: Kurosu, M. (ed.) HCII/HCI 2013, Part III. LNCS, vol. 8006, pp. 49–58. Springer, Heidelberg (2013)
38. Raymundo, T.M., da Silva Santana, C.: Factors influencing the acceptance of technology by older people: how the elderly in Brazil feel about using electronics. IEEE Consum. Electron. Mag. **3**, 63–68 (2014)
39. Wilkowska, W., Ziefle, M.: Perception of privacy and security for acceptance of e-health technologies: exploratory analysis for diverse user groups. pp. 593–600 (2011)
40. Scott, J.E., Walczak, S.: Cognitive engagement with a multimedia ERP training tool: assessing computer self-efficacy and technology acceptance. Inf. Manag. **46**, 221–232 (2009)

The Role of Technology Self-efficiency on Technology Product Acceptance and Usage: A Study on Chinese Older People

Jing Pan[1], Hua Dong[2(✉)], and Weining Ning[2]

[1] College of Architecture and Urban Planning,
Tongji University, Shanghai, China
2901candy@tongji.edu.cn
[2] College of Design and Innovation, Tongji University, Shanghai, China
{donghua,123ning}@tongji.edu.cn

Abstract. Aging is one of the most significant population trends in the world while technology is developing at an unprecedented rate. Technology products inevitably enter people's life, but many older people experience difficulty, frustration, or exclusion when using them. Therefore, the acceptance and usage of technology products among older people is relatively low. This study focuses specially on Chinese older people (aged between 50 and 70), using mobile phone as the research tool, to investigate whether self-efficacy would affect one's desirability and ability of using technology products.

Keywords: Technology · Self-efficacy · Acceptance · Older people

1 Introduction

Nowadays, technology products can be found in all the domains of our life (Wang and Liu 2014). Many research have proved that technology products can improve older people's life quality. They benefit older people in different aspects such as social integration and adaption, searching for information, everyday tasks, and entertainment, keeping active mind (Malla 2014).

However, numerous studies suggest that older people experience difficulty, frustration, or exclusion when using technology products. (Burnett 2009; Demiris 2004). Thus, many older people prefer to be left behind instead of learning the foreign technology that they have never encountered before. (Mieczakowski and Clarkson 2013; Kang 2009).

Self-efficacy is raised and applied in psychological domain initially. It describes individual's perception of his or her capabilities to perform and complete a task (Bandura 1997). A person who has high self-efficiency degree could be more active and confident in handling different issues. So we raise the general hypothesis that high technology self-efficacy would affect one's desirability of using technology products positively.

Also, some researchers have explored the relation between self-efficacy and task performance (Combe et al. 2013; Wolters et al. 2010) but report different results.

© Springer International Publishing Switzerland 2016
J. Zhou and G. Salvendy (Eds.): ITAP 2016, Part I, LNCS 9754, pp. 209–215, 2016.
DOI: 10.1007/978-3-319-39943-0_20

Specifically, this study aimed to explore the role of self-efficacy on the acceptance and usage of technology products among Chinese older people.

The "older people" in this study were set from age 50 to 70. Usually, we define people over 60 years old as the older people while 60 is the age that people are going to retired in China. We included people between 50–60, whom we define as the 'young-old', for the consideration that this group of people are experiencing the evolvement of Internet and have been involved in different technologies to some degree, which may gives us some predictive inspiration in future design and research work. We excluded people over 70 in this study, because they are more likely to be failed in the task performance due to their physical and cognitive competence decline in aging process.

The "acceptance" is evaluated by "the frequency of technology usage" and "usage" is evaluated by "task performance".

2   Methods

This study is part of a multiple capability-related data survey conducted by the Inclusive Design Research Group at Tongji University. Seven interviewers are recruited into this survey. They have received unified training and are familiar with the process of testing. Face-to-face questionnaire and performance test are applied in this study.

2.1   Participants

There are 130 respondents aged 50–70 (mean = 57.4, male = 60, female = 70) who were recruited from seven cities in China (Fuzhou, Shanghai, Nanjing, Yulin, Lanzhou and Fuzhou). 127 respondents (Table 1) had mobile phone and completed the whole test. Most of them have an education level above high school.

Table 1. Basic information of the respondents

Age	50-59	60-69	All
Gender			
Male	31	28	59
Female	47	21	68
Education			
Primary school or below	0	4	4
Middle school	10	20	30
High school	40	8	48
Secondary technique school	6	9	15
Junior college	12	4	16
Bachelor degree or above	10	4	14

2.2   Technical Self-Confidence

Self-efficacy does not refer to people's general beliefs in themselves, such as self-esteem does. It refers to people's beliefs about their abilities in more specific realms. Therefore, in this study, Technical Self-Confidence Scale invented by Combe et al. was adopted instead of Ralf Schwarzer's General Self-Efficacy Scale (GSES). This scale is based on the Subjective Technical Competence (STC) scale used by Arning and Ziefle (2007) and the Affinity to Technology Scale used by Wolters et al. (2010). It consists of ten statements: seven positive ones and three negative ones. It is used in the research of designing technology for older people, which fits this study quite well. This scale has been carefully translated to fit the Chinese background.

The respondents rated the statements from 1 to 5 as to whether they totally disagree (1) or totally agree (5). The higher the total score is, the higher the technology self-efficacy the respondent has.

2.3   Frequency of Technology Usage

Mobile phone, computer and Internet have been widely used in China today. The "the frequency of technology usage" is evaluated by the summing up the frequency of using all these three. The respondents rated the frequency with number 1 to 4:

1 = Never
2 = Occasionally
3 = Everyday within 4 h
4 = Everyday more than 4 h

2.4   Performance Test

GALAXY Trend 3 was used as a unified tool in the performance test. The product interaction tasks consisted of making a phone call, texting and sending a message, taking a photo and sending photo through social network app (Wechat). The testing results are coded as '0' or '1' depending on whether the tasks were successfully completed. Overall performance is calculated base on the scores respondents got in all these four tasks.

3   Results and Analysis

3.1   Technical Self-confidence

The results show that the average score of all the respondents is 28 (Min = 10, Max = 48, SD = 7.932). The technology self-confidence of male (M = 29) is a little higher than that of female (M = 26).

Technology self-efficacy is most significant correlated with education (correlation coefficient = 0.282, p < 0.01).

Older people with higher education level have higher technology self-efficacy but people at different age within 50–70 do not show much difference in technology self-efficacy (Table 2).

Table 2. Correlation coefficient between technology self-efficacy and demographic variables

	Gender	Age	Education
Correlation coefficient	−.175*	−.118	.282**
p	.046	.181	.001

*. Correlation is significant at the 0.05 level (2-tailed).
**. Correlation is significant at the 0.01 level (2-tailed).

3.2 Frequency of Technology Usage

The average score of frequency of technology usage is 8.65 (SD = 2.562). Female respondents (Mean = 8.76) use technology a little more frequently than male respondents (Mean = 8.52).

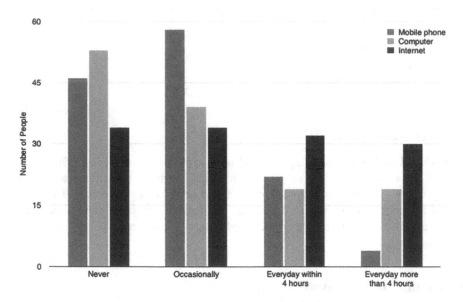

Fig. 1. Usage of Mobile phone/Computer/Internet

Figure 1 illustrates the frequency of technology products usage among the respondents and the detailed data can be seen in Table 3.

Generally, respondents use mobile phone more frequently than computer.

Table 3. Descriptive statistic of frequency of usage

Frequency of Usage	Min	Max	Mean	SD
Mobile phone	1	4	3.12	.797
Computer	1	4	2.55	1.114
Internet	1	4	2.97	1.071
Technology (overall)	3	12	8.65	2.570

3.3 Task Performance

In the performance test, 90.6 % of the respondents successfully completed the task of making telephone call; 52 % of them had successfully texted and sent message; 72 % of them had completed taking photo and 34.6 % completed Wechat testing task (Table 4).

For the older people in China, making phone calls (M = 0.91, SD = 0.294) seems to be the easiest task for the respondents in this test while sending a photo through Wechat seems to be the most difficult one (M = 0.34, SD = 0.480).

Table 4. Task performance

TASK	Fail (0)	Success (1)	Mean	SD
Make a phone call	12	115	.91	.294
Text and send a message	61	66	.52	.502
Take a photo	35	92	.72	.449
Send a photo through Wechat	82	45	.35	.480
Overall performance			2.5	1.214

3.4 Technical Self-confidence, Frequency of Technology Usage and Task Performance

The results show that older people's technology self-efficacy is significant correlated with the frequency of technology usage (correlation coefficient = 0.362, p < 0.01) and task performance (correlation coefficient = 0.315, p < 0.01). The frequency of technology usage also significant correlates with task performance (correlation coefficient = 0.563, p < 0.01) (Table 5).

Table 5. Correlation coefficient between technology self-efficacy, frequency of usage and task performance

	Technical Self-confidence	Frequency of Technology Usage	Task Performance
Technical Self-confidence		.362[**]	315[**]
Frequency of Technology Usage			.563[**]
Task Performance			

[**]. Correlation is significant at the 0.01 level (2-tailed).

4 Discussion and Conclusion

In this study, we explore the role of technology self-efficiency on technology product acceptance and usage, trying to figure out whether self-efficacy would affect one's desirability and ability of using technology products.

The elderly's technology self-efficacy is positive and significant correlated with the frequency of technology usage (correlation coefficient = 0.362, p < 0.01). People with higher self-efficacy use technology products more frequently. And in turn, using technology products frequently may contributes to higher technology self-efficacy as well.

In this study, the older people with higher technology self-efficacy reported a better task performance (correlation coefficient = 0.315, p < 0.01). This result is consistent with the finding of Wolters et al. (2010) but opposite to that of Combe et al. (2013).

Since task performance also significantly correlates with the frequency of technology usage (correlation coefficient = 0.563, p < 0.01). We analysis the correlation between technology self-efficacy and task performance again after the frequency of technology usage is controlled (Table 6).

Table 6. Correlation coefficient between technology self-efficacy and task performance after frequency of technology usage is controlled

Control Variables		Task Performance
Frequency of Technology Usage	Correlation coefficient	.170
	P	.057

This time, technology self-efficacy shows no significant correlation with task performance. Therefore, we assume that the different task performance may be resulted from the different frequency of technology usage instead of technology-self efficacy.

In conclusion, technology self-efficacy is expected to be an effective and predictive tool to evaluate the older people's acceptance of technology products while it's not very effective in predicting older people's performance of technology products usage.

This also raised a possible approach to improve older people's acceptance by improving their technology self-efficacy efficiency.

5   Limitation of This Study

Several limitations should be noted for this study. First, the study population was based on a convenience sample and the education level of the respondents in this study is relatively high. Second, the performance test used GALAXY Trend 3 as a unified tool instead of respondents' own mobile phones, in order to test how these older people performance when they using this GALAXY Trend 3 for the first time. Although none of the respondent's mobile phone is GALAXY Trend 3, but the respondent whose commonly used mobile phone has the same software system (Android) with GALAXY Trend 3 will be more likely to succeed in the task test than those whose commonly used mobile phone has a different software system (e.g. IOS). The effect of this factor on the results of this study cannot be ruled out.

References

Burnett, J.S., et al.: Older adults' attitudes towards computers, the Internet, and email (2009)

Arning, K., Ziefle, M.: Understanding age differences in PDA acceptance and performance. Comput. Hum. Behav. **23**, 2904–2927 (2007)

Bandura, A.: Self-Efficacy: The Exercise of Control. Freeman, New York (1997)

Birren, J.E., Schaie, K.W.: Handbook of the Psychology of Aging. Gulf Professional Publishing, London (2001)

Combe, N., Harrison, D., Dong, H.: Designing technology for older people – the role of technical self-confidence in usability of an inclusive heating control. In: Marcus, A. (ed.) DUXU 2013, Part III. LNCS, vol. 8014, pp. 49–56. Springer, Heidelberg (2013)

Demiris, G., Rantz, M., Aud, M., Marek, K., Tyrer, H., Skubic, M., Hussam, A.: Older adults' attitudes towards and perceptions of "smart home" technologies: a pilot study. Med. Inform. Internet Med. **29**(2), 87–94 (2004)

Kang, J.: Technology phobia of old people. Today Panorama of Mod. Sci. **13**, 16–18 (2009). (in Chinese)

Malla, R.: Information and Communication Technology for Elderly: A Literature Review (2014)

Mieczakowski, A., Clarkson, P.: Ageing, Adaption and Accessibility: Time for the Inclusive Revolution! (2013)

Wolters, K.M., Engelbrecht, K.P., Gödde, F., Möller, S., Naumann, A., Schleicher, R.: Making it easier for older people to talk to smart homes: the effect of early help prompts. Univ. Access Inf. Soc. **9**(4), 311–325 (2010)

Wang, Y., Liu, J.: Study on status and problems of information and communication technologies (ICT) intervening in elderly life in china. Sci. Res. Aging **2**(10), 42–50 (2014). (in Chinese)

The Transformation of Reading Among the Ageing Population in the Digital Age

Dobrinka Peicheva[1] and Lilia Raycheva[2(✉)]

[1] Faculty of Philosophy, The Neophyte Rilski Southwest University, Blagoevgrad, Bulgaria
peichevad@gmail.com
[2] Faculty of Journalism and Mass Communication, The St. Kliment Ohridsky Sofia University,
Sofia, Bulgaria
lraycheva@yahoo.com

Abstract. The processes of globalization, the Internet, the broadband technologies, and the convergence are among the main milestones tracing the dimensions of humankind's development in the 21st century. They are also the fundamental points that trace the basis of social transformations. Today these transformations are catalyzed by the intense development of information and communication technologies. As positive as their impact might be on progress in all areas of life, it is no less true that they pose challenges for the social stratification of society. The trend of population ageing determines the need for urgent prevention of elderly people's social exclusion from the modern information environment.

The proposed paper examines the European policies in this respect and presents the results of a social survey on changing reading practices (with respect to texts on paper and electronic support) of elderly people in Bulgaria.

Keywords: Ageing population · ICT · E-reading · Transformation

1 Introduction

"Our life is a hybrid between virtual and physical space", Manuel Castells pointed out at the second international forum on The Media of the Future, conducted in RIA Novosti in 2012.

Indeed, humanity today is facing a new stage of its development. Now the local particularities and local interests are a function of the shared goals and tasks of global processes, which are without ideological basis. Modern globalization tendencies are inevitably influenced by multifarious ICT.

The text is developed within the framework of the research programs COST Action IS1402: *Ageism - a multi-national, interdisciplinary perspective* and COST Action IS1404: *Evolution of Reading in the Age of Digitization (E-READ).*

© Springer International Publishing Switzerland 2016
J. Zhou and G. Salvendy (Eds.): ITAP 2016, Part I, LNCS 9754, pp. 216–225, 2016.
DOI: 10.1007/978-3-319-39943-0_21

In hypermodern times, when technologies are revolutionizing culture, which is no longer in the representations but in the objects, the brands and the technologies of information society [1], information and communication defines the parameters of the mediatized society.

The processes of globalization, the Internet, the broadband technologies, and the convergence are among the main milestones tracing the dimensions of humankind's development in the 21st century. They are the vectors that outline the basic social transformations [2]. Today these transformations are being catalyzed by the potential of the blogosphere and the social networks, as well as of the mobile ICT. The exclusion of analog television broadcasting was accompanied by a number of communication innovations: Facebook appeared in 2004, Twitter – two years later, in 2006, Instagram – in 2010. The most popular site for sharing video YouTube was created in 2005. Smartphone has been on the market since 2007, and iPad – since 2010. The generations of the so-called digital natives Y and Z, i.e., according to the classification by Mark McCrindle and Emily Wolfinger, i.e. the generation of those born after the 1980s, are dictating the new trends in communication processes and the technological platforms in those processes [3].

Many detailed expert studies and public discussions have focused on the problem of overcoming prejudices and negative stereotypes concerning the differences between generations and the degree of capacity of elderly people to take part in, and contribute to social development.

2   European Policies on Ageing

In 2015, mankind commemorated two significant anniversaries – the tenth year since May 17 was proclaimed *World Information Society Day* and 25 years since October 1 was proclaimed *International Day of Older Persons*. Lately the demographic collapse is seen as one of the greatest challenges to the economic and social system of the EU. Perhaps that is why 2012 was proclaimed, unprecedentedly for the second time (the first was 1993), as European Year for Active Ageing and Solidarity between Generations. The aim of these and other initiatives is to enhance the public awareness of the many-sided contribution of older people, and to promote measures that create better opportunities for their active life.

The section on "Silver Surfers" in the statistical portrait of the European Union for 2012, prepared by Eurostat on that occasion, is devoted to the better use of the potential of ICT for a healthy and independent ageing. ICT have a special role in our times as an instrument for dealing with the specific problems caused by population ageing. In order for the life of elderly people to have a better quality, the physical and psychological, but also the social, dimensions of their life are important; these include: social inclusion, access to public services, lifelong learning, social and economic activeness.

Statistics show a growing use of the Internet, in the age groups 55–64 and 65–74, for electronic mail correspondence, for seeking information for goods and services, for health information, for reading online newspapers and acquainting with the news, for inclusion in education activities, etc. E-banking and e-shopping have become increasingly popular lately [4].

Information and communication technologies can help elderly people improve the quality of their lives, preserve their health and live longer independent lives.

In the communication "Ageing Well in the Information Society" published in 2007, the European Commission presented an action plan for enhanced application of ICT in dealing with problems caused by ageing of the European population. The action plan is oriented to several areas:

- at the workplace – through development of electronic skills and electronic training so that older people may remain active and productive for a longer time;
- in society – through new ICT solutions for contacts in the social media and through more effective supply of access to public and commercial services which lead to better quality of life and reduce social isolation;
- at home – by providing healthier and better quality of life, assisted by ICT for maintaining a higher degree of independence.

The aim of the plan is to give political and industrial impetus to the making considerable efforts for creating and enlarging instruments and ICT services accessible to users, in stressing the need of elderly users, supporting other policy areas, and seeking solutions to the challenges of ageing [5].

The population trends are alarming. Although it is expected that the overall population of the European Union will grow to 532 millions by 2060, the population in half of the member states (Bulgaria, Croatia, Germany, Greece, Estonia, Hungary, Latvia, Poland Portugal, Rumania, Slovakia, Slovenia, and Spain) will decrease. The prognoses show that the ratio of people above 65 to those between 15 and 64 will increase from 27.8 % to 50.1 %. This will practically mean that the ratio between persons of working age and those in retirement age will decrease from 4:1 to 2:1 [6].

It is on these prognoses that many serious political debates about "the graying of Europe" are based, including the comprehensive Europe 2020 Strategy for Smart, Sustainable and Inclusive Growth. The strategy envisages development of technologies that enable elderly people to live independently and to take an active part in society. The program in the field of digital technologies for Europe (A Digital Agenda for Europe) is fundamental for the Strategy and aims to accelerate high-speed access to the Internet and to increase the benefit ensuing from the creation of a unified digital market for households. The ambitious aim is that by 2015, 60 % of disadvantaged people, including those aged 55–74, will regularly use the Internet [7].

The increase of average life expectancy is viewed as the basic cause of population ageing. The demographic challenges that the EU is expected to face in the coming decades can be overcome by introducing a wide range of ICT initiatives at three different levels: the professional – developing new markets based on ICT products and services aimed at the specific needs of ageing individuals; the social - ensuring more effective management and supply of key services for the elderly, such as healthcare and social care; the individual – improving the quality of life of elderly people and supporting their social participation.

The technical options for communication means are increasing in the contemporary information environment, characterized by developing new electronic media forms. Also increasing are the possibilities to choose different reading supports and consequently, the possibility of satisfying specific individual needs. In order to improve the quality of life, elderly people today have a larger choice of means to attain equality through inclusion – a choice provided by the new communication technologies – and hence, to attain individual and social satisfaction.

3   Transformations of Reading

The new media e-forms are constantly enlarging the options for reading. The content can be read in a printed book or magazine, but also on an e-reader, on a computer that has Internet access, on a notebook, tablet, mobile smartphone, etc. Today, the temporal and spatial distance for making media contact is very much reduced. Communication restructurings in the area of reading are becoming increasingly sustainable. But are they irrevocable?

Viewed in a historical perspective – they are. The whole history of culture is a history of restructuring of cultural-communicational artifacts. These restructurings are indicators of reception of the content of the concrete media and forms of communication, and they are the features under which entire historical-cultural epochs are labeled: the age of traditional written culture, the age of electronic culture, etc. Yet the modern restructuring of communications is wider in scope and far more dynamic.

Mobility is identified as the basic measure of modern communication tools; it is an invariable part of communication restructurings. Mediatized mobile communications have proven to be emblematic for mediatized society [8, 9]. Paradoxically, mobility is the stable element of modern media constructs, while reading and writing are the prevalent communication activities.

Transformations are taking place in the cultural models of reading and writing as well. A new written culture is emerging, which uses a national and international vocabulary and combines verbal and non-verbal signs and symbols.

Reading is the activity that is undergoing unprecedented transformation. It is gradually shifting towards electronic forms and Internet sources, thus reducing contacts with paper support – and this can be traced down, not only in professional activities and interaction but in leisure activities as well. People today read far more on their mobile communication devices than on traditional supports. Reading itself is becoming increasingly fragmentary; it is made more complex through the use of specifying terminological and informational links and references that accompany reading, with options for additional search for facts, events, other authors who have written on a given issue, etc.

4   Survey Methodologies

The data on which the present analysis and conceptualization are based are drawn from a complex social survey conducted in April-October 2015 under a research project.[1] The project comprises two types of interconnected surveys (quantitative and qualitative) conducted by the research team:

1. QUANTITATIVE: A representative survey among 1120 people across the whole country, selected on a quota principle.

The results have been verified by means of data from a representative social survey on "Reading Practices in Bulgaria, 2014", conducted by the social survey agency Alfa Research, headed by Prof. Dr. Boryana Dimitrova, in the framework of a research project with the same name.[2]

2. QUALITATIVE: Focus groups specified in one of its variants – the "world café", with moderators Dilyana Keranova and Violeta Nikolova, members of the research team. The world café was realized in the months of September and October 2015 in two meetings, and it included 23 students and 22 older people having attitudes towards electronic reading.

The foremost research questions addressed in the quantitative survey are: what are the changing cultural models and media reading practices; what is being practiced by whom and how; what are the modern proportions and restructurings; what are the preferences; what are the advantages and shortcomings of electronic reading? These questions were aimed at revealing the situation and establishing the regularities and future trends.

The focus group discussions in the qualitative study are related to the search for in-depth information about the causes of the growth of e-reading and e-writing, as well as of the limited use of e-readers.

5   Results

The e-book and its carriers, e-readers, are not largely present in the everyday life of the Bulgarians, especially of the older generation. Even though they have the character of library depositories and are meta-media constructs, as yet few people own them, and they are mainly used when a person is mobile. In Bulgaria, about 70 % of respondents have never handled an e-reader. The reading of books on an e-reader applies to 3.4 % of elderly people and a total of 5.4 % of all respondents.

In fact, only 4.4 % of respondents in the Alfa Research survey indicated they mostly read on an e-reader.

---

[1] Research project: "Transformations of Reading in Mediatized Society" (2015). The Neophyte Rilski Southwestern University - Blagoevgrad. Team Leader: Assoc Prof. DSc Dobrinka Peicheva.

[2] Research project: "Reading Practices in Bulgaria" (2014). The St. Kliment Ohridski Sofia University. Team Leader: Prof. Dr Aleksandar Kyosev.

The relatively high prices of electronic readers, as well as the decreasing desire to read literary texts, are factors that limit the spread of e-readers. In fact, it is a well-known fact that traditional reading is decreasing throughout the world and in Bulgaria as well (Table 1).

Table 1. Most customary ways for people to read

Which of these ways of reading are most customary for you?	I mostly read on paper	67,3 %
	I hardly read at all	19,9 %
	I mostly read on a computer	17,3 %
	Usually I don't read on a computer but do various things	7,6 %
	I mostly read on a tablet or smartphone	6,9 %
	I mostly read on an elec- tronic reader	4,4 %
	I mostly listen to audio books	0,5 %

Respondents chose more than one answer, so the sum of percentages exceeds 100. The above-mentioned social survey of reading practices conducted in 2014 confirmed the continuing decrease of reading in Bulgaria. It was found that only about 1/3 of Bulgarians read books several times a week, and others read a maximum of 5 books per year. It was also found that half of the respondents have not read a single book [17].

However, it was also found that nearly 30 % of readers of books prefer e-reading.

5.1 In the Quantitative Survey, the Following Important Conclusions Were Drawn

1. For all age groups, electronic reading is now predominant over reading on paper. Over 50 % of the respondents above the age of 60 also communicate through the Internet and read and write by electronic devices. The reasons for which the educated elderly population accepts communication innovations are related to facility of access to a much larger variety of sources than the traditional means provide. Given the low income of pensioners in Bulgaria, electronic reading is preferable for financial reasons as well. The ample supply of newspapers and books makes it possible to choose and to fill one's leisure time, which, understandably, is growing among the elderly population.
2. The predominant reading preferences are still for texts on paper. This is characteristic for all age groups in Bulgaria. Forty-four percent of respondents definitely agree with this, and older people are a majority by this indicator.

The answer to the question, "Do you have preferences in reading?" shows that the majority of people prefer to read on paper.

It is interesting to see the causes of preference for reading texts on paper.

This preference is related to habits (36.4 %) of older people. Some leading motives for this preference are that it is easier to assimilate text printed on paper (32.6 %) and easier to remember the contents of reading (29. 8 %).

We also see that when reading on paper, it is much easier to concentrate on the text, to experience the content, to encompass and reread texts. 51.5 % of elderly respondents have indicated this (Fig. 1).

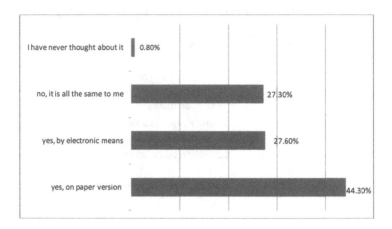

Fig. 1. Reading preferences

Elderly people also indicate the advantages of electronic reading. Over 40 % of them declare they have used this tool (Fig. 2).

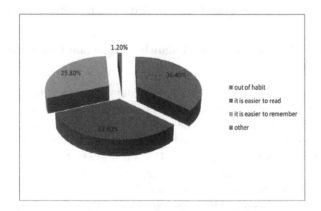

Fig. 2. Reasons for preferring paper support in reading

The preference for electronic reading and respectively, not attaching importance to the support of content (paper or electronic support), are connected to the possibilities provided by e-reading through the Internet, namely: connecting to other texts by using links, the possibility of making all kinds of references, the possibility of feedback through participation in forums, expressing one's opinion in blogs, on specialized sites, by sending messages to authors, etc.

The preference for e-reading is also due to the possibility of making contact in combination with other communication activities. The respondents have singled out several factors as especially significant: receiving (11.9 %) and writing (12 %) e-messages, combining reading with other activities in the Internet (17.2 %), combining reading with talking with friends (6.2 %) or with creative activity (5.5 %) (Fig. 3). The remaining 47% did not pointed out preference for e-reading.

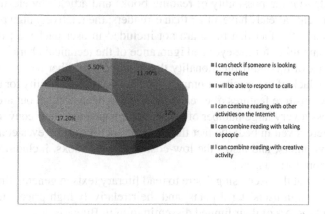

Fig. 3. Combining reading with other communication activities

Electronic reading has both advantages and disadvantages [10–16].

One shortcoming is the overloaded quantity of contacts. Also, it is harder to memorize information. Both of these disadvantages are related to the striving to receive more information, and a large share of electronic texts is of a multi-media nature. Multi-media products make it possible to follow links to other media products containing other types of audio-visual content, and they combine different formats of information. The "fragmentation" of reading and the non-linear perception on one hand, and the possibility of quickly enhancing and checking information through other media products on the other, are some of the factors that "frustrate" the memorizing of this type of information.

Older people, like younger ones, want to receive as much information on the Internet as possible within a given amount of time. They are particularly curious to follow all the references available in a text.

5.2 Discussions in the Qualitative Study Led to Several Important Findings

Apart from nuances, the focus group respondents in the two focus groups had similar representations about electronic reading and writing, and they explained these as due to several causes, among them: the increased media literacy of the population in all age groups; the accessible cost of most electronic carriers disseminated in society; the facilitation offered by the new communication means, which overcome space and time; the simultaneous realization of interpersonal contact and mass communication; the combining of written text with sound, image and picture; the possibility for achieving various kinds of creativity; the possibility of overcoming isolation; the possibility for personal involvement and solidarity. The respondents also pointed out the compatibility of electronic reading and writing with other communication means as well as their being mutually interchangeable in different spaces and also - their multi-functionality, which includes reading, writing, listening, viewing, recording, etc.

The concrete explanations of focus group participants regarding the limited use of e-readers pointed to several issues such as the decreased amount of reading of books in general in Bulgaria; the possibility of reading books and articles by electronic means that the respondents already have, other than e-readers; the relatively high price of electronic readers and the fact that these are not included in user packages; the idea that e-readers are damaging for the eyes and ignorance of the technical characteristics of e-readers; the lack of the multi-functionality that is typical of other means of e-reading; and finally - the lack of the specific aroma of paper and of the possibility for underlining.

Among the positive features of e-readers that have been pointed out are: the possibility to possess a very large number of books and magazines; their convenience to be used everywhere, even in bed; the fact that they are better for the eyes compared with tablets and computers; and also - the low-cost access to books, including free books downloaded from torrents, etc.

It is evident that the decreasing desire to read literary texts in general, the non-inclusion of these texts in users' tariff plans, and their relatively high price, emerge as the most important factors of their limited dissemination in Bulgaria.

6 Conclusion

The impetuous spread of e-media formats in daily life, as an evolutionary development of mobile and interactive communication means, has brought about a continuous increase in reading and writing in our time. The new media forms, such as blogs, Vlogs, e-books, e-newspapers, electronic radio, television, newspapers, magazines, profiled and institutional sites, social networks, etc., are involving a growing number of people and positioning them in unlimited spatial trajectories. The mediatized reality is becoming filled with unprecedented and incomparable cultural transformations and communication centers, with new cultural and behavior practices. The model of traditional searching for and reading of books, magazines, newspapers, reference literature, etc., at home, in the office, in transport means, etc., has shifted to electronic versions. E-reading and e-writing are the prevalent communication activities and are the new structure-forming elements of communication. It is a challenge for every researcher to know what direction these transformations will take and what will be their effect on the intellectual and physical health of people.

Prejudices and negative stereotypes are current challenges concerning the life of the ageing population in the modern information environment; identifying the ways in which these prejudices may be overcome will help neutralize the rise of barriers to the full participation of older people in socio-cultural processes, including the labor market. Social distancing, discrimination based on age in key spheres of the labor market, in healthcare, education, access to services and information, are not, and cannot be, productive for society. Communication skills, including reading and writing skills that use the new means of communication, are a prerequisite for inclusion of ageing people and for the use of the elderly population's potential.

References

1. Lash, S.: Criticism of Information. Kota Publ. House, Sofia (2004)
2. Tomov, M., Raycheva, L.: The facebook image of the 2013/2014 social protests in Bulgaria. In: Dobek-Ostrowska, B., Głowacki, M. (eds.) Democracy and Media in Central and Eastern Europe 25 Years on, pp. 166–181. Peter Lang Edition, Wroclaw (2015)
3. McCrindle, M., Wolfinger, E.: The ABC of XYZ: Understanding the Global Generations. UNSW, Sydney (2009)
4. EUROSTAT statistical books: active ageing and solidarity between generations. A statistical portrait of the European Union (2012). http://ec.europa.eu/eurostat/documents/3217494/5740649/KS-EP-11-001-EN.PDF/1f0b25f8-3c86-4f40-9376-c737b54c5fcf
5. European Commission: Ageing well in the Information society: action plan on information and communication technologies and ageing. http://eur-lex.europa.eu/legal-content/BG/TXT/?uri=URISERV:l24292
6. European Commission: The 2015 Ageing Report. Economic and budgetary projections for the 28 EU Member states (2013-2060). http://ec.europa.eu/economy_finance/publications/european_economy/2015/pdf/ee3_en.pdf
7. European Commission: Europe 2020: A European strategy for smart, sustainable, and inclusive growth. http://eur-lex.europa.eu/LexUriServ/LexUriServ.do?uri=COM:2010:2020:FIN:EN:PDF
8. Peicheva, D.: The Mediatized Reality. The Neophyte Rilski University Publ. House, Blagoevgrad (2011)
9. Peicheva, D.: Restructuring of communications and transformations of reading in the digital age. In: Peicheva, D., Serafimova, M. (eds.) Sociological Spaces. The Neophyte Rilski University Publ. House, Blagoevgrad (2015)
10. Sparrow, B., Liu, J., Wenger, D.M.: Google effects on memory: cognitive consequences of having information at our fingertips. Science 333(6043), 776–778 (2011). doi:10.1126/science.1207745
11. Alexander, P.A.: The disciplined reading and learning research laboratory: reading into the future: competence for the 21st century. Educ. Psychol. 47(4), 259–280 (2012)
12. Benedetto, S., Drai-Zerbib, V., Pedrotti, M., Tissier, G., Baccino, T.: E-readers and visual fatigue. PLoS ONE 8(12), e83676 (2013). doi:10.1371/journal.pone.0083676
13. Lauterman, T., Ackerman, R.: Overcoming screen inferiority in learning and calibration. Comput. Hum. Behav. 35, 455–463 (2014)
14. Mol, S.E., Jolles, J.: Reading enjoyment amongst non-leisure readers can affect achievement in secondary school. Front. Psychol. 5(1214), 1–10 (2014)
15. Rouet, J.-F., Britt, M.A.: Learning from multiple documents. In: Mayer, R.E. (ed.) Cambridge Handbook of Multimedia Learning, 2nd edn, pp. 813–841. Cambridge University Press, Cambridge (2014)
16. Jacobs, A.M.: Towards a neurocognitive poetics model of literary reading. In: Willems, R. (ed.) Towards a Cognitive Neuroscience of Natural Language Use. Cambridge University Press, Cambridge (2015)
17. Kyosev, Al.: Readers' practices in Bulgaria. www.abk.bg/attachments/download/420

Changing Patterns of ICT Use in Finland – The Senior Citizens' Perspective

Pekka Räsänen[(⊠)] and Ilkka Koiranen

Economic Sociology/Department of Social Research,
University of Turku, Turku, Finland
pekras@utu.fi

Abstract. The purpose of our paper is to provide an overview of the development of Finnish society in relation to senior citizens' online activities. As in many other countries, the proportion of 'grey consumers' is constantly growing as its society is ageing. Thus, we argue that the investigation of older people's online activities provides useful information for a more general understanding of some of the key features of the contemporary information society. The empirical portion of the paper consists of an analysis of nationally representative surveys (n = 7,810) collected between 2006 and 2014. The data represent individuals aged 55 to 74. Our results indicate that Finnish seniors have, on average, become more active online. However, it also seems that online activity nonetheless declines as people grow older. In addition, differences in Internet use purposes continue to be associated with education and income.

Keywords: Internet use purposes · Senior citizens · Temporal changes

1 Introduction

Over the last few decades, people in Western and Asian societies have experienced improved opportunities for consumption and leisure activities. In general, this has become possible due to a higher level of material wealth and education, the diffusion of mass media and modern household appliances, and increased life expectancy and health [1–3]. Indeed, many social scientists recognise the late 20th and the early 21st centuries as a period of mass consumption, during which we have witnessed a sharp rise in spending on various non-housing expenditures and recreational activities, such as holidays, eating out and cultural events [4–6]. More recently, we have also witnessed the rise of the new information and communication technologies known as ICTs.

ICTs are in many ways crucial for the future of advanced societies. The Internet in particular offers increased opportunities for information retrieval, social interaction and consumer expenditure. It can also provide possibilities for acquiring new skills, such as learning languages or finding novel past-time activities. In addition, the Internet is also considered as a vital tool in improving the services offered by public sector organisations. For example, it is believed that in future, Internet-based systems will soon provide the primary platform for receiving professional support on everyday health [2, 7].

The older population segments could offer us a feasible look at recent developments. In other words, the experiences of older people may have greater value on the

© Springer International Publishing Switzerland 2016
J. Zhou and G. Salvendy (Eds.): ITAP 2016, Part I, LNCS 9754, pp. 226–237, 2016.
DOI: 10.1007/978-3-319-39943-0_22

societal level than the experiences of younger segments when mapping recent changes in ICT use. People who have recently retired or are retiring now, and have participated in the post-war consumer culture, are especially important in these respects. They play a key role here as they have more time to engage in various social activities than other age groups. Furthermore, many scholars across the world argue that attitudes towards consumption are changing rapidly and that one's life course is losing its role as a major determinant of consumer behaviour [8–10]. Because of this, a profound investigation into older people's online activities would provide useful information for a more general understanding of some of the key features of the ongoing information revolution.

Finland can provide a topical research context for studying the changing patterns of ICT use and social inequalities associated with the use of ICTs. This is because Finland is one of the Nordic countries that are often considered as welfare societies possessing social and economic equality [11, 12]. From a comparative perspective, Finland and other Nordic societies are characterised by a commitment to full employment for men and women, equality in terms of free participation in higher education, and the promise of universal social benefits for all citizens. Further, economic and social inequalities within Nordic societies are often considered to be relatively small. For instance, somewhat weak structural disparities have been found when the patterns of household expenditure on culture and recreation have been examined [3, 13, 14].

Focusing on an average consumer in Finland would probably offer us a relatively reliable measure of all consumers in the country. Regarding older population segments, however, we may also notice that Finland is currently ageing very rapidly. The current population projections suggest that by 2030, nearly half of the Finnish population will consists of those aged 50 and over [15]. In this article, we examine what kind of temporally durable, structural differences there are in the Internet use patterns among senior Finns. The empirical part of the article consists of the results of a nationally representative 'ICT use by household and individuals' survey (n = 7,810) collected by Statistics Finland. We examine the popularity of four different Internet use purposes (overall access, email, online banking and online shopping) from 2006 to 2014. In the analysis, we focus on respondents aged 55 to 74. This examination gives us a feasible opportunity to address some of the basic characteristics of ICT activity among the older population segments in Finland.

The article proceeds as follows. We first discuss the kinds of societal changes that have taken place in the Finnish information society in the early 2000s. This is followed by our empirical section where we describe the data analysed, the logic behind our analysis, and comment on the results. In the concluding section, we will summarise our results and refer to certain theoretical implications in our research, which deal with ageing and the use of the Internet.

2   Leisure, ICT, and the Aging Society

It has been noted that the fruits of affluence now take the form of time spent in distinctive leisure-time activities. It is also believed that leisure activities have become more important in expressing the individual's place in social hierarchies and in the construction of social identities [4, 16, 17]. During the past decades, the Finns' relationship with leisure has changed significantly in relation to attitudes, time-use and consumption expenditure. Spending on leisure has increased significantly [18–20] as well as the appreciation of leisure time in Finland [21, 22] as well as in many other countries [23, 24].

Several studies have indicated that the amount of leisure time has, generally speaking, increased during the past few decades across Western societies [25–27]. Additionally, the time use statistics from Finland demonstrate this trend when comparing the early 2000s to the 1980s. Nowadays, less time is spent working, while more time is devoted to leisure time than 20 years ago. Watching TV is still the most time-consuming leisure-time activity in Finland, although time spent watching TV has only increased among older Finns. The popularity of watching TV is followed in preference by social interaction, computer use, outdoor activities and exercising, reading and other leisure-time activities. However, it is also argued that leisure-time habits have, to some extent, changed over the last ten years. On the population level, Finns these days are less socially active and read less but do take part in more outdoor activities, while spending significantly more time at the computer [28–30].

Following the vigorous economic growth during the late 1990s, a rapid increase in the supply of ICT services can be witnessed in Finland and in many other countries. After the turn of the century, the Internet user rates have blossomed. We can observe this by simply looking at the statistics on the penetration of Internet access. For example, in 2001, the proportion of individuals aged 15 and over who had used the Internet at least once in past 3 months was approximately 50 % in Finland. By 2014, however, the share of the Finns aged 16 and over was 87 %, respectively. This indicates an increase of almost 40 % points in less than 15 years [15, 31].

However, we can argue that there are also other recent developments in Finnish society, which also require our attention. Namely, we also need to understand the changing role of ageing and the individual's activities in later life. As it is well-known, recent improvements in working life, education and health care have transformed the population structures in Western societies. The first evidence of this comes from demography; the proportion of the retired population compared to those of working age has increased considerably in Finland over the last decades. In 1950, people under the age of 14 made up 30 % of the whole population, while those who were 65 and over accounted for only 6.7 % of the Finnish population. In 2014, the respective percentages were 16.4 for under 14-year-olds and 19.9 for those aged 65 and over [32, 33].

This demographic change results from the fact that the life expectancies of men and women born in Finland towards the late 1950s were 63 years and 69 years respectively; currently the respective life expectancies of Finns are 78 years for men and 84 years for women. Given this, Finland's population is currently one of the most rapidly ageing of all EU countries [15, 34, 35]. However, in addition to having a longer life expectancy, people also have more opportunities after their retirement. This is to say that a relatively new life phase is emerging for older adults in which there is no longer employment or child rearing to take up one's time and limit their activities [36]. According to many scholars, this 'third age' means, for many, a period for engaging in new cultural and educational pursuits [2, 37, 38]. What is most relevant is that today's older people do not want to adopt consumption styles and leisure activities that are typical for older people, but rather, they want to actively participate in and keep up with contemporary consumer culture and also with new technology. Thus, age differences in leisure consumption might be blurring, as older people also want, in many respects, to take part in the similar activities that younger people do [39].

The general prosperity brought about in recent decades has provided an increased standard of living for almost everyone in Finland. In general, a higher standard of living has also served to diminish economic inequality between population segments; both the more and less educated, the old and the young alike. At the same time, however, socio-demographic differences still associate with the use of the ICTs. Indeed, a constant finding reported in research literature is that young, highly educated and well-off individuals are often the most frequent Internet users [3, 40, 41]. Older age groups, particularly those who are aged over the retirement age, are the least likely to ever access the Internet. But what kinds of disparities can we witness among senior citizens when examining the Internet use patterns by use purpose during the past few years?

3 Research Questions, Data and Methods

The aim of this paper is to examine some of the central characteristics of Internet use among the senior citizens in Finland during the time period between 2006 and 2014. Our main interest relates to the interconnections between Internet use purposes and the basic sociodemographic background of older population segments. The following three research questions were therefore formulated:

1. How did the senior citizens' Internet use patterns change in general and according to age in Finland between 2006 and 2014?
2. How did the Internet use patterns connect with other basic socio-demographic factors in 2006 and 2014?

The data utilised were derived from the official Finnish statistics dataset 'ICT use by individuals and households' collected by Statistics Finland (n = 7,810). The data were primarily collected by phone interviews, however, data also include information derived from the population statistics, such as information on respondents' age, gender, education, residence and income [33]. In our analysis, we focus on the older population segments, namely those aged 55 to 74.

As dependent measures, we utilise a total of four Internet use variables in the analysis: overall access, email, ebanking, and online purchases during the past 12 months or earlier. Each of these activities were measured using the dichotomous options 'yes' and 'no'. Thus, these items only offer us a rough overview of information on Internet use patterns. For instance, they do not reveal anything about the frequency of the given use purposes. At the same time, however, this measurement is the most straightforward way to make a distinction between the online users and non-users.

Our independent variables include age, gender, education and income. Age was categorised into three groups, '55–64-year-olds', '65–69-year-olds' and '70–79-year-olds'. The 60–64-year olds are usually considered as representing the economically active population, although only approximately two out of five Finns in that age group are actually participating in working life. By the age of 65, most Finns have already retired. Education reflects the three educational levels of Statistics Finland's official education categorisation, which are 'bachelor/higher', 'secondary' and 'primary'. Income is also a relevant independent measure, as people younger than 65-years of age are typically in a better financial position than those who are older. However, older age contributes to greater possibilities for increased leisure time. In our analysis, we use a coarse classification of income quartiles, based on income from all household members. Finally, the variable 'gender' reports the sex of the respondents.

We may generally assume that the participation in most online activities will decline according to age. At the same time, we may also assume that the online activities have also become more common over time. However, is this really the case in Finland? As stressed in earlier studies, it is clear that age itself is interlocked with Internet activities [3, 38, 40], but we do not necessarily know what kind of associations actually exist among Finnish senior citizens. Therefore, we will use descriptive and explanatory techniques in order to understand this phenomenon slightly better. First, the aim of the analysis is to describe the interconnections between Internet use purposes and age over time. Afterwards, logistic regression models will be applied in the explanatory analysis.

4 Findings

The starting point of our analysis can be found in Fig. 1, which gives us the temporal trends of Internet penetration rates before and after 2006 (in percentages). In the figure, national penetration rate averages are calculated on the basis of citizens aged 15 and over [for details, see 33]. In addition, we also show a polynomial trend line for the actual annual increase. Starting from 2006, we also show three trends for the older age groups, 55–64-year-olds, 65–69-year-olds, and 70–79-year-olds, which are our focus here. As the figure shows, Internet use has indeed increased very rapidly in Finland since the turn of the millennium.

Figure 2 offers us a closer look at how different online activities among Finnish senior citizens have changed over time in the period between 2006 and 2014. The figure shows the differences between age categories. In overall Internet use, for instance, the difference between the 55–64-year-olds and the oldest age group, has diminished from 46 % to 24 % over the past 12 years. This means that the proportion of those who are using the Internet is growing faster within the oldest age groups. For example, between the years 2006 and 2014, the proportion of those who have used the Internet has increased from 67 % to 94 % among 55–65-year-olds, while at the same time, the proportion of Internet users has grown from 21 % to 70 % in the oldest age group. This means that the growth for 55–64-year-olds is about 27 % points between the years 2006 and 2014, while the growth for the oldest age group is over 50 % points in that time period.

Similar trends also hold true for email use, the use of ebanking services and online purchases. The proportions of those who have performed the activities in question have grown faster in the very oldest group. It can be seen that the oldest citizens are catching up with the others in Internet use activities. In general, these findings are consistent with recent research on how digital divides change when time passes. It can be said that

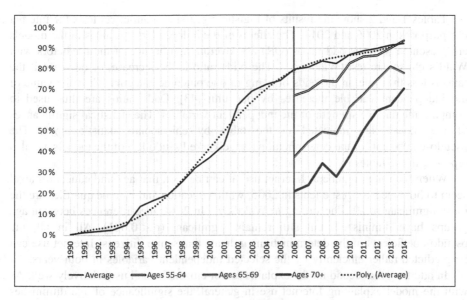

Fig. 1. Internet penetration rates in Finland, 1990–2014 (%)

when new digital activities appear, they are first adopted by young, well-off and educated citizens. Over time, however, the older, disadvantaged and people with a lower education level also start to use the technology and services [41, 42]. These changes describe how digital divides grow wide and deep at first and then start to narrow when time goes by. However, this does not mean that the divides between different groups are going to disappear permanently, because these divides are always transformed again when new technologies or innovations emerge [42].

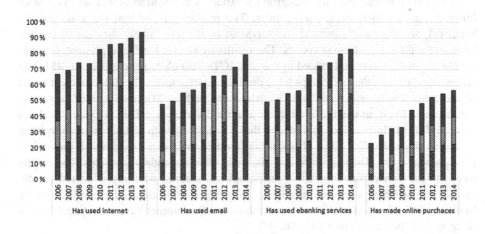

Fig. 2. Senior citizens Internet use purposes by age, 2006–2014 (%)

Tables 1 and 2 show the results of logistic regression main-effect tests for Internet use purposes in 2006 and 2014. The effects of the independent variables in the models are presented with the odd ratios (OR) and overall significance of the predictors with Wald's chi square test (Wald's χ^2). The odds ratio is the increase, or decrease if the ratio is less than one, in the odds of being in one outcome category when the value of the independent variable increases by one unit [43]. Odds ratios are thus used to compare the relative strength of the independent variables. The statistical significances of the models are indicated in the table by chi square statistics (χ^2). The pseudo-coefficients of the determination (Nagelkerke Pseudo R^2) of the models are also reported in the tables.

When focusing on general Internet use, it can be seen that age and education level seem to hold the strongest effects in 2006, while education and income quartiles are the most significant in 2014 according to Wald's χ^2. In 2014, the differences between age groups have diminished, but still remain significant (p < 0,001). All in all, the pseudo-coefficients of the determinations indicate that senior citizens' Internet use can be predicted rather efficiently by the selected independent variables in both years.

In addition, the second model explains senior citizens' email use relatively well. As with the model explaining Internet use in general, the significance of age diminishes between 2006 and 2014. However, the significance of income and education increases between the ensuing years. In practice, this means that the differences between different income quartiles and education categories have increased. In the third model, we investigated senior citizens' use of digital banking services. As in the models portraying Internet use in general and email use, in this model the significance of age also decreases in the latter model. Further, the significance of the education level decreases, while the income quartile's significance increases slightly. Unlike the other models, the model representing online shopping better explains the share of variation in the year 2014 than in 2006. Further, the income quartile and education are also stronger in 2014 than in 2006.

The tables reveal that all background variables are statistically associated with Internet use activities, except for gender. The results indicate that the younger, the better off, and the more educated an individual is, the more likely they are to use the Internet for the selected use purposes. The results by age are hardly surprising; younger people are usually more interested in the new ICTs than older people [42, 44, 45]. The differences between the age groups have diminished over time. The differences in terms of education also demonstrate that those who have graduated from college or university are the most likely to use the Internet in a more diverse way. This is evident in both 2006 and 2014. In practice, this means that the citizens with tertiary education have over nine times the likelihood of using the Internet compared to seniors in the lowest education category. The pattern is also visible in other dependent variables. The results were in line with earlier theoretical and empirical studies, whereby educated people usually use and have used the Internet more regularly at work. Additionally, in many 'white-collar' jobs, personal computers, email and the Internet have been regular tools since end of the last century [42, 46, 47].

Differences according to income levels are also partly consistent with preceding research. However, we can witness an interesting temporal change here. The income quartile has become a more significant predictor of internet use activities in the year

Table 1. Internet use purposes among senior citizens in 2006 (logistic regression models with Wald's χ^2 and odds ratios [OR])

Main effects	Internet use OR	Email OR	Online banking OR	Online shopping OR
Age, χ^2	**49,42*****	**41,89*****	**35,07*****	**19,52*****
55-64 years	6,21***	5,18***	4,90***	5,12***
65-69 years	2,87***	3,65***	2,68***	3,01***
+70 years (a)	1	1	1	1
Gender, χ^2	**1,43(ns)**	**0,98(ns)**	**0,01(ns)**	**0,03(ns)**
Female	0,8(ns)	0,83(ns)	1,01(ns)	1,04(ns)
Male (a)	1	1	1	1
Education, χ^2	**63,43*****	**46,14*****	**41,37*****	**32,67*****
BA/higher	9,46***	4,84***	4,34***	3,69***
Secondary	5,54***	3,60***	3,26***	3,65***
Primary (a)	1	1	1	1
Income quartiles, χ^2	**29,14*****	**40,52*****	**42,96*****	**13,55****
Highest	4,84***	7,06***	5,84***	3,77***
Third	2,76**	3,54***	3,60***	2,36**
Second	1,42(ns)	1,75(ns)	1,48(ns)	1,41(ns)
Lowest (a)	1	1	1	1
-2 Log Likelihood (b)	**712,1*****	**707,1*****	**728,5*****	**543,0*****
df	7	8	8	8
Nagelkerke R²	**.395**	**.359**	**.331**	**.229**

Note: *** = $p < 0.001$; ** = $p < 0.01$; * = $p < 0.05$; (ns) = $p > 0.05$; (a) = reference category; (b) = indicates the difference in the chi square statistic between the model and a reduced model. *Source:* Statistics Finland 2015.

Table 2. Internet use purposes among senior citizens in 2014 (logistic regression models with Wald's χ^2 and odds ratios [OR])

Main effects	Internet use OR	Email OR	Online banking OR	Online shopping OR
Age, χ^2	**20,57*****	**18,63*****	**22,64*****	**32,35*****
55-64 years	3,77***	2,75***	2,93***	3,93***
65-69 years	3,09***	1,70*	2,085***	1,67**
+70 years (a)	1	1	1	1
Gender, χ^2	**1,49(ns)**	**1,36(ns)**	**1,24(ns)**	**1,27(ns)**
Female	1,36(ns)	1,24(ns)	1,24(ns)	0,83(ns)
Male (a)	1	1	1	1
Education, χ^2	**35,20*****	**53,84*****	**35,79*****	**57,99*****
BA/higher	15,01***	7,78***	5,088***	4,10***
Secondary	5,58***	5,05***	3,78***	3,67***
Primary (a)	1	1	1	1
Income quartiles, χ^2	**36,27*****	**47,82*****	**48,24*****	**33,99*****
Highest	13,52***	7,21***	7,00***	4,22***
Third	5,88**	4,54***	3,52***	2,14***
Second	2,21(ns)	1,89(ns)	1,54(ns)	1,14(ns)
Lowest (a)	1	1	1	1
-2 Log Likelihood (b)	**427,9*****	**726,7*****	**710,9*****	**912,5*****
df	8	8	8	8
Nagelkerke R²	**.366**	**.335**	**.295**	**.288**

Note: *** = $p < 0.001$; ** = $p < 0.01$; * = $p < 0.05$; (ns) = $p > 0.05$; (a) = reference category; (b) = indicates the difference in the chi square statistic between the model and a reduced model. *Source:* Statistics Finland 2015.

2014 than it was in 2006. The odds for using the Internet in general, or for email, ebanking or shopping online, increase steadily from the lowest to the highest income quartile in both years. The odds ratio against the lowest income quartile in the second one is not statistically significant in any of the Internet use activities either in 2006 or 2014. However, the odds against the lowest and the highest income quartile grew in all Internet use activities between 2006 and 2014.

5   Conclusion

Earlier research suggests that the Internet plays a major role in terms of social participation by providing relatively easy access to information on various activities and events. In the near future, we expect to witness a remarkable extension of the software and application market, particularly in relation to services aimed at 'grey consumers'. On the population level, the significance of this extension is significant because the Finnish population is ageing rapidly.

While the Internet and other ICTs are in many ways useful, their proliferation can also connect to pre-existing inequalities. In this context, such conceptions as 'information haves' and 'information have-nots' have been referred to. These conceptions basically mean that the new technologies are creating social problems simply because some individuals are less likely than others to use the new technology. The discussion on the digital divide is also relevant for the older segments of population. Technology gaps between those who have access to the new resources and those who do not are still being established. In this respect, governmental and other public online services, as well as commercial online activities, should be the most widely discussed topics when reflecting on the future development of the ICT for senior citizens.

Based on theoretical discussion about the changing faces of the digital divide, it can be said that all online activities examined in this study can be understood as 'mature Internet activities'. This is because the growth of the proportion of users has slowed significantly or almost stopped among the youngest age groups in Finland. Despite the fact that the growth rate has slowed down among the younger citizens, the proportion of those who use the ICT is still growing among the older population segments.

In this study we relied on data from one country alone. In other words, further, comparative research is required both from an international and a domestic perspective. In general, however, the persisting connections between common online activities and socio-demographic characteristics provide us with an interesting finding in terms of the ageing welfare society. By encouraging senior citizens with tools and the means to use these services, there can be a pay off in the societal context, as general activity is usually associated with a better quality of life and life satisfaction.

Acknowledgements. This research was funded by the Strategic Research Council of the Academy of Finland (research consortium Digital Disruption of Industry DDI).

References

1. Freedman, M.: Prime Time: How Baby Boomers will Revolutionize Retirement and Transform America. Public Affairs, New York (1999)
2. Jones, I.R., Hyde, M., Victor, C.R., Wiggins, R.D., Gilleard, C., Higgs, P.: Ageing in a Consumer Society: From Passive to Active Consumption in Britain. Polity Press, London (2008)
3. Räsänen, P.: The consumption disparities in information society: comparing the traditional and digital divides in Finland. Int. J. Sociol. Soc. Policy 25(1–2), 48–62 (2006)
4. Bauman, Z.: Work, Consumerism and the New Poor. Milton Keynes: Open University Press, Buckingham (1998)
5. Blow, L., Leicester, A., Oldfield, Z.: Consumption Trends in the UK, 1975–1999. IFS Reports R65. Institute of Fiscal Studies, London (2004)
6. Giddens, A.: Europe in the Global Age. Polity Press, Cambridge (2007)
7. Rashidi, P., Mihailidis, A.: A survey on ambient-assisted living tools for older adults. IEEE J. Biomed. Health Inf. 17(3), 579–590 (2013)
8. Bennett, A.: Subcultures or neo-tribes? rethinking the relationship between youth, style and musical taste. Sociology 33(3), 599–617 (1999)
9. Harrison, J., Ryan, J.: Musical taste and ageing. J. Ageing Soc. 30(4), 649–669 (2010)
10. Räsänen, P.: In the Twilight of Social Structures: A Mechanism-Based Study of Contemporary Consumer Behaviour. University of Turku, Turku (2003)
11. Esping-Andersen, G.: The Three Worlds of Welfare Capitalism. Polity Press, Oxford (1990)
12. Ferrera, M.: The "Southern Model" of Social Welfare in Europe. J. Eur. Soc. Policy 6(1), 17–37 (1996)
13. Purhonen, S.: Televisio ja kulttuuripääoma: ohjelmatyyppien ja mieliohjelmien sosiaalinen eriytyminen nyky-Suomessa [Television and Cultural Capital: Social Segregation According to Program Type and Favourite Programs in Contemporary Finland]. In: Sosiologia 48. 2 (2011)
14. Wilska, T.A.: Survival with Dignity?: The Consumption of Young Adults During Economic Depression; a Comparative Study of Finland and Britain, 1990-1994. Turku School of Economics and Business Administration, Turku (1999)
15. Statistics Finland, Väestörakenne [Population structure] (2015b). http://www.stat.fi/til/vaerak/tau.html
16. Giddens, A.: Modernity and Self-Identity: Self and Society in the Late Modern Age. Stanford University Press, Stanford (1991)
17. Featherstone, M.: Consumer Culture and Postmodernism. Sage, London (1991)
18. Statistics Finland, Finns consume eleven times more now than 100 years ago (2007). http://www.stat.fi/tup/suomi90/heinakuu_en.html
19. Statistics Finland, Väestörakenne, Väestö iän mukaan vuosina 1875–2009 [Population structure, population according to age from the years 1875-2009] (2009). http://www.stat.fi/til/vaerak/2009/vaerak_2009_2010-03-19_tau_003_fi.html
20. Statistics Finland, Kotitalouksien kulutus [Household consumption] (2014). http://www.stat.fi/til/ktutk/2012/ktutk_2012_2014-02-28_tie_001_fi.html
21. Liikkanen, M.: Vapaa-aika – työn vastakohta, harrastuksia vai vapautta? Hyvinvointikatsaus [Leisure – the Opposite of Work, Hobbies or Freedom? A Review of Wellbeing] 2/2004. Statistics Finland, Helsinki (2004)
22. Liikkanen, M.: Suomalainen vapaa-aika: arjen ilot ja valinnat [Finnish Leisure: Everyday Joys and Choices]. Gaudeamus, Helsinki (2009)

23. Halman, L., Inglehart, R., Díez-Medrano, J., Luijkx, R., Moreno, A., Basáñez, M.: Changing Values and Beliefs in 85 Countries: Trends from the Values Surveys from 1981 to 2004. Brill, Boston (2007)
24. Chatzitheochari, S., Arber, S.: Class, gender and time poverty: a time-use analysis of British workers' free time resources. Br. J. Sociol. 63(3), 451–471 (2012)
25. Aguiar, M., Hurst, E.: Measuring trends in leisure: the allocation of time over five decades. Q. J. Econ. 12(3), 969–1006 (2007)
26. Gershuny, J.: Changing Times: Work and Leisure in Post-industrial Societies. Oxford University Press, Oxford (2000)
27. Robinson, J.P., Godbey, G.: Time for Life: the Surprising Ways Americans Use Their Time. Pennsylvania State University Press, State College (1999)
28. Statistics Finland, Ajankäyttötutkimus [Survey on use of time] (2011). http://www.stat.fi/til/akay/2009/05/akay_2009_05_2011-12-15_tie_001_fi.html
29. Pääkkönen, H.: Perheiden aika ja ajankäyttö. Tutkimuksia kokonaistyöajasta, vapaaehtoistyöstä, lapsista ja kiireestä [Family Time and Use of Time: Studies about Total Working Hours, Volunteer Work, Children and Tumult]. Tutkimuksia 254. Statistics Finland, Helsinki (2010)
30. Pääkkönen, H., Hanifi, R.: Ajankäytön muutokset 2000-luvulla [Changes of use of time in the 2000s]. Statistics Finland, Helsinki (2011)
31. Statistics Finland, Vapaa-ajan merkitys lisääntynyt [The importance of leisure has increased] (2005). http://www.stat.fi/ajk/tiedotteet/v2005/tiedote_005_2005-01-26.html
32. Statistics Finland, Väestörakenne, Väestö iän mukaan vuosina 1875–2009 2009 [Population structure, population according to age from the years 1875-2009] (2009). http://www.stat.fi/til/vaerak/2009/vaerak_2009_2010-03-19_tau_003_fi.html
33. Statistics Finland, Väestön tieto- ja viestintätekniikan käyttö, Internetin käytön muutoksia 2015 [The population's use of ICTs, changes in the use of the Internet 2015] (2015a). http://www.stat.fi/til/sutivi/2015/sutivi_2015_2015-11-26_kat_001_fi.html
34. Eurostat: Population structure and ageing (2014). http://ec.europa.eu/eurostat/statistics-explained/index.php/Population_structure_and_ageing
35. Myrskylä, M.: Elämme toistakymmentä vuotta elinajanodotetta pidempään [We Will Live a couple of Decades Longer than Life-Expectancy]. In: Tieto & trendit 1 (2010)
36. Weiss, R.S., Bass, S.A.: Challenges of the Third Age: Meaning and Purpose in Later Life. Oxford University Press, Oxford (2002)
37. Karisto, A.: Finnish baby boomers and the emergence of the third age. Int. J. Ageing Later Life 2(2), 91–108 (2007)
38. Näsi, M., Räsänen, P., Sarpila, O.: ICT activity in later life: internet use and leisure activities amongst senior citizens in Finland. Eur. J. Ageing 9(2), 169–176 (2012)
39. Gilleard, C., Higgs, P.: Contexts of Ageing: Class, Cohort and Community. Polity Press, Cambridge (2005)
40. Peacock, S.E., Künemund, H.: Senior citizens and internet technology: reasons and correlates of access versus non-access in a European comparative perspective. Eur. J. Ageing 4, 191–200 (2007)
41. Van Dijk, J.A., van Deursen, A.J.: Digital Skills: Unlocking the Information Society. Palgrave Macmillan, New York (2014)
42. Van Dijk, J.A.: The deepening Divide: Inequality in the Information Society. Sage Publications, London (2005)
43. Tabachnick, B.G., Fidell, L.S.: Using Multivariate Analysis. Harper Collins College Publishers, California State University Northridge, Northridge (2001)
44. Rice, R.E., Katz, J.E.: Comparing internet and mobile phone usage: digital divides of usage, adoption, and dropouts. Telecommun. Policy 27(8), 597–623 (2003)

45. Hargittai, E.: Digital na(t)ives? variation in internet skills and uses among members of the "net generation". Sociol. Inq. **80**(1), 92–113 (2010)
46. Blom, R., Melin, H., Nikula, J.: Changes in the work situation: proliferation of good working life or just the same old pall? In: Blom, R., Melin, H. (eds.) Economic Crisis Social Change and New Divisions in Finland, pp. 25–52. Publications of Department of Sociology and Social Psychology. University of Tampere, Tampere (1998)
47. Florida, R.: The Rise of the Creative Class. Basic Books, New York (2002)

Elders' Perceptions on the Role of ICTs on Their Lives

Charo Sádaba[✉]

Institute for Culture and Society, School of Communication, University of Navarra,
31080 Pamplona, Spain
csadaba@unav.es

Abstract. Elders have embraced the technology at a later stage than the rest of population due, mainly, to their difficulty to keep pace of the evolution of the technology, life situations that usually do not require a big exposure to the internet, and the age-related physical limitations such as failing eyesight or reduced dexterity. But in a context of promotion of active aging, the internet offers a real option to fight social isolation and, in consequence, to improve elderly well-being. A theoretical reflection about how computer mediated communication could help this age group to increase social capital is offered. As Western governments are designing inclusion programs for the elderly the social perspective and potential benefits of the technology should be taken into account.

Keywords: Elderly · Technology · Internet · Social capital · Social isolation · Computer mediated communication · Active aging · Inclusion · Digital divide

1 Introduction

On May 22nd 2009 Maria Amelia López, the world oldest blogger at that time, passed away in her hometown, a small village in the North of Spain, Muxia. She was introduced to the internet by her granchildren two years before that and since then she blogged about her political memories but also about her own life. While doing so, as she stated in one of her last posts "I forget about my illness. The distraction is good for you– being able to communicate with people. It wakes up the brain, and gives you great strength." Her blog[1] was during those years a global success with more than 1.5 million visits.

Some years later, on March 2014, Peter Oakley, the "Internet GranDad" died in the UK at the aged of 86[2]. His YouTube channel was once the most popular of this video platform. Between 2006 and 2014 Mr. Oakley uploaded more than 400 videos covering subjects as his childhood memories or his everyday events. One of the most surprising effects of his presence on the YouTube was that thousands of users "adopted" him as GranDad and talked to him sharing hours of online conversations. Later on, he recognized that "there are millions of people without grandparents who find small comfort in

---

[1] http://amis95.blogspot.com.
[2] http://www.independent.co.uk/news/people/internet-grandad-peter-oakley-dies-aged-86-9214952.html.

© Springer International Publishing Switzerland 2016
J. Zhou and G. Salvendy (Eds.): ITAP 2016, Part I, LNCS 9754, pp. 238–244, 2016.
DOI: 10.1007/978-3-319-39943-0_23

old, simple, stories. I have had my 15 min of fame - and enjoyed every minute of it."[3] In one of his videos he also stated that "being online has alleviated my loneliness"[4].

These two cases received a wide interest from worldwide media. Both were frequently interviewed by newspapers and television stations from all over the world. Their stories were relevant due to its exceptionality: elders are far away of technology and it is not usual to see them in the center of the digital stage.

But one the most interesting things about these stories is that both of them recognized how being connected to the world through the technology alleviated some of the ailments they were suffering because of their age: it was good to forget about health problems and it helped them to fight loneliness and social isolation.

2   Elders in a Connected World

As both Mrs. López and Mr. Oakley stated several times, being online could be a source of benefits for elderly people that should be actively explored. Inclusion policies in Western countries in the last years have focused on this particular group and research has been lately focused on finding out the main functionalities and profits that technology could offer to active aging lifestyles [1].

But in fact these efforts also recognize that older population has had more difficulties to embrace technology than other demographic groups and this is why they need extra resources now. This probably will change in the next few years quite radically with the retirement of a generation of able technology users that would use technology to manage a new life stage full of social activities.

In the meanwhile, and when implemented, one of the objectives of the policies is fighting social isolation and loneliness through technology as an effective way to improve older people's well being and quality of life [2].

2.1   Elders Online

In 2014, according to Pew Internet Research, 57 % of citizens aged 65 or more in the US used the internet, email or access the internet via a mobile device[5], while a 74 % of those owned a cell phone. Consultancy firm McKinsey&Company report [3] found out that in October 2014, 18 % of the 4,4 billion offline individuals worldwide were seniors (55 and up). This group is disproportionately represented as it supposes, according to this study, the 7 % of the online population worldwide. In the particular case of Spain, for example, latest available data shows that 74,6 % of elderly people (age 65 and up) has never used the internet[6].

---

[3] http://www.independent.co.uk/news/people/internet-grandad-peter-oakley-dies-aged-86-9214952.html.

[4] http://www.telegraph.co.uk/news/uknews/10389336/Peter-Oakley-being-online-has-allevi-ated-my-loneliness.html.

[5] http://www.pewinternet.org/data-trend/internet-use/latest-stats/.

[6] Imserso, Barómetro Mayores UDP, January 2015, ref. 14089-14223/III-2.

When using the technology, cognitive age, technology-related anxiety and adventurousness are the psychological variables relevant to their online behavior [4]. According to Rogers [5] it could be said that, as a group, elders' innovativeness is lesser than in other age groups as children or young adults, for example, that have adopted the technology at a quicker pace and in a more pervasive way.

There are several reasons to explain this weak relation between this age group and digital technology: elders are less familiar with computers and mobile devices than the younger generations, and it can be difficult for them to keep pace of the rapid evolution of the technology. Seniors, who are more likely to be retired or unemployed, have because of this life situation less exposure to the internet and the latest technologies on a everyday basis. And, besides that, there are also physical limitations such as failing eyesight or reduced dexterity that can also present issues for this age group.

While it is true that internet penetration amongst this group is, all over the world, less significant than the rest of population, during the last five years some technological advances, as the touch-based screen devices, have had a relevant and positive impact on the number and the extent of activities older people is embracing in Western countries.

From a theoretical point of view, and based on previous research, this article offers a reflection on how and why elderly is coping with a highly digital social environment, with and intensive culture of sharing personal information with others. Cultivating social capital [6], creating and maintaining social bonds, emerges as a feasible explanation to the actual practices and a promising reality for those elders who are not still online.

3 Social Media Use: Potential Benefits and Risks

In November 2015 Facebook had more than 1.5 billion accounts (almost 1 billion of these were accounts of active users)[7]. Spending time on social media platforms or applications is one of the most popular activities for internet users all over the world. But understanding the reasons behind this behavior is a very complex issue.

Kietzmann et al. [7] propose a honeycomb of seven blocks to explain social media functionalities. According to them social media users are revealing their identity (the real or the ideal one), having conversations, sharing content with others, maintaining a public presence, establishing relationships, managing reputation and trust, and taking part in groups or communities. The blocks are not exclusive and most users are doing several of these things at the same time.

Exploring the reasons behind elders' social media use is still a novel field, as this age group has only recently joined the social networking sites in a significant way. As Peral et al. [4] explained, the existing preconceptions about elders are not valid anymore and cognitive age, feeling younger, is probably the most important driver to be present online.

Besides this, establishing and maintaining social ties is also very important for this age group. As families are spread in different physical locations, technology offers the elderly an effective and cheap way to be in contact with their children and, above all,

---

[7] http://www.internetworldstats.com/facebook.htm.

their grandchildren. Real time video applications, as Skype, Google Hangout or Face-Time, are some of the most popular tools to satisfy this particular need. And once they are online, creating new social connections is very natural for this age group.

Fighting boredom and loneliness have been two the main objectives to explain elderly media usage: this target group is heavy user of television content as a way to entertain themselves and pass the time [8]. The internet offers them a new way to discover and consume content but it also adds a valuable social component that potentially makes it very attractive to this group.

3.1 Benefits: Building Social Capital

Social capital has been mentioned as one of the potential benefits of social media use. That engagement and participation in social groups have positive consequences for both the individual and the community is not a novel idea as it refers to Durkheim's suggestion of group life as an antidote to anomie and self destruction [9].

According to Portes (2000: 44) two elements may help to explain the popularity of the concept of social capital in the last decades: firstly, it focuses on the positive consequences of sociability ignoring the less attractive ones; but it also relates those consequences with a broader discussion where social capital can be a source of power and influence as if it were a financial asset.

Social capital could be bridging (and inclusive) and/or bonding (or exclusive). The former is formed through open social connections including several people who can join a single common interest, while the second refers to those tighter forms present on homogeneous groups, with a strong identity. Although inclusive social capital allows a greater number of relationships in the wider environment, they may be weaker than those typical of most closed or exclusive groups.

One of the main functions of social capital is being a source of network-based support beyond the immediate family: in an aggressive and very individualistic society, where lifestyles push individuals to be away from the family unit, social networks become a good substitute for human support.

It is Putnam [10] who advocates in a more determined way that also virtual social networks can add to social capital as they also create value, both individual and collective, and users can "invest" in building a network of relationships.

In recent years it has become clear the crucial role of communication technologies helping people to create social and emotional connections; also as internet can improve our communication skills it has an immediate effect on the enrichment of social communities. There is agreement on the ability of computer mediated communication to generate a sense of intimacy similar to face to face communication, which explains how research has consistently related internet usage with higher levels of general wellness [11–13].

The ability of mediated communication to increase or at least maintain social capital has been widely studied by Katz et al. [14]. Social capital increases with the development of virtual communities while the physical ones are still extending. An increase in virtual social relationships should not imply a reduction of the physical social life, but can complement and expand internet community relations, and consequently the social capital. Thus, a greater computer mediated communication should be followed by more social contact, civic participation and a greater sense of community.

It could be argued that computer mediated communication presents a clear barrier for elderly as sometimes it is difficult for this age group to deal with technological devices and applications. Learning curve is slower for them as their use is less intensive and usually not associated to work tasks and pressures. And, of course, physical limitations also are important: reading on small screens could be challenging when facing failing eyesight, and interacting with content, even through touch-based screens, could be a difficult with reduced dexterity. But in the last years several advances are being developed to allow an easier user experience despite of the age and physical conditions. Accessibility is today a must for software and hardware companies and it could be foreseen a clear improvement in this area, so the technology mediation would be everyday less relevant from the practical point of view.

It is relatively easy to find arguments to support how the use of social networking sites can increase social capital, but these benefits can only be achieved when, as Katz et al. note. (2004: 13) subjects are aware of the online /offline duality and are mature enough to understand and take advantage of the social networks' benefits.

And in this particular point elderly are better equiped than other age groups. Their life experience, not an asset in the case of younger users [15], allows them to have an increased awareness of the online/offline duality and, at the same time, they are able to understand the real benefits of social networking sites because they have a real need to satisfy.

In fact some researchers have found out a compensatory use of social networking sites due to the existence of weak or unsatisfactory social relations rather than an online investment countered by a strong social capital offline [16].

So, in terms of cultivating social capital, and being a fact that the physical barriers avoiding a more general use of the technologies by this age group are being reduced, it could be said that elders are in a very good position to explore the social media and social networking sites as a way to develop social capital. They have the need to foster the use, but also have the experience to understand what the real benefits are. And, at the same time, they do not have the eagerness of some younger internet users.

3.2   Social Media Risks: Privacy and Trust

While building social capital could be a potential benefit for elders' usage of social media, it is also true that there is not always a direct and positive correlation between this use and an increase in social capital. In fact, and according to Katz et al. [14], physical distance produces more fragmented and less dinamic communities.

The emergence of social media in the last decade has also led to a scenario where social convergence has become the norm online [17] and personal information is the currency. While privacy concerns around this issue are clear and very important, internet users are disclosing a huge amount of personal information in order to create, establish or maintain personal relationships. The potential benefits, such as an increase in social capital [18, 19], seem to balance the risks perceived by users [20].

Social networking sites, as Facebook or Twitter, or other types of social platforms as dating sites, invite their users to set up a personal profile first and then share personal information with their friends and followers. Previous research about how individuals present themselves in cyberspace has demonstrated that they can be strategic managing their self image online [21].

In the case of elders, their usually slower publication pace, due to lower technical abilities, protects them from some of the risks that younger and more able users are facing.

A possible risk this age group could face when developing virtual relationships is related to the cues that a more experienced user has to understand a behavior and, therefore, to trust or not a particular user who wants something from him or her [22]. While none seems to be free of this risk, and emotions can sometimes lead to take unsafe decisions regarding disclosure of personal information, more experienced users have at least previous examples or ways to quickly read misconducts and act accordingly.

4 Discussion

Since the arrival of the internet to the general population, elder people has had a complicated relationship with technology even in the more developed world. Western countries are fighting to make this digital divide everyday less significant through the promotion of inclusion programs, but it is still an important barrier in most developing countries.

Probably due in part to their apparent lack of interest, and their real lack of presence online, research about the motivations and drivers for elders' social media usage is yet in its first steps. While there are a good number of researchers working on the relation between health and technology, are mainly the functional abilities of the devices the ones that are being explored.

From a social sciences point of view there is room for improvement and implementation of research projects dealing with their inner motivations, and the psychological barriers that older users are facing when dealing with technology. An interdisciplinary effort is required to properly cover this, as it is a fact that there are physical elements that can constitute barriers higher enough to deter these users to try or repeat an experience with technology.

Social capital has emerged as a natural result of the social media explosion we are living in. While researchers are trying to measure the real impact of its usage over social capital, it seems that elders are in a very good position to explore this potential benefit: they have a real need of social contact and at the same time have the maturity to embrace the use of social media minimizing the risks and maximizing the opportunities.

References

1. Llorente, C., Viñarás, M., Sánchez, M.: Internet and the elderly: enhancing active ageing. Comunicar 23(45), 29–36 (2015)

2. Cattan, C., White, M., Bond, J., Learmouth, A.: Preventing social isolation and loneliness among older people: a systematic review of health promotion interventions. Ageing Soc. **25**, 41–67 (2005)
3. McKinsey&Company: "Offline and falling behind: Barriers to Internet Adoption", October 2014
4. Peral, B., Arenas, J., Villarejo, A.F.: From digital divide to psycho-digital divide: elders and online social networks. Comunicar **23**(45), 57–64 (2015)
5. Rogers, E.: Diffusion of Innovations. The Free Press, New York (1971)
6. Bourdie, P.: The forms of capital. In: Richardson, J.C. (ed.) Handbook of Theory and Research for the Sociology of Education, pp. 241–258. Greenwood, NY (1985)
7. Kietzmann, J.H., Hermkens, K., McCarthy, I.P., Silvestre, B.S.: Social media? get serious! understanding the functional building blocks of social media. Bus. Horiz. **54**, 241–251 (2011)
8. Haddon, L.: Social exclusion and information and communication technologies: lessons from studies of single parents and the young elderly. New Media Soc. **2**(4), 387–406 (2000)
9. Portes, A.: Social capital: its origins and applications in modern sociology. In: Lesser, E.L. (ed.) Knowdlegde and Social Capital: Foundations and Application, pp. 43–67. Butterworth-Heinemann, Boston (2000)
10. Puttnam, R.: Bowling Alone. Simon & Schuster, New York (2000)
11. Gibbs, J.L.: Self-presentation in online personals: the role of anticipated future interaction, self-disclosure, and perceived success in Internet dating. Commun. Res. **33**, 152–177 (2006)
12. McKenna, K.Y.A., Green, A.S., Gleason, M.: Relationship formation on the internet: what's the big attraction? J. Soc. Issues **58**, 9–31 (2002)
13. Valkenburg, P.M., Peter, J.: Social consequences of the internet for adolescents: a decade of research. Curr. Dir. Psychol. Sci. **18**, 1–5 (2009)
14. Katz, J.E., Rice, R.E., Acord, S., Dasgupta, K., David, K.: Personal mediated communication and the concept of community in theory and practice. In: Kalbfleisch, P. (ed.) Communication and Community, Communication Yearbook 28, pp. 315–371. Erlbaum, Mahwah (2004)
15. Sadaba, Ch.: Use of information and communication technologies by Latin American children and adolescents. The interactive generations case. Media@LSE Working Paper Series **29** (2014)
16. Colombo, F., Aroldi, P., Carlo, S.: New elders, old divides: ICTs, inequalities and well-being amongst young elderly italians. Comunicar **23**(45), 47–55 (2015)
17. Boyd, D.: Facebook's privacy trainwreck. exposure, invasion, and social convergence. Convergence: Int. J. Res. New Media Technol. **14**(1), 13–20 (2008)
18. Ellison, N., Steinfield, C., Lampe, C.: The benefits of facebook friends: Social capital and college students' use of online SNSs. J. Comput. Mediated Commun. **12**(4), 1143–1168 (2007)
19. Sádaba, Ch., Vidales, M.J.: El impacto de la comunicación mediada por la tecnología en el capital social: adolescentes y teléfonos móviles. Virtualis **6**(11), 75–90 (2015)
20. Ibrahim, Y.: The new risk communities: social networking sites and risk. Int. J. Media Cult. Polit. **4**(2), 245–253 (2008)
21. Walther, J.B., Slovacek, C., Tidwell, L.: Is a picture worth a thousand words? Photographic images in long-term and short-term computer-mediated communication. Commun. Res. **28**, 105–134 (2001)
22. Whitty, M.: Revealing the 'real' me, searching for the 'actual' you: presentations of self on an internet dating site. Comput. Hum. Behav. **24**, 1707–1723 (2008)

A Usability Research for Developing and Deploying Chronic Pain Relief Treatment Applications for Older Adults

Wang-Chin Tsai[1(✉)], Chia-Ling Chang[2], and Cheng-Min Tsai[3]

[1] Department of Product and Media Design, Fo Guang University, Yilan, Taiwan
forwangwang@gmail.com
[2] Department of Education Industry and Digital Media, National Taitung University,
Taitung, Taiwan
idit007@gmail.com
[3] Department of Creative Product Design and Managerment, Far East University, Tainan, Taiwan
ansel.tsai@gmail.com

Abstract. Chronic Pain relief treatment strategies have been shown to improve health outcomes and decrease the cost of healthcare for older adults living with chronic illness. Reliable health informatics applications, which allow older individuals to manipulate and review personal chronic pain related information have, in turn, been shown to improve chronic pain relief treatment outcomes by supporting learning and reflection. We identify the need for a handheld device infrastructure that facilitates the creation and deployment of such applications and describe our progress in developing and making available such an infrastructure, which we call "Pain Free and Fly". We discuss how the content of Pain Free and Fly. Follows from key strategies and results in the chronic pain relief treatment literature, and how its application programming application and related services can be leveraged by other researchers wishing to build an older adults' chronic pain health treatment applications. This investigation analyzed several tasks and collects the related information and opinion from observation and interview. Research findings are based on the outcome of the usability testing and investigation.

Keywords: Chronic pain · Older adults · Treatment · Usability testing

1 Introduction

Persistent pain is common among the aging population, much more so than in younger cohorts. Recent studies on pain found that 17 % of adults under 30 in Taiwan experience pain often compared with 57 % of older adults. The prevalence of pain in older persons (typically defined as 65 years or older by demographers, insurers, and employers) consistently demonstrates a substantial burden of pain, with reports of 28 % to 39 % of older adults in the community experiencing daily pain and 42 % to 73 % of older persons residing in nursing homes experiencing pain. Furthermore, undertreated pain has many potential detrimental consequences that affect the individual in question but also can

© Springer International Publishing Switzerland 2016
J. Zhou and G. Salvendy (Eds.): ITAP 2016, Part I, LNCS 9754, pp. 245–252, 2016.
DOI: 10.1007/978-3-319-39943-0_24

burden their family, friends, and even society. These consequences include depression, anxiety, falls, malnutrition, reduced cognition, impaired sleep, functional disturbances, declines in socialization and recreational activities, increased health care costs, and reduced quality of life. Higher postoperative pain scores are related to longer hospital stays, increased time to ambulation, and chronic functional impairment, indicating that pain has a more potent impact than simply patient discomfort and needs to be addressed early.

Although it is clear that chronic pain can markedly impair physical function, emotional well-being and general quality of life for a large portion of the population, it is far less clear how sufferers of chronic pain can effectively manage their experience of pain. In particular, people may have difficulty identifying factors that trigger or finding method reduce their pain. In addition, current pain treatment programs may be limited to treating symptoms through medication and may ignore other contributing factors. Moreover, despite evidence that actively involving and educating patients about their care helps reduce pain levels [1]. It was not clear whether commercially available tools for pain treatment actually support people's understanding of the relevant factors and present this information in a useful tool.

Therefore, pain relief treatment strategy and technology tool seeks to empower older individuals living with chronic illness to improve their quality of life and health outcomes by making informed decisions and useful tool about actions and behaviors that affect older adults' health. In the past time, older patient taking part in such pain treatment educational programs are taught problem-solving skills which, combined with the disease-specific information and technical skills taught in patient education, enable them to identify health problems and take the actions necessary to overcome them [2]. Pain relief treatment strategies and technology tool have been shown to be effective in improving the health outcomes of older individuals living with diabetes, asthma, arthritis and other chronic illnesses.

Various pain relief treatment strategies and technology tool help older patients understand relationships between their health status and condition. As such, personal technology tool that helps older patients track and present this type of pain information can help improve their health outcomes and quality of life [3]. Such tools, which include network-aware medical devices, online remedy diaries, digital pedometers and a wide variety of other hardware and software, have received a great deal attention from academia and industry in recent years.

The purpose of the present investigation was to focus on the factors and design element critical to the effective treatment of chronic pain and to evaluate pain treatment tools currently available to the general public using these criteria as well as general human factors principles. To clarify the problems most relevant to pain treatment, we conducted structured interviews with two subject matter experts (SMEs). In addition, a usability analysis of an available pain relief and treatment tool names "Pain Free and Fly" was conducted with fifteen older adults and a heuristic analysis of two additional pain treatment tools available on the market was also performed.

2 Literatures

2.1 The Concept of Chronic Pain Treatment

Treating chronic pain can be challenging. And it may take several types or combinations of treatments before you find relief. Passive therapy (those treatment modalities that do not require energy expenditure on the part of the patient) can provide short term and instant relief during chronic pain flare-ups and is directed at controlling symptoms such as pain, inflammation, and swelling [2, 5]. These therapies can include massage, ultrasound, iontophoresis, paraffin (wax) treatment, light therapy, or traction. Passive therapies may be useful over the short term but have limited benefit for chronic pain conditions overall. The key to effective treatment, however, is still a combination of avoidance of migraine triggers, stress treatment and relaxation techniques, and non-medication symptom relief through the use of locally applied heat or cold, massage, hot showers, and rest in a quiet, darkened room [4]. Older adults benefit from complementary or alternative therapies such as relaxation techniques, training in relief hypnosis, biofeedback, yoga, aromatherapy, acupuncture, spinal manipulation, and homeopathic remedies is useful for relieving different kinds of pain. Moreover, traditional pain acupressure is most popular selection for facing chronic pain in Taiwan,

2.2 The Current Application to Chronic Pain Relief Treatment

Chronic Pain is complex, so there are many treatment options -medications, therapies, and mind-body techniques. Acupuncture and acupressure are types of traditional Chinese medicine. It needs to determine trigger points that the areas within the body's muscle groups that cause pain to be felt elsewhere in the body. It helps individuals and massage practitioners alike identify the relevant trigger points and focus on them for pain relief. These remedies relieve pain by manipulating the skin at key points. This prompts the body to release endorphins which can block messages of pain from being delivered to the brain. This preliminary research discuss some of the existing pain relief applications and clarify the continued works of usability testing.

Muscle Trigger Points Massage Therapy. The Muscle Trigger Points Massage Therapy application is an extensive compilation of common trigger points in a human body and their related referral patterns. When pain exists in a human body, it can generally be alleviated or mitigated through massage therapy by focusing on key trigger points that cause the pain. Unfortunately, most people do not know where these trigger points are. Many massage therapists also often struggle to truly pin point the appropriate areas of the body to work on in order to relieve specific types of pain in specific areas of the body. This application helps overcome all such challenges. This application is great for individuals who are interested in relief healing methods, massage therapists, physical therapists, chiropractors, or anyone else interested in finding the cause of their muscular pain and how to relieve it. This application features hundreds of trigger points throughout the entire body and shows you each trigger point's corresponding referral patterns (where the pain could exist in the body. Not only will users be able to visually see the pain areas and trigger points, user will also be able to read about each (their causes and remedies). Further, you will find recommended exercises to prevent or mitigate such pain (Fig. 1).

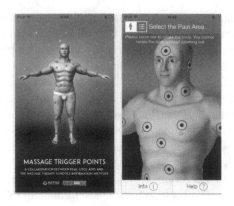

Fig. 1. Muscle trigger points massage therapy

Simply Health Back Care. The simply health Back Care app offers health information and advice to help user manage and prevent back pain. There are graphics and videos of exercises for user to follow and user can input the area and strength of user's pain to keep own pain diary. User can also search for practitioners near user from thousands of physiotherapists, chiropractors, osteopaths and acupuncturists. All information and exercises are supplied by the UK charity Back Care. With this app user will be able to record where and how severe own back pain is in the 'Me and My Back' diary. It can also watch and follow exercise videos and animated illustrations of common back pain relief and prevention exercises. Moreover, searching for qualified practitioners near user. User can also find information on preventing back pain: At home, in the office, When driving, When cycling exist (Fig. 2).

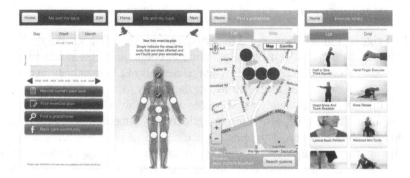

Fig. 2. Muscle trigger points massage therapy

3   Method

This research was conducted by means of usability experiment, structured questionnaire and interview. Each program's features were evaluated based on a set of common benchmark tasks. The experiment investigated the performance of chronic pain treatment programs on questionnaire. A structured questionnaire was utilized as a research tool for use opinion collection. The structured questionnaire consisted of three major dimensions: basic personal information, scale of computer skill knowledge, scale of instant message programs attitudes. Finally, the research conducted some short interview to discuss detailed behavior data and needs in order to be the references for the human factors concept development.

3.1   Participants

The sample for the usability investigation was composed of healthy, diverse older adults. Fifteen participants, four males and eight females, volunteered for this research. The mean age of the participants was 66.5 years (from 62 to 67 years, standard deviation 2.48 years). The participants were recruited from community classes for the elderly and through personal contacts. The older participants were asked to rate their computer skills on a Likert Scale from 1–5 (i.e., 1 = Not Skilled, 5 = Highly Skilled). One participant rate at level 1; nine at level 2; one at level 3; and one at level 4. These scores indicated a range of skills that could be discussed of this research. Although all but three participant had an Internet connection at home, their experience levels as information searchers were varied. Just only one participant was expert in using a variety of health-informedica application, while the rest were inexperienced as users, and had mainly head those titles. During the search session, all of the participants used the Android operating system to use the chronic pain relief and treatment application in Chinese. The sizes of the tablet monitors and resolutions were selected. The protocol was explained and informed consent was obtained from each participant.

3.2   Testing Procedure

The testing procedures consisted of the following steps:

1. The detailed program content was introduced to the individual participants.
2. Participants were given 10–15 min of free conducting the pain relief treatment programs to allow them to become familiar with the content.
3. Usability testing on chronic pain relief and treatment applications was conducted. Participants were required to perform tasks of the application. This research wanted to ascertain if there were additional problem areas that hindered interaction between participants. This research also wanted to gather data about how the participants encounter problems while using the application to accomplish interaction tasks. The tasks are shown as below:
   (1) Search for type of the pain
   (2) Take a photo to manipulate the location of pain
   (3) Acupressure of the pain location

3.3   Application for experiment-Pain Free and Fly

Chronic Pain is a highly complex disease that can have different characteristics for each person that struggles with it. In order to smoothly decrease and effectively treat chronic pain, older patients rely on such acupressure information and methods about personal condition as possible. Traditional pain acupressure that document a rough paper simply don't give the necessary details and procedure. The current Pain Free application with 18 different pain and remedy acupressure modules, chronic Pain Free and Fly provide health acupressure solution. It gives older patients the tools needed to capture, aggregate, and analyze this wide array of information into a format that older adults can use to best relieve chronic pain (Fig. 3).

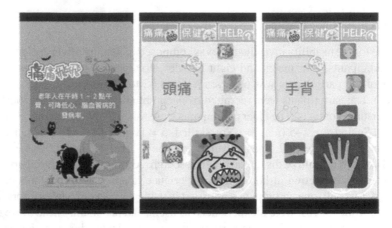

Fig. 3. Pain free and fly

4   Discussion and Results

This study was carried out to find out the kinds of errors made by older novice users of a "**Pain Free and Fly**" Application of tablet computer. Due to the nature of the study it was impossible to identify with certainty the definitive causes of the errors from the users' side, but some errors may be related to the age of the participants, such as reduced visual capability: e.g. the text information on some of the controls was too illegible for older participants to see or be able to recognize. Another problem was reduced dexterity and muscle control (and in some cases in appropriate finger characteristics to operate a capacitive touchscreen reliably). The acupressure controls required very specific photo inputs to operate correctly, whether for press duration time, accuracy, speed or simply, the touchscreen capacitance range was calibrated to limited area. Other problems seemed to because by inexperience, older users having not enough transfer able prior technology experience, or by conflicting prior experiences. For example, there is sometimes a lack of explicit confusion on finger and palm controls, so older users do not have a clue what the control is meant to do. Another problem seemed to be a lack of confidence, making older participants hesitant to engage in a 'trial and error' exploration approach (Fig. 4).

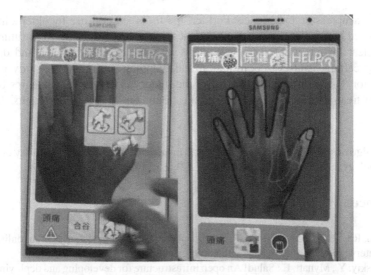

Fig. 4. The manipulation of area for acupressure

The main generic problems the participants encountered can be categorized as follows:

- Problems with operating the touchscreen reliably –both failed and repeated activations. The operation of the touchscreen appeared to be incorrectly calibrated for older users' fingers and palm capacitances, and so despite them carrying out what appeared to be the requisite length of time tapping, the device would simply not register a tap event.
- Confusion about how to move the finger and palm to the designated location. The touchscreen photo capture area required that older adults match to locations where they wanted the outline to be, rather than using the tab key in certain situations. This seemed problematic for older users who did not find it easy to learn to touch the screen to move the tablet, when was present.
- Conceptual problems, such as confusion between the concepts of acupressure modules (select and swipe to the left) and back (go to previous screen/back out of application). Older Participants seemed to transfer knowledge from prior experiences with non-digital applications (such as camera) and their limited digital experiences.

5   Conclusions

The information gleaned from the SME interviews helped identify the variables critical to pain relief treatment application, including physical acupressure guidance, area of acupressure, the acupressure quality, and side effect taking behavior. With such a large and complex body of knowledge, it is important to have some method of recording and clarifying the acupressure information. However, the usability and heuristic analyses revealed that current pain relief tool are limited in their ability to improve pain treatment and hence quality of life because of the absence of capabilities to support learning about one's pain acupressure experience. Further, the tools' ease of use by older adults was compromised by various design characteristics that must be considered in future tools, such as clear layout, uninformative anchors on acupressure modules, and difficulty modifying certain hand-eye coordination and mapping settings. This study provides guidance for design of tools that facilitate the understanding of relationships between pain-relief treatment factors to improve pain treatment through older adults' lifestyle changes.

Acknowledgements. This study received partly financial support from the Ministry of Science and Technology, under Grant No. MOST 104-2221-E-431-002.

References

1. Berman, R.L.H., Iris, M.A., Bode, R., Drengenberg, C.: The effectiveness of an online mind-body intervention for older adults with chronic pain. J. Pain **10**(1), 68–79 (2009)
2. Medynskiy, Y., Mynatt, E.: Salud! An open infrastructure for developing and deploying health self-management applications. In: 4th International ICST Conference on Pervasive Computing Technologies for Healthcare, Munich (2010)
3. Blondal, K., Halldorsdottir, S.: The challenge of caring for patients in pain: from the nurse's perspective. J. Clin. Nurs. **18**(20), 2897–2906 (2009)
4. Park, J., Cho, B., Paek, Y., Kwon, H., Yoo, S.: Development of a pain assessment tool for the older adults in Korea: the validity and reliability of a Korean version of the geriatric pain measure (GPM-K). Arch. Gerontol. Geriatr. **49**(2), 199–203 (2009)
5. McBride, S.E., Tsai, W., Knott, C.C., Rogers, W.A.: Supporting the management of osteoarthritis pain: a needs analysis. In: 55th Annual Meeting of the Human Factors and Ergonomics Society, Las Vegas (2011)

Understanding Age-Related Differences in Privacy-Safety Decisions: Acceptance of Crime Surveillance Technologies in Urban Environments

Julia van Heek$^{(\boxtimes)}$, Katrin Arning, and Martina Ziefle

Human-Computer Interaction Center, RWTH Aachen,
Campus-Boulevard 57, 52074 Aachen, Germany
{vanheek, arning, ziefle}@comm.rwth-aachen.de

Abstract. Although crime surveillance technologies (CST) are incrementally used in cities all over the world to improve safety, critics and data privacy specialists fear a rising violation of urban residents' privacy. So far, research on CST neither focuses in-depth on their acceptance nor addresses different user diversity factors. To reach a high degree of CST acceptance, not only technical parts are of importance but also human aspects and the way in which CST meet the residents' needs. In this paper, we present the results of a conjoint analysis (CA) study regarding the acceptance of CST with special focus on the residents' age and including the attributes *locations, reduction in crime rates (safety), handling of recorded footage (privacy)*, and *camera type*. Age-specific similarities and differences in respondents' preferences were revealed.

Keywords: Crime surveillance acceptance · Aging · Safety · Privacy · Conjoint analysis

1 Introduction

In recent years, the use of CST for the purpose of crime surveillance in urban environments has been controversially discussed: on the one hand, more and more different types of CST are installed in cities all over the world to enhance safety, driven by increasing numbers of terrorist attacks and criminal offenses [1–3]. On the other hand, critics and data privacy specialists fear a rising violation of the urban residents' privacy [4, 5]. In the course of urbanization processes and demographic change, by 2030 more people will live in cities than in other regions [6]. Thus, it will be an increasingly important challenge of modern societies to meet the complex requirements of urbanization processes as well as wishes and needs of future residents and to do justice to the trade-off between individual needs for safety and privacy. For this reason, research concerning acceptance of CST is required to determine at which locations and on what terms they are accepted and which conditions may lead to changes in needs for privacy and safety.

© Springer International Publishing Switzerland 2016
J. Zhou and G. Salvendy (Eds.): ITAP 2016, Part I, LNCS 9754, pp. 253–265, 2016.
DOI: 10.1007/978-3-319-39943-0_25

1.1   Crime Surveillance Technologies (CST)

Aiming for increasing safety in terms of higher rates of crime prevention and detection, a rising number of CST is currently used in almost every city in the world [7, 8]. This is heavily criticized by data protection specialists, who view the recording and storage of data as a violation of a human's privacy and personal rights [5, 9]. In particular, an absence of transparency is raising concerns pertaining to usage or processing of recorded data material, because, in most instances, it is unclear what exactly happens with recorded data. Thus, the relationship between privacy and safety is often understood as conflict or trade-off [10] and leads to central questions regarding the implementation of CST in urban areas: at which locations and on what terms is privacy or safety more important and to what extent do the requirements of city residents differ depending on individual characteristics? So far, it is a common practice to use CST without considering the requirements and needs of city residents [e.g., 11, 12]. A long-term acceptance and adoption of surveillance technologies in urban environments will only be achieved if residents are included into implementation processes and their wishes, fears, and needs are taken into account.

1.2   Acceptance of CST

Previous research essentially focuses on technical and functional features of CST such as localization and detection technologies or drones [13, 14] as well as the effectiveness of CST [5, 15]. These technologies are usually implemented into urban environments without considering opinions and needs of city residents and acceptance of CST is, if anything, comparatively superficially addressed. Attempts were made to understand crime surveillance acceptance by means of theoretical models or to determine whether crime surveillance is generally accepted or rejected [e.g., 16, 17].

So far, potential impact factors in terms of user diversity factors were only sporadically investigated: e.g., perceived safety [18], perceived crime threat [19], and gender [20] were emphasized to be important impact factors on the acceptance of CST and safety measures. Facing demographic change and aging societies, it is of great importance to examine if residents' age influences the acceptance of crime surveillance, which – to the best of our knowledge - has not been specifically examined yet. Besides user diversity factors, an understanding of determinants that affect technology acceptance is essential for a successful adoption and integration of innovative technologies [21]. Perceived safety and protection of one's own privacy [5, 22] as well as locations of surveillance and the type of inserted technologies [22] were proved to be influencing determinants for crime surveillance acceptance. Thus, an empirical approach is necessary, that investigates the acceptance of CST as a function of important determinants (locations, type of technology, and different needs for privacy and safety) and age as possible influencing user factor. Previous models like TAM or UTAUT are well-established theoretical approaches to explain and predict the adoption of technologies [23, 24]. However, they are not transferrable to the context of crime surveillance: questionnaires, designed on the basis of TAM and UTAUT, since they do not allow to holistically portray complex decision scenarios, in which several decision criteria are weighted against each other. Moreover, it is not possible to draw conclusions about relative importance, relationships, and inter-actions of factors concerning crime surveillance acceptance. By combining a conjoint analysis with a traditional questionnaire, more information can be obtained and different attributes' acceptance as well as their interrelations can be analyzed in detail.

2 Methodology

In this study, we assumed that the acceptance of CST is especially influenced by age. Thus, the results of a conjoint analysis study were analyzed with a particular focus on the respondents' age. The conjoint analysis approach included four attributes that had been identified as important impact factors on crime surveillance acceptance in a preceding study [22]: locations of surveillance, increase in privacy operationalized as reduction in crime rates, privacy in terms of different handlings of the recorded data material, and different camera types. The aim of this study was to examine whether and to which extent crime surveillance scenario decisions based on these attributes were linked to age.

2.1 Conjoint Analysis

Conjoint Analyzes (CA) combine a measurement model with a statistical estimation algorithm. They were developed in the 1960s and first deployed for assessments of products and product configurations as well as the determination of product prices [25]. Within a CA, respondents evaluate specific product or scenario configurations that consist of multiple attributes and differ from each other in the attribute levels.

Using CA data, simulations of decision processes as well as fragmentations of scenario preferences into separate part-worth utilities of attributes and their levels are enabled [26]. Relative importance of attributes provides information about the pro-portion an attribute contributes to the decision for or against a scenario and which attribute influences the respondents' selection most. Part-worth utilities indicate which levels are accepted or rejected most. Preference shares can be interpreted as indicator of acceptance. For this study, the choice-based-conjoint (CBC) analysis approach was chosen, because it mimics a complex decision process in which several attributes influence the final decision [26].

2.2 Attributes and Levels

Based on a literature analysis and a preceding quantitative study, we selected relevant influencing factors for video-based crime surveillance acceptance [22]:

- *Location:* private home environment was contrasted to public and semi-public locations as place for camera installation.
  - *Levels:* train station, market, department store, and home.

- *Reduction in crime rate (safety):* increase in safety as major benefit of crime surveillance, which was operationalized as a reduction in crime rate.
  - *Levels: 0 %, 5 %, 10 %,* and *20 %.*
- *Handling of recorded footage (privacy):* violation of one's own privacy as major barrier to crime surveillance, which was operationalized as different intensities of handling of recorded data material.
  - *Levels: archiving by police, storage in profile databases, location determination,* and *face recognition.*
- *Camera type:* refers to different camera types, which differ in features of size, visibility, and conspicuity.
  - *Levels: large & tracking, dome, mini-dome,* and *hidden & integrated.*

2.3 Experimental Design and Questionnaire

The questionnaire was composed using the SSI Web Software [27] and consisted of four parts. First, demographic data was assessed, e.g., age, gender, experience as a victim of crime. Second, respondents had to evaluate their needs for privacy and safety as well as their perceived crime threat (PCT) at different places (each four items on a six-point Likert-scale). For further analysis, sum scores were calculated relating to privacy needs, safety needs, and PCT (each: min = 4; max = 24). In a third step, the attributes and their levels were introduced. Afterwards, the scenario was presented and participants were to imagine that they would be alone during the day at one of the introduced locations. Then, participants should select the scenario that meets their needs for safety and privacy best and most. In the fourth part, the CBC choice tasks with four attributes and four levels each (see Sect. 2.2) were presented.

Since a combination of all corresponding levels would have led to 256 (4 × 4 4 × 4) possible combinations, the number of choice tasks was reduced. Thus, each respondent rated 10 random tasks and one fixed task. A test of design efficiency confirmed that the reduced test design was comparable to the hypothetical orthogonal design (median efficiency of 99 %).

2.4 Sample

Data was collected in an online questionnaire in Germany. Participants were invited via e-mail and were forwarded to the questionnaire that took approximately 15 min to complete. In total, 273 participants took part in the study. Since only complete questionnaires could be used for further analysis (i.e., no missing answers especially in the choice tasks), 162 data sets were analyzed (return rate: 59.3 %). The mean age of the participants was 35.5 years (min = 16, max = 80, SD = 14.6) and gender was evenly spread with 49.4 % males and 50.6 % females. Concerning their type of residence, the majority of participants (53.7 %) indicated to live in an apartment building, 28.4 % specified to live in a detached house, 11.1 % in a row house and 6.8 % in a semi-detached house. Regarding their residential area, 37.0 % of the respondents reported to live in the city center and 22.8 % on the outskirts, 22.2 % in suburbs and

17.9 % in a village. In terms of previous experiences with crime, 67.1 % have already fallen victim to *"slight offenses,"* e.g., theft or burglary, and 11.3 % to *"serious offenses,"* e.g., assault, robbery, rape. Altogether (each: min = 4; max = 24), an average need for safety (M = 12.2; SD = 4.7) and an average perceived crime threat (M = 11.2; SD = 4.4) were present. Needs for privacy were generally on an markedly higher level (M = 19.1; SD = 6.8).

2.5 Data Analysis

Data analysis was carried out by using Sawtooth Software [27, 28]: In a first step, relative importance of attributes and part-worth utilities were computed on the basis of Hierarchical Bayes estimation. In a second step, preference simulations were calculated, which estimate the influence on preferences if certain attribute levels change or are consciously kept constant within a specific scenario [26, 28]. The simulation of preferences allows for specific "what-if"-examinations, e.g., the influence of the privacy-safety trade-off on respondents' preferences can be analyzed in detail within a predefined scenario.

3 Results

This chapter presents the results of the conjoint analysis, differentiating between age effects among respondents. General results of the conjoint analysis have already been published [29]. In the present study we focused on the impact of age on scenario decisions in terms of crime surveillance preferences.

3.1 Segmentation and Characteristics of Age Groups

In order to understand age-related differences perceptions as well as diverse needs for safety and privacy depending on the age, we especially focus on a younger group (up to 25 years; n = 55; M = 22.6; SD = 2.5) and on an older group of participants (50 years and older; n = 34; M = 58.9; SD = 8.4). The results of the middle age group (between 26 and 49 years; n = 73) were also analyzed, but they are not reported here in detail, since they did not differ from the results of the "young group".

As the group characterization in Table 1 shows, both age groups did not differ significantly in terms of gender. However, they differed with regard to respective living circumstances: the majority of the "young group" lived in an apartment building and, for the most part, in city centers while on the other hand, the majority of the "old" group lived in houses (detached, semi-detached, row) primarily in rather rural areas outside the city center. Younger and older adults reported the same experiences with crime (i.e. have already become victims of "slight" or "serious" offenses). The same applied to safety needs, which did not differ significantly among young and older adults. In contrast, both groups differed strongly in their needs for privacy and perception of criminal threat: the participants of the "young" group had a significantly

Table 1. Characterization of both age groups

	"young" group (n=55)	"old" group (n=34)	P
age (M,(SD))	22.6 (2.5)	58.9 (8.4)	<.01
gender (male; female in %)	45.5% m ; 54.5% f	64.7% m ; 35.3% f	n.s.
type of residence in %	detached house 20% semi-detached house 9.1% row house 12.7% apartment building 58.2%	detached house 47.1% semi-detached house 5.9% row house 14.7% apartment building 32.4%	<.01
residential area in %	city center 49.1% outskirts 23.6% suburbs 16.4% village 10.9%	city center 5.9% outskirts 23.5% suburbs 35.3% village 35.3%	<.01
exp. "slight offenses"(%)	65.5% yes; 34.4% no	61.8% yes; 38.2% no	n.s.
exp. "serious offenses" (%)	12.3% yes; 87.7% no	9.1% yes; 90.9% no	n.s.
need for safety (M,(SD))	12.0 (4.2)	13.6 (5.5)	n.s.
need for privacy (M,(SD))	20.8 (4.1)	14.8 (9.0)	<.01
perceived crime threat (M,(SD))	9.5 (3.5)	13.9 (5.1)	<.01

higher need for privacy than the participants of the "old" group whereas the participants of the "old" group showed a clearly higher perception of criminal threat than the "young" group.

3.2   Importance of Attributes for Scenario Selection

By means of Hierarchical Bayes analysis, the importance of attributes was determined and, thus, main factors influencing the acceptance of crime surveillance acceptance were discovered depending on age groups (see Fig. 1).

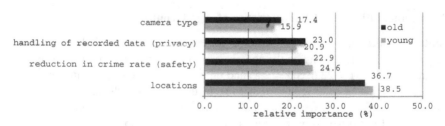

Fig. 1. Relative importance of attributes depending on age groups

In total, there were differences between the age groups regarding attributes and levels, but not very strongly pronounced. For both groups, *locations* was the most important attribute and influenced the decisions for or against a scenario the most. For the "young" (38.5 %) this attribute was slightly more important than for the "old" group (36.7 %). In contrast, the attribute *camera type* was least important for both groups and had the lowest impact on scenario decisions, whereas it was a little more important for the "old" (17.4 %) than for the "young" group (15.9 %). Interestingly, the importance of the attributes *reduction in crime rate (safety)* and *handling of recorded data (privacy)* showed comparatively unexpected results: although the "young" group was characterized by a stronger need for privacy, the *attribute reduction in crime rate (safety)* (24.6 %) was more important for the scenario decisions of this group than the attribute *handling of recorded data (privacy)* (20.9 %). In contrast, the "old" group showed an almost equal importance of *handling of recorded data (privacy)* (23.0 %) and *reduction in crime rate (safety)* (22.9 %). Accordingly, the privacy-attribute was slightly more important to the "old" group, while the safety-attribute was a bit more important to the "young" group. A more accurate idea of differences and similarities between the age groups can be demonstrated by the results of the utilities of attribute levels.

3.3 Utilities of Attribute Levels

In Fig. 2, the average part-worth utilities are shown for all attribute levels. Based on the part-worth utilities, attribute levels with highest positive and negative evaluations and, therefore, scenarios with highest and lowest potential of acceptance can be identified. The best scenario configuration for both age groups would be: crime surveillance at a "train station," with a "reduction in crime rate of 20 %," "archiving by police" as way of data handling, and using a "large & tracking camera."

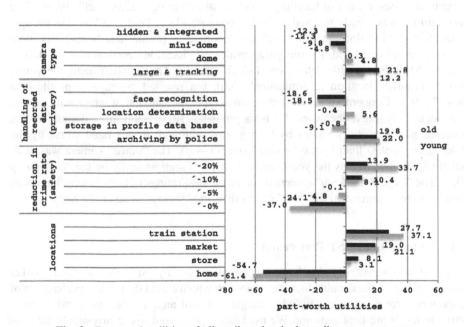

Fig. 2. Part-worth utilities of all attribute levels depending on age groups

Concerning absolute utility values, the levels of the attribute *locations* reached the largest span and, thus, the highest and lowest utility values for both age groups, which is explained by the high relative importance score of this attribute. Within this attribute, crime surveillance was rejected at "home," with the "young" group (–61.4) declining it a bit more strongly than the "old" group (–54.7). All public locations were rated positively and, therefore, they contributed to a favorable decision for a scenario, but to varying degrees. Surveillance at a "store" reached slightly positive utility values in the "young" group (3.1) and only marginally higher values in the "old" group (8.1). "Market" received clearly higher positive values from both groups ("young": 21.1; "old": 19.0). Crime surveillance at a "train station" reached the highest positive utility values in both groups, but it was unexpectedly (see Sect. 4.1) more important to the "young" (37.1) than to the "old" group (27.7). The safety-attribute *reduction in crime rate* received the second largest span and a nearly linear function of utility values (from the young group). The higher the reductions in crime rate (gain in safety), the higher were the utility values. A "reduction in crime rate of 0 %" was rated worst and it was more strongly rejected by the "young" (–37.0) than by the "old" group (–24.1). "5 % reduction in crime rate" was slightly rejected by the "young" group (–4.8) and evaluated as almost neutral by the "old" group (–0.1). A reduction of "10 %" resulted in positive evaluations by both groups ("young": 8.1; "old": 10.4). This positive evaluation quadrupled for a crime reduction of "20 %" in the "young" group (33.7), but 20 % less crime it was only rated slightly higher than 10 % by the "old" group (13.9). Within the privacy-attribute *handling of recorded data,* initial similarities of both age groups existed in relation to the worst and best evaluations: "archiving by police" was perceived as best option of handling recorded data ("young": 22.0; "old": 19.8); "face recognition" was clearly rejected by both ("young": –18.5; "old": –18.6). The groups' evaluation of "location determination" and "storage in profile data bases" was more diverse: on the one hand, the old group evaluated "location determination" (–0.4) as well as "storage in profile data bases" (–0.8) neutrally. On the other hand, the young group accepted "location determination" (5.6), but rejected "storage in profile data bases" (–9.1). Concerning the attribute camera type, the "hidden & integrated" camera was identically rated the worst by both groups (–12.3). The "mini-dome" camera received negative utility values by both groups, although it was rated worse by the "old" group (–9.8) than by the "young" group (–4.8). The "dome" camera was evaluated slightly positive by the young group (4.8), and seen neutrally by the "old" group (0.3). The "large & tracking" camera received the best ratings of both groups, but it was clearly more important to the "old" (21.8) than the "young" group (12.2).

3.4   Simulation of CST Preferences

In a next step, sensitivity simulations were carried out by using the Sawtooth market simulator [27]. In the simulation, we examined to which extent the relative preferences of respondents for a scenario vary when single levels of an attribute change while other attribute levels are kept constant. We used this type of analysis to investigate the relationship between safety and privacy for both age groups in more detail, because the relative importance of the attributes *reduction in crime rate (safety)* and *handling of recorded data (privacy)* were rather similar. Based on the findings in previously reported part-worth utilities, two constant safety and privacy scenarios of attributes levels were constructed: (1) "high safety" (and low privacy) with the levels "crime reduction of 20 %"

and "face recognition"; (2) "high privacy" (and low safety) with the levels "archiving by police" and "crime reduction of 0 %". These levels were kept constant while the levels of the other attributes (locations and camera type) changed. Outcomes are pictured in Fig. 3 for the "young" group and in Fig. 4 for the "old" group. In the "young" group, the "high safety" scenario reached a higher average preference (62.5 %) compared to the "high privacy" scenario (37.5 %) (see Fig. 3). For all single attribute levels, the "young" group's preference for "high safety" was clearly higher than for "high privacy." The acceptance of the "high safety" scenario (max. at train station +16.4 %) and, even more so, of the "high privacy" (max. at train station: +32 %) scenario rose, when surveillance was provided and carried out at public locations. There was only a small difference between the various public locations. However, at the private location (home), there was the largest difference between both scenarios and "high safety" was clearly preferred. Concerning all camera types, the "young" group favored the "high safety" scenario consistently by at least 21 %.

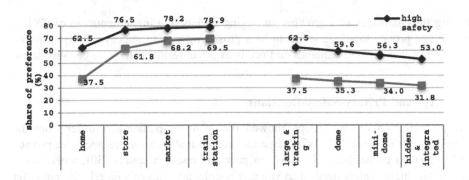

Fig. 3. Relative preferences for the scenarios "high safety" vs. "high privacy" ("young" group)

In contrast, the "old" group's decisions were not as explicitly unambiguous, because the preference ratings of both scenarios were closer together (see Fig. 4). Also in the "old" group, there was a higher average preference for the "high safety" (54.2 %) than the "high privacy" (45.8 %) scenario. The acceptance of the "high safety" scenario reached a maximum of 67.9 % for surveillance at a market (+13.7 %) and of the "high privacy" scenario a maximum of 72.3 % for surveillance at a train station (+26.5 %). Both scenarios were rated better when surveillance was carried out at public places. The "old" group preferred the "high safety" scenario (54.2 %) to the "high privacy" scenario at their home. At more public locations (store and market), the "old" group slightly favored the "high privacy" scenario. At a "train station" the "old" group preferred the "high privacy" scenario (72.3 %) clearly more than the "high safety" scenario (64.5 %). However, the "high safety" scenario was slightly preferred for all camera types.

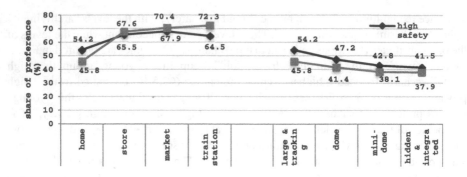

Fig. 4. Relative preferences for the scenarios "high safety" vs. "high privacy" ("old" group)

4   Discussion

Facing the challenges of a growing and aging society, the implementation of CST at public and private locations seems to be a promising way to improve safety in future cities. However, diverse demands and needs of urban residents have to be considered.

4.1   Age and Privacy-Safety-Decisions

The investigation of age groups showed that younger participants differ from the elderly, in particular in their living circumstances, but also in various needs for privacy and perceived crime threat. Contrary to previous research results [30], where older people had higher safety needs than younger people, this sample's elderly did not differ significantly from the younger generation in this regard. In general, results showed that crime surveillance decisions differ only slightly with respect to the participants' age. Crime surveillance seems to be such a central and engaging scenario that similar decision patterns occur regardless of age and are presumably driven by motives such as perceived threat and self-protection. When it comes to surveillance in urban areas, the location of surveillance is of great importance regardless of age.

Crime surveillance is accepted at public locations and rather rejected at private locations, although this could be driven by motives such as a greater perceived need for protection at public locations. In detail, younger participants rejected surveillance at home even more strongly than the elderly, which may be due to the fact that the elderly indicated a significantly stronger perceived crime threat "at home" ($p < 0.01$). Contrary to our expectations, surveillance at a "train station" was more important for younger participants. This was inasmuch unexpected as the elderly's total perceived crime threat was significantly higher and, thus, we assumed that all locations but especially public locations were favored by older participants. The camera type was of minor importance to both age groups and, thus, technical features of *cameras* such as visibility or conspicuity were comparably unimportant. However, if camera technology is used for surveillance, it should be visible and striking. Nowadays common seamless integration of surveillance systems into the private or public environment is not desirable from the users' perspective. Overall, participants' feedback showed that it comparatively does not matter how data is collected, it is more important what happens to the data and how long it is stored. Besides the location of surveillance, the trade-off between safety and privacy is important for crime surveillance acceptance and holds the most obvious differences between the age groups. Unexpectedly, for the younger group, the attribute safety was more important for scenario decision than the privacy-attribute, although this group was characterized by a higher need for privacy and a lower perceived crime threat. Using sensitivity analyzes in the market simulator, a direct decision situation between safety and privacy could be simulated, in contrast to previous findings, in which safety and privacy were usually evaluated in isolation [10]. The sensitivity analysis showed that younger participants decided clearly in favor of safety in a direct comparison between safety and privacy. Therefore, privacy is becoming less important and is abandoned to some extent in favor of safety, if it has to be explicitly decided between both. For the elderly, privacy and safety hold a similar importance. Only when considering the trade-off in the sensitivity analysis, trends are detectable: privacy is favored at home while safety is preferred at public locations. The elderly's decisions between safety and privacy are clearly more influenced by the location of surveillance than by the camera type. Results show the importance of considering safety and privacy in the context of urban crime surveillance: safety and privacy are both of great importance and the right balance between those aspects is different for diverse groups of urban residents.

4.2   Limitations and Further Research

The applied conjoint analysis approach was useful for evaluating preferences of different crime surveillance scenarios. However, it has some limitations in methodology and content, which should be considered in future studies. For example, the limited number of attributes has to be criticized. Participants' feedback showed a request for integrating other privacy aspects into the study, e.g., duration of data storage. In this study, a compromise had to be made between an economic research design with a limited number of attributes and the complexity of the research issue. Thus, in future studies, we will use adaptive conjoint approaches (e.g., ACBC) allowing for bigger attribute numbers. Furthermore, a comparatively young sample was under study, and thus, the size of the older group was slightly smaller than the younger group's size. This could have possibly resulted in an underestimation of barriers, concerns, or preferences. Thus, the study should be repeated in larger and regarding age, more representative samples. Additionally, the results mirror a European perspective with only one cultural context. Thus, we aspire a replication in other countries to compare crime surveillance needs and wishes of city residents depending on their cultures and backgrounds.

References

1. La Vigne, N.G., Lowry, S.S., Markman, J.A., Dwyer, A.M.: Evaluating the use of public surveillance cameras for crime control and prevention. Final Technical report, The Urban Institute, Justice Policy Centre, Washington, DC (2011)
2. Lyon, D., Haggerty, K.D.: The surveillance legacies of 9/11: recalling, reflecting on, and rethinking surveillance in the privacy era. Can. J. Law Soc. 27(3), 291–300 (2012)
3. Deflem, M., McDonough, S.: The fear of counterterrorism: surveillance and civil liberties since 9/11. Society 52(1), 70–79 (2015)
4. Whitaker, R.: The End of Privacy: How Total Surveillance is Becoming a Reality. The New Press, New York (1999)
5. Welsh, B.C., Farrington, D.P., Taheri, S.A.: Effectiveness and social costs of public area surveillance for crime prevention. Annu. Rev. Law Soc. Sci. 11(1), 111–130 (2015)
6. Ziefle, M., Schneider, C., Valeé, D., Schnettler, A., Krempels, K.H., Jarke, M.: Urban Future outline (UFO) a roadmap on research for livable cities. ERCIM News 98, 9–10 (2014)
7. Dailey, K.: The rise of CCTV surveillance in the US. BBC News Mag. (2013)
8. Barrett, D.: One surveillance camera for every 11 people in Britain, says CCTV survey. Telegraph (2013)
9. Schwartz, A.: Chicago's video surveillance cameras: a pervasive and poorly regulated threat to our privacy. Nw. J. Technol. Intell. Prop. 11(2), 45–60 (2012)
10. Friedewald, M., van Lieshout, M., Rung, S., Ooms, M., Ypma, J.: Privacy and security perceptions of european citizens: a test of the trade-off model. In: Camenisch, J., Fischer-Hübner, S., Hansen, M. (eds.) Privacy and Identity Management for the Future Internet in the Age of Globalisation, pp. 39–53. Springer, Heidelberg (2014)
11. Jho, W.: Challenges for e-governance: protests from civil society on the protection of privacy in e-government in Korea. Int. Rev. Adm. Sci. 71(1), 151–166 (2005)
12. Joh, E.E.: Privacy protests: surveillance evasion and fourth amendment suspicion. Ariz. Law Rev. 55, 997–1029 (2013)
13. Hampapur, A., Brown, L., Connell, J., Ekin, A., Haas, N., Lu, M., Merkl, H., Pankati, S., Senioa, A., Shu, C., Tian, Y.L.: Smart video surveillance – exploring the concept of multiscale spatitemporal tracking. IEEE Signal Process. Mag. 22(2), 38–51 (2005)
14. Sarre, R., Brooks, D., Smith, C., Draper, R.: Current and emerging technologies employed to abate crime and to promote privacy. In: Arrigo, B., Bersot, H. (eds.) The Routledge Handbook of International Crime & Justice Studies, pp. 327–349. Routledge, Abingdon (2013)
15. Cameron, A., Kolodinski, E., May, H., Williams, N.: Measuring the effects of video surveillance on crime in Los Angeles. Report for California Research Bureau, School of Policy Planning and Development, May 2008
16. Sousa, W.H., Madensen, T.D.: Citizen acceptance of police interventions: An example of CCTV surveillance in Las Vegas. Crim. Justice Stud. 29(1), 40–56 (2016)
17. Wiecek, C., Saetnan, A.R.: Restrictive? Permissive? The contradictory framing of video surveillance in Norway and Denmark. Report, Department of Sociology and Political Science, Norwegian University of Science and Technology, Trondheim (2002)
18. Boomsma, C., Steg, L.: Feeling safe in the dark: examining the effect of entrapment, lighting levels & gender on feelings of safety & lighting policy acceptability. Environ. Behav. 49(2), 193–212 (2012)
19. Van Heek, J., Arning, K., Ziefle, M.: How fear of crime affects needs for privacy & safety. Acceptance of crime surveillance technologies in smart cities. In: 5th International Conference on Smart Cities and Green ICT Systems, Rome, 23–25 April 2016

20. Sochor, J., Wester, M.: Gendered perceptions of positioning technologies. In: 5th International Conference on Women's Issues in Transportation (2014)
21. Rogers, E.: Diffusion of Innovations. New York Free Press, New York (2003)
22. Van Heek, J., Arning, K., Ziefle, M.: Safety and privacy perceptions in public spaces: an empirical study on user requirements for city mobility. In: Giaffreda, R., Caganova, D., Li, Y., Riggio, R., Voisard, A. (eds.) LNICST 151. Springer, Heidelberg (2015)
23. Davis, F.D., Bagozzi, R.P., Warshaw, P.R.: User acceptance of computer technology: a comparison of two theoretical models. Manage. Sci. 35(8), 982–1003 (1989)
24. Venkatesh, V., Morris, M.G., Davis, G.B., Davis, F.D.: User acceptance of information technology. MIS Q. 27(3), 425–478 (2003)
25. Luce, R.D., Tukey, J.W.: Simultaneous conjoint measurement. J. Math. Psychol. 1, 1–27 (1964)
26. Orme, B.: Interpreting the Results of Conjoint Analysis, Getting Started with Conjoint Analysis, pp. 77–89. Res. Pub. LLC Madison, WI (2010)
27. SSI Web,Version 8.2.0. Sawtooth Software Inc., Sequim (2013)
28. SMRT: Market Research Tools. Sawtooth Software Inc., Sequim (2013)
29. Van Heek, J., Arning, K., Ziefle, M.: "All eyes on you!" Impact of location, camera type, and privacy-security-tradeoff on the acceptance of crime surveillance technologies. J. Urban Stud. 253–265 (submitted 2016)
30. Dickerson, A.E., Molnar, L.J., Eby, D.W., Adler, G., Bé-dard, M., Berg-Weger, M., Trujillo, L.: Transportation and aging: a research agenda for advancing safe mobility. Gerontologist 47(5), 578–590 (2007)

Intentions to Use Smart Textiles in AAL Home Environments: Comparing Younger and Older Adults

Martina Ziefle[✉], Philipp Brauner, and Julia van Heek

Human-Computer Interaction Center, RWTH Aachen University,
Campus Boulevard 57, 52074 Aachen, Germany
{ziefle,brauner,vanHeek}@comm.rwth-aachen.de

Abstract. The vision of ubiquitous computing is increasingly picking up pace. An increasing number of everyday objects are equipped with smart technology and start to form the Internet of Things. Yet, interacting with these devices is based on conventional surfaces made of glass, metal, or plastic. We believe that textile interaction surfaces will be the next frontier of ubiquitous computing and identified many blank spots in the research landscape. Peoples' perception and acceptance of smooth and soft interaction surfaces is insufficiently understood. In this paper we present a study in which 90 people of a wide age range evaluated the suitability of smart textiles in different usage scenarios in the home environment. Overall, a solid willingness to use smart textiles as input devices was found, even though there were conditional acceptance criteria which should be given before participants would be willing to buy them. In contrast to many other technology contexts, however, age is not decisive in the evaluation of the usefulness of smart textiles. Younger and older adults seem to have a quite similar evaluation, hinting at a quite generic acceptance pattern.

Keywords: Smart textiles · Age · AAL · Technology acceptance · User diversity

1 Motivation

In 1991 Marc Weiser's and his team at Xerox Parc envisioned the tremendous shift caused by computers shrinking in size and growing in number and capacity [1]. The once bold vision of Ubiquitous Computing is increasingly becoming reality, as more and more everyday objects and devices are equipped with sensors, actuators, computing, and communication technology. The growing number of increasingly intermeshed set of smart objects is slowly but surely forming the Internet of Things [2]. While the increasing penetration of everyday objects with smart information and communication is a relatively new development, one should also consider mankind's past. Humanity uses textiles for at least 30.000 years [3, 4] and they still accompany us every day. Textiles are usually positively connoted and rely on inherent characteristics of the tissue - soft, flexible, elastic, warm, chic, pleasurable, smooth, velvety, multicolored – what makes this technology quite ubiquitous for many different usage contexts [5–7]. As smart technical devices will be increasingly used within home environments [8–10], these

© Springer International Publishing Switzerland 2016
J. Zhou and G. Salvendy (Eds.): ITAP 2016, Part I, LNCS 9754, pp. 266–276, 2016.
DOI: 10.1007/978-3-319-39943-0_26

aspects are likely to gain additional importance in the future [11, 12]. This is of special importance against the background of the demographic change [13, 14]. The challenges raised by the demographic change have been broadly recognized and well formulated in the last decade. In the near future, an increasingly number of older persons need extended long-term care in many societies, and traditional health care systems are not prepared to meet the increased demands, neither with regard to financial necessities, nor with regard to the medical care situation and the care supply chain [11, 15]. The enormous progress in information and communication technology as well as developments in medical engineering open up novel chances for supporting older patients in keeping mobility and maintaining independency at old age [8].

Studies show that older adults wish to maintain their independence as long as possible [16, 17] and to stay longer at home (rather than to move in a senior home), reaching a perceived gain in the quality of life in a familiar environment. In the last few years, the concept of Ambient Assisted Living formed a new understanding of technologically supported living at home [18, 19]. The integration of different kinds of smart sensors in the home environment is able to support seniors in maintaining independent life styles at home, e.g. by monitoring and control health-related information [20]. From a technical point of view, the integration of information and communication technology is basically feasible [21, 22]. From a social point of view, the integration of technology into the sanctuary of the own four walls is fragile [23, 24].

Recent research revealed that "home" is a synonym for retreat and protection in which technology is difficult to become an integral part. Also, rooms are quite differently seen regarding privacy and intimacy and the openness to integrate technology [25].

In order to reach a high degree of user acceptance, the users' perspectives should be considered as well as their requirements towards an accepted technology and their needs with respect to social values (e.g., privacy, dignity, connectedness, communication styles). In short: The success of Ambient Assisted Living necessitates an understanding of people and their willingness to use and integrate technical devices in their personal spaces [26].

2 The Research Context: Textiles in the Home Context

"Intuitex" is the framework of the research presented here, an interdisciplinary project at RWTH Aachen University, funded by the German Ministry of Education (http://www.comm.rwth-aachen.de/index.php?article_id=923&clang=0).

The project aims at the development of user-centered textiles as input devices to be integrated in ambient assisted living environments that adapts to the residents' requirements and which is a seamless and natural part of the daily living space of people. A specific focus is directed to the older and frail people and their requirements for usable and well-accepted technical products that can be used in the home environment. This claim includes an understanding of users' acceptance and the natural and intuitive use of textiles in context. In Fig. 1, schematic drawings of a potential application scenario are pictured, in which textiles are used as input devices to control light or room temperature.

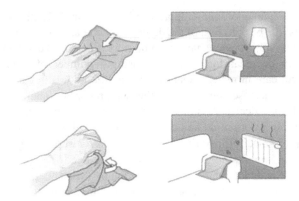

Fig. 1. Schematic drawings of potential applications of smart textiles within the home environment ® Intuitex, RWTH Aachen University.

The input devices need to be easy to use (in order to reach a high user acceptance), and should adapt to age-related difficulties in the manual control of input devices. Also the textiles should have attractive designs with suitable fabrics that fit seamlessly into the living spaces at home. Iteratively, users' requirements are empirically assessed and integrated into the technological development in order to produce prototypes in iterative cycles, with users evaluating the usability, the design, the aesthetics and the functionality in each of the iterative cycles.

In order to understand the perceived utility of smart textiles within the home context, we conducted a questionnaire study, in which users' attitudes towards the use of smart textiles are collected.

3 Method

The questionnaire study was directed to users' attitudes with respect to the perceived or envisioned use of smart textiles in different rooms and contexts at home. The study was assumed to catch a broad view on the topic, quantifying the benefits and barriers. Items used were based on previous empirical work in our workgroup, in which we collected argumentation patterns as well as user experience of users of a wide age range [5–7]. The questionnaire was delivered online and completing it took about 20 min.

3.1 Participants

A total of 90 persons volunteered to take part in the study (58.9 % female). Participants were reached through the social networks of younger and older adults. In order to analyze age effects, the whole sample was split in three age groups. Age group 1 - "the younger (≤ 30 years)" – consisted of 53 persons, with a mean age of 24.1 years (SD = 3.2). In age group 2, – "the middle-aged (>30 up to <50 years)" – were 20 persons with a mean age of 34.3 years (SD = 3.7) and in age group 3 – "the older (≥ 50 years)"– 17 persons, with a mean age of 57.2 years, SD = 6.5).

With increasing age, participants showed a significantly lower technical self confidence (as measured by the short scale of Beier [27], $r = -.276$; $p < 0.01$; $F (2,88) = 5.6$; $p < 0.05$). Regarding the needs with respect to usable and easy to learn devices, no age effects were found (n.s.). Nearly all participants – independently from their age – expressed a specific claim for usable devices (from 48 points to be reached, all age groups ranged at about 44 points). Participants were not gratified for their efforts. Only a small fraction (2 %) had previous experience with smart textiles. 40 % had heard about the possibility to use smart textiles (mainly from the sports area). Mostly, participants were not aware that textiles could be also used as input devices for the home context.

3.2 Questionnaire

After a short demographics section in which age, gender and previous experience of participants with smart textiles were assessed, an introduction part was presented, in which smart textiles were explained as well as the idea to use smart textiles as input devices. A next section then addressed *perceived requirements (conditional acceptance criteria), but also benefits and barriers.* The items were based on previous studies in this context [6, 7] (Table 1).

Table 1. Items within the section "requirements, benefits and barriers". The items had to be answered on a 6-point Likert scale (1 = I do not at all agree; 6 = I completely agree).

Statements	
Positive	"These devices simplify my life."
	"I will gladly use these smart textiles."
Negative	"Such a device will complicate my life."
	"These devices will probably break easy."
	"I doubt such a device will work properly if hands are wet or dirty."
	"I'm afraid this device will be quickly stolen."
Conditionals	"The handling must be easy to learn."
	"The textiles have to last for a long term."
	"The handling has to be fun."
	"The textiles have to be stylish."
	"Using such a textile must not exhaust me."
	"The textiles and the functions they can control must be useful."

Furthermore, it was of interest if smart textiles would be evaluated differently, depending on different usage contexts and home spaces, in which the textiles could be used. We contrasted four different scenarios: kitchen, living room, bedroom, and clothing (i.e., wearables). For all these different scenarios, the following statements had to be evaluated (Table 2).

Table 2. Use of smart textiles in kitchen, living room, bedroom, and clothing. Items were answered on a 6-point Likert scale (1 = I do not at all agree; 6 = I completely agree).

Scenario statements
"I think the presented scenario make sense."
"I would like to buy such a textile."
"I'd be concerned that a casual touch is interpreted as an operating gesture."
"I believe the necessary gestures to control the device are easy to learn."
"I believe I'd enjoy the handling."
"My friends will envy me this textile."
"I believe gestures will be reliably recognized by the textile."
"I will be able to quickly perform learned gestures."
"I would be embarrassed to use the smart textile in front of others."
"I'd be afraid of inadvertently damaging the textile (e.g., by spilling drinks over it)"

4 Results

In order to analyze age effects, ANOVA respectively MANOVA procedures were run, with age as independent and acceptance items as dependent variables.

4.1 Conditional Acceptance Criteria, Benefits and Barriers

In a first step, participants evaluated the conditional requirements for an accepted use of smart textiles. In Fig. 2, descriptive outcomes are depicted. Items were arranged in three categories: Items that support the use (positive), items which express a negative attitude (negative) and those items which depict conditional acceptance, thus requirements which should be given in order to reach acceptance. From Fig. 2, two things are noteworthy:

(1) The agreements to the positive statements as well as the negative statements was much lower than the agreement to the conditionals, which should be given before participants would use smart textiles. Neither do participants fully agree to the positive items, according to which devices simplify life, nor do participants fully agree to the negative statements that were directed to an uncomfortable and bothersome use of smart textiles. When it comes to the conditional acceptance criteria, usability, usefulness, and ease of using the textiles are in the foreground for all participants. Interestingly, the design and the stylishness of the textiles are not so important.

(2) Age effects in the evaluation of the conditional acceptance criteria, but also the perceived benefits and barriers were mostly not present, revealing a quite unique view on smart textiles. Regarding the claim that the devices must last for a long time, a significant age effect was found ($F(2,89) = 4.9$; $p < .001$), with the younger participants agreeing to this claim much more strongly than the middle-aged and the older participants. A next age difference referred to the belief that those textile input devices might complicate the lives ($F(2,89) = 3.2$; $p < .001$), which is more frequently confirmed by older adults.

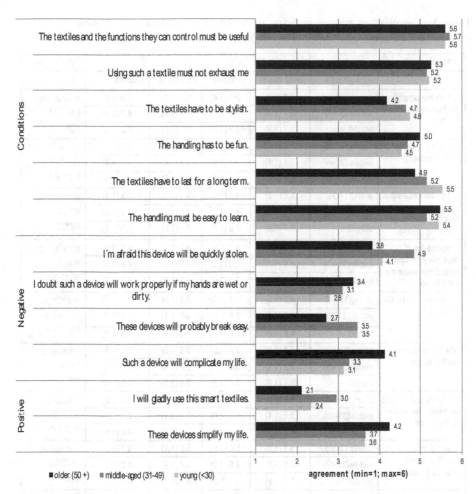

Fig. 2. Mean evaluations of requirements in the three age groups

4.2 Use of Smart Textiles in Different Home Scenarios

In a second step, participants evaluated the acceptance for the use of smart textiles in the kitchen, the living room, the bedroom as well as integrated into the clothes. It was analyzed if the perceived usefulness of smart textiles differs across scenarios, and, second, if age groups show a different evaluation.

In Table 3, descriptive outcomes (means, standard deviations) are given for all items, as well as the significance outcome for the main effect "scenarios" and "age". As can be seen from Table 3, the evaluation **across scenarios** differ in most of the cases. Textiles in the kitchen were perceived as less useful compared to the other scenarios ($F(3,83) = 7.5$; $p < .001$) and participants would not buy it for the use in the kitchen ($F(3,83) = 5.6$; $p < .001$).

Participants indicated to be to a lesser extent concerned that a casual touch would be interpreted as an operating gesture for clothes – while they are more concerned when

Table 3. Use of smart textiles in living room, kitchen, bedroom, and clothing. Items were answered on a 6-point Likert scale (1 = I do not at all agree; 6 = I completely agree).

Scenario Statements		Scenarios (M, (SD))				Significance
	Age-groups	living room	kitchen	bedroom	clothes	
"I think the presented scenario make sense."	Young (17-30)	3.3 (1.7)	2.4 (1.4)	3.3 (1.4)	3.9 (1.6)	scenarios: p<0.01; age: n.s.
	Middle (31-49)	3.1 (1.3)	2.8 (1.7)	3.1 (1.7)	4.0 (1.8)	
	old (50, +)	3.7 (1.7)	3.7 (1.8)	4.0 (1.6)	4.2 (1.6)	
"I would like to buy such a textile. "	Young (17-30)	3.1 (1.6)	2.5 (1.4)	3.1 (1.6)	3.3 (1.6)	scenarios: p<0.01; age: n.s.
	Middle (31-49)	2.8 (1.4)	2.4 (1.6)	2.5 (1.6)	3.5 (1.5)	
	old (50, +)	3.8 (1.7)	3.2 (1.7)	3.4 (1.6)	3.9 (1.5)	
"I´d be concerned that a casual touch would be interpreted as an operating gesture."	young(17-30)	4.8 (1.2)	4.8 (1.4)	5.1 (1.3)	3.3 (1.6)	scenarios: p<0.01; age: p<0.1
	middle(31-49)	4.2 (1.7)	4.1 (1.5)	4.6 (1.5)	3.1 (1.6)	
	old (50, +)	3.7 (1.6)	2.9 (1.6)	3.5 (2.0)	3.0 (1.7)	
"I believe the necessary gestures to control the device are easy to learn."	young(17-30)	4.9 (1.1)	4.7 (1.3)	4.7 (1.2)	4.8 (1.2)	scenarios: n.s. age: n.s.
	middle(31-49)	4.8 (1.4)	4.6 (1.3)	4.2 (1.4)	4.8 (1.5)	
	old (50, +)	4.9 (1.1)	5.1 (0.9)	5.2 (0.8)	5.3 (0.7)	
"I believe I´d enjoy the handling. "	young(17-30)	4.1 (1.5)	3.8 (1.5)	3.9 (1.5)	4.1 (1.5)	scenarios: p<0.01; age: n.s.
	middle(31-49)	4.0 (1.5)	3.8 (1.6)	3.6 (1.5)	4.3 (1.7)	
	old (50, +)	4.8 (1.6)	4.4 (1.7)	4.4 (1.4)	4.5 (1.4)	
"My friends will envy me this textile."	young(17-30)	3.6 (1.6)	2.9 (1.5)	3.3 (1.5)	3.5 (1.5)	scenarios: p<0.01; age: n.s.
	middle(31-49)	3.2 (1.5)	3.0 (1.7)	2.7 (1.6)	3.5 (1.5)	
	old (50, +)	3.1 (1.3)	3.0 (1.3)	2.8 (1.3)	3.6 (1.5)	
"I believe gestures will be reliably recognized by the textile."	young(17-30)	3.5 (1.5)	3.4 (1.5)	3.0 (1.4)	3.8 (1.8)	scenarios: p<0.05; age: p<0.01
	middle(31-49)	3.5 (1.4)	3.8 (1.6)	2.9 (1.1)	2.9 (1.7)	
	old (50, +)	4.3 (1.3)	4.5 (1.4)	4.5 (1.4)	2.6 (1.5)	
"I will be able to quickly perform learned gestures."	young(17-30)	5.1 (1.0)	5.0 (1.0)	5.0 (1.1)	3.7 (1.4)	scenarios: p<0.01; age: n.s.
	middle(31-49)	4.9 (1.1)	4.8 (1.2)	4.7 (1.3)	4.2 (1.3)	
	old (50, +)	5.3 (0.6)	5.2 (0.8)	5.1 (0.7)	4.6 (1.1)	
"I would be embarrassed to use the smart textile in front of others."	young(17-30)	1.9 (1.3)	2.0 (1.3)	1.9 (1.4)	1.8 (1.0)	scenarios: p<0.01; age: p<0.01
	middle(31-49)	1.4 (0.6)	1.4 (0.6)	1.8 (1.1)	2.2 (1.3)	
	old (50, +)	1.5 (0.9)	1.4 (0.6)	1.4 (0.6)	3.5 (1.9)	
"I´d be afraid of inadvertently damaging the textile (e.g., by spilling drinks over it)"	young(17-30)	4.3 (1.5)	4.8 (1.4)	3.9 (1.7)	4.7 (1.6)	scenarios: p<0.01; age: p<0.05
	middle(31-49)	3.1 (1.7)	3.3 (1.7)	2.7 (1.6)	5.3 (1.3)	
	old (50, +)	3.1 (1.6)	3.2 (1.5)	2.4 (1.1)	2.9 (2.1)	

the textiles are used in the different rooms (F(3,83) = 7.2; p < .001). In addition, the use of textiles in the kitchen and bedroom are perceived as less enjoyable (F(3,87) = 4.8; p < .004). Scenarios do also differ significantly regarding the belief that gestures will be reliably recognized by the textile (F(3,88) = 3.2; p < .005) and participants are differently convinced that they are able to quickly learn the gestures to control the smart textiles (F(3,88) = 8.7; p < .001). Age, in contrast, revealed to be a

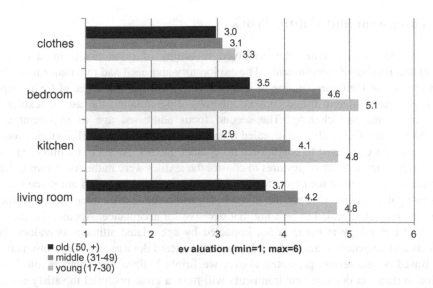

Fig. 3. Age differences: "I believe that the gestures will be reliably recognized by the textile"

not that decisive for acceptance. In contrast to younger age groups, older adults do not believe that the gestures will be reliably recognized by the textile ($F(3,87) = 3.3$; $p < .004$, Fig. 3).

On the other hand older adults are quite fearless that they inadvertently damage the textile ($F(3,87) = 4.8$; $p < .005$) when using it, in contrast to younger adults which are more afraid in this regard ($F(3,82) = 4.2$; $p < .005$, Fig. 4).

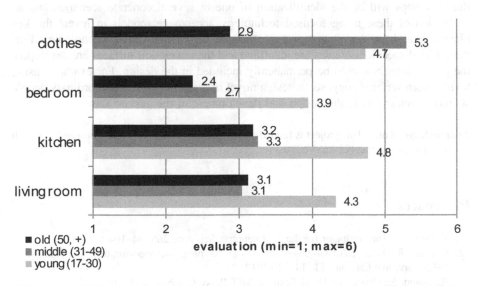

Fig. 4. Age differences for the item "I'd be afraid of inadvertently damaging the textile"

5 Discussion and Future Work

In this study, we examined the perceived suitability of smart textile input devices integrated into home environments. The exploratory approach had two major foci: One was directed to the understanding of users' attitudes towards the usage of textile input devices within different usage contexts, thereby differentiating the use of textiles in different rooms and clothing. The second focus addressed age as important user diversity factor. Generally, we revealed a basic openness to use novel devices, though the usage was connected to conditional acceptance factors. As such, usability, ease of use and high learnability of gestures to control the textiles were in the foreground. With respect to the different scenarios, textiles in the kitchen and bedroom are perceived as less enjoyable in contrast to textiles in the living room and textiles integrated in clothes. Age, in contrast, revealed to be a not that decisive for acceptance. Apparently, the use of novel technology at home is not impacted by age-related attitudes or values, but reflects a more generic claim for usable and easy to learn devices that is age-insensitive.

Based on the results presented above, we firmly believe that smart textile inter-action surfaces in domestic environments will have a great potential to satisfy a wide range of people's needs. However, the road towards this vision is long and full of stones, especially if the people's perspective should be integrated and the design and development of should follow a participatory design approach. One should critically have in mind that the attitudes users report in questionnaires, might be quite artificial, at least as long as users do not have the chance to really interact with the textile tech-nology and develop hands-on experience respecting the handling of smart textiles. Studies [28, 29] show that persons might overemphasize the fears and concerns against a novel technology (e.g., in terms of privacy and security violations), if evaluations exclusively only rely on the imagination of using it [30].

As the results here thus might lack mostly practical knowledge and factual validity, the next steps will be the identification of one or several concrete scenarios and an evaluation of these using focused technology acceptance models to reveal the key players that shape acceptance and rejection of theses innovative technologies. Fur-thermore, if specific use cases are identified and the interaction surfaces are developed, the potential users should be permanently included in the design. For example, using textile touch surfaces suggests to design novel interaction gestures and ordinary people should be integrated in the design and development of the gesture sets.

Acknowledgements. This project is funded by the German Ministry of Education and Research under the reference number 16SV6270.

References

1. Weiser, M.: The computer for the 21st century. Sci. Am. **265**, 94–104 (1991)
2. Caceres, R., Friday, A.: Ubicomp systems at 20: progress, opportunities, and challenges. IEEE Pervasive Comput. **11**, 14–21 (2012)
3. Robinson, S.: History of Dyed Textiles. MIT Press, Cambridge (1970)

4. Kvavadze, E., Bar-Yosef, O., Belfer-Cohen, A., Boaretto, E., Jakeli, N., Matskevich, Z., Meshveliani, T.: 30,000-year-old wild flax fibers. Science **325**, 1359 (2009)
5. Schaar, A.K., Ziefle, M.: Smart cloths: perceived benefits vs. perceived fears. In: 5th ICST/IEEE Conference on Pervasive Computing Technologies for Healthcare 2011, pp. 601–608 (2011)
6. Ziefle, M., Brauner, P., Heidrich, F., Möllering, C., Lee, K., Armbrüster, C.: Understanding requirements for textile input devices individually tailored interfaces within home environments. In: Stephanidis, C., Antona, M. (eds.) UAHCI 2014, Part III. LNCS, vol. 8515, pp. 587–598. Springer, Heidelberg (2014)
7. Hildebrandt, J., Brauner, P., Ziefle, M.: Smart textiles as intuitive and ubiquitous user interfaces for smart homes. In: Zhou, J., Salvendy, G. (eds.) Human Computer Interaction International - Human Aspects of IT for the Aged Population, pp. 423–434. Springer, Switzerland (2015)
8. Ziefle, M., Röcker, C.: Acceptance of pervasive healthcare systems: a comparison of different implementation concepts. In: 4th ICST Conference on Pervasive Computing Technologies for Healthcare 2010, pp. 1–6 (2010)
9. Heidrich, F., Golod, I., Russell, P., Ziefle, M.: Device-free interaction in smart domestic environments. In: Proceedings of Augmented Human 2013, pp. 65–68. ACM Press, New York (2013)
10. Katterfeldt, E.-S., Dittert, N., Schelhowe, H.: Textiles as ways of relating computing technology to everyday life. In: Proceedings of the 8th International Conference on Interaction Design and Children, pp. 9–17. ACM Press, New York (2009)
11. Leonhardt, S.: Personal healthcare devices. In: Mekherjee, S., et al. (eds.) Malware, Hardware Technology Drivers of AI, pp. 349–370. Springer, Dordrecht (2006)
12. Scheermesser, M., Kosow, H., Rashid, A., Holtmann, C.: User acceptance of pervasive computing in healthcare: main findings of two case studies. In: Proceedings of 2nd International Conference on Pervasive Computing Technologies for Healthcare, Tampere, pp. 205–213 (2008)
13. Park, S., Jayaraman, S.: Enhancing the quality of life through wearable technology the role of a personalized wearable intelligent information infrastructure in addressing the challenges of healthcare. IEEE Eng. Med. Biol. **22**(3), 41–48 (2003)
14. Ziefle, M., Wilkowska, W.: Technology acceptability for medical assistance. In: 4th ICST Conference Pervasive Computing Technologies for Healthcare, pp. 1–9 (2010)
15. Wilkowska, W., Ziefle, M.: User diversity as a challenge for the integration of medical technology into future home environments. In: Ziefle, M., Röcker, C. (eds.) Human-Centred Design of eHealth Technologies. Concepts, Methods and Applications, pp. 95–126. IGI Global, Hershey (2011)
16. Dewsbury, G., Edge, M.: Designing the home to meet the needs of tomorrow... today: smart technology, health and well-being. Open House Int. **26**(2), 33–42 (2001)
17. Mynatt, E.D., Melenhorst, A.-S., Fisk, A.D., Rogers, W.A.: Aware technologies for aging in place: understanding user needs and attitudes. Pervasive Comput. **3**(2), 36–41 (2004)
18. Nehmer J., Becker M., Karshmer A., Lamm R.: Living assistance systems: an ambient intelligence approach. In: Proceedings of the 28th International Conference on Software Engineering, pp. 43–50. ACM, Shanghai (2006)
19. Strese, H., Seidel, U., Knape, T., Botthof, A.: Smart Home in Deutschland - Untersuchung im Rahmen der wissenschaftlichen Begleitung zum Programm Next Generation Media (NGM) des Bundesministeriums für Wirtschaft und Technologie [Smart Home in Germany, Study accompanying the program Next generation Media of the German Ministry of Economics and Technology] (2010)

20. Klack, L., Schmitz-Rode, T., Wilkowska, W., Kasugai, K., Heidrich, F., Ziefle, M.: Integrated home monitoring and compliance optimization for patients with mechanical circulatory support devices. Ann. Biomed. Eng. **39**(12), 2911–2921 (2011)
21. Lee, M.: Embedded assessment of wellness with smart home sensors. UbiComp 2010, Copenhagen, 26–29 September 2010
22. Eloy, S., Plácido, I., Duarte, J.P.: Housing and information society: integration of ICT in the existing housing stock. In: Braganca, et al. (eds.) SB 2007, Suistainable Construction, Materials, Practices. IOS Press, Portugal (2007)
23. Mann, W.C. (ed.): Smart Technology for Aging, Disability, and Independence: The State of the Science. Wiley, Hoboken (2005)
24. Stronge, A.J., Rogers, W.A., Fisk, A.D.: Human factors considerations in implementing telemedicine systems to accommodate older adults. Telemed. Telecare **13**, 1–3 (2007)
25. Ziefle, M., Himmel, S., Wilkowska, W.: When your living space knows what you do: acceptance of medical home monitoring by different technologies. In: Holzinger, A., Simonic, K.-M. (eds.) USAB 2011. LNCS, vol. 7058, pp. 607–624. Springer, Heidelberg (2011)
26. Holzinger, A., Searle, G., Auinger, A., Ziefle, M.: Informatics as semiotics engineering: lessons learned from design, development and evaluation of ambient assisted living applications for elderly people. In: Stephanidis, C. (ed.) Universal Access in HCI, Part III, HCII 2011. LNCS, vol. 6767, pp. 183–192. Springer, Heidelberg (2011)
27. Beier, G.: Kontrollüberzeugungen im Umgang mit Technik [Locus of control when interacting with technology]. Rep. Psychol. **24**, 684–693 (1999)
28. Woolham, J., Frisby, B.: Building a local infrastructure that supports the use of assistive technology in the care of people with dementia. Res. Policy Plann. **20**(1), 11–24 (2002)
29. Cvrcek, D., Kumpost, M., Matyas, V., Danezis, G.: A study on the value of location privacy. In: Proceedings of the ACM Workshop on Privacy in the Electronic Society, pp. 109–118. ACM, New York (2006)
30. Wilkowska, W., Ziefle, M., Himmel, S.: Perceptions of personal privacy in smart home technologies: do user assessments vary depending on the research method? In: Tryfonas, T., Askoxylakis, I. (eds.) HAS 2015. LNCS, vol. 9190, pp. 592–603. Springer, Heidelberg (2015)

Psychological and Cognitive Aspects
of Interaction and Aging

Interactive, Multi-device Visualization Supported by a Multimodal Interaction Framework: Proof of Concept

Nuno Almeida[1,2], Samuel Silva[1,2(✉)], Beatriz Sousa Santos[1,2], and António Teixeira[1,2]

[1] DETI – Department of Electronics, Telecommunications and Informatics, University of Aveiro,
Aveiro, Portugal
[2] IEETA – Institute of Electronics and Informatics Engineering of Aveiro, University of Aveiro,
Aveiro, Portugal
{nunoalmeida,sss,bss,ajst}@ua.pt

Abstract. Nowadays, users can interact with a system using a wide variety of modalities, such as touch and speech. Nevertheless, multimodal interaction has yet to be explored for interactive visualization scenarios. Furthermore, users have access to a wide variety of devices (e.g., smartphones, tablets) that could be harnessed to provide a more versatile visualization experience, whether by providing complementary views or by enabling multiple users to jointly explore the visualization using their devices. In our effort to gather multimodal interaction and multi-device support for visualization, this paper describes our first approach to an interactive multi-device system, based on the multimodal interaction architecture proposed by the W3C, enabling interactive visualization using different devices and representations. It allows users to run the application in different types of devices, e.g., tablets or smartphones, and the visualizations can be adapted to multiple screen sizes, by selecting different representations, with different levels of detail, depending on the device characteristics. Groups of users can rely on their personal devices to synchronously visualize and interact with the same data, maintaining the ability to use a custom representation according to their personal needs. A preliminary evaluation was performed, mostly to collect users' first impressions and guide future developments. Although the results show a moderate user satisfaction, somehow expected at this early stage of development, user feedback allowed the identification of important routes for future improvement, particularly regarding a more versatile navigation along the data and the definition of composite visualizations (e.g., by gathering multiple representations on the same screen).

Keywords: Multi-device applications · Multimodal interaction · Interactive visualization

1 Introduction

Human-Computer Interaction has known considerable advances in recent years. The widespread availability of mobile and multimodal devices boosted the proposal of novel interaction modalities and the exploration of multimodal interaction. These new

© Springer International Publishing Switzerland 2016
J. Zhou and G. Salvendy (Eds.): ITAP 2016, Part I, LNCS 9754, pp. 279–289, 2016.
DOI: 10.1007/978-3-319-39943-0_27

interaction capabilities, although currently used and explored in different application areas, have not been much considered for Interactive Visualization [1]. Nevertheless, it is of the utmost relevance to explore and understand the strengths and weaknesses of multimodality when used in this context [2], exploring the potential advantages deriving from a richer interaction scenario, allowing adaptability to different contexts [3], and a wider communication bandwidth between the user and the application [4, 5]. In this regard, aspects such as interaction modality choice, adaptability (e.g., different ways of displaying data depending on the hardware or environment), and the combination of modalities assume particular relevance. Furthermore, deriving from the wide range of devices available (smart TVs, tablet, smartphones, etc.), it is also relevant to explore how these may be used to support Visualization [6], whether individually, providing different views, adapted to the device characteristics [3], or simultaneously, providing multiple (complementary) views of the same dataset [7], fostering a richer interaction experience, or as the grounds for collaborative work [8].

One of the application scenarios guiding our efforts in this context is provided by the ongoing Marie Curie IAPP project IRIS[1]. The aim of this project is to provide a natural interaction communication platform accessible and adapted for all users, particularly for people with speech impairments and elderly in indoor scenarios. The particular scenario under consideration, a household, where a family lives (parents, two children and a grandmother), and where different devices exist around the house, and are owned by the different family members, is a perfect match to the challenges identified above. In our view, communication can go beyond the exchange of messages through these media and profit from the dynamic multi-device environment, where similar contents (e.g., a vacation memoir or the family agenda) can be viewed in different manners, adapted to the device and user preferences, and supporting a collaborative interaction effort.

While we have previously presented an approach to a multi-device multimodal application [1], where one user could profit from multiple devices to have complementary views of the same contents, we have yet to explore the use of one application by different users simultaneously, through multiple devices, tackling how each user visualizes contents and interacts, and how each user's interactions are reflected in the overall state of the application.

In line with these ideas, our main goal is to explore multimodal interactive visualization in multi-device settings and the first challenge, addressed in this article, resides on how to best support these features. We do not aim to mimic existing dedicated conference room collaborative systems, where applications are specifically tailored for that purpose. Instead, we want to bring the availability of this kind of features to everyday life devices and applications, enabling its availability in any application.

To that purpose, in Sect. 2 we present related work on multimodal and multi-device applications, in Sect. 3 we consider a W3C based multimodal interaction architecture, in line with our previous work [9–12], and explore its components to serve multimodal interactive visualization. A proof of concept application is then described in Sect. 4 illustrating a set of basic features made possible by the proposed

---

[1] http://iris-interaction.eu.

solution. Section 5 presents the outcomes of a preliminary evaluation, conducted with six participants, to elicit user feedback to guide future efforts. Finally, Sect. 6 presents a brief discussion and conclusions concerning the outcomes and prospective lines of future work.

2 Related Work

A review of recent literature shows several works focusing on multi-display and other multi-device related topics such as ubiquitous multi-device and migratory multimodal interfaces. PolyChrome [13] is a web based application framework that enables collaboration across multiple devices by sharing interaction events and managing the different displays. Another similar solution is the Tandem Browsing Toolkit [14] that allows developers to rapidly create multi-display enabled applications. Conductor [15] and VisPorter [7] are other examples of multi-display frameworks. Thaddeus [16] is a system which enables information visualization for mobile devices.

WATCHCONNECT [17] is a toolkit for prototyping applications that enables interaction through smartwatches. This work presents a different way of interaction that uses the hardware capabilities of smartwatches.

Several works focus on ubiquitous multi-device scenarios, Kernchen et al. [18] explore the processing steps needed to adapt multimedia content and define framework functionalities. HIPerFace [19], from 2011, is a multichannel architecture that enables multimodal interaction and multi-device scenarios, enabling its use in multiples devices.

Other topic related to the use of multimodal and multi-device scenarios is migratory multimodal interfaces. Berti and Paternò [20] describe migratory interfaces as interfaces enabling users to switch between devices while seamlessly continuing their ongoing task. Blumendor et al. [21] describe a multimodal system with several devices, from TVs to smartphones, where the user interface dynamically adapts to the new context and change the used modalities.

Paterno [22] addresses and discusses some aspects that should be considered while designing multimodal and multi-device interfaces.

Shen et al. [23] propose three modes for multi-surface visualization and interaction, namely: independent, reflective, and coordinated. In the first, devices work independently, while in the second each device shows the same content, and in the last it basically shows the same content but from different viewpoints. Alemayehu Seyed [24] presents a study to identify better interaction design for multiple displays, resulting in a set of guidelines to improve user experience.

From this short overview of recent literature we can highlight the community's interest in exploring multimodal interaction in multi-device scenarios, but there seems to be only very few attempts to address it based on existing standards. While the different proposals provide solutions to tackle the required features, their widespread use may be limited by the adoption of specific architectures, in each case. Furthermore, there is no particular focus on how multimodal interaction and multi-device support can be harnessed for interactive visualization.

3 Multi-device Support

This section presents a brief overview of the architectural aspects involved in supporting multimodal multi-device interaction, discussing the main aspects of the adopted multimodal architecture, and briefly describing the devised multi-device approach.

Multimodal Architecture. Our architecture proposal is based on the W3C multimodal architecture recommendations [25] and on previous efforts to create multi-device systems [10].

The W3C standard for multimodal architectures is divided into four modules (see Fig. 1): the interaction manager (IM), responsible to receive all event messages and generate actions; the data model, that stores the information of the IM; input and output modalities, capturing the users' interaction events or presenting information to the user; the runtime framework, the module responsible for the communication between the modules and the necessary services to run multimodal applications.

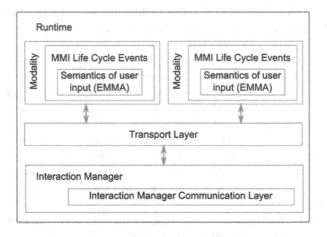

Fig. 1. Multimodal architecture main modules

Going Multi-device. Figure 2 presents the overall architecture of our proposal and possible modalities. Modalities can only communicate with the IM using MultiModal Interaction (MMI) life cycle events [26] carrying EMMA (Extensible MultiModal Annotation markup language) [27], the events information. On the bottom, several classes of devices supported are presented: a computer connected to a large screen, a tablet or a smartphone. Whenever the same modality is connected to the IM, the IM must send a copy of the event to each modality, i.e., interaction is propagated through the different devices and representations.

Aiming for a more ubiquitous approach, we use a cloud based IM capable of managing different modalities in different devices and multiple users.

Each device must run the visualization modality; the touch modality is connected to the visualization modality in order to obtain the objects that the user is interacting with.

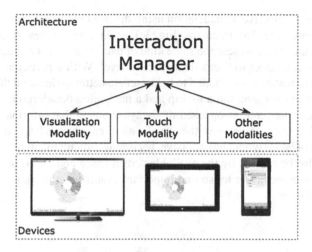

Fig. 2. Architecture and Devices

As a natural outcome of adopting a multimodal architecture, other modalities can be added such as speech [9].

4   Proof of Concept

To support our work and illustrate the capabilities of the proposed approach, we considered a usage scenario extracted from our work on the evaluation of ubiquitous interactive scenarios [28] and created an application prototype to serve as a proof of concept.

Usage Scenario. Dynamic Evaluations as a Service (DynEaaS) is a framework to support the evaluation of multimodal applications in dynamic contexts [28]. Without entering into detail regarding its full range of features, each evaluation session results in data describing all user actions, his/her responses to evaluation tools (e.g., questionnaires) presented during system usage, and all relevant environmental properties and changes. In this context, the considered usage scenario envisages a meeting among three experts to discuss the results of an evaluation session, focusing on the data containing information about the user interaction with a tele-rehabilitation system [28].

The interactions data is organized hierarchically: in the first level are the main components of the application (login, exercise, chat, video and application); in the intermediate levels, subcomponents (e.g., the exercise component has the presentation and list subcomponents); the lower level refers to events and actions (e.g., during exercise presentation there are pause and repeat actions). Each expert has a device capable of running the visualization application (also other modalities can be added to control the application).

Prototype Application. For the development of the proof-of-concept application, the effort was focused in the visualization modality, different modes of visualization were selected based on the data nature. A new modality for the framework was created using

D3.js supporting Interactive Visualization using different representations: the sunburst (Fig. 3a), tree view (Fig. 3b), treemaps (Fig. 3c), and a timeline view (Fig. 3d). Any of these representations can present the same kind of data. The data is organized hierarchically and users can select to focus on a specific level. With a particular focus on the first level, a set of features were added to help users to better understand the data. While moving the mouse over a region a tooltip and a navigation breadcrumb are displayed. This option was considered as opposed to always showing that information as part of the representation since, sometimes, the visualizations encompass large amounts of data and the number of labels would be excessive, becoming difficult to interpret. The number of labels can also be limited by the available screen space and based on the degree of interest of the data they refer to, so that important events are always shown and some labels may be hidden.

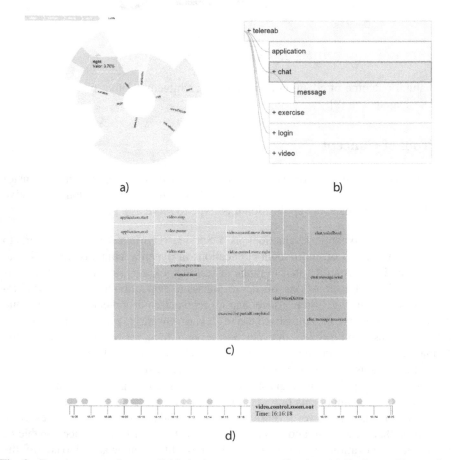

Fig. 3. Data representations available in the prototype application: (a) Sunburst, (b) tree view, (c) treemap, and (d) timeline view.

All devices share a synchronized view of the data, loading the data from the same location. Depending on the device, the modality may default to a representation that best suits it, depending on various criteria. For example, tree views are used instead of the sunburst for small screen sizes, e.g., smartphones.

5 Preliminary Evaluation

At this point, since we only have a first prototype, serving as a proof-of-concept, our main goal was not to put a strong emphasis on usability results (although not excluding them), since the prototype complexity is still low, and our main concern was to provide a basic set of technical features. Therefore, we were particularly interested in performing a preliminary formative evaluation that could elicit user feedback and suggestions, yielding requirements to guide further developments. The study was conducted with 6 participants, all male, aged between 25 and 35 years old.

5.1 Method

Based on Pinelle et al. [29], we created a plan to evaluate the prototype's usability. First, the system was explained to the users. Then, users were asked to complete two sets of

Table 1. Evaluation tasks

Individual tasks	
Task 1	Find which of the components was most used
Task 2	Find if the user made a mistake dictating or the recognition didn't worked well
Task 3	What was the total time of the session? Compare with the time the user took to perform the exercises
Task 2 (Tablet)	Select the exercises events and verify if the user concluded every exercise.
Task 3 (PC)	Change the view to see each individual event, filter the chat events and observe the time when the user received messages. When were the messages received?
Task 4 (Smartphone)	Select each event until "exercise.Presentation". What is the percentage?
Task 5 (Tablet)	View all names in the visualization.
Task 6 (Smartphone)	Select video.control. What was the most used control?
Group tasks	
Task 1 (PC)	Compare the number of interactions between the video control and chat control. What is the value of each?
Task 2 (Tablet)	Select the exercises events and verify if the user concluded every exercise.
Task 3 (PC)	Change the view to see each individual event, filter the chat events and observe the time when the user received messages. When were the messages received?
Task 4 (Smartphone)	Select each event until "exercise.Presentation". What is the percentage?
Task 5 (Tablet)	View all names in the visualization.
Task 6 (Smartphone)	Select video.control. What was the most used control?

tasks, as described in Table 1. The first set of tasks, was to be conducted once, individually, using a single device, while the second set should be performed in group, with each user working on a different device (PC, tablet or smartphone). In the second task set, each user had his/her own task, but others could also interact to find the result faster.

A subjective evaluation approach was considered, in which users were observed performing the tasks, incidents were registered, and users were encouraged to think aloud. In the end, users were asked to fill a questionnaire, based on the System Usability Scale (SUS) [30]. The scale goes from one to five where one is strong disagreement and five strong agreement. Furthermore, using the same scale as the SUS, other items were added to the questionnaire (Table 2) to analyse the users' preferences concerning the visualizations and their usage in multi-device contexts. Also, users were asked to order visualizations according to their preferences.

Table 2. Questions added to SUS, answered in the same scale

Q1	Different visualizations helped to better understand the data?
Q2	Different visualization helped to navigate through the data?
Q3	It is easy to get information from the "sunburst"?
Q4	It is easy to get information from the "timeline"?
Q5	It is easy to get information from the "treemap"?
Q6	The "breadcrumb" helps to locate the information?
Q7	The "Tooltips" and highlight helps to locate the information?
Q8	Combining visualizations helped to understand the information?
Q9	The smartphone is helpful in this context?

5.2 Results

The calculated SUS score was 58 %. While the score was not a great result, this was somehow expected since our main focus, at this stage, was on a first prototype including all the basic technical features supporting the multimodal multi-device interactive visualization. Nonetheless, the other evaluation methods allowed to identify the users' difficulties and retrieve suggestions. Users had some difficulties understanding the data at first since they were not acquainted with the specificities of the application from where the data were retrieved. They always looked for the information using the predefined visualization when, for instance, in the second task, they needed to change to the timeline, which is a complementary visualization, to obtain the results. Users also showed some difficulties finding how to select a different visualization. Also, they struggled to find an event in the timeline. Most of these difficulties were in the first set of tasks, where tasks were individual, and the participants were using them for the first time. In the second set, they were able to communicate and help each other finishing the tasks.

Figure 4 presents the results of the questionnaire. In the users' opinion, the treemap visualization and breadcrumb did not help much. On the other side, the sunburst and the timeline, as well as the tooltips, helped understand the data. Users found the possibility of having different visualizations and the use of the smartphone helpful.

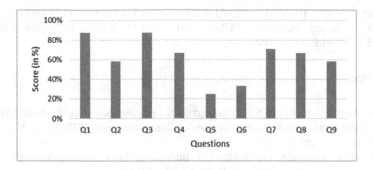

Fig. 4. Overall results obtained from the questionnaire. Please refer to Table 2 for the considered questions.

Resulting from the 'think aloud' use of the prototype, several interesting suggestions were gathered, such as:

Provide a way to differentiate error events from general events
Be able to display the sunburst and timeline on the same screen
Zoom in the timeline in the horizontal
Use the breadcrumb to navigate to previous levels

6   Conclusions

In this first stage of our work, we show how a multimodal architecture, adopted to support multimodal interaction, can also easily encompass the features needed to support multi-user, multi-device interactive visualization. A proof of concept application shows how the visualization modality can work, enabling users to simultaneously interact with the same data and entities while choosing their own representation preferences in the context of the used device. A preliminary evaluation of the application prototype has been carried out to assess the users' overall opinion regarding the provided features (e.g., different representations and synchronous functioning among devices, possibly using different representations for each device) with positive outcomes and ideas for further work.

By taking advantage of a multimodal framework to provide the multi-device features, we are also potentially bringing visualization into multimodality. At its current stage, apart from the visualization modality, the presented proof of concept still does not explore multiple modalities in service of visualization. Nevertheless, inherent to the features of the adopted architecture, a speech synthesis based output modality, for example, would be easy to add [9] along with gaze, as we recently showed for another application domain [31, 32]. This obviously does not mean that innovative approaches to interactive visualization appear automatically, but that the technical effort to add support for those modalities is considerably reduced, leaving room for their creative use in service of visualization, a path we will continue pursuing.

Addressing how the visualization adapts to the characteristics of the data and device is also one of our current lines of work, in line with the proposal of generic interaction modalities aligned with the MMI architecture standard (e.g., for speech interaction [9, 33]).

Acknowledgements. The work presented in this chapter has been partially funded by IEETA Research Unit funding (Incentivo/EEI/UI0127/2014) and Marie Curie IAPP project IRIS (ref. 610986, FP7-PEOPLE-2013-IAPP).

References

1. Lee, B., Isenberg, P., Riche, N.H., Carpendale, S.: Beyond mouse and keyboard: expanding design considerations for information visualization interactions. IEEE Trans. Vis. Comput. Graph. **18**, 2689–2698 (2012)
2. Ward, M.O., Grinstein, G., Keim, D.: Interactive Data Visualization: Foundations, Techniques, and Applications. CRC Press, Natick (2010)
3. Roberts, J.C., Ritsos, P.D., Badam, S.K., Brodbeck, D., Kennedy, J., Elmqvist, N.: Visualization beyond the desktop–the next big thing. IEEE Comput. Graph. Appl. **34**, 26–34 (2014)
4. Jaimes, A., Sebe, N.: Multimodal human-computer interaction: a survey. Comput. Vis. Image Underst. **108**, 116–134 (2007)
5. Lee, J.-H., Poliakoff, E., Spence, C.: The effect of multimodal feedback presented via a touch screen on the performance of older adults. In: Altinsoy, M., Jekosch, U., Brewster, S. (eds.) HAID 2009. LNCS, vol. 5763, pp. 128–135. Springer, Heidelberg (2009)
6. Schmidt, B.: Facilitating data exploration in casual mobile settings with multi-device interaction (2014). http://elib.uni-stuttgart.de/opus/volltexte/2014/9420
7. Chung, H., North, C., Self, J.Z., Chu, S., Quek, F.: VisPorter: facilitating information sharing for collaborative sensemaking on multiple displays. Pers. Ubiquitous Comput. **18**, 1169–1186 (2014)
8. Isenberg, P., Elmqvist, N., Scholtz, J., Cernea, D., Ma, K.-L., Hagen, H.: Collaborative visualization: definition, challenges, and research agenda. Inf. Vis. **10**, 310–326 (2011)
9. Almeida, N., Silva, S., Teixeira, A.: Design and development of speech interaction: a methodology. In: Kurosu, M. (ed.) HCI 2014, Part II. LNCS, vol. 8511, pp. 370–381. Springer, Heidelberg (2014)
10. Almeida, N., Silva, S., Teixeira, A.J.S.: Multimodal multi-device application supported by an SCXML state chart machine. In: Workshop on Engineering Interactive Systems with SCXML, the Sixth ACM SIGCHI Symposium on Computing Systems (2014)
11. Almeida, N., Teixeira, A.: Enhanced interaction for the elderly supported by the W3C multimodal architecture. In: Proceedings of 5ª Conferência Nacional sobre Interacção (2013)
12. Teixeira, A.J.S., Almeida, N., Pereira, C., e Silva, M.O.: W3C MMI architecture as a basis for enhanced interaction for ambient assisted living. In: Get Smart: Smart Homes, Cars, Devices and the Web, W3C Workshop on Rich Multimodal Application Development. Metropolitan Area, New York (2013)
13. Badam, S., Elmqvist, N.: PolyChrome: a cross-device framework for collaborative web visualization. In: Proceedings of Ninth ACM International Conference on Interactive Tabletops and Surfaces (2014)
14. Heikkinen, T., Goncalves, J., Kostakos, V., Elhart, I., Ojala, T.: Tandem browsing toolkit: distributed multi - display interfaces with web technologies, pp. 142–147 (2014)
15. Hamilton, P., Wigdor, D.J.: Conductor: enabling and understanding cross-device interaction. In: Proceedings of the 32nd Annual ACM Conference on Human Factors in Computing Systems - CHI 2014, pp. 2773–2782. ACM Press, New York (2014)

16. Woźniak, P., Lischke, L., Schmidt, B., Zhao, S., Fjeld, M.: Thaddeus: a dual device interaction space for exploring information visualisation. In: Proceedings of the 8th Nordic Conference on Human-Computer Interaction, pp. 41–50 (2014)

17. Houben, S., Marquardt, N.: WATCHCONNECT: A toolkit for prototyping smartwatch-centric cross-device applications. In: Proceedings of 33rd Annual ACM Conference on Human Factors in Computing Systems (2015)

18. Kernchen, R., Meissner, S., Moessner, K., Cesar, P., Vaishnavi, I., Boussard, M., Hesselman, C.: Intelligent multimedia presentation in ubiquitous multidevice scenarios. IEEE Multimed. 17, 52–63 (2010)

19. Weibel, N., Oda, R.: Hiperface: a multichannel architecture to explore multimodal interactions with ultra-scale wall displays. In: ICSE 2011: Proceedings of the 33rd International Conference on Software Engineering (2011)

20. Berti, S., Paternò, F.: Migratory multimodal interfaces in multidevice environments. In: Proceedings of 7th International Conference Multimodal interfaces. ACM (2005)

21. Blumendorf, M., Roscher, D., Albayrak, S.: Dynamic user interface distribution for flexible multimodal interaction. In: International Conference on Multimodal Interfaces and the Workshop on Machine Learning for Multimodal Interaction on - ICMI-MLMI 2010. p. 1. ACM Press, New York (2010)

22. Paterno, F.: Multimodality and multi-device interfaces. In: W3C Workshop on Multimodal Interaction, Sophia Antipolis (2004)

23. Shen, C., Esenther, A., Forlines, C., Ryall, K.: Three modes of multisurface interaction and visualization. In: Information Visualization and Interaction Techniques for Collaboration Across Multiple Displays Workshop associated with CHI (2006)

24. Seyed, A.: Examining user experience in multi-display environments (2013)

25. Dahl, D.A.: The W3C multimodal architecture and interfaces standard. J. Multimod. User Interfaces 7(3), 171–182 (2013)

26. Bodell, M., Dahl, D., Kliche, I., Larson, J., Porter, B., Raggett, D., Raman, T., Rodriguez, B.H., Selvaraj, M., Tumuluri, R., Wahbe, A., Wiechno, P., Yudkowsky, M.: Multimodal architecture and interfaces: W3C recommendation (2012)

27. Baggia, P., Burnett, D.C., Carter, J., Dahl, D.A., McCobb, G., Raggett, D.: EMMA: Extensible multimodal annotation markup language (2009)

28. Pereira, C., Almeida, N., Martins, A.I., Silva, S., Rosa, A.F., Oliveira e Silva, M., Teixeira, A.: Evaluation of complex distributed multimodal applications: evaluating a telerehabilitation system when it really matters. In: Zhou, J., Salvendy, G. (eds.) ITAP 2015. LNCS, vol. 9194, pp. 146–157. Springer, Heidelberg (2015)

29. Pinelle, D., Gutwin, C., Greenberg, S.: Task analysis for groupware usability evaluation. ACM Trans. Comput. Interact. 10, 281–311 (2003)

30. Lewis, J.R., Sauro, J.: The factor structure of the system usability scale. In: Kurosu, M. (ed.) HCD 2009. LNCS, vol. 5619, pp. 94–103. Springer, Heidelberg (2009)

31. Vieira, D.: Enhanced multimodal interaction framework and applications. Master thesis, Aveiro, Universidade de Aveiro, (2015)

32. Vieira, D., Freitas, J.D., Acartürk, C., Teixeira, A., Sousa, L., Silva, S., Candeias, S., Dias, M.S.: Read That Article: Exploring synergies between gaze and speech interaction, pp. 341–342 (2015)

33. Almeida, N., Teixeira, A., Rosa, A.F., Braga, D., Freitas, J., Dias, M.S., Silva, S., Avelar, J., Chesi, C., Saldanha, N.: Giving voices to multimodal applications. In: Kurosu, M. (ed.) Human-Computer Interaction. LNCS, vol. 9170, pp. 273–283. Springer, Heidelberg (2015)

The Gamification of Cognitive Training: Older Adults' Perceptions of and Attitudes Toward Digital Game-Based Interventions

Walter R. Boot[1]([✉]), Dustin Souders[1], Neil Charness[1],
Kenneth Blocker[2], Nelson Roque[1], and Thomas Vitale[1]

[1] Department of Psychology, Florida State University, Tallahassee, FL, USA
{boot, charness, souders, roque, vitale}@psy.fsu.edu
[2] Department of Psychology,
Georgia Institute of Technology, Atlanta, GA, USA
kblocker3@gatech.edu

Abstract. There has been recent excitement over the potential for commercial and custom digital games to reverse age-related perceptual and cognitive decline. The effectiveness of digital game-based brain training is controversial. However, a separate issue is, should digital game-based interventions prove effective, how best to design these interventions to encourage intervention engagement and adherence by older adults (ages 65 +). This study explored older adults' perceptions and attitudes toward game-based interventions after they were asked to play digital games (experimental or control games) for a month-long period. Clear differences in attitudes toward game-based interventions were observed, as assessed by post-intervention surveys, with older adults finding games in the control condition (word and number puzzle games) more enjoyable and less frustrating compared to a digital game that consisted of gamified brain training interventions that have demonstrated some degree of success in the literature. Interestingly, older adults perceived the control condition as more likely to boost perceptual and cognitive abilities (e.g., vision, reaction time), as assessed by a post-intervention survey of expectations. Although predicting intervention adherence was challenging, overall motivation to do well in the intervention was significantly related to perceptions of cognitive benefit. Not surprisingly, game enjoyment also predicted motivation. Finally, older adults who perceived the game they were assigned to play as more challenging were more likely to believe the game would boost cognition. These findings identify attitudes and beliefs that could be targeted to motivate older adults to adhere to digital game-based interventions found to boost cognition. To better explore factors related to intervention adherence in the future we propose studies of longer duration (e.g., 6–12 months) and studies that allow more flexibility and choice with respect to amount of gameplay (instead of gameplay being dictated by a fixed schedule determined by the experimenter, leaving less variability to be explained by individual difference factors).

Keywords: Older adults · Video games · Digital games · Perceived benefits · Adherence

© Springer International Publishing Switzerland 2016
J. Zhou and G. Salvendy (Eds.): ITAP 2016, Part I, LNCS 9754, pp. 290–300, 2016.
DOI: 10.1007/978-3-319-39943-0_28

1 Introduction

A major focus of research has been the degree to which certain activities can reduce or reverse the perceptual and cognitive declines associated with advancing age [1]. More specifically, over the past decade the potential for commercial [e.g., 2, 3] and custom [e.g., 4] digital game interventions to improve cognition has generated a great deal of excitement. While initial results appear promising, the idea that digital games and commercial brain training software packages can meaningfully improve the cognition of older adults remains controversial [5, 6]. Relatedly, others have investigated whether digital games, specifically exergames that involve physical activity, might be used to improve physical fitness and health [e.g., 7, 8].

A separate issue is the degree to which digital game-based interventions intended to improve cognitive or physical health are motivating to older adults and encourage intervention adherence. Effective digital game-based interventions are not possible unless older adults are willing and able to engage with these games for an extended period of time. While much work has explored the potential benefits of digital game-based interventions, far fewer studies have attempted to uncover the general principles related to older adults' motivation to engage in digital game-based interventions and factors related to intervention adherence. This is crucial information needed in order to maximize benefits should these types of interventions prove effective.

Digital games are a form of technology, and technology adoption models exist that help guide predictions related to the factors that influence the intention to use digital game-based interventions by older adults. For example, the Unified Theory of Acceptance and Use of Technology (UTAUT, [9]), and the earlier Technology Acceptance Model (TAM, [10]), propose that the perceived benefits (e.g., usefulness) and perceived costs (e.g., ease of use) from technology influence both intention to use technology and subsequent use. An older adult who believes strongly that digital game interventions are effective at improving cognition is predicted, according to these models, to be more likely to adopt this technology. Perception of effort required to learn and use a new technology also plays an important role. In this case, effort expectancy may be partly shaped by previous experience with technology platforms on which these interventions are typically delivered (personal computer, tablet, smartphone). If an older adult has little or no previous experience with these technologies, he or she may perceive substantial costs with respect to the adoption of digital game-based interventions, or may not have the prerequisite knowledge to engage in such interventions. Experience successfully using similar technology may influence self-efficacy, which has also been found to influence technology adoption [11].

Fast-paced action video games have been promoted as one of the most effective types of digital games with respect to improving cognition [12]. Unfortunately, these games are among the games that older adults are least interested in playing [13]. Boot and colleagues [14] attempted to assess whether a fast-paced action game might improve the perceptual and cognitive abilities of an older adult sample. The action game chosen was a popular racing game on the Nintendo DS system (*Mario Kart*). A control group played the brain fitness focused game *Brain Age 2*. Participants in each group were asked to play the game they were assigned for a total of 60 h (5 h a week over 3 months). However, the effect of the action game could not be assessed because of the extremely low rate of adherence in this condition. The intervention having stronger evidence in support of it (action game) was adhered to significantly less by older adults ($M = 22$ h for *Mario Kart* vs. 56 h for *Brain Age*). Various analyses explored reasons for this lack of adherence and found that, compared to participants in the brain fitness game group, participants in the action game intervention were significantly less likely to believe the intervention they received would have a meaningful impact on their ability to perform everyday tasks. Furthermore, older adults found this intervention less enjoyable. In subsequent analyses, individual differences in enjoyment and perceived benefit predicted adherence as well as motivation to perform well on training tasks. A follow-up study of shorter duration (10 days) found much higher levels of adherence for *Mario Kart*, suggesting that intervention duration may play an important role [15]. These initial results highlight the importance of understanding adherence, but also provide suggestions as to the important factors that determine individual differences in adherence and motivation.

At this point, it is clear that the games that older adults prefer are not the same types of games that are most popular among younger, more active gamers, and game-based cognitive interventions need to take this into account. A number of studies have explored both older adult digital game preferences and the reasons older adult gamers play. For example, although violent first-person shooters are generally a popular game genre, older adult focus group research suggests a general aversion toward games with violent content [16]. This research also indicates a perception by older adults that games provide stimulation that might serve as a form of "brain training." Motivation for gaming among older adults may also be shaped by feelings of wellbeing associated with gameplay [17]. Casual games, including puzzle games and computerized versions of non-digital games (e.g., card and board games) were among the most popular games reported by a Dutch older adult gamer sample, with the need for challenge reported as the primary appeal of gaming [18]. Similarly, in a sample of both gaming and non-gaming older adults, puzzle and educational games were rated as the most interesting genres, and challenge and intellectual stimulation were rated as being among the most important features of a game [13]. In sum, the types of games that older adults appear to have the most interest in may be different from those most enjoyed by younger gamers, and a variety of factors (challenge, perceived benefits to cognition and wellbeing) appear to motivate game play in this population.

The current paper attempts to replicate previous relationships observed between intervention motivation and adherence and various perceptions, attitudes, and individual difference factors in two different digital game conditions to explore the generalizability of previous findings. Specifically, our primary hypotheses predicted that adherence (number of sessions completed) and self-reported motivation to perform well while playing the intervention games would be related to self-reported perceived benefits to cognition from the intervention and intervention enjoyment. This would be consistent with our previous findings, and also consistent with models of technology adoption. Participants were randomly assigned to play 30 sessions of gameplay over the course of one month. One group received a brain fitness game made up of gamified versions of interventions that have been reported in the literature as improving cognition (e.g., N-back training, memory updating training). The control group received word and number puzzle games. After initial training in the laboratory on how to access their assigned intervention on a tablet computer, and how to play the digital games that they were assigned, participants completed training at home and used a diary to keep track of their gameplay. Upon returning to their lab after this one-month period, their attitudes toward the game they were assigned to play and their perceptions of game benefits were assessed.

2   Method

Our goal was to have 60 U.S. participants (ages 65 +) randomly assigned to either the intervention brain training group or a control game condition ($N = 30$ each), complete the digital game-based condition they were assigned, and complete a battery of perceptual and cognitive tasks before and after training. In total, 78 participants were recruited and randomly assigned to meet this goal, with 18 participants dropping out at various points during the study. Because game perceptions and attitudes were assessed during the second lab visit, no data were available for these measures for participants who dropped out. Additionally, some participants had incomplete survey data (2), and some participants did not record adherence as requested (3). As a result, analyses reported here included a minimum of 55 participants.

Both the experimental and control interventions were tablet-based (Acer Iconia A700 10 inch). The brain training intervention consisted of gamified versions of task-switching, N-back, memory updating, reasoning, planning, and spatial reasoning tasks that were adaptive in nature (i.e., if the participant was successful on a level, the tasks were made more difficult). These were gamified in the sense that appealing graphics were added, goals were set for players, and motivating feedback was given in the form of game scores. Progress was graphed over time. A "Wild West" theme connected these games (see [19] for a more detailed description). The control intervention consisted of three common puzzle games (crossword, Sudoku, and word search) and followed the same structure of the intervention condition. Participants in both groups were asked to play seven sessions of gameplay each week for about forty-five minutes each session for one month, and were given a diary to keep track of their gaming sessions. Both groups were asked to divide their time during each gaming session between three different games within their intervention. For the control group, these three games were crossword, Sudoku, and word search. In the brain training intervention, this was a balanced subset of three games out of a total of seven that varied from session to session.

Perceptions and attitudes toward the game participants were assigned to play were assessed with surveys at the end of the intervention. Participants rated the degree to which they thought games like the ones they were assigned to play might improve various abilities: vision, reaction time, memory, hand-eye coordination, reasoning ability, multi-tasking ability, and the ability to perform everyday tasks such as driving. Participants also rated the degree to which they found their intervention enjoyable, challenging, and frustrating. Motivation was assessed with a question that asked participants to rate the following statement: "I was motivated to perform well on the games

I was given to play." All of these questions were rated on a 1–7 scale, from very strongly disagree to very strongly agree.

3 Results

Adherence. Our primary measure of adherence was the number of sessions (out of 30) that each group completed according to their diary records. Adherence was generally good for both interventions (> 70 % of sessions completed), though slightly below the 80 % figure generally judged acceptable for medication adherence. The control group completed 22 sessions on average ($SD = 9.02$) and the brain training games group completed 23 ($SD = 7.67$).

Game Perceptions. Participants were asked to rate how enjoyable, challenging, and frustrating the intervention they were asked to engage in was (Fig. 1). These questions were phrased in the manner of "I found the games I was given to play enjoyable." These data were entered into an ANOVA and a significant game group by game perception interaction was observed ($F(2, 112) = 3.87, p < .05$). As depicted in Fig. 1, participants assigned to the brain training digital games group found their intervention less enjoyable and more frustrating compared to the control group, and both groups found their games equally challenging. Potential reasons for these differences in ratings are discussed later.

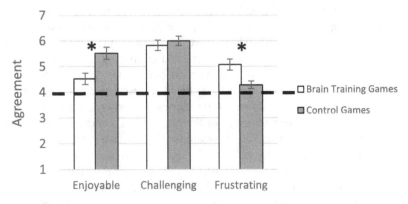

Fig. 1. Game perceptions as a function of group assignment. Error bars represent ±1 SEM. * = p < .05 between groups. 4 = Neutral (Neither agree nor disagree).

Intervention Expectations. Participants were asked to rate how likely the intervention they were asked to engage in would improve a variety of perceptual and cognitive abilities (Fig. 2). These questions were phrased in the manner of "Digital games like the ones I was given to play have the potential to improve vision." Expectation data were entered into an ANOVA and a significant game group by ability interaction was observed ($F(6, 342) = 3.87, p < .01$). As depicted in Fig. 2, participants in general expected the intervention they were assigned would result in broad improvement, but

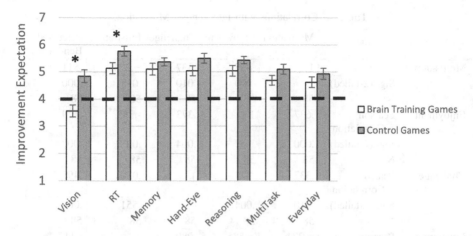

Fig. 2. Improvement expectations as a function of group assignment. Error bars represent ± 1 SEM. * = p < .05 between groups. 4 = Neutral (Neither agree nor disagree).

participants in the control group believed that their intervention was more likely to improve vision and reaction time compared to the brain training intervention.

Intervention Motivation. Intervention motivation was assessed with a single item: "I was motivated to perform well on the games I was given to play." No difference in motivation was observed between the two interventions ($M = 5.82$, SD = 1.14 for Control; $M = 5.28$, SD = 1.19 for Brain Training; $t(56) = 1.80$, $p = .08$).

Next we turned to the best predictors of intervention motivation. A previous study [14] found that digital game enjoyment and perceived benefits to perceptual and cognition abilities predicted motivation. Since motivation was similar for both groups, these data were collapsed. A Principal Components Analysis reduced perceived benefits to a single score for analysis. Similar effects were observed in the current data set, with enjoyment, challenge, and perceived cognitive benefits positively related to motivation, and frustration negatively related to motivation (Table 1). Interestingly, higher perceptions of intervention challenge were associated with a greater belief that the intervention would improve cognition.

When all predictors were induced (including group as a control variable) in a multiple regression analysis, enjoyment appeared to have the largest independent effect on motivation to do well in the intervention (Table 2). There was also still a trend for perceived benefits to perceptual and cognitive abilities to be predictive of motivation, though this effect was no longer significant.

Predictors of Adherence. We examined whether we could predict intervention adherence (number of sessions completed) with similar factors that predicted intervention motivation, and also examined a potential relationship between adherence and motivation itself. Unfortunately, no significant predictors of intervention adherence were observed (Table 3). There was a trend for a positive relationship between intervention adherence and motivation ($r = .24$, $p = .08$).

Table 1. Correlations with Intervention Motivation.

		Motivation	Enjoyment	Challenge	Frustration	Perceived Benefit
Motivation		1	.637**	.337**	−.274*	.511**
	Sig. (2-tailed)		.000	.010	.038	.000
	N	58	58	58	58	58
Enjoyment	Pearson Correlation	.637**	1	.373**	-.385**	.529**
	Sig. (2-tailed)	.000		.004	.003	.000
	N	58	58	58	58	58
Challenge	Pearson Correlation	.337**	.373**	1	.080	.495**
	Sig. (2-tailed)	.010	.004		.551	.000
	N	58	58	58	58	58
Frustration	Pearson Correlation	−.274*	−.385**	.080	1	-.117
	Sig. (2-tailed)	.038	.003	.551		.382
	N	58	58	58	58	58
Perceived Benefit	Pearson Correlation	.511**	.529**	.495**	−.117	1
	Sig. (2-tailed)	.000	.000	.000	.382	
	N	58	58	58	58	59

** Correlation is significant at the 0.01 level (2-tailed).
* Correlation is significant at the 0.05 level (2-tailed).

Tablet Computer Proficiency. Finally, given the technological nature of the intervention we examined whether tablet proficiency at the beginning of the trial predicted either motivation or adherence. We used a measure under development called the *Mobile Device Proficiency Questionnaire* to assess tablet proficiency, based largely on the Computer Proficiency Questionnaire [20]. The average score on this measure was 18.87 (SD = 9.74) out of 40, consistent with very low proficiency. Floor on this scale is a score of 8. Tablet proficiency was unrelated to intervention motivation ($r(55)$ = .02, p = .89) and intervention adherence ($r(53)$ = -.09, p = .52). This can be interpreted

Table 2. Regression model for intervention motivation.

Model	Unstandardized		Standardized	t	Sig.
	B	Std. Error	Beta		
(Constant)	2.937	1.262		2.328	0.024
Condition	0.133	0.268	0.057	0.497	0.621
Enjoyment	**0.455**	**0.13**	**0.484**	**3.509**	**0.001**
Challenge	0.074	0.177	0.051	0.419	0.677
Frustration	−.066	0.096	−.080	−.686	0.496
Perceived Benefit	0.279	0.155	0.237	1.804	0.077

Table 3. Correlations with Intervention Adherence

		Adherence	Motivation	Enjoyment	Challenge	Frustration	Perceived Benefit
Adherence	Pearson Correlation	1	.237	.161	.025	−.001	.195
	Sig. (2-tailed)		.081	.241	.854	.996	.150
	N	56	55	55	55	55	56
Motivation	Pearson Correlation	.237	1	.637**	.337**	−.274*	.511**
	Sig. (2-tailed)	.081		.000	.010	.038	.000
	N	55	58	58	58	58	58
Enjoyment	Pearson Correlation	.161	.637**	1	.373**	−.385**	.529**
	Sig. (2-tailed)	.241	.000		.004	.003	.000
	N	55	58	58	58	58	58
Challenge	Pearson Correlation	.025	.337**	.373**	1	.080	.495**
	Sig. (2-tailed)	.854	.010	.004		.551	.000
	N	55	58	58	58	58	58
Frustration	Pearson Correlation	−.001	−.274*	−.385**	.080	1	−.117
	Sig. (2-tailed)	.996	.038	.003	.551		.382
	N	55	58	58	58	58	58
Perceived Benefit	Pearson Correlation	.195	.511**	.529**	.495**	−.117	1
	Sig. (2-tailed)	.150	.000	.000	.000	.382	
	N	56	58	58	58	58	59

** Correlation is significant at the 0.01 level (2-tailed).
* Correlation is significant at the 0.05 level (2-tailed).

positively in that the amount of tablet training provided in the laboratory was sufficient to allow participants to engage in the intervention for an extended period of time.

4 Conclusion and Discussion

Hypotheses with respect to adherence and motivation were developed based on previous adherence findings of a similar study and models of technology adoption. We found that several factors predicted intervention motivation (but not adherence). Perhaps not surprisingly, enjoyment of the intervention assigned was most strongly related to motivation. However, perceived benefits to perceptual and cognitive abilities also tended to be related to motivation. These findings largely replicated patterns observed in a previous study evaluating different games [14]. To the extent possible, when designing digital game-based interventions, these games should be fun and enjoyable. However, this might not always be possible. In order for cognitive training to be effective, it may need to push the limits of an individual's abilities and require effortful engagement that might not be perceived as pleasant. There may be a tension between what produces cognitive benefits and what results in an enjoyable game experience. Thus, it is important to uncover factors other than enjoyment that might contribute to motivation. Our previous findings, along with the findings reported here, suggest that belief in the efficacy of digital game-based cognitive interventions may also play a role.

The brain fitness game condition was perceived as more frustrating and less enjoyable. This again may be attributed to the fact that these games were designed to challenge participants' abilities and weren't designed specifically for entertainment purposes (as the word and number puzzle games in the control condition were). However, that is not to say that the gamification of these brain training tasks was not effective at increasing enjoyment. In order to test this hypotheses, gamified and non-gamified versions of the same cognitive training tasks would need to be compared head-to-head.

Interestingly, participants expected greater benefits in the control condition compared to the intervention condition. This is ideal with respect to being able to eliminate placebo effects as a potential explanation for differences in performance on cognitive outcome measures. If participants demonstrate greater cognitive improvement in the brain training digital game group compared to the control group, despite lesser expectation for improvement, the presence of a placebo effect is unlikely [21].

Limitations. Our analyses focused on participants who completed the intervention (in the sense that they came back to the lab approximately one month later to complete surveys and the cognitive assessment battery). We did not have perception and motivation data for participants who did not return to the lab to complete this post-training session. Our analyses excluded participants who may be the least adherent (participants that never played their assigned game or had extreme difficulty doing so, and thus dropped out of the study without competing any additional study components). Hence, the results presented here may represent a biased view of the factors that influence motivation and adherence.

This intervention was also relatively short with respect to duration (30 days). Ideally we would like to understand the factors that relate to long-term intervention adherence as it is assumed that greater intervention dose may result in larger benefits. Due to the limited duration of the study, and the knowledge that they were part of a study and they were expected to follow a specific training schedule and record their adherence, intervention adherence may be overestimated in the current study. A similar intervention that asked participants to participate for 3 months found much lower rates of adherence [14].

Future Directions. Future studies of adherence would likely benefit from a longer study duration (e.g., 6 months or more). Without a greater amount of variability in adherence data it may be difficult to uncover predictive individual difference factors. Future studies might also consider imposing a less strict training schedule, allowing participants more choice with respect to how often to engage with the intervention [e.g., 22]. In our study the imposed training schedule may have largely overridden what an individual might have naturally done. To the extent possible, future studies should also rely on automatic recording of adherence rather than diary data to make the adherence aspect of the study less salient to participants, and potentially, more accurate.

Acknowledgments. We gratefully acknowledge support from the National Institute on Aging, NIA 3 PO1 AG017211, Project CREATE III – Center for Research and Education on Aging and Technology Enhancement (www.create-center.org).

References

1. Hertzog, C., Kramer, A.F., Wilson, R.S., Lindenberger, U.: Enrichment effects on adult cognitive development can the functional capacity of older adults be preserved and enhanced? Psychol. Sci. Public Interest **9**(1), 1–65 (2008)
2. Green, C.S., Bavelier, D.: Action video game modifies visual selective attention. Nature **423** (6939), 534–537 (2003)
3. Strobach, T., Frensch, P.A., Schubert, T.: Video game practice optimizes executive control skills in dual-task and task switching situations. Acta Psychol. **140**(1), 13–24 (2012)
4. Anguera, J.A., Boccanfuso, J., Rintoul, J.L., Al-Hashimi, O., Faraji, F., Janowich, J., Gazzaley, A.: Video game training enhances cognitive control in older adults. Nature **501** (7465), 97–101 (2013)
5. http://longevity3.stanford.edu/blog/2014/10/15/the-consensus-on-the-brain-training-industry-from-the-scientific-community/
6. http://www.cognitivetrainingdata.org/
7. Hall, A.K., Chavarria, E., Maneeratana, V., Chaney, B.H., Bernhardt, J.M.: Health benefits of digital videogames for older adults: a systematic review of the literature. Games Health. Res. Devel. Clin. Appl. **1**(6), 402–410 (2012)
8. Wiemeyer, J., Kliem, A.: Serious games in prevention and rehabilitation—a new panacea for elderly people? Eur. Rev. Aging Phys. Act. **9**(1), 41–50 (2012)
9. Venkatesh, V., Morris, M.G., Davis, F.D., Davis, G.B.: User acceptance of information technology: Toward a unified view. MIS Q. **27**, 425–478 (2003)
10. Davis, F.D., Bagozzi, R.P., Warshaw, P.R.: User acceptance of computer technology: a comparison of two theoretical models. Manage. Sci. **35**, 982–1003 (1989)
11. Czaja, S.J., Charness, N., Fisk, A.D., Hertzog, C., Nair, S.N., Rogers, W.A., Sharit, J.: Factors predicting the use of technology: findings from the Center for Research and Education on Aging and Technology Enhancement (CREATE). Psychol. Aging **21**(2), 333–352 (2006)
12. Green, C.S., Bavelier, D.: Action video game training for cognitive enhancement. Current Opin. in Behav. Sci. **4**, 103–108 (2015)
13. Blocker, K.A., Wright, T.J., Boot, W.R.: Gaming preferences of aging generations. Gerontechnology **12**, 174–184 (2014)
14. Boot, W.R., Champion, M., Blakely, D.P., Wright, T., Souders, D.J., Charness, N.: Video games as a means to reduce age-related cognitive decline: Attitudes, compliance, and effectiveness. Front. Psychol. **4**, 1–9 (2013)
15. Souders, D.J., Boot, W.R., Charness, N., Moxley, J.H.: Older adult video game preferences in practice: investigating the effects of competing or cooperating. Games Cult. **11**(1–2), 170–200 (2016)
16. Nap, H.H., De Kort, Y.A.W., IJsselsteijn, W.A.: Senior gamers: preferences, motivations and needs. Gerontechnology **8**(4), 247–262 (2009)
17. Loos, E.F., Zonneveld, A.: Silver gaming: serious fun for seniors. In: Proceedings of the Human Aspects of IT for the Aged Population. Design for Aging, Second International Conference, ITAP 2016, Held as Part of HCI International 2015, Toronto, 17–22 July, 2016. Springer, Berlin (2016) (accepted)

18. De Schutter, B.: Never too old to play: the appeal of digital games to an older audience. Games Cul. **6**(2), 155–170 (2010)
19. Baniqued, P.L., Allen, C.M., Kranz, M.B., Johnson, K., Sipolins, A., Dickens, C., Kramer, A.F.: Working memory, reasoning, and task switching training: transfer effects, limitations, and great expectations? PLoS ONE **10**(11), e0142169 (2015)
20. Boot, W.R., Charness, N., Czaja, S.J., Sharit, J., Rogers, W.A., Fisk, A.D., Nair, S.: Computer proficiency questionnaire: assessing low and high computer proficient seniors. Gerontologist **55**(3), 404–411 (2015)
21. Boot, W.R., Simons, D.J., Stothart, C., Stutts, C.: The pervasive problem with placebos in psychology why active control groups are not sufficient to rule out placebo effects. Perspect. Psychol. Sci. **8**(4), 445–454 (2013)
22. Nagle, A., Riener, R., Wolf, P.: High user control in game design elements increases compliance and in-game performance in a memory training game. Frontiers Psychol., **6** (2015)

Age-Differentiated Analysis of the Hand Proximity Effect by Means of Eye-Tracking

Christina Bröhl[✉], Sabine Theis, Matthias Wille, Peter Rasche,
Alexander Mertens, and Christopher M. Schlick

Institute of Industrial Engineering and Ergonomics,
RWTH Aachen University, Aachen, Germany
{c.broehl,s.theis,m.wille,p.rasche,
a.mertens,c.schlick}@iaw.rwth-aachen.de

Abstract. Research focusing on the position of the hands with regard to visual stimuli has recently received a great deal of attention. One of the main findings is that stimuli that are close to the hands are perceived and processed more precisely than those that are more distant. In this study, the effect of hand proximity was studied using a visual search task and analyzed regarding fixation durations. The hands were placed in varying positions: directly at the screen, on the table and on the lap. As performance in information processing is highly dependent on the subject's age, effects were analyzed in an age-differentiated manner. Results showed a significant effect regarding hand positions moderated by age: Fixation durations were shorter for positions of the hands at the screen and longer for positions away from the screen in the younger age group. In the older age group the effect was vice versa, fixation durations were longer for the position of the hand at the screen and shorter for positions away from the screen.

Keywords: Peripersonal space · Hand proximity · Nearby hands · Ergonomic design · Age-robust design · Visual search · Eye-tracking

1 Introduction

Due to technological progress, the means of interacting with input devices in computing changed from indirect, as the motion of the devices had to be translated to the motion of a pointer on a screen, to direct, as touch technologies were introduced into the market. When using direct input devices, the space directly surrounding the body called peripersonal space is crucial. As input devices are mainly used by hand, this paper aims at studying cognitive processes with regard to hand presence.

1.1 The Effects of Proximal Hands

Recent studies have suggested that the location of the hand has an influence on perceptual processes. This effect may be explained by the fact that objects near the body, especially near the hands, may be candidates for manipulation in potential actions and therefore are be perceived differently. Research focusing on the perception of stimuli near the hands found out that the direction and strength of the effect is mainly

© Springer International Publishing Switzerland 2016
J. Zhou and G. Salvendy (Eds.): ITAP 2016, Part I, LNCS 9754, pp. 301–308, 2016.
DOI: 10.1007/978-3-319-39943-0_29

dependent on task context, resulting in a positive effect in some tasks, while for other tasks the effect might change to a negative outcome. With regard to visual working memory, for example, a positive effect was found, as more elements could be kept in mind when the hands were near a stimulus. Another positive effect exists when processing visual stimuli while searching for a specific target. The results of five experiments administered by Reed et al. [1] showed that subjects detected target items which appeared near the hand in a covert attention task more quickly than targets away from the hand. This effect was also present for hands, which were not visible and only proprioceptive information about the location of the hand was given. Regarding tasks dealing with specific cognitive mechanisms, results showed that placing the hands near a stimulus can lead to a preference for focusing on details [2], a delay in attentional disengagement [3] and an enhancement in cognitive control mechanisms [4]. The effects caused by hand presence were also analyzed in lesion studies with patients having damages in specific brain areas. In this context, Schendel and Robertson [5] examined the post-stroke vision loss of a hemianopia patient by performing a detection task experiment in which three different conditions were compared. In the first condition, the patient's left arm lay on his lap, in the second condition, the left arm was positioned in the left visual field and the stimulus presentation took place within reach of the arm, while in the third condition the stimulus presentation was varied in distance, namely out of the reach of the arm. The results showed that a reduction in the severity of the visual deficit can be noticed in the case the arm of the patient acted in the "blind" field during condition two although the patients' inability to "see" the stimulus.

In summary, study results demonstrate a preferential processing of visual objects near the hands. Apart from the effects just described, engaging to stimuli more fully may also be non-facilitative for tasks requiring the processing of words and sentences. For example, Davoli et al. [6] let subjects judge the sensibleness of sentences and found that subjects are slower and less effective when their hands are near a visual display compared to when their hands were on the lap. In line with this result, Le Bigot and Jaschinski [7] found more errors in a letter detection task while subjects read pseudo text when the hands were near a computer screen than when the hands were further away from the screen on a desk.

Besides the distance between stimulus presentation and hand, the way how tasks are processed has an influence on the strength of the effect. Most of the studies analyzed tasks where hands were in a task congruent position. However, Brown et al. [8] studied a setting where the palm of the hand was rotated in the direction of the display and compared this position to a setting where the hand was rotated away from the display. The authors found a stronger effect of hand proximity when the hand was in a task congruent position, namely rotated with the palm in direction of the display. In another study, Festman et al. [9] studied the effect of hand proximity with moving hands. In grasping movements and pointing tasks a meaningful movement would be in the direction of the stimulus which needs to be attended to. Thus, the authors studied this movement direction and compared it to a movement which went the opposite way. Their results showed a stronger effect for movements into the direction of the stimulus and this was also true when the hands were not visible but covered under a table. Reed et al. [10] added a tool, specifically a rake, into their study setting. In the first condition they placed this tool in a meaningful position according to the original context of usage, whereas it was placed in an incongruent position in the second condition. This study again showed a stronger effect for the condition with the tool being in a task congruent position. These studies have shown that the effect which is engendered through the proximity of the hand not only originates from the presence of the hand or the tool, but also through the functional relation of the hand or the tool to the task context.

Evidence for the effect comes from Rizzolatti et al. [11] and their contribution to the bimodal neuron hypothesis. These researchers studied monkeys with lesions in specific brain regions and found partially separate neural circuits for differing distances around the body. Monkeys with lesions in the unilateral frontal lobe were not able to detect stimuli which were in their reaching distance and monkeys with unilateral lesions in the parietal lobe failed to attend to stimuli beyond reaching distance. Further, these neural systems are bimodal neurons responding to both visual stimuli, which are in the space immediately surrounding the body, called peripersonal space, and tactile information. As the hand moves, the receptive fields of the neurons in the brain move with the hand [12]. As the effect of proximal hands is stronger for task congruent hand positions and movements, it is not caused solely by a difference in attentional engagement to stimuli in peripersonal space but in a change in the process of object perception [13].

1.2 Peripersonal Space of the Elderly

Past studies of the influence of age on movement tasks have found that differences in hand motion are attributable to differences in the perception of peripersonal space, not to deficits in motor skills [14]. Based on studies administered by Tipper et al. [15], which found that while executing grasping movements the position of the object is automatically encoded in reference to the hand in younger subjects, Bloesch et al. [14] showed that in older subjects the reference frame is not specifically attributed to the hand but to the body as a whole. By means of reach-and-point actions, such as the movement needed to dial on a phone, Bloesch et al. found that distractor objects placed along a movement path slowed participants' performance more than distractors outside the movement path in younger subjects but not in older subjects. Instead older subjects' performance was slowed down when a distractor was placed near their bodies. Therefore, the authors concluded that young subjects adopt an action-centered refer-ence frame while older aged subjects make use of a body-centered reference frame. One of the key findings from these papers is that older people have more problems in performing actions in peripersonal space and these shortfalls are not only caused by impairments in motor skills.

1.3 Eye-Tracking Metrics

The cognitive processes associated with search processes are covered and cannot be observed directly. However, by using eye-tracking measures, eye movements can be analyzed. The basic idea behind analyzing eye movements is that cognitive processes can be inferred from gaze behavior. A way to assess the visual focus is by utilizing fixation durations of the eyes regarding the stimulus in question. Thereby, longer fixation durations are an indicator for the difficulty to extract information from a display [16].

Concerning age differences in mean fixation durations most studies report higher mean fixation durations for older subjects. When analyzing navigational behavior on web pages, for example, Fukuda and Bubb [17] found that subjects aged between 62 and 74 years had longer fixation durations than younger participants aged between 17 and 29 years. Moreover, Hill et al. [18] investigated computer expertise when using the internet among older subjects (70–93 years) and found that older novices had significant higher mean fixation durations than older experts. However, there are a few studies that reported no age differences regarding the fixation durations. For example, Veiel et al. [19] investigated age differences in the perception of visual stimuli and found no age difference regarding the fixation durations. This is in line with the results of Maltz and Shinar [20], who studied visual performance while driving.

1.4 The Present Study

In order to examine age-related declines in human-computer interaction, this study focusses on cognitive processes in a visual search task, as searching for icons or functions on a screen is an essential part while interacting with software. Therefore, three different distances of the hand in reference to the screen were studied as independent variables: hands placed on the screen, hands placed on the table and hands placed on the lap. As dependent variable fixation durations were analyzed. As there are age-related declines in the perception of peripersonal space, results are studied in an age-differentiated manner. With regard to prior work which found longer search times [3, 21] and slower attentional disengagement [3] when hands are near a stimulus it is hypothesized that fixation durations are longer for positions of the hands at the screen.

2 Method

2.1 Participants

Altogether, 69 right-handed subjects with normal or corrected-to-normal vision participated in the study. The age ranged from 20 to 60 years (mean = 34.67, SD = 12.83 yrs.)

2.2 Apparatus

The experiment was conducted with a 17-inch LCD monitor. Eye–movements were measured during the task using the SMI eye-tracking glasses 2.0. In reference to Rayner [22] the criterion for fixations of the eye in order to count as fixation duration was set to 50 ms.

2.3 Procedure and Task

Subjects were seated at a desk in front of a computer with a viewing distance of 500 mm from the screen. The three hand conditions are shown in Fig. 1. In each condition, a computer mouse located under the subject's right hand served as input device. In the first condition, both hands were placed at the sides of the display and the arms were supported by an elbow rest. In the second condition hands were placed on the table in front of the participant and in the third condition, the hands were placed on a wooden slat resting on the subject's lap. The horizontal distance between the hands was kept constant for all conditions.

Fig. 1. Visualization of the study conditions: hands on the screen (left), hands on the table (center) and hands on the lap (right).

The search display consisted of a matrix containing 48 rectangles with different alphanumeric characters. Characters that look similar in upper case and lower case were presented only once. In total, each of the 48 rectangles needed to be searched in a random order for each hand position to ensure that every part of the display would be included in the task, resulting in 3 × 48 trials of the visual search task. During every trial, one character that needed to be searched was presented first. After that, a blank screen was shown as a masking stimulus for three seconds, followed by the search matrix in which alphanumeric characters were arranged randomly in every trial. At the beginning, instructions for the task were given and five practice trials were carried out per condition. After locating the search stimulus, participants were instructed to click the mouse with the right index finger.

3   Results

Tests of Normality revealed that fixation durations for the three positions of the hands were not normally distributed. However, according to the findings of e.g. Lumley et al. [23] and Norman [24] ANOVA is robust concerning the violation of normality for sample sizes larger than n = 30. Therefore, repeated-measures analysis of variance was used to study the overall effect of hand position statistically. In the case Mauchly's test of sphericity showed a significant effect, within-subject effects were analyzed by means of the values corrected by Greenhouse-Geisser. The level of significance was set to $\alpha = 0.05$. Effect sizes are categorized according to the guidelines from Cohen and Cohen [25] into small (< .01), medium (< .06) and high (< .14).

3.1   Fixation Durations

A one-way repeated-measures ANOVA was conducted to compare the effect of hand position on fixation durations. Generally, the effect showed no significant result (F (2,126) = 2.52, p = .084; η_{p^2} = .038). However, after controlling for age by including it as a covariate, results revealed significant differences in the three hand positions with respect to fixation durations (F(2,124) = 4.17, p = .018; η_{p^2} = .063) and no significant interaction effect (F(2,124) = 2.66, p = .074; η_{p^2} = .041). In order to study the effect visually, error bar graphs were created for two different age groups (Fig. 2).

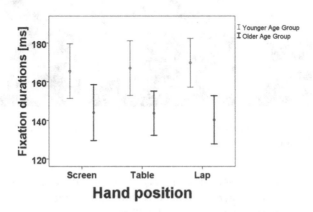

Fig. 2. Mean fixation durations (in msec.) for young subjects aged between 20 and 39 (n = 41) years and for an old group aged between 40 and 60 years (n = 23).

4   Discussion

Prior work has documented effects of hand proximity on perceptual processes. Abrams et al. [3] for example showed that subjects shift their attention between several items more slowly when their hands are near a display, resulting in longer search times. However, these effects were only studied with simple search tasks and did not take eye-tracking measures and age differences into account. In this study, we tested the effect of three different hand positions on fixation durations in a visual search task.

Overall, repeated-measures ANOVA showed no significant effect for the general model. However, after age was added as a covariate, results showed a significant effect with regard to the position of the hand. Fixation durations were shorter for the positions of the hands at the screen in comparison to the positions of the hands on the table and on the lap in the younger age group. However, for the older age group this effect was vice versa: Fixation durations were longer for the hands at the screen in comparison to the two other conditions. Studying the interaction effect showed no significant result but as the p-value was about p = .074 it can be concluded that there is a tendency in the values for an interaction in the scores of hand position depending on age.

This study therefore indicates that there are differences with regard to the position of the hands and eye-tracking measures and that these differences vary with regard to age for fixation durations. However, some limitations are worth noting. Although we found statistically significant results, we were not able to compare age groups due to different group sizes. As the eye-tracker we used only works for people not wearing glasses we had problems finding older aged subjects for our study. Another limitation is the fact that prior studies found longer search times for positions of the hands near a stimulus [21] which is not supported by the eye-tracking measures in our study for the young age group. An explanation may be the fact that although search times are longer, the process of searching may be less straining resulting in shorter fixation durations for nearby hands in the young age group. Therefore, further analysis concerning age differences is needed as well as an analysis of the amount of fixations found for the different hand positions. Furthermore, the dilation of the pupil will be studied with regard to the position of the hand as pupil diameter can be used as a measure of task difficulty.

Based on the results of the study, the effect evoked by proximal hands should be analyzed in a second study in a different task context. While in this study the effect was studied in a directional search task where the item that was searched was defined ahead, in the follow-up study the search task should be non-directional. Therefore, two parts of a display (one left and one right) should be compared regarding differences in items while effects generated by the hands are studied. In line with prior studies [3, 21], it is hypothesized that search times are longer for positions of the hands at the screen and that the effect of proximal hands is stronger for the right side of the screen for right-handed people as there may be more task interference by the prominent hand.

Acknowledgements. This publication is part of the research project "TECH4AGE", which is funded by the German Federal Ministry of Education and Research (BMBF, Grant No. 16SV7111) supervised by the VDI/VDE Innovation + Technik GmbH.

References

1. Reed, C.L., Grubb, J.D., Steele, C.: Hands up: attentional prioritization of space near the hand. J. Exp. Psychol. Hum. Percept. Perform. **32**(1), 166 (2006). doi:10.1037/0096-1523. 32.1.166
2. Davoli, C.C., Brockmole, J.R., Goujon, A.: A bias to detail: how hand position modulates visual learning and visual memory. Mem. Cognit. **40**(3), 352 (2012). doi:10.3758/s13423-013-0514-0
3. Abrams, R.A., Davoli, C.C., Du, F., Knapp III, W.H., Paull, D.: Altered Vision Near Hands. Cognition **107**(3), 1035 (2008). doi:10.1016/j.cognition.2007.09.006
4. Weidler, B.J., Abrams, R.A.: Enhanced cognitive control near the hands. Psychon. Bull. Rev. **21**(2), 462 (2014). doi:10.3758/s13423-013-0514-0
5. Schendel, K., Robertson, L.C.: Reaching out to see: arm position can attenuate human visual loss. J. Cogn. Neurosci. **16**(6), 935 (2004). doi:10.1162/0898929041502698
6. Davoli, C.C., Du, F., Montana, J., Garverick, S., Abrams, R.A.: When meaning matters, look but don't touch: the effects of posture on reading. Mem. Cognit. **38**(5), 555 (2010). doi:10.3758/MC.38.5.555

7. Le Bigot, N., Jaschinski, W.: Hand position at computer screens. In: Dittmar, A., Forbrig, P. (eds.) The 29th Annual European Conference, p. 85 (2011)
8. Brown, L.E., Morrissey, B.F., Goodale, M.A.: Vision in the palm of your hand. Neuropsychologia 47(6), 1621 (2009). doi:10.1016/j.neuropsychologia.2008.11.021
9. Festman, Y., Adam, J.J., Pratt, J., Fischer, M.H.: Both hand position and movement direction modulate visual attention. Front. Psychol. 4, 657 (2013). doi:10.3389/fpsyg.2013.00657
10. Reed, C.L., Betz, R., Garza, J.P., Roberts, R.J.: Grab it! Biased attention in functional hand and tool space. Atten. Percept. Psychophys. 72(1), 236 (2010). doi:10.3758/APP.72.1.236
11. Rizzolatti, G., Matelli, M., Pavesi, G.: Deficits in attention and movement following the removal of postarcuate (area 6) and prearcuate (area 8) cortex in macaque monkeys. Brain 106(3), 655 (1983)
12. Gross, C.G., Bender, D.B., Rocha-Miranda, C.E.: Visual receptive fields of neurons in inferotemporal cortex of the monkey. Science 166(3910), 1303 (1969)
13. Cosman, J.D., Vecera, S.P.: Attention affects visual perceptual processing near the hand. Psychol. Sci. 21(9), 1254 (2010). doi:10.1177/0956797610380697
14. Bloesch, E.K., Davoli, C.C., Abrams, R.A.: Age-related changes in attentional reference frames for peripersonal space. Psychol. Sci. 24(4), 557 (2013) doi:10.1177/0956797612457 385
15. Tipper, S.P., Lortie, C., Baylis, G.C.: Selective reaching, Evidence for action-centered attention. J. Exp. Psychol. Hum. Percept. Perform. 18(4), 891 (1992). doi:10.1037/0096-1523.18.4.891
16. Goldberg, J.H., Kotval, X.P.: Computer interface evaluation using eye movements, Methods and constructs. Int. J. Ind. Ergon. 24(6), 631 (1999). doi:10.1016/S0169-8141(98)00068-7
17. Fukuda, R., Bubb, H.: Eye tracking study on web-use: comparison between younger and elderly users in case of search task with electronic timetable service. PsychNology J. 2003 (3), 202 (2003)
18. Hill, R.L., Dickinson, A., Arnott, J.L., Gregor, P., McIver, L.: Older web users' eye movements. In: Tan, D., Fitzpatrick, G., Gutwin, C., Begole, B., Kellogg, W.A. (eds.) The 2011 Annual Conference. p. 1151 (2011)
19. Veiel, L.L., Storandt, M., Abrams, R.A.: Visual search for change in older adults. Psychol. Aging 21(4), 754 (2006) doi:10.1037/0882-7974.21.4.754
20. Maltz, M., Shinar, D.: Eye Movements of Younger and Older Drivers. Hum. Factors J. Hum. Factors Ergon. Soc. 41(1), 15 (1999). doi:10.1518/001872099779577282
21. Bröhl, C., Antons, C., Bützler, J., Schlick, C.: Age-differentiated analysis of the hand proximity effect in a visual search paradigm. In: Lindgaard, G., Moore, D. (eds.) Proceedings 19th Triennial Congress of the IEA, Melbourne, 9-14 August 2015
22. Rayner, K.: Eye movements in reading and information processing, 20 years of research. Psychol. Bull. 124(3), 372 (1998). doi:10.1037/0033-2909.124.3.372
23. Lumley, T., Diehr, P., Emerson, S., Chen, L.: The importance of the normality assumption in large public health data sets. Annu. Rev. Public Health 23(1), 151 (2002). doi:10.1146/annurev.publhealth.23.100901.140546
24. Norman, G.: Likert scales, levels of measurement and the "laws" of statistics. Adv. Health Sci. Educ. 15(5), 625 (2010). doi:10.1007/s10459-010-9222-y
25. Cohen, J.: Statistical power analysis for the behavioral sciences, p. xxi, 567. L. Erlbaum Associates, Hillsdale (1988). ISBN 0805802835

Combinations of Modalities for the Words Learning Memory Test Implemented on Tablets for Seniors

Erika Hernández-Rubio[1], Amilcar Meneses-Viveros[2(✉)],
Erick Mancera-Serralde[3], and Javier Flores-Ortiz[3]

[1] Instituto Politécnico Nacional, SEPI-ESCOM, México D.F., Mexico
ehernandezru@ipn.mx
[2] Departamento de Computación, CINVESTAV-IPN, México D.F., Mexico
ameneses@cs.cinvestav.mx
[3] School of Computing, Instituto Politeécnico Nacional, México D.F., Mexico

Abstract. Mnesic problems in older adults is a global health problem. Some proposals have been made to support health care in older adults using mobile technologies. In particular,there are analysis and design of mobile applications focusing on the elderly to apply memory tests Luria. For example, in word learning test, multiple words or numerical figures unraleted are shown to the patient. The number of item exceed the numer that the patient can remember. Usually the serie consist of ten or twelve words or numerical digits. After this task, the patient is asked to repeat the series in any order. In one hand, the physical deterioration of the elderly makes it difficult the usability of the user interface of mobile applications. These deteriorations can be auditory, visual and motor. They are particular to each elderly. For this reason, a traditional user interface loses effectiveness when it has interaction with older people. In another hand, some studies suggest that Tablets are the best mobile devices for older adults, because the size of their screen and usability of their user interface. However, tablets have different modes of interaction and it is not yet clear how the elderly respond to them. One solution to this problem is to provide different modalities for interaction. This modalities they must be presents in applications for tablets. In this work, we present the implementation of the test world learning Luria memory test. And we implemented several combinations of modalities for the test. Finally we present the result of interaction with the older adults.

1 Introduction

Old age is a natural occurrence in the biological development of humans. It involves a series of physiological changes caused by the sensitive, perceptive, cognitive and motion control impairment in older adults. Humans who reach this stage of life develop diseases of natural degeneration of the body such as Alzheimer and Parkinson, among others [1–5].

The various problems of vision, hearing, cognition and movement presenting the elderly, hinder the use of existing technological resources because software

© Springer International Publishing Switzerland 2016
J. Zhou and G. Salvendy (Eds.): ITAP 2016, Part I, LNCS 9754, pp. 309–319, 2016.
DOI: 10.1007/978-3-319-39943-0_30

applications are not designed to cover these deficiencies. Older adults have limitations on the use of technology. The 47 % of the problems reported for older adults due to financial and health difficulties. About 25 % of the above difficulties can be resolved by designing systems that take into account these limitations [3].

Some proposals have been made to support health care in older adults using mobile technologies. Several of these proposals focus on the monitoring of patients [1,6]. Monitoring relates to the evolution of a disease, or to ensure that it is following a treatment [7–9]. In particular in the case of memory tests they have been developed for dementia [4,9–12].

In particular, there are analysis and design of mobile applications focusing on the elderly to apply memory tests Luria [5,10,11,13,14]. For example, in word learning test, multiple words or numerical figures unrelated are shown to the patient. The number of item exceed the number that the patient can remember. Usually the serie consist of ten or twelve words or numerical digits. After this task, the patient is asked to repeat the series in any order.

In one hand, the physical deterioration of the elderly makes it difficult the usability of the user interface of mobile applications [2,3,15]. These deteriorations can be auditory, visual, motor and cognitive. They are particular to each elderly. For this reason, a traditional user interface loses effectiveness when it has interaction with older people. In another hand, severals works say that Tablets are the best mobile devices for older adults, because the size of their screen and usability of their user interface [4,14]. One solution to this problem is to provide different modalities for interaction. This modalities they must be presents in applications for tablets.

In this work, we present the implementation of the test world learning Luria memory test. And we implemented four combinations of modalities for the test:

Vision-Haptic. In this combination of modalities, the application presents the serie on the touch screen and after the presentation, the user must type the words using the virtual touch keyboard.

Vision-Voice. In this case, the application displays the words on the touch screen and the user indicates the words by voice.

Audition-Haptic. In this combination, the applications says the serie and the user must type the serie using the virtual touch keyboard.

Audition-Voice. In this case, the applications says the words and the user indicates the words by voice.

Finally we present the result of interaction with the older adults.The application was tested in 27 people: 24 women and 3 mens. The age average of the sample is 70 years old. We notice that older adults neither read or write could not be tested. Older adults who have no experience with the use of mobile devices showed no reluctance to use.

2   Related Work

The work related to this work focuses on several aspects: Interaction modalities, tele rehabilitation and monitoring to help older adults.

From the perspective of modalities. Several studies have been developed to compare the effectiveness and efficiency of multimodal interfaces against unimodal interfaces as well as to clarify some wrong use of multimodal interfaces assumptions [16,17]. In the literature it has been reported work to find patterns that suit the capabilities of the end user or the context of use of a particular application [18]. And it has been found that low specific tasks use the multimodal communication can handle complex tasks. These tests multimodal include speech input and pen input [18]. Uni modal interfaces are adequately assessed for seniors, such as touch [19]. The use of multimodal interfaces is still not clear to seniors in some cases may be beneficial [6,20,21] and other not much [22], although reports of failures in over 70 years old.

Furthermore, many of these studies focus on the effectiveness of using mobile technology and augmented reality for remote rehabilitation and severals authors have reported encouraging results [6]. This rehabilitation ranging from rehabilitation systems for different types of disabilities or motor, visual and cognitive problems to name a few [6,21].

Acceptance of older adults to use technology to support them in monitoring and rehabilitation process has been reported in several studies [1]. Several authors show that older adults are supported in Internet consultations on health, also they are easy to adopt the use of new technologies such as smartphones, tablets and smart TVs. Monitoring systems can range from the use of cameras in a house, to the use of sensors in devices that are adapted to the body of information acquired by mobile devices using the elderly [1,7,8,23–25].

3   Prototype Design

The design of the prototype should be focused on the elderly. It is known that older adults have changes in their mental and physical faculties that may affect the acceptance of the technology. Therefore considered the prototype design guidelines aimed at seniors. The guidelines for designing displays for seniors are taken from [2,3]. With these guidelines, they developed mockups for testing Luria and subsequently implemented in Tablets using Android OS. There were two evaluations of the prototypes, the first with specialists. This helped us to correct the prototype. In the second phase, the prototype was evaluated by an elderly driver to know that changes had to be made in the prototype group. The third prototype was used for testing.

3.1   GUI Design for Older Adults

Interface design for seniors considered possible natural damage they may have. These impairments are visual, auditory, movement and cognitive.

Vision. Physiological changes to the eye related to aging result in less light reaching the retina, yellowing of the lens (making blue a difficult to discern color), and even the beginning stages of cataracts result in blurriness.

312 E. Hernández-Rubio et al.

The eye muscles are also affected; it can be more difficult for older adults to quickly change focus or get used to fast-changing brightness. Some solutions for design include: conspicuity can be enhanced by enhanced contrast and taking advantage of preattentive processes, and effortful visual search can be lessened through application of Gestalt laws.

Effect of vision. How the visual aspects of the web can interact with aging to produce difficulties.

Background images should be used sparingly if at all because they create visual clutter in displays. High contrast should be maintained between important text or controls and the background. Older users vary greatly in their perceptual capabilities; thus interfaces should convey information through multiple modalities (vision, hearing, touch) and even within modalities (color, organization, size, volume, texture). Within a website, consistency should be the highest priority in terms of button appearance and positioning, spatial layout, and interaction behavior. Older users are likely to have a reduced tolerance for discovery and quit instead of hunting

Information should be presented in small, screen-sized chunks so that the page does not require extensive scrolling. If this cannot be helped, alternative ways of navigating (such as table of contents) or persistent navigation that follows the user as they scroll be provided.

Hearing. A wide variety of changes can occur to hearing. A good auditory design considers both the physical changes in sound perception and the congnitive changes in the comprehension that comes from initial perception. Keeping informational sounds above background noise requires a study of the display environments. The loudness of a sound is truly individual, but can be approximated through the sound pressure levels (dB) and frecuencies typically maintained in the aging ear. When hearing loss is severe enough that users wear an aid, consider how those aids interact with the interface.

List of general design guidelines that can be used to improve the design of auditory menus. Calculate loudness levels. Consider potential background noise For tones, use low-tom-mid-range frequencies When designing a display device, consider physical proximity ti the ear and interactions with hearing aids. Avoid computer-generated voices Use prosody Provide succinct prompts Provide context

Cognition. The main objective in the design of displays is that they are easy to understand. It is intended that the interface is effective, that is, to help users to complete tasks with less confusion and less possible error. To achieve this, we consider some user skills such as: working memory, spatial skills and perceptual speed. Working memory allows the user to recall situations or things in a short period of time. Spatial ability refers to the user to have a location-based representation of the environment where it interacts, in our case, the state of the application. The perceptual speed indicates the rate at which it perceives and processes information. It is known that these skills decline with age, so the design should not be confused with the instructions or the information presented.

For this reason they have only information related to the test. It ensures that each task selection, display, are associated with their own display. Generating an intuitive workflow, as shown in Sect. 3.3. In each display the action to take as a central element occurs, this allows the user to hold the attention.

Movement. The movement is an essential part of many means of interaction, because a series movements, perform an action to complete a task. Motion control refers to the accuracy and response time of a movement of a human. The accuracy and response time decay with age, for various reasons, mainly due to illness, such as Parkinson or arthritis. From [2], it is suggested that there is sufficient time for inputs, have feedback by other means (auditory, visual, haptic). Simplifying the number of target elements with which the user must interact. And use words instead of images.

3.2 Words Learning Luria Memory Test

For this test, the patient is shown several words or numbers not linked to each and whose number exceeds the amount that can remember. Usually the series consist of 10 to 12 words o 8 to 10 numbers. The patient is asked to recall and repeat the series in any order. After recording the number of items retained, presents to the patient again the series and re-record the results. This process is repeated 8 to 10 times and the data obtained are shown in graphical form called "memory curve". After complete all repetitions and spent 50 to 60 min, the specialist must ask to the patient the series of words without mentioning it to the patient again.

The application must download the series of words in a database containing common series for this test. Must have a variety of these series, so that no repetition between tests. The test shows that words can be read to the patient or in the form of text. In this analysis we consider two cases.

– For the case in which the words are presented in the form of text, must take the general considerations of a text in this analysis. The words are displayed on screen with an appearance time for the user to have a chance to read the word and hold it. In this analysis it is proposed that the time of occurrence for word is 5 to 10 s.
– For the case in which the words are presented in the form of audio, playback of sound files is required in the mobile devices. This represents a higher data download and use more features. This form is recommended for this test, because it's similar to testing experience between the patient and the specialist.

Once the series of words presented to the patient, the application indicates that the patient must enter the words that were presented above. These instructions can be displayed as text on screen. The test suggests that the reproduction of the words to be spoken instead of being written. This requires a hearing user interface. The implementation of a speech recognition algorithm for mobile devices solves this problem. When the user pronounce the words that recalls, the application transform the received audio into text, allowing to store as a string the words the patient recalls. Once record a word, the application must request more words until the user indicates that they no longer remember more words or reached the total words. The application should display a button to indicate that the user does not remember more words and will terminate the test process. A simpler way to implement this phase of the test is to apply the words through a text input, that is, the user will write the words remember and these strings register for the test. Incorrect orthography is a problem when validating a user input word belongs to the series of words.

3.3   Prototype Design

The prototype is designed to have support for Luria Memory test with four modalities. A female voice was used for audio messages. The prototype design considers the user to select the mode of interaction. Depending on different displays that are presented. As shown in Fig. 1, the first display allows the user to select the interaction modality.

When the user select Vision-Haptic modality option, the user is asked to look at the words that he showed. This instruction is presented in both audio and alert panel for a few seconds. After each word is presented for a period of time

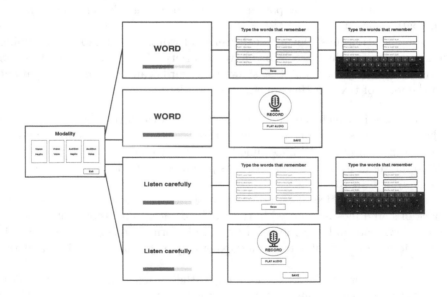

Fig. 1. Prototype design mockup

(shown in a progress bar). This display will be many times as words is displayed to the user. Then, it prompted the user to type the words to remember. This instruction is also presented in both audio and alert panel. After a display is shown in a form where they should write the words to remember. The writing is done through the touch qwerty keyboard. This whole process is repeated three times, increasing the number of words in each iteration.

When the user choose Vision-Voice modality option the user sees the words and to repeat recording them. First, the user is asked to look at the words that he showed. After each word is presented for a period of time (shown in a progress bar). Then, it prompted the user to repeat the words to remember. After a display is presented to record the words to remember. This whole process is repeated three times, increasing the number of words in each iteration.

When the user select Audition-Haptic option the user hears the words and remember to write. First, it prompted the user to listen carefully to the words. Then a display with a progress bar appears while the application plays audio with the words. Then, it prompted the user to type the words to remember. The writing is done through the touch qwerty keyboard. As in previous cases, this process is repeated three times, increasing the number of words in each iteration.

When the user select Audition Voice option the user hears the words and must record the words to remember. First, it prompted the user to listen carefully to the words. This instruction is presented in both audio and alert panel for a few seconds. Then a display with a progress bar appears while the application plays audio with the words. Then, it prompted the user to repeat the words to remember. After a display is presented to record the words to remember. This whole process is repeated three times, increasing the number of words in each iteration.

4 Test and Results

The prototype test Luria learning 10 words applied to 27 seniors with an average age of 70 years. The 90 % is female and 10 % is male. All seniors in our sample can read and write, are at healthy mental condition, and in a 25 % had visual problems (caused by diabetes) and 25 % had hearing problems. An adult in our sample suffers from Alzheimer and other three are diagnosed with a condition of arthritis. Only three users had experience using tablets.

The prototype we used had two phases of review. These phases included review by a specialist in the field of neuropsychology and a pilot group of older adults. The prototype was developed for the Android platform version 4.2 and was implemented in 7-inch tablets.

To apply the test, first it is shown and explained to users running prototype. They were then asked to do the test. And finally users answered a questionnaire usability and effectiveness.

Figure 2 shows the problems with the GUI components detected by the users. It can seen that the prototype have minors errors in the GUI design for older adults. 21 users had no problems in using the prototype. Three users have problems with the directions and one user have problem with de size of letter o size of button.

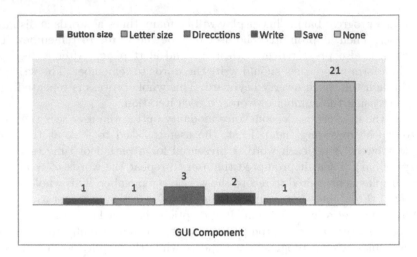

Fig. 2. Problems with the GUI design. This graphic shows the number of older adults that have some problem with the prototype GUI.

Figure 3 shows the modality that was easier to use. It can be seen that the Audition-Voice and Vision-Voice were more acceptance. The Audition-Haptic mode had little acceptance and Haptic-Vision modality had no acceptance. This graph was obtained by asking users which modality they preferred. The modality more acceptable to the user is the voice.

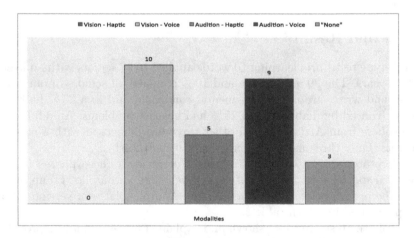

Fig. 3. Preferences modalities for older adults. This graphic shows the number of older adults that prefer use the different interaction modalities.

5   Conclusion

In this paper we have presented the prototype test Luria learning 10 words. We have focused more on the effectiveness of the interface, rather than on the effectiveness of the test. However, this helps us to trust the results of effectiveness of the test in future work.

We can see that for healthy older adults who can read and write, there is no problem in using the modalities. However, we note that older adults prefer to use the modality of voice instead of the haptic modality. Ninety-five percent of user of our sample have the basic education level, making it possible for spelling problems that had caused rejection of the haptic modality.

Eventhough only three users had experience using tablets, 100 % of users were able to complete the tasks of the prototype. Older adults without mental illness, as is most of the sample used in this work, not present reluctance to use technology. We attribute this largely to the use of the tablet and design guidelines for older adults who use the prototype. Our experiment shows the sizes of buttons and letters were adequate. This was no reason for users will use the haptic mode. But older adults prefer to use the voice mode [26].

References

1. Czaja, S., Beach, S., Charness, N., Schulz, R.: Older adults and the adoption of healthcare technology: opportunities and challenges. Technologies for active aging. International Perspectives on Aging, pp. 27–46. Springer, New York (2013)
2. Pak, R., McLaughlin, A.: Designing Displays for Older Adults. CRC Press, Boca Raton (2010)
3. Fisk, A.D., Rogers, W.A., Charness, N., Czaja, S.J., Sharit, J.: Designing for Older Adults: Principles and Creative Human Factors Approaches. CRC Press, Boca Raton (2009)
4. Yamagata, C., Kowtko, M., Coppola, J.F., Joyce, S.: Mobile app development and usability research to help Dementia and Alzheimer patients. In: Systems, Applications and Technology Conference (LISAT), 2013 IEEE Long Island, pp. 1–6. IEEE (2013)
5. Mandala, P.K., Saharana, S., Khana, S.A., Jamesa, M.: Apps for dementia screening: a cost-effective and portable solution. J. Alzheimers Disease **47**, 869–872 (2015)
6. Pereira, C., Almeida, N., Martins, A.I., Silva, S., Rosa, A.F., Oliveira e Silva, M., Teixeira, A.: Evaluation of complex distributed multimodal applications: evaluating a telerehabilitation system when it really matters. In: Zhou, J., Salvendy, G. (eds.) ITAP 2015. LNCS, vol. 9194, pp. 146–157. Springer, Heidelberg (2015)
7. Demiris, G., Rantz, M.J., Aud, M.A., Marek, K.D., Tyrer, H.W., Skubic, M., Hussam, A.A.: Older adults' attitudes towards and perceptions of "smart home" technologies: a pilot study. Med. Inform. Internet Med. **29**(2), 87–94 (2004)
8. Demongeot, J., Virone, G., Duchêne, F., Benchetrit, G., Hervé, T., Noury, N., Rialle, V.: Multi-sensors acquisition, data fusion, knowledge mining and alarm triggering in health smart homes for elderly people. Comptes Rendus Biologies **325**(6), 673–682 (2002)

9. Boletsis, C., McCallum, S., Landmark, B.F.: The use of smartwatches for health monitoring in home-based dementia care. In: Zhou, J., Salvendy, G. (eds.) ITAP 2015. LNCS, vol. 9194, pp. 15–26. Springer, Heidelberg (2015)
10. Sawyer, P., Sutcliffe, A., Rayson, P., Bull, C.: Dementia and social sustainability: challenges for software engineering (2015)
11. Span, M., Hettinga, M., Vernooij-Dassen, M., Eefsting, J., Smits, C.: Involving people with dementia in the development of supportive it applications: a systematic review. Ageing Res. Rev. **12**(2), 535–551 (2013)
12. Novitzky, P., Smeaton, A.F., Chen, C., Irving, K., Jacquemard, T., O'Brolcháin, F., O'Mathúna, D., Gordijn, B.: A review of contemporary work on the ethics of ambient assisted living technologies for people with dementia. Sci. Eng. Ethics **21**(3), 707–765 (2015)
13. Ancient, C., Good, A., Wilson, C., Fitch, T.: Can Ubiquitous devices utilising reminiscence therapy be used to promote well-being in Dementia patients? An exploratory study. In: Stephanidis, C., Antona, M. (eds.) UAHCI 2013, Part III. LNCS, vol. 8011, pp. 426–435. Springer, Heidelberg (2013)
14. Miranda, J.A.H., Hernàndez Rubio, E., Meneses Viveros, A.: Analysis of luria memory tests for development on mobile devices. In: Duffy, V.G. (ed.) DHM 2014. LNCS, vol. 8529, pp. 546–557. Springer, Heidelberg (2014)
15. Lund, H.H.: Play for the elderly - effect studies of playful technology. In: Zhou, J., Salvendy, G. (eds.) ITAP 2015. LNCS, vol. 9194, pp. 500–511. Springer, Heidelberg (2015)
16. Oviatt, S.: Ten myths of multimodal interaction. Commun. ACM **42**(11), 74–81 (1999)
17. Turk, M.: Multimodal interaction: a review. Pattern Recogn. Lett. **36**, 189–195 (2014)
18. Oviatt, S., Coulston, R., Lunsford, R.: When do we interact multimodally?: cognitive load and multimodal communication patterns. In: Proceedings of the 6th International Conference on Multimodal Interfaces, pp. 129–136. ACM (2004)
19. Bush, E.: The use of human touch to improve the well-being of older adults a holistic nursing intervention. J. Holist. Nurs. **19**(3), 256–270 (2001)
20. Teixeira, V., Pires, C., Pinto, F., Freitas, J., Dias, M.S., Rodrigues, E.M.: Towards elderly social integration using a multimodal human-computer interface. In: Proceeding International Living Usability Lab Workshop on AAL Latest Solutions, Trends and Applications, AAL (2012)
21. Hackney, M.E., Hall, C.D., Echt, K.V., Wolf, S.L.: Multimodal exercise benefits mobility in older adults with visual impairment: a preliminary study. J. Aging Phys. Act. **23**(4), 630–639 (2015)
22. Patil, R., Uusi-Rasi, K., Tokola, K., Karinkanta, S., Kannus, P., Sievänen, H.: Effects of a multimodal exercise program on physical function, falls, and injuries in older women: a 2-year community-based, randomized controlled trial. J. Am. Geriatrics Soc. **63**(7), 1306–1313 (2015)
23. Sixsmith, A., Johnson, N.: A smart sensor to detect the falls of the elderly. IEEE Pervasive Comput. **3**(2), 42–47 (2004)
24. Sorwar, G., Hasan, R.: Smart-tv based integrated e-health monitoring system with agent technology. In: 26th International Conference on Advanced Information Networking and Applications Workshops (WAINA), pp. 406–411. IEEE (2012)
25. Aal, K., Ogonowski, C., von Rekowski, T., Wieching, R., Wulf, V.: A Fall Preventive iTV Solution for Older Adults. Siegen, Germany (2014)

26. Li, R., Zhu, X., Yin, S., Niu, Y., Zheng, Z., Huang, X., Wang, B., Li, J., et al.: Multimodal intervention in older adults improves resting-state functional connectivity between the medial prefrontal cortex and medial temporal lobe. Front Aging Neurosci. **6**, 39 (2014)

Exploring the Antecedents of Technostress and Compulsive Mobile Application Usage: Personality Perspectives

Kuo-Lun Hsiao[1](✉), Chun-Hsiung Lee[2], Hsiu-Sen Chiang[1], and Ju-Yun Wang[1]

[1] Department of Information Management,
National Taichung University of Science and Technology,
Taichung City, Taiwan, ROC
{klhsiao,hschiang,s1810331108}@nutc.edu.tw
[2] Department of Information Management,
Cheng Shiu University, Kaohsiung City, Taiwan, ROC
Leech@csu.edu.tw

Abstract. Mobile social applications make people's communication easier, but the overuse of smartphones will bring negative effects on our lives. Past research has demonstrated that personality traits were associated with excessive mobile phone use. However, few studies use personality theory to explore the antecedents of compulsive mobile application usage. There, this study explored the effects of the big five personality traits on compulsive usage of mobile social application and examined the influence of compulsive usage on technostress. A total of 389 valid questionnaires were collected by online survey method. The seven hypotheses proposed were examined by SmartPLS software. The results showed that neuroticism, extraversion, and conscientiousness had significant effects on compulsive usage of mobile social applications. In addition, neuroticism, openness to experience, and compulsive usage significantly influenced technostress. Finally, this study discussed the implications of these findings and offered directions for future research.

Keywords: Personality traits · Compulsive usage · Mobile application · Technostress

1 Introduction

With the development of mobile technology, mobile devices have become a necessity for many people. More and more services are provided through mobile devices and Internet to help people with their daily lives. For example, people can shop, make payments, book tickets, and watch videos via these devices. In particular, the software designed to run on mobile services is called mobile application (mobile APP). Mobile APP can be put into categories such as games, social networking, entertainment and finance. People can choose and download the mobile APP they need to accomplish works that can only be done by computer (Hung et al. 2015).

Although mobile APP eases our lives, it could cause many concerns when not properly used. Some researchers have indicated that personality traits are related to

© Springer International Publishing Switzerland 2016
J. Zhou and G. Salvendy (Eds.): ITAP 2016, Part I, LNCS 9754, pp. 320–328, 2016.
DOI: 10.1007/978-3-319-39943-0_31

smartphone use. Person with specific personalities will overuse smartphone (Lee et al. 2014). Roberts et al. (2015) examined the relationship between the big five personality traits and smartphone addiction. The big five personality dimensions include openness, neuroticism, extraversion, agreeableness and conscientiousness. The study demonstrated that personality traits influence addictive use of smartphone. Therefore, it is important to explore the antecedents of compulsive behavior and its influence on technostress. Though past studies have demonstrated the relationships between personality traits and compulsive behavior (Hung et al. 2015; Lee et al. 2014), little research have used personality traits to explore the factors influencing compulsive use of mobile APP. Hence, this study adopts personality traits to investigate the antecedents of compulsive use of social mobile APPs, and examine the relationships between such behavior and technostress.

2 Research Model

We adopted the big five personality traits in our research model, shown in Fig. 1. This research model is based on the model proposed by (Hirschman 1992) in which traits theory was used to explain the relationship between personality and compulsive behavior. Several studies have examined the relationship between personality, problematic use of cell phone, and addiction (Bianchi and Phillips 2005; Takao et al. 2009). In psychological literature, extraversion and materialism were used to predict compulsive behavior (Chak and Leung 2004; İskender and Akin, 2010). According to past literature reviewed, we assume personality is correlated to compulsive use of mobile APP. Furthermore, we focus on the most popular mobile APPs: social APPs. In this study, the five personality traits mentioned above are used to explore the relationship between personality and compulsive use of mobile APP. The definitions of each construct and hypotheses are presented below.

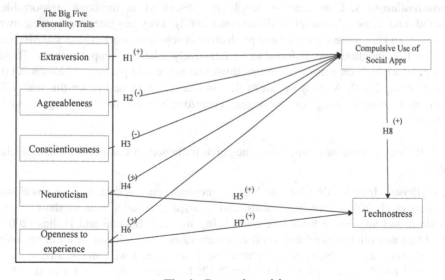

Fig. 1. Research model

Extraversion. Extraversion reflects the extent to which people are comfortable with direct social interaction (Costa and McCrae 1992b). Extraverted people are dominant in social interaction, enthusiastic, talkative, and gregarious. They also tend to be impulsive and venturesome. Individuals who rate high on extraversion tend to use virtual social services and have more online social experiences (Gosling et al. 2011). Ross et al. (2009) stated that extraversion is positively related to communication through social networking sites. Ryan and Xenos (2011) confirmed that extraversion is highly associated with Facebook use. In terms of cell phone use, extraverts always carry their cell phone anytime, and are hardly disturbed by others when using smartphones in public places (Roberts et al. 2015). Therefore, we expect that extraverted persons will be addicted to mobile devices and mobile APP, especially social APP and games APP, and these addictive habits will eventually become compulsive. We therefore proposed the following hypotheses:

H1: Extraversion will have a positive influence on compulsive use of social APP.

Agreeableness. Agreeableness is defined as being sympathetic, considerate, kind, trusting, and tolerant (Costa and McCrae 1992b). Researchers found that low agreeableness may be associated with cell phone misuse and other problematic cell phone use. A recent study showed a significant negative correlation between agreeableness and addiction to smartphone (Andreassen et al. 2013). People low on agreeableness spend more time using instant message service (Butt and Phillips 2008; Ehrenberg et al. 2008) and are more likely to use their mobile phones to play games (Phillips et al. 2006). Based on the above findings, we posit that agreeableness is related to cellphone misuse, and could result in compulsive use. Thus, we proposed the following hypotheses:

H2: Agreeableness will have a negative influence on compulsive use of social APP.

Conscientiousness. Conscientious people are described as thorough, responsible, ordered, and show self-discipline (Baumeister 2002). They pay attention to their own behavior, and are more organized and productive at school or work (Costa and McCrae 1992a). Conscientiousness is found to be negatively related to impulsiveness. Those who measure high on conscientiousness think and act less impulsively (Mowen 2000; Roccas et al. 2002). A study on adults demonstrated that those low on this trait will spend more time sending text messages. Therefore, we ask the following research questions:

H3: Conscientiousness will have a negative influence on compulsive use of social APP.

Neuroticism. Individuals who rate high on neuroticism are described as emotional (Roberts et al. 2015), moody, anxious, and worried. Neurotics tend to show strong emotions and aggressive behaviors when being irritated. Bianchi and Philips (2005) found that neuroticism is related to extreme behaviors and addiction. A lot of research has suggested that problematic cell phone use is associated with stress, anxiety, and emotional instability (Augner and Hacker 2012; Beranuy et al. 2009; Ha et al. 2008;

Jenaro et al. 2007; Reid and Reid, 2007). Therefore, it is predicted that neurotic or emotionally unstable people may be sensitive to technostress and will use smartphone to reduce stress and anxiety (Roberts et al. 2015).

H4: Neuroticism will have a positive influence on compulsive use of social APP.

H5: Neuroticism will have a positive influence on technostress.

Openness to Experience. Costa and McCrae (1992b) define openness to experience as being curious and receptive of new ideas. People who score high on this trait tend to be imaginative, artistically sensitive, active, intelligent, broad-minded, and adventurous. They have broad interests, long for new experiences, and are willing to try new media tool (Butt and Phillips 2008; Tuten and Bosnjak, 2001). When Facebook was first launched, it was an innovation for people having high openness score. This could explain why openness is positively related to using Facebook as a communication tool (Ross et al. 2009). Consistent with this finding, openness has been found to be correlated to use of instant message and SNS (Butt and Phillips 2008; Correa et al. 2010). Wang et al. (2012) also discovered that people high in openness are more likely to play online games. Accordingly, it is expected that individuals high on openness are more likely to install different kinds of mobile APP. Moreover, developers of social APP keep launching promotional activities and release new versions of APPs to attract users. Driven by curiosity and openness to experience, individuals may start using new functions of APPs or participating in activities, increasing the frequency and the amount of time they use mobile devices, and thus develop compulsive use and technostress. Hence, we proposed the following hypotheses:

H6: Openness will have a positive influence on compulsive use of social APP.

H7: Openness will have a positive influence on technostress.

Compulsive Usage and Technostress. Smartphones provide an efficient way for users to receive and reply to messages instantly, which encourages people to check their mobile devices more frequently. Constant phone checking has been seen as a compulsive behavior (Oulasvirta et al. 2012). Nowadays mobile APPs are a leading trend, which makes people overuse mobile APP and causes pressure and depression (Matusik and Mickel 2011). In this study, we define compulsive use of social APP as using these APPs continuously, repeatedly, and excessively. Studies exploring relationship between compulsive behaviors and negative emotions have found that compulsive behaviors have negative influence on patients' physical health, mental health, and social ability (Eisen et al. 2006; Hauschildt et al. 2010). Hence, compulsive use of social APP could make users feel irritated and mentally fatigued, and finally experience technostress (Lee et al. 2014). Therefore, we proposed the following hypotheses:

H8: Compulsive use of social APP will have a positive influence on technostress.

3 Measurement Development and Data Collection

The questionnaire contained two sections: demographic profile and construct items. The items used to operationalize the constructs included in the model were adapted from relevant prior studies and were slightly modified to fit the target context. Items for measuring Big Five personality traits were adapted from John et al. (1991). Items for measuring compulsive usage of mobile app were adapted from Lee et al. (2014). Items for measuring technostress were taken from Tarafdar et al. (2007). All items were measured using a 5-point Likert scale, ranging from "strongly disagree" (1) to "strongly agree" (5). In order to modify ambiguous expressions, the wording of the scales, and the length of the instrument, a pretest was performed with 2 experts and 12 respondents familiar with mobile apps.

The data for this study were collected via an online survey questionnaire. This research targeted the users of mobile social and game applications in Taiwan. Participants were recruited via popular virtual communities of mobile apps, and participation was encouraged by offering a raffle. They spent 12 min to fill a questionnaire out averagely. After incomplete responses and duplicates were eliminated, 389 usable responses remained. Analysis of the sample shows that 56 % of the respondents were female, most respondents were between 18 and 25 years of age, and 73 % used Android smartphones. About 120 of the respondents had more than one smart device.

4 Results

4.1 Tests of the Measurement Model

To test the proposed research model, this study used SEM to examine the hypotheses. The estimation of the proposed casual models in SEM involves two components: the measurement and the structural models. The two components were assessed by AMOS 23.0 software package.

A confirmatory factor analysis, using AMOS, was conducted to test the proposed measurement model. Several fit indicators in Table 1 were evaluated to assess how well the model fitted the data. The results show that the model fit was good: ratio of chi-square statistics to the degree of freedom (df), the standardized root mean squared residual (SRMR), and root mean square error of approximation (RMSEA) are less than the recommended values while goodness-of-fit index (GFI), adjusted goodness-of-fit index (AGFI), comparative fit index (CFI), incremental fit index (IFI) are greater than

Table 1. Measures of the model fit

Goodness of fit measures	χ^2/df	GFI	AGFI	CFI	IFI	RESEA	SRMR
Recommended value	≤5.00[a]	≥0.85[b]	≥0.9[b]	≥0.9[b]	≥0.9[b]	≤0.08[c]	≤0.1[d]
CFA model	2.56	0.862	0.829	0.904	0.905	0.064	0.065
Structural model	2.37	0.858	0.827	0.903	0.904	0.059	0.065

Source: [a]Bentler (1989) [b]Bagozzi and Yi (1988) [c]Browne and Cudeck (1993) [d]Hoang et al. (2006)

the suggested threshold. According to the above test outcomes, it can be summarized that the hypothesized measurement model fits the data well.

4.2 Structural Model and Hypothesis Testing

AMOS 23.0 was used to access the structure model and hypotheses by examining the path coefficients and R^2 values. The fitness measures of the structure model also indicated a good level of fit (see Table 1). The path coefficients are standardized regression coefficients and are used to explain the direction of relationships among variables. R^2 values represent the proportion of variance in the endogenous variables and are shown as a representation of the explanatory power of the structure model. The results are showed in Fig. 2 with non-significant paths as dotted lines, the path coefficients next to each line between constructs.

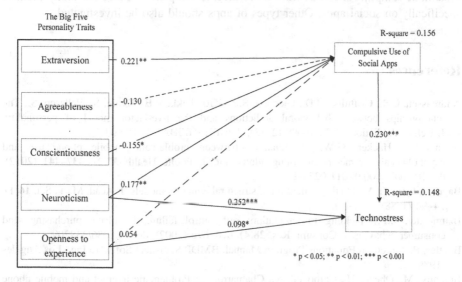

Fig. 2. Analysis results

With regard to the big five personality traits, only extroversion and neuroticism had significant positive effects on compulsive social application usage whereas only conscientiousness had negative impact on compulsive social application usage, supporting H1, H3, and H4 ($\beta = 0.2219$, p < 0.01; $\beta = 0.177$, p < 0.01; $\beta = -0.155$, p < 0.05), but not H2 and H6. In line with expectations, extroversion and neuroticism were found to have significant positive effects on compulsive social and game application usage ($\beta = 0.252$, p < 0.001; $\beta = 0.098$, p < 0.05), supporting H5 and H7. In addition, the results revealed that compulsive usage had positive direct effects on technostress ($\beta = 0.230$, p < 0.001), thereby supporting H8. Finally, the results show that 15.6, and 14.8 percent of the respective variance of compulsive social application usage and technostress can be explained by the research model.

5 Discussion

This study proposed eight hypotheses to understand the relationships among personality traits, technostress, and compulsive mobile application usage. According to the analysis results, six hypotheses were supported but two hypotheses were not supported. The similar result was also found in the past research. For example, Marshall et al. (2015) indicated that agreeableness did not influence Facebook users' behaviors of updating their profiles and messaging. In addition, social apps do not count for new services anymore and have become less attractive for those who rate high in openness.

This study is subject to certain limitations and results should be interpreted and accepted with caution. First, our survey was conducted using online questionnaires and employed nonrandom sampling. The online survey method was appropriate for collecting data from a sample which was free of geographical constraints and included only respondents with mobile app experience. Future studies could implement more systematic sampling methods from more diverse samples. Second, our study focused specifically on social apps. Other types of apps should also be investigated.

References

Andreassen, C.S., Griffiths, M.D., Gjertsen, S.R., Krossbakken, E., Kvam, S., Pallesen, S.: The relationships between behavioral addictions and the five-factor model of personality. J. Behav. Addictions 2(2), 90–99 (2013). doi:10.1556/JBA.2.2013.003

Augner, C., Hacker, G.W.: Associations between problematic mobile phone use and psychological parameters in young adults. Int. J. Public Health 57(2), 437–441 (2012). doi:10.1007/s00038-011-0234-z

Bagozzi, R.P., Yi, Y.: On the evaluation of structural equation models. J. Acad. Mark. Sci. 16(1), 74–94 (1988)

Baumeister, R.F.: Yielding to temptation: self-control failure, impulsive purchasing, and consumer behavior. J. Consum. Res. 28(4), 670–676 (2002). doi:10.1086/338209

Bentler, P.: Structural Equations Program Manual. BMDP Statistical Software Inc., Los Angeles (1989)

Beranuy, M., Oberst, U., Carbonell, X., Chamarro, A.: Problematic internet and mobile phone use and clinical symptoms in college students: the role of emotional intelligence. Comput. Hum. Behav. 25(5), 1182–1187 (2009). doi:10.1016/j.chb.2009.03.001

Bianchi, A., Phillips, J.G.: Psychological predictors of problem mobile phone use. CyberPsychol. Behav. 8(1), 39–51 (2005). doi:10.1089/cpb.2005.8.39

Browne, M., Cudeck, R.: Alternative ways of assessing model fit. In: Bollen, K.A., Long, J.S. (eds.) Testing Structural Equation Models, pp. 136–162. Sage, Newbury Park (1993)

Butt, S., Phillips, J.G.: Personality and self reported mobile phone use. Comput. Hum. Behav. 24(2), 346–360 (2008)

Chak, K., Leung, L.: Shyness and locus of control as predictors of internet addiction and internet use. CyberPsychol. Behav. 7(5), 559–570 (2004). doi:10.1089/cpb.2004.7.559

Correa, T., Hinsley, A.W., De Zuniga, H.G.: Who interacts on the web?: the intersection of users' personality and social media use. Comput. Hum. Behav. 26(2), 247–253 (2010)

Costa, P.T., McCrae, R.R.: Neo PI-R professional manual (1992a)

Costa, P.T., McCrae, R.R.: Normal personality assessment in clinical practice: the NEO personality inventory. Psychol. Assess. **4**(1), 5 (1992). doi:10.1037/1040-3590.4.1.5

Ehrenberg, A., Juckes, S., White, K.M., Walsh, S.P.: Personality and self-esteem as predictors of young people's technology use. CyberPsychol. Behav. **11**(6), 739–741 (2008)

Eisen, J.L., Mancebo, M.A., Pinto, A., Coles, M.E., Pagano, M.E., Stout, R., Rasmussen, S.A.: Impact of obsessive-compulsive disorder on quality of life. Compr. Psychiatry **47**(4), 270–275 (2006). doi:10.1016/j.comppsych.2005.11.006

Gosling, S.D., Augustine, A.A., Vazire, S., Holtzman, N., Gaddis, S.: Manifestations of personality in online social networks: self-reported facebook-related behaviors and observable profile information. Cyberpsychol. Behav. Soc. Networking **14**(9), 483–488 (2011). doi:10.1089/cyber.2010.0087

Ha, J.H., Chin, B., Park, D.-H., Ryu, S.-H., Yu, J.: Characteristics of excessive cellular phone use in Korean adolescents. CyberPsychol. Behav. **11**(6), 783–784 (2008). doi:10.1089/cpb.2008. 0096

Hauschildt, M., Jelinek, L., Randjbar, S., Hottenrott, B., Moritz, S.: Generic and illness-specific quality of life in obsessive-compulsive disorder. Behav. Cogn. Psychother. **38**(04), 417–436 (2010)

Hirschman, E.C.: The consciousness of addiction toward a general theory of compulsive consumption. J. Consum. Res. **19**(2), 155–179 (1992)

Hoang, D.T., Igel, B., Laosirihongthong, T.: The impact of total quality management on innovation: findings from a developing country. Int. J. Qual. Reliab. Manage. **23**(9), 1092–1117 (2006)

Hung, W.-H., Chen, K., Lin, C.-P.: Does the proactive personality mitigate the adverse effect of technostress on productivity in the mobile environment? Telematics Inform. **32**(1), 143–157 (2015). doi:10.1016/j.tele.2014.06.002

İskender, M., Akin, A.: Social self-efficacy, academic locus of control, and internet addiction. Comput. Educ. **54**(4), 1101–1106 (2010). doi:10.1016/j.compedu.2009.10.014

Jenaro, C., Flores, N., Gómez-Vela, M., González-Gil, F., Caballo, C.: Problematic internet and cell-phone use: psychological, behavioral, and health correlates. Addict. Res. Theory **15**(3), 309–320 (2007). doi:10.1080/16066350701350247

John, O.P., Donahue, E.M., Kentle, R.L.: The Big Five Inventory—Versions 4a and 54. University of California, Institute of Personality and Social Research, Berkeley (1991)

Lee, Y.-K., Chang, C.-T., Lin, Y., Cheng, Z.-H.: The dark side of smartphone usage: psychological traits, compulsive behavior and technostress. Comput. Hum. Behav. **31**, 373–383 (2014). doi:10.1016/j.chb.2013.10.047

Marshall, T.C., Lefringhausen, K., Ferenczi, N.: The big five, self-esteem, and narcissism as predictors of the topics people write about in facebook status updates. Personality Individ. Differ. **85**, 35–40 (2015)

Matusik, S.F., Mickel, A.E.: Embracing or embattled by converged mobile devices? Users' experiences with a contemporary connectivity technology. Hum. Relat. **64**(8), 1001–1030 (2011). doi:10.1177/0018726711405552

Mowen, J.C.: The 3M Model of Motivation and Personality: Theory and Empirical Applications to Consumer Behavior. Springer Science & Business Media, New York (2000)

Oulasvirta, A., Rattenbury, T., Ma, L., Raita, E.: Habits make smartphone use more pervasive. Pers. Ubiquit. Comput. **16**(1), 105–114 (2012). doi:10.1007/s00779-011-0412-2

Phillips, J.G., Butt, S., Blaszczynski, A.: Personality and self-reported use of mobile phones for games. CyberPsychol. Behav. **9**(6), 753–758 (2006). doi:10.1089/cpb.2006.9.753

Reid, D.J., Reid, F.J.: Text or talk? Social anxiety, loneliness, and divergent preferences for cell phone use. CyberPsychol. Behav. **10**(3), 424–435 (2007). doi:10.1089/cpb.2006.9936

Roberts, J.A., Pullig, C., Manolis, C.: I need my smartphone: a hierarchical model of personality and cell-phone addiction. Pers. Individ. Differ. **79**, 13–19 (2015). doi:10.1016/j.paid.2015.01.049

Roccas, S., Sagiv, L., Schwartz, S.H., Knafo, A.: The big five personality factors and personal values. Pers. Soc. Psychol. Bull. **28**(6), 789–801 (2002). doi:10.1177/0146167202289008

Ross, C., Orr, E.S., Sisic, M., Arseneault, J.M., Simmering, M.G., Orr, R.R.: Personality and motivations associated with Facebook use. Comput. Hum. Behav. **25**(2), 578–586 (2009). doi:10.1016/j.chb.2008.12.024

Ryan, T., Xenos, S.: Who uses facebook? An investigation into the relationship between the big five, shyness, narcissism, loneliness, and facebook usage. Comput. Hum. Behav. **27**(5), 1658–1664 (2011). doi:10.1016/j.chb.2011.02.004

Takao, M., Takahashi, S., Kitamura, M.: Addictive personality and problematic mobile phone use. CyberPsychol. Behav. **12**(5), 501–507 (2009). doi:10.1089/cpb.2009.0022

Tarafdar, M., Tu, Q., Ragu-Nathan, B.S., Ragu-Nathan, T.S.: The impact of technostress on role stress and productivity. J. Manage. Inform. Syst. **24**(1), 301–328 (2007). doi:10.2753/MIS0742-1222240109

Tuten, T.L., Bosnjak, M.: Understanding differences in web usage: the role of need for cognition and the five factor model of personality. Soc. Behav. Pers. Int. J. **29**(4), 391–398 (2001)

Wang, J.-L., Jackson, L.A., Zhang, D.-J., Su, Z.-Q.: The relationships among the big five personality factors, self-esteem, narcissism, and sensation-seeking to Chinese University students' uses of social networking sites (SNSs). Comput. Hum. Behav. **28**(6), 2313–2319 (2012). doi:10.1016/j.chb.2012.07.001

Impact of Website Complexity and Task Complexity on Older Adult's Cognitive Workload on Mobile Devices

Jincheng Huang[✉] and Jia Zhou

Department of Industrial Engineering,
Chongqing University, Chongqing 40044, China
cquhcijc@cqu.edu.cn, zhoujia07@gmail.com

Abstract. This study focused on older adults' cognitive workload of mobile devices. An experiment was conducted to investigate the influence of website complexity and task complexity on users' visual search behavior. 15 older adults needed to perform a simple shopping task and a complex shopping task on different mobile websites in this experiment. Three findings were derived. First, compared with simple tasks, participants spent more time on complex tasks and experienced heavier mental workload; Second, the color of mobile websites did affect participants' workload on the websites with fewer links whereas it did not affect participants' workload on the websites with more links, and 85 % of the participants preferred the mobile websites with color; Third, as the number of links on the mobile websites increased, participants spent more time in finding the target and experienced heavier mental workload.

Keywords: Older adults · Website complexity · Task complexity · Mobile devices

1 Introduction

Mobile devices were promising tools to provide many opportunities to meet the need of older adults in an aging society [1]. Older adults would like to use mobile technology (e.g. E-readers and tablets) when they found it useful, as they wanted to keep in touch with family members [2]. However, older adults had some disadvantages in effectively utilizing those technical products because of their cognitive decline. For instance, older adults experienced age-related decreases in the speed of information processing [3], and they were less able to resolve details and were less sensitive to critical environmental characteristics such as color and luminance [4]. Therefore, considering the growing number of older technical product users [5], it was instructive to take older adults' cognitive decline into account in the website design process.

Website complexity was one of the common factors that designers needed to consider in the website design process. Besides, mobile devices were expected to perform different tasks in a more complicated environment than personal computer. Therefore, task complexity was another factor which needed to be considered in the website design process. Previous studies mostly aimed at the influence of task type and

J. Zhou and G. Salvendy (Eds.): ITAP 2016, Part I, LNCS 9754, pp. 329–338, 2016.
DOI: 10.1007/978-3-319-39943-0_32

task complexity [6, 7] on users' visual search behavior of websites on the personal computer, however, there were limited studies investigating how task complexity influenced older adults' visual search behavior on mobile devices. In order to tailor website complexity and task complexity to older adults' ability for the mobile surfing environment, an experiment was conducted. Results of this study presented suggestions to improve the design for older adults' visual behavior on mobile devices websites for designers.

2   Literature Review

Previous studies had found that website complexity did affect users' attitudes and visual search behavior [8]. However, the relationship between website complexity and user experience was still unclear. There were researchers believed that websites with lower complexity were more effective [9, 10], whereas others thought that websites with high complexity increased the richness of the information and thereby strengthened the requirement and satisfaction of users [11, 12].

The website complexity was somehow related to the visual complexity and the amount of information. Previous study had found that visual complexity of websites influenced users' cognition and emotion in different ways (e.g. facial expression, task performance, and memory) [13]. Sicilia and Ruiz (2010) had found that participants' information processing followed a pattern "inverted U-shape", where workload first increased and then decreased as the amount of information increased [14].

Task complexity was related to the "increase in information load, information diversity, or rate of information change" [15]. Considering the task complexity from the perspective of devices, compared with watches, PDAs (personal digital assistant) could represent the situation with a high level of task complexity, because the PDA had 17 experiential features (e.g. address book, notepad, and mail) whereas watches only had six experiential features [16].

Age-related perceptual changes in vision such as visual acuity, color vision, and useful field of view were happened in older adults [4]. Previous studies had found that older adults' ability to discriminate and perceive shorter wavelength light (e.g. blues and greens) decreased [17]. Fisk et al. (2009) had found that perceptual speed of older adults decreased more than younger adults as task complexity increased. And they recommended designer to avoid information overload for older learners according to their past experience of developing computer training programs for older adults [18].

3   Methodology

An experiment was conducted to investigate the influence of website complexity and task complexity on users' visual search behavior. Participants' performance was observed, and the self-report of cognitive workload and System Usability Scale (SUS) were collected.

3.1   Participants

A total of 15 older adults from Yuzui Citizen School in Jiangbei District of Chongqing, China were recruited as participants. Older adults who were literate and aged above 60 were eligible for this study. The age of the participants ranged from 60 to 74 years old (Mean = 65.3, SD = 5.31). In total, there were eight male participants and seven female participants.

3.2   Dependent Variables

The dependent variables of the experiment were task completion time, scores of SUS, and scores of NASA Task Load Index (NASA-TLX) [19]. Specifically, the task completion time was analyzed through video playback, which was recorded through the application - *Mirroring360* (version 1.5.1.4). The SUS questionnaire was used to measure the satisfaction of the participants and usability of websites. The NASA-TLX was used to measure participants' cognitive workload. Figure 1 showed that a participant was doing a simple shopping task on the mobile website with low complexity and the synchronous application was recording participant's operation on the mobile devices.

Fig. 1. A participant was doing a simple task on the low-complexity website

3.3   Independent Variables

The independent variables of the experiment were website complexity and task complexity. There were three factors in this experiment. Visual complexity (with or without color) and the number of links (fewer or more links) were two factors to measure website complexity. Simple tasks (find and match without decision making) and complex tasks (find and compare with decision making) were used to measure task complexity.

The levels of website complexity were mainly varied by page length, the number of pictures and links, and the amount of animation of websites on the personal computer [20]. Considering the screen size of mobile devices, the experiment here mainly took the number of links (fewer or more links) and the visual complexity (with or without

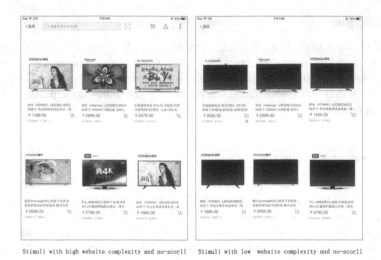

Stimuli with high website complexity and no-scorll   Stimuli with low website complexity and no-scorll

Fig. 2. Two mobile websites with high (left) and low (right) visual complexity

color) as the factors to distinguish different website complexity (low and high level). Specifically, there were six pictures and links on the low-complexity website, where the product overview page was one page and could not be scrolled. And there were 24 pictures and links on the high-complexity website, where the product overview page were four pages and could be scrolled. Visual complexity (with or without color) was the other factor to distinguish different levels of website complexity. Figure 2 showed the websites with high and low visual complexity.

Simple and complex tasks as Leuthold et al. (2011) did in their study [21] would be manipulated in this experiment through two scenarios, and detailed information would be presented in the next section.

3.4   Experimental Design and Task

The purposes of this study were tested through a laboratory experiment with a 2*2*2 within-subject design (i.e., 2 level of task complexity * 2 level of number of links * 2 level of visual complexity). During the experiment, participants were asked to buy a product on the mobile websites. Specifically, they needed to perform one simple task and one complex task, which represented two online shopping scenarios in real life.

In the situation of simple shopping task, participants were asked to buy a specific product on the mobile websites. This task represented a scenario in real life where users knew clearly what they needed to buy before shopping on the mobile websites. In the situation of complex tasks, participants were given a series of features of the products (e.g. price, product size, and brand) to shop online. Those limited features would ask them to make comparisons before making shopping decisions. There were multiple eligible products that matched the features on the mobile websites, which would force participants to make comparisons and considerations among different products and to find a product that matched the features.

4 Equipment and Procedures

The websites were running on an iPad with iOS 7.1 operating system. A notebook computer (MacBook Air) with OS X EI Capitan operating system and a synchronous recording application (*Mirroring360,* version 1.5.1.4) was used to record participants operation on the iPad in the experiment.

The experiment took each participant about 40 min. Firstly, each participant began the experiment by filling out a consent form and a general questionnaire about his/her demographic information and experience of using technology products and online shopping. Secondly, a short introduction of the experiment was conducted. Thirdly, participants started to perform the experimental tasks, and they were asked to conduct two tasks on different websites separately. Finally, a five-minute exploratory interview was conducted.

5 Results and Discussions

5.1 Descriptive Statistics

There were a total of 15 participants in this experiment (eight males, seven females). 80 % of the participants were junior high school education and 20 % were primary school education. Basically most of the participants had little online shopping experience. 20 % of the participants had two-year experience with smart phones. However, all of the participants had not experience with tablets. On average, participants spent 3.6 h (SD = 2.23) in watching TV per day.

5.2 Statistic Analysis of Performance and Cognitive Workload

Repeated ANOVA was used to analyze data. Table 1 showed the means and standard deviation of task completion time, scores of cognitive workload, and scores of SUS when participants performed different tasks on mobile websites with different levels of website complexity.

Visual complexity (with or without color) and the number of links (fewer or more links) were chosen as the factors to distinguish different levels of website complexity. Results of repeated ANOVA for testing the effects of three factors (task complexity, visual complexity, and the number of links) on task completion time, scores of cognitive workload, and scores of SUS were shown in Table 2. And the paired t-test was conducted for the purpose of fully understanding the interaction effects of three factors.

As to the task completion time, Fig. 3 showed the estimated marginal means of task completion time in different treatments. Compared with simple tasks, participants spent more time on complex tasks. As the number of links on the mobile websites increased, participants spent more time in finding the target. Specifically, under the simple task, the task completion time increased while the number of links increased and visual complexity decreased. Under the complex task, the task completion time increased

Table 1. Descriptive statistics of dependent variables

Dependent variables	Task complexity	Website complexity			
		Mean (standard deviation)			
		Fewer links with color	More links with color	Fewer links without color	More links without color
Task completion time (s)	Simple	35.60(16.715)	51.40(24.555)	36.07(10.559)	60.13(27.126)
	Complex	50.27(32.471)	89.67(41.684)	34.67(15.810)	77.67(29.635)
Scores of cognitive workload	Simple	2.54(0.875)	3.52(1.035)	3.12(1.114)	3.20(1.515)
	Complex	3.01(1.044)	4.95(2.117)	3.51(1.461)	3.90(1.170)
Scores of SUS	Simple	4.07(0.608)	3.75(0.651)	3.64(0.961)	3.12(1.114)
	Complex	3.67(0.866)	3.26(0.778)	3.83(0.737)	3.27(0.984)

Table 2. Results of repeated measures of ANOVA for independent variables

Independent variables	df	Dependent variables		
		Task completion time (s)	Scores of cognitive workload	Scores of SUS
Task complexity	1	F = 9.624 p = 0.008*	F = 17.581 p = 0.001*	F = 2.130 p = 0.167
Visual complexity	1	F = 1.678 p = 0.216	F = 0.107 p = 0.748	F = 1.748 p = 0.207
The number of links	1	F = 31.135 p < 0.001*	F = 10.603 p = 0.006*	F = 19.869 p = 0.001*
Task complexity * visual complexity	1	F = 3.723 p = 0.074	F = 1.150 p = 0.302	F = 9.074 p = 0.009*
Task complexity * the number of links	1	F = 4.392 p = 0.055	F = 5.975 p = 0.028*	F = 0.218 p = 0.648
Visual complexity * the number of links	1	F = 1.721 p = 0.211	F = 13.983 p = 0.002*	F = 0.616 p = 0.446
Task complexity * visual complexity * the number of links	1	F = 0.101 p = 0.756	F = 0.459 p = 0.509	F = 0.035 p = 0.854

Note: *Significant at 0.05 level.

while the number of links and visual complexity increased. Task completion time and the cognitive workload were kept in a similar tendency.

As to the cognitive workload, Fig. 4 showed the estimated marginal means of scores of cognitive workload in different treatments. The interaction effects of task complexity and the number of links for cognitive workload were found significant. Participants experienced heavier mental workload to complete complex task than the simple task. As the number of links on the websites increased, participants experienced heavier mental workload to complete the tasks. And the influence caused by the changes of these two factors was different.

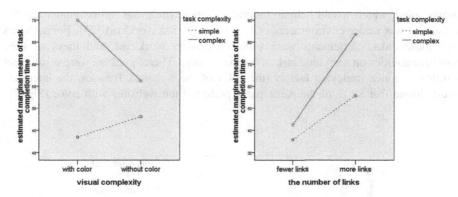

Fig. 3. The marginal means of task completion time

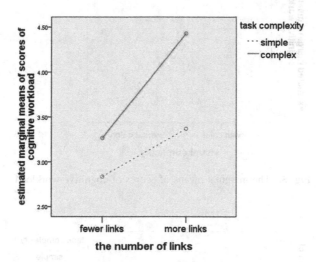

Fig. 4. The marginal means of scores of cognitive workload

The interaction effects of visual complexity and the number of links for cognitive workload were found significant. On the websites with fewer links, from the results of paired t-test, participants experienced heavier workload on the websites without color than the websites with color (t = 2.850, p = 0.008). On the websites with more links, there was no significant difference between websites with color and websites without color. This indicated that website color did not affect participants' visual behavior on the websites with more links.

Previous study had found that website color would affect users' satisfaction within different cultures on a personal computer website [22]. This finding was fitted to the situation where participants performed tasks on the websites with fewer links. However, it could not work on the websites with more links. According to the load theory of attention proposed by Lavie et al. [23], a cognitive selection mechanism existed in the human mind, which would help an individual ignore irrelevant information when the individual was under environments of heavier cognitive workload [24]. For websites with more links, participants were suffering heavier workload, and they put their cognitive abilities on searching task in the experiment. Therefore there were insufficient abilities to notice irrelevant factors (the color of the website). Besides, the interview results found that 85 % of the participants preferred the websites with color (Fig. 5).

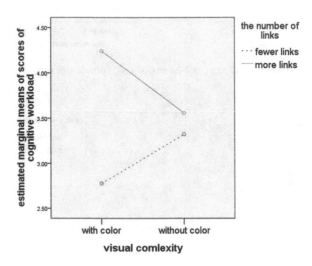

Fig. 5. The marginal means of scores of cognitive workload

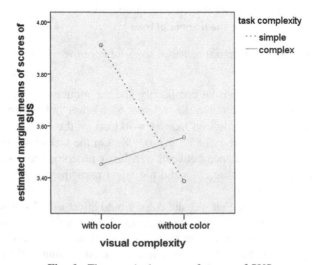

Fig. 6. The marginal means of scores of SUS

As to the scores of SUS, the interaction effects of task complexity and visual complexity for SUS were found significant. On the websites with color, compared with complex tasks, participants' scores of SUS were higher than simple tasks ($t = 2.861$, $p = 0.008$). As shown in Fig. 6, under the simple task, scores of SUS decreased while visual complexity decreased ($t = 3.107$, $p = 0.004$).

6 Conclusion

This study investigated older adults' cognitive workload of mobile devices. To provide good user experience of mobile devices for older adults, an experiment was conducted to investigate the influence of website complexity and task complexity on users' visual search behavior. Based on the results, three main findings were derived.

First, compared with simple tasks, participants spent more time on complex tasks. As the number of links on the mobile websites increased, participants spent more time in finding the target.

Second, participants experienced heavier mental workload to complete the complex task than the simple task. As the number of links on the websites increased, participants experienced heavier mental workload to complete the tasks. Besides, the influence caused by the changes of task complexity and website complexity was different.

Third, the color of mobile websites did affect participants' workload using the websites with fewer links (six links) whereas it did not influence participants' workload using the websites with more links (24 links). And the interview results also found that 85 % of the participants preferred the websites with color.

There were two limitations of this study. First, the sample size was small and the participants had low education level. It could not be considered as very representative for the whole group of older users. Second, websites in the prototypes were different from the real situation of mobile devices websites.

Acknowledgment. This work was supported with funding from a National Science Foundation China grant 71401018.

References

1. Plaza, I., Martín, L., Martin, S., et al.: Mobile applications in an aging society: status and trends. J. Syst. Softw. **84**(11), 1977–1988 (2011)
2. Bracken, C.C., Yang, H., Pettey, G.: "What I Love about Technology": older adults and mobile communication technologies. Stud. Media Commun. **3**(1), 127–133 (2015)
3. Josephson, S., Holmes, M.E.: Age differences in visual search for information on web pages. In: Proceedings of the 2004 symposium on Eye tracking research & applications, pp. 62–62 (2004)
4. Salvendy, G.: Handbook of Human Factors and Ergonomics. Wiley, Hoboken (2012)
5. Olson, K.E., O'brien, M.A., Rogers, W.A., et al.: Diffusion of technology: frequency of use for younger and older adults. Ageing Int. **36**(1), 123–145 (2011)

6. Wang, Q., Yang, S., Liu, M., et al.: An eye-tracking study of website complexity from cognitive load perspective. Decis. Support Syst. **62**, 1–10 (2014)
7. Şendurur, E., Yildirim, Z.: Students' web search strategies with different task types: an eye-tracking study. Int. J. Hum.-Comput. Interact. **31**(2), 101–111 (2015)
8. Nadkarni, S., Gupta, R.: A task-based model of perceived website complexity. MIS Quart. **31**(3), 501–524 (2007)
9. Agarwal, R., Venkatesh, V.: Assessing a firm's web presence: a heuristic evaluation procedure for the measurement of usability. Inform. Syst. Res. **13**(2), 168–186 (2002)
10. Venkatesh, V., Morris, M.G., Davis, G.B., et al.: User acceptance of information technology: toward a unified view. MIS Quarterly **27**(3), 425–478 (2003)
11. Deng, L.: Affect in web interfaces: a study of the impacts of web page visual complexity and order. Urbana **51**, 61801 (2010)
12. Palmer, J.W.: Web site usability, design, and performance metrics. Inform. Syst. Res. **13**(2), 151–167 (2002)
13. Tuch, A.N., Bargas-Avila, J.A., Opwis, K., et al.: Visual complexity of websites: Effects on users' experience, physiology, performance, and memory. Int. J. Hum Comput Stud. **67**(9), 703–715 (2009)
14. Sicilia, M., Ruiz, S.: The effects of the amount of information on cognitive responses in online purchasing tasks. Electron. Commer. Res. Appl. **9**(2), 183–191 (2010)
15. Wedel, M., Pieters, R.: A review of eye-tracking research in marketing. Rev. Mark. Res. **2008**(4), 123–147 (2008)
16. Jiang, Z., Benbasat, I.: The effects of presentation formats and task complexity on online consumers' product understanding. Mis Quart. **31**(3), 475–500 (2007)
17. Said, F.S., Weale, R.A.: The variation with age of the spectral transmissivity of the living human crystalline lens. Gerontology **3**(4), 213–231 (1959)
18. Fisk, A.D., Rogers, W.A., Charness, N., et al.: Designing for Older Adults: Principles and Creative Human Factors Approaches. CRC Press, Boca Raton (2009)
19. Hart, S.G., Staveland, L.E.: Development of NASA-TLX (Task Load Index): results of empirical and theoretical research. Adv. Psychol. **52**, 139–183 (1988)
20. Geissler, G.L., Zinkhan, G.M., Watson, R.T.: The influence of home page complexity on consumer attention, attitudes, and purchase intent. J. Advertising **35**(2), 69–80 (2006)
21. Leuthold, S., Schmutz, P., Bargas-Avila, J.A., et al.: Vertical versus dynamic menus on the world wide web: eye tracking study measuring the influence of menu design and task complexity on user performance and subjective preference. Comput. Hum. Behav. **27**(1), 459–472 (2011)
22. Cyr, D., Head, M., Larios, H.: Colour appeal in website design within and across cultures: a multi-method evaluation. Int. J. Hum Comput Stud. **68**(1), 1–21 (2010)
23. Lavie, N., Hirst, A., De Fockert, J.W., et al.: Load theory of selective attention and cognitive control. J. Exp. Psychol. Gen. **133**(3), 339 (2004)
24. Klemz, B.R., Gruca, T.S.: Dueling or the battle royale? the impact of task complexity on the evaluation of entry threat. Psychol. Mark. **20**(11), 999–1016 (2003)

Experiencing Computer Anxiety Later in Life: The Role of Stereotype Threat

Loredana Ivan and Ioana Schiau[(✉)]

Faculty of Communication, National University of Political Science and Public Administration,
Bucharest, Romania
{loredana.ivan,ioana.schiau}@comunicare.ro

Abstract. In the current paper we use semi-structured interviews ($N = 12$) to reveal instances which trigger age-based stereotype threat and subsequent computer anxiety for older individuals, and potential impact on their technological self-efficacy. The results show that situation-specific anxiety arises in situations when older people were faced with children or younger adults who presented higher ICT skills. We argue that when the situation is "powerful enough" to increase older people's awareness of the negative stereotypes associated to their group in relation to technology, this would increase computer anxiety and could have a negative influence on technology appropriation and performance.

Keywords: Stereotype threat · Computer anxiety · Older people · Age-based stereotype

1 Introduction

1.1 Computer Anxiety and Age Differences

The widespread use of information and communication technologies (ICT) seems to lead to the assumption that most individuals feel comfortable using them. Research on the human-computer interaction is currently focused on technology dependence, a phenomenon that occurs when individuals are deprived of their desired use of ICT devices [1]. However, there are individuals who use computers and other ICT devices reluctantly, and those who do not feel comfortable at the thought of using them. Computer anxiety is a negative emotional feeling or evaluation experienced when an individual encounters a real or estimated task which requires the use of computers or of other computer mediated technology [2]. This type of anxiety is often compared to test anxiety or math anxiety [3, 4]. Authors [5, 6] agree that such negative feelings impact performance or at least have negative effects on the individuals': competence with computers, ability to enjoy computer related tasks, self-evaluation of people's own ability to handle computer tasks, ability to focus when using new technologies or receiving training in using them (getting easily distracted), and ability to overcome the initial reluctance to try new devices.

Studies on feelings of anxiety towards computer and computer use go back to the early 1980s, when computers were mainly depicted as instruments to achieve higher

© Springer International Publishing Switzerland 2016
J. Zhou and G. Salvendy (Eds.): ITAP 2016, Part I, LNCS 9754, pp. 339–349, 2016.
DOI: 10.1007/978-3-319-39943-0_33

efficiency and productivity [7]. The feeling of fear, unease and tension towards computer use proved to be shared by large segments of population, both old and young and with varying degrees of familiarity and skill in using ICT. Traditionally, older people, those less trained in using technologies or less educated in general, are seen as more intimidated, hostile and worried about computer use and are perceived as more likely to experience anxiety to computers, according to Beckers and colleagues [8]. Still, there is inconsistent evidence that age is a predictor for computer anxiety [9]. In a previous study [10], we found a potential explanation for the inconsistencies in studies that approached the relation between age and computer anxiety. The direct effect of age on computer anxiety was rather low, whereas the mediated effect of age through socio-economic status and computer experience was significantly higher, proving that the two predictors – socio-economic status and experience – could play a more important role in explaining individual differences in computer anxiety. Moreover, studies conducted with students [2] suggest a paradoxical situation: "the current generation of undergraduate students exhibit more psychological discomfort with computers than individuals who represent the previous generation in terms of exposure to computerization" (p. 221). This probably happens due to high social pressure for new generations of students to be continuously up to date with the latest technologies.

There are several estimates on the percentage of people that experience strong feelings of anxiety towards computer, on different age groups [11, 12]. Still we lack longitudinal studies and cross-cultural data. Moreover, computer anxiety could be experienced by everyone, depending on the context and situations that might trigger such feelings, or due to social pressure surrounding technology adoption.

In the current paper we argue that, instead of focusing on age as a predictor of computer anxiety and analyzing how feelings of anxiety are experienced by different age groups, we could focus on specific instances that trigger computer anxiety. We discuss instances which create feelings of discomfort, social embarrassment or the fear of looking inept, that negatively impact older people's performance and willingness to try to use ICT.

1.2 Stereotype Threat and Computer Anxiety

The term "stereotype threat" was first used by Steele and Aronson [13] to describe a situation in which one feels at risk of confirming a negative stereotype about one's own social group. Such instances appear when one views oneself in terms of salient group membership (e.g. "I am old and old people are not expected to be good at technology use, so using this application might be really difficult"). Such feelings and evaluations can undermine people's performance, due to concerns about the possibility of confirming a negative stereotype. The stereotype threat was originally studied by Steele and Aronson [13] on African American students, by analyzing their performance on a standardized cognitive test, as compared to Caucasian students, when the situation was "powerful enough" [14] to trigger awareness of racial stereotypes. Subsequent studies conducted on different social groups proved that any individual is vulnerable to stereotypes threat in situations that increase the salience of group identity, as the group is presented in negative terms, relevant to the tasks [15]. Several studies found gender differences in the performance of men and women, in situations where gender had been highlighted before the task completion. This influenced the performance of women on math tests [16, 17], and resulted in gender differences in social competence tasks [18], with men scoring lower than women. Similarly, students with a lower socio-economic status performed worse on cognitive tasks than children with a higher socio-economic status, when background differences were highlighted [19, 20]. And, similarly to the first quoted study, Caucasian men performed worse than Asian men on mathematics tasks, when racial aspects were triggered [21].

Stereotype threat is experienced as a state of psychological discomfort arising "when individuals are confronted with an evaluative situation, in which one's group is associated with a negative stereotype" [22]. Therefore, "stereotype threat" impacts performance by raising individual anxiety level, when one becomes aware of the negative stereotypes [23].

We depart from an earlier observation made by Steele [24] concerning situational anxiety as a potential moderator of stereotype threat effect. It was suggested that stereotype threat effects could be noticed particularly in social anxiety situations [25]. More recently, experimental manipulations proved that, in stereotype threat situations, individuals experienced higher situational-specific anxiety, confirming the potential moderator role of situational anxiety in the way stereotype thereat impacts performance. This was measured by psycho-physiological parameters: skin conductance, skin temperature, blood pressure – resulting, for example, in differences in cognitive efficiency. Overall, researchers agree that anxiety accompanies stereotype threat [26]. People facing stereotype threat reported higher levels of anxiety in relevant tasks, self-doubt and lower self-efficacy, negative expectations and lower motivations in pursuing the tasks.

In the current paper, we argue that stereotype threat in computer related tasks could raise computer anxiety and undermine individual performance or cause reluctance to technology. Moreover, we argue that this assumption is valid for the situation is which an individual is aware of belonging to a group that is negatively evaluated in terms of technology use, such as women or old people.

There are several studies investigating stereotype threat and computer performance on women [27], proving that the stereotype effect impacts women's' attribution of failure and success in computer related tasks; causing a gender gap in science, technology, engineering and mathematics (STEM) through self-perception of technology efficacy, technology anxiety and expectations about future performance in STEM education. Still, we lack studies to investigate the role of stereotype threat in acquiring ICT skills for older adults. Only one study the authors know of approached the topic of age-based stereotype threat and its effect on older adults' performance in acquiring computer skills [28].

Nevertheless, the age-based groups have not been neglected in studies that investigate stereotype threat effect –see [29] for a review. Studies have focused on the way older adults underperformed on memory, cognitive and physical tasks, as result from age-based stereotype threat [30–32]. In fact, the meta-analysis of Lamont and colleagues [29] shows that age-based stereotype threat investigations have been conducted in four stereotyped performance domains: memory, cognitive, physical, and driving. The article [29] also included the study of Fritzsche et al. [28] to argue for a potential fifth domain for age-based stereotype threat investigation: new skills acquisition. In this particular study, participants were trained to learn to use a new computer-based library system, being randomly assigned in a stereotype threat versus pacing condition, and then tested on the skills they acquired. Contrary to expectations, stereotype-threat was found to improve participants' performance both during training sessions and at the final test. Fritzsche and collaborators [28] argued that, contrary to similar studies in which performance testing occurred immediately following the stereotype threat conditions, in their study, training intervention happened in-between the treatment condition and performance testing. Nonetheless, here we argue that computer anxiety could be used to explain contradictory findings, as feeling of anxiety could moderate the effect of stereotype threat on performance. There are studies showing that a moderate level of computer anxiety, for example, has a positive impact on performance [33]. Beckers [34] discuss "the threshold effect", indicating that computer anxiety would hinder perform-ance when it is severe and depending of some contextual factors – such as, for example, the ambiguity of the computer tasks, or the level of individuals' experience with that particular task.

2   The Present Study

The current study departs from the meta-analysis conducted by Lamont et al. [29] on age-based stereotype threat. We look for arguments that, in the case of studies regarding older adults and computer use, computer anxiety could be investigated as a moderator factor of stereotype threat on performance. In other words, we predict that stereotype threat situations would influence people performance in technology use to the extent to which such situations trigger high levels of computer anxiety. As previous studies have used experimental manipulations of age-based stereotypes, in the current study we use semi-structured interviews to explore older people's way of depicting "comfortable" and "uncomfortable" situations of technology use in everyday activities. We looked for specific cues regarding computer anxiety: such as the feelings of helplessness, unease, social embarrassment and tension, as well as for the way people overcome such feelings and describe their self-efficacy in handling computer tasks in everyday routine. The present study aims to describe instances which trigger age-based stereotype threat and subsequent computer anxiety for older individuals, and the potential impact on their technological self-efficacy.

Three characteristics are found by Lamont et al. [29] in their study to moderate age-based stereotype threat: (1) age, as for the young-old (60 to 65) the stereotypes seem to be less salient compared to old-older adults (65–70). Moreover, the age-based stereotype threat seems to be diminished on the 70 to 80 group; (2) gender – as ageing stereotypes are more self-relevant for women; (3) cultural and social-economic background, as the experience of being old or the self-relevance of ageing stereotype is different from a socio-cultural community to another. As a result, we approach these three criteria in our sample selection.

2.1 Method

We used semi-structured interviews to collect data and both authors conducted interviews with participants from two urban areas in Romania (Bucharest and Braşov). Semi-structured interviews were voice-recorded and then transcribed for further analysis. The interviewers took notes of participants' social economic status, age, gender, the number of devices they use and experience in using these devices. For the current paper we focus on participants' descriptions of uncomfortable situations when using ICT in daily life activities and we looked for specific signs of situation-based anxiety.

2.2 Participants

Participants were selected based on age, gender, and level of education. We conducted 12 interviews with people over 60 years of age in Bucharest (the largest city in Romania) and in Braşov (a medium-sized town in the west part of the country). The study is exploratory and focuses on urban areas, as the level of people over 60 having access to internet in rural areas is rather small (less than 2 %). Thus, we conducted 2 interviews per each category built from the combination of the three selection axes: gender (women, and men); age (60 to 65, and 66 and above) and education (medium – up to 8 classes and more, and high education-college graduation). Fieldwork was conducted in Romanian between October and December 2015.

2.3 Results

2.3.1 Instances Which Trigger Age-Based Stereotype

Participants showed awareness of age-related stereotypes regarding ICT use. Being faced with children or younger adults who present higher ICT skills is an instance that triggered awareness of belonging to the group of older adults that these stereotypes address:

"My friend told me one of her nieces said - she had asked something and the niece said: <<oh, why do you need to know that, Auntie, at your age!>> (…) Yes, I feel the younger generation has this attitude. This is my sensation and this is what I feel." (Woman, higher education, 60, Braşov)[1]

"Older people were not used to these instruments and especially not now, when the transition is so sudden, and so they are afraid. For the young, for young people, even from second grade they already know. My neighbor, when he started kindergarten, he had a tablet and was tapping on it and saying <<here is the teddy bear>>. He was half a meter tall". (Male, higher education, 68, Braşov)

Some of the participants repeated the stereotype, stressing the fact that younger adults are the ones who possess knowledge about ICT and are the ones in charge of disseminating it to older adults:

---

[1] Own translation.

"Children are the ones who stimulate us with the mobile phones, how else would an old person know how to use them? Young people have made old people smart too." (Woman, lower education, 71, Bucharest)

This participant seemed aware of the age-related ICT-use stereotype, already expecting that younger adults will be impatient regarding her needs to use technology:

"When I bought my speakers, I went to the shop one Friday evening, it was raining, and I told a young man who worked there, I said <<Listen, dear, are you patient? I want to buy something, but will you be patient with me?>>" (Woman, higher education, 60, Braşov)

When asked what they believe others think about individuals in their age group using ICT, answers revealed the participants' awareness of the group stereotype threat:

"I think young people laugh about it: <<look at that old hag with a phone, or with such-and-such device>>". (Woman, higher education, 60, Braşov)

"I think that, at a certain age, I mean when people are young, they do not understand why older people also want to do things, to use this and that... they think <<why does she need this?>>". (Woman, higher education, 60, Braşov)

"Sometimes they say <<would you look at her, look what a phone she has, look at her using it, look what she's learned>>. Things like that. When they see an older person they say <<look what she's bought, looks like she had money>>" (Woman, medium education, 76, Bucharest). This participant mentions the effect of socio-economic status, which, correlated with older age, can act as a trigger of stereotype threat. This shows older adults in Romania are aware they are not expected to be able to afford new technologies.

"Some consider that we do not know enough." (Woman, higher education, 60, Braşov)

Moreover, it could be argued that several participants had internalized these stereotypes and were now, in turn, replicating them in their answers when discussing themselves or, generally, people in their age group. For instance, a participant described being in the hospital and wanting to use a tablet, but being unable to:

"I couldn't ask them for help with my tablet, they were old and sick people, and I don't think they would have handled such things. (...) They wouldn't know how to use them, because they've not had the opportunity to use them, they have no children, live alone." (Woman, medium education, 76, Bucharest).

The participant reinforces the stereotype that younger adults are the ones who possess the knowledge about ICT use and that it is only through their dissemination of information that older adults could acquire these new skills:

"Older people are afraid to even hold such devices, because they don't know how to work them. But they can slowly ease up, I've seen old people learn to use a computer when they are 55–60, well, the ones who aren't afraid to." (Male, higher education, 68, Braşov)

"For older people it is a handicap, for those who did not need to learn... you know younger people learn faster, for old people it is a handicap." (Woman, higher education, 70, Braşov)

"I mean it's a little difficult, well, one's mind is not used to this new system, I mean, until you try it a little and then it grips you and you like it." (Woman, higher education, 70, Braşov)

"Those who have managed to use them feel proud, but the others yearn to learn and the abilities of their mind do not help them anymore, the mind is lazier at a certain age, and there is nobody to help them, but I think on some level everyone would want it." (Woman, higher education, 70, Braşov, medium sized town)

"One time, P. (son-in-law) even said I was an example: <<Look, C. uses Facebook, and my mother does not; C. uses so-and-so, my mother does not>>, so I thought I am keeping up pretty well, better than other people my age." (Woman, higher education, 60, Braşov) – Even though the participant seems pleased with her own level of ICT skills, she also shows to be aware of the stereotype that other people in her own age group do not perform as well.

We also found that several of the individuals we interviewed brought up not only age-related stereotypes, but also gender stereotypes regarding ICT use. This could be relevant, as Romania is a society with rather traditional gender roles, where not only could there be an aged-based stereotype regarding use of ICT, but also a gender one, as it is assumed that men are more likely to be in charge of technology-related tasks in the family.

"Usually men our age know more, this is what I have seen and that is the way it was in my family too, if there was someone else to concentrate on it, then I let them do it." (Woman, higher education, 60, Braşov)

"I was not used to it, you know, there was always my husband to handle these things and I did not overload my memory with these things if someone else could do it." (Woman, higher education, 60, Braşov)

Talking about her mobile phone: "The first few times I used it it was easy because my husband knew how to and he taught me, otherwise, if it were up to me to do it myself… he took care of all my settings and put in all my contacts." (Woman, higher education, 70, Braşov)

"My wife is afraid to use the TV receiver (i.e. a device that permits the reception of digital television), <<why work on the television and the receiver too>>? If her television is broken, I'm the one who fixes it, and so on. But that's that." (Man, higher education, 68, Braşov)

2.3.2 Computer Anxiety Cues

Participants described numerous situational anxiety cues in daily situations when they were aware of the age-based negative stereotypes.

"My children were discussing for a long time about buying me a tablet and I told them they were crazy. They joked about the fact that I will not be able to use it. And indeed I receive it for Christmas. I felt lost and I started to use it only when they were gone." (Woman, medium education, 60, Bucharest)

"I try to keep up but it is very hard, it is very difficult. And when you get a new phone or so, you feel like you need a training course. It's difficult, it's difficult." (Woman, higher education, 60, Braşov)

Therefore, new skills acquisition is quoted as a trigger of stereotype threat, consistent with the observations of Lamont and collaborators [29].

"The first one was the computer and I was so nervous. Now I have a laptop, but the first one was a computer, it also had a keyboard and I struggled to type. It was harder in the begining, it was emotional, a psychological barrier." (Woman, higher education, 60, Braşov)

One individual describes being in the hospital and having asked her granddaughter for the tablet. Being unable to use it triggered feelings of frustration: "I said give it to me, I could look over some games, because I was bored (…) and it wasn't working, it didn't work, it either wasn't working well, or it worked for a bit and then stopped. I said take it away, I don't want it anymore! It felt bad, because I was sorry, it would have taken up my time, helped me forget I was in hospital". (Woman, medium education, 76, Bucharest)

The feelings of anxiety are more situational specific – as they tend to arise during first experiences with the device, usually in the presence of others of by comparison with others.

"Oh, very difficult. I am not very skilled with it [mobile phone] now either, but I can make calls and talk, that I'm able to do, to call someone. Otherwise, to look around it, well, I have grandchildren who can use the phone as though it were… I don't know what; I have grandchildren who save me, because I cannot, I can't figure it out, how to work it, what if I break something? Not that I don't want to, if I broke one I could learn how to use it, to use it and look around it, but I don't have the heart to, what if I break it? I am afraid, my grandchildren say <<you won't break it, grandmother, press this key, and this one>> but it's difficult". (Woman, lower education, 71, Bucharest)

Discussing the use of computers by general practitioners, one participant discussed the anxiety her older adult doctor experienced, and the way her younger doctor views those who do not have ICT skills: "I noticed this with doctors too, our doctor was about ten years younger than me, not young-young, but he was not old and the poor man, it was torture for him at first, he said <<it's driving me mad, I put in all my data and I made a mistake and it was an ordeal>>. Our current doctor, he has no problem with it, it's natural to him, it was natural from the beginning and he said <<whoever can't manage can just stay home>>". (Women, higher education, 70, Braşov). This once more seems to reinforce the stereotype that older adults have a harder time using ICT and that younger adults believe those who are unable to use them efficiently might as well give up.

The way anxiety impacts performance and willingness to adopt ICT is described by most of the interviewers. The cues of anxiety are associated with reluctance, rejection or compliance:

"I don't need anything too sophisticated, to be honest, I get confused trying to use it. I know that if you get used to it, it is not that difficult. It was easier with the laptop because I had used a computer at work, but I still have problems now, if I get stuck I need someone to come and help me (…) I can't say I feel fully in control now either, but I manage with the things I need, I only use it to write." (Woman, higher education, 70, Braşov)

"Last year I accidentally erased all the data on my old phone, when I got this new one, then I was very upset, and I had to learn how to save my files, but I still don't know how to and I keep postponing, I should at least save them online, I lost all the pictures from my old house, I was sorry about the pictures, of spring, summer, colors, leaves, so all the memories gone". (Woman, higher education, 60, Braşov)

3 Discussion and Conclusion

In the current study we investigated the role of stereotype threat in triggering computer anxiety for older individuals. By means of semi-structured interviews with people aged 60 and above, we revealed instances which create feelings of discomfort, social embarrassment, when individuals were aware of negative stereotypes about their age group in relation to the use of ICT. We start from the assumption that fear of negative evaluation can undermine people's performance, due to concerns about the possibility of confirming a negative stereotype. We looked for cues of such feelings and instances that could trigger computer anxiety in the way older people describe the ICT use in daily routine.

The results show situation-specific anxiety arises when older people faced children or younger adults who possess higher ICT skills. Older people depicted such instances as triggering awareness of being a member of the group with a negative stereotype. Such instances also seem to create reluctance and alienation from technology. As a result, they feel less willing to have initiative in using particular devices, considering it is the role of younger people to disseminate the information. Older people perceived themselves more as "objects" then "subjects" of the information regarding technology and they depicted the younger people as impatient and sarcastic in such situations. As a result, more feelings of awkwardness, social embarrassment and ineptitude arise triggering withdrawal and decreased interest in new communication technology.

The results of the interviews indicate that contextual factors should also be considered, whenever we have contradictory findings of the relation between computer anxiety and performance in older individuals. We argue that when the situation is "powerful enough" to increase older people's awareness of the negative stereotypes associated to their group in relation to technology, this would increase computer anxiety and could have a negative influence of technology appropriation and performance. We noticed that during our data collection, the interviews conducted by the second author of the paper (younger author) managed to collect more information on cues of anxiety towards ICT than the second author, possibly due to the same effect of stereotype thereat. Although a limit of the current research procedure, this could also be considered another indicator that the stereotype threat phenomenon can be activated though subtle contextual cues that sometimes we are not aware of.

Acknowledgement. This project was supported by UEFISCDI, project grant PN-II-RU-TE-2014-4-0429, AGETECH: Understanding Technology Later in Life, 2014–2017.

References

1. Rosen, L.D., Whaling, K., Carrier, L.M., Cheever, N.A., Rokkum, J.: The media and technology usage and attitudes scale: an empirical investigation. Comput. Hum. Behav. **29**, 2501–2511 (2013)
2. Bozionelos, N.: Socio-economic background and computer use: the role of computer anxiety and computer experience in their relationship. Int. J. Hum. Comput. Stud. **61**(5), 725–746 (2004)
3. Fletcher, W.F., Deeds, J.P.: Computer anxiety and other factors preventing computer use among United States Secondary Agricultural Educators. J. Agric. Educ. **35**(2), 16–21 (1994)
4. Gibson, P.A., Stringer, K., Cotten, S.R., Simoni, Z., O'neal, L.J., Howell-Moroney, M.: Changing teachers, changing students? the impact of a teacher-focused intervention on students' computer usage, attitudes, and anxiety. Comput. Educ. **71**, 165–174 (2014)
5. Maurer, M.M.: Computer anxiety correlates and what they tell us: a literature review. Comput. Hum. Behav. **10**(3), 369–376 (1994)
6. Parayitam, S., Desai, K.J., Desai, M.S., Eason, M.K.: Computer attitude as a moderator in the relationship between computer anxiety, satisfaction, and stress. Comput. Hum. Behav. **26**(3), 345–352 (2010)
7. Powell, A.L.: Computer anxiety: Comparison of research from the 1990s and 2000s. Comput. Hum. Behav. **29**, 2337–2381 (2013)
8. Beckers, J.J., Schmidt, H.G., Wicherts, J.: Computer anxiety in daily life: Old history? In: Loos, E.F., Mante-Meijer, E.A., Haddon, L. (eds.) The Social Dynamics of Information and Communication Technology, pp. 13–23. Ashgate, Aldershot (2008)
9. Fuller, R.M., Vician, C., Brown, S.A.: E-learning and individual characteristics: the role of computer anxiety and communication apprehension. J. Comput. Inform. Syst. **46**, 103–115 (2006)
10. Fernández-Ardèvol, M., Ivan, L.: Why age is not that important? An ageing perspective on computer anxiety. In: Zhou, J., Salvendy, G. (eds.) ITAP 2015. LNCS, vol. 9193, pp. 189–200. Springer, Heidelberg (2015)
11. King, J., Bond, T., Blandford, S.: An investigation of computer anxiety by gender and grade. Comput. Hum. Behav. **18**, 69–84 (2002)
12. Dutton, W., Helsper, E.J., Gerber, M.M.: The Internet in Britain. Oxford Internet Institute, University of Oxford, Oxford (2009)
13. Steele, C.M., Aronson, J.: Stereotype threat and the intellectual test performance of African Americans. J. Pers. Soc. Psychol. **69**(5), 797–811 (1995)
14. Zimbardo, P.G.: Revisiting the stanford prison experiment: a lesson in the power of situation. Chronicle High. Educ. **53**(30), B6–B7 (2007)
15. Schmader, T., Johns, M., Forbes, C.: An integrated process model of stereotype threat effects on performance. Psychol. Rev. **115**(2), 336–356 (2008)
16. Huguet, P., Régner, I.: Stereotype threat among schoolgirls in quasi-ordinary classroom circumstances. J. Educ. Psychol. **99**, 545–560 (2007)
17. Marx, D.M., Roman, J.S.: Female role models: protecting women's math test performance. Pers. Soc. Psychol. Bull. **28**, 1183–1193 (2002)
18. Koenig, A.M., Eagly, A.H.: Stereotype threat in men on a test of social sensitivity. Sex Roles **52**(7–8), 489–496 (2005)
19. Spencer, B., Castano, E.: Social class is dead. Long live social class! Stereotype threat among low socioeconomic status individuals. Soc. Justice Res. **20**(4), 418–432 (2007)

20. Croizet, J.C., Claire, T.: Extending the concept of stereotype threat to social class: the intellectual underperformance of students from low socioeconomic backgrounds. Pers. Soc. Psychol. Bull. **24**(6), 588–594 (1998)
21. Aronson, J., Lustina, M.J., Good, C., Keough, K., Steele, C.M., Brown, J.: When white men can't do math: necessary and sufficient factors in stereotype threat. J. Exp. Soc. Psychol. **35**(1), 29–46 (1999)
22. Appel, M.: Kronberger, N: Stereotypes and the achievement gap: stereotype threat prior to test taking. Educ. Psychol. Rev. **24**(4), 609–635 (2012)
23. Osborne, J.W.: Gender, stereotype threat and anxiety: psychophysiological and cognitive evidence. J. Res. Educ. Psychol. **8**, 109–138 (2006)
24. Steele, C.M.: A threat in the air: how stereotypes shape intellectual identity and performance. Am. Psychol. **52**(6), 613–629 (1997)
25. Spencer, S.J., Steele, C.M., Quinn, D.M.: Stereotype threat and women's math performance. J. Exp. Soc. Psychol. **35**(1), 4–28 (1999)
26. Osborne, J.W.: Testing stereotype threat: does anxiety explain race and sex differences in achievement? Contemp. Educ. Psychol. **26**(3), 291–310 (2001)
27. Koch, S.C., Müller, S.M., Sieverding, M.: Women and computers. Effects of stereotype threat on attribution of failure. Comput. Educ. **51**(4), 1795–1803 (2008)
28. Fritzsche, B.A., DeRouin, R.E., Salas, E.: The effects of stereotype threat and pacingon older adults' learning outcomes. J. Appl. Soc. Psychol. **39**(11), 2737–2755 (2009)
29. Lamont, R.A., Swift, H.J., Abrams, D.: A review and meta-analysis of age-based stereotype threat: negative stereotypes, not facts, do the damage. Psychol. Aging **30**(1), 180–193 (2015)
30. Abrams, D., Crisp, R.J., Marques, S., Fagg, E., Bedford, L., Provias, D.: Threat inoculation: experienced and imagined intergenerational contact prevents stereotype threat effects on older people's math performance. Psychol. Aging **23**, 934–939 (2008)
31. Hess, T.M., Auman, C., Colcombe, S.J., Rahhal, T.A.: The impact of stereotype threat on age differences in memory performance. J. Gerontol. B Psychol. Sci. Soc. Sci. **58**, 3–11 (2003)
32. Hess, T.M., Emery, L., Queen, T.L.: Task demands moderate stereotype threat effects on memory performance. J. Gerontol. B Psychol. Sci. Soc. Sci. **64**, 482–486 (2009)
33. Chua, S.L., Chen, D.T., Wong, A.F.: Computer anxiety and its correlates: a meta-analysis. Comput. Hum. Behav. **15**(5), 609–623 (1999)
34. Beckers, J.J., Rikers, R.M.J.P., Schmidt, H.G.: The influence of computer anxiety on experienced computer users while performing complex computer tasks. Comput. Hum. Behav. **22**(3), 456–466 (2006)

Control with Hand Gestures by Older Users: A Review

Sheau-Farn Max Liang$^{(\boxtimes)}$ and Yun-Ju Becker Lee

Department of Industrial Engineering and Management,
National Taipei University of Technology,
1, Sec. 3, Zhong-Xiao E. Rd., Taipei 10608, Taiwan
maxliang@ntut.edu.tw

Abstract. While the quantity and proportion of aging population has been increased rapidly around the world, new means of Human Computer Interaction (HCI), such as control with hand gestures has been introduced and gained its popularity in everyday activities. These trends create opportunities and challenges of gestural user interface design for elderly people. Old people not only increase in chronological age but also relate to various degrees of deterioration in abilities of perception, cognition, and psychomotor. Old population also differs from other age groups in terms of prior experience and knowledge, social status, and interpersonal relationship. In this paper, we first reviewed issues about age and its related characteristics. We then summarize the findings from reviewed literature. Two major applications of gestural user interfaces, "gesture-on-surface" and "gesture-in-midair," were included in this review. While gesture-on-surface refers to gesture control on touchscreens, gesture-in-midair denotes that hand gestures are performed without touching anything. A discussion was provided at the end of this paper to suggest that gestural interfaces for older users should be simple and intuitive, and with necessary instruction and feedback. To differentiate age-related attributes in future studies was also recommended.

Keywords: Gestural interface · Age · Elderly people

1 Introduction

With the advance of technology, control by hand gestures has been applied in our daily lives. This is evident in the cases of controlling a smart phone with gestures on the surface of its touch screens and controlling a smart TV with gestures in midair recognized by its sensors.

Two major applications of gestural user interfaces were identified in this paper as "gesture-on-surface" and "gesture-in-midair." Gesture-on-surface refers to gesture control on touchscreens. Common applications found in literature are mobile phones, tablet computers, and public information kiosks with different sizes of display screens and angles of inclination. The tasks performed in previous research involved object selection and manipulation, text and digit entry, and function control commands. These tasks could be performed by one or more fingers with one or two hands, or by a stylus

J. Zhou and G. Salvendy (Eds.): ITAP 2016, Part I, LNCS 9754, pp. 350–359, 2016.
DOI: 10.1007/978-3-319-39943-0_34

held by hand. On the other hand, gesture-in-midair denotes that hand gestures are performed without touching anything. The gestures are usually detected through cameras, gyroscopes, or motion sensors. Applications studied in literature are inter-active televisions, video games, and smart appliances. Same as the research on gesture-on-surface, the tasks performed were object selection and manipulation, text and digit entry, and function control commands. These tasks could be performed by one of the three main types: freehand, handheld, and hand-worn. Freehand gestures were often the gestures made in air with an exception of using a finger of one hand as a pointer to pointing the palm of the other hand as a control panel. Handheld means performing gestures by holding a device, such as a mobile phone or the Wiimote controller. Hand-worn is to performing gestures by wearing a device, such as a ring or bracelet. Freehand gestures could be performed by one or two hands, whereas handheld and hand-worn gestures were often performed one-handed.

Most studies in the field of gesture control have only focused on young users. However, according to the statistics report of World Health Organization (WHO), the quantity and proportion of aging population has been increased rapidly around the world. In some developed countries, the percentage of old people has reached 21 % (World Health Organization 2015). Therefore, it is important to further explore the potential opportunities and challenges of gestural user interface design for elderly people. This paper is the first step of this attempt by reviewing related literature on control with hand gestures by older users. Twenty-four journal and conference papers published from 2009 to 2015 were included in this review. The remaining part of the paper proceeds as follows: Sect. 2 presents issues about age and its related charac-teristics. The findings from reviewed literature were then summarized in Sect. 3. Finally, a discussion was provided in Sect. 4.

2 Age and Related Characteristics

There is no standard definition of old age. The United Nations has agreed that the 60 years old is as the beginning of old age, whereas the onset of old age is delayed until 65 years old in most of the developed countries, and is advanced to 50 years old in a World Health Organization (WHO) project in Africa. As can be seen from the data in Table 1, the ages of older participants in our reviewed 24 papers varied from one to another paper, but they were within the range of 52 to 91 years old.

Old people not only increase in chronological age but also relate to various degrees of deterioration in abilities of perception, cognition, and psychomotor (ISO/IEC Guide 71 2001). Old population also differs from other age groups in terms of prior experi-ence and knowledge, social status, and interpersonal relationship. Seventeen out of the reviewed 24 papers collected data about participants' background information including previous experience on the use of electronic products, physical and mental conditions, education levels, or job status.

There has been a gradual decrease in older participant's experience of using newly-introduced technologies. Only few papers reported their older participants had no experience of using computers (Hwangbo et al. 2013; Leonardi et al. 2010), whereas older participants in the other reviewed papers had experience in using computers

Table 1. Summary of reviewed papers

Reference	Number and age of participants	Independent variable	Dependent variable
McLaughlin et al. (2009)	24 Y: 18–25 (20.1, 1.3) 24 O: 60–70 (65.2, 3.0)	Age; Control device/task; Attention allocation	Response time
Chung et al. (2010)	12 Y: 20 s-30 s (25.6, 3.2) 12 O: 60 s-70 s (69.0, 3.4)	Age; Control device/task	Entry speed; Error rate; Ease of use
Leonardi et al. (2010)	15 O: 62–93 (77.0, —)	Observation	
Stößel and Blessing (2010)	22 Y: 20–35 (26.1, 3.5) 20 O: 60–75 (67.0, 3.9)	Age	Perceived suitability
Stößel et al. (2010)	18 Y: 21–33 (26.0, 3.4) 18 O: 60–71 (63.0, 3.2)	Age; Device size; Gesture complexity	Error; Speed
Bhuiyan and Picking (2011)	16 G: 18–30 (—, —) 16 G: 31-40 (—, —) 8 G: 41–50 (—, —) 8 G: 51–60 (—, —) 7 G: 61–70 (—, —) 8 G: 71–80 (—, —) 1 G: 80+	Age group; Control task	Completion time; Success rate; Usability
Kobayashi et al. (2011)	20 O: 60 s-70 s (—, —)	Practice duration; Object size; Screen size; Gesture type	Completion time
Bobeth et al. (2012)	24 O: 65–73 (68.3, 2.4)	Control type	Completion time; Error rate; Acceptance
Gerling et al. (2012)	I: 15 O: 60–90 (73.7, 9.9) II: 12 O: 60–91 (76.7,10.6)	Gesture type	Completion rate; Perceived suitability; Affect

(Continued)

Table 1. (*Continued*)

Reference	Number and age of participants	Independent variable	Dependent variable
Pham and Theng (2012)	24 O: — (74.0, 6.4)	Control device	Perceived performance; User experience
Lepicard and Vigouroux (2012)	12 Y: 23–33 (28.1, 3.5) 12 O: 63–89 (77.6, 7.9)	Age; Gesture type; Control task	Completion time; Error rate
Rice et al. (2013)	20 Y: 15–20 (18.0, 1.9) 20 O: 55–74 (61.3, 5.1)	Age group	User experience
Gerling et al. (2013)	16 Y: 18–27 (23.9, 2.5) 17 O: 62–86 (71.5, 7.3)	Age; Control task; Control device	Performance; User experience
Hwangbo et al. (2013)	22 O: 65 + (70.6, 3.7)	Object Size; Object Spacing	Completion time; No. of errors; Perceived suitability; Ease of use; Mental effort; Physical effort; Recognizability; Usability; Satisfaction
Findlater et al. (2013)	20 Y: 19–51 (27.7, 8.9) 20 O: 61–86 (74.3, 6.6)	Age; Control task; Control device	Movement time; Error rate; Perceived difficulty
Marinelli and Rogers (2014)	No participant	Heuristic evaluation	
Page (2014)	4 O: 66–88 (78.0, 11.2)	Structured observation	
Mihajlov et al. (2014)	17 O: 54–82 (67.3, —)	Gesture type	Completion time; No. of error
Bobeth et al. (2014)	15 Y: 19–38 (26.8, 4.4) 15 O: 66–80 (71.3, 3.9)	Age; Control device; Control task	Completion time;; No. of error; User experience
Wulf et al. (2014)	20 Y: 25–45 (33.9, 6.2) 20 O: 65–85 (71.9, 5.1)	Age; Device orientation; Gesture type	Performance
Liu et al. (2014)	I: 10 O: 65–80 (—, —) II: 6 O: 55–80 (—, —)	Interview	

(*Continued*)

Table 1. (*Continued*)

Reference	Number and age of participants	Independent variable	Dependent variable
Gao and Sun (2015)	40 Y: 19–24 (21.6, 1.1) 40 O: 52–81 (64.5, 7.4)	Age; Gesture type; Screen type; Object size; Object spacing; Device inclination angle	Completion time; No. of error rate; User experience
Ferron et al. (2015)	6 O: 65–83 (—, —)	Interview	
Sáenz-de-Urturi et al. (2015)	14 O: 65–94 (81.3, 8.9)	Questionnaire	

Note: Format of "participant" column: [no. of participant] [group: Y: young, O: old, G: group]: [range] (mean, standard deviation); —: no data

(Chung et al. 2010; Ferron et al. 2015; Findlater et al. 2013; Gerling et al. 2013; Kobayashi et al. 2011; Mihajlov et al. 2014). For the technologies of gesture-on-surface and gesture-in-midair, low proportions of older participants with related experience were reported in the majority of the papers (Bobeth et al. 2014; Gerling et al. 2012, 2013; Kobayashi et al. 2011; Mihajlov et al. 2014; Sáenz-de-Urturi et al. 2015; Wulf et al. 2014). However, higher percentages of older participants with the experience of gesture-on-surface were found in very recent studies (Ferron et al. 2015; Gao and Sun 2015). From results of interviews, Page (2014) found that older participants' experience of using mobile phones was affected by their previous experience. However, there was no significant effect of older participants' previous experience on the results in the study by Hwangbo et al. (2013).

Older participants' sensory conditions and mobility were examined in some papers, such as vision (Chung et al. 2010; Kobayashi et al. 2011; Lepicard and Vigouroux 2012), hearing (Kobayashi et al. 2011), and the abilities of hands and upper-extremities (Gao and Sun 2015; Gerling et al. 2013; Lepicard and Vigouroux 2012; Mihajlov et al. 2014; Pham and Theng 2012; Wulf et al. 2014).

Participants' education levels were reported in some papers (Leonardi et al. 2010; Gao and Sun 2015). Gao and Sun (2015) speculated that, compared to participants with lower education level, the participants with higher education levels might be more familiar with and have more positive attitude to new technologies. The data about the status of retirement had also been collected (Stößel and Blessing 2010). Ziefle and Bay (2005) argued that participants' perceptions about high-tech products were influenced by whether they were retired or not.

3   Summary of Findings in Previous Research

The findings of previous research were summarized under five headings: Older Vs. Younger Age Groups, Control Tasks and Devices, Sensory Feedback, Physical Abilities, and Cognitive Abilities.

3.1   Older Vs. Younger Age Groups

The differences in gesture control between older and younger user groups have been found in a number of respects. McLaughlin et al. (2009) revealed that the attention resources of old users were affected more than the ones of young users by the design of control. Gerling et al. (2013) found that old users experienced difficulty in controlling directions with the midair gestures, and this caused the increase in their mental workloads. On the other hand, Stößel and Blessing (2010) found that the control gestures with multi-fingers were used less by old people than by the young. In addition, control gestures for the rotating and zooming of an object on touchscreens were more difficult for old users than for the young (Gao and Sun 2015; Lepicard and Vigouroux 2012). By applying 42 touchscreen control gestures with different levels of complexity, Stößel et al. (2010) found that young participants performed faster than old participants, but there was no significant difference in accuracy between the two groups. Similar result was reported in the study by Bhuiyan and Picking (2011). They grouped particiants according to their ages and found that the younger the group was, the less time they needed to complete the control tasks with midair gestures, but all the groups could perform the tasks without any error.

In summary, gesture-on-surface may be a better means of control compared to other conventional control methods, especially for older people (Findlater et al. 2013). For gesture-in-midair, old users seemed to need more instructions or hints for operation (Bobeth et al. 2014; Rice et al. 2013).

3.2   Control Tasks and Devices

The performance of older users was affected by different control tasks and devices. McLaughlin et al. (2009) reported that old users would benefit from the matching tasks, such as using a touchscreen for pointing and ballistic tasks but not for the dismatching repetitive and precision tasks. Findlater et al. (2013) found that old users performed better by gestures on touhcscreens than by conventional control devices such as mouses. Bobeth et al. (2014) showed that old people could effectively and efficiently perform gsture-on-surface control, but they were more interested in gesture-in-midair control since it could get more excercise. For gesture-in-midair, Pham and Theng (2012) compared freehand control to handheld control and revealed that handheld control was easier to be performed than freehand by old users. Furthermore, Gerling et al. (2013) demonstrated that older user preferred handheld control to freehand control since they liked the feeling of something being held during the control.

In general, elderly persons could do gesture control with ease on touchscreens for simple tasks, such as dragging or tapping an object, but not for more complex tasks, such as rotating or resizing an object (Findlater et al. 2013; Gao and Sun 2015; Kobayashi et al. 2011; Lepicard and Vigouroux 2012; Mihajlov et al. 2014; Stößel and Blessing 2010; Wulf et al. 2014). Some research results showed that control with single finger might be more suitable than with multi-finger for older users (Lepicard and Vigouroux 2012; Mihajlov et al. 2014; Stößel and Blessing 2010; Wulf et al. 2014).

However, Kobayashi et al. (2011) pointed out that older users preferred multi-finger control to single-finger control if they received appropriate instruction of operation.

For gesture-in-midair, direct and simple manipulation with gestures was suitable to old people (Bobeth et al. 2012; Gerling et al. 2012). For gesture-on-surface, bigger object size (Kobayashi et al. 2011; Hwangbo et al. 2013; Gao and Sun 2015), larger screen (Stößel et al. 2010; Kobayashi et al. 2011), and vertical but not horizontal device orientation (Wulf et al. 2014) could enhance old users' performance.

3.3 Sensory Feedback

Sensory feedback is important for old people to do the control with gestures. Chung et al. (2010) demonstrated that the performance of old users have been enhanced as virtual keyboard being located near to the output display on the screen. Kobayashi et al. (2011) concluded that visual feedback could reduce error rates. Gerling et al. 2013 compared two game consoles and found that elderly players could play more efficiently with the one showing players' locations on the screen than the other without this feedback.

In addition to visual feedback, auditory or haptic feedback has been suggested for gesture control (Chung et al. 2010; Hwangbo et al. 2013). Hwangbo et al. (2013) suggested including both auditory and haptic feedback. However, for single type of feedback, auditory feedback was better than haptic (vibration) feedback for old people using smart phones since it might be difficult for old users to hold the phones during vibration. For gesture-in-midair, Sáenz-de-Urturi et al. (2015) recommended adding auditory feedback. Freehand type of control appears to provide less haptic feedback so it was not as preferred as handheld type of control (Gerling et al. 2013).

3.4 Physical Abilities

Physical abilities of older users affect their performances of control with gestures. Page (2014) found most of the older participants could not perform the scrolling task on touchscreens and this might be due to the physical design of user interfaces. Older users also had difficulty to do the object rotating on touchscreens since it demanded higher level of physical coordination (Mihajlov et al. 2014). Lepicard and Vigouroux (2012) reported that older participants seemed to sacrifice speed for accuracy about the gesture control on touchscreens. Moreover, this paper showed that multi-finger gestures led to more deviation from standard actions than single-finger gestures. Several studies noticed that a slow speed of performing a gesture for older users might be due to the decline of their physical abilities (Bhuiyan and Picking 2011; Chung et al. 2010; Hwangbo et al. 2013; Stößel et al. 2010). Besides, older participants were easier to feel fatigue than younger ones during their performance (Lepicard and Vigouroux 2012), especially performing gestures in midair (Gerling et al. 2012).

3.5 Cognitive Abilities

Instructions or hints about operation procedures were found necessary to assist older users in gesture control for both gesture-in-midair (Bhuiyan and Picking 2011; Marinelli and Rogers 2014; Rice et al. 2013) and gesture-on-surface (Bobeth et al. 2014; Gao and Sun 2015). Page (2014) argued that the failure of operation of older participants might because of a lack of related experience and knowledge, as well as the deterioration of working memory. Therefore, the operation procedures should be simple and intuitive (Bobeth et al. 2014; Ferron et al. 2015), such as single-finger gestures (Mihajlov et al. 2014; Stößel and Blessing 2010) or gestures without the need to learn (Bobeth et al. 2012; Gao and Sun 2015). For example, the dragging gesture on touchscreens (Mihajlov et al. 2014). The speed of older user's performance might be influenced by the decline of working memory (Chung et al. 2010; Hwangbo et al. 2013). Also, the performance seemed to be impacted more by the effect of cognitive abilities than physical abilities (Hwangbo et al. 2013).

4 Discussion

This paper has reviewed literature related to gesture control by older users. Suggestions of gestural interface design have been summarized as follows:

Considering the decline in mental and physical abilities and various backgrounds of older people, gestural interface should be simple and intuitive. While the term of simple means less physical and mental effort to perform gestures, and fewer steps to be memorized or learned, the term of intuitive refers to meet users' expectations according to their previous experience and knowledge. More specifically, gestural interface should be designed with suitable number, size, spacing and layout of objects on display screens for older users to manipulate them directly under their own pace. The mappings between control commands and corresponding gestures should be designed to reflect older users' previous experience and abilities in perception, cognition, and psychomotor. Physical demand of gestures, especially gesture-in-midair, should be examined to avoid older users suffering from fatigue. Finally, control instruction and feedback should be considered in the design of gestural interfaces.

Chronological age is not the only indicator to define whether a person is old. Further research should collect more data about participant's backgrounds, such as previous experience, mental and physical abilities, and social status, so that the cause-and-effect relationships between age-related attributes and performances of gesture control can be identified and applied to the design of gestural interfaces.

This review of literature concludes that research on gestural interfaces for elderly people is worthwhile for further exploration. Research on the design of gestural interfaces, control tasks, devices, and gesture types, as well as the evaluation of user experience and usability is recommended.

References

Bhuiyan, M., Picking, R.: A gesture controlled user interface for inclusive design and evaluative study of its usability. J. Softw. Eng. Appl. 4(09), 513 (2011)

Bobeth, J., Schmehl, S., Kruijff, E., Deutsch, S., Tscheligi, M.: Evaluating performance and acceptance of older adults using freehand gestures for TV menu control. In: Proceedings of 10th European conference on Interactive TV and Video, pp. 35–44. ACM (2012)

Bobeth, J., Schrammel, J., Deutsch, S., Klein, M., Drobics, M., Hochleitner, C., Tscheligi, M.: Tablet, gestures, remote control? Influence of age on performance and user experience with iTV applications. In: Proceedings of 2014 ACM International Conference on Interactive Experiences for TV and Online Video, pp. 139–146. ACM (2014)

Chung, M.K., Kim, D., Na, S., Lee, D.: Usability evaluation of numeric entry tasks on keypad type and age. Int. J. Ind. Ergon. **40**(1), 97–105 (2010)

Ferron, M., Mana, N., Mich, O.: Mobile for older adults: towards designing multimodal interaction. In: Proceedings of 14th International Conference on Mobile and Ubiquitous Multimedia, pp. 373–378. ACM (2015)

Findlater, L., Froehlich, J.E., Fattal, K., Wobbrock, J.O., Dastyar, T.: Age-related differences in performance with touchscreens compared to traditional mouse input. In: Proceedings of SIGCHI Conference on Human Factors in Computing Systems, pp. 343–346. ACM (2013)

Gao, Q., Sun, Q.: Examining the usability of touch screen gestures for older and younger adults. Hum. Factors: J. Hum. Factors Ergon. Soc. 0018720815581293 (2015)

Gerling, K., Livingston, I., Nacke, L., Mandryk, R.: Full-body motion-based game interaction for older adults. In: Proceedings of SIGCHI Conference on Human Factors in Computing Systems, pp. 1873–1882. ACM (2012)

Gerling, K.M., Dergousoff, K.K., Mandryk, R.L.: Is movement better? Comparing sedentary and motion-based game controls for older adults. In: Proceedings of Graphics Interface 2013, pp. 133–140. Canadian Information Processing Society (2013)

Hollinworth, N., Hwang, F.: Investigating familiar interactions to help older adults learn computer applications more easily. In: Proceedings of 25th BCS Conference on Human-Computer Interaction, pp. 473–478. British Computer Society (2011)

Hwangbo, H., Yoon, S.H., Jin, B.S., Han, Y.S., Ji, Y.G.: A study of pointing performance of elderly users on smartphones. Int. J. Hum.-Comput. Interact. **29**(9), 604–618 (2013)

Kobayashi, M., Hiyama, A., Miura, T., Asakawa, C., Hirose, M., Ifukube, T.: Elderly user evaluation of mobile touchscreen interactions. In: Campos, P., Graham, N., Jorge, J., Nunes, N., Palanque, P., Winckler, M. (eds.) INTERACT 2011, Part I. LNCS, vol. 6946, pp. 83–99. Springer, Heidelberg (2011)

Leonardi, C., Albertini, A., Pianesi, F., Zancanaro, M.: An exploratory study of a touch-based gestural interface for elderly. In: Proceedings of 6th Nordic Conference on Human-Computer Interaction: Extending Boundaries, pp. 845–850. ACM (2010)

Lepicard, G., Vigouroux, N.: Comparison between single-touch and multi-touch interaction for older people. In: Miesenberger, K., Karshmer, A., Penaz, P., Zagler, W. (eds.) ICCHP 2012, Part I. LNCS, vol. 7382, pp. 658–665. Springer, Heidelberg (2012)

Liu, Z., Liao, C., Choe, P.: An approach of indoor exercise: kinect-based video game for elderly people. In: Rau, P. (ed.) CCD 2014. LNCS, vol. 8528, pp. 193–200. Springer, Heidelberg (2014)

Ijsselsteijn, W., Nap, H.H., de Kort, Y., Poels, K.: Digital game design for elderly users. In: Proceedings of 2007 Conference on Future Play, pp. 17–22. ACM (2007)

ISO/IEC Guide 71: Guidelines for Standards Developers to Address the Needs of Older Persons and Persons with Disabilities (2001)

Marinelli, E.C., Rogers, W.A.: Identifying potential usability challenges for Xbox 360 Kinect exergames for older adults. In: Proceedings of Human Factors and Ergonomics Society Annual Meeting, vol. 58, no. 1, pp. 1247–1251. SAGE Publications (2014)

McLaughlin, A.C., Rogers, W.A., Fisk, A.D.: Using direct and indirect input devices: attention demands and age-related differences. ACM Trans. Comput.-Hum. Interact. (TOCHI) **16**(1), 2 (2009)

Mihajlov, M., Law, E.L.C., Springett, M.: Intuitive learnability of touch gestures for technology-naïve older adults. Interact. Comput. iwu044 (2014)

Page, T.: Touchscreen mobile devices and older adults: a usability study. Int. J. Hum. Factors Ergon. **3**(1), 65–85 (2014)

Pham, T.P., Theng, Y.L.: Game controllers for older adults: experimental study on gameplay experiences and preferences. In: Proceedings of International Conference on the Foundations of Digital Games, pp. 284–285. ACM (2012)

Rice, M., Tan, W.P., Ong, J., Yau, L.J., Wan, M., Ng, J.: The dynamics of younger and older adult's paired behavior when playing an interactive silhouette game. In: Proceedings of SIGCHI Conference on Human Factors in Computing Systems, pp. 1081–1090. ACM (2013)

Sáenz-de-Urturi, Z., García Zapirain, B., Méndez Zorrilla, A.: Elderly user experience to improve a Kinect-based game playability. Behav. Inf. Technol. **34**(11), 1040–1051 (2015)

Stößel, C., Blessing, L.: Is gesture-based interaction a way to make interfaces more intuitive and accessible. In: HCI 2009 Electronic Proceedings: WS4–Prior Experience. British Computer Society, Cambridge (2009)

Stößel, C., Blessing, L.: Mobile device interaction gestures for older users. In: Proceedings of 6th Nordic Conference on Human-Computer Interaction: Extending Boundaries, pp. 793–796. ACM (2010)

Stößel, C., Wandke, H., Blessing, L.: Gestural interfaces for elderly users: help or hindrance? In: Kopp, S., Wachsmuth, I. (eds.) GW 2009. LNCS, vol. 5934, pp. 269–280. Springer, Heidelberg (2010)

World Health Organization: World Health Statistics 2010. World Health Organization, Geneva (2015)

Ziefle, M., Bay, S.: How older adults meet complexity: aging effects on the usability of different mobile phones. Behav. Inf. Technol. **24**(5), 375–389 (2005)

A Preliminary Study on How the Icon Composition and Background of Graphical Icons Affect Users' Preference Levels

Hsuan Lin[1(✉)], Yu-Chen Hsieh[2], and Wei Lin[3]

[1] Department of Product Design,
Tainan University of Technology, Tainan, Taiwan
te0038@mail.tut.edu.tw
[2] Department of Industrial Design,
National Yunlin University of Science and Technology, Yunlin, Taiwan
chester@yuntech.edu.tw
[3] Department of Interior Design,
Hwa Hsia University of Technology, Taipei, Taiwan
weilin@cc.hwh.edu.tw

Abstract. Currently, it is a common scene that users click on-screen graphical user interfaces (GUI), or visual icons, to operate computers, tablet computers and smartphones as well as to execute program instructions. Employing eye-trackers as experimental tools, this study aimed to explore how different presentation modes of graphical icons affect users' preference levels. The experiment was designed to investigate two variables: icon composition and background. Through permutation and combination, six presentation modes were obtained as follows: line + positive background (M1), plane + positive background (M2), line + negative background (M3), plane + negative background (M4), line + no background (M5), and plane + no background (M6). With the help of eye-trackers, seven participants were demanded to view thirty stimuli, or the contour drawings of graphical icons, presented simultaneously in the six above-mentioned modes. The participants' fixation duration and fixation frequency were analyzed through two-way ANOVA. The analytical results showed that in terms of the two performance indicators above, M4 performed the best among the six presentation modes. Moreover, negative background performed better than positive background. The findings herein can serve as a reference when icons are researched or designed in the future.

Keywords: Icon composition · Background · Icon border · Fixation · Eye-tracking

1 Introduction

With the rise of cellphones and tablet computers, the market of mobile applications (App) has been increasingly booming, so graphical icons have been commonly found in smart mobile devices. While working with the help of computers, tablets or smartphones, users simply click on-screen graphical user interfaces (GUI), or visual

© Springer International Publishing Switzerland 2016
J. Zhou and G. Salvendy (Eds.): ITAP 2016, Part I, LNCS 9754, pp. 360–370, 2016.
DOI: 10.1007/978-3-319-39943-0_35

icons, which allow them to operate computers or execute program instructions [1]. With graphical icons presented in a relaxing way, users can locate their desired functions or objects more easily and quickly [2, 3]. That working mode enables users to manipulate the main menus, control buttons, and charts in a highly visual way; therefore, the software is used with much more ease [4]. Also, users can intuitively input instructions to be executed and interact with devices [5]. Graphical icons are more suitable for a smaller display space, such as the small screen on a handheld device. It's because graphical icons can convey more information or show the minimum instructions in the limited space [6]. Being more diversified as well as convenient, applications in cellphones, tablets, and computers are increasing constantly, with the number of corresponding icons increasing. Under such a situation, designers tend to make icons more and more complex so that icons may provide large amounts of information in a limited space and enhance users' attention [3]. Well-designed icons can achieve such positive effects as drawing users' attention, shortening search time, reducing operational errors, and relieving users' burden. In consequence, icon presentation design of a GUI has remained an important consideration to interface designers.

In the past, research on visual icons mainly focused on their sizes, distances, background, [2, 7, 8] as well as contrast [9]. As for icon-searching, much emphasis was put on how subjective evaluation of usability is affected by brightness, contrast, sharpness [1], position, number, color, and shape [10]. However, there has been little research on how presentation modes of icons can affect users' preference levels. This study explored icon presentation modes; specifically, through eye trackers, the participants' fixation duration and fixation frequency were measured while the icons were being viewed; besides, subjective evaluation of preference was conducted and analyzed. The findings herein can be used as a reference by interface designers to design icons.

2   Experiment on Preference Levels

In this study, a 13-inch tablet was employed to explore how users' preference levels are affected by the two independent variables of icon presentation: icon composition and background. According to previous research, icon composition is subdivided into lines and planes, while background is subdivided into positive background, negative background, and no background [11]. Based on icon composition and background, six presentation modes were obtained through permutation and combination as follows: line + positive background (M1), plane + positive background (M2), line + negative background (M3), plane + negative background (M4), line + no background (M5), and plane + no background (M6). In the experiment, an eye tracker was utilized to measure each participant's fixation duration and fixation frequency while the viewed icons were presented in the six modes mentioned above; in addition, how preference levels were affected by icon presentation modes would be investigated. The whole experiment was modeled on the experimental procedures propounded by Ho and Lu [12].

2.1 Participants

To perform the experiment, seven college students were recruited as the participants, whose ages ranged from eighteen to twenty-two. Because the participants were different in height, the location and height of each chair had to be realigned to match its occupant. Besides, the height of each participant's head was fixed so that his or her sight line was parallel with the center of the screen right in front of him or her. The participant's eyes should be kept at 60 cm away from the screen; meanwhile, each participant had to feel relaxed in a sitting posture throughout the experiment. Immediately after entering the laboratory, each participant sat in front of a computer. After being properly seated, each participant started to read the instructions. When the visual fixation experiment was performed with the help of an eye-tracker, the participant's vision and attention would affect his or her judgment. Therefore, each participant had to pass a procedure called "correction of the visual fixation point." Moreover, his or her vision had to conform to the standard vision before or after correction. The seven participants followed the within-subjects design, and the order in which they conducted the experiment was in compliance with the counterbalanced measures design. In other words, the order in which each participant operated the experimental interfaces varied with his or her predetermined sequence. After an individual experiment was finished, its result was automatically recorded in the system. As the whole experiment was completed, each participant was rewarded with NT$300.

2.2 Icon Stimuli

The thirty icons selected by Lin et al. [13] were used as icon stimuli in this study. The colors, backgrounds, and decorative lines of the sample icons were removed so that such factors as color, brightness, contrast, and shadow might have no effect on preference levels or image recognition. After that, the icon stimuli were converted into contour drawings presented in their optimum views, with the line width of icon borders being 2 pixels, or 0.05 cm. The stimuli were arranged in accordance with the experiment conducted by Huang and Chiu [14]. Each stimulus was presented concurrently in six different modes, or a group of six icons. In addition, the distance between the screen center and each icon was equal; likewise, the distance between the centers of two adjacent icon stimuli was equal. Consequently, after being connected, the centers of the six icons formed a regular hexagon, as shown in Fig. 1. Through permutation and combination, the six presentation modes were randomly displayed so that they might appear in six different positions as many times as possible. Each presentation mode of any of the thirty icon stimuli was compared with the other five modes. The accurate shape, location and partition of an icon could not be determined based on visual fixation during the eye-tracking experiment. As a result, the experiment focused on the overall shape of the icon to make a judgment, without showing its detailed features.

Fig. 1. Six presentation modes of an icon stimulus

2.3   Experimental Tools and Conditions

With a resolution of 1024*768 pixels, the 22-inch screen was employed and connected with an eye tracker to record visual tracks. As for image presentation, the HP desktop computer was used to control graphical software. Furthermore, GazeTracker (GT), a piece of interface software in the HP desktop computer, was responsible for detecting the number of first fixations measured by FaceLabTM v4, which is an eye tracking system. The sampling frequency of FaceLabTM eye tracker is 60 Hz; meanwhile, the FaceLabTM software was used to calculate the mean delay time of 30 ms.

2.4   Experimental Procedures

The experimental procedures in this study are described as follows. (1) The experimental goals, methods, and procedures were explained to all participants. (2) Each participant started to write down his or her basic information, including name, age, gender, and college major. (3) After reading the experimental instructions, each participant was requested to observe the graphical icons which attracted much attention. (4) Both vision examination and correcting visual fixation points were carried out. (5) At the beginning of the experiment, each participant was exposed to a gray screen for six seconds. (6) Then, the participant was exposed to a fixation plus sign ("+") on the screen for two seconds. (7) The participant was demanded to put his or her index finger on the Enter key and to start viewing a target image on the screen. Next, the contour drawing of an icon in six presentation modes appeared at the same time. After choosing the favorite icon in a particular presentation mode, the participant had to press the Enter key. (8) The participant went on to experiment with the next icon, repeating steps 5 to 8 above until all the thirty icon stimuli were tested. (9) Each participant was required to fill out a subjective questionnaire of preference in accordance with a scale of seven levels, with score 1 meaning extremely negative, score 4 meaning neutral, and score 7 meaning extremely positive, as shown in Fig. 2. For an individual participant, the whole experiment lasted between twenty-five and thirty minutes.

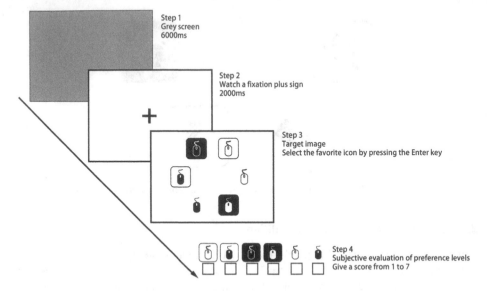

Fig. 2. The flow chart of the experiment

2.5   Analysis of the Collected Data

Eye-trackers were employed to record the experimental data while seven participants were viewing thirty icon stimuli presented simultaneously in six modes. As each icon was viewed repeatedly by the participants, thirty groups of fixation duration and fixation frequency were obtained. Next, the two-way ANOVA with dependent samples was conducted. Finally, the statistical software, Windows SPSS 12.0, was used to analyze the results, with p < .05 set as the level of a significant difference.

3   Result

3.1   Fixation Duration

To explore the effect of icon presentation modes on preference, the eye-tracker was employed to measure fixation duration and fixation frequency; meanwhile, a questionnaire was used to measure subjective preference levels. Afterwards, the effects exerted by icon composition and background were analyzed.

The interaction of icon composition and background produced a statistically significant effect on fixation duration ($F_{(2, 12)} = 6.124$, $p < 0.05$). Table 1 shows the result of ANOVA concerning fixation duration. The longest fixation duration, or 9785.3 (SD = 6073.65) ms, belonged to plane + negative background (M4) while

Table 1. ANOVA result of fixation duration

Source	df	SS	MS	F
Within subjects	6	279.414	46.569	
Icon composition (C)	1	26.870	26.870	1.985
C × Subject within group	6	81.205	13.534	
Background (B)	2	135.839	67.920	5.180*
B × Subject within group	12	157.357	13.113	
C × B	2	24.224	12.112	6.124*
Subject within group	12	23.734	1.978	

Significant at * ≦0.05; **≦0.01; ***≦0.001

Table 2. Mean fixation duration under each level of the independent variables and LSD's multiple range tests on significant factors.

Source	n	Fixation duration (ms)	Std. Error	LSD
Icon composition (C)				
Line	7	5014	884	
Plane	7	6614	1443	
Background (B)				
Positive	7	4431	878	Negative>Positive
Negative	7	8354	1953	
Non	7	4657	769	

line + negative background (M3) ranked second, with fixation duration of 6923.0 (SD = 4921.83) ms. Ranked third was plane + no background (M6), with fixation duration of 5893.6 (SD = 3294.55) ms. Ranked fourth was line + positive background (M1), with fixation duration of 4699.7 (SD = 2188.36) ms. Ranked fifth was plane + positive background (M2), with fixation duration of 4163.1 (SD = 3165.87) ms. The shortest fixation duration, or 3420.1 (SD = 1231.34) ms, went to line + no background (M5). As shown in Table 1, the effect of icon composition alone on fixation duration did not reach a significance level ($F_{(1, 6)}$ = 1.985, $p>0.05$); on the contrary, the effect of background on fixation duration reached a significance level ($F_{(2, 12)}$ = 5.180, $p < 0.05$). After being analyzed through LSD multiple range test, it was discovered that the mean fixation duration of positive background, negative background, and no background was 4431 ms, 8354 ms, and 4657 ms respectively, as shown in Table 2. In other words, the participants spent more time viewing the icons with negative background than those with positive background, as shown in Fig. 3.

3.2 Fixation Frequency

Similarly, the interaction of icon composition and background had a statistically significant effect on fixation frequency ($F_{(2,12)}$ = 7.895, $p < 0.01$), as shown in Table 3. Plane + negative background (M4) ranked first, getting 49.8571 (SD = 28.7195) times

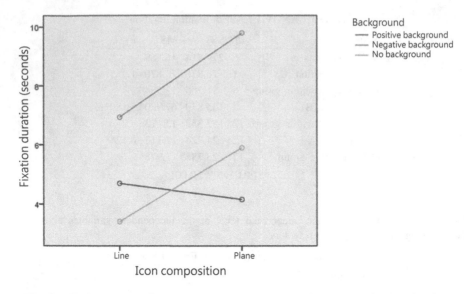

Fig. 3. The interactive effect of icon composition and background on fixation duration

Table 3. ANOVA result of fixation frequency

Source	df	SS	MS	F
Within subjects	6	5642.571	940.429	
Icon composition (C)	1	648.241	648.241	2.474
C × Subject within group	6	1572.286	262.048	
Background (B)	2	3403.857	1701.929	5.199*
B × Subject within group	12	3928.143	327.345	
C × B	2	778.429	389.214	7.895**
Subject within group	12	591.571	49.298	

Significant at * $\leqq 0.05$; **$\leqq 0.01$; ***$\leqq 0.001$

while line + negative background (M3) ranked second, getting 35.1429 (SD = 23.6462) times. In the third group ranked plane + no background (M6), line + positive background (M1), and plane + positive background (M2), getting 30.5714 (SD = 15.92542) times, 25.0000 (SD = 10.69268) times, and 20.7143 (SD = 13.37553) times respectively. The lowest fixation frequency, or 17.4286 (SD = 4.99524) times, went to line + no background (M5), as shown in Fig. 4.

The effect of icon composition on fixation frequency did not reach a significance level ($F_{(1, 6)} = 2.424$, $p > 0.05$). Contrarily, the effect of background on fixation frequency reached a significance level ($F_{(2, 12)} = 5.199$, $p < 0.05$), as shown in Table 3. After being analyzed through LSD multiple range test, it was discovered that the mean fixation frequency of positive background, negative background, and no background was 22.857, 42.5, and 24 times respectively, as shown in Table 4. Namely, in terms of

Table 4. Mean fixation frequency under each level of the independent variables and LSD's multiple range tests on significant factors.

Source	n	Fixation frequency	Std. Error	LSD
Icon composition (C)				
Line	7	25.857	4.127	
Plane	7	33.714	6.343	
Background (B)				
Positive	7	22.857	3.579	Negative>Positive
Negative	7	42.500	9.376	
Non	7	24.000	3.637	

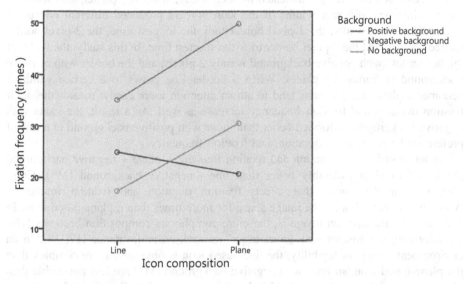

Fig. 4. The interactive effect of icon composition and background on fixation frequency

fixation frequency, the icons with negative background performed better than those with positive background.

4 Dissection

4.1 Fixation Duration

The interactive effect of icon composition and background on fixation duration reached a significance level. Fixation duration and fixation frequency were similarly influenced by the six icon presentation modes. In terms of both fixation frequency and fixation frequency, plane + negative background (M4) ranked first while line + negative background (M3) ranked second. In the third group ranked plane + no background (M6), line + positive background (M1), and plane + positive background (M2). It was line + no background (M5) that ranked last. M4 and M3 performed considerably better than M2, M1, M6, and M5. That is because negative background combined with icon borders is considered to be a part of the icon. The white target icon with negative background and borders is likelier to be noticed than that with positive background and borders. It was suggested that when the background is almost the same color as the searched target, the search speed will be lowered [15]. In this study, the background of some target icons is white, such as the icons in modes M2 and M1.

As shown in this study, there was no significant difference in search speed either between no background and positive background or between no background and negative background. The above result corresponded with the conclusion reached by Huang and Chiu [14], who investigated how the width of the icon border and the icon size affected search time. As indicated by their study, when the participants searched for certain icons, different widths of the icon borders produced different effects on search time. Specifically, the 1-pixel border took the longest time, the 2-pixel border ranked second, and the 3-pixel border took the shortest time. In this study, the width of the border line with positive background is only 2 pixels, and the border with negative background is framed by planes. When a border line grows to a certain width, it becomes a plane. Larger icons tend to attract attention more easily; meanwhile, their fixation duration and fixation frequency increase as well. As a result, the icons with negative background performed better than those with positive background in terms of preference levels, fixation duration, and fixation frequency.

In terms of fixation duration and fixation frequency, plane + negative background (M4) performed considerably better than line + negative background (M3). Complexity is another factor that affects fixation duration and fixation frequency. A line-based icon dissects the image space for more times than a plane-based icon. In consequence, the finer an image is, the more complex its composition becomes [16]. Visually complex images may lower users' recognition performance [17, 18]. In an environment with poor legibility, the line-based icon is obviously more complex than the plane-based icon, so lines with negative background (M3) are less noticeable than planes with negative background (M4). Furthermore, the plane-based icon has a larger area, looking more vivid than the line-based icon [19]. By contrast, the fine lines of a line-based icon render itself unclear. Consequently, the participants in this study had more difficulty recognizing line-based icons, with their preference levels lowered.

4.2   Fixation Frequency

As suggested in previous studies, an icon includes its background and image, with the border regarded as a part of the icon. The image with negative or positive background is larger than the image with no background. A larger image helps to upgrade its own recognizability [20] and is easily captured by vision [21]. As indicated by the experimental results herein, the effects of M2, M6, and M1 on fixation duration and fixation frequency show no statistically significant difference regardless of different sizes of the same icon. The conclusion is similar to that reached by Fleetwood & Byrne [6], who explored icon borders. According to the two researchers, having no border, round borders, and square borders showed no significant difference in their effects on users' search speed. Similarly, this study presumes that line-based and plane-based images catch the participants' eye easily, for the focus of fixation is the line or plane rather than the border. Although the icon with positive background, such as M1 and M2, is larger than the icon with no background (M6), the participants concentrate too much attention on the image itself to notice the fine lines of the border with positive background. Therefore, M6, M1, and M2 show no significant difference in terms of fixation duration and fixation frequency.

Among the six icon presentation modes, line + no background (M5) gets the shortest fixation duration and the lowest fixation frequency. It is probably because the area of an icon in M5 appears smaller. Besides, though M5 and M6 are icons with no border, the line-based icons in M5 looks more complex than the plane-based icon in M6. Accordingly, the recognizability of M5 is poorer than that of M6, with the participants' preference for M5 lowered.

5 Conclusions

This study explored how different icon presentation modes affected users' preference levels. While the icons were being viewed by the participants, eye trackers were employed to record their fixation duration and fixation frequency. The findings herein indicate that icon composition and background have an effect on users' preference for the viewed icons. Specifically, the icon in M4 (plane + negative background) performs the best, getting the highest preference level. Moreover, icon composition has no effect on users' preference levels. In terms of fixation duration and fixation frequency, negative background performs better than positive background. The findings herein can be used as a reference by interface designers to design icons.

Acknowledgements. The authors hereby extend sincere thanks to Ministry of Science and Technology (MOST) of the Republic of China (ROC) for their financial support of this research, whose project code is MOST 104-2221-E-165-001. It is thanks to the generous patronage of MOST that this study has been smoothly performed.

References

1. Näsänen, R., Ojanpää, H.: Effect of image contrast and sharpness on visual search for computer icons. Displays **24**, 137–144 (2003)
2. Huang, K.-C.: Effects of computer icons and figure/background area ratios and color combinations on visual search performance on an LCD monitor. Displays **29**, 237–242 (2008)
3. Lindberg, T., Näsänen, R.: The effect of icon spacing and size on the speed of icon processing in the human visual system. Displays **24**, 111–120 (2003)
4. Memon, A., Banerjee, I., Nagarajan, A.: GUI ripping: reverse engineering of graphical user interfaces for testing. In: Proceedings. 10th Working Conference on Reverse Engineering 2003, WCRE 2003, pp. 260. IEEE (2003)

5. Wu, F.-G., Lin, H., You, M.: The enhanced navigator for the touch screen: a comparative study on navigational techniques of web maps. Displays **32**, 284–295 (2011)
6. Fleetwood, M.D., Byrne, M.D.: Modeling icon search in ACT-R/PM. Cogn. Syst. Res. **3**, 25–33 (2002)
7. Legge, G.E., Pelli, D.G., Rubin, G.S., Schleske, M.M.: Psychophysics of reading—I normal vision. Vis. Res. **25**, 239–252 (1985)
8. Legge, G.E., Rubin, G.S., Luebker, A.: Psychophysics of reading—V. the role of contrast in normal vision. Vis. Res. **27**, 1165–1177 (1987)
9. Näsänen, R., Ojanpää, H., Kojo, I.: Effect of stimulus contrast on performance and eye movements in visual search. Vis. Res. **41**, 1817–1824 (2001)
10. Huang, H., Lai, H.-H.: Factors influencing the usability of icons in the LCD touchscreen. Displays **29**, 339–344 (2008)
11. Lin, H., Lin, W., Tsai, W.-C., Cheng, Yune-Yu., Wu, F.-G.: Effect of the color tablet computer's polarity and character size on legibility. In: Stephanidis, C., Antona, M. (eds.) UAHCI 2014, Part II. LNCS, vol. 8514, pp. 132–143. Springer, Heidelberg (2014)
12. Ho, C.-H., Lu, Y.-N.: Can pupil size be measured to assess design products? Int. J. Ind. Ergon. **44**, 436–441 (2014)
13. Lin, H., Lin, W., Tsai, W.-C., Hsieh, Y.-C., Wu, F.-G.: How different presentation modes of graphical icons affect viewers' first fixation and attention. In: Antona, M., Stephanidis, C. (eds.) UAHCI 2015. LNCS, vol. 9176, pp. 226–237. Springer, Heidelberg (2015)
14. Huang, K.-C., Chiu, T.-L.: Visual search performance on an lcd monitor: effects of color combination of figure and icon background, shape of icon, and line width of icon border. Percept. Mot. Skills **104**, 562–574 (2007)
15. Wolfe, J.M., Oliva, A., Horowitz, T.S., Butcher, S.J., Bompas, A.: Segmentation of objects from backgrounds in visual search tasks. Vis. Res. **42**, 2985–3004 (2002)
16. Shieh, K.-K., Huang, S.-M.: Effects of pictorial size and circle-slash thickness on glance legibility for prohibitive symbols. Int. J. Ind. Ergon. **33**, 73–83 (2004)
17. Curry, M.B., McDougall, S.J., de Bruijn, O.: The effects of the visual metaphor in determining icon efficacy. In: Proceedings of the Human Factors and Ergonomics Society Annual Meeting, pp. 1590–1594. SAGE Publications (1998)
18. Dewar, R.: Design and evaluation of public information symbols. Visual information for everyday use: Design and research perspectives, pp. 285–303 (1999)
19. Wong, W.: Principles of form and design. John Wiley & Sons, New York (1993)
20. Bullimore, M., Howarth, P., Fulton, J.: Assessment of visual performance. Evaluation of human work: a practical ergonomics methodology, pp. 804–839 (1990)
21. Mirzoeff, N.: The Visual Culture Reader. Psychology Press, New York (2002)

Tests of Cognitive Training as Archetypes in Elderly People

Identifying Design Categories for Cognitive and Communicative Interaction

Claudia Isabel Rojas R.[1] and Juan Alberto Castillo M.[2(✉)]

[1] Taller 11 Group Design Research,
Universidad Pedagógica y Tecnológica de Colombia, Duitama, Colombia
claudia.rojas@uptc.edu.co
[2] ErgoMotion-Lab, Medicine and Health Sciences School,
Rosario University, Bogota, Colombia
Juan.castillom@urosario.edu.co

Abstract. This paper describes the tests were used to identify useful categories to be integrated into an interactive learning test for use in the design of interactive devices for seniors.

The inquiry sought to understand from a broad view as they occur in the elderly, some of the cognitive and communicative processes, mainly those in which mediates the interaction with technology. Test of cognitive training used with older adults, they selected taken as a reference two criteria of relevance: first tests aimed at strengthening processes of care and guidance; and secondly, tests have proven to be efficient in activating processes of memory and executive functions, which are directly involved in the interaction with technology.

As a result of this process categories are obtained, for the development and evaluation aimed at optimizing interaction processes in older adults. Retained categories were: identify and describe, relate group or associate and work sequences.

Keywords: Older people · Interaction · User experience · Cognitive process · Learning task

1 Introduction

The process of internalization and cognitive appropriation is mediated by social interaction and intercommunication, where the type of communication language used is critical, and even more in the digital environment where screens have changing processes. "According to Vygotsky (1987, 1988), in the words of Pino Sirgado (2000), unlike animals, subject to the instinctive adaptation mechanisms, humans create instruments and systems of signs whose use enables them to transform and see the world, share their experiences and develop new psychological functions", Moreira (2004). For him, in the process of cognitive development man it goes reconstituting

© Springer International Publishing Switzerland 2016
J. Zhou and G. Salvendy (Eds.): ITAP 2016, Part I, LNCS 9754, pp. 371–377, 2016.
DOI: 10.1007/978-3-319-39943-0_36

internally, approaching what has already been developed by the species and then progressed to contribute to the creation of new tools and signs.

From these assumptions and considering the differences in response obtained depending on how content is presented and affecting performance levels, three useful skills for interactive processes were evident, and better yet regarding any communication process, which were defined mannered sub-categories of analysis for communication skills: a first abilities relating to the resolution of semantic content where words and general text are privileged, a second ability related to resolution of abstract contents primarily numerical operations and a final equally transverse to the applied tests and essential in interactive processes corresponding to resolution of symbolic content, supported mainly in pictures. These categories are defined on the ground that the main interest of this work is in the interactive mediation, as well as raises Scolari (2008) corresponds to this subject a change of perspective on communication processes, a paradigm "that it may not works from the theories of reception, if not from a communication concept that is approached from the new possibilities of interactive digital communication."

From these theoretical assumptions, since the Lotca test was applied in order to stimulate some conscious cognitive capacities of human beings, and considering how the content is grouped and activities of standardized tests, a second review of the contents of the tests was conducted in order to determine this time relevant aspects of cognitive order.

1.1 Cognitive Skills

According to Reed (2007), cognitive skills are the abilities and processes of mind needed to perform a task, and they are the working of the mind and enabling knowledge being responsible for acquiring and retrieve it for later use; according to data collected with the tests, it was found that these tests include thought processes that are common to the use of interactive technologies relating mainly to identify or describe images, relate figurative elements and associated or group elements because of their morphological characteristics, and other activities where sequences are performed to achieve some end.

Since there is currently no single taxonomy of cognitive skills, it was considered useful to classify them into two groups: basic and higher skills. This proposed division, basic or simple cognitive abilities are to observe, remember, compare, sort, group, label, classify, infer, analyze, reason and higher cognitive skills are aimed at problem solving, decision making, critical thinking and creative thinking. (Ramos et al. 2010).

Also considered, thinking skills sorted Trujillo and Salcedo (2012), in relation to the functional cognitive abilities that can be associated with the interaction, and the changes in the mode of information processing by humans while performing tasks related to the understanding of the environment, the content in the second category of analysis was defined as: cognitive aspects, and decided that would include the sub-categories of analysis: identify, relate, grouping and processing sequences.

2 Subject and Methods

For the development of experimental tests a group of volunteers of both sexes, some with an active working life and other retired with age of 60, was formed; according to the guidelines referred to the years of experience of interaction with technologies that bring together the population born before 1960, which is known in sociology as electro-mechanical interfaces characterized by mostly using analog type. The volunteers were grouped into three subgroups, a sub-group consisting of attending therapy activities in the Meredi Barrios Unidos hospital, another made up his companions, and a third group attending the Senior Center in the "La Caracola" Activity Center in Bogotá.

In total, data from 12 aged adult's volunteers, who performed all the selected tests were recorded. All participants were informed of the interest of the study, the final use of the data and consented in writing their participation; and the tests were applied under ethical standards within the premises of the two institutions, considering the rhythms of each person to advance or delay the process voluntarily.

2.1 Assess Test and Evaluation Plans and Procedures

The initial activity consisted in apply a base test aimed to establish the overall capabilities of the participants and their relevance to shape the sample. The entry base test corresponded to excerpts from the general health survey reported by the group of Gerontology at the University of Caldas. The evaluated items were selected in consideration of the aspects established by theory as determinants of cognitive decline in adults: health conditions, social relationships, education, dependence, autonomy and depression.

This test determines the average age was 68, the predominant language in the group is the Spanish and live mainly with children or relatives. It was also determined that all trial participants were literate, however large differences in educational level is presented as some have completed only primary, other intermediate levels and another group reached higher levels of education. Most participants were women with 83.3 %, since only two men involved in the study, 58.3 % of these are single, 16.7 % married and 25 % of the participants are widowed.

In assessing the cognitive decline of the group, since the exercises in the test it was found that in general the spatial orientation in the group performed well with 94.75 % accuracy. In identifying images the result was correct for the overall group, but in relation to the recall of observed images it was found a large decrease, because only 75 % was successful. The other aspect evaluated by the test is related to the understanding and linguistic memory, for this aspect to be evaluated by reading stories and texts, a precision level of 84 % was identified in the responses for adult group. After reviewing these data, it was determined that the group complied with the basic skills needed to be part of the study, and proceeded to apply standardized tests selected for the approach.

From a quantitative exploratory perspective that considers these instruments as archetypes and useful tools for approach to understanding the cognitive reality of seniors, the following tests were selected: Brief Neuropsychological Assessment Neuropsi; this test explores nine areas: orientation, attention/concentration, language, memory, executive functions, visuospatial processing, reading, writing and arithmetic, the second test used was Loewenstein Occupational Therapy Cognitive Assessment (LOTCA) battery, for seniors. In all cases, the test results from the tests were registered into the registration protocols, that for this purpose are pre-designed and from which the assessment and monitoring of each individual is made when is relevant.

3 Results

3.1 Data Communication Skills

For semantic communication skills, the results of the activities of the battery "Neuropsi" were considered referring to spontaneous verbal memory, sentence repetition, verbal fluency, reading and writing as well as evocative mainly verbal, key memory and recognition of series. Due to memory can store experiences and perceptions to evoke subsequently, initially spontaneous verbal memory was assessed. There was noted that performance in these skills is not entirely satisfactory since only 54 % of participants correctly pronounced the words of the exercise, and praying obtained generally a percentage of 79.13.

Regarding verbal fluency two aspects were measured, one semantic and the other phonological, obtaining better results in semantic aspects (49.4 % shooting percentage) than in the phonological (36.3 % shooting percentage). Two other items were assessed to the research participants related to reading (77.8 % correct) and writing (91.65 % correct), here, unlike previously evaluated aspects, participants performed better. Finally in semantic aspect some evocation exercises related to verbal memory were performed, the results are presented in Table 1.

Table 1. Data communication skills

	General	GROUP		
		G1	G2	G3
Spontaneous verbal memory	30,55 %	33,3 %	61,1 %	13,9 %
Key memory	45,82 %	50,0 %	66,7 %	33,3 %
Recognition	61,1 %	61,1 %	88,9 %	47,2 %

From the results in the application of these exercises was observed that people performed better in recognizing words they had memorized earlier, followed by the review using keys. The table also presents that trend until this point of the analysis G2 group integrated by accompanying persons, obtained the best results in the exercises. The G1 group corresponding to those in training therapy Meredi hospital, and G3 group attending the La Caracola adult center.

To analyze the abstract communication skills some items evaluated on the battery "Neuropsi" were considered, especially those related to operations of regression digits,

Table 2. Data communication skills

	Percentage of correct answers
Inverted numbers	52 %
Consecutive subtraction	81,65 %
Problems with basic operations	66,7 %
Logic reasoning	72,5 %

consecutive mental arithmetic subtraction, and those responsible for evaluating executive functions mainly through increasing calculation operations. Likewise the results of logical reasoning exercises from Battery "LOTCA" were reviewed for this purpose. The results of these activities are recorded in Table 2, where it is evident that the lower performance was in operations of inverted numbers. Generally participants fared well in this type of logical questions.

For the analysis of the figurative abilities sub-category, items from "Neuropsi" related to visual detection, perception and visuospatial memory, naming and understanding figurative and graphic sequencing were considered. From the "LOTCA" Battery points related to sequencing activities of shapes and forms. The first test focuses on the symbolism, especially in image recognition, in the first part identification of figures according to a given model was made, here it was established that the average number of figures recognized for the participants was 9, the highest number of figures a participant recognized was 16 out of 21.

Measurements related to visuospatial processes were performed through copying figures of average complexity, where good conservation was evident in research, reflected in the 80 % of hits returned by the group in the test. Another evidence of this subcategory was to name the images to be presented, where was obtained a 91.65 % of correctly identifying pictures by participants. Similar results were obtained when asking participants to point out some ways to assess comprehension instruction, 84.7 % of participants noted the successful forms.

In reviewing the activities in which people should follow a pictorial sequence it was determined that in the Neuropsi test only 58.3 % of the group follow the sequence logically, compared with LOTCA test where they reach 90.8 %. In contrast to the presentation of a sequence of geometric figures, in which individuals obtained a more homogeneous development, obtaining a general average of 81.25 % for the two tests. For the evocation exercises made regarding visuospatial memory was identified that only a 42.38 % of the participants achieved successes in this type of activity, in contrast to the perception of the spatial image, where it was found that 93.3 % of people understood and properly developed the exercises.

4 Cognitive Skills Data

To start, there is the case of spatial perception, which considered three aspects: body awareness, spatial relationships and spatial relationships in the picture, here, the percentage of accuracy in most aspects were quite high as evidenced by the in Table 3.

Table 3. Perception data

	Percentage of correct answers
Body awareness	**97,9 %**
Spatial relationships	**97,5 %**
Spatial relationships in the picture	**93,3 %**

Regarding motor praxias three aspects were measured; motor imitation which was expressed in a percentage of 91.7 % success, Using 100 % objects and symbolic actions 97.5 % and was identified that all individuals retain their motor praxis in the use of objects, and the other two areas assessed also performed well. In the measurement of visual motor skills organization, six aspects were considered: Copy shapes 90.8 %, reproduction of models in 2D 90.8 %, board construction 82.5 %, design with colorful blocks 77.5 %, play puzzle 73.3 % and clock drawing 80.8 % over these issues is identified that there is a slight decrease in cognitive activities, being puzzle play the lowest performance.

Regarding rational operations four aspects were measured; Categorization, pictorial sequence, geometric sequence and logical questions, the percentages of accuracy in each of the aspects are presented in the Table 4.

Table 4. Rational data operations

	General
Categorization	**85,9 %**
Pictorial sequence	**90,8 %**
Geometric sequence	**81,2 %**
Logical questions	**72,5 %**

Comparing the four items evaluated, it was found that the best performance achieved those involved in the investigation was in spatial perception, followed by motor praxis and where lower performance was obtained in rational operations. This could indicate that these seniors have retained more cognitive abilities related or associated with images and motor imitation.

On the other hand, considering the way the content and activities of standardized testing is clustered, it was revealed that these include thought processes common to the use of interactive technologies, as cognitive skills are the abilities and processes of the mind necessary to perform a task, and responsible for acquiring the knowledge and recover it for later use. In this sense a second category of analysis was formulated called: Cognitive aspects, with its analysis sub-categories: identify, relate, grouping and processing sequences.

When comparing the average percentages of success was found that in the best performance obtained corresponded to the activity of identification with 88.13 % and the lowest in the preparation of sequences with 70.6 % success, this may mean that people find it easier to relate to explicit and visible figures than recalling previously observed images. To conclude this category, it was established that cognitive processes assessed showed a good performance in the group of participants, and by comparing the average percentages of success that cast the four criteria set could say that the best performance obtained is the ability to identify and lower performance in elaborating sequences.

5 Conclusion

The collected data were used as support for the design of an interactive learning experience, this experience served to validate the categories and the approach to a formulation of a knowledge based and referred to interaction design for senior citizens. The elements of the designed solution consist of a set of semantic and figurative elements, purpose was to achieve a minimization of the elements of abstract order in the design, in consideration of the difficulties encountered in this experience.

Since the purpose of the research study was to review the proposal of actions on the designed interfaces, not from the menu concept, thus not to offer a semantic or symbolic scale of options, usually sorted on operability and functionality criteria; to achieve this objective the most important processes identified in the results of the tests were applied, identify and describe, relate, group or associate and develop sequences, since it was found that these factors favor the emergence and stimulation of functions: the use of these elements in the development of interaction algorithms stimulate attention and memory, and also strengthen the capacity of the elderly to plan, make judgments and decisions, cognitive aspects directly involved in the interactive processes.

Acknowledgements. This study was conducted in the framework of a research internship at the Ergonomics Laboratory of the Universidad del Rosario in Bogota Colombia.

References

Moreira, M.A.: Meaningful learning and lenguage. Moreira, Caballero y Rodríguez. Aprendizaje significativo: interacción personal, progresividad y lenguaje Significant learning: personal interaction, escalation and language. Publications Service of the University of Burgos, Burgos, pp. 67–86 (2004)

Ramos, A.I., Herrera, J.A., Ramírez, M.S.: Development of cognitive skills and mobile learning: a case study. Comunicar **34**, 201–209 (2010)

Reed, S.K.: Cognición. Theory and Applications. Thom son Wadsworth, USA (2007)

Scolari, C.: Hipermediations: elements for a theory of interactive digital communication. Gedisa Editorial (2008)

Trujillo, M.A.P., Salcedo, M.R.: Implementation and enforcement of the ECA strategy to develop the basic skills of thought 'comparison'. Basic Sci. J. Bolivarian University Simon Bolivar **13**, 9–26 (2012)

Eye Movements on Assessing Perceptual Image Quality

Cheng-Min Tsai[1(✉)], Shing-Sheng Guan[2], and Wang-Chin Tsai[3]

[1] Department of Creative Product Design and Management, Far East University, Tainan, Taiwan
ansel.tsai@gmail.com
[2] School of Design, Fujian University of Technology, Fuzhou, China
[3] Department and Graduate School of Product and Media Design, Fo Guang University,
Yilan, Taiwan

Abstract. The purpose of this study is focusing on "Analysis for human's Region of Interest (ROI) on complex images", and collected the subject's eye movement and 'scan path' when assessing perceptual image quality task by using eye tracking method. The participants in this study were 30 students with convenience sampling from design, management and engineering college in National Yunlin University of Science and Technology. 11 stimulus of this experiment was selected from ISO standard image by focus group, and the type of image was divided into still image, portrait, landscape and architecturally image. The two tasks in this experiment are 'assessing perceptual image quality' and 'assessing perceptual color quality'. And analysis the 'Fixation duration' and 'Amplitude of saccade' of ROIs from eye movement when assessing perceptual image quality task. The results show 1. when the 'perceptual color quality' is higher and the 'perceptual image quality' is higher, too; 2. The subjects were tended to browse the still and landscape image widely when assess the perceptual image quality and perceptual color quality task; 3. In contrast to the still image, the subjects were focus on the face of portrait image; 4. The subjects' eye movement was tended to stabilize and homogenize when assess the 'perceptual color quality task'.

Keywords: Image quality · Eye tracking · Visual assessment

1 Introduction

The factors composing image quality are highly complex. From the perspective of research and development, human factors engineering must also be taken into account in addition to the physical attributes of images. The ultimate purpose of displays is to correctly transmit all image content to human visual systems. However, many past studies have emphasized the physical attributes of images as a basis, using algorithms to calculate video compression or video coding to examine the physical quality of images. Studies examining the subjective assessment of perceptual image quality from a psychological perspective are a more recent development. Newell [1] has figure out the three levels for information processing system (IPS). Those were included Physical implementation, Algorithmic manipulation, and Semantic understanding. Maeder and Eckert [2] figure out the three levels for cognition processing system with human's

© Springer International Publishing Switzerland 2016
J. Zhou and G. Salvendy (Eds.): ITAP 2016, Part I, LNCS 9754, pp. 378–388, 2016.
DOI: 10.1007/978-3-319-39943-0_37

cognition. Those were included Mathematical, Psychovisual, and Task oriented. Thus, the aim of this study was focusing on the perceptual image quality base on the information processing system and cognition processing system. As the Fig. 1 showed the inverted triangle is the research scope of perceptual image quality in user-centered approach. The cognition level is widely research approach by implementing human factor research to perform empirical study [1, 2].

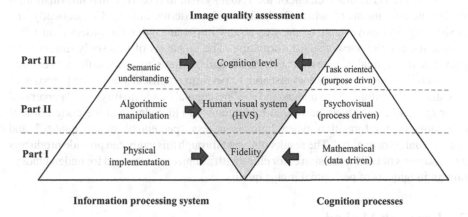

Fig. 1. The research scope of perceptual image quality in user-centered approach (Color figure online)

Over the past ten years, many studies have begun to examine assessments of image information and visual quality through human visual systems based on perspective of human factors engineering and perception psychology. Some studies have examined the relationship between image information and regions of interest (ROI) [3–5]. Other studies have established predictive models or derived algorithms based on the focuses of visual attention during the viewing of images [6, 7]. In the past five years, a number of studies involving visual assessment methods have attempted to examine the primary factors in static perceptual image quality based on human visual systems [3, 4, 8, 9]. However, these studies have yet to reach a consensus. Over the past 20 years, many studies on complex images have emphasized the physical measurement of image quality, most commonly using peak signal-noise ratio (PSNR) and root mean square error (RMSE) statistical analysis techniques to assess differences in image quality. However, these image quality measurement methods are primarily intended to calculate the fidelity of processed images to original images. Consequently, it may be that calculated image quality cannot be directly analogized or applied to the perceptual image quality judgment standards of the human eye. In recent years, many visual psychology studies have attempted to use mathematical algorithms to predict the location or positions of interest within a specified space. Privitera et al. [6] used a series of studies to predict the scan-paths of eye movement. His studies involved the use of geometrical spatial kernels and linear filter models for analysis, calculating algorithms of regions of interest (aROIs) to predict the regions focused on by humans when they viewing the images (human ROIs, hROIs). Nguyen et al. [10] established and grouped hROIs based on analysis of scan-paths and sequences of fixation occurring when humans viewing grayscale images; they further performed local image compression based on the ROIs. However, the images normally viewed by humans through their visual systems are all color images. Whether the results of the relevant research described above can be generalized to all visual focuses remains to be clarified.

As the eye is the first element of the visual system to receive visual information, it is also the only means by which the brain obtains external images. Consequently, the positioning and movements of the eye are an important index for observation when people focus on or view visual information. The emphasis of this study differs from previous image quality assessment methods and attempts to use a different research approach by using human factors research to perform empirical study. The purposes of this study are twofold: (1) to understand the "perceptual image quality" and "perceptual color quality" subjectively perceived by humans; (2) to understand the correlation of eye movement information when humans assess "perceptual image quality" and "perceptual color quality." The results obtained through this study can provide producers and designers of LCD television color chips with a subjective standard for understanding human judgments of perceptual image quality.

2   Research Method

2.1   Experiment Material and Environment

The LCD-TV was adopted as the sample-displaying monitor. Moreover, GretagMacbeth Eye-One was adopted to conduct the characterization correction and establish the ICC profile. The study was conducted in a laboratory with fixed luminance control as 233 lx and the color temperature set as 6,500 k.

2.2   Eye Tracking Technique

The video-based, pupil/corneal reflection eye tracking apparatus used was an infra-red eye movement recording system (EyeLink II) manufactured by SR Research Ltd, Canada. The subjects were seated facing a calibrated 30 in. Sharp LCD-TV (30 cm high and 40 cm wide) which was 120 cm away. The visual angle of the whole screen is 36.8 degrees wide, 28.1 degrees high. The visual angle of each single stimulus is 6 degrees wide and 6 degrees high. The monitor has a vertical scan frequency of 60 Hz, and a resolution of 1280×768 pixels. Subjects wore a headset containing a camera which monitored and recorded their eye movements and fixation locations (Fig. 2).

2.3   Image Stimuli

There were 11 stimuli have been selected from ISO standard image by focus group that were study in our color and image lab, and those image including still image, portrait, landscape and architecturally image (Table 1). All the images were be selected from

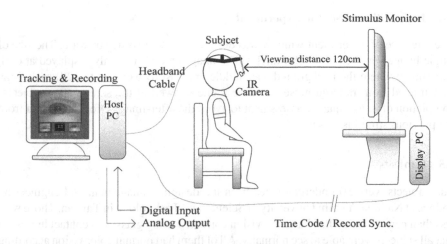

Fig. 2. The eye tracking apparatus set for experiment condition (Color figure online)

ISO 12640-1 (1997), ISO 12640-2 (1997), ISO 12640-3 (2004), ISO 12640-3 (2007) and Kodak standard image database by focus group. Each stimulus was displayed for 5 s, and then a calibration point popped up for drift correction to avoid systematic shift and after-image effects.

Table 1. The image stimuli set for experiment

No.	1	2	3	4
Image				
No.	5	6	7	8
Image				
No.	9	10	11	
Image				

2.4   Image Stimuli Set for Experiment

The interface of experiment window was design by Visual Basic software. The size of single image was 1280 by 768 (pixels). The images were randomly displayed at each experiment where the background was middle grey (RGB were set to 128) each time. Constructed from random noises, a noise frame showed at the screen after subjects' completion of image quality assessment to avoid the after-image effect generated from the previous stimulus image.

2.5   Subjects

The subjects were 30 undergraduates from the design, management and engineering college at National Yunlin University of Science and Technology in Taiwan. Those with less than perfect vision had had their vision corrected using glasses or contact lenses, so that all subjects were able to see normally. All of them had normal color vision according to the Ishihara color vision test.

2.6   Experimental Procedure

Two stage were be set for experimental procedure. First, after subjects reported to the laboratory and passed the color vision test, they should read the instructions of the experiment and practiced participating in it. A process to calibrate and validate the eye tracker was performed by having each subject fix the location of 9 points on the calibration screen. Once the calibration and validation was done, the subject started to view each of the displayed frames. Second, each participant should to assess 11 images with 7 scale of Likert scale on two tasks those were "perceptual image quality" and "perceptual color quality".

Fig. 3. Sample of fixation duration (left); Sample of amplitude of saccade (right) (Color figure online)

2.7   Data Analysis of Eye Movement

The serial order in which the images were projected was randomized by the computer so that the image order changed every trial. The data of eye position were collected into host PC with eye tracking system. Two raw data from eye position were "Fixation Duration (FD)" and "Saccade Amplitude (SA)". The FD is mean that "The time that subject gaze the point of image, such as regions of interest of image (as left image of Fig. 3, the blue point was count for fixation duration)"; The SA is mean that "The amplitude of saccade when subject viewing the image (as right image of Fig. 2, the yellow arrow line was the amplitude between two gaze point)".

3 Data Analysis and Results

3.1 Subjective Assessment Analysis

Data analysis was according to participants' subjective assessment the perceptual image quality and perceptual color quality. One-way ANOVA results demonstrated that was no significant variation between the assessment results for "perceptual image quality" and "perceptual color quality" ($F_{(1, 660)} = 3.331, p > .05$). On the other hand, correlation analysis performed between the two revealed that the assessments of "perceptual image quality" and "perceptual color quality" exhibited significant direct correlation ($r = .684$, $p < .001$). These subjective assessment results suggest that higher color quality will lead to correspondingly higher overall image quality. Particularly, for the four images of "Images 5, 7, 8, and 2," subjects gave these images relatively high scores whether they were performing the assessment tasks for "perceptual image quality" or for "perceptual color quality." Conversely, when subjects performed "perceptual image quality" and "perceptual color quality" assessment tasks for the two portraits in "Images 11 and 10," the images were assessed as being of lower quality.

3.2 Eye Movement Analysis

This study also analyzed the scan-paths exhibited by subjects as they viewed images in the image assessment process; the scan-path analysis included the two indices of 'fixation duration' (FD) and 'saccade amplitude' (SA). The former refers to the continuous time for which the eyes fix upon a specific location during repeated visual search processes (ex. Scan-paths) when viewing images. Scan-paths also include other important information such as SA. SA can reflect whether image viewing consists of fixation on localized regions or global browsing.

SA Variance Analysis. As eye movement information is massive, outlier tests and SA standardization must be taken into account prior to statistical analysis in order to ensure the accuracy of the information. Analysis was performed for the SA produced in scan-paths when subjects viewed images of different qualities. One-way ANOVA revealed that significant differences did exist in SA ($F_{(10, 9771)} = 57.288, p < .001$); at the same time, the Duncan test showed that when subjects assessed perceptual image quality, the SA was greatest when they viewed "image 5" (see Fig. 4). In other words, when subjects assessed the perceptual image quality of "image 5," they tended to browse the image in a global fashion. In addition, in perceptual color quality assessment, One-way ANOVA showed that there were significant differences in the SA for different images ($F_{(10,}$

7090) = 37.921, *p* < .001). The Duncan test revealed that when subjects assessed perceptual color quality, SA was the greatest when "image 4" was viewed (see Fig. 5). In other words, when subjects assessed the perceptual color quality of "image 5," they tended to view the image more globally and also spent more time evaluating the image. These results are consistent with those produced when subjects assessed the perceptual image quality of "Image 5."

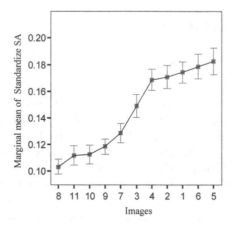

Fig. 4. SA variance analysis for "perceptual image quality" assessment of different images

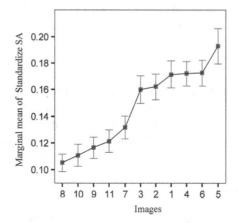

Fig. 5. SA variance analysis for "perceptual color quality" assessment of different images

FD Variance Analysis. Analysis of the visual fixation duration exhibited by users when viewing images of different qualities reveals that there are significant differences in FD between different images ($F_{(10, 9806)} = 3.366$, $p < .001$). At the same time, Duncan testing showed that when subjects assess perceptual image quality, FD was shortest for "images 5 and 4." In contrast, the greatest FD was associated with "image 11" (308 ms on average) (see Fig. 6). In addition, in assessment of perceptual color quality, One-way ANOVA showed that there are significant differences in FD between different images

$(F_{(10, 7108)} = 3.167, p < .001)$. Duncan testing showed that when subjects assess perceptual color quality, "image 7" had the shortest FD (see Fig. 7); by contrast, "image 11" had the longest FD (307 ms). This result is consistent with the result obtained from subjects evaluating the perceptual image quality of "image 11."

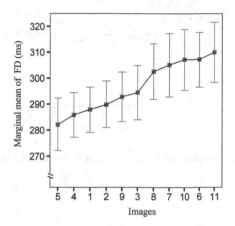

Fig. 6. FD variance analyses for "perceptual image quality" of different images

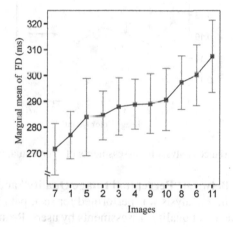

Fig. 7. FD variance analyses for "perceptual color quality" of different images

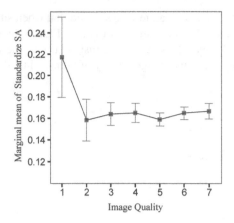

Fig. 8. SA variance analysis for assessments of "perceptual image quality"

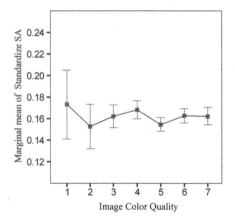

Fig. 9. SA variance analysis for assessments of "perceptual color quality

Correlation Analysis Between "Perceptual Image Quality" and "Perceptual Color Quality" in SA. Variance analysis was performed for scan-path in "perceptual image quality" and "perceptual color quality" assessments by users. Results showed that there was no significant variation between SA of scan-paths when subjects assessed "perceptual image quality" and "perceptual color quality" ($F_{(1, 16861)} = .910, p > .05$). In other words, correlation potentially existed between the SA of scan-paths in "perceptual image quality" and "perceptual color quality." Consequently, correlation analysis was performed for the relationship between those two; results showed that there was significant direct correlation between the SA of "perceptual image quality" and "perceptual color quality" ($r = .447, p < .001$). These results demonstrate that when subjects assessed "perceptual image quality" and "perceptual color quality," a certain degree of consistency existed in the browsing behaviors associated with the two types of assessments. In addition, One-way ANOVA showed that when subjects gave lower "perceptual image quality" assessments, SA was significantly higher than in other assessment results ($F_{(6,}$

$_{6344)}$ = 1.881, p < .001) (See Fig. 8). In other words, speaking generally, when subjects believed that an image had lower quality, their scan-paths browsed images with large amplitudes of saccade; by contrast, when subjects assessed "perceptual color quality," image browsing strategies were not affected by the assessment of "perceptual color quality" ($F_{(6, 5597)}$ = 1.385, p = .217) (See Fig. 9).

4 Conclusion

4.1 Results of Subjective Assessment for "Perceptual Image Quality" and "Perceptual Color Quality"

A summary of the experimental results from this study reveals that "perceptual image quality" and "perceptual color quality" were directly correlated. In other words, in subjective assessments, overall image quality increases if color quality increases. This result also begins to substantiate the claim of Trémeau and Charrier [11] that "the color appearances of images are related to perceptual image quality". This study primarily emphasized "examination of human's regions of interest in complex images." Whether or not regions or objects with relatively high frequency domain attracted greater attention remains to be tested by in future research.

4.2 Results of Correlation Analysis for "Perceptual Image Quality" and "Perceptual Color Quality" on Eye Movement

Generally, when subjects assessed the "perceptual image quality" and "perceptual color quality" of static object and landscape images, they tended towards broader browsing; for human images, visual attention was typically focused on faces. These results are consistent with the research of Nguyen et al. [10]. However, this study found that subjects in general did not approve of the "perceptual image quality" or "perceptual color quality" of human images. We posit that because experimental tasks did not require subjects to assess the skin tones of human images, the majority of subjects focused their visual attention on facial regions when they assessed images. Consequently, the facial features of the subjects photographed in the images may have interfered with the assessment of image quality of subjects. In addition, the time required to assess perceptual image quality was significantly higher than the time needed to assess perceptual color quality. This result suggests that the concept of perceptual image quality is broader and vaguer in the cognitive processes of subjects compared to the concept of perceptual color quality. At the same time, in addition to subjective assessment results showing that high perceptual color quality were consistent with high overall image quality, eye movement information for perceptual color quality assessments were also directly correlated with eye movements in overall image assessments. Furthermore, the tasks for evaluating "perceptual color quality" were significantly clearer and more specific than tasks for evaluating "overall image quality." At the same time, when individuals assessed "perceptual color quality," their eye movement information was also more stable and consistent than in "perceptual image quality" assessments. As a result, we suggest that future studies regarding "perceived image quality" also consider "perceptual color quality" assessment criteria in order to reduce cognitive differences between subjects regarding "perceptual image quality" which affect the accuracy of assessment results.

Acknowledgments. The authors would like to thank the participants and TTLA (Taiwan TFT LCD Association) for supporting this research and providing insightful comments.

References

1. Newell, A.: Unified Theories of Cognition. Harvard University Press, Cambridge (1990)
2. Maeder, A.J., Eckert, M.: Medical image compression: quality and performance issues. In: Pham, B., Braun, M., Maeder, A.J, Eckert, M.P (eds.) New Approaches in Medical Image Analysis, Proceedings of SPIE, vol. 3747, pp. 93–101 (1999)
3. Sheikh, H.R., Bovik, A.C.: Image information and visual quality. IEEE Trans. Image Process. **15**(2), 430–444 (2006)
4. Ginesu, G., Massidda, F., Giusto, D.D.: A multi-factors approach for image quality assessment based on a human visual system model. Sig. Process. Image Commun. **21**, 316–333 (2006)
5. Fedorovskaya, E.A., Ridder, H., Blommaert, F.J.: Chroma variants and perceived quality of color images of natural scenes. Color Res. Appl. **22**(2), 96–110 (1996)
6. Privitera, C.M., Fujita, T., Chernyak, D., Stark, L.W.: On the discriminability of hROIs, human visually selected regions of interest. Biol. Cybern. **93**(2), 141–152 (2005)
7. Santella, A., DeCarlo, D.: Robust clustering of eye movement recordings for quantification of visual interest, In: The proceeding of Eye Tracking Research and Applications (ETRA) Symposium (2004)
8. Calabria, A.J., Fairchild, M.D.: Perceived image contrast and observer preference I: the effects of lightness, chroma, and sharpness, manipulations on contrast perception, Munsell Color Science Laboratory, Rochester Institute of Technology (2003)
9. Sheedy, J.E., Smith, R., Hayes, J.: Visual effects of the luminance surrounding a computer display. Ergonomics **48**(9), 1114–1128 (2005)
10. Nguyen, A., Chandran, V., Sridharan, S.: Gaze tracking for region of interest coding in JPEG 2000. Sig. Process. Image Commun. **21**, 356–377 (2006)
11. Trémeau, A., Charrier, C.: Influence of chromatic changes on the perception of color image quality. Color Res. Appl. **25**(3), 200–213 (1999)

A Study of Human Behavior and Mental Workload Based on Neural Network

Lan Xiao, Jing Qiu[✉], and Jun Lu

School of Mechatronics Engineering, University of Electronic Science and Technology of China,
Chengdu, Sichuan, People's Republic of China
qiujing@uestc.edu.cn

Abstract. Human mental activities could be displayed by human behavior, which are observable directly in work environment. In current study, a method based on human behavior not directly related to task execution in work is proposed to assess the workload in mental work situations. Ten subjects were recruited and asks to perform various levels of a mental task. The link between human behavior and mental workload for four mental tasks completed on a computer were studied based on Neural Network. The result indicates that the relationship between human behavior and mental workload could be well described in a non-linear model.

Keywords: Human behavior · Mental workload · Neural Network

1 Introduction

Mental workload is a crucial issue of the ergonomic research for human mental work. In general, the wide-accepted assessment and measurement of the mental workload mainly include the following 4 methods: subjective questionnaires, physiological measures, performance or errors, and task-performing-related body actions measure. However, each of them could only reflect one aspect of the human mental states. In some respects, there are a number of limitations for the intrusiveness and discontinuity in these methods (O'Donnell and Eggemeier 1986; Wierwille and Eggemeier 1993; Meshkati et al. 1995; Farmer and Brownson 2003; Cain 2007). The results of some previous studies indicated that the specific facial muscle activity are correlated to mental status (Veldhuizen et al. 2003; Capa et al. 2008). Based on the performance and error for workload measurement, the performance of both primary and secondary tasks has been analysed. The performance of primary and secondary tasks is dependent on the strategy of task performance. O'Donnell and Eggemeier (1986) pointed out that underload may enhance performance and overload may result in a floor effect. Task-performing body behaviour only reflects the input to and the output from the person, rather than the entirety of internal activities in the brain. Moreover, the effect of the workload on an operator in a mental work setting is generally interpreted by the integration of all of the measurements used.

With gradually increasing automation in the human-machine system, the role of an operator has been moved to supervisory controller from manual worker (Sheridan 1987).

© Springer International Publishing Switzerland 2016
J. Zhou and G. Salvendy (Eds.): ITAP 2016, Part I, LNCS 9754, pp. 389–397, 2016.
DOI: 10.1007/978-3-319-39943-0_38

Hence, motor actions of the operator are being gradually decreasing and may only be episodic, while sensory-perceptual and mental activities are increasing (Bedny and Karwowski 2006). Thus, it can be difficult to observe task-performing body behaviors in such work settings due to their infrequent occurrence. Hence, the total activity (both mental and external activities) of the operator would not be entirely revealed if only their sensory-motor actions were analysed. Currently, the analysis of actions directly involved in the test tasks, such as eye movements and gross motor actions, have been widely and comprehensively accepted for workload assessment. Non-task-performing and nonverbal body behavior (e.g. face behavior) occur to accompany and support task-performing body behavior. Although human-machine interaction is different from human-human communication, nonverbal behavior can be elicited by machines during human-machine interaction in the close-loop human-machine system, which is similar to human-human communication (King 1997). Hence, the same behavior in terms of rates for tasks and types can occur as in human-human communication, where facial expression is the most innate (Argyle 1998, cited from King 1997). Furthermore, as Feyer (2007) concluded that both task performing and non-task performing body behaviours (activities) makes an influence on the interactions and human performance. Also, observable body behaviour can reflect mental processes (Keijze 2005). To date, face behavior, as one part of body behavior, has not gained much interest in workload assessment in mental work settings. The studies of King (1996; 1997) are relative early for the effect of cognitive activity on facial expression. King (1997) made a survey of facial expression in human-computer systems. The results showed that rates of facial expressions were higher for computer-based tasks. Based on his study, King (1996) argued that facial expressions were related to cognitive activities based his study. In the model of Guhe et al. (2006), mouth openness is a parameter for the predictor of mental workload. Recently, a study by Stone and Wei (2011) indicated that facial expression can be a effective index of workload for arithmetic tasks. They used FACS (Facial Action Coding System) approach by Ekman and Friesen (1978) to code face behavior. However, this face coding approach needs a well-trained coder and is very time-consuming. Meanwhile, the relationships between the facial muscle activity and workload were investigated in previous studies. The results of these studies indicated that the specific facial muscle activity are correlated to mental status (Veldhuizen et al. 2003; Capa et al. 2008). They showed indirectly the correlation between face behavior and workload in the mental settings.

In current study, the range of the human activity had been expanded to contain the head position and the upper body skeleton. Human behavior (head position, face behavior and the upper body skeleton), as an activity which is easy to observe, was used to be a parameter to verify the correlation between the human behavior and the mental workload.

The previous studies have used the linear model or the simple non-linear model to describe the link of the human behavior and the mental workload, which is not entirely linear. Hence, the purpose of this study was to figure out the relationship between human behavior and mental workload using the Neural Network algorithm.

2 Method

2.1 Subjects

A total of 10 subjects (male, mean age: 22.4 years, SD of age: 1.1 years) were recruited for the study from our university setting. They were all right-handed and have various experience on computer games. And all of them reported that they had no mental or physical health problems or diseases.

2.2 Experimental Design

Subjects would be given 4 typical psychological tests which were selected to simulate various mental activities. The 4 tests were used to represent 4 four stages of information processing (information acquisition, information analysis, decision selection, and action implementation). So the amounts to the whole workload would be affected when the major factors based on information processing changed.

- Digit span task (DIG). DIG is a simulation of information acquisition. A series of numbers are sequentially displayed on the screen. Participants were required to duplicate the number sequence in a limited amount of time (10 s) after all the numbers were displayed. The length of the next number sequence was increased by one digit upon completion of the current task. On the other hand, the length of the next number sequence was reduced by one digit when the study participant failed in the current task. The length of the number sequence was 3–6 digits in level 1 (easy task) and 7–10 digits in level 2 (complicated task). The interface of the DIG task is shown in Fig. 1(a).

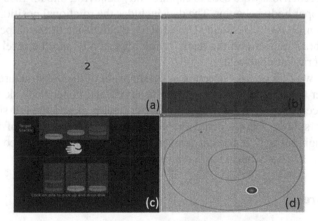

Fig. 1. Snapshots of each task. (a) DIG. (b) TIME. (c) TOL. (d) DEXT

- Time wall task (TIME). TIME is a simulation of information analysis. A dot was shown moving downward from the top of the screen to the bottom at a constant speed. The screen was divided into two parts; the dot in upper two-thirds of screen was visible.

However, the lower one-third screen was covered by "red wall", which renders the dot invisible. The study participants were asked to observe and analyze the speed of the dot as it moves downward, estimate the exact time that the dot reach the bottom, then press the space bar in the keyboard. The speed of the moving dot was randomly generated. Furthermore, the speed of the moving dot was higher in level 2 (complicated task) than that in level 1 (easy task). The interface of the TIME task is shown in Fig. 1(b).

- The Tower of London test (TOL). The TOL simulates decision selection. Various disks of different colors that represent target styles and muddled styles were shown on the screen. The study participants were asked to put a disc across the muddled style to target another disk as it moves. However, only one disk was moved each time by clicking a mouse, and the task should be completed within a given time. The number of disks was 3–4 in level 1 (easy task) and 5–6 in level 2 (complicated task), and these randomly appeared at each task. The interface of the TOL task is shown in Fig. 1(c).

- Dexterity task (DEXT). The DEXT simulates decision selection. A jumping green dot and a big circle were displayed on the screen. The study participants were asked to try their best to control and place the small jumping dot at the center of a big circle by using a mouse. The jumping range of the dot was determined by an elasticity function. The jumping range was wider in level 2 (complicated task) than that in level 1 (easy task). The interface of the DEXT task is shown in Fig. 1(d).

2.3   Experimental Equipment and Material

The data of the face behavior and the upper body skeleton is captured by Kinect, a low-cost sensor could be a tool with continuous, and supplementary approach function. There were two Kinect sensors were used to capture body behavior, one for face behavior and the other for upper body behavior. The data includes the rotational position of the head, 6 Animation Units (AUs), 11 Shape Units (SUs), the distance of the palpebral superior and the palpebral inferior and the angle of the upper body and the level ground with respect to the gravitational field.

The top view of laboratory structure and a snapshot of the lab structure as shown in Fig. 2, In order to collect the subject's face behavior and upper body skeleton, one of the device placed in front of the subject. Another device placed the left side of the lab to capture the subject's body behavior, it can analysis the change of human body behavior through infrared. It also can convert each joint data into space coordinates and record the subject's body behavior in real-time.

2.4   Procedure

The experimental procedure started with an explanation of the tasks and the procedure to each subject. First, the subject was required to fill in a biographical questionnaire. Then, the subject was seated on the chair and asked to find his/her normal seating position for working in front of the display by moving the table and adjusting chair or display. The subjects practiced the four tasks until achieving a constant performance. After the training period, the subjects were asked to fill out a questionnaire regarding their state

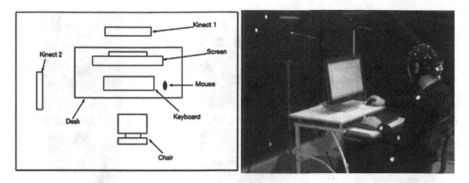

Fig. 2. Lab structure

of mind using the positive affect/negative affect scale. Each task lasted 4 min. The 4 tasks were performed by the subjects. The order of tasks was randomized for each of the subjects. At the end of the experiment, the subjects were asked to assess their state of mind again.

2.5   Data Collection and Analysis

As mentioned earlier, a Kinect sensor is very low-cost compared with other commercial tools for face behavior analysis. The Kinect sensor can track the head pose and face behavior. A right-handed coordinate system is used to quantize tracking results1 in the Kinect. The origin of the coordinate system is located at the Kinects optical center. Z axis is pointing towards a user and Y axis is pointing up, as Fig. 3 shows. The X, Y, and Z position (rotation and translation) of the users' head are captured as well based on the Kinect coordinate system. 87 two dimensions and 13 additional points on the face can be tracked. A Kinect sensor can also provide a subset defined in the Candide3 model2, which are weights of six Animation Units (AUs) (Fig. 4). The means and SDs of AUs of each task levels were used for statistical analysis.

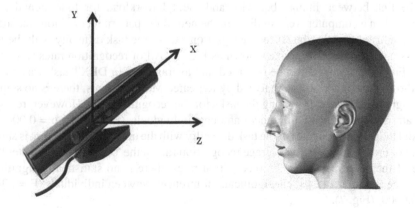

Fig. 3. Kinect coordinate system

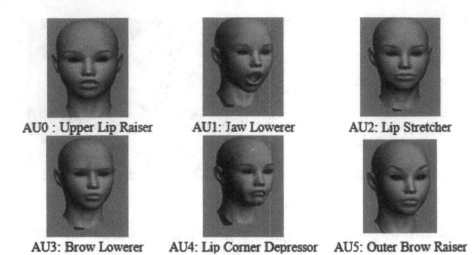

AU0 : Upper Lip Raiser   AU1: Jaw Lowerer   AU2: Lip Stretcher

AU3: Brow Lowerer   AU4: Lip Corner Depressor   AU5: Outer Brow Raiser

Fig. 4. Definition of AUs in Kinect

The distance between upper and lower lids and the angle of spine has been calculated in current study as two parameters.

Neural Network Toolbox provides functions and apps for modeling complex nonlinear systems that are not easily modeled with a closed-form equation. In the current study, we use the neural network pattern recognition tool in Matlab software and the neural net fitting tool to analyze data, and the statistical analysis was performed using SPSS 21 software with the significance level set to 0.05. The Repeated Measurement Test was used to analyze the recognition rate on subjects.

3   Results

Using the neural net fitting, the relationship between the facial behavior and the work-load calculated based on the NASA-TLX be fitted perfectly, as Fig. 5 shows.

The link between human behavior and mental workload for four mental tasks completed on a computer were studied. In the neural net pattern recognition, according to the confusion matrix, the correct recognition rate of the task difficulty with the face expression could be 90 % above (shown as Fig. 5). All of recognition rates were over 90 %. From the Fig. 5, it can be observed that average rate in DEXT task was greater than those of the other tasks. Analyzed by Repeated Measurements, there is no statistically significant difference among the tasks for the recognition rate. However, recognition rates were significant differences amongst individuals. (F = 24202, p = 0.0000).

And the recognition rates of the task difficulty with the upper body skeleton, is shown as Fig. 6. From the Fig. 6, the average recognition rate in the TOL task was greater than those of the other tasks. For the recognition rates, there is no statistically significant difference among the tasks, but significant differences between individuals (F = 294.2, p = 0.0000) (Fig. 7).

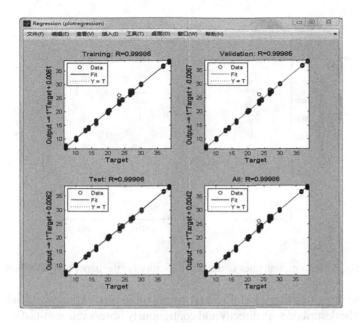

Fig. 5. Regression of the workload

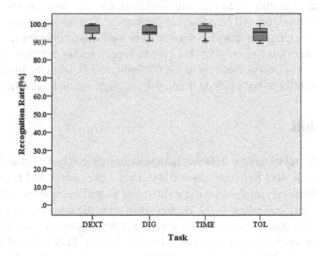

Fig. 6. Recognition rates of the task difficulty for the face expression

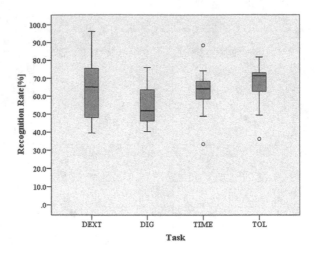

Fig. 7. Recognition rates of the task difficulty for the upper body skeleton

Although previous literature of mental workload indicated that workload measurement could be described with directly and contiguously observable non-task-performing behaviors, the workload measurement still has a few challenges. In the present study, the relationships between task difficulties and human behavior were studies during simulated mental tasks. Except for the upper body behavior, the body behavior should be studied more in its entirety to measure workload, e.g. the subjects' shoulder breadth while they were working will be a feasible parameter. The results of the present study show that the differences in human behavior were well discernible for midrange workload levels. It shows the possibility that non-task-performing behavior is nonlinearly correlated with workload as Bedny et al. (2000) indicated. To rich the method for measuring workload through body behavior analysis, further research is required.

4   Conclusion

In this study, the relationships between human behavior and task demand were investigated using the Kinect-base tracking method. Facial expression and upper body skeleton were quantitatively analyzed using a video-based analysis system. In the neural net pattern recognition, according to the confusion matrix, the correct recognition rate of the task difficulty, could contain a high level, and the relationship between the facial behavior and the workload calculated based on the NASA-TLX be fitted accurately by the neural net fitting. The result indicates that the relationship between human behavior and mental workload could be described well in a non-linear model. Based on these findings of the current study, human behavior may be used as an indicator of the workload in mental work settings. It is recommended that different levels of the same type of mental task be used in further research to develop a supplementary method for workload assessment based on human behavior.

References

Argyle, M.: Bodily Communication C, 2nd edn. Methuen & Co., Ltd., London (1998)

Cain, B.: A Review of the Mental Workload Literature. Technical reports, RTO-TR-HFM-121-Part-II, Defence Research and Development Toronto, Canada (2007)

Capa, R.L., Audiffren, M., Ragot, S.: The interactive effect of achievement motivation and task difficulty on mental effort. Int. J. Psychophysilogy **70**, 144–150 (2008)

Ekman, P., Friesen, W.V.: Facial Action Coding System. Consulting Psychologists Press, Palo Alto (1978)

Famer, E., Brownson, A.: Review of workload measurement, analysis and interpretation methods. European Organisation for the Safety of Air Navigation 33 (2003)

Feyen, R.G.: Bridging the gap: exploring interactions between digital human models and cognitive models. In: Duffy, V.G. (ed.) HCII 2007 and DHM 2007. LNCS, vol. 4561, pp. 382–391. Springer, Heidelberg (2007)

Keijzer, F.: Theoretical behaviorism meets embodied cognition: twotheoretical analyses of behavior. Philosophical Psychology **18**, 123–143 (2005)

King, W.: Reflections of thought: cognitive facial expressions in the human interface. In: Proceedings of the 5th IEEE International Workshop on Robot and Human Communication, Tsukuba, Japan, 11–14 November, 1996

King, W.: Human - computer dyads? A survey of nonverbal behavior in human-computer systems. In: Proceedings of Workshop on Perceptural User Interfaces (PUI 1997), Banff, Cananda, Los Alamitos, CA, 19–21 October, 1997

Meshkati, N., Hancock, P.A., Rahimi, M., Dawes, S.M.: Techniques in mental workload assessment. In: Wilson, J., Corlett, E. (eds.) Evaluation of Human Work: A Practical Ergonomics Methodology, pp. 749–782. Taylor and Francis Ltd., Bristol (1995)

O'Donnell, R., Eggemeier, F.T.: Workload assessment methodology. In: Boff, K., Kaufman, L., Thomas, J., Boff, K., Kaufman, L., Thomas, J. (eds.) Handbook of Perception and Human Performance, pp. 41–49. Wiley, New York (1986)

Sheridan, T.: Supervisory control. In: Salvendy, G. (ed.) Handbook of Human Factors, pp. 1243–1268. Wiley, New York (1987)

Stone, R.T., Wei, C.-S.: Exploring the linkage between facial expression and mental workload for arithmetic tasks. In: Proceedings of 55th Annual Meeting of the Human Factors and Ergonomics Society, Las Vegas, USA, 19–23 September, 2011

Veldhuizen, I.J.T., Gaillard, T., De Vries, A.W.K.J.: The influence of mental fatigue on facial EMG activity during a simulated workday. Biol. Psychol. **63**, 59–78 (2003)

Wierwille, W.W., Eggemeier, F.T.: Recommendations for mental workload measurement in a test and evaluation environment. Hum. Factors **35**, 263–285 (1993)

Mobile and Wearable Technologies
for the Elderly

Designing a Smart Watch Interface for a Notification and Communication System for Nursing Homes

Haneen Ali and Huiyang Li[✉]

State University of New York at Binghamton, Binghamton, NY, USA
{halil,hli}@binghamton.edu

Abstract. Among the unique challenges faced by nursing homes is poor communication and notification. An analysis of the work system showed that a mobile device-based system that rely less on auditory display is promising. We proposed a smartwatch interface as part of communication and notification system for nursing homes. A user-centered design approach was adopted in the design and evaluation of the interface. The application integrates call light system, chair and bed alarms, wander guard, and calling for help functions and uses multi-modal interfaces to provide informative alarms for nursing home staff. Through a process of iterative testing and refinement with prospective users (through cognitive walkthrough, heuristic evaluation and usability testing of low-fidelity prototypes), a final design was well received by nursing experts in geriatric care and at local nursing homes. The effects of the system will be tested in the future using a high-fidelity prototype through simulation experiment.

Keywords: Nursing homes · Smartwatch · Interface

1 Introduction

The number of Americans elderly over the age of 65 is expected to increase form 40.2 million in 2010 to 88.5 million in 2050 [1]. This means there will be an increase in the need for long-term care services and facilities, such as nursing homes. Nursing home residents usually have physical or cognitive impairment, and complex health conditions, and thus are at high risk of medical errors and adverse events [2], such as falls. For example, one-in-three residents in nursing homes suffered from a medication error, infection or some other type of harm related to their treatment. A typical nursing home with 100 beds reports 100–200 fall annually [4], and about 1,800 older adults living in nursing homes die from fall-related injuries each year [5]. Nationwide, there is a growing concern about the quality and safety of residents in nursing homes [6].

One contributing factors to those events is the poor communication and notification system in nursing homes. The aim of this paper is to design a smartwatch interface for a notification and communication system for nursing homes, as a part of a multidisciplinary project "developing a fall prevention and notification system for nursing homes" [22, 23].

© Springer International Publishing Switzerland 2016
J. Zhou and G. Salvendy (Eds.): ITAP 2016, Part I, LNCS 9754, pp. 401–411, 2016.
DOI: 10.1007/978-3-319-39943-0_39

1.1 Mobile Devices in Healthcare

In healthcare settings, different mobile technologies have been used for communication, including mobile phones, smartphone, and hands-free devices [7]. Hands-free communication devices were proposed and implemented in healthcare settings to improve the communications efficiency and nursing workflow [8, 10]. Hands-free communication devices were introduced to the healthcare industry because of their light weight, and are intended for verbal communication through local network. Those devices allow the user to freely use his or her hands while communicating [9]. One example of such hands-free devices is Vocera. It is a simple touch device worn around the user's neck. The user can make calls by simply saying the name of the recipients [10, 11]. Despite of the promising features, literature showed negative effects of using this type of hands-free devices, such as the potential loss of control, reliability, and some technical issues, such as dropped calls, poor reception, and communication privacy and confidentiality [9, 12, 13]. Smartphones have also been used for communication in healthcare. One study found that using the smartphones can actually reduce physicians' response time compared with using pagers [14]; other studies found that using the smartphones for communication improved the perception of the users of an effective communication, increase the staff satisfaction, and made them believe the work is easier and more efficient [15, 16].

The Smartwatch is a new type of mobile and wearable devices. The primary use has been monitoring exercises and collecting biometric data, such as steps, distance, and calories consumption [17]. Smartwatch offer more convenient way of direct monitoring, and its acceptance by everyone [18]. Smartwatch have also been used as a continuous monitoring device in health care settings. For example, Samsung Gear smartwatch was used to monitor heart rate using the multi-sensors embedded in the watch and send the information to a host through a wireless networks [19]. It was used for patients with advanced Parkinson's disease, who are at high risk of falls. Those patients need a real-time gait monitoring to reduce the chance of falls. Smartwatch serve as a promising candidate of the monitoring device because it is easier to wear than other sensors placed at foot, ankle, and thigh [20]. Epic Haiku app, developed for Apple iWatch, notifies doctors about lab results and provides doctors with access to patient's information [27]. AirStrip, another app for iWatch, allows doctors to remotely monitor their patients by receiving a real-time stream of that patient's vital signs [29]. Although the application of smartwatch in healthcare industry is at its early stage, but the literature shows it is promising especially in communication, and it can improve the efficiency of workflow. Smartwatch allows staff such as nurses to use voice control while navigating the interface, send updates quickly, and receive alarms on different types of events [28]. This way nurses will always have access to up-to-date critical information about patients' conditions, without compromising any comfort as smartwatch are socially acceptable and comfortable to wear [21]. This is why we chose smartwatch as the mobile device for the proposed communication and notification system.

2   Methods

A User-Centered Design (UCD) methodology was used in consultation with healthcare professionals at local nursing homes. We began by interviewing clinical nursing professors who have extensive experience with nursing homes, and nursing home staff such as registered nurse (RNs), certified nurse aids (CNAs), unit managers and other administrative staff. We also conducted observations in local nursing homes to analyze the work system and identify human factors challenges in fall prevention. We particularly paid attention to the call light systems and how staff interacts with the system. The analysis of the work system showed that a mobile device-based system that relied less on auditory displays would be necessary for communication and notification in nursing homes. We chose smartwatch as the mobile device because of hands-free, personal, and wearable nature. The analysis also helped us define the types of tasks the smartwatch should do/provide, the action sequences, specific flow of alarming process, and level of information that should be provided with each alarm. The details of the interviews and observations can be found in [22]. In this and next section, we only provide the most relevant information.

2.1   Observations

A structural observations were conducted in four nursing homes in upstate New York. Three of the facilities were proprietary, one was public, and one was voluntary. The number of beds ranges between 150–380 beds. The authors conducted around 200 h of observations during the three shifts to collect information about (1) general information about the units such as the layout, (2) the type of call light systems each nursing home use, (3) how the system notify the staff about a call light, (3) how the staff locate the room of call light, (4) how the staff is notified about other alarms in the unit, and how they locate the alarms, (5) the call light system and other alarms in use to identify usability issues. During the observations, detailed notes were taken using a notebook, and then transformed into an electronic version immediately. Then the data were analyzed and sorted into themes.

2.2   Iterative Design

We used an iterative design and evaluation approach. Three iterations were completed. For each iteration, we used heuristic evaluation and cognitive walkthrough to evaluate the prototype. The first two prototypes were generated using PowerPoint, and the third one was made using InVision. A paper prototype was made based on the first design and was evaluated and tested by the research team using a real scenario. A brain storming session was conducted with the research team to discuss all the issues identified with the first prototype. The design was modified and improved and then tested again. The second design was tested with a nursing student who had experience working in nursing homes, and a nursing professor has extensive clinical and research experience with geriatric care particularly in nursing home care. Significant changes to the display design were made after the second iteration (see Smartwatch Interface section). For the third iteration, we transformed our static screens into an interactive interface using InVision. The prototype was then evaluated by the team, and by the same nursing professor.

2.3   Cognitive Walkthrough

In a cognitive walkthrough, the "user" interacted with the design to explore the product and to identify factors that contribute to errors. The cognitive walkthrough consists of six steps: (1) to develop full understanding to users knowledge, (2) to identify the tasks they perform, (3) to create a detailed scenarios about the tasks, (4) To walkthrough the correct action sequence to finish the task, (5) to identify the cognitive process the users need to go through to accomplish the tasks successfully, (6) identify the learning and adaptive responses while doing the tasks [29].

Cognitive walkthrough was completed using paper prototypes and a case scenario. The scenario was done in unit with an L-shape hallway. The unit had 36 residents, 4 CNAs and 1 LPN. Each CNA was assigned 9 residents. The scenario specified the location of each one of the residents in the floor. The subject played the role of a CNA and was assigned 1 resident with a bed exit alarm, 4 with a chair exit alarm. The subjects had multiple tasks that required responding to 2 bed exit alarm, 3 chair exit alarm, and 5 call lights from the bedroom, 1 call light from the bathroom, and 1 fall incident.

3   Results

3.1   Observation Results

Nursing homes usually use many fall-prevention technologies, that send an alarm to notify the nurses about the residents conditions and if they are at risk of fall. Chair pads and bed mats are thin sheet with pressure sensors, which are able to send an alarm when the residents attempt to stand or exit bed [22]. Clip alarm, is a string clipped to the shoulder of a resident's shirt. When the residents' trunk moves forward while sitting, the string will pull the magnet off the base and trigger the alarm.

In addition to the sensors above, the call light system is another notification system extensively used in nursing homes. The call light system consists of an auditory alarm broadcast at the nurse station or loudly from speakers at different locations of nursing homes to inform the nurses of a call light, and a light with two parts (a white light to indicate call light from the bedroom, and a red light to indicate call light from the bathroom) above the door to each resident's room to help the nurse to locate the room of alarm. One of the nursing homes is using a console placed at nurse station, this console is able to display the room number to help the nurses in locating the room more easily. Another one is using pagers that displays call lights and room numbers.

Many human factors challenges are associated with those systems. Noises from the auditory systems are almost constant. This causes discomfort of the residents and the staff. Staff can also develop alarm fatigue and thus tend to ignore the alarm as they assume resident do not need. With a system that use only auditory alarms at the nurse station instead of broadcasting the alarms, the noise is less in the unit, however the response time to call light is long because the nurse station is not staffed most of the time. Using a pager can reduce the noise and also display the room number, but nursing home staff is always busy providing service for residents, and they cannot grab the pager to see the room number. In most the nursing homes, CNAs tend to locate the room by looking at lights on the top of the doors, which is also challenging at times due to the layout. Nurses and CNAs have to walk to the middle of the hallway to see the light because of beams and door frames block some lights from being seen.

Call light systems in nursing homes also have many usability issues. All the call light system that were observed provide an auditory signal, but none of them provide any directional information for the staff [22, 23]. In addition, the auditory signal does not distinguish call light from the bedroom from call light from the bathroom, which is often represents more urgent needs. In one of the nursing homes, they use a console at the nurse station that has a display, but it can only display one room number at a time. In case of new alarm comes in, it will "cover" the pervious room number from the display and keep the newest one without any indication of the previous ones. Chair and bed mats have similar usability issues: lack of directional information, nuisance alarms and false alarms.

In summary, the staff are always busy taking care of residents thus are not hands free. They have difficulties hearing the auditory alarms, particularly from the end of the hallway. The nurse station is not always occupied, thus a central display may not work for monitoring. Smartwatches can be a creative solution for most of the problems and issues associated with call light system, and the communication breakdowns in nursing homes.

3.2 Proposed Design

We proposed a system for fall prevention and notification in nursing homes. The system uses smart sensors for predicting falls by detecting resident's intention to stand up at its early stage (see details in [23]) and includes a central display and smartwatch interfaces to present this and other alarms. The alarms include chair pads and bed mats, call lights, wander guard system, and clip alarms. They will be sent to a server in the facility then displayed based on the nature and time.

3.3 Smartwatch Interface

Design Version One. The representation of any alarms on the smartwatch (Fig. 1A) displays information about the resident, type of alarm, room number, time passed after the alarm was triggered, and the assigned CNA. The smartwatch will also present an auditory signal and a vibrotactile signal to inform the CNA of any new alarm. The CNA will be instructed to look at his/her watch to locate and identify the alarm. The display size was designed based on Samsung Gear S2 smartwatch. Three alarms can be displayed at the same time, since it is not common to have more than three alarms at the same time. CNAs can delete the alarm by swipe the alarm message to the left or to the right. After several brainstorming session with the research team/the observers at nursing homes, we added a feature that informs the CNA about her assigned residents by highlighting the name of the CNA first (Fig. 1B). This then was changed to highlighting the entire message to become more salient (Fig. 1C).

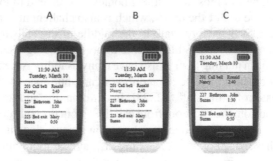

Fig. 1. Smartwatch display design. Version one, first Stage

A cognitive walkthrough was conducted to evaluate the paper prototype of the first version of the proposed design. With a case scenario, feedback was collected on the size of the smartwatch, whether the displayed information was enough and clear to be understood by the CNAs, the logic of the action sequences, and the specific flow of alarming process.

One important comment from the cognitive walkthrough was to add an icon that represents each type of the alarms to support at-a-glance monitoring. A brainstorming session with the team was conducted again, the icons were chosen and placed at the middle of the alarm message first (Fig. 2A) then they were moved to the right or to the left side of the message (Fig. 2B), and then the team decided to be consistent with the different smartphones in the market, and place the icons at the left side of the alarm message (Fig. 2C). In addition to the position of the icons, the team decided to highlight the chair exit alarm since it is very critical one and to make it more noticeable by the CNAs.

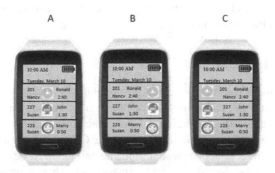

Fig. 2. Smartwatch Design. Version one, second stage

Design Version Two. The second paper prototype was prepared, and tested using a real case scenario from one of the team members based on their experience in nursing homes. Many usability issues were identified at this stage such as lack of error tolerance if the user deleted the wrong alarm; too many highlighted alarm messages in the display (assigned residents, bed exit alarm) which might confuse the CNAs; lack of solution for more than three alarms; and what if one resident need something urgent and pushed the call light again. A few significant changes were introduced to the design. A scroll down/ scroll up feature was added in case there were more than three alarms at the same time (Fig. 3A and B). In addition to adding the option of using the call light for a second time after certain wait time, a second timer was added, which would flash to be more salient (Fig. 3C). A confirmation message was added when deleting an alarm to reduce the chance of deleting another alarm by mistake. The color of the bed exist alarm icon was changed to be red because it is one of the most urgent alarms in nursing homes (Fig. 3D). Three different auditory alarms and vibro-tactile signals will also be used for notifying CNAs about different events such as bed exit alarm, chair exit alarm, and call bell alarm.

Fig. 3. Smartwatch design. Version two

The third paper prototype was created and tested by experts in nursing home care.. The prototype was tested by nursing students who already had experience working in nursing homes, and faculty members who had extensive clinical and research experience with nursing home setting. Cognitive walkthrough was conducted with the participants using specific tasks designed based on work scenarios observed in nursing homes. Participants were also asked specific questions about their understanding of the alarms and the events through the scenario. Based on the evaluation process and their own clinical experience, the participants suggested that the icons for both bed and chair exit alarm should be red and they should look the same since both indicate urgent nursing alarms (Fig. 3B).

Design Version Three. The third version of the design was well received by nursing experts in geriatric care and staff at local nursing homes. They suggested that the smart-watch be used for more communication and notification functions, such as the Wander Guard system, contacting colleagues, and calling for help. The new design shown in Fig. 4 includes a main display that consists of icons of all functions, including (1) "Assignment" that allows CNAs choose residents assigned to him/her; (2) "Alarms", for informing and notifying CNAs about different call bells and nurse alert alarms; (3) "Contacts" that contains all important phone numbers; (4) "Wander Guard" for notifying about residents who might be exiting the building; (5) "Help", with which CNAs can send a message calling for help from other CNAs; and (6) "Emergency", for notifying the staff about any emergency in the facility such as a fall.

Fig. 4. Smartwatch design. Version three

When the staff receive their smartwatch at the beginning of the shift, the first step is to sign in to their account. They will fist click on the 'Assignment' icon to open the resident list, and choose their assigned residents by clicking on their names, and then done to exit the 'Assignment' App. Any new alarm, emergency, or any notifications will be appear at the upper left corner of the screen (Fig. 5A). The CNA then would need to swipe down to open the new notification, or she can click on the icon for App. For example, if she received an alarm about a fall, she can swipe down or she can click on the "ER" icon to see more details about the incident (Fig. 5A and B).

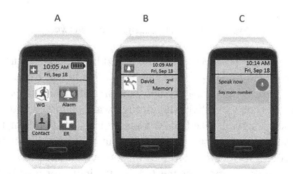

Fig. 5. Smartwatch. Version three

The "Alarm" App will be used to notify the staff about any alarm in their unit, such as chair/bed exit and call lights. It will display all the alarms in the unit and highlight alarms from residents assigned to the CNA who uses the App. This highlighting is customized for each user. Each staff member is supposed to respond to any alarms in the unit, no matter whether the resident was assigned to them or not. So, the same auditory sound will be used to notify the CNA about all the alarms in the unit, with only different sound for the bed or chair exit as they are considered more urgent.

The 'WG' App notifies the staff about any residents who wear an ankle band approaching exits or exiting the building. In the current system, when a resident with high risk of wander is close to an exit when the exit door is open, a very loud auditory alarm is triggered and can be heard throughout the entire unit or floor. Sending the signal to the watch can again help reduce noise level.

The 'Contact' App will provide the speed dial for all the important contacts in the facility such as the RN on duty, unit manager, physician, or the administrators. The staff can use voice command to call in case of emergency.

'Help' App. will be used to ask for help in the same unit. It was observed in many cases CNAs looking for help from another staff member in the unit, (e.g. asking for help in using lifting machine). CNAs can use voice command after clicking on the icon to send the room number. A message will be sent to all the staff in the unit (Fig. 5C).

4   Conclusions

Poor quality of care and safety in nursing homes is an ongoing problem that is growing nationwide [6, 25, 26]. Poor communication is found to be a major contributor to errors that affect safety and quality of care. Effective staff-resident communication, sharing patient's data, and collaboration among the staff were found to be important in improving the outcomes. Smartwatch are hands-free devices that facilitate communication and notification in nursing homes. We designed a smartwatch interface as part of a communication and notification system for nursing homes. The interface presents informative visual, auditory and tactile alarms on various types of events to the user without causing too much noise for non-users (the residents or other staff members). It allows the staff to access the right information at the right time, and to be informed about the residents' conditions and any updates on their condition all the time, to be informed about any adverse events or alarms in the unit, and to communicate with their colleagues.

The effects of the system will be tested using a high-fidelity prototype through simulation experiment. Nursing home staff such as CNAs will use the smartwatch and receive alarms while performing hypothetical tasks. Their behavior, particularly response to alarm messages, will be recorded and analyzed. The system is expected to reduce response time to call lights and other alarms, and help nursing home staff to manage interruptions such as call light requests, and prioritize multiple ongoing tasks.

Acknowledgement. The authors would like to thank the participants for their time and help. We would also like to thank Dr. Ann Myers and the administrative staff at the nursing homes for their advice and support. This work was supported by Binghamton University's Interdisciplinary Collaboration Grants (Project No. 1119297).

References

1. Vincent, G.K., Velkoff, V.A.: The next four decades: The older population in the United States: 2010 to 2050. Current population reports P25-1138. US Census Bureau, Washington (2010)
2. Decker, F.H.: Nursing homes, 1977–99: What has Changed, What has not? National Center for Health Statistics, Hyattsville (2005)
3. Wagner, L., McDonald, S., Castle, N.: Relationship between nursing home safety culture and joint commission accreditation. Jt. Comm. J. Qual. Patient Saf. **38**(5), 207–215 (2012)

4. Rubenstein, L.Z., Josephson, K.R., Robbins, A.S.: Falls in the nursing home. Ann. Intern. Med. **121**, 442–451 (1994)
5. Rubenstein, L.Z., Robbins, A.S., Schulman, B.L., Rosado, J., Osterweil, D., Josephson, K.R.: Falls and instability in the elderly. J. Am. Geriatr. Soc. **36**, 266–278 (1988)
6. Chung, G.: Nursing assistant views on nursing home regulatory inspection knowledge and attitudes regarding the state nursing home survey. J. Appl. Gerontol. **31**(3), 336–353 (2012)
7. Wu, R.C., Tran, K., Lo, V., O'Leary, K.J., Morra, D., Quan, S.D., Perrier, L.: Effects of clinical communication interventions in hospitals: a systematic review of information and communication technology adoptions for improved communication between clinicians. Int. J. Med. Inf. **81**(11), 723–732 (2012)
8. Richardson, J.E., Ash, J.S.: The effects of hands free communication devices on clinical communication: balancing communication access needs with user control. In: AMIA Annual Symposium Proceedings, pp. 621–625 (2008)
9. Richardson, J.E., Shah-Hosseini, S., Fiadjoe, J.E., Ash, J.S., Rehman, M.A.: The effects of a hands-free communication device system in a surgical suite. J. Am. Med. Inf. Assoc. JAMIA **18**(1), 70–72 (2011)
10. Yang, Y., Rivera, A.J.: An observational study of hands-free communication devices mediated interruption dynamics in a nursing work system. Health Policy Technol. **4**(4), 378–386 (2015)
11. Breslin, S., Greskovich, W., Turisco, F.: Wireless technology improves nursing workflow and communications. Comput. Inf. Nurs. CIN **22**(5), 275–281 (2004)
12. Jacques, P.S., France, D.J., Pilla, M., Lai, E., Higgins, M.S.: Evaluation of a hands-free wireless communication device in the perioperative environment. Telemed. J. E Health **12**(1), 42–49 (2006)
13. Vandenkerkhof, E.G., Hall, S., Wilson, R., Gay, A., Duhn, L.: Evaluation of an innovative communication technology in an acute care setting. Comput. Inf. Nurs. **27**(4), 254–262 (2009)
14. Aziz, O., Panesar, S.S., Netuveli, G., Paraskeva, P., Sheikh, A., Darzi, A.: Handheld computers and the 21st century surgical team: a pilot study. BMC Med. Inf. Decis. Making **5**, 28 (2005)
15. O'Connor, C., Friedrich, J.O., Scales, D.C., Adhikari, N.K.J.: The use of wireless e-mail to improve healthcare team communication. J. Am. Med. Inf. Assoc. JAMIA **16**(5), 705–713 (2009)
16. Wu, R.C., Morra, D., Quan, S., Lai, S., Zanjani, S., Abrams, H., Rossos, P.G.: The use of smartphones for clinical communication on internal medicine wards. J. Hosp. Med. **5**(9), 553–559 (2010)
17. Stegemann, S.: The future of pharmaceutical manufacturing in the context of the scientific, social, technological and economic evolution. Eur. J. Pharm. Sci. http://dx.doi.org.proxy.binghamton.edu/10.1016/j.ejps.2015.11.003
18. Bradway, M., Årsand, E., Grøttland, A.: Mobile health: empowering patients and driving change. Trends Endocrinol. Metab. **26**(3), 114–117 (2015)
19. Varga, N., Bokor, L., Takács, A.: Context-aware IPv6 flow mobility for multi-sensor based mobile patient monitoring and tele-consultation. Procedia Comput. Sci. **40**, 222–229 (2014)
20. Mazilu, S., Blanke, U., Calatroni, A., Gazit, E., Hausdorff, J.M., Tröster, G.: The role of wrist-mounted inertial sensors in detecting gait freeze episodes in Parkinson's disease. Pervasive Mob. Comput. http://dx.doi.org.proxy.binghamton.edu/10.1016/j.pmcj.2015.12.007
21. Johnson, K.: Literature review: an investigation into the usefulness of the smart watch interface for university students and the types of data they would require (2014). http://img1.wikia.nocookie.net/__cb20140801120101/mobile-computing-prediction/images/c/c7/Literature_Review_KMJ.pdf (2014)

22. Li, H., Ali, H.: Human factors considerations in the design of falls prevention technologies for nursing homes: a case study. In: Proceedings of 2015 Symposium on Human Factors and Ergonomics in Health Care (2015)
23. Ali, H., Li, H.: Developing a fall prevention system for nursing homes. In: Proceedings of Human Factors and Ergonomics Society's 59th Annual Meeting. Human Factors and Ergonomics Society, Los Angeles (2015)
24. Smith-Jackson, T.L.: Cognitive walkthrough method (CWM). In: Stanton, N., Hedge, A., Brookhuis, K., Salas, E., Hendrik, H. (eds.) Handbook of Human Factors and Ergonomics Methods. CRC Press, Boca Raton (2005)
25. Castle, N.G., Wagner, L.M., Ferguson, J.C., Handler, S.M.: Nursing home deficiency citations for safety. J. Aging Soc. Policy **23**, 34–57 (2011)
26. Gruneir, A., Mor, V.: Nursing home safety: current issues and barriers to improvement. Ann. Rev. Publ. Health **29**, 369–382 (2008)
27. Ochsner health System. http://www.apple.com/business/ochsner/
28. American Sentinel University: Is Wearable Technology the Future of Nursing? http://www.americansentinel.edu/blog/2014/12/10/is-wearable-technology-the-future-of-nursing/
29. Apple shows off AirStrip's vital sign monitoring Apple Watch app. http://mobihealthnews.com/46687/apple-shows-off-airstrips-vital-sign-monitoring-apple-watch-app

Tactile Interaction for Novice User

Uncolocated Gestures

Denis Chêne[1]([⊠]), Vincent Pillot[2], and Marc-Éric Bobillier Chaumon[2]

[1] Orange Labs, 28 Ch. du Vieux Chêne, 38243 Meylan, France
denis.chene@orange.com
[2] GRePS (EA 4163), 5 av. P. Mendès-France, 69676 Bron, France
vincent@pacmail.fr, marc-eric.bobillier-chaumon@univ-lyon2.fr

Abstract. This paper introduces the concept of tactile interaction for novice elderly users. Cognitive difficulties, motor constraints, visual overloads and lacks of feedback lead to hardly usable tactile smartphone among elderly users. An optimized tactile interface was produced, offering continuous and secure gestures, and introducing "uncolocated gestures". Comparative tests to a classic tactile interface show that those gestures solves interaction problems but generates other difficulties. Uncolocation is a solution of interest but has to be learned and has to be progressively acquired through activity. A final enhanced profile for Elderly users was set and solves this situation, enabling uncolocation manipulation for Back and Up-Down commands and preventing it for Validation command, until it is totally acquired by the user.

Keywords: Handheld devices for the elderly · Use and design of smart phones for the elderly · Novice profile · MenuDFA · Tactile interaction

1 Introduction

Elderly users are often novices in smart phones use and they face touchscreen use as a hard experiment [1]. One may talk of illectronism, a kind of numerical world illiteracy. In fact, taps, multi-finger taps, repeated taps, slides, swipes, multi-touch gestures and others abstract interface objects are certainly many sources of confusion [2, 3]. Indeed, to interact tactilely on a touchscreen is not so easy and it requests good visual-motor abilities. Due to this, hence elderly user and other novices are left out. Firstly, this paper analyzes why tactile interaction generates troubles. Secondly an alternative tactile interaction mechanism is described. Then a user comparative user test between a classical tactile interface and an optimized tactile interface for novice user is described. Finally results and limitations of the innovative interaction method are discussed and solved.

2 Limitations of Classical Tactile Interface

Standard interaction method pushes novice user (and also expert user) to do numerous types of errors. Indeed many inadvertent actions are done by novice use. As the "tap"

© Springer International Publishing Switzerland 2016
J. Zhou and G. Salvendy (Eds.): ITAP 2016, Part I, LNCS 9754, pp. 412–423, 2016.
DOI: 10.1007/978-3-319-39943-0_40

gesture required by standard touchscreen devices is short delayed it leads to many missed validations and missed backward navigation. This is direct consequence of merging selection and validation phases in a single operation. Through a personal computer interaction mediated with a mouse, it is not really a problem as user can point out, move his mouse over an item (pointing phase), and then clicks it (selection phase) or double-clicks it (selection-validation phase). During web browsing through hyperlinks the double click is useless as in this case selection-validation phase is achieved through a single click. But the user can still move is mouse over the item before acting, in order to obtain some information about the pointed item.

Tactile Device. On the opposite on a tactile device, the user loses this opportunity to point over the item[1]. In parallel he is losing as well the choice to have a single or a double click. Touching the screen is a trigger threshold. Or, on the contrary, novice user is in a situation of discovering and learning. He needs time to decide and clear information about available functions. How to be aware about new elements if they are directly triggered? He needs time to ask for information before execution, and even time during the command execution. Finally, on a classical tactile interface the user will have probably to get that information himself, mainly through errors and missed actions. He has to go there, in order to know where he goes. This lack of division between information, selection and validation phases leads to an interaction style that could be named "blind arbitrarily exploration".

Moreover, the gesture itself of "doing a tap" on a screen is not so easy to operate for a novice user. It needs some cognitive, motor and visual accuracy. Novice users start from real buttons metaphor and apply it to tactile buttons. Real buttons are much easier to operate as they offer many feedbacks (pressure, abutment). But tactile buttons are refrained from giving any details and finally mislead user. Indeed, despite of their "real button" affordance, that should lead to push them, they are not push-able but push-off-able. Main action is triggered after the tap-off phase, not before. But second level action (as Edit mode or Contextual menu) is triggered after a long duration tap-on phase. Then novice users are frequently doing a long press as they will do for a "real button", but are faced with a non-expected second level action. Tap nature (on or off) and tap duration are not the only trap. Lack of information about requisite pressure leads novice user to press too hard, generating side effect of a wider contact zone, and pointing errors.

Pointing errors have many other causes. Ergonomics real buttons are often curved and have a concave shape in order to help the finger to fit in and to feel the limits. That is not the case on a tactile interface where, in addition, items are smaller. To slip even slightly is not recommended. Moreover on a tactile phone the hand hide a part of the pointed item, which further accentuates pointing errors. Moreover, tactile virtual buttons at the bottom of the phone are often invisible and are erroneously activated. Consequently, standard tactile interface overstretch cognitive, motor and visual user capacities.

User Capacities. If that is not bad enough, user capacities themselves may be altered. It is often the case with elderly users [3]. Finger shaking, lack of finger sensibility, low

---

[1] Some recent new technologies will offer to detect that the finger is just over the screen, without touching it. It may be an outcome.

pointing capacities, or finger electrical conductivity, visual impairment, and audio disabilities are minor and major disabilities that often goes hand in hand with elderly. Largely speaking short and localized gestures should be avoided in case of accessibility needs [4].

Situation of Use. Situation of use has also to be taken into account. Indeed even if novice users are often trying to use their mobile phone with two hands, they are often glad to do it with a single hand [5] as mobility is related to multitask activities. By example user will make a call and will walk at the same time, sharing is attention between the street interactional path and the virtual tactile one [6]. Daily, users will also hold something in one hand and have to answer a call with the other one. When user is sited, his mobile phone use is totally different from a standing use [7].

Such contextual use leads generally to one-handed use [8]. In such situation, interaction is achieved through thumb activity and this has consequences on comfort of use [9] and on performance [10]. Indeed, comfort of use may be severely altered. As an example dramatic increase of thumb interaction may multiply the occurrence of related musculo-skeletal disorders [11]. Indeed a pointing interface where interaction items to be pointed out are spread all over the screen is not really adapted to thumb limitations.

Divided in 12 parts (Fig. 1) the screen shows structural deficiencies for tap activity through the thumb. Only 5 and 8 zones seem accurately tap-able [12]. But researchers explored other kinds of gestures: horizontal and vertical swipes. 3, 5, 6, 7, & 8 zones seem accurately swipe-able [13]. It has to be noted that this is true for novice users as well as for expert users.

Fig. 1. Partition in 12 zones of the smartphone screen [10]

Classical tactile interface displays tiny items all over the screen, and use short time-lapse gestures, that are also strongly localized and that finally lead to many execution and pointing constraints. On the contrary vertical and horizontal swipe may be more easily executed, through the thumb with one hand, or through other fingers in case of a two-handed use. Metatla et al. even recommend using a "no direct pointing" interface [14]. It means to be able to act without being dependent from the item and the finger co-location (uncolocation command). Moreover, such continuous gestures are not generating any trouble in case of disability user constraints [3], provided that they are not too long [15].

3   An Optimized Tactile Interface for Novice Users

What could be an optimized tactile interface for novice user? First, classical tactile interface need to be optimized in terms of cognition. Few interface objects are easier to understand than many. Vertical list component is a good candidate to better understanding as it is quite the only component that can be a substitute to every kind of interface objects.

It needs also to be optimized in terms of available basic commands. Information phase need to be available and usable before command execution. If Selection and Validation phases are dissociated one from each other, hence, after Selection phase achievement, user has the choice to choose between Information or Validation phase.

Such an optimized interface needs as well to be optimized in terms of gesture execution through continuous gestures (as drag and swipes gestures), through uncolocated items manipulations or at least few pointing constraints, and with sufficient time delays.

Taking into account all those arguments leads to define a tactile interface that is managed only through cascading lists components, with a user-controlled focus, and a secure tactile manipulation made of long presses and swipes. Such a tactile interface optimized for novice elderly users (N interface) was designed based on the MenuDfA component [16]. It applies to user interfaces whose functions (e.g. list items, menu options, settings) can be organized in a hierarchical way (e.g. top levels lists and sub lists). As there is no "average" user it offers several interaction profiles optimized to each kind of user. Beyond the "Design for All" principle, MenuDfA technique provides a mean for adjusting finely each interaction profile, and more specifically gestures that can be executed through continuous focus handling or in a discrete manner (shortcut gesture, as a rapid swipe). It organizes the various items of the intended application in the form of a set of hierarchical lists where the items of each list are displayed vertically. It provides a sequential access to the interface elements, as well as a direct access. In both cases selection and validation may be set to two separated operations. Interaction mode can be set to pointless or pointed at, and in this case, uncolocated or colocated actions can be chosen. Thus it covers a large diversity of user needs and situations.

A selection focus enables user to navigate the entire application just by moving the focus in the four directions. Vertical displacements are used for moving through the items of the current list, and horizontal displacements for moving through the hierarchy of lists. A slide towards Up moves the focus up, to the previous item; a slide towards Down moves the focus down to the next item; a slide towards Right validates the current item and goes down into list hierarchy; and a slide toward Left goes back and up in the hierarchy. In such a context, absolute positioning isn't mandatory. Indeed, all the gestures make use of relative positioning. It means that they can begin anywhere on the screen, the finger and the focus has no colocation constraint.

A dedicated profile to novice users was set. It is called hereafter "N interface". Tactile interaction in the N interface was designed to answer to novice constraints. They need time to ask for information and to be secured thus selection time was separated from validation time. This is achieved through a replacement of tap-shot by continuous focus manipulation. They need time then standard tap was replaced by a long tap delay (800 ms). They need support to pointing inaccuracy then large items were designed and inaccuracy pointing square was added. They need access to any screen zone through the thumb, then uncolocation of the finger and the aimed item was allowed. Available navigation commands of the N interface are the following: the user has to first move the focus to the aimed item, with a continuous vertical gesture (Up or Down) or a Short Press in case of direct pointing (less than 800 ms). But no validation occurs at this time. Only a vocalization of the current focused item is displayed to the user. The Up or Down gestures may be colocated (Fig. 2) or uncolocated (Fig. 3).

Fig. 2. Colocated continuous up-down focus manipulation (selection) and colocated right gesture (validation)

Fig. 3. Uncolocated continuous up-down focus manipulation (selection) and uncolocated Right gesture (validation)

When the short press is executed on a previously selected item, then it repeats vocalization of the focused item. It enables user to ask for information as many as he likes. Then he can validate the focused item with his choice of a continuous colocated (Fig. 2) or uncolocated (Fig. 3) gesture to the right. This validation can also be done with a colocated-only long press (Fig. 4).

Fig. 4. Colocated Press (less than 800 ms) for selection and Hold (more than 800 ms) for validation

The back command is a continuous gesture to the left similar to the right one. It can be either colocated to the focused item or uncolocated. We will see that even if Left and Right gestures are similar, their inherent commands attribution (respectively Back and Validation commands) has a great impact on understanding and manipulation. Note that there is no need of a Back button, and consequently such Back button wasn't displayed at all on the N interface.

4 Comparative User Test

In order to perform a meaningful comparison of the tactile interaction modes, an equivalent classical tactile interface was also designed (C interface). On the C interface only the Short Press (Tap) is available to achieve validation, and back action (on the back button) in a unique selection/validation phase. It needs precise pointing and fine motor abilities and has a high potential for unintended mistakes. Back action is available on the screen with a back button on the top left part of the screen. C and N interfaces are designed with the same functionalities enabling making a phone call from number dialing, or from contact selection, or from past phone call list. Contact list is available and contacts are editable.

The only visual differences between those two interfaces (Fig. 5) is the existence in the N interface of a focus element (a rectangle), of some visual feedbacks associated to continuous manipulation, and the lack of any back button. This novice optimized tactile interface (N) was compared to classical tactile interface (C). Experimental plan was the following: $S_{10}<I_2*T5>$. N and C interfaces (I factor) were both used one after another by 10 elderly touchscreen expert users and 10 elderly touchscreen novice users (S). Users were from 70 years old (expert average; $\sigma = 6{,}70$) to 74 years old (novice average; $\sigma = 7{,}63$). Novice users had never touched any touchscreen devices. Expert users were used to use a tactile mobile phone. 5 tasks (T) had to be made on each interface. First they had to find a recent call in the call history list. Second they had to find a radio station in the radio list hide in the sub-level of the Menu item. Third they had to dial a number and to call someone. Fourth they had to find a specific contact in the call history list and to add it to the contact list, but they had to do it in a one-handed situation. Fifth, they had to modify a contact in the contact list.

Fig. 5. N and C interfaces comparison

N and C interfaces order was counterbalanced. And before each of them some explanations about the tactile interaction mode was given to user. For the N interface the explanation was: «you have to move the focus in order to select the item you want. Then validate it doing a gesture to the right side». If the user had some difficulties to execute this pre-test, then it was added: «you can also do a long press to validate». For the C interface the explanation was: «you have to tap on the screen in order to validate the item you want». Time, task achievement, and errors were recorded on log files, and on videotapes. In the N condition 9 types of errors were coded. Type 1 is when the user wants to validate an item X, but forget to manipulate the focus that is still on item Y, and thus validates Y instead of X. Type 2 is when the user wants to validate an item X, points at it, but due to pointing inaccuracy during press, validates another close item. Type 3 is when the user tries to validate the selected item by a Right gesture, but switches to another one because its gesture starts too slowly and with inaccuracy. Actually its gesture has generated a Press & Hold on another item, leading to a missed validation. Type 4 is when the user tries a Tap in order to validate the current focused item. Type 5 is when the user operates a Tap or another gesture on the title zone of the screen that has no linked command. The user probably seeks for the Back button of the C interface. Type 7 is when the user wants to validate with a Right gesture and makes a Left one. Conversely for Type 8, the user wants to do a back with a Left gesture and makes a Right one. Type 9 is when the user wants to glide the focus over items but due to a too slow execution the item underneath finger is unfortunately selected.

In the C condition 10 types of errors were coded. Type 1 is about pointing inaccuracy: another item than the one aimed to is validated during a Tap. Type 2 is a missed vertical manipulation (up-in-the list with drag Down gesture) of the list that generates an unexpected validation. Type 3 is the same for down-in-the list (drag Up gesture). Type 4 is when the user does a wrong validation of an item during an attempt to go back with the back button softkey. Type 5 is the same in case of the use of the back button in the Title zone. Type 6 error is when the user tries to do a validation with a Right gesture that is totally inoperative in this C condition (persistence of the N interface procedure for part of the users that start with N condition). Type 7 is similar to the previous one, but for the Left gesture. Type 8 is when the user tries to navigate vertically in the list but is stopped by the list end or top abutment. Type 9 is when user tries to do a Tap on the title (inoperative). Type 10 is when the user tries to activate another non-actable item. Those errors where merged in more generic categories in order to be compared. Pointing inaccuracies (N types 2, 3 and C types 1,2,3,4,5), focus adjustment difficulties (N types 9 and C types 2,3,8), interaction methods confusion (N types 4 and C types 6,7), non-actable items (N types 5,6 and C types 9, 10), specific N condition errors, types 7,8 about laterality confusion and type 1 missed validations due to uncolocation.

4.1   Results

A Wilcoxon signed ranks test shows that in N condition novice errors were as numbered as in C condition (novice N errors M = 1.75, SD = 2.37 and C errors M = 1.78, SD = 2.34) whatever was the task (Fig. 6). That was not expected as uncolocation and Selection-Validation dissociation were here to solve gesture inaccuracies and unintended mistakes in the N condition.

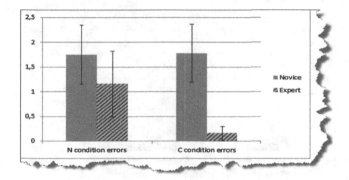

Fig. 6. Means (all) errors comparison between N and C condition for novice and expert users

And even expert users are doing more errors in N condition. That was expected as some gestures (up and down) are reversed compared to C condition but we can see in the details results that it's mainly due to other causes. Detailed results show that new kinds of error appear in N condition, and are mainly due to uncolocated actions, for novice and expert users. One main observation of this study is that uncolocated actions are very difficult to understand for both novice and expert user. Both are constantly stuck to direct pointing. This behavior was awaited for expert user of standard tactile pointing interface, as they are used to directly point at items, but it wasn't for novice users. But at the beginning of the task the "focus" element existence is not so obvious for them. They manipulate it clearly with vertical slides ($\wedge\vee$), but in a located manner. They put precisely their finger on the focus and start to drag it to another item. They start to acquire that sliding vertically the focus may be done in an uncolocated way only when they are facing long lists and have to scroll them. At this point they understand slightly that they can move the focus without being stuck to it. But this possibility is not easily extended to validation phase. And many missed validations occur because the user was rapidly doing a right slide gesture directly on an item (that was not already focused). Doing so, they were validating another item without realizing that it was not the focused one. The Right gesture without colocation constraint ($\rightarrow$) is a trap for novice and expert users until they have not acquired that the focus can be used in an uncolocated manner. On the contrary the Left uncolocated gesture ← doesn't generate error at all, as it is never dependent to location. Indeed it just goes back to the previous level. Starting from the focused item or not doesn't change anything in that case.

Details results show also that those errors due to Right gesture hide the effect of other interesting points of the N interface. If one centered on other expected errors than errors due to uncolocated Right gesture (uRg), then the N condition fulfills his goal. Indeed Mann-Whitney test shows, that expected errors (as gesture inaccuracies and located missed validation and pointing located errors) are significantly in a smaller amount ($z = 2.42$, $p < .01$) for novice in N condition (errors without uRg errors M = 0.31, SD = 0.77) than for novice in C condition (errors without uRg errors M = 1.78, SD = 2.34). In brief that is to say these usual errors due to short press gestures combining validation and selection (classical Tap) are mainly done on C prototype but not on N prototype, as expected (Fig. 7).

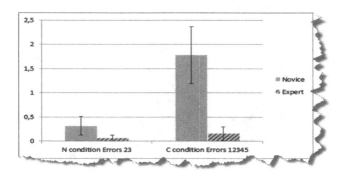

Fig. 7. Mean of expected errors (without uRg errors) in N condition vs C condition for novice and expert users

N condition with its "Selection & Validation" dissociation and its numerous facilitations has served its purpose to substantially reduce expected usual errors. Moreover, on a descriptive point of view, even expert users are doing fewer errors in N condition than in C condition (even if there is no significant difference in their case).

One of the task asked users to operate one-handed with the thumb. Similarly, centered on expected errors without uncolocation errors, results show that in N condition, novice users (M = 0.5, SD = 0.93) are doing quite as much errors as expert users (0), namely almost peanuts. In thumb interaction mode, N condition made the glass ceiling disappear between novice and expert users. It is not the case in the C condition where novice users (M = 3.75, SD = 3.54) are doing significantly more errors ($z = 2.383$, $p < .02$) than expert users (M = 0.625, SD = 1.06). Usual pointing interface (C) is still a trap for novice users, and also for expert users in on-handed situation. On the contrary N condition is well suited both for novice and expert users in a one-handed situation.

4.2 Novice Profile Adjustment

Accordingly to this study the novice profile was easily enhanced. Uncolocation errors on validation command (uRg) were quickly annihilated, switching colocation factor on "off" for the Right gesture. Square incertitude (4 mm) and zoom level were augmented a few in order to reduce even more imprecision errors. Medium tap delay was reduced from 800 ms to 500 ms (some users declare 800 ms was a little bit too long) in order to increase a little bit efficiency. Those user tests lead us also to improve displays specifications (size, contrast, and legible "Accessible DfA" font[2]), audios and tactile feedbacks type and timings.

5 Discussion

Uncolocation is very useful for novice and expert users, mostly in one-handed situation but this focus uncolocation concept needs to be understood in use. N condition experiment was only half an hour and this was a short delay to learn both for novice and expert users. Nevertheless Metatla proposal to use uncolocated navigation has to be carefully implemented. Uncolocation can be used in order to limit pointing errors and to facilitate back command. Indeed Left gesture enables to do a Back without asking for a lot of precision and generates very few manipulation errors. Up and Down command enabling to navigate inside the current list is also enhanced by uncolocation as user needs less precision. Of course, all this needs adequate continuous manipulations and clear feedbacks, feedforwards and affordances.

However, uncolocation for the validation command is a trap for novice and expert user that have not totally acquired this practice. Nevertheless both of them start to acquire it as they were easily doing uncolocated Left gesture and uncolocated Up-Down gestures. As a matter of fact, operative learning transfer was ongoing during this half an hour use of N interface. It starts clearly from the Up-Down navigation inside the current list, at the limits of the screen, when users were trying to reach the next item outside the screen. It was confirmed when users were more and more operating a less controlled Left gesture for going back, thereby freeing their own pointing constraints. The chances are better than not that the next operative learning transfer will be for the validation command. But it has to be brought progressively following a personalized learning curve, perhaps after some hours of use, or some days. Waiting that moment, a solution has to be set for validation command. And this solution must be compatible with a future availability of an uncolocated right gesture that is clearly well suited for thumb usage. This solution is to first reduce validation only to a long Press, and to keep other uncolocated gestures (Up-Down and Left). After some time of use, the adaptative interface will be able to offer to user to add this Right uncolocated gesture. Of course, some user ecological user tests have to be done in order to confirm this assertion.

---

[2] Available at https://github.com/Orange-OpenSource/font-accessible-dfa.

6   Conclusion

Through this experimental study, innovative touchscreen interaction optimized to novice users was defined, tested and adjusted. Right validation gesture, as source of many errors wasn't kept in the final profile. The separation of selection from validation phase was confirmed as appropriate. Long press of 800 ms delay was validated for secure navigation but will gain in efficiency to be a bit shorter. Left for back command was validated. Dragging focus Up and Down was also appropriate for novice users. Simple Tap for getting information about the current focused item was estimated as really useful.

Enhancement of the novice profile was easily done after the test thanks to the general great flexibility offered by the MenuDfA component. Other profiles are currently underway (low vision, blind, illiteracy, motor, cognitive) and should be useful for answering diversity usually found in elderly population.

References

1. Hwangbo, H., Yoon, S.H., Jin, B.B., Han, Y.S., Ji, Y.G.: A study of pointing performance of elderly users on smartphones. Int. J. Hum. Comput. Interact. 29(9), 604–618 (2013)
2. Trewin, S., Swart, C., Pettick, D.: Physical accessibility of touchscreen smartphones. In: Proceedings of the 15th International ACM SIGACCESS Conference on Computer and Accessibility, vol. 19, pp. 1–8 (2013)
3. Kobayashi, M., Hiyama, A., Miura, T., Asakawa, C., Hirose, M., Ifukube, T.: Elderly user evaluation of mobile touchscreen interactions. In: Campos, P., Graham, N., Jorge, J., Nunes, N., Palanque, P., Winckler, M. (eds.) INTERACT 2011, Part I. LNCS, vol. 6946, pp. 83–99. Springer, Heidelberg (2011)
4. MacGookin, D., Brewster, S., Jiang, W.: Investigating touchscreen accessibility for people with visual impairments. In: Proceedings of the 5th Nordic Conference on Human-Computer Interaction: Building Bridges, pp. 298–307 (2008)
5. Karlson, A.K., Bederson, B.B.: ThumbSpace: generalized one-handed input for touchscreen-based mobile devices. In: Baranauskas, C., Abascal, J., Barbosa, S.D.J. (eds.) INTERACT 2007. LNCS, vol. 4662, pp. 324–338. Springer, Heidelberg (2007)
6. Bergstrom-Lehtovirta, J., Oulasvirta, A., Brewster, S.: The effects of walking speed on target acquisition on a touchscreen interface. In: Proceedings of the 13th International Conference on Human Computer Interaction with Mobile Devices and Services, pp. 143–146 (2011)
7. Chourasia, A.O., Wiegmann, D.A., Chen, K.B., Irwin, C.B., Sesto, M.E.: Effect of sitting or standing on touch screen performance and touch characteristics. J. Hum. Factors Ergon. Soc. 55(4), 789–802 (2013)
8. Karlson, A.K., Bederson, B.B., Contreras-Vidal, J.L.: Understanding single-handed mobile device interaction. In Lumsden, J., (Ed) Handbook of Research on User Interface Design and Evaluation for Mobile Technologie, pp. 86–101 (2008)
9. Trudeau, M.B., Young, J.G., Jindrich, D.L., Dennerlein, J.T.: Thumb motor performance varies with thumb and wrist posture during single-handed mobile phone use. J. Biomech. 45, 2349–2354 (2012)
10. Trudeau, M.B., Udtamadilok, T., Karlson, A.K., Dennerlein, J.T.: Thumb motor performance varies by movement orientation, direction, and device size during single-handed mobile phone use. Hum. Factors J. Hum. Factors Ergon. Soc. 54(1), 52–59 (2012)

11. Berolo, S., Wells, R.P., Amick, B.C.: Musculoskeletal symptoms among mobile hand-held device users and their relationship to device use: a preliminary study in a Canadian university population. Appl. Ergon. **42**(2), 371–378 (2011)

12. Park, J., Han, S.H.: Defining user value: a case study of a smartphone. Int. J. Ind. Ergon. **43**(4), 274–282 (2013)

13. Wobbrock, J.O., Myers, B.A., Aung, H.H.: The performance of hand postures in front-and back-of-device interaction for mobile computing. Int. J. Hum. Comput. Stud. **66**(12), 857–875 (2008)

14. Metatla, O., Martin, F., Stockman, T., Bryan-Kinns, N.: Non-visual menu navigation: the effect of and audio-tactile display. In: Proceedings of the 28th International BCS Human Computer Interaction Conference on HCI 2014-Sand, pp. 213–217 (2014)

15. Kane, S.K., Wobbrock, J.O., Ladner, R.E.: Usable gestures for blind people: understanding preference and performance. In: Proceedings of the SIGCHI Conference on Human Factors in Computing System, pp. 413–422 (2011)

16. Petit, É., Chêne, D.: MenuDfA: navigation gestuelle tactile sans contrainte dans un menu linéaire hiérarchique. Article de recherche, Orange Labs. 2014. Archive ouverte HAL <hal-01056978> (2014)

Mobile Technology for Older Adults: Protector, Motivator or Threat?

Lynne Coventry[(✉)] and Pam Briggs

PaCT Lab, Department of Psychology,
Northumbria University, Newcastle upon Tyne, UK
{lynne.coventry, p.briggs}@northumbria.ac.uk

Abstract. New technologies offer an opportunity to improve the wellbeing and independence of older adults, but many of the potential benefits, have not yet been realised. Some technologies suggest a lifestyle of constant monitoring, controlling and nudging - transformations that could be perceived as threatening. To better understand older adult perceptions and attitudes to adoption of such systems, we describe a 3 week field trial of an application and view the results through the lens of protection motivation theory. Our participants identified a number of threats including not being able to live independently, fear of getting lost, being stigmatised and lack of privacy. Usability, accessibility, reliability, costs and usefulness all negatively impacted coping appraisal that would result in non-adoption, despite their stated intention to adopt the technology in the future.

Keywords: Older adults · Service design · Behaviour theories

1 Introduction

Many aspects of social policy address the ageing population, especially in relation to health, social care and housing [1] as the so called 'Golden Generations', e.g. individuals born between 1925 and 1945 [2] are living longer than those born prior to these decades [3]. The aging population is perceived as a burden on current health and social services and people are turning to technology as a possible solution.

Advances in wireless networks and mobile devices has supported the emergence of mobile health services. Technologies including smart homes [4] (Rodrigues and Rui 2013), personal alarms, GPS tracking and smart assistive and mobile technologies [5] offer the potential to support older adults remaining in their own homes for longer and may even lead to healthier behaviours.

More generally, computer use has been associated with a range of benefits for older adults, including: decreased feelings of loneliness [6, 7]; decreased levels of depression [8]; decreased feelings of stress [9]; increased feelings of personal growth and purpose in life [10]; and an increased feeling of independence [11]. While younger, higher-income, and more highly educated older adults in the US use the internet and broadband at rates similar to the general population; internet use and broadband adoption drop off dramatically around age 75 [12]. In this paper we explore these issues by capturing user attitudes and behaviours during a three week field trial of a mobile information support system for older adults, developed during the 'Freedom to Roam' project.

© Springer International Publishing Switzerland 2016
J. Zhou and G. Salvendy (Eds.): ITAP 2016, Part I, LNCS 9754, pp. 424–434, 2016.
DOI: 10.1007/978-3-319-39943-0_41

Freedom to Roam explored the services that would support older adults in maintaining independence and good local community engagement. The aim was to support most commonly held perceptions of aging well: having/maintaining physical health and functioning; taking part in leisure and social activities; maintaining mental functioning and activity and maintaining social relationships and contacts [13]. The project utilized a mobile tablet, linked to a carer control centre (market place) to provide a client (older adult) application that could be personalized with applications based on the location, interests and needs of the individual user. There was also a carer' application that provided the facility to communicate, monitor and manage user devices and that also provided the ability to monitor multiple devices. This system was deployed in a field trial as part of a participatory design study, where we worked with older adults to identify the services that might best support older adults. The aim of the field trial was to evaluate acceptance of this system by clients and carers and this paper presents the clients' experience, seen through the lens of protection motivation theory [14].

2 Background

Older adults do not just adopt new technology because it is 'out there' [15]. Whilst there may be good adoption if they see a use for it [16] the general opinion is that they prefer to stick to the tried and tested traditional approaches. Some designers stress the importance of the value or worth of offerings [17–20], where the emphasis is on creating services and systems that users perceive as worthwhile.

Early work on acceptance stressed both the usefulness and usability of a system was important for adoption [21]. Thus much of the research with older adults has been focused upon age-related perceptual and motor changes (usability/accessibility issues) with resulting designs that, *inter alia*, allowed users to enlarge text and button size or provide audio output. In other words, there has been a focus on mitigating the vision, hearing, and physical disabilities that accompany ageing rather addressing any of the cognitive impairments, perhaps because there has been little consensus as to how best to support the cognitive declines that accompany aging [22, 23].

However, usefulness and usability may tell only part of the story. Nutbeam [24] states that adopting services or an activity to promote, protect or maintain health should be considered within a health behavior framework rather than a technology acceptance framework, which suggests that theories such as Protection Motivation Theory may be a more appropriate lens through which to investigate these technologies for older adults.

Protection motivation theory (PMT) was first posited by Rogers [14] as a framework for understanding the impact of fear appeals and coping appraisals on attitudes and behaviours. The fundamental idea is that people may be motivated to change behaviour if they fear the consequences of inaction, but later versions of PMT [25] also recognize that other triggers to behaviour change involve the belief that the individual has both the resources and the self-belief to initiative and maintain a change. In short, then, people make a threat appraisal in which they assess both the severity of a threat (e.g. getting cancer from smoking) and their own vulnerability to it. They also make a coping appraisal where they assess their ability to deal with that threat. This in turn requires a belief that the behaviour change will reduce the threat (response efficacy) and a belief that one is capable of performing the recommended behavior (self-efficacy). These are discussed in more detail, with relevant examples below.

2.1   Threat Appraisal

Presently, technologies for older adults general focus on accessibility and are marketed as a response to the negative aspects of ageing – e.g. "what if you have an accident and there is no one is around to help?" In other words, there is a fear appeal which means that an older adult must first make a judgement about their own vulnerability to the threat and secondly they must assess whether the response (pressing an alarm button) would constitute an adequate and effective coping response. They must also weigh up other costs –financial ('it costs too much') identity ('it looks ugly') or social ('my friends don't use one'). All these issues come into play as part of a health decision-making process.

We should not underestimate the role of fear in driving older adult behaviour. Consider fear of falling, for example, as an area where fear has been shown to lead to a maladaptive coping response. While previously changes in gait were cited as risk factors for falling, i.e., decreased stride length and speed and prolonged double support [26], illustrated that these adaptations were essentially maladaptive responses born out of a fear of falling. Contrary to common belief, a wider stride does not necessarily increase stability but instead seems to predict an increased likelihood of experiencing falls.

To take a different example, we see claims that GPS tracking systems are useful for people with dementia, but many individuals simply don't see themselves in these terms – i.e. there is no perceived vulnerability and hence uptake is relatively poor even for people who would benefit from these services. Further, and counter-intuitively, adoption of the device itself can evoke fears of vulnerability, mistrust and lack of privacy Thomas et al. [27].

2.2   Coping Appraisal

Self-efficacy, i.e., the belief that one can complete tasks and reach goals [28], seems to be related to technology adoption [29–31]. This is closely related to a construct named "obsolescence", defined as a gradual loss of social integration and perceived lack of competence to deal with the demands of modern society. Obsolescence is also related to technology use [32] and can mediate the relationship of technological experience and loneliness. People with higher feelings of obsolescence (for instance: "being anti-quated") make more errors, need more time to complete technology-based tasks and report more usability concerns [33]. Typically, feelings of obsolescence increase with age [34]. In effect, this can mean that the 'response costs' of adopting new technologies are simply too high (e.g. [35]).

We should also consider whether any rewards accrue from a maladaptive response, in this case, technology avoidance. These are often overlooked in research, but there are benefits in not having to learn new technology, not feeling stigmatized, not being monitored and individuals may often claim that they avoid new technologies because they prefer the rewards of face to face contact.

These are the kinds of issues we explore in this study. In the following sections we present more information on the design and functionality of the Freedom to Roam system before presenting data gained during a three week field trial. We use protection motivation theory as a framework for analysis, asking questions about how well mobile technologies could engage older users and address some of their fears.

3   System Design

The intention behind the Freedom to Roam application was to encourage older adults to engage in activities outside of the home through the provision of location and client specific applications which encourage social integration and activity, while providing communications between a carer and a client and between a client and friends with the aid of a remote tracking service. To encourage continued use some applications for use within the home entertainment applications were also provided.

The Freedom to Roam application provided a carer application called Marketplace and a mobile client device, managed by the carer application. It was designed to function on a tablet, with each client being in possession of a bespoke dashboard of applications depending on their interests and daily activities and independent living support needs.

The Marketplace application provided the capacity to manage multiple clients from a single care control centre. It had the following functionality:

Question and answer: broadcast multiple choice, questions, to one or several clients and coordinate answer, e.g. gather requests for meal options for the day.

Update client applications: install or remove applications from clients' devices. Applications can be selected for clients from a general app store (e.g. Google play) and added to the approved (for older adults) Freedom to Roam Marketplace. Thus each device is personalized to its owner.

Follow Organisations: This service allows carers to follow other care groups or individuals to see the applications they are recommending. For instance, Age UK may set up recommendations for older adults or the RNIB for visually impaired users.

Receive call-back/contact requests: The one touch call facility alerts the carer that their client requires a call back.

Track Freedom to Roam devices: The physical location of the device can be monitored. This can be used to check if the client is moving around as normal, or to find the client, should there be cause for concern.

3.1   Client Applications

Previous research had identified that certain activities interested older adults, such as reporting issues to their local council [36]. In addition we recognized a range of apps that could aid both mental and physical well-being and promote increased mobility [37, 38].

Further applications were identified through tea party focus groups with older adults [39]. Tea parties are considered to be an appropriate method as they provide a relaxing environment which encourages participants to engage with the technology and provide genuine opinions as opposed to feeling constrained by possible formal perceptions of social acceptable behaviour in a university environment. The final client applications were selected from the following themes;

- Health: health symptoms information, health location, order repeat prescriptions
- Entertainment: games, news, TV Guide
- Communication: Skype, email call back request, Multiple choice messaging
- Local Information: what's on in the vicinity, Report It
- Out and About: Local transport applications; My Nearest, I am Here, Where am I

4   Field Trial Method

Forty two older adults, with experience of using a computer took part in the trial (M = 14, F = 29) aged between 56 and 85 years (mean = 69.5 years). Experience of technology varied amongst the group with 40 participants having access to the internet at home and 7 being in possession of a mobile smart device. Twenty five Motorola Xooms were utilized in protective casing to encourage participants to take them with them at all times.

Pre-trial questionnaires ascertained technology use, types of online activities and attitudes towards using the device over the following three weeks. Diaries consisted of one daily task over a 21 day period for individuals to conduct and record their experiences, including ability to complete the task, ease of use, likelihood to use again and any general comments about what they particularly liked or disliked or would change. General overviews of the apps or internet sites were also obtained at the end of each week of the trial. Each week focused on a different set of applications. Of course they could use any of the applications at any point, but they had to complete at least the daily task. A post-trial questionnaire investigated opinions, attitudes and the impact of the device on their behaviour. Some participants then took part in a discussion group at the end of the trial.

4.1   Procedure

Stage 1 involved inviting the individuals to the lab to complete the pre-trial demographic questionnaires and introduce them to the technological device they were going to be using for the following three weeks. A training session lasting between 90–120 min was provided. Messages were sent twice daily throughout the trial. The researcher monitored the message responses and the time to respond throughout as an indicator of trial engagement, possible problems users may face and whether users were keeping the devices switched on. The researcher acted as the carer and users contacted the researcher when there were issues – either via telephone, the 'Callback' facility or via an email On return of each device and diary participants completed the post-trial questionnaire, took part in the focus group (if they so wished).

5 Findings

In making an analysis of participant responses, we asked two particular questions about the system that came from protection motivation theory, a threat question about how adoption might be motivated by the fears associated with ageing and a coping question about whether people felt empowered by the system or whether they felt the costs of using the system were simply too great.

Q1: Might the threat of ageing motivate people to adopt Freedom to Roam?

In a PMT framework, we would expect participants to be motivated to adopt assistive technology in part because they are fearful of the risks associated with ageing. We found that our participants were generally well aware of threats to health either through their own experiences or through friends with declining health. They acknowledged that ageing had affected general health, memory, dexterity and walking ability and recognized that the aging process was a threat to their independence. They were clear that some of the major threats associated with ageing were loneliness, being house bound, being unable to care for self and eventually ending up depending on other people or in a care home. This was certainly a future state they did not want for themselves – and so they were convinced of the overall severity of the threat, however they were much less convinced about their own personal vulnerability to that threat. In other words, they generally felt that they were ageing well, despite their lists of health issues, and in some cases, didn't want to be reminded through the Freedom to Roam Apps that they were, indeed, ageing. Thus, we saw some distancing of participants from the Newcastle Older Peoples Website, as they disliked the fact that it was for 'older people'.

One area which did tap into perceived threat in an interesting way was location tracking. Previous research has reported that older adults are resistant to location awareness and tracking [25], but in our own post-trial questionnaires over 90 % of individuals provided positive or neutral affirmations to the question "*It is good that my location is known to others.*" Participants could see that location tracking had the potential to support them if anything went wrong when they were out, however, this perception was modified by the system's lack of accuracy (response efficacy) which, in practice, meant that there was no way to mitigate the threat.

> "*If somebody has a heart problem and could collapse or something, it would be a way of finding where they are. Mind, mine wasn't very accurate.*"

> "*It wasn't terribly accurate that 'I am here', we could be 90 yards away.*"

In addition, one of the maladaptive effects of our system was that system use actually increased feelings of vulnerability associated with ageing. Thus, over a third of our sample reported that they felt that ownership of the device made them a target for crime whilst they were using it in public places.

"I felt a bit vulnerable when out, especially if sitting on a bench trying to do something. You hear about people pinching phones and this [device] is quite big & visible" "Because it's so big, it attracts attention"

"... I felt terrible with this thing. Terribly self-conscious and vulnerable. I photographed this lamppost and thought, "oh, I'm not sending it from here",

"The only thing I didn't like was having to take it out. I would lock it in the boot for security if I had taken it out – maybe if it was my own I wouldn't be as paranoid".

To a certain extent these issues were related to the size of the device, however they recognized that a smaller device would create accessibility issues – these were large devices that were meant to support ease of use, but in fact, as we can see below, this particular aspect backfired and became a usability problem.

Q2: Did people feel empowered by Freedom to Roam or were the costs too great?

Overall, people enjoyed many of the elements in the new system, but were most appreciative of those playful or newsy elements that were associated with positive ageing. Thus, for example, they viewed the games as useful with suggestions to incorporate more games such as Solitaire or Scrabble and some acknowledgement that they could play certain games for hours:

"I loved Word Push, the feedback was like a ray of the sun."

Many also enjoyed the daily messages which were generally seen as a positive element of the system:

"I sat up watching and waiting for it to come on."

The Top 3 apps enjoyed were those allowing individuals to keep up to date with the news (BBC News –48 %), obtaining information, (Information Now –43 %) and reporting issues to the local councils (Report It –29 %)

"I like Information Now, I thought that was really good...... kind of feel they're in the business of supporting you in some way."

"Easy to use, the pothole I photographed had been filled in, within 2 days."

However, the usability costs of the system were generally considered very high and not all apps were seen as useful. Picking up the point about device size above, the device was considered too heavy by 75 % of participants and too big by 50 % and many felt they were unable to carry it around on a daily basis with comments such as

"would you really be wanting to wander round the supermarket carrying this."

Glare was also an issue, surprisingly over 90 % claimed the device to be 'free from glare', one assumes they were answering from the perspective of using it indoors, as 55 % could not conduct the task that involved taking a photograph of a pothole and sending it to their local council due to sunshine glare:

"Took the photograph, sunny day, hardly could see pothole with the glare"

"The outside brightness/contrast of the screen made it difficult to use the camera."

Accessories created accessibility issues with the cases used highlighting dexterity issues and demonstrating accessibility issues.

"It's the device I found irritating actually; I couldn't easily take it out of its case to start it. That was a bit of a pain."

Reliability of the 3G access was also problematic, with 5 individuals experiencing difficulties within their homes, either due to overpopulated blackspots or due to living in semi-rural locations. In addition, a couple who were keen to take the device on outings with them became frustrated as they lost 3G connectivity,

"When I turned it on there was no coverage."
"Couldn't find me because I was beyond Rothbury."
"Mine didn't seem to connect to the internet at all"
"But I went for a walk and then nothing"

Some of the applications rated as less popular were also deemed hard to use or irritating. For example, Shopping List (scan items as they are used to build a shopping list) was the least favourite because it simply did not work effectively, i.e. *"nothing would scan"* and it was faster to *"just write my shopping list."* The messaging app was perceived as having limited usefulness for the more independent older adults, and receiving messages, to which they had to respond was irritating. When participants did not respond, it was not always clear to the carer if the message had been received or not and could create anxiety and, for some, the messages themselves were a source of irritation;

"one of the frustrations of the whole three weeks was your messages, morning and night, especially the ones that were asking about have you done so-and-so, and you can only tick one box. You can't then add to your answer, and I found that very frustrating, you know."

Overall, then, the response costs of using the system were simply seen as too high.

6 Conclusions

The issues with the different applications highlighted the benefit of a marketplace for older adults, that would highlight the most useful and usable technologies for older adults. The appropriateness, reliability and quality of applications is extremely variable. The marketplace would provide a sign post to the best applications rather than the current trial and error approach. This approach supports informal carers, who may not have the awareness of technologies available and save their time and effort.

Location Awareness was viewed as both a potential protector and a threat to personal privacy and so has to be well managed. There was evidence of a change of attitude towards location awareness within a single focus group session as one individual, initially resistant to the notion had *"distinct reservations, from a civil liberty point of view"* then shifted their opinion slightly to consider the notion, albeit conservatively, stating a need for *"tremendous guarantees of who controlled the information."*

Researchers and developers should consider a mixed methods approach to the evaluation of any technology. The general attitude towards the technology was quantitatively measured as positive. 75 % of the trial users responding positively to using this type of technology in the future and rated features highly. However this must be interpreted with caution as a PMT lens on the comments suggests that this is probably not the case with the current instantiation of the device, but rather improvements on a number of dimensions are assumed to make this level of acceptance a reality. These issues include universal network coverage, size of device, usability, functionality offered and a change in attitude of older adults towards using technology in public.

When working with older adults in the future, it is important to consider when to involve older adults in the process. At the moment, they are brought in to respond to an existing solution, however, it may be more appropriate for the older adults to help decide what should be designed: i.e. don't bring them into a participatory design process when the decision about what to design has already been made. Consider participatory research, where the older adult supports the research to decide what problem should be addressed and how it should be addressed.

References

1. Harding, E.: Sustainable planning for housing in an ageing population: a guide for regional-level strategies. International Longevity Centre UK (2008). http://www.ilcuk.org. uk/files/pdf_pdf_49.pdf
2. Malley, J., Hancock, R., Murphy, M., Adams, J., Wittenberg, R., Comas-Herrera, A., Curry, C., King, D., James, S., Morciano, M., Pickard, L.M.: The effect of lengthening life expectancy on future pension and long-term care expenditure in England, 2007 to 2032. Health Stat. Q. **52**(1), 33–61 (2011)
3. Dunnell, K.: Ageing and mortality in the UK – national statistician's annual article on the population. Popul. Trends **134**, 6–23 (2008)
4. Rodrigues, H., Rui, J.: System implications of context-driven interaction in smart environments. Interact. Comput. **26**, 105–117 (2013)
5. Jara, A.J., Lopez, P., Fernandez, D., Zamora, M.A., Ubeda, B., Skarmeta, A.F.: Communication protocol for enabling continuous monitoring of elderly people through near field communications. Interact. Comput. **26**, 145–167 (2014)
6. Sum, S., Mathews, R.M., Hughes, I., Campbell, A.: Internet use and loneliness in older adults. CyberPsychol. Behav. **11**(2), 208–211 (2008)
7. White, H., McConnell, E., Clipp, E., Branch, L.G., Sloane, R., Pieper, C., Box, T.L.: A randomized controlled trial of the psychosocial impact of providing internet training and access to older adults. Aging Ment. Health **6**(3), 213–221 (2002)
8. Cotten, S.R., Ford, G., Ford, S., Hale, T.M.: Internet use and depression among older adults. Comput. Hum. Behav. **28**(2), 496–499 (2012)
9. Wright, K.: Computer-mediated social support, older adults, and coping. J. Commun. **50**(3), 100–118 (2000)
10. Chen, Y., Pearson, A.: Internet use among young and older adults: relation to psychological well-being. Educ. Gerontol. **28**, 731–744 (2002)
11. Stark-Wroblewski, K., Edelbaum, J.K., Ryan, J.J.: Senior citizens who use e-mail. Educ. Gerontol. **33**, 293–307 (2007)
12. Smith, A.: Older adults and technology use (2014). http://www.pewinternet.org/2014/04/03/older-adults-and-technology-use/
13. Bowling, A.: Enhancing later life: How older people perceive active ageing? Aging Ment. Health **12**, 3 (2008)

14. Rogers, R.W.: A protection motivation theory of fear appeals and attitude change1. J. Psychol. **91**(1), 93–114 (1975)
15. Hanson, V.L.: Influencing technology adoption by older adults. Interact. Comput. **22**, 502–509 (2010)
16. Hogeboom, D.L., McDermott, R.J., Perrin, K.M., Osman, H., Bell-Ellison, B.A.: Internet use and social networking among middle-aged and older adults. Educ. Gerontol. **36**, 93–111 (2010)
17. Cockton, G.: A development framework for value-centred design. In: Extended Abstracts on Human Factors in Computing Systems CHI 2005, pp. 1292–1295. ACM (2005)
18. Cockton, G.: Designing worth is worth designing. In: Proceedings of the 4th Nordic Conference on Human-Computer Interaction: Changing Roles, pp. 165–174. ACM (2006)
19. Norman, D.A.: Human-centered design considered harmful. Interactions **12**(4), 14–19 (2005)
20. Sellen, A., Rogers, Y., Harper, R., Rodden, T.: Reflecting human values in the digital age. Commun. ACM **52**(3), 58–66 (2009)
21. Davis, F.D.: Perceived usefulness, perceived ease of use, and user acceptance of information technology. MIS Q. **13**(3), 319–340 (1989)
22. Czaja, S.J., Lee, C.C.: The impact of aging on access to technology. Univ. Access Inf. Soc. **5** (4), 341–349 (2007)
23. Gillespie, A., Best, C., O'Neill, B.: Cognitive function and assistive technology for cognition: a systematic review. J. Int. Neuropsychol. Soc. **18**, 1–19 (2012)
24. Nutbeam, D.: Health promotion glossary. Health Promotion Int. **13**(4), 349–364 (1998)
25. Maddux, J.E., Rogers, R.W.: Protection motivation and self-efficacy: a revised theory of fear appeals and attitude change. J. Exp. Soc. Psychol. **19**(5), 469–479 (1983)
26. Maki, B.E.: Gait changes in older adults: predictors of falls or indicators of fear? J. Am. Geriatr. Soc. **45**(3), 313–320 (1997)
27. Thomas, L., Little, L., Briggs, P., McInnes, L., Jones, E., Nicholson, J.: Location tracking: views from the older adult population. Age Ageing **42**(6), 758–763 (2013)
28. Bandura, A.: Self-efficacy: toward a unifying theory of behavioral change. Psychol. Rev. **84** (2), 191–215 (1977)
29. Bennett, J.: Online communities and the activation, motivation and integration of persons aged 60 and older. A literature review. Version 1.1 (2011)
30. Oudshoorn, N., Pinch, T.J. (eds.): How Users Matter: The Co-construction of Users and Technologies. The MIT Press, Cambridge (2003)
31. Silverstone, R., Hirsch, E. (eds.): Consuming Technologies, Media and Information in Domestic Spaces. Routledge, London (1992)
32. Chang, S.E.: Computer anxiety and perception of task complexity in learning programming related skills. Comput. Hum. Behav. **21**, 713–728 (2005)
33. Loos, E., Haddon, L., Mante-Meijer, E. (eds.): Generational Use of New Media. Ashgate, Farnham (2012)
34. Fagan, M., Neill, S., Wooldridge, B.: An empirical investigation into the relationship between computer self-efficacy, anxiety, experience, support and usage. J. Comput. Inf. Syst. **44**, 95–104 (2003)
35. Coleman, G.W., Gibson, L., Hanson, V.L., Bobrowicz, A., McKay, A.: Engaging the disengaged: how do we design technology for digitally excluded older adults? In: Proceedings of the 8th ACM Conference on Designing Interactive Systems, pp. 175–178. ACM, August 2010
36. Greathead, D., Arief, B., Coventry, L., van Moorsel, A.: Deriving requirements for an online community interaction scheme, In: CHI 2012, Austin, pp. 1541–1546, 5–10 May 2012

37. Resnick, B.: Health promotion practices of older adults: testing an individualized approach. J. Clin. Nurs. **12**(1), 46–55 (2003)
38. Aresu, M., Bécares, L., Brage, S.: Health Survey for England: Physical Activity and Fitness, vol. 1 (2008)
39. Coventry, L., Jones, E.: The role of tea parties to elicit technology requirements to support the mobility of older adults. In: Proceedings of the 5th International Conference on Pervasive Technologies Related to Assistive Environments, PETRA 2012 (2012)

The Effect of Screen Size of Mobile Devices on Reading Efficiency

Yu-Chen Hsieh[1(✉)], Chien-Ting Kuo[1], and Hsuan Lin[2]

[1] Graduate School of Industrial Design, National Yunlin University of Science and Technology,
Yunlin, Taiwan
chester.3d@gmail.com
[2] Department of Product Design, Tainan University of Technology, Tainan, Taiwan
te0038@mail.tut.edu.tw

Abstract. Past research has shown that academia has no consensus on the advantages and disadvantages between paper-based reading and digital reading, which is why this research is an investigation of the differences between the two mediums for reading, whether it affects the performance of reading, and how do the different sizes of digital reading devices compare to the traditional paper. This researcher utilized questionnaires and behavioral observation as methods of investigation. The use of questionnaires was mainly to understand the operational habits of digital device users and the kinds of writing they read, and the behavior observation entailed asking 40 subjects to read on a given device or paper medium for an experiment on reading comprehension to gather data on user reading speed, comprehension, fatigue and other parameters. The results from this study will be used as a basis to formulate a more comprehensive research framework for a future study that more accurately measures the difference between digital devices of various sizes and paper medium.

Keywords: Digital reading · Reading efficacy · Screen-size

1 Introduction

Ever since Apple Inc. introduced the first iPhone in 2007, the sizes of smart phones and tablet PCs, particularly concerning the screen, have been diverging in order to meet consumer needs. Smart phones have had gradual size increase through periodic updates (Yang 2014) and the most popular of phones have gone from 3.5 in. (screen size) devices in 2010 to 4.3 in. devices in 2011, to the iPhone 6 Plus launched by Apple in September 2014 which has reached a size of 5.5 in. For tablet devices, however, it has developed from early 9.7 in. devices and both shrunken to 7–8 in. and enlarged to 10 in. or even 12 in. for more recent devices. The divergence of device sizes satisfies the demands of users with different needs, and has also given life to novel device usage habits. It used to be that bus stops and mass-transit stations would be filled with people waiting for transport who are reading books and magazines and newspapers. Today, the same places can be seen filled with heads looking down at phones and tablets. This ubiquity of personal handheld devices has affected the reading habits of people, and has transitioned

© Springer International Publishing Switzerland 2016
J. Zhou and G. Salvendy (Eds.): ITAP 2016, Part I, LNCS 9754, pp. 435–445, 2016.
DOI: 10.1007/978-3-319-39943-0_42

the habit of reading for many from one that used to be paper-based to one that is practiced with electronic material on handheld devices. Does this new reading behavior improve reading performance? Does this result in a difference in reading comprehension? How else does this new reading habit differ from reading on traditional paper mediums? These are the key points which this research tried to investigate.

This research hoped to reveal the difference in the ability to gather information between different sizes of digital devices and paper-based medium and primarily involved the following goals:

1. To investigate the difference in reading performance between different device screen-sizes.
2. To compare the ability of readers in how they extract information from different device screen-sizes and paper medium.
3. To investigate the fatigue levels of reading on devices of different screen-sizes and paper medium.

2 Literatures

2.1 The Change in the Size of Digital Devices

The Change in Smart Phone Screen Size. The size of the smart phone has grown gradually from the earliest 3.5 in. iPhone introduced in 2007 as various device makers made bigger and bigger products. In 2011, Samsung introduced the Galaxy note that pushed the boundaries of smart phone sizes to 5.3 in., the first device of its enlarged size. 2012 was the year when competition in the smart phone market was at its height. Various makers came out with plus-size products that sparked a 'battle of the phones'. The poster-child device for plus-size phones in this time was the Samsung Galaxy Note 2; it raised the benchmark of screen-size to an incredible 5.5 in. and a couple of years later devices between 5 to 5.5 in. was the market mainstream (Appier 2014a, b). Asian regions when compared to other regions significantly preferred plus-size devices; In China, 39 % of all devices sold were over 5 in., and in the entire Asia-Pacific region the figure reached 43 %. The trend of phones over 5 in. being mainstream by the end of 2014 (Appier 2014a, b) meant that even Apple Inc. who strongly resisted plus-size phones eventually introduced 6 in. devices in order to meet consumer demand.

The Change in Tablet Computer Screen Size. The tablet computer started thriving in 2010 when Apple introduced the 9.7 in. iPad. Due to the convenience and portability of its size – over laptops – it quickly became a highly sought-after product, and other makers responded with similar tablets of their own. When the size of these larger-than-phone devices were deemed by their users to be still too heavy to carry or to read with, iPad introduced the 7.9 in. iPad mini in 2012, and Amazon introduced the Kindle Fire small tablet. According to a survey done by advertising firm Appier of cross-device usage habits of Asian users in the first half of 2014, consumers are preferring tablets under 8 in. and smart phones over 4.7 in., and in their survey of the second half of 2014, they discovered that users of 9.7 in. large tablets have significantly dropped, with most users preferring small tablets between 7 and 8.9 in. (Appier 2014a, b)

Research Related to Screen Size and Effect on Reading. Lin et al. (2013) found that reading 12 pt font on devices between 6 in. and 9.7 in. took the shortest amount of time, and that reading 12 pt and 14 py font on 8.1 in. and 9.7 in. produced higher reading accuracy. Wang et al. (2012) on the other hand conducted experiments on three different sizes of reading devices in their investigation of the performance of reading Chinese articles from the devices and found that screen size does not affect reading performance, and that users preferred devices less than 7 in. in screen size and also devices that are 10.1 in. size.

2.2   The Advantages of Both Types of Mediums

The Advantages of Digital Reading.

Interactivity. Digital reading inherently contains the interactivity that paper based reading lacks. Content designers are able to incorporate pictures, sound, color, and animation to present ideas that are more complex, and this can also generate a sense of involvement for the user (Shneiderman and Plaisant 2010). In addition, for readers with special needs, such as those who are visually impaired, the content on the screen can be enlarged for easier reading, or a device could even convert the text into sound and read the text out loud (Blenkhorn et al. 2003).

Readability. Siegenthaler et al. (2011) compared the eye movement of reading on paper and on digital reading devices to study their difference. The experiment involved reading the same article on paper and 5 different devices while the eye movement of the readers were recorded. It revealed that there was no significant difference in the reading habit itself, and that reading on paper was very similar to reading on a digital device. This was due to the fact that digital readers had available the function to adjust font size and letter spacing, and allowed the reader to make further adjustments according to preference, while the same adjustments weren't possible on paper-based materials. Results also revealed that the fixation time on paper-based medium was longer than that on a digital reading device, which indicates that while readability of paper-based medium is lower than that of digital devices, their reading speeds were not significantly different.

The Advantage of Reading on Paper-Based Medium.

Reading on Paper Produces a Better State of Mind. A portion of scholars believe reading on paper to be better. Norwegian researchers (Mangen et al. 2012) gave Norwegian students an article to read on paper and digital medium then gave them a reading comprehension test on the computer. Results showed that digital reading produced poorer comprehension than paper, and the length of the article was an important factor of comprehension. The human mind is more adept at remembering images than it is at remembering text, and we tend to assist the memory storage of text by their visual position on a page or a book and try to recall the content based on that position. However, since digital content can scroll up and down the screen or be presented on a page to page basis, the user is unable to use the same fixed position trick or the feel of the thickness of the book at a certain page number to aid in this process, and this interruption can make comprehension poorer.

More Suited for Reading Longer Text. In the regard of the length of a piece of text, a research by Macedo-Rouet et al. (2009) in which 122 college students were asked to answer 18 mathematical questions revealed that printed class notes and test-papers were more efficient to read on than computer screens. The study also suggested that reading a piece of text that is excessively long on screen should be avoided, as longer text requires a higher cognitive load, which lowers reading efficacy. This research suggests that it is possible to read longer text on paper than on a screen.

The research into the trend of device sizes for this study revealed that smart phones are increasing in size while tablets are both increasing and decreasing in size. Do the varieties of screen sizes affect reading efficiency and comprehension? What reading habits are exhibited by users of different device sizes? Does the preference of a certain font size make a difference? And what are the differences in reading performance and comprehension between the various device sizes and paper-based medium? As mentioned above are questions that this research delved into.

3   Method

This research is intended as a preliminary study before a formal study is conducted. A smaller scale experiment was used to examine the experiment process and observe data trends in order to make adjustments and later construct an experiment that can highlight the relevant effects. This study planned on using three sizes of devices and a book of a widely available size for comparison for a total of 4 groups. Each subject was asked to read a length and layout controlled passage while their operation and browsing process were observed and recorded. Then, they were asked to fill out tests and questionnaires once the reading was completed. The primary observations and recordings will be made of the following:

1. Reading behavior: posture when operating, font size of choice
2. Reading comprehension and efficacy: total reading time, reading comprehension test score
3. Reading fatigue: Based on the subjective visual fatigue questionnaire designed by Heuer et al. (1989)

3.1   Digital Devices for Experiment

To minimize the deviation that can be caused by software or hardware differences, this research used smart phones and tablets all made by the same maker. These mobile devices are a Samsung Galaxy Note Pro 12.2 (12 in.), a Samsung Galaxy Tab A (9.7 in.), and a Samsung Galaxy Note 3 (5.5 in.) for the coverage of devices that are commonly used today (as Table 1).

Table 1. Handheld devices used in this study

Model	Samsung Galaxy Note Pro 12.2	Samsung Galaxy Tab A	Samsung Galaxy Note 3
Device size	295.6 mm × 204 mm × 7.95 mm	242.5 mm × 166.8 mm × 7.5 mm	153.5 mm × 78.6 mm × 8.5 mm
Screen size	12.2 in.	9.7 in.	5.5 in.
Weight	750 g	487 g	176 g

3.2 Choice of Software and Reading Content for Experiment

This research had selected Google Play Books App (as Fig. 1) as the reading software. This is a pre-installed software on all Android devices by Google Inc. that allows the user to access over 4 million eBooks. It is able to process PDF and EPUB file formats, and provides free trial-read and purchasing functions. The research was conducted using the EPUB format, its advantage being that it allows adjustment of font sizes for easier reading. Google Play Books also gives the user the following controls of EPUB files: a choice of three types of display (white text on black background, black text on white background, and black text on yellow background), screen brightness, font, font size, line spacing, etc. For this experiment, the subject was allowed to adjust the font size only and no other adjustments including the line spacing was allowed.

Fig. 1. Adjustments available on Google Play Books

To better suit general interest, This chosen passage to read was a passage from the book, '*Big Data*', written by Viktor Mayer-Schönberger and Kenneth Cukier (Mayer-Schönberger and Cukier 2014), and for simplicity the passage in the digital as well as the paper version of the book were identical, including the reading from left to right layout. The passage is from early in the chapter 'Now-Letting the data speak' on pages 10 to 13, totally 1540 words.

3.3 Experimental Variables

The independent and dependent variables in the experimental design are as explained below:

Independent Variables. The type and size of the content carriers: three sizes of mobile devices: Samsung Galaxy Note Pro (12.2 in.), Samsung Galaxy Tab A (9.7 in.), Samsung Galaxy Note 3 (5.5 in.), and a book within normally acceptable dimensions (A5, 148×210 mm) are the four comparison groups.

Dependent Variables.

1. Reading comprehension variables: Total read time, comprehension test score.
2. Reading fatigue levels are 6 criteria's, in question form, from Heur's questionnaire: "I am having difficulty seeing", "A strange feeling is surrounding my eye", "I feel my eyes are tired", "I feel numb", "I am having a headache", "I feel dizzy when I stare at the screen" which are answered on a 10-point scale (Heuer et al. 1989).
3. Font size: This research let the subjects select a font size of their choice before they commence reading. In addition to making setting adjustments on the device, a font size chart is overlaid on the screen and books in order to obtained a standardized font size figure. Google play Books displays font size as a percentage, which was then converted to a 'pt' measurement using a standard conversion chart.

3.4 Subjects and the Experiment Procedure

This research was intended as a preliminary study before a formal experiment is conducted in order to verify preliminary experiment design and reveal a data trend. Ever group was assigned 10 subject for a total of 40 subjects for the experiment. Each subject was a college student with experience of at least one year with a mobile device. The experiment was conducted with one group given the book and 3 groups each given a different size device for a total of 4 groups. All subjects were required to participate in each step of the test, and in order to prevent memory from interfering with results, each subject conducted the experiment only once. The experiment proceeded in a quiet, well lit, and uninterrupted laboratory.

The experiment procedure was as follows:

1. The subject was asked to be seated, and given a briefing of the research objective.
2. The subject was then provided with a tablet while given explanation and precautions of the task, and then instructed on the functions of Google Play Book, including user interface functions and EPUB format inherent functions. Subjects were then allowed to make adjustments to the font size suitable to them, and the font size setting was then announced to the researcher for recording.
3. Researcher then asked the subject to turn or move or scroll to the cover page on their device or book, ready to begin the test.
4. Timer begins when the subject had turned to the appropriate page containing the passage to begin reading. The researcher observed and recorded reading behavior

and method of handling the device of the subject while the subjects were reading, and the timer stops when the subject has finished reading.

5. When reading was done, the researchers gave 5 questions relevant to the passage content for the subject to answer. The questions were 4-choice multiple choice questions. Once that was done, the subject was asked to fill out a Heuer's subjective visual fatigue questionnaire and basic personal information.

4   Results

4.1   Reading Speed

The average reading time for the 3 different device groups and paper are displayed on Fig. 2. As can be seen, the book took the longest to read through, at around 4 min, and the 9.7 in. tablet took the shortest, at less than 3 min. The 12.2 in. and 5.5 in. devices were about the same at just over 3 min.

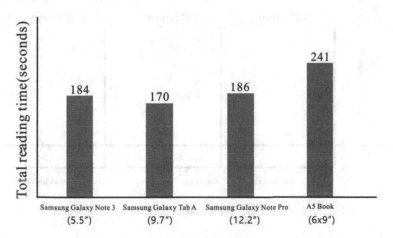

Fig. 2. Average read time on the different devices and paper

One-way ANOVE is then applied to compare each variable, the F-value of the variables and their significance are as Table 2.

Table 2. Experimental results through One-way ANOVA

Comparisons	F Value	P
Screen size and read time	0.130	.879
Content carrier type and read time	5.649	.023[a]
Content carrier type and comprehension score	5.523	.024[a]
Screen size and comprehension score	.233	.794

[a]$P < 0.05$ significant.

As seen in Table 2, screen size and read time showed no significance(F = 0.130, p = 0.879 > 0.05), indicating that the size of the screen did not affect read time significantly. But if the digital devices were combined into one group in comparison with the paper group, statics show a significant difference (F = 5.649, p = 0.023 > 0.05). It can therefore be postulated that reading on paper takes longer than reading on screens, as the reading time on a screen is between 170 and 186 s while on paper it is 241 s.

4.2 Font Size Selection

In regards to screen size and the selection of the font size, Chart 5 shows that most users in the 5.5 in. smart phone group selected 11 pt to conduct their reading, and 9.7 in. tablet users mostly had 14 pt as their font size of choice. The 12.2 in. tablet users were less grouped, with some opting for large 19 pt font which allowed them to read every word with ease, while there were ones who preferred 9 pt font that allowed them to fit the entire passage on one page (see Fig. 3).

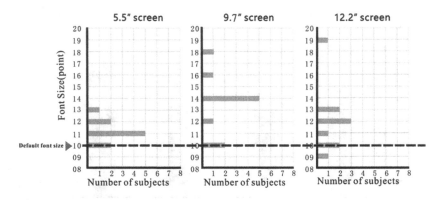

Fig. 3. Font size selection numbers in relation to screen size

4.3 Reading Comprehension

As Table 3 indicates, in regards to whether the two types of content carrier, digital screen and paper, had a substantial effect on reading comprehension, results showed a significant difference (F = 5.523, p = 0.024 < 0.05), which confirms a difference between comprehension reading on the two mediums. The average comprehension rate of reading on paper was higher, at a score of 4.6 out of 5, and according to the definition of comprehension as described, is a fairly high level. Meanwhile, the digital devices scored an average of 3.6 out of 5, signifying the higher level of comprehension of reading on paper. Chart 3 indicates that the size of the screen itself does have a significant relations to comprehension levels (F = 0.233, p = 0.794 > 0.05), it can therefore be said that regardless of screen size, those who read on digital devices had about the same level of comprehension.

4.4   Visual Fatigue Questionnaire

This research uses Heuer's visual fatigue questionnaire to obtain the figures in Fig. 4, in which can be seen that out of the 6 assessment questions, paper scored the lowest for everyone, signifying that reading on paper causes the least amount of fatigue. Of the three mobile device sizes, the 9.7 in. tablet scored the lowest, meaning that 9.7 in. tablets is the most suitable size of the three device sizes for reading due to the least amount of fatigue that it generates.

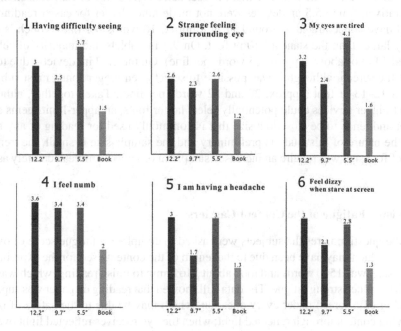

Fig. 4. Average scores from the visual fatigue questionnaire for the different device sizes and paper.

5   Discussion

5.1   Reading Efficiency and Comprehension of the Content Carriers

According to the preliminary experiment in this study, in terms of reading speed, reading on a mobile device happens faster than on paper regardless of the size of the device. The figures from this experiment showed reading on screen to be up to 33.33 % faster than reading on paper, but we cannot conclude that reading on screen is better performance wise than reading on paper because, in terms of comprehension, reading on paper is superior to reading on screen, with an average difference of 27.78 % in favor of paper. Our researchers have therefore inferred that, when reading on screen and using a mobile device, because of the properties of the digital screen, behaviors such as speed-reading or skim-reading can occur, speeding up the reading process but at the same time lowering comprehension of what was read. This portion of the results concurs with past research which showed similar results, which is that reading on screen will generate a poorer comprehension of the content than reading on paper, and therefore digital screens are less suited for reading long passages.

5.2   Font Selection on the Content Carriers

Examining the relationship between screen size and font size revealed that the size of the screen can affect the font size that the user selects. The size of font chosen on the comparatively small 5.5 in. devices were not made much larger for easier reading but instead have concentrated at around 11 pt (approx. 16 words per line), which is only slightly larger than the standard 10 pt font. On 9.7 in. tablets, the majority of subject selected 14 pt or above (approx. 25 words per line). On the 12.2 in. devices, due to the size of the screen, although it was possible to select even bigger fonts, most subjects selected 12–13 pt font (approx. 28 and 32 words per line). Taken together, although users of bigger devices could potentially select larger fonts, an upper-limit seems to be present and tends to be close to a size that is commonly used for reading of any type. Since the nature of this study is preliminary and the sample size is small, the trend in terms of font size will require an increased sample in order to be more accurately ascertained.

5.3   Visual Fatigue of the Content Carriers

From the questionnaires the subjects were asked to complete, a fatigue score of over 8 was rare, which may have been due to the length of the content used for the experiment. The passage was 1540 words and took about 3 to 5 min to finish reading, which was not enough to induce strong fatigue. The data still showed that reading on paper was superior to reading on a screen under every question, which may be due to the nature of paper displaying content through reflected light; when the eye receives reflected light over an extended period of reading, visual fatigue is not easily generated. The screen on digital devices today, however, emits light from its light emitting diodes (LED) behind the liquid crystal panel, which produces more flare and can cause higher visual fatigue over an extended period of reading. Furthermore, of the three device sizes, 9.7 in. devices produced less fatigue across the board compared to the other two device types. Our researchers postulated that the 9.7 in. device is closest to conventional book sizes of the three device types, which means that the experience perceived by the user in terms of searching on page, perceived font size, paragraph layout, the behavior of glancing, etc. most closely approximate the experience of reading on book, and therefore generates the least fatigue. We can infer that screens that most closely simulate conventional book sizes can avert a greater amount of fatigue.

6   Conclusions

The preliminary experiments performed in this study shows that screen size does not affect reading performance, but readers obtain a higher level of comprehension reading on paper compared to reading on screen, and therefore the paper is still the more optimal medium of conveying information. Iin terms of fatigue from reading, the book is still a more comfortable form of content carrier, although out of the three device sizes used in this experiment, the 9.7 in. tablet produced less visual fatigue compared to the other two device sizes, and so 9.7 in. is the optimal screen size for a device when reading a extended piece of text, and any increase in screen size would not be able to increase reading performance or reduce fatigue.

Furthermore, under conditions where letters are plainly readable, people will tend to make adjustments to the font size according to the size of the screen, primarily due to the need to closely approximate traditional paper-based reading in terms of the ratio of font size and word count to the page, whereby users with smaller screens will shrink the font, and those with larger screen will enlarge it accordingly in order to maintain an acceptable layout in terms of number of words per line that is found in books and paper articles.

This research was intended as a preliminary run prior to formal testing, and so the sample size was set to 40. In order to bolster the credibility and persuasiveness of this line of study, a sample size of at least 120 is planned for the formal experiment, allowing the related data to be more definite as well as more objective.

References

Appier: Appier Research Report: Cross-Screen User Behavior Insights, Asia 1H 2014 (2014a)
Appier: Appier Research Report: Cross-Screen User Behavior Insights, Asia 2H 2014 (2014b)
Mayer-Schönberger, V., Cukier, K.: Big Data: A Revolution That Will Transform How We Live, Work, and Think. Eamon Dolan/Mariner Books; Reprint edition, 4 March 2014 (2014). ISBN-10:0544227751, ISBN-13:978-0544227750
Blenkhorn, P., Evans, G., King, A., Kurniawan, S.H., Sutcliffe, A.: Screen magnifiers: evolution and evaluation. IEEE Comput. Graph. Appl. 23(5), 54–61 (2003)
Lin, H., Wu, F.G., Cheng, Y.Y.: Legibility and visual fatigue affected by text direction, screen size and character size on color LCD e-reader. Displays 34, 49–58 (2013)
Heuer, H., Hollendiek, G., Kröger, H., Römer, T.: Die Ruhelage der Augen und ihr Einfluß auf Beobachtungsabatand und visuelle Ermüdung bei Bildschirmarbeit. Zeitschrift für experimentelle und angewandte psychologie 36, 538–566 (1989)
Mangen, A., Walgermo, B.R., Brønnick, K.: Reading linear texts on paper versus computer screen: effect on reading comprehension. Int. J. Educ. Res. 2013(58), 61–68 (2012)
Macedo-Rouet, M., Ney, M., Charles, S., Lallich-Boidin, G.: Students' performance and satisfaction with Web vs. Paper-based practice quizzes and lecture notes. Comput. Educ. 53(2), 375–384 (2009)
Siegenthaler, E., Wurtz, P., Bergamin, P., Groner, R.: Comparing reading processes on e-ink displays and print. Display 32(5), 268–273 (2011)
Wang, Y, Zhao, Z.H., Wang, D., Feng, G.H., Luo, B.: How screen size influences Chinese readability. State Key Laboratory for Novel Software Technology, Nanjing University (2012)
Yang, C.Y.: An observation on the trend of Tablet Design from CES 2014, Nankang IC Design Incubation Center, Taiwan (2014)
Shneiderman, B., Plaisant, C.: Designing the User Interface: Strategies for Effective Human-Computer Interaction, vol. 5. Addison-Wesley, Reading (2010)

Design of Smart Watch for Old People Based on the Benchmark of Consumers' Kansei Intention

He Huang[✉], Yixiang Wu, Jianxin Cheng, and Minggang Yang

School of Art, Design and Media, East China University of Science
and Technology, M. BOX 286, NO. 130, Meilong Road, Xuhui District,
Shanghai 200237, China
{1983222hh,wuyixiang_15,yangminggang}@163.com,
cjx.master@gmail.com

Abstract. Current product design is dependent on designers' experiences, knowledge and shaping ability excessively. But consumers' demand changes owing to rapid growth of market economy. The focus of the product transforms from original basic demand to deeper level of Kansei. Consumers' Kansei appeal should be reflected more and presented by shape, material, color or other shaping element of smart watch besides considering health, comfort and other elements because the relation of watch and human are relatively intimated. Old people are different from general consumer group physically and psychologically, which embodies in the degeneration of visual sense, auditory sense, reaction capacity, the force of hands and the memory ability of text and graphic. Old people are greatly different from other group in Kansei intention and user experience of using smart watch. Therefore whether appearance design or interaction design for watch should embody our care for the special group-old people to improve the product satisfaction degree and bring convenience for them. If the parameters relative to consumers' Kansei intention can be found, they can assist designers in accurately positioning the shaping and functional design features of products to improve the efficiency of design. The author conducts design evaluation on survey samples combining with Kansei engineering taking "smart watch for old people" as an example in this study to verify the idea that the shaping design of product is dependent on Kansei intention. The main results and completed work in this paper includes: Survey on shaping, interview and questionnaire appraisal of smart watch targeting at old people consumer group are carried out firstly; relative data information and picture sample pool are collected; shaping of smart watch for old people is broken down using Morphological Analysis method and survey contents to determine shaping design elements which influence image of consumers; representative image words describing the shaping of smart watch for old people are determined with cluster analysis method; and then multivariate linear relation model between consumers' Kansei intention and the shaping design of smart watch for old people is built. Quantification relation between Kansei image meaning evaluation value and shaping design elements are built and multivariate regression analysis is conducted with Quantification Theory Type I method on the basis of performing statistical analysis on image meaning evaluation experiment result of representative sample to obtain correlated category score, item range, constant,

J. Zhou and G. Salvendy (Eds.): ITAP 2016, Part I, LNCS 9754, pp. 446–456, 2016.
DOI: 10.1007/978-3-319-39943-0_43

multiple correlation coefficient and determination coefficient. And on this basis mathematic relation model between all Kansei intention and design elements are built so that the aim of estimating consumers' Kansei intention is reached. Finally sample is selected to verify it, Paired-sample T check analysis on the estimation value of correlation model and the mean value of subjective evaluation is conducted and the result shows that the estimation model has reliability.

Keywords: Kansei Engineering · Smart watch · Quantification theory type I

1 Introduction

Current aging of population is not only a huge problem faced by the developing countries like China, but also a difficulty that the whole world should be faced with together. In the next five decades, world's aging tendency of population is speeding up and becoming more and more critical. According to the medium program of the United Union, the global old age population coefficient will increase from 6.9 % in 2000 to 21.4 % in 2050. The growth range is even higher than ever (2002). The increase proportion of aging population makes the social pension, life quality of elder people, products for the elder become popular topics among scholars in recent years. The rapid development of Internet, big data and artificial intelligence, especially the frequent update of electronic product, leads to huge changes in elder people's daily life. For example, there are more and more wearable smart devices for the elder people and the new functions features emerge in an endless stream, like all sorts of smart Bracelet and smart watch, etc. Therefore, these are important topics to master the general rule of elderly consumers' psychology, design products based on consumers' demands, reflect caring for the elders and increase their satisfactions ratio.

2 Research Background

As a newly rising electronic device, smart watch contains not only plentiful functions but also close connection with human body. So the designer should give more responses to consumer's emotional appeal besides considering health and comfortableness factors, and deliver through the modeling elements like shape, material and color. The former products design is more dependent on the subjective judge and thought of designer, while along with the emerging of experience economy, consumers' position is becoming more and more important in product design. The rapid development of market economy causes changes in consumers' demand and their focus point varies from the original basic needs to a deeper emotional level. As a consumer oriented human engineering technology, Kaisei Engineering (KE) focus more on users' experience and demands, which is why it is called the "Emotional Design"(Nagamachi 1995). KE is the first choice of development methods by conversing consumers' impression, feeling and demands on existing or concept products into specific design parameters (Nagamachi 1995; Schütte, 2004). This article would analyze the elder's perceptual demand for smart watch by Kaisei Engineering method.

3 Literature Review

The explosive development of intelligent products and the rapid expansion of the scope of application in recent years make the scholars pay more and more attention back to the real needs of consumers, usability, ease of use and user experience and so on. For example, Han, along with some others, took consumable electronic products as example, carried out some case studies and proposed a usability evaluation system of some meaning (2001); Beom and Kyeyoun (2009) discussed the basic framework of product usability evaluation from the customer's perceptual perception of product design taking dishwasher as the example. Costas Boletsis analyzed the feasibility of using smart watches to monitor the health of the elderly in the family (2015). According to Hartono's view (2012), the perceptual engineering is considered to be essentially superior to other similar methods. It establishes a mathematical model of the perceptual response through human sensory and external stimuli, which can reduce subjectivity to the maximum extent. The application of perceptual engineering covers many aspects nowadays, such as products and services, including interior design, automobile designs (i.e. Mazda, Nissan, NISSAN, TOYOTA, MITSUBISHI, Honda, Ford, Fiat and Hyundai, etc.), bra (i.e. Wacoal), residence (see Llinares and Page, 2011), beverage (i.e. beer), consumer electronic and service, etc. The research by Huang Cheng (2014) on the design of smart watches adopts the theory of kansei engineering quantification, combines with consumer psychology and finally concludes a professional and targeted result.

4 Research Methods and Procedure

4.1 Investigation and Analysis of Product Function

This study designs a product survey questionnaire on the smart watch function and performance for the elderly consumer groups. The questionnaire contains 16 projects in total: Time reminder, heart rate monitoring, double talk, sleep monitoring, sports step counting, weather forecast, GPS positioning, emergency assistance(SOS), medication reminders, blood pressure monitoring, electronic fence, long standby, voice control, waterproof function, camera, Bluetooth music. Measure consumers' expectation value by Likert scale: "−2, −1, 0, 1, 2" for "Strongly unwanted, unwanted, neutral, wanted, strongly wanted". The questionnaire is carried out in two ways: on-site give-out and recycle, and the network questionnaire survey. The on-site way gives out 120 pieces of questionnaire and recycles 105 valid pieces in the parks, where the elder exercise in the morning. The number of network survey participant is 652 and valid questionnaire quantity is 611. Statistical data contributes to understand the general situation of the elderly consumer demand for smart watches, which helps designers to plan and make decisions when they are developing new products. See Table 1:

We can see from the data that the expectation value of the elders is higher in SOS, long standby, medication reminders, time reminder, blood pressure monitoring and heart rate monitoring. It means that the elder care more for these functions and would like these to be realized in products. See Fig. 1:

Table 1. Consumers' intention to the functions of smart watch

Time reminder	Heart rate monitoring	Double talk	Sleep monitoring	Sports step counting	Weather forecast	GPS positioning	SOS
1.328	1.175	1.017	0.986	0.928	0.876	0.936	1.622
Medication reminders	Blood pressure monitoring	Electronic fence	Long standby	Voice control	Waterproof function	Camera	Bluetooth music
1.393	1.282	0.937	1.414	1.124	0.906	0.815	0.753

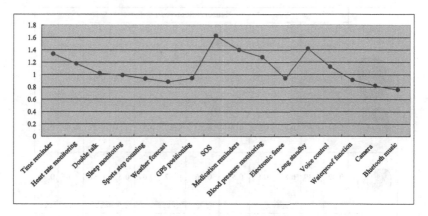

Fig. 1. Data ordering of kansei intent towards product function

Certainly there is demand for the other functions, which requires the designers to pay attention to and choose when designing. As the elder prefer something of habits and regular, their memory and response decrease correspondingly, and it is often difficult and slow to accept new things, so it is not proper to pursuit more and comprehensive in smart watch function quantity but to keep the main and necessary functions, add some new features to help them to use and learn. In addition, due to the degradation of the physiological function of the elder, the operation of electronic equipment, especially some small devices like watch, will cause a lot of inconvenience. The design of buttons and interfaces is worth our attention. They should be easy to master to avoid frustration caused by operation error. We will be able to understand the elderly consumers' preliminary kansei intention towards smart watches through the investigation and analysis of the product function, conclude a clear design objective and initial direction and form the keynote of the product function design.

4.2   Product Modeling Intention Survey

This study collects a variety of brands and styles of smart watches for elder, total 120, as experimental samples through manufacturers' website, brochure and shopping mall, etc. Classify similar products by Delphi method and KJ method and screen to 32. Remove other interference factors, such as color and brand, and display in black and white pictures to facilitate consumers' kansei evaluation of product modeling. Select 50 adjectives by online survey, references and interviews, screen to 12 and code them by expert analysis and group discussion. Set 5 scales for each adjective according to Likert scale: very 2, better 1, neutral 0, not very −1, worst −2. Let the elderly consumers, as the test subjects, give grades to the 12 intention adjectives of the 32 experimental samples. Add up the grades and calculate the average score. See Table 2:

Table 2. Table of kansei evaluation score (average)

Sample	Kansei Adjectives											
	1	2	3	4	5	6	7	8	9	10	11	12
	Concise	Steady	Graceful	Modern	Comfortable	Technological	Fashion	Practical	Upscale	Elaborate	Demotic	Safe
	1.25	0.89	0.95	0.92	0.90	0.87	0.75	0.86	0.57	0.62	1.05	1.17
	1.01	0.52	0.83	0.91	0.76	0.97	0.88	0.71	0.60	0.52	0.63	0.72
	0.92	0.49	0.81	0.85	0.59	0.56	0.57	0.67	0.52	0.68	0.66	0.70
...	...	...	...	...	...	...	...	...	...	...	...	...
	0.82	0.86	0.70	0.69	0.60	0.64	0.60	0.54	-0.32	0.55	0.69	0.80
	0.35	0.51	0.62	0.82	0.46	0.68	0.81	-0.39	0.61	0.69	0.64	0.77
	0.79	0.63	0.72	0.84	0.49	0.58	0.69	0.55	0.51	0.71	0.60	0.66

4.3   Spatial Analysis on Kansei Semantics

In order to facilitate the cluster analysis of the sample afterwards, we will carry out the factor analysis of the statistical data of kansei evaluation score. The main function of factor analysis is to reduce dimension. After the factor analysis, the original variables form a small number of comprehensive indicators or dimensions. Then the cluster analysis is implemented on the basis of a few comprehensive indexes or dimensions, which will make the effect more concise and clear. It can also be said that clustering within a space with fewer dimensions is easier to be understood compared with the space with more dimensions. This is mainly due to the limited information processing and perception of human beings. So the final number of factors (kansei adjectives) should be as less as possible on the precondition that "less but fine". Through factor

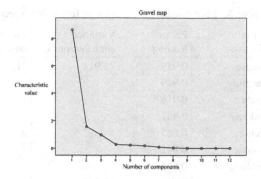

Fig. 2. Factor analysis — gravel map

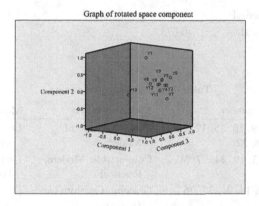

Fig. 3. Factor analysis — graph of rotated space component (three dimensional)

analysis, we get the gravel map as Fig. 2, three dimensional graph of rotated space component in Fig. 3 and common factor data sheet in Table 3.

Through the data results of factor analysis, we can choose 4 representative adjectives according to the level of the factor load: concise, graceful, comfortable and practical.

4.4 Modeling Element Analysis

Next, we use morphological analysis, assisting with the research content, to analyze the morphology of the smart watch of the elder in this study. We set the design elements into the dial, screen, watch strap, button and frame preliminarily, then we determine the modeling designing elements impacting on consumer intention by cluster analysis as dial, watch strap and button, see Table 4.

Number dial, watch strap and button as X1, X2 and X3, which are the main modeling elements in smart watch for elders. Mark their general modeling distribution as C11, C12, C13, C14, C21, C22, C23, C31, C32, C33, C34 and C35, see Table 5.

Table 3. Factor analysis — common factor data sheet

Common factor	Kansei adjectives	Factor loading	Variance contribution/%	Cumulative contribution rate/%
Factor 1 (Style)	Concise	0.959	71.911	71.911
	Graceful	0.949		
	Steady	0.916		
	Modern	0.887		
	Fashion	0.865		
	Demotic	0.842		
	Comfortable	0.865		
Factor 2 (Quality)	Technological	0.713	13.103	85.014
	Elaborate	0.681		
	Safe	0.632		
Factor 3 (Value)	Practical	0.842	8.105	93.119
	Upscale	0.678		

Table 4. Cluster analysis result

Category	Sample number	Kansei intention	Modelling feature
1	1, 5, 6, 9, 10, 15, 17, 20, 25, 28, 32	Concise, Graceful, Modern	Dial, screen, watch strap, button
2	2, 11, 13, 19, 24, 27, 30, 31	Comfortable, Modern, Practical	Dial, watch strap, button
3	7, 8, 12, 14, 21, 22, 26	Graceful, Comfortable, Demotic	Dial, frame, screen, watch strap
4	3, 4, 16, 18, 23	Concise, Practical	Dial, frame, watch strap

Table 5. Modeling designing element classification sheet

Designing Element	Classification (Modeling Distribution)
Dial (X1)	C11 Rounded square C12 Rounded rectangle C13 Circle Others C14
Strap (X2)	C21 Integral C22 Separated C23 Others
Button(X3)	C31 Circle C32 Ellipse C33 rectangle C34 Large rounded rectangle Others C35

4.5   The Establishment of Kansei Evaluation Matrix and Mathematical Model

According to the results of cluster analysis, select 12 typical samples from collective product samples, conclude 4 representative adjectives by factor analysis, quantify design elements into quantitative data of 1 and 0 and construct kansei evaluation matrix. We can design elements as independent variables and the average value of the kansei evaluation as the dependent variable according to the matrix. The mathematical model is established as the multiple regression equation, see Table 6.

Table 6. Kansei evaluation matrix

Sample NO.	Kansei evaluation adjectives				Designing elements											
					Dial(X1)				Strap(X2)			Button(X3)				
	Concise	Graceful	Comfortable	Practical	C11	C12	C13	C14	C21	C22	C23	C31	C32	C33	C34	C35
1	0.92	0.95	0.90	0.86	1	0	0	0	0	1	0	0	0	1	0	0
2	0.71	0.83	0.76	0.71	0	0	1	0	1	0	0	0	1	0	0	0
3	0.64	0.81	0.59	0.67	0	1	0	0	0	1	0	0	0	0	1	0
4	0.91	0.82	0.62	0.69	1	0	0	0	1	0	0	0	0	0	0	1
5	0.53	0.74	1.09	0.88	0	0	0	1	0	1	0	0	0	0	1	0
6	0.50	0.76	0.87	-0.27	0	0	1	0	0	1	0	0	0	0	1	0
7	0.66	0.59	0.97	0.72	1	0	0	0	0	1	0	1	0	0	0	0
8	0.63	0.68	-0.13	0.91	0	1	0	0	1	0	0	0	0	1	0	0
9	0.37	0.90	0.87	0.75	1	0	0	0	0	1	0	1	0	0	0	0
10	-0.19	0.57	0.63	1.10	0	1	0	0	0	0	1	0	0	0	0	1
11	0.75	0.52	0.66	0.90	1	0	0	0	1	0	0	1	0	0	0	0
12	0.76	0.90	0.56	0.75	0	1	0	0	0	1	0	0	0	1	0	0

4.6   Solution and Analysis of Mathematical Model

Solving models by quantifying theory I and obtaining important values like item scores, scope of projects (partial correlation coefficient), constant terms, multiple correlation coefficients and coefficients of determination with the help of calculation software. See it in Table 7:

Thus, taking kansei intention "concise" as an example, we can obtain its regression equation:

$$Y_{Concise} = 14C11 + 0.377C12 - 206C13 + 0.186C14 + 0.728C21 + 0.26C22 - 0.062C3 + 0.219C31 - 0.178C32 + 0.353C33 + 0.208C34 - 0.252C35 + 3.751;$$

Relevant values concerning the three kansei adjectives "graceful", "comfortable" and "practical" can be obtained in the same method. See the numbers in Table 8:

And mathematical models of which the coefficients between groups of kansei intentions and designing elements are explicit can be made according to this, so as to achieve the purpose of predicting the kansei intentions of consumers, facilitating the design of models.

Table 7. Relevant data obtained by regression analysis (kansei intentional word "concise")

Designing elements	Categories	Item scores	Scope of projects (Partial correlation coefficient)	Constant terms	Coefficients of determination	Multiple correlation coefficients
Dial (X1)	C11	0.514	0.573	3.751	0.793	0.891
	C12	0.377				
	C13	−0.206				
	C14	0.186				
Strap (X2)	C21	0.728	0.288			
	C22	0.260				
	C23	−0.062				
Button (X3)	C31	0.219	0.396			
	C32	−0.178				
	C33	0.353				
	C34	0.208				
	C35	−0.252				

Table 8. Scores of designed items about kansei intentional adjectives

Kansei adjectives	Dial(X1)	Strap(X2)	Button(X3)
Concise	0.573	0.288	0.396
Graceful	0.461	0.138	0.221
Comfortable	0.602	0.376	0.559
Practical	0.668	0.257	0.473

5   Results and Test

We can conclude from the previous research results from 4.1 to 4.6 about older consumers' rough intention or preference: that the elders pay more attention to some practical functions in smart watch, like long standby time, time reminding and medicine reminding, as well as some health care functions such as SOS, medicine reminding, blood pressure monitoring and heart rate monitoring, while some other functions are relatively inferior. Concerning appearance, the elders prefer concise, elegant, comfortable and practical watch, and the dials and buttons have greater effects on the appearance kansei intention, which require special focus of the product developers when designed. Watchband doesn't affect the appearance too much, while it does affect the degree of comfort to some extent.

Finally, select 24 samples to take verification. Obtaining one set of data through kansei predictions by modeling. Meanwhile, select another 30 testers to give kansei scores, which produce another set of data. T-Test analysis were carried out towards the predicted value and subjective evaluation means of the relational model, and the results showed that the T value in paired sample verification is 0.183, which is a bit low, while the sig (significance impact level) is 0.857, which is kind of big, illustrating there is no great difference between predicted value(calculated from the equations) and subjective evaluation means(re-evaluation), therefore indicating that the intention-predicting model is credible. See it in Table 9.

Table 9. T-Test data analysis (scores about the kansei adjective "concise")

Paired sample correlation coefficient				
		N	Correlation coefficient	Sig.
Pair1	Relational model predicted value & Subjective evaluation score	24	0.876	0.000

Paired sample test								
		Paired difference						
		Mean value	Standard deviation	Standard error of mean	95% confidence interval of difference		t	df	Sig (Paired sample test)
					Lower limit	Upper limit			
Pair1	Predicted value of the relational model- Subjective evaluation score	0.00375	0.10060	0.02053	-0.03873	0.04623	0.183	23	0.857

6   Conclusions and Discussions

This study shows that consumer research can help the designers set up the functions on target and reasonably. Meanwhile, analyzing older consumers' model design towards electronic products by the means of Kansei engineering could increase the designer's accuracy, making them to know better what the products should be like. We may conclude from the above two points that designing products with the older people as center along with full investigations based on their kansei intention make the designing intention more accurate and more practical, the appearance and shape more correspond to consumers' kansei cognition and physiological characteristics, and help bring convenience and pleasure, increasing elder consumers' satisfaction.

References

Population Division, DESA, United Nations, World Population Ageing 1950–2050 (2002)

Nagamachi, M.: Kansei engineering: a new ergonomic consumer-oriented technology for product development. Int. J. Ind. Ergon. **15**, 3–11 (1995)

Norman, D.A.: Emotional Design: Why Do We Love (or Hate) Everyday Things. Basic Books, New York (2004)

Han, S.: Usability of consumer electronic products. Int. J. Ind. Ergon. **28**, 143–151 (2001)

Beom, S., Yong, G., Kyeyoun, C.: Development of a usability evaluation framework with quality function deployment: from customer sensibility to product design. Hum. Factors Ergon. Manuf. **19**, 177–194 (2009)

Boletsis, C., McCallum, S., Landmark, B.F.: The use of smartwatches for health monitoring in home-based dementia care. In: Zhou, J., Salvendy, G. (eds.) ITAP 2015. LNCS, vol. 9194, pp. 15–26. Springer, Heidelberg (2015)

Hartono, M., Tan, K.C., Ishihara, S., Peacock, B.: Incorporating Markov chain modeling and QFD into kansei engineering applied to services. Int. J. Hum. Factors Ergon. **1**, 74–97 (2012)

Nagamachi, M., Lokman, A.M.: Innovation of Kansei Engineering. CRC Press, Taylor & Francis Group, Boca Raton (2011)

Huang, C., Tang, W., Shao, J.: Research on intelligent watch modeling based on consumer psychology and perceptual engineering. Mech. Des. Manuf. Eng. **11**, 32–37 (2014)

A Study of the Factors Affecting the Usability of Smart Phone Screen Protectors for the Elderly

Shuo-Fang Liu, Ching-Fen Chang[✉], Ming-Hong Wang, and Hsin-Hsi Lai

Department of Industrial Design, National Cheng-Kung University, No. 1, University Road, Tainan City 701, Taiwan, ROC
P38041067@mail.ncku.edu.tw

Abstract. The issues arising from ageing societies have received worldwide attention. Many studies have pointed out that mobile technology can positively assist the elderly with smartphones being the most prevalent. The low sensitivity of finger touch and the slow response of a smartphone's interface may affect the finger coordination and stability of the elderly on the touch screen interface. A large number of studies suggest that the sense of touch can provide smartphone users to experience richer interaction than audio visual communications alone. Therefore, the reason for using the four different smartphone screen protector materials (Anti-Smudge (AS), Anti-Smudge and Glare (ASG), Blue Light Cut (BLC), and Tempered Glass (TG)) for this experiment on smartphone users aged 50 and above. Each material is scored with a usability evaluation method in order to obtain the superior screen protector in regards to usability for the elderly. The results from the experiments found that TG was the most suitable for elderly, followed by ASG, and then AS. It also showed that the thickness of the smartphone screen protectors do not affect elderly users when manipulating the screen surface. However, smooth surfaced, matte touch material with a translucent visual exterior seems to be the most suitable for elderly smartphone users.

Keywords: Elderly · Smart phone · Screen protectors · Usability

1 Background

The phenomenon of increased living age and ageing population is one that impacts the global society. According to the World Population Ageing 2015 Highlights statistics report from the United Nations, the global number of people aged over sixty has reached nine hundred million, and this number is predicted to increase to fourteen hundred million in 2030 [1]. When the ageing population issue becomes serious, a society is labeled a "Super Aged Society". In an ageing society, the elderly might have physiological deteriorations which can lead to disabilities. These disabilities, which may be associated with their psychological and social adaptation issues, will require new solutions.

© Springer International Publishing Switzerland 2016
J. Zhou and G. Salvendy (Eds.): ITAP 2016, Part I, LNCS 9754, pp. 457–465, 2016.
DOI: 10.1007/978-3-319-39943-0_44

Research indicates that mobile technology not only stimulates the ageing positively, but also provides them with a powerful assistive technology, which can help
them to maintain their own independency and self-esteem. In addition, this technology
enables the ageing to remain connected to society. Mobile technology has the potential
to provide new opportunities to enhance the health and the quality of life of the elderly,
especially when they begin suffering from health issues. Many studies have found that
as a person ages, their physical functions, including reaction speeds and the ability to
receive and assess information, deteriorate and regress. These regressions can negatively impact on their daily lives, and may lead to increased psychological issues [2, 3].
Mobile devices have been integrated with more digitized functions which enable them
to exchange and interact with information more efficiently, and as a result, the market
share of smartphone have seen a considerable growth. The following chapters will
investigate the usability of smartphones for the elderly.

1.1   How Ageing Affects the Use of the Hands

As people age, their muscle fibers decrease and shorten. Muscle contractions weaken,
which affects of the elderly by making their movements slower. As a result of this
muscle deterioration, it may be difficult for people to press the small icons or buttons as
they age and their abilities of control and manipulation decrease [4, 5]. Elderly people
may, therefore, struggle to use devices and applications which require small movements. Moreover, slower mental reactions may affect the ability to receive and process
information in the brain which could in turn impact the coordination and stability on
their movements.

1.2   Receiving Information System

As people receive the information through visual images, ageing increases the difficulty
to receive information via the eyes. The eyes may suffer from several impairments,
such as lesions, yellowing, cloudy and blurred vision, and poor color sensitivity
(especially to the color blue and yellow) [6]. Hyperopia, or farsightedness, is another
health issue that may develop as a person ages. This impairment can also result in
difficulty when receiving and reacting to visual stimulation [7, 8]. Because of the
effects that these numerous health issues resulting in the degradation of vision have on
the elderly, fatigue while staring at a small, lit screen is quite a common complaint [9].

Another method of receiving messages is through the tactile sense. The tactile sense
conveys information, such as the feeling of pain and temperature, by processing
external stimulations through the skin [10]. As skin ages, a rough surface develops.
This results in a lower quantity of sensory cells, which in turn decreases the sensitivity
of the tactile sense, which often results in the person being able to endure more pain
[11, 12]. The tactile sense is important because it not only allows one to react to their
environment immediately, but it can also help with psycho-social development to
encourage interpersonal relationship communications [10, 13].

1.3   Usability Design

Usability design is a user-base oriented approach to creating the criteria of product designs. The main purpose is to investigate and analyze the positives and negatives of a design to improve the product. In 1980, many designers, scholars, and experts suggested that the "user friendly" concept should be emphasized on product designs with "user-base orientation" to meet the users' demands, as opposed to requiring users to learn the functions of the product [14]. Furthermore, "Quality Attribute" and "Ease of Use" are the required concepts to adjust and improve the simplicity for the users [15]. The Usability Metrics (Errors, Efficiency, Learnability, Memorability, and Satisfaction) are used to ensure that the design processes can meet the users' requirements.

1.4   Investigating Problems and Assessment

Smartphones work through touch and, in most cases, commands are executed by using the fingers to touch and slide across the surface of the screen. However, because of the low sensitivity of the sense of touch and slow reactions to the visuals on the screen, the elderly often have difficulty using smartphones. The literature found that richer interactive experiences can be created by enhancing the tactile sense on the screen while using the smartphone. These experiences can be more rewarding than traditional audio visual communications [16]. Therefore, this research will investigate the effect of different screen protectors on the elderly focusing on the tactile sense. From the findings, this study will make a recommendation for the ideal screen protectors for use by the elderly.

2   Method

2.1   Experimental Setup

As previously discussed, ageing creates problems for people. One study showed that the sensitivity of the sense of touch starts to deteriorate from the age of fifty [17], while another study showed that the clarity of sight begins to weaken as age increases [18].

- Participants: The thirty participants, who were over fifty years old, were recruited from various community centers in Taiwan for this research.
- Material Sample: The four most popular types of screen protectors for smartphones in the current market were selected for the questionnaire (see Table 1).
- Experimental Tool: All participants used the same five-inch screen Android smartphone to maintain a level of experimental accuracy and consistency.
- Conducting Experiment: The experiment was conducted on a one-to-one basis. Before the experiment, the topic and the experiment process were reviewed. Some ground rules were also introduced at the beginning. Next, the participants used the smartphones without screen protectors for five minutes. After these five minutes, the participants used each of the four different screen protectors in order. These screen protectors were scored with a usability evaluation questionnaire. Each section lasted twenty minutes.

Table 1. The experimental subjects

Material Sample	AS (Anti-Smudge)	ASG (Anti-Smudge & Glare)	BLC (Blue Light Cut)	TG (Tempered Glass)
Material	PET	PET	PET	Glass
Thickness	0.2mm	0.22mm	0.22mm	0.35mm
Visual characteristics	Glossy	Matte	Glossy with yellow color	Translucent

2.2 Experimental Process

Using the actual smartphone with each of the four different material protectors allowed the participants to be able to define the differences between them precisely. The experimental process was as follows:

- Participants were asked to enter a list of specific number to unlock the screen, and make a phone call using a method familiar to them. This could help to provide an evaluation of the error rate.
- The study found that minimizing, rotating, sliding and enlarge objects on the screen were the most common commands input by touch [19]. However, the methods of minimizing, enlarging, and rotating objects on the screen are more complicated. These commands are associated with the Learnability and memory evaluation.

2.3 Usability Questionnaire

The questionnaire content contained seven Usability Metrics which were: Errors, Efficiency, Learnability, Memorability, Satisfaction, Visual, and Sense of Touch. A Likert Scale was used to evaluate the level of the participants' satisfactions. A lower score represented lower satisfaction, while a higher score represented higher satisfaction.

3 Result

3.1 Comparative Analysis of Each Marital Sample

After compiling all of the statistical data of the four material samples, it was analyzed in ANOVA. The results showed that the different screen protectors had significant differences in performance (P<0.05) (see Table 2). After this the results of each material sample were compared, and examining the inner factors that influenced each other, to obtain the relative merits for the participants (see Table 3). The results found that the most recommended screen protector for the elderly was the material sample TG, follow by ASG, then AS.

Table 2. Usability statistics results

			Evaluation items						
			Errors	Efficiency	Learnability	Memorability	Visual	Sense of Touch	Overall Satisfaction
Sample	AS	Number	30	30	30	30	30	30	30
		Mean	2.4	2.8	2.4	2.1	3.4	2.8	3.1
		S.D.	0.9	1.1	1.1	0.9	1.0	1.2	1.2
	ASG	Number	30	30	30	30	30	30	30
		Mean	2.9	3.0	2.9	2.4	2.9	3.3	3.3
		S.D.	1.2	1.0	1.3	1.3	1.1	1.0	1.2
	BLC	Number	30	30	30	30	30	30	30
		Mean	2.8	2.8	3.8	3.2	3.1	2.6	3.3
		S.D.	1.1	1.3	1.1	1.3	1.2	1.3	1.2
	TG	Number	30	30	30	30	30	30	30
		Mean	3.3	3.7	3.6	3.2	4.2	4.2	4.1
		S.D.	1.1	1.1	1.1	1.4	0.7	0.8	0.9
F value			3.078	4.636	9.775	6.585	9.897	13.259	4.533
P value (significance)			0.03	0.004	0.000	0.000	0.000	0.000	0.005

Moreover, the results indicate that the smooth-surfaced, matte touch, translucent material is probably the most suitable screen protector for elderly smartphone users. One interesting finding was that the thickness of the screen protector seemed to have no difference on the user. The further discussions on the differences of results with the (*) symbol (see Table 3) as follow:

1. TG>AS has significant differences on Errors (p=0.016<0.05)
2. TG>AS, and TG>BLC shows noticeable differences on Efficiency and Sensitivity (Both p=0.009<0.05)

3. BLC>AS shows the most outstanding differences than other comparisons on Learnability (p=0.000<0.05)
4. BLC>AS, and TG>AS both shows great differences on Memorability of hand/finger gestures (p=0.002<0.05)
5. TG shows the highest differences on Overall Satisfaction on the comfort of visual and sense of touch (p<0.05)

Table 3. The usability of analysis of variance on the different smartphone screen protectors

Variable	(I) gesture	(J) gesture	The average difference (I-J)	Standard error	Significance	Comparison result	Variable	(I) gesture	(J) gesture	The average difference (I-J)	Standard error	Significance	Comparison result
Errors	AS	ASG	-0.467	0.276	0.334		Efficiency	AS	ASG	-0.233	0.29	0.852	
		BLC	-0.367	0.276	0.547				BLC	0.000	0.29	1.000	
		TG	*-0.833**	*0.276*	*0.016*				*TG*	*-0.933**	*0.29*	*0.009*	
	ASG	AS	0.467	0.276	0.334			ASG	AS	0.233	0.29	0.852	
		BLC	0.1	0.276	0.984				BLC	0.233	0.29	0.852	
		TG	-0.367	0.276	0.547	TG>ASG>BLC>AS			TG	-0.700	0.29	0.080	TG>ASG>BLC,AS
	BLC	AS	0.367	0.276	0.547			BLC	AS	0.000	0.29	1.000	
		ASG	-0.1	0.276	0.984				ASG	-0.233	0.29	0.852	
		TG	-0.467	0.276	0.334				*TG*	*-0.933**	*0.29*	*0.009*	
	TG	*AS*	*0.833**	*0.276*	*0.016*			TG	*AS*	*0.933**	*0.29*	*0.009*	
		ASG	0.367	0.276	0.547				ASG	0.7	0.29	0.080	
		BLC	0.467	0.276	0.334				*BLC*	*0.933**	*0.29*	*0.009*	
Learnability	AS	ASG	-0.467	0.293	0.386		Memorability	AS	ASG	-0.367	0.313	0.647	
		BLC	*-1.367**	*0.293*	*0.000*				*BLC*	*-1.133**	*0.313*	*0.002*	
		TG	*-1.233**	*0.293*	*0.000*				*TG*	*-1.133**	*0.313*	*0.002*	
	ASG	AS	0.467	0.293	0.386			ASG	AS	0.367	0.313	0.647	
		BLC	*-0.9**	*0.293*	*0.014*				BLC	-0.767	0.313	0.074	
		TG	*-0.767**	*0.293*	*0.048*	BLC>TG>ASG>AS			TG	-0.767	0.313	0.074	BLC,TG>ASG>AS
	BLC	*AS*	*1.367**	*0.293*	*0.000*			BLC	*AS*	*1.133**	*0.313*	*0.002*	
		ASG	*0.9**	*0.293*	*0.014*				ASG	0.767	0.313	0.074	
		TG	0.133	0.293	0.968				TG	0.000	0.313	1.000	
	TG	*AS*	*1.233**	*0.293*	*0.000*			TG	*AS*	*1.133**	*0.313*	*0.002*	
		ASG	*0.767**	*0.293*	*0.048*				ASG	0.767	0.313	0.074	
		BLC	-0.133	0.293	0.968				BLC	0.0	0.313	1.000	

Visual	AS	ASG	0.433	0.263	0.355		Sense of Touch	AS	ASG	-0.5	0.286	0.310
		BLC	0.3	0.263	0.664				BLC	0.2	0.326	0.928
		TG	-0.867*	0.263	0.007				TG	-1.433*	0.267	0.000
	ASG	AS	-0.433	0.263	0.355			ASG	AS	0.5	0.286	0.310
		BLC	-0.133	0.263	0.957				BLC	0.7	0.298	0.100
		TG	-1.3*	0.263	0.000	TG>AS>BLC>ASG			TG	-0.933*	0.232	0.001
	BLC	AS	-0.300	0.263	0.664			BLC	AS	-0.2	0.326	0.928
		ASG	0.133	0.263	0.957				ASG	-0.7	0.298	0.100
		TG	-1.167*	0.263	0.000				TG	-1.633*	0.280	0.000
	TG	AS	0.867*	0.263	0.007			TG	AS	1.433*	0.267	0.000
		ASG	1.3*	0.263	0.000				ASG	0.933*	0.232	0.001
		BLC	1.167*	0.263	0.000				BLC	1.633*	0.280	0.000

Sense of Touch note: TG>ASG>BLC>AS

Satisfaction	AS	ASG	-0.2	0.286	0.898	
		BLC	-0.167	0.286	0.937	
		TG	-0.967*	0.286	0.005	
	ASG	AS	0.2	0.286	0.898	
		BLC	0.033	0.286	0.999	
		TG	-0.767*	0.286	0.042	TG>ASG,BLC>AS
	BLC	AS	0.167	0.286	0.937	
		ASG	-0.033	0.286	0.999	
		TG	-0.80*	0.286	0.031	
	TG	AS	0.967*	0.286	0.005	
		ASG	0.767*	0.286	0.042	
		BLC	0.8*	0.286	0.031	

4 Discussion

Generally, the translucent screen protector seemed to hold more beneficial characteristics to assist the smartphone users. However, the results indicate that the TG material sample was superior to the ASG material, which had different characteristic than others (see Table 1). Moreover, a majority of the participants agreed that the touch and visual differences of the ASG material sample were obvious. These findings are as follow:

1. The characteristic of visual translucent

There was a higher score on the visual translucent characteristic showed for the TG material sample than ASG and BLC. This could imply that the elderly prefer a translucent screen and clean than soften lights.

2. The characteristic of smooth in the feeling of touch

The TG material sample was observed to have the smoothest feeling of all of the material samples. This was followed by ASG, AS, and BLC (see Table 1). However, it is interesting to note that most participants preferred ASG which had a rougher surface.

3. Increasing the sensitivity in sense of touch properly

In this research, most participants agreed that most of the difficulties of using smartphones were from learning new instructions. However, most participants indicated that they felt the responses were more sensitive when using the TG material sample, which seemed to negatively impact on Learnability. Surprisingly, this seemed to increase the level of difficulty when using the smartphone as the participants felt that they had to respond quicker.

5   Conclusion

5.1   Implication

The aim of this study was to discover which material would suit the needs and requirements of elderly smartphone users. The researcher's interpretation of the findings clearly recommend the use of two different materials. The findings suggest that the two most suitable materials were the TG and ASG screen protector material samples. Therefore, by applying the proper screen protector, elderly people could be encouraged use smartphones. The findings of this research could, therefore, be of use to organizations or companies that want to make smartphones more accessible and attractive to the elderly.

5.2   Limitations and Suggestions for Further Study

This study was not without limitations. For one, each experiment demanded much from the participants. Each participant had to use four different material samples and had to feedback on each of the usability metrics. This made each experiment somewhat lengthy. Therefore, a more effective method of data collection, such as through using by metrology equipment, could increase accuracy and decrease the duration of each experiment.

Another limitation could be age group. Different age groups would provide different sensitivities of touch and sight, which could offer a more varied insight into the requirements of the elderly compared to other age groups. A study investigating the preferences of different age groups may provide information for people interested in marketing screen protectors and smartphones for the elderly.

References

1. Department of Economic and Social Affairs. World Population Ageing 2015 Highlights. United Nations (2015). http://www.un.org/en/development/desa/population/publications/pdf/ageing/WPA2015_Highlights.pdf. Accessed 04 Feb 2015
2. Hardill, I., Olphert, C.W.: Staying connected: exploring mobile phone use amongst older adults in the UK. Geoforum **43**(6), 1306–1312 (2013)
3. Plaza, I., Martin, L., Martin, S., Medrano, C.: Mobile applications in an aging society: status and trends. J. Syst. Softw. **84**(11), 1977–1988 (2011)

4. Lee, C.-F., Kuo, C.-C.: Difficulties on small-touch-screens for various ages. In: Stephanidis, C. (ed.) HCI 2007. LNCS, vol. 4554, pp. 968–974. Springer, Heidelberg (2007)
5. Seidler, R., Stelmach, G.: Motor Control, Encyclopedia of Gerontology: Age, Aging and the Aged. Academic Press, San Diego (1996)
6. Schneck, M.E., Haegerstrom-Portnoy, G., Lott, L.A., Brabyn, J.A.: Comparison of panel D-15 tests in a large older population. Optom. Vis. Sci.: Official Publication of the American Academy of Optometry 91(3), 284–290 (2014)
7. Czaja, S.J.: Microcomputers and elderly. In: Helander, M. (ed.) Human-computer Interaction, pp. 584–598. Elsevier, New York (1988)
8. Zajicek, M.: Interface design for older adults. In: Proceedings of the 2001 EC/NSF Workshop on Universal Accessibility of Ubiquitous Computing: Providing for the Elderly, 21–25 May, Alcácer do Sal (2001)
9. Welford, A.T.: Changes of performance with age. In: Charness, N. (ed.) Aging and Human Performance, pp. 333–369. Wiley, Chichester (1985, 1987)
10. Sallnäs, E.L., Rassmus-Gröhn, K., Sjöström, C.: Supporting presence in collaborative environments by haptic force feedback. ACM Trans. Comput. Hum. Interact. (TOCHI) 7(4), 461–476 (2000)
11. 沙, 依仁.: 高齡學. Wu-Nan Book Inc., Taipei (1995)
12. Peng, C.H.: Gerontology. Yang-Chih Book Co., Ltd., Taipei (1999)
13. Chellali, A., Dumas, C., Milleville-Pennel, I.: Influences of haptic communication on a shared manual task. Interact. Comput. 23(4), 317–328 (2011)
14. Bevan, N., Kirakowski, J., Maissel, J.: What is usability? In: Proceedings of the 4th International Conference on HCI, Stuttgart, 1–6 September 1991
15. Nielsen, J.: Usability Engineering. AP Professional, Cambridge (1993)
16. Banter, B.: Touch screens and touch surfaces are enriched by haptic force-feedback. Inf. Display 26(3), 26–30 (2010)
17. Fisk, A.D., Rogers, W.A., Charness, N., Czaja, S.J., Sharit, J.: Designing for Older Adults: Principles and Creative Human Factors Approaches. CRC Press, New York (2004)
18. Saxon, S.V., Etten, M.J., Perkins, E.A.: A Guide for the Helping Professions: Physical Change and Aging, 5th edn. Springer Publishing Company, New York (2010)
19. Wang, M.-H., Chang, Y.-C., Liu, S.-F., Lai, H.-H.: Developing new gesture design mode in smartphone use for elders. In: Zhou, J., Salvendy, G. (eds.) ITAP 2015. LNCS, vol. 9193, pp. 519–527. Springer, Heidelberg (2015)

Effect of Icon Amount and Visual Density on Usability of Smartwatches

Fan Mo[✉], Shuping Yi, and Jia Zhou

Department of Industrial Engineering, Chongqing University, Chongqing 400044, China
mofan1992@gmail.com, ysp@cqu.edu.cn, zhoujia07@gmail.com

Abstract. Appropriate design for smartwatches menu on the tiny touchscreen is desired and, hence, this study aims to explore the effect of icon amount and visual density on older adults' performance and satisfaction. To achieve this goal, an experiment was conducted. A total of 15 older adults participated in this study. The results of this study showed which combination of visual density and icon amount was better on the tiny screen (e.g., 40 mm wide and 40 mm high). First, a small number of icon amount (e.g., 8 icons) was generally better used in smartwatches menu. In that case, both visual density of 4 icons per page and 8 icons per page caused better performance. Second, compared with 1 icon and 8 icons per page, the visual density of 4 icons per page might was the best choice if the number of icon amount was large (e.g., 24 icons and 48 icons). Finally, the study also indicated that older adults' gestures of wearing smartwatches on the back of wrist, taping with the index finger and closing hand related to better performance.

Keywords: Smartwatches menu · Icon amount · Visual density · Older adults · Users' gestures

1 Introduction

Smartwatches are in dilemma about how to display abundant applications on a tiny display with the increasingly used by older adults. They have the potential to seamlessly integrate with human body and integrate functions of health care and personal safety, which could benefit older adults in particular. But displaying functions on a tiny display is a great challenge for older adults. To solve this problem, the menu is widely used in smartwatches to organize applications.

The icon amount and visual density of menus might influence older adults' performance and satisfaction. Icon amount is the total number of applications in the menu, and visual density is the number of applications from per page. A large number of icon amount could result in long and complex menus, and a large number of visual density could increase older adults' cognitive load. Previous research found that proper smartphones menu' icon amount and visual density could improve interface usability. However, there is a lack of study on the icon amount and visual density of smartwatches. Therefore, this paper proposed different icon amount and visual density of smartwatches, developed prototypes, and tested their effect on older adults' performance and satisfaction through experiment.

© Springer International Publishing Switzerland 2016
J. Zhou and G. Salvendy (Eds.): ITAP 2016, Part I, LNCS 9754, pp. 466–477, 2016.
DOI: 10.1007/978-3-319-39943-0_45

2 Literature Review

In previous research, the menus of smartphones and smartwatches were studied. The limited display size could increase users memory load [1]. In order to reduce the memory burden on the users, the depth, breadth of menus should appropriate [2, 3]. There could be conflict with between menu breadth and font size. A study on feature phones showed that displaying five menu items per page was better than displaying one menu item per page, and 12pt font size was better than 8pt [4]. As to the smartwatch, four most common menus (one-line list, two-line grid menu, rotating menu, and clustered menu) were tested. The results showed that two-line grid menu and clustered menu were more efficient at performance [5].

As to the interaction of smartwatches, most of studies focused on the input of smartwatches. Existing studies can be classified as two branches: interaction outside the display or interaction inside the display. As to interaction outside the display, Perrault, Lecolinet, Eagan and Guiard [6] proposed a novel gesture technique for wristband interaction, in order to avoid the visual occlusion and the fat finger problem. And then, Knibbe et al. [7] extended the interactive surface for a smartwatch to the back of the hand and defined a range of supported bimanual gestures. As to interaction inside the display, text entry was redesigned to adapt to the tiny input screen and obtained a better result than the original interface [8, 9]. However, when users taped on the screen, the error rates became higher as the buttons became smaller [10]. In addition, Shen, Xue, Li and Zhou [11] indicated that the number of the icons should not be more than 25 in one area, and for small number of the icons, the interelement spacing should be more than 1/2 icon.

The study of the output of smartwatches is needed. This research chose icon amount and visual density as two factors, to find out their effect on performance and satisfaction of smartwatches.

3 Methodology

3.1 Variables

The independent variables were icon amount and visual density. Both of them were within-subject variables. Three levels of icon amount were 8 icons, 24 icons, and 48 icons. Three levels of visual density were 1 icon per page, 4 icons per page, and 8 icons per page.

Recent investigations indicated that there were average 95 installed apps on smartphones around the world [12], and there were average 36 installed third-party apps on smartphones in China [13]. Further, the existing smartwatches (Moto 360, Apple Watch, and Samsung Gear) showed that the available number of icon amount ranged from 6 to 64, and visual density of 1, 2 and 9 icons per page were appropriate choices. To ensure that visual density was appropriate and would not change in every page, icon amount of 8, 24 and 48 icons and visual density of 1, 4 and 8 icons per page were chosen.

The stimulus displayed nine prototypes on a smartwatch, and prototypes of three levels of visual density are shown in Fig. 1. The icon's dimensions were 6.30 mm (60px) wide and 6.30 mm (60px) high. The distance between two icons was 3.78 mm (36px) in the prototypes with 4 icons per page, and was 1.58 mm (15px) in the prototypes with 8 icons per page.

Fig. 1. The stimulus of three levels of visual density on Moto 360

The dependent variables were task effectiveness, efficiency and users' satisfaction. In total, six different dependent variables were surveyed. Two measures referred to effectiveness, three of the measures addressed efficiency, and one measure was related to users' satisfaction of using prototypes. The measures are described in detail below.

Effectiveness can be measured by the success rates of solving tasks, and the success rates of taping. Efficiency can be measured by the number of necessary swiping left in the menu, the number of swiping right, and task completion time. Every task started with the first page, so users needed to keep swiping left to complete the tasks. The measure of number of swiping right indicated that users in the belief of having crossed the correct position went back to a previous position within the menu.

Users' satisfaction was measured by questionnaire (PSSUQ). It has seven items. Six items measures user's perceived usability [14], and the last item is an overall question to measure usage intention [15]. Five-point Likert scale was used.

Four demographic variables were taken into account. User' basic information (age, education, etc.) was measured by questionnaire. User's finger dexterity and vision were measured by finger dexterity test and near vision test. Moreover, users' gestures of using the smartwatch were recorded.

3.2   Participants

Sixteen older adults (9 males and 6 females) took part in this experiment. Their average age was 65.47 (SD = 5.29, range 59 to 74). They were recruited from Chongqing Jiangbei district Yuzui aged community. Older adults who had poor eyesight were encouraged to wear presbyopia glasses. 73.3 % of older adults had Junior High School diploma. 26.67 % of them had used smartphones for 2 years. 33.33 % of them used to wear watches until they started to use mobile phones. Participants were highly interested in their performance and enjoyed this experiment very well.

3.3   Equipment

One pilot test was conducted in older adult' home. Formal experiment was conducted in an office of the Citizen School of Yuzui, Jiangbei, Chongqing. Prior to the task, a Finger Dexterity Tester (Beida Jade Bird, 2-601) and a Near Vision Test Card were used to measure the participants' finger dexterity and vision. In the experiment, a smartwatch (Moto 360; screen: 1.56″, 320 × 290, round; OS: Android Wear OS 5.1.1) and a smartphone (Xiaomi 2; screen: 4.3″, 1280 × 720; OS: Android OS 5.0.2, MIUI Global 7.1) were used. Moto 360 connected to Xiaomi 2 via Bluetooth, and the nine prototypes were running on them. Prototypes were developed by Java language. The coordinates and times of every tap and swipe were listened and recorded.

3.4   Experimental Tasks

These prototypes were tested in a random order. Participants were required to complete 45 tasks, and five tasks for each prototype. Each participant was requested to search for a target number in each task. The numbers were in a random arrangement.

In order to know the target number they were going to search in a task, participants needed to look at the smartphone screen at first (shown in Fig. 2). They searched for the target number by swiping left and right within prototypes and taped the icon with the correct number. Then, the number on the smartphone screen changed into the next target number of tasks. When a tap was detected, the background color of icon turned green to alert the participants. Meanwhile, the smartphone played the sound of a beep in order to draw participants' attention to the change of target number.

Fig. 2. Illustration of the display conditions in the smartphone and smartwatch

These prototypes were designed for simulating the scenario of using real smartwatches menu, so each task started with the first page. To record the start time in a prototype, each prototype contained a dialog box that was displayed before all tasks began, and participants taped to start the first task. After participants completed the tasks of one prototype, a dialog box of "End and Congratulations" displayed.

3.5 Procedures

The experiment took each participant about 60 min. The experiment process was listed as follows. First, participants were given an overall introduction of the experiment and were required to complete a questionnaire in order to provide their personal details. Under the Finger Dexterity Tester (shown in Fig. 3), participants were required to align steel pins at holes, and put them in the holes one by one from "Start" to "End". Participants' finger dexterity was measured through the total time taken to complete. Further, participants' vision was measured. Second, participants were shown a basic demonstration of the system. They practiced about the basic operation of prototypes and completed the tasks in this tutorial demonstrate. And then, participants were required to complete the 45 tasks. The details of user action in every task were recorded. Each participant was encouraged to complete the experiment individually, and was not allowed to talk with experimenters. After completing each prototype, participants filled in the PSSUQ. In the final of the experiment, participants were interviewed briefly. Two experiment field scenes are shown in Fig. 3.

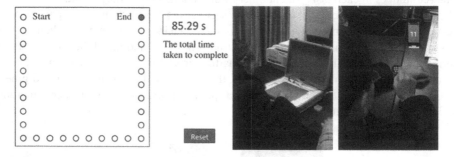

Fig. 3. Instruction of Finger Dexterity Tester and experiment field scenes (finger dexterity test and fulfilling tasks in the smartwatch)

4   Results and Discussion

4.1   Overall Performance

The influences of icon amount and visual density on effectiveness and efficiency were tested through MANOVA. The results showed that they did not significantly affect effectiveness. Regarding efficiency, there were significant differences in the number of swiping left ($F(2,126) = 100.3$, $p < 0.001$), the number of swiping right ($F(2,126) = 10.3$, $p < 0.001$), and task completion time ($F(2,126) = 88.2$, $p < 0.001$) among three levels of icon amount. What's more, there were significant differences in the number of swiping left ($F(2,126) = 168.2$, $p < 0.001$), the number of swiping right ($F(2,126) = 11.6$, $p < 0.001$), and task completion time ($F(2,126) = 55.4$, $p < 0.001$) among three levels of visual density. Therefore, multiple comparison was conducted.

As shown in Fig. 4, there were significant differences between icon amount of 8 and 24 icons ($t < 0.001$), 8 and 48 icons ($t < 0.001$), 24 and 48 icons ($t < 0.001$), and there were significant differences between visual density of 1 and 4 icons per page (t < 0.001), 1 and 8 icons per page (t < 0.001), 4 and 8 icons per page (t = 0.019) in the number of swiping left. Prototypes with larger number of icon amount or lower visual density had larger number of swiping left than the opposite prototypes. One possible reason was that breadth of the menu was increased, so participants needed to search the page one by one within the menu through swiping left.

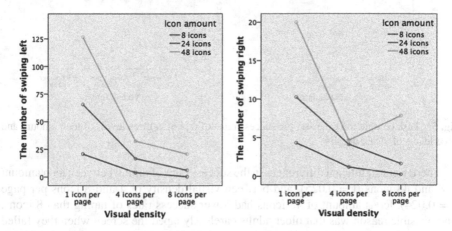

Fig. 4. The number of swiping left and the number of swiping right in three levels of icon amount and three levels of visual density

There were significant differences between icon amount of 8 and 48 icons (t < 0.001), 24 and 48 icons (t = 0.006), and between visual density of 1 and 4 icons per page (t < 0.001), 1 and 8 icons per page (t < 0.001) in the number of swiping right. Users went back to a previous position within the menu by swiping right, when they in the belief of having crossed the correct position. Which meant that icon amount of 48 icons or visual density of 1 icon per page led to that users were more likely to miss the target page.

As shown in Fig. 5, there were significant differences in the task completion time between icon amount of 8 and 24 icons (t < 0.001), 8 and 48 icons (t < 0.001), 24 and 48 icons (t < 0.001). That is, participants spent more time to search the target page with the increasing numbers of icon amount. There were significant differences in the task completion time between visual density of 1 and 4 icons per page (t < 0.001), 1 and 8 icons per page (t < 0.001). Similarly, low visual density led to the increasing of breadth of the menu, so participants spent more time when searching the target page. However, 4 icons per page had no significant differences with 8 icons per page. Which meant that searching in visual density of 4 and 8 icons per page were similar in task completion time for older adults.

The results indicated that icon amount and visual density has apparent influence on some aspects of efficiency. Further, multiple comparison was conducted to analysis the influence on effectiveness.

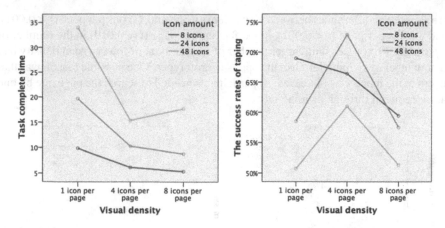

Fig. 5. Task completion time and the success rates of taping in three levels of icon amount and three levels of visual density

There were significant differences in the success rates of taping between icon amount of 8 and 48 icons (t = 0.025), and between visual density of 4 and 8 icons per page (t = 0.024). Icons amount of 48 icons had lower success rates of taping than 8 icons. One possible reason was that older adults carelessly taped the screen when they failed to swipe. That's one of the reasons why visual density of 1 icon per page had higher success rates of taping with the icon amount of 8 icons, but had lower success rates with 24 and 48 icons. Moreover, visual density of 8 icons per page was likely to lead to visual occlusion and the fat finger problem, which may further resulted in low success rates. And visual density of 4 icons per page had the highest success rates of taping compared with 1 and 8 icons per page. However, there were no significant differences in the success rates of solving tasks.

4.2   Users' Judgments with Respect to the Ease of Use

The average score of three levels of icon amount and three levels of visual density are shown in Fig. 6. The results indicated that participants preferred a menu with less number of icon amount or high visual density.

To dig into the reasons of the difference of users' satisfaction, results of interview were analyzed. Participants expressed their dissatisfied with the prototype with 24 total icons and 1 icon per page, and the prototype with 48 total icons and 1 icon per page. They generally felt tired to continuously swipe left within the menu, particularly when the number of icon amount was large. Surprisingly, older adults expressed no dissatisfied with the high visual density, although the success rates of taping were reduced. For the reason of older adults' less experience of using smartphones, they preferred the operation of taping rather than swiping, especially on a tiny touchscreen.

The influences of icon amount and visual density on users' satisfaction were tested through MANOVA. There were significant differences in satisfaction among three levels

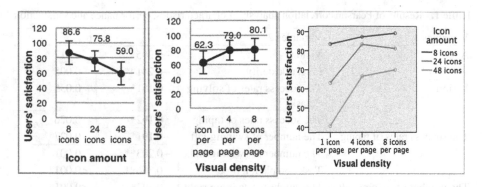

Fig. 6. Users' satisfaction in three levels of icon amount and three levels of visual density

of icon amount (F(2,126) = 35.2, p < 0.001), and among three levels of visual density (F(2,126) = 17.9, p < 0.001). Then, multiple comparison was conducted.

As shown in Fig. 6, there were significant differences between icon amount of 8 and 24 icons (t = 0.001), 8 and 48 icons (t < 0.001), 24 and 48 icons (t = 0.006), and between visual density of 1 and 4 icons per page (t < 0.001), 1 and 8 icons per page (t < 0.001) in users' satisfaction. The results indicated that older adults were sensitive to the increasing numbers of icon amount. Also, they were dissatisfied with the visual density of 1 icon per page. And visual density of 4 icons per page had no significant difference with 8 icons per page in users' satisfaction.

4.3   Interrelations Between User Characteristics, Performance, and Satisfaction

A further consideration refers to the impact of user characteristics, performance and satisfaction (shown in Table 1), which of them might possibly cause or at least interact with each other on tiny touchscreen. This is especially meaningful in the aging group, as aging is going along with the decreases in body flexibility and vision.

Age, vision and finger dexterity did not show meaningful correlations with efficiency and satisfaction. However, there was no surprised that age was significantly correlated to vision and finger dexterity. Further, vision showed significant correlation with effectiveness, meant that reduction of vision led to low success rates of taping and solving tasks.

The success rates of taping were significantly correlated to efficiency (number of swiping left, number of swiping right and tasks completion time). However, the success rates of solving tasks did not affect the efficiency and satisfaction in the different display conditions, which was confirmed by the fact that all tasks were easy to solve. Three aspects of efficiency had significant correlations with each other respectively, showed that with higher efficiency the tasks were solved faster and simpler. Also, satisfaction showed to have a similar effect on efficiency than the success rates of taping, which might mean that older adults judged the prototypes in accordance with their feeling of efficiency.

Table 1. Results of Pearson correlation analysis of characteristics, performance and satisfaction

Variables 1	Variables 2	r	p
Age	Vision	−0.205*	0.017
	Finger dexterity	−0.241**	0.005
Vision	The success rates of solving tasks	0.181*	0.035
	The success rates of taping	0.192*	0.026
The success rates of taping	The number of swiping left	−0.191*	0.027
	The number of swiping right	−0.283**	0.001
	Task completion time	−0.306**	<0.001
The number of swiping left	The number of swiping right	0.597**	<0.001
	Task completion time	0.897**	<0.001
	Users' satisfaction	−0.643**	<0.001
The number of swiping right	Task completion time	0.635**	<0.001
	Users' satisfaction	−0.408**	<0.001
Task completion time	Users' satisfaction	−0.639**	<0.001

Note: *Correlation is significant at the 0.05 level (2-tailed)
** Correlation is significant at the 0.01 level (2-tailed)

4.4 Users' Gestures of Using Smartwatches

The final consideration refers to analysis users' gestures of using the smartwatch. Users' gestures were consisted of the posture of the wrist with a smartwatch, the finger gesture of taping and swiping, and hand gesture of the watch operation.

Regarding the posture of wrist, most of older adults wore the smartwatch on the back of their wrists in the experiment. But three of them wore the smartwatch on the front of the wrist. One participant changed the posture to wear the watch on the front of his wrist in the experimental process. The results of interview showed that they used to wear watches like this and they thought this posture was more suitable for looking and operating the watches. However, correlation analysis indicated that wearing the watch on the front of wrist had low success rates of solving tasks.

Regarding the finger gesture, older adults used their index finger, middle finger and thumb to tap (and swipe) the smartwatch screen in the experiment. Three participants used middle finger, and two of them changed to use index finger in the experimental process. Only one participant used thumb and then changed to use index finger eventually. Correlation analysis indicated that participants who taped with middle finger or thumb had low finger dexterity, and tended to wear the watch on the front of the wrist. However, there were no reasons showed that finger gesture had significant effect on performance and satisfaction.

Regarding the hand gesture, approximately half of participants closed their hands when taping the smartwatch screen with finger, especially middle finger. Positive correlations were found between hand gesture and finger gesture to support that view. There also was significant correlation between hand gesture and posture of wrist, showed that participants who wore the watch on the front of wrist generally tended to close their hands. Moreover, correlation analysis showed that opening hand had low success rates of taping. One possible reason was that opening hand blocked participants' line of sight. Results of Pearson correlation analysis were shown in Table 2.

Table 2. Results of Pearson correlation analysis of Users' gestures and performance

Variables 1	Variables 2	r	p
The posture of wrist	The finger gesture	0.308**	<0.001
	The hand gesture	0.421**	<0.001
	The success rates of solving task	0.257**	0.003
The finger gesture	The hand gesture	0.352**	<0.001
	Finger dexterity	0.469**	<0.001
The hand gesture	The success rates of taping	0.327**	<0.001

Note: ** Correlation is significant at the 0.01 level (2-tailed)

All the tap of prototypes with three levels of visual density was recorded (shown in Fig. 7). Results showed that participants generally tended to tap the bottom right corner of icons. And some of tap crossed the border of icons, especially the icons located at the right side of the screen. As to the tap in prototypes with 1 icon per page, many point of tap were located outside of the icon, which was a demonstration that older adults may carelessly tap the screen when they failed to swipe. What's more, if the visual density was high, participants would probably carelessly tap the icon located at the bottom right corner of the target icon.

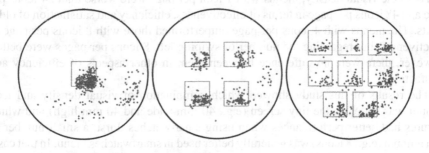

Fig. 7. All point of the tap in prototypes with three levels of visual density (from left to right: 1 icon per page, 4 icons per page, 8 icons per page)

All the swipe of a representative participant was shown in Fig. 8. The difference among the swiping trajectory of three levels of visual density was that participants took obviously fewer number of swiping, no matter swiping left and right, if visual density was higher. And participants only swiped up and down in the prototypes with 1 icon per page. The reason was that they thought low visual density might mean the pages on which they could swipe in both vertical direction and horizontal direction. Moreover, the distance of swiping left (blue line) was longer than the distance of swiping right (red line) in all prototypes. The angle (formed of swiping trajectory and horizontal direction) of swiping right was less than the angle of swiping right.

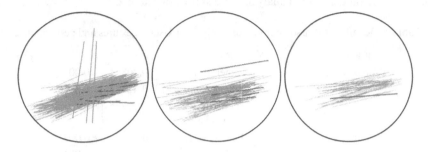

Fig. 8. All swiping trajectory in prototypes with three different levels of visual density (from left to right: 1 icon per page, 4 icons per page, 8 icons per page)

5 Conclusion

Appropriate menu design on the round tiny screen is desired and, hence, this study aims to explore the effect of icon amount and visual density within smartwatches menu on older adults' performance and satisfaction. To achieve this goal, the study proposed different icon amount and visual density of smartwatches and carried out an experiment.

As to the icon amount, menus with 8 icons were better than those with 24 icons and 48 icons in terms of efficiency and satisfaction of older adults. Regarding effectiveness, icon amount of 8 icons was significantly better than 48 icons.

As to the visual density, menus with 1 icon per page were worse than 24 icons per page and 48 icons per page in terms of effectiveness, efficiency and satisfaction of older adults. The menus with 4 icons per page outperformed those with 8 icons per page in effectiveness, but regarding the number of swiping left, 8 icons per pages were better. However, there were no difference between them in other aspects of efficiency and satisfaction.

The results of this study showed which combination of visual density and icon amount was better on the tiny screen (e.g., 40 mm wide and 40 mm high) and which gestures had better performances when using smartwatches. First, a small number of icon amount (e.g., 8 icons) was generally better used in smartwatches menu. In that case, both visual density of 4 icons per page and 8 icons per page had strong qualifying performance. Designers even can used visual density of 1 icon per page if they wanted older adults see icons more clearly. Second, compared with 1 icon and 8 icons per page, the visual density of 4 icons per page might was the best choice if the number of icon amount was large (e.g., 24 icons and 48 icons).

The results indicated that there were relationships between the posture of the wrist with a smartwatch, the finger gesture of taping and swiping, and hand gesture of the watch operation. Wearing the watch on the back of wrist, taping with the index finger and closing hand related to better performance when using smartwatches.

Two limitations of this study also need to be considered. First, icons in the prototypes were different from real icons of smartwatches' applications. Second, the older participants had low education level and cannot be considered as a very representative sample of older users.

Acknowledgment. This work was supported with funding from a National Science Foundation China grant 71401018.

References

1. Chae, M., Kim, J.: Do size and structure matter to mobile users? an empirical study of the effects of screen size, information structure, and task complexity on user activities with standard web phones. Behav. Inf. Technol. **23**, 165–181 (2004)
2. Zhou, J., Rau, P.L.P., Salvendy, G.: Older adults' use of smart phones: an investigation of the factors influencing the acceptance of new functions. Behav. Inf. Technol. **33**, 552–560 (2014)
3. Ziefle, M.: Instruction formats and navigation aids in mobile devices. In: Holzinger, A. (ed.) USAB 2008. LNCS, vol. 5298, pp. 339–358. Springer, Heidelberg (2008)
4. Ziefle, M.: Information presentation in small screen devices: the trade-off between visual density and menu foresight. Appl. Ergon. **41**, 719–730 (2010)
5. Kim, M.J., Yoon, S.K., Choi, J.H.: A study of menu structure on smartwatch for effective navigation - focused on types of menu and color cues. J. Digit. Des. **15**, 395–406 (2015)
6. Perrault, S.T., Lecolinet, E., Eagan, J., Guiard, Y.: Watchit: simple gestures and eyes-free interaction for wristwatches and bracelets. In: the SIGCHI Conference on Human Factors in Computing Systems, pp. 1451–1460. ACM, New York (2013)
7. Knibbe, J., Martinez Plasencia, D., Bainbridge, C., Chan, C.K., Wu, J., Cable, T., Coyle, D.: Extending interaction for smart watches: enabling bimanual around device control. In: The CHI 2014 Extended Abstracts on Human Factors in Computing Systems, pp. 1891–1896. ACM, New York (2014)
8. Cho, H., Kim, M., Seo, K.: A text entry technique for wrist-worn watches with tiny touchscreens. In: The 27th Annual ACM Symposium on User Interface Software and Technology, pp. 79–80. ACM, New York (2014)
9. Komninos, A., Dunlop, M.: Text input on a smart watch. IEEE Pervas. Comput. **13**, 50–58 (2014)
10. Hara, K., Umezawa, T., Osawa, N.: Effect of button size and location when pointing with index finger on smartwatch. In: Kurosu, M. (ed.) Human-Computer Interaction. LNCS, vol. 9170, pp. 165–174. Springer, Heidelberg (2015)
11. Shen, Z., Xue, C., Li, J., Zhou, X.: Effect of icon density and color contrast on users' visual perception in human computer interaction. In: Harris, D. (ed.) EPCE 2015. LNCS, vol. 9174, pp. 66–76. Springer, Heidelberg (2015)
12. Yahoo. How android users interact with their phones. http://yahooadvertisingca.tumblr.com/post/95821374980/yahoo-aviate-has-teamed-up-with-the-data
13. TalkingData. 2014 China mobile Internet report. http://www.talkingdata.com/index/#/datareport/-1/zh_cn
14. Lewis, J.R.: Psychometric evaluation of the PSSUQ using data from five years of usability studies. Int. J. Hum.-Comput. Interact. **14**, 463–488 (2002)
15. Zhou, J., Rau, P.L.P., Salvendy, G.: Use and design of handheld computers for older adults: a review and appraisal. Int. J. Hum.-Comput. Interact. **28**, 799–826 (2012)

Generational Comparison of Simultaneous Internet Activities Using Smartphones and Computers

Andrea Rosales[✉] and Mireia Fernández-Ardèvol

Internet Interdisciplinary Institute (IN3),
Universitat Oberta de Catalunya (UOC), Barcelona, Spain
{arosalescl,mfernadezar}@uoc.edu

Abstract. Computers and smartphones are multipurpose devices with overlapping capacities. Thus, users end up interacting with the same information through different devices, sometimes simultaneously (or within a short timeframe). As our artifact ecologies grow, it is clear that the use of multipurpose devices cannot be understood in isolation, and diverse uses are widely influenced by personal interests. However, personal interests change over a lifetime. Tracking the online smartphone and computer activities of 178 Spanish users aged 17 to 76, we make an intergenerational comparison of simultaneous activities on both devices. We demonstrate that simultaneous activities are common to people of all ages, tending to happen more during working hours. While age stereotypes say that older people are less active users of technologies, some are also engaged in simultaneous smartphone–computer use, evidence that they are making the most of the devices available to them.

Keywords: Smartphones · Computers · Multitasking · Synchronization · Generational approach

1 Introduction

With the emergence of diverse multipurpose digital devices, it has become clear that the use of one device cannot be understood fully in isolation, but rather as part of its device ecology (or artifact ecology [1]). Similarly, the use of one service (for example, email) cannot be understood fully by only looking at its use on one device; the focus should be on its distributed use across different devices. Moreover, communication and information activities should be understood as a complete structure of "communicative ecologies" [2].

The increasing complexity of device ecologies challenges the formation of new ideas on how different digital devices (we will refer to them simply as "devices") can be used together to better support communicative ecologies. Some current features for supporting multiple device interaction include cloud computing, to allow content synchronization (e.g. Dropbox); setup synchronization of the same app in multiple devices (e.g. syncing a browser's history, tabs and settings); or remotely controlling a second device (e.g. using "AllShare Play" to control audio and video content), among others.

© Springer International Publishing Switzerland 2016
J. Zhou and G. Salvendy (Eds.): ITAP 2016, Part I, LNCS 9754, pp. 478–489, 2016.
DOI: 10.1007/978-3-319-39943-0_46

Moreover, there are services available on a single device (free phone calls through the fixed line) and multiplatform services (e.g. email). There are single-service devices (e.g. cameras, ebooks or music players) and multipurpose devices (e.g. smartphones, tablets, PCs and smartwatches). Thus, diverse devices are combined in different ways according to personal choices. These combinations of device affordances and available services as well as interests influence how people interact with their device ecology. Research in the area of multiple device interaction includes spatially-aware interactions [3] or using smartphones to interact collaboratively with tablets [4] and using a toolkit to allow rapid setup of device ecologies [5]. However, there is a "need for interfaces, applications, and services that better support multi-device use" [6, p. 3903].

In these complex times of personal device ecology, communication, work and entertainment services are mediated through the same devices. While one can appreciate the pervasiveness of multipurpose devices, there is a tension between the boundaries separating work and private domains [7]. In this sense, time use is becoming less structured and more fragmented and overlapped [8]; however, these practices vary depending on age, occupation and interests, because personal values and interests change over the course of a lifetime [9].

While there is a wide variety of services to support multi-device interaction – either already on the market or currently under research – there are fewer studies focusing on how people actually interact with their device ecology (some exceptions include [6, 10]). Yet, understanding how individuals interact with their device ecology is key when it comes to designing Internet experiences that match individuals' interests.

In this paper we focus on the simultaneous use of computers and smartphones, as they are the most popular multipurpose devices [11]. Specifically, our research questions are: When and how often does a sample of active Internet users in Spain make simultaneous use of their computers and smartphones? How does this use differ by age and sex?

Previous studies on how individuals interact with their device ecologies either do not involve older people or do not include age in their analysis of different behaviors [6, 10]. We take a generational approach [12] to understanding how age influences a person's interaction with the device ecology. In addition, while previous studies have focused mostly on qualitative and self-reported data, we use a quantitative approach using activity logs in order to create a dialog between, on the one hand, previous research reporting declarative results collected by means of qualitative techniques and, on the other hand, (presumably) more objective information collected via log data tracking and behavioral data [13]. Thus, we tracked the Internet activities of 178 smartphone and computer users and quantified simultaneous activities on both devices. This combination of methods allows us to show emergent habits that have not been incorporated in the public discourse on the topic.

According to our analysis, simultaneous activities are common among people of all ages, and they tend to happen more during working hours. Results also show that there are no significant differences in simultaneous activities conducted by men and women, and there is no correlation between age and weighted simultaneous activities with respect to all user Internet activities. It shows that, despite ageist assumptions such as "older people are not interested in" or "are not avid users of", there are in fact older people who are making the most of the devices available.

2　Related Work

Simultaneous activities are somewhat related to other concepts used in HCI research, including user multitasking [14] and multi-device use or combined use [6]. While Ames uses the concept of "multitasking" to refer to the use of smartphones while carrying out other activities [14], Jokela et al. use the term "multi-device use" to describe "all situations and tasks where users used multiple information devices together" [6, p. 3905]. Although in most cases it is not possible for humans to conduct two divergent activities at the same time, we will use the term "simultaneous activities" to refer to activities conducted on more than one multipurpose device at the same time or within a short timeframe.

Different forms of simultaneous activities have been described, including convergent and divergent activities [15], which is similar to the concept of related and unrelated use [6, 16]. Convergent activities refer to one main task comprising an arrangement of tasks conducted through different devices; for example: "Participants explained that their tablets can enhance the TV experience by extending that activity through, for example, looking up related information about the program that they were watching" [16, p. 6]. Divergent activities refer to different tasks conducted on different devices in a short period of time; for example: some users are "constantly switching their focus between the TV program and their (divergent) tablet activity" [16, p. 6].

According to the reports of participants in previous studies, simultaneous activities are not made fortuitously. Availability, affordances, costs as well as personal choices and opportunity usually account for their decision to combine the use of multiple devices. Thus, users "mixed and adapted existing functions to meet their own priorities" [17, p. 629].

It is possible that the two services required are not available to the user on their different devices. *I googled the phone number of my physiotherapist with the tablet and called with my phone* [6, p. 3907]. Sometimes is more comfortable, convenient or easy to use each device for certain services or situations. *I read email on the computer if I can. The keyboard is better, and there is multitasking. But it is good to know that those things can be done on the iPhone* [10, p. 453]. Due to the service price, users are inclined to use certain services and devices. *I use WhatsApp extensively, as I have a limited number of phone calls a month* [18]. Sometimes it is a personal choice in order to separate activities. *I have decided only to access Facebook from the iPhone. That's because it used to distract me and take too much of my time. Now I have better control over that* [10, p. 453]. It is possible that the combination of two available devices provides the users with a better service. *My friend called me and asked me to the movies. I checked my calendar and information about the movie with my laptop while talking on the phone* [6, p. 3909]. *While watching TV, I checked the translation of a word with my phone,* or *While watching a movie on TV, I opened the IMDB page with my phone* [6, p. 3909].

However, most of the activities reported by participants in different studies [6, 18] include the combined use of the smartphone and TV, or phone calls and computers, amongst others. The combined use of other functions of the smartphone and the computer is reported less often, particularly when talking about divergent activities: "It is possible that the participants did not recognize many common situations as Parallel

Use of multiple devices, as the unrelated parallel tasks may not always be conscious" [6, p. 3909]. Divergent activities could be associated with an intrusion of private life in the work routine, and vice versa; engaging in personal chats while trying to write a paper could be a common case of divergent use. Thus, because they could be considered a negative behavior or because users are not conscious of divergent activities, individuals will tend not to include them in subjective reports. Thus, tracked data can help to identify simultaneous use of smartphone and computer activities.

3 Methods

We relied upon a market research panel focusing on the Spanish population to track the Internet activities of a set of already registered panelists (to whom we will refer simply as "panelists") using smartphones and (laptop or desktop) computers. Panelists were active Internet users who, before starting the project, had been invited to join the panel precisely because of this active use. An app was installed on their computers and smartphones that allowed the panel members to track their Internet activities as well as receive non-monetary rewards for their participation in what were mainly surveys and tracking activities. Non-monetary rewards depended on participation in the different studies, accumulating points that could be exchanged for commercial products delivered to the home. The dataset corresponded to one month of activity between November 17 and December 16, 2014. The software registered 4 types of Internet activity: (1) computer website visits; (2) computer searches; (3) smartphone app accesses; and (4) smartphone website visits. Each time users conducted an Internet activity, the system registered the type of activity, the date and access time, session length and connection type (Wi-Fi or mobile data). Here there was one main difference between smartphone and computer activities. While the smartphone registered only one activity at a time, the one shown on the screen, the computer could register multiple activities at the same time, which corresponded to all the URLs open in the browser. For example if a panelist opened a fitness app in their smartphone (i.e. Endomondo) to track their running, the tracking software would count one access when they activated it and then log the length of the session until the panelist moved on to another app or their phone returned to the idle mode. However, on the computer, if a panelist opened their Facebook account it would keep counting them as being active until they closed it. In other words, due to the differences in their respective systems, smartphones have been understood as non-multitasking devices while computers have been tracked as multitasking devices.

The sample reflected the characteristics of active Internet users among the Spanish population [19]. The sample of smartphone and computer users included 178 panelists. There were 84 women (47.2 %) and 94 men (52.8 %) ranging from 17 to 76 years of age. We classified panelists in 5 age cohorts: individuals aged 17 to 24 (32 panelists, 18 % of the total sample); individuals aged 25 to 34 (43 panelists, 24 %); individuals aged 35 to 44 (41 panelists, 24 %); individuals aged 45 to 54 (35 panelists, 19 %); and individuals aged 55 to 76 (27 panelists, 15 %).

There were analytical challenges in lumping together different age cohorts of older people under a unique label [20, 21], but given the current limitations in the demographics of the Spanish online population, with older age cohorts being underrepresented, the approach proposed here was more appropriate. In addition, there has been extensive debate on what it means to be old or who can be described as being old [22], so we used a quantitative approach as an indicator of a new social and physical context. Thus, we only built one group of older people, individuals 55 and over, since in Spain it is at this age that it is common to start experiencing the first advanced age-related social (e.g. retirement, ageism, widowhood) or health (e.g. physical and cognitive issues) changes. In this sense, people over 55 have special needs and interests that should be taking into account in the design of new ICTs.

3.1   Data Analysis

Within the dataset, we analyzed the emergence of simultaneous activity. Similar to Böhmer's definition of an app chain [23], simultaneous activities are a sequence of Internet activities conducted on the computer and the smartphone. Such Internet activities could be related or not and are issued by a single user within a short time period. With the tracked data it was impossible to actually know if the user had been interacting actively with and/or watching the webpage or app the entire time that the webpage was open or the app active. Thus, similar to Carrascal, we used a delimiter measured in seconds to characterize when two Internet activities should have happened simultaneously or within a short period of time. While Carrascal used 30″ as a delimiter [24], we adjusted the delimiter to the type of Internet activities conducted, namely desktop web session, desktop search session, mobile web session and mobile app session, because the length of activities in the 4 different types of Internet activity varied significantly. We explored three scenarios to define the delimiter to be used, including mean, truncated mean and median. Each scenario led to different simultaneous activities (see Table 1). We selected the second scenario, in order to have a moderated perspective. Moreover, this scenario used the truncated mean, the mean without outliers, which was particularly relevant in regard to desktop web sessions, as

Table 1. Scenarios to identify simultaneous activities

	Scenario 1	Scenario 2	Scenario 3
Activity indicators			
Activities	778,999	778,999	778,999
Simultaneous activities	39,705	21,376	12,838
%	5.10 %	2.74 %	1.59 %
Individuals with simultaneous activities	174	167	161
Criteria for defining scenarios			
	Mean	Truncated mean	Median
Web desktop delimiter	4'01"	1'22"	36"
Search desktop delimiter	30"	15"	10"
Web smartphone delimiter	39"	15"	0"
App smartphone delimiter	1'26"	25"	12"

people could leave email or social network sites open for up to 12 h, a timeframe that could not be considered as active.

Simultaneous activities included at least two activities, one on the smartphone and the other on the computer, separated according to the time delimiter of the first activity. Panelists could have used other devices during the tracking period, which we were not able to track or analyze. Consequently, this ratio of simultaneous device activities responds to the collected data, the definition we applied and the equation we used to calculate it. In this paper it has been used as an indicator of simultaneity and in order to make gender, hour and generational comparisons.

4   Results

Here we present a selection of descriptive statistics related to simultaneous activities, followed by their analysis according to gender, age and time of the day.

4.1   Frequency of Simultaneous Activities

Out of the 778,999 total Internet activities conducted by the 178 panelists, 21,376 (2.7 % of the total) were part of simultaneous activities. These 21,376 activities were distributed across 9,861 sessions, of which 8,474 included one device change, while the rest included up to 6 device changes. Of the sample of 178 panelists, 167 (93.8 %) conducted simultaneous activities. They conducted a mean of 4.8 simultaneous activities per day (see Table 2).

Table 2. Number of panelists by number of simultaneous activities

Number of panelists	Simultaneous activities during the tracked month	Simultaneous activities per day
11	0	0
23	2–8	0.14
27	9–29	0.63
25	30–59	1.41
30	60–99	2.78
42	100–299	5.79
20	>300	16.51
Total: 167	Mean: 145	Mean: 4.8

Eleven panelists did not conduct simultaneous activities in the tracked devices during the analyzed period. Five were women and six were men aged 28 to 71, and they typically showed a low level of Internet activity on one or both of their devices, that is, below the mean for smartphone activities (M = 116.06, SD = 94.78), computer activities (M = 29.82, SD = 98.30) or both.

While we cannot assume any causality direction between simultaneous activities and Internet activities, we proved a one-tailed Pearson correlation between the two variables. According to the Pearson correlation, the greater the use of the Internet, the greater the number of simultaneous activities, and vice versa, and therefore there is a correlation between the number of simultaneous activities ($M = 4.003$, $SD = 5.61$) and Internet accesses (145.88 Internet accesses per person, per day, $SD = 98.30$), $r(159) = 0.680$, $p < 0.001$. This is also true within each age cohort; 18 to 24 ($r(24) = 0.569$, $p < 0.000$), 25 to 34 ($r(36) = 0.736$, $p < 0.000$), 35 to 44 ($r(39) = 0.808$, $p < 0.000$), 45 to 54 ($r(33) = 0.640$, $p < 0.000$), and 55 to x ($r(27) = 0.549$, $p < 0.005$) (Fig. 1).

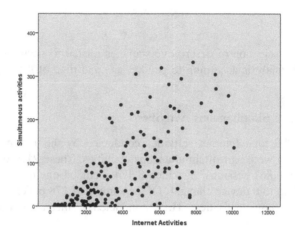

Fig. 1. Simultaneous activities **out of** all **Internet** activities by user

4.2 Simultaneous Activities by Gender

There are no significant differences in the amount of Internet activities conducted by men and women (p-value $= 0.982 > 0.05$). Similarly, there are no significant differences in the amount of simultaneous activities conducted by men and women (p-value $= 0.636 > 0.05$). Consequently, there are no significant differences in the percentage of simultaneous activities from daily activities by gender (p-value $= 0.686 > 0.05$), which represents weighted simultaneity according to the level of each panelist's Internet activity (see Table 3).

Table 3. Mean daily activities by gender. Comparing daily activities by gender, including simultaneous, non-simultaneous and total activities and the percentage of simultaneous activities out of total activities. The p-value refers to the one-way ANOVA, comparing the data for females and males.

Mean daily activities	Female	Male	p-value	Total
All internet activities	146.05	145.73	0.982	145.88
Non-simultaneous activities	141.84	141.91	0.996	141.87
Simultaneous activities	4.21	3.81	0.636	4.003
% of simultaneous activities out of total daily activities	2.8	2.6	0.686	2.7

4.3   Generational Comparison

Age and mean daily simultaneous activities are negatively correlated ($r = -0.215$, $p < 0.01$, $n = 178$); similarly, age and mean daily non-simultaneous activities are negatively correlated ($r = -0.239$, $p < 0.01$, $n = 178$). The younger the panelists are, the more simultaneous and non-simultaneous activities they carry out, and vice versa. However, there is no correlation between age and the percentage of simultaneous activities from daily activities ($r = -0.147$, $p > 0.01$, $n = 178$), which represents weighted simultaneity according to the level of each panelist's Internet activity. Thus, we can conclude that the percentage of simultaneous activities from all Internet activities is not related to age. Breaking activities by age, significant differences can be seen in some cases (Table 4):

Table 4. Daily activities by age cohorts. Comparing daily activities by age cohort, including simultaneous, non-simultaneous and total activities and the percentage of simultaneous activities out of total activities. The p-value refers to the one-way ANOVA, comparing the data for females and males. * Significant at a 0.005 level.

Mean daily activities	17 to 24	25 to 34	35 to 44	45 to 55	55 to 76	p-value	Total
Total	**193.81**	146.27	141.56	143.71	97.82	0.006*	145.88
Non simultaneous activities	**187.89**	141.39	137.69	140.69	96.0	0.007*	141.87
Simultaneous activities	**5.92**	4.88	3.86	3.03	1.82	0.039*	4.00
% of Simultaneous activities from daily activities	3.15	**3.45**	2.80	2.15	1.89	0.251	2.70

- There are significant differences between mean daily simultaneous activities and age groups (p-value = 0.039 < 0.05). Yet there are two age groups that stand out: individuals aged 17 to 24, with the highest levels of simultaneous activities ($M = 5.91$, $SD = 5.52$); and individuals aged 55 to 76 ($M = 1.82$, $SD = 2.05$), with the lowest levels.
- There are significant differences between mean daily non-simultaneous activities and age groups (p-value = 0.007 < 0.05). However, there are only differences between individuals aged 17 to 24 ($M = 187.89$, $SD = 117.81$) and individuals aged 55 to 76 ($M = 96.00$, $SD = 68.55$). Again, more activity is observed among young users.
- However, there are no significant differences among the percentages of simultaneous activities out of total activities by age cohorts (p-value = 0.251 > 0.05).

4.4   When? Daily Distribution

Daily Internet activities (see total Table 5) are concentrated mostly during active hours (9 h to 24 h) with a considerable decrease late night/early morning (1 h to 8 h). However, simultaneous activities tend to cover typical office hours (9 h to 20 h), while non-simultaneous activities cover office and evening hours (11 h to 22 h) (see Table 5).

Table 5. Hourly percentage of simultaneous and non-simultaneous Internet activities. Each cell value refers to the percentage of simultaneous or non-simultaneous Internet activities by hour. Colors are normalized by row, with black indicating each category's maximum and white indicating each category's minimum percentage.

Time of day	6h	7h	8h	9h	10h	11h	12h	13h	14h	15h	16h	17h	18h	19h	20h	21h	22h	23h	24h	1h	2h	3h	4h	5h	Total
Total	0.7	1.9	3.0	4.1	4.8	5.5	5.9	6.2	5.8	6.1	5.8	5.8	6.2	6.4	6.4	6.0	5.8	4.9	3.9	2.0	1.1	0.6	0.5	0.6	100
Simultaneous	0.5	1.5	2.9	5.1	5.9	6.2	6.3	6.5	6.7	6.5	6.0	5.8	6.4	6.0	5.4	4.8	4.8	4.0	3.9	1.7	1.2	0.5	0.4	0.4	**100**
Non-simultaneous	0.7	1.9	3.0	4.1	4.8	5.4	5.9	6.1	5.8	6.1	5.8	5.8	6.2	6.4	6.4	6.0	5.8	4.9	3.9	2.0	1.1	0.6	0.5	0.5	**100**

There is little difference in the percentage of simultaneous activities by hour among age cohorts. Individuals aged 17 to 24 tend to start simultaneous activities later in the morning and stay active until later in the night (see Table 6).

Table 6. Hourly percentage of simultaneous Internet activities by age cohort. Each cell value refers to the percentage of simultaneous Internet activities by age cohort and hour. Colors are normalized by row, with black indicating each category's maximum and white indicating each category's minimum percentage.

	6h	7h	8h	9h	10h	11h	12h	13h	14h	15h	16h	17h	18h	19h	20h	21h	22h	23h	24h	1h	2h	3h	4h	5h	Total
16 to 24	0.5	1.6	2.2	3.0	4.2	5.2	6.0	6.3	6.2	6.4	5.6	5.3	5.9	6.3	6.2	6.1	5.8	5.6	5.1	2.9	1.9	1.0	0.5	0.4	100
25 to 34	0.9	1.8	2.8	4.1	4.4	5.4	5.7	6.2	5.8	5.7	5.7	5.9	6.5	6.8	6.4	5.5	5.6	5.4	4.2	2.3	1.1	0.7	0.6	0.6	100
35 to 44	0.7	2.0	3.2	4.9	5.5	5.9	6.3	6.1	5.7	6.3	6.3	6.2	6.6	6.3	6.2	6.5	6.0	4.0	2.6	1.1	0.4	0.3	0.3	0.5	100
45 to 54	0.9	2.5	3.8	4.6	4.9	5.5	5.3	6.1	5.8	6.3	5.8	6.0	6.2	6.2	6.6	6.0	5.3	4.4	3.4	1.6	1.0	0.6	0.5	0.7	100
55 to 76	0.6	1.6	3.3	4.1	5.7	5.2	6.1	6.2	5.6	5.6	5.9	5.9	5.7	6.2	6.5	5.9	6.6	5.3	4.0	1.4	0.7	0.7	0.5	0.5	100

5   Limitations

The sample included in the study is not representative of the entire Spanish population, as it only deals with the online Spanish population. In addition, panelists are active Internet users, a fact which under represents the older Spanish population. However, due to a generational change and the widespread use of mobile devices, active older Internet users are a population segment on the rise with their own particular interests and habits. Thus, HCI should considerer the particular interests of active older Internet users when designing future technologies with them in mind.

Moreover, the panelists in this study were all panelists of the market research tool used and common users of other market research tools, a fact that should be considered as a bias of the sample. In a future study, this data could be contrasted with real-life experiences reported by users in order to gain a better understanding of the topic.

6 Discussion, Conclusion and Implications

By tracking the Internet activities of a set of 178 panelists aged 17 to 76, we were able to present a generational study of simultaneous activities, namely Internet activities conducted on smartphones and computers within a short period of time (one month). Specifically, we described when and how often these individuals made simultaneous use of computers and smartphones and how this use was different according to age and sex.

While previous studies have focused mostly on disaggregated use of computers and smartphones [14] or other combinations of multi-device use [6], we have shown that simultaneous activities using smartphones and computers are common for panelists of all ages, as 93 % of participants were involved in simultaneous activities. We have also shown that there are no differences in the percentage of simultaneous activities out of total activities by gender or age. In addition, simultaneous activities were found to be concentrated mostly during central working hours, from 11 h to 16 h.

By means of simple descriptive indicators, we were able to demonstrate the richness of the data and the nuances brought about by each indicator. We would highlight that, while common age stereotypes depict older people as less avid users of technologies, with many HCI studies portraying them accordingly [18], there are also older people who engage in simultaneous use of smartphones and computers, which shows how some older people are making the most of the devices available to them. Results show that, regardless of the level of Internet activity, simultaneous activity practices have the same relative importance at any age.

Moreover, simultaneous activities are a part of everyday life. Therefore, providing better support for this transition among different devices will be a key factor in supporting divergent and convergent activities in devices commonly used simultaneously. Future research could include an analysis of the most popular categories of apps or websites used during simultaneous activities to characterize the activities related with simultaneous use of multipurpose devices.

References

1. Jung, H., Stolterman, E., Ryan, W., Thompson, T., Siegel, M.M.: Toward a framework for ecologies of artifacts: how are digital artifacts interconnected within a personal life? In: Proceedings of the 5th Nordic Conference on Human-Computer Interaction, pp. 201–210, Lund (2008)

2. Tacchi, J.A., Slater, D., Hearn, G.N.: Ethnographic action research: a user's handbook. New Delhi, India (2003)
3. Rädle, R., Jetter, H., Schreiner, M., Lu, Z., Reiterer, H., Rogers, Y., Raedle, R., Schreiner, M., De, H.R.: Spatially-aware or spatially-agnostic ? elicitation and evaluation of user-defined cross-device interactions. In: Proceedings of CHI 2015, pp. 3913–3922 (2015)
4. McAdam, C., Brewster, S.: Using mobile phones to interact with tabletop computers. In: Proceedings of the ACM International Conference on Interactive Tabletops and Surfaces ITS, vol. 11, pp. 232–241 (2011)
5. Bellucci, A., Aedo, I., Diaz, P.: ECCE toolkit: prototyping UbiComp device ecologies. In: Proceedings of 2014 International Working Conference on Advanced Visualisation and Interfaces - AVI 2014, pp. 339–340 (2014)
6. Jokela, T., Ojala, J., Olsson, T.: A diary study on combining multiple information devices in everyday activities and tasks. In: Proceedings of the 33rd Annual ACM Conference on Human Factors in Computing Systems - CHI 2015, pp. 3903–3912, Seoul (2015)
7. Lowry, D., Moskos, M.: Hanging on the Mobile Phone: Experiencing Work and Spatial Flexibility. Working Paper Series, National Institue of Labour Studies, Flinders University, Australia, 153, 0–19 (2005)
8. Castells, S., Fernández-Ardèvol, M., Linchuan Qiu, J., Sey, A.: Mobile Communication and Society: A Global Perspective. MIT Press, Cambridge (2006)
9. Neugarten, B.L., Neugarten, D.A.: The Meanings of Age: Selected Papers of Berenice L. Neugarten. University of Chicago Press, Chicago (1996)
10. Bødker, S., Klokmose, C.N.: Dynamics in artifact ecologies. In: Proceedings of the 7th Nordic Conference on Human-Computer Interaction Making Sense Through Design, pp. 448–457 (2012)
11. Clarke, J., Montesinos, M., Montanera, R., Bermúndez, A.: Estudio Mobile. Interactive Advertising Bureau - Spain. Retrieved December 8, 2015. http://www.iabspain.net/wp-content/uploads/downloads/2015/09/Estudio-Mobile-2015.pdf
12. Loos, E., Haddon, L., Mante-Meijer, E. (eds.): Generational Use of New Media. Ashgate, Burlington (2012)
13. Möller, A., Kranz, M., Schmid, B., Roalter, L., Diewald, S.: Investigating self-reporting behavior in long-term studies. In: Proceedings of SIGCHI Conference on Human Factors in Computing Systems - CHI 2013, pp. 2931–2940 (2013)
14. Ames, M.: Managing mobile multitasking: the culture of iPhones on stanford campus. In: Computer Supported Cooperative Work, pp. 1487–1498 (2013)
15. Brown, B., McGregor, M., Laurier, E.: iPhone in vivo: video analysis of mobile device use. In: Proceedings of the SIGCHI Conference on Human Factors in Computing Systems (CHI 2013), pp. 1031–1040 (2013)
16. Müller, H., Gove, J., Webb, J.: Understanding tablet use: a multi-method exploration. In: International Conference on Human Computer Interaction with Mobile Devices Services – MobileHCI, pp. 1–10 (2012)
17. Barkhuus, L., Polichar, V.E.: Empowerment through seamfulness: smart phones in everyday life. Pers. Ubiquit. Comput. 15, 629–639 (2011)
18. Rosales, A., Fernández-Ardèvol, M.: Beyond whatsapp: older people and smartphones. Accept. to be Publ. Rom. J. Commun. Public Relations (RJCPR) (2016)
19. INE: Population at 1st January 2014. Municipal Register. http://www.ine.es/jaxi/menu.do?type=pcaxis&path=%2Ft20%2Fe260&file=inebase&L=1
20. Sawchuk, K., Crow, B.: Into the grey zone: Seniors, cell phones and milieus that matter. WI: J. Mob. Media 5(1) (2011)
21. Bytheway, B.: Ageism and age categorization. J. Soc. Issues 61, 361–374 (2005)
22. Higgs, P., Gilleard, C.: Rethinking Old Age. Palgrave Macmillan, London (2015)

23. Böhmer, M., Hecht, B., Schöning, J., Krüger, A., Bauer, G.: Falling asleep with angry birds, facebook and kindle – a large scale study on mobile application usage. In: Proceedings of the International Conference on Human-Computer Interaction with Mobile Devices and Services, vol. 47 (2011)
24. Carrascal, J.P., Church, K.: An in-situ study of mobile app & mobile search interactions. In: Proceedings of the SIGCHI Conference on Human factors in Computing Systems (CHI 2015), pp. 2739–2748, Seoul (2015)

Using the Smartphone to Support Successful Aging: Technology Acceptance with Selective Optimization and Compensation Among Older Adults

Yao Sun$^{(\boxtimes)}$, Margaret L. McLaughlin, and Michael J. Cody

University of Southern California, Los Angeles, USA
{yaosun, mmclaugh, cody}@usc.edu

Abstract. Aging populations and the rapid dissemination of technological innovations both underscore the importance of the use and adoption of new technologies among older adults. Most studies have focused primarily on the barriers older adults face in adopting new technologies without paying much attention to how seniors might purposefully make use of new technologies to handle age-related changes. In this study, we filled both theoretical and empirical gaps by focusing on the roles smartphones might play in helping older adults handle challenges in their daily lives. Drawing upon a web-based survey of older adults 55–75 years old, our study revealed that having a positive attitude is key to successful aging and that this positive attitude toward aging motivates the elderly to utilize smartphones to compensate for aging-related deficits in daily life. We conclude our paper with a discussion of the theoretical implications of these results and directions for future research.

Keywords: Aging · Smartphone · Deficit · Technology acceptance · Selective optimization with compensation

1 Introduction

Since the last century, a substantial increase in life expectancy in conjunction with the post-World War II population bulge has created a large proportion of older adults living in the United States. According to the World Population Ageing 2013 report[1] published by the United Nations, from 2013 to 2050, the number of people aged 60 years or older is expected to increase from 841 million to over 2 billion. Despite the inevitable diseases and declines that are commonly associated with aging, the elderly can increasingly live independently and support themselves in many aspects of life. Like other developmental stages in life, aging can be successfully traversed. For example, although one experiences losses in some domains of functioning as one ages, one also enjoys growing wisdom. From young to old adulthood, what people tend to want in life

---

[1] http://www.un.org/en/development/desa/population/publications/pdf/ageing/
WorldPopulationAgeing2013.pdf.

© Springer International Publishing Switzerland 2016
J. Zhou and G. Salvendy (Eds.): ITAP 2016, Part I, LNCS 9754, pp. 490–500, 2016.
DOI: 10.1007/978-3-319-39943-0_47

dramatically changes [12]. Considering biological and environmental conditions, individuals increasingly seek to balance losses rather than strive for higher-level goals.

Aging populations and the rapid dissemination of technological innovations together underscore the importance of the use and adoption of new technologies among older adults; however, most studies have focused only on the barriers older adults face in adopting new technologies without paying much attention to how these older adults might purposefully make use of new technologies to better handle their age-related challenges. We filled these theoretical and empirical gaps in the present study by focusing on the roles smartphones might play in how older adults approach their specific challenges in daily life.

2 Technology Acceptance Among Older Adults

The technology acceptance model (TAM) is one of the fundamental and influential theories to explain how individuals adopt and use new technologies. Proposed by Davis in 1989, this model is based on the theory of reasoned action [14] and has been expanded to a number of different topics and research areas.

The perceived usefulness and perceived ease of use of new technologies are two fundamental attitudinal constructs in the TAM [10]. Perceived usefulness is the degree to which an individual's performance is enhanced by adopting a new technology, while perceived ease of use refers to how effortless an individual finds adopting and using a new technology. Previous studies have confirmed the positive impacts of perceived usefulness and perceived case of use on actual technology use. Although originally aimed at investigating Internet use, the TAM has been further developed and widely employed to examine the use of cellphones and smartphones [26, 28, 34].

The TAM has also been expanded to study continuing users, e.g., some studies surveyed current users of mobile Internet and found that both perceived usefulness and perceived ease of use positively predicted their intention to continue using the given technology [22]. Similarly, the results of earlier studies that investigated mixed types of users showed the positive effects of these two key constructs on both initial adoption and continued use of telemedicine technology [23]. Other studies have demonstrated similar effects on the adoption and use of email [1], online shopping systems [18], and online investing technologies [27]. Taken together, i.e., for both initial adoption and continued use of a new technology, both perceived usefulness and perceived ease of use strongly influence attitudes toward new technologies.

3 Attitudes Toward Aging: Glass Half Full or Half Empty?

Several specific terms have been coined to describe the physical, psychological, and cognitive characteristics of human aging [6, 21]. For example, "pathological" aging is used to describe aging-related chronic disease states [40], whereas "normal" aging refers to aging that occurs without disease or disability, but with the loss of some general functions [4]. "Usual" or "successful" aging emphasizes a state in which symptoms of diseases are not exhibited, but some physical or cognitive changes are experienced [40]. More specifically, "successful" aging has been conceptualized as aging with a "low risk of disease and disease-related disability; high mental and physical functioning; and active engagement with life" (p. 38) [41]. In other words, aging is not necessarily negative; people can be proactive in response to growing old. As older adults successfully manage aging, they develop new attitudes toward aging and discover new possibilities available to them.

A growing body of literature has shown that older people tend to have different perceptions of aging [31]. On the one hand, early research tended to presume aging to be negative; therefore, such research focused on the inevitability of losses and fear of death [7, 30, 31]. Some research has found that older adults tend to develop negative self-stereotypes and perceive themselves as being less able in many domains of functioning [32]. Conversely, to take one example, scholars interviewed 32 long-term care residents regarding their perceptions of aging, finding that participants perceived aging as successful. Their approaches to successful aging were identified as being adaptive to change, not letting things get them down, and never giving up hope for a better situation [20]. Likewise, other studies also demonstrated that engaging with friends and learning to cope with change were crucial in achieving successful aging [11].

Previous studies have also found that the perception older adults have of aging is distinct from impairment. For instance, studies have found that such perceptions of aging are related to but independent of specific experiences of impairments and deficits [43]. Research studies have also explored subjective aging-related deficits. According to these subjective reports, aging may cause several functional changes, such as memory decline [8] or vision impairment [24].

For older adults, technology can be viewed as both good and bad. Some individuals perceive many unavoidable barriers to the use and adoption of new technologies. Due to physical impairments or psychological resistance, these aging adults may try to circumvent new technologies. For example, a loss of flexibility or a decline in one's hearing may hinder the use and adoption of new technologies [39]. Conversely, new technologies can present new opportunities for learning and socializing. Studies have reported that when seniors are taught how to use computers, their psychological barriers diminish such that they are more willing to engage in the virtual world [13]. Other research indicated that social networks play a critical role in promoting Internet use by seniors, since the elderly still want to maintain social relationships [25]. Numerous studies have confirmed that older adults are more willing to use new technologies when they are in positive psychological states or need to complete routine daily tasks. Therefore, we offer the hypotheses below.

H1a: Older people with positive attitudes toward aging are more likely to have positive attitudes toward smartphones as compared to those with negative attitudes toward aging.

H1b: Older people who perceive themselves as having aging-related deficits are more likely to have positive attitudes toward smartphones as compared to those not having this perception.

H2: Older people with positive attitudes toward aging perceive fewer deficits as compared to those who have negative attitudes toward aging.

4 Successful Aging: Selective Optimization with Compensation

Unlike most conventional gerontology research, the meta-model of selective optimization with compensation (SOC) views the late stage of life as a satisfying period. In this model, adaptive and successful aging are proposed with a focus on how older people make decisions in their daily lives through selection, optimization, and compensation [5].

In laying the foundation for this model, Baltes and Baltes (1990) depicted the aging process as occurring "under development-enhancing and age-friendly environmental conditions" (p. 8) and integrated this process into goal-oriented personal development. Taking a global view based on this integration, the SOC model argues that individuals across all life stages manage their life development through three processes, i.e., selection, optimization, and compensation. Selection, by definition, refers to setting goals. Individuals face a broad range of alternatives and domains of functioning throughout their entire lives; hence, focusing on a few specific goals will help them take better advantage of available resources to reach personal objectives.

Two types of selection have been identified, i.e., elective and loss-based selection [15]. Elective selection aims at reaching a desired state or goal, such as knowing what to pursue in one's career and what to avoid. Loss-based selection refers to consequential behaviors that stem from experiencing a possible loss of particular maintaining functions. For example, one may stop taking part in sports when one's legs hurt.

Optimization is tightly linked to goal-oriented means, such as focusing on a few very important goals and devoting oneself completely to them. Compensation is defined as "the use of alternative means to maintain a given level of functioning when specific goal-relevant means are no longer available" (p. 644) [15]. In other words, to maintain a certain level of functioning requires the availability of compensatory means such that individuals can substitute lost means for new ones.

SOC-related behaviors have been tested in many studies on aging and life-management issues. For example, studies have found that the elderly employ SOC, because doing so enables them to reach better states of functioning, such as memory and locomotor functioning [6, 33]. Similarly, Freund (2006) compared younger and older adults by using a sensorimotor task, demonstrating that the older participants, in contrast to the younger ones, were more persistent in terms of compensation versus optimization. Based on a postural control task comparison between older and younger adults, some studies have also reported an extension of SOC to include pathologic aging research [38]. In other words, as people age, they tend to stop pursuing a "better" state, but rather compensate to maintain an existing state that may not be the best, yet seems fine to the individual. Instead, of striving for gains, people start to counteract their losses as they step into the later stages of life. Previous literature has confirmed that SOC is at work in regulating the behaviors of the aging. Therefore, combined with technology acceptance and attitudes toward aging, we proposed the two hypotheses below.

H3a: Older people who have positive attitudes toward aging are more likely to use smartphones as compared to those who have negative attitudes toward aging.

H3b: Older people who perceive themselves as having aging-related deficits are more likely to use smartphones as compared to those who do not have this perception.

5   Method

Our methodology centered on a web-based Qualtrics survey completed by 160 participants 55 years of age and older. Of this group, 60.6 % were between the ages of 55 and 65 and 39.4 % were between the ages of 66 and 75. Males and females constituted 38.5 % and 60.9 % of the participants, respectively. With respect to geographical regions, all within the United States, 36.6 % of the participants were from the South, followed by 23 % from the West, 21.7 % from the Midwest, and 18 % from the Northeast. Regarding smartphone use, 52.8 % of the participants were current smartphone users, while 46 % were non-users. Data analysis for this study was mainly based on 85 smartphone users. Data were collected on other demographic indicators, including marital status, employment status, and living arrangements. Except for the demographic questions, all of the questions were randomized during distribution.

The respondents were asked to assess their current statuses with respect to several possible areas of age-related decline, including vision, hearing, mobility, and memory. If they noted that they had experienced changes in one or more of these areas, they were then asked to indicate strategies they use to face any resulting daily challenges, e.g., using their smartphones for online shopping if their mobility was impaired or taking notes on their smartphones to support their own memory. Strategies proposed as alternatives included non-technological solutions (e.g., having a family member shop for me), as well as simply opting not to pursue the given activities.

5.1   Measures

Attitude toward Aging. The attitude toward aging items were each measured on a five-point Likert Scale, including such statements as "I am as happy now as when I was younger" and "Things keep getting better than I thought as I get older." The items were adopted from several prior studies on the self-perception of aging [30, 42] with a Cronbach's alpha of 0.848.

Perceived Aging Deficits. The perceived aging deficit items measured attitudes toward aging-related deficits, showing the degree to which the individuals perceived that they had certain types of aging-related deficits. Items were adopted from several subjective tests regarding vision, hearing, memory, and motion impairments [8, 24, 35–37], including such items as "As I age, I repeat more often to someone what I have just told them than previously" and "I have more difficulty reading newspapers than I did several years ago." The overall reliability of this scale was 0.902.

Attitude toward Smartphones. The attitude toward smartphones items were measured in terms of perceived usefulness and perceived ease of use of smartphones, again using a five-point Likert Scale. Items were adopted from the seminal work on the TAM [10], proposing such statements as "I find the smartphone easy to use" or "I find the smartphone useful in my life." The reliability of this scale was 0.979.

Using Smartphones as Compensation. The use of smartphones as selective optimizations with compensation items were mainly generated based on the SOC scale [15], integrating items from the Instrumental Activities of Daily Living form that measures an elderly person's daily activities [29]. The items in this section generally focused on smartphones' roles in the older adults' responses to the loss of certain abilities involved in completing daily tasks, such as "I cannot get out to meet my friends as much as I did before, so I use my smartphone to keep in contact with them." This scale's reliability was 0.866.

6 Results

Applying the ordinary least squares (OLS) method, we detected significant associations among all four of the measures defined in Sect. 5, i.e., attitude toward aging, perceived aging deficits, attitude toward smartphones, and using smartphones as compensation. In addition, statistical analysis using PROCESS with 1,000 bootstraps and a 95 % confidence interval suggested conditional indirect effects among these variables [21], indicating more complicated relations between aging status and smartphone adoption among older adults.

Hypotheses 1a and 1b were supported by the data. More specifically, older adults reported significantly more positive attitudes toward using smartphones as compensation when they viewed aging positively ($\beta = .345$, $p < .001$) and when they perceived themselves as having aging-related deficits ($\beta = .077$, $p < .01$). This result indicated that older adults who have positive attitudes toward new technologies are those viewing life from the "glass half full" perspective rather than from the "glass half empty" perspective. Likewise, those who acknowledged their aging-related deficits tended to prefer to compensate for them with smartphones (Tables 1 and 2).

Table 1. Stepwise regressions of effects on attitude towards the smartphone

	Model 1		Model 2	
	Coefficient	Std. Error	Coefficient	Std. Error
Intercept	11.368	3.257	−.993	3.721
Age	−.031	.402	−.013	.362
Gender	.358	.789	.005	.687
Region	.298	.358	.318	.323
Ethnicity	−.033	.403	.028	.350
Marital status	−.010	.187	−.106	.163
Education	−.166	.139	−.121	.137
Employment	11.368	3.257	.345	.068
Aging attitude			.077***	.024
Perceived deficits			−.993**	3.721
R2	.032		.296	

*$p < .05$, **$p < .01$, ***$p < .001$

Hypothesis 2 was also supported by the data, indicating a meditating effect among attitudes toward aging and smartphones versus perceived aging deficits. The standard regression coefficient between attitudes toward aging and perceived aging deficits was significant (b = − 1.33, SE = .29, p < .001), as was the coefficient between perceived aging deficits and attitudes toward smartphones (b = .07, SE = .02, p < .01). Therefore, the standardized indirect effect was the product (−1.33)(.07) = − .093. The direct effect attitudes toward aging had on attitudes toward smartphones was significant (b = .35, SE = .06, p < .001). The results of normal theory tests indicated that the overall meditational effect was significant (Z = − 2.54, p < 0.05) (Figs. 1 and 2).

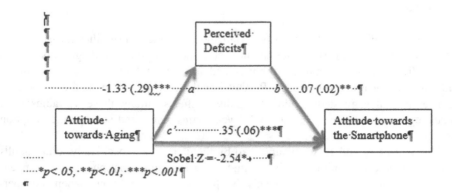

Fig. 1. Conditional indirect effects on attitude towards the smartphone

Hypotheses 3a and 3b were also supported. The statistical results indicated that older adults who believe they had certain aging-related deficits (β = .28, p < .05) and who had positive attitudes in response to the aging process (β = .19, p < .001) were more likely to adopt smartphones to compensate for their deficits. The conditional indirect effect, again, was found to be significant. The standard regression coefficient between attitudes toward aging and perceived aging deficits was significant (b = − 1.33, SE = .29, p < .001), as was the coefficient between perceived deficits and using smartphones as compensation (b = .27, SE = .06, p < .001). Consequently, the standardized indirect effect was the product (−1.33)(.27) = − .354. The direct effect attitudes toward aging had on attitudes toward smartphones was significant (b = .49, SE = .17, p < .01). As with Hypothesis 2, the results of normal theory tests indicated that the overall meditational effect was significant (Z = − 3.22, p < .01).

7   Discussion

How do older adults manage their lives in the digital era? Too many studies have emphasized the barriers they face in adopting new technologies; yet, little is known regarding the role new technologies have in successful aging. Drawing upon the results of an online survey of older adults, in this study, we set out to reveal the effects of physical and psychological aging on the adoption of smartphones in terms of compensating for aging deficits. All of the hypotheses were supported by the data, with three major themes emerging from our analysis, i.e., the attitudes of older adults toward

Table 2. Stepwise Regressions of Effects on Use of Smartphone

	Model 1		Model 2	
	Coefficient	Std. Error	Coefficient	Std. Error
Intercept	26.985	8.261	1.430	7.008
Age	−1.082	1.019	−1.038	.637
Gender	.354	2.002	1.466	1.213
Region	−.746	.908	.462	.729
Ethnicity	.381	1.021	.631	.633
Marital status	−.593	.474	−.205	.303
Education	.077	.353	−.236	.256
Employment	26.985	8.261	.279	.114
Aging attitude			.190*	.045
Perceived deficits			1.430***	7.008
R2	.052		.194	

*p < .05, **p < .01, ***p < .001

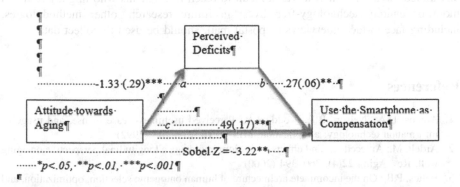

Fig. 2. Conditional indirect effects on use of the smartphone to compensate for deficits

aging impact their (1) self-perceptions of aging-related deficits, (2) attitudes toward smartphones, and (3) use of smartphones to compensate for deficits.

First, older adults exhibited different attitudes toward aging, leading their perceptions of aging deficits to vary. Those who reported feeling better about themselves now as opposed to when they were younger tended to see themselves as having few deficiencies in terms of vision, hearing, memory, and mobility as a result of aging. Conversely, older adults focused on the nostalgia of their youth tended to report more deficits caused by aging. Positive attitudes and wisdom can protect older people from declining life situations and health [2].

The attitudes the older adults had toward aging resulted in different viewpoints regarding smartphones. By relating these attitudes to their perceived deficits, our study demonstrated that older people who believe aging is not a depressing issue tended to consider smartphones to be useful and enjoyable. In other words, positive attitudes toward aging gave rise to more confidence in handling changes in their daily lives [11], thus reducing their psychological resistance to adopting smartphones to compensate for deficits (except that more confidence also led to fewer perceived deficits to compensate for).

Through the lens of SOC, our current study further demonstrated that older adults were actually able to make deliberate choices to cope with their life issues, especially regarding the question of whether to adopt and use smartphones. For those with positive attitudes toward growing old, using smartphones to compensate for deficits was simply an alternative means of solving problems. Yet, seniors who resisted aging and getting old tended to avoid using new technologies (such as smartphones) to facilitate their activities even though they reported experiencing certain physiological deficits. Shedding light on successful aging through SOC, our findings suggest that whether or not aging can be successful largely depends on how older adults treat aging.

Similar to other studies, our present research has several limitations that call for scholarly attention in future research. First, it focused only on cross-sectional survey reports rather than longitudinal data in measuring the causations among variables; further studies should attempt to address this issue. Second, since the survey was distributed via the Internet, it was difficult to reach respondents who might live much more or entirely technology-free lives; in future research, other methodologies, including face-to-face interviews or postal mail, should be used to collect data.

References

1. Adams, D.A., Nelson, R.R., Todd, P.A.: Perceived usefulness, ease of use, and usage of information technology: a replication. MIS Q. **16**, 227–247 (1992)
2. Ardelt, M.: Antecedents and effects of wisdom in old age a longitudinal perspective on aging well. Res. Aging **22**(4), 360–394 (2000)
3. Baltes, P.B.: On the incomplete architecture of human ontogeny: selection, optimization, and compensation as foundation of developmental theory. Am. Psychol. **52**(4), 366 (1997)
4. Baltes, P.B., Baltes, M.M.: Psychological perspectives on successful aging: the model of selective optimization with compensation. Successful Aging: Perspect. Behav. Sci. **1**, 1–34 (1990)
5. Baltes, M.M., Carstensen, L.L.: The process of successful ageing. Ageing Soc. **16**(04), 397–422 (1996)
6. Baltes, M.M., Lang, F.R.: Everyday functioning and successful aging: the impact of resources. Psychol. Aging **12**(3), 433 (1997)
7. Becker, G.: Age bias in stroke rehabilitation: effects on adult status. J. Aging Stud. **8**(3), 271–290 (1994)
8. Calabria, M., Manenti, R., Rosini, S., Zanetti, O., Miniussi, C., Cotelli, M.: Objective and subjective memory impairment in elderly adults: a revised version of the Everyday Memory Questionnaire. Aging Clin. Exp. Res. **23**(1), 67–73 (2011)
9. Cotelli, M., Calabria, M., Manenti, R., Rosini, S., Zanetti, O., Cappa, S.F., Miniussi, C.: Improved language performance in Alzheimer disease following brain stimulation. J. Neurol. Neurosurg. Psychiatry **82**(7), 794–797 (2011)
10. Davis, F.D.: Perceived usefulness, perceived ease of use, and user acceptance of information technology. MIS Q. **13**, 319–340 (1989)

11. Duay, D.L., Bryan, V.C.: Senior adults' perceptions of successful aging. Educ. Gerontol. **32**, 423–445 (2006)
12. Ebner, N.C., Freund, A.M., Baltes, P.B.: Developmental changes in personal goal orientation from young to late adulthood: from striving for gains to maintenance and prevention of losses. Psychol. Aging **21**(4), 664 (2006)
13. Eastman, J.K., Iyer, R.: The elderly's uses and attitudes towards the Internet. J. Consum. Mark. **21**(3), 208–220 (2004)
14. Fishbein, M., Ajzen, I.: Predicting and Changing Behavior: The Reasoned Action Approach. Taylor & Francis, New York (2011)
15. Freund, A.M., Baltes, P.B.: Life-management strategies of selection, optimization and compensation: measurement by self-report and construct validity. J. Pers. Soc. Psychol. **82**(4), 642 (2002)
16. Freund, A.M.: Successful aging as management of resources: The role of selection, optimization, and compensation. Res. Hum. Dev. **5**(2), 94–106 (2008)
17. Freund, A.M.: Age-differential motivational consequences of optimization versus compensation focus in younger and older adults. Psychol. Aging **21**(2), 240 (2006)
18. Gefen, D., Karahanna, E., Straub, D.W.: Trust and TAM in online shopping: an integrated model. MIS Q. **27**(1), 51–90 (2003)
19. Grønland, M.: User Acceptance of Information Technology: An Empirical Study of It's Learning. Master Thesis, Norwegian University of Science and Technology (2010)
20. Guse, L.W., Masesar, M.A.: Quality of life and successful aging in long-term care: perceptions of residents. Issues Mental Health Nurs. **20**(6), 527–539 (1999)
21. Hayes, A.F.: Beyond Baron and Kenny: statistical mediation analysis in the new millennium. Commun. Monogr. **76**(4), 408–420 (2009)
22. Hill, C.M., Solomon, C.J., Gibson, S.J.: Aging the human face-A statistically rigorous approach. In: The IEE International Symposium on Imaging for Crime Detection and Prevention, ICDP 2005, pp. 89–94. IET, June 2005
23. Hong, S., Thong, J.Y., Tam, K.Y.: Understanding continued information technology usage behavior: a comparison of three models in the context of mobile internet. Decis. Support Syst. **42**(3), 1819–1834 (2006)
24. Hu, P.J., Chau, P.Y., Sheng, O.R.L., Tam, K.Y.: Examining the technology acceptance model using physician acceptance of telemedicine technology. J. Manage. Inf. Syst. **16**, 91–112 (1999)
25. Iecovich, E., Isralowitz, R.E.: Visual impairments, functional and health status, and life satisfaction among elderly Bedouins in Israel. Ageing Intl. **29**(1), 71–87 (2004)
26. Jung, Y., Peng, W., Moran, M., Jin, S.A.A., McLaughlin, M., Cody, M., Silverstein, M.: Low-income minority seniors' enrollment in a cybercafé: psychological barriers to crossing the digital divide. Educ. Gerontol. **36**(3), 193–212 (2010)
27. Kim, S.H.: Moderating effects of job relevance and experience on mobile wireless technology acceptance: adoption of a smartphone by individuals. Inf. Manag. **45**(6), 387–393 (2008)
28. Konana, P., Balasubramanian, S.: The social–economic–psychological model of technology adoption and usage: an application to online investing. Decis. Support Syst. **39**(3), 505–524 (2005)
29. Kwon, H.S., Chidambaram, L.: A test of the technology acceptance model: the case of cellular telephone adoption. In: Proceedings of the 33rd Annual Hawaii International Conference on System Sciences, p. 7. IEEE, January 2000
30. Lawton, M.P., Brody, E.M.: Assessment of older people self maintaining and instrumental activities of daily living. Nurs. Res. **19**(3), 278 (1970)

31. Levy, B.R., Slade, M.D., Kunkel, S.R., Kasl, S.V.: Longevity increased by positive self-perceptions of aging. J. Pers. Soc. Psychol. **83**(2), 261 (2002)

32. Levy, B.R., Slade, M.D., Kasl, S.V.: Longitudinal benefit of positive self-perceptions of aging on functional health. J. Gerontol. Ser. B: Psychol. Sci. Soc. Sci. **57**(5), P409–P417 (2002)

33. Levy, B.R.: Mind matters: cognitive and physical effects of aging self-stereotypes. J. Gerontol. Ser. B: Psychol. Sci. Soc. Sci. **58**(4), P203–P211 (2003)

34. Li, K.Z., Lindenberger, U., Freund, A.M., Baltes, P.B.: Walking while memorizing: age-related differences in compensatory behavior. Psychol. Sci. **12**(3), 230–237 (2001)

35. Lu, J., Yu, C.S., Liu, C., Yao, J.E.: Technology acceptance model for wireless Internet. Internet Res. **13**(3), 206–222 (2003)

36. Mart, T., Fiorella, M., Heidrun, M., Isto, R., Zsuzsa, S.: Temporal aspects of the out-of-home activities of elderly people. In: The International MOBILATE Survey: Enhancing Mobility in Later Life. Conference paper presented at the 10th International Conference on Travel Behaviour Resaerch, Lucerne, pp. 10–15, August 2003

37. Mollenkopf, H.: Ageing and Outdoor Mobility: A European Study, vol. 13. IOS Press, Amsterdam (2004)

38. Nobel, W.G.: The hearing measurement scale as a paper-pencil form: preliminary results. Ear Hear. **5**(2), 95–106 (1979)

39. Rapp, M.A., Krampe, R.T., Baltes, P.B.: Adaptive task prioritization in aging: selective resource allocation to postural control is preserved in Alzheimer disease. Am. J. Geriatr. Psychiatry **14**(1), 52–61 (2006)

40. Rogers, W., Fisk, A.D.: Human factors, applied ognition, and aging. In: Craik, F.I.M., Salthouse, T.A. (eds.) The Handbook of Aging and Cognition, 2nd edn. Lawrence Erlbaum Associates Publishers, Mahwah (2000)

41. Rowe, J.W., Kahn, R.L.: Human aging: usual and successful. Science **237**(4811), 143–149 (1987)

42. Rowe, J.W., Kahn, R.L.: Successful aging: The MacArthur Foundation Study. Pantheon, New York (1998)

43. Slagle, C.: Psychometric construction and validation of a measure of positive aging. Doctoral Dissertation, The University of Utah (2011)

44. Strawbridge, W.J., Wallhagen, M.I., Cohen, R.D.: Successful aging and well-being self-rated compared with Rowe and Kahn. Gerontologist **42**(6), 727–733 (2002)

Author Index